SUPREME SCALE ATLAS
BRITAIN

Contents

Map pages	inside front cover
Route planner	*II–V*
London district map	*VI–VII*
Smart motorways	*VIII*
Atlas symbols	1
Road maps 1:160,000 scale	2–152
Channel Islands 1:113,000 scale	12–13
Isle of Man 1:200,000 scale	102
Orkney and Shetland Islands 1:605,000 scale	147
Western Isles 1:528,000 scale	152

Ferry ports

Aberdeen Harbour....................133	Holyhead Harbour....................72	Poole, Port of..........................11
Channnel Tunnel.......................17	Hull, Port of..............................87	Port of Tyne............................101
Dover, Port of...........................17	Liverpool Docks........................74	Portsmouth Harbour.................13
Fishguard Harbour....................36	Newhaven Harbour...................16	Southampton, Port of...............13
Harwich International Port.........47	Pembroke Dock........................36	
Heysham Harbour.....................82	Plymouth, Port of.......................4	

Town plans

Aberdeen................................133	Liverpool..................................74	St Andrews.............................125
Aberystwyth..............................48	Llandudno.................................73	Scarborough............................93
Blackpool..................................82	Middlesbrough..........................93	Southend-on-Sea.....................35
Dundee....................................125	Newcastle upon Tyne..............101	Sunderland..............................101
Exeter...9	Newquay.....................................3	Swansea...................................26
Great Yarmouth.........................71	Plymouth.....................................4	
Ipswich......................................47	Ramsgate...................................35	

Restricted junctions	153
Index to place names	154–184
County, administrative area map	154
Distances and journey times	inside back cover

14th edition June 2019

© AA Media Limited 2019

Revised version of atlas formerly known as *Maxi Scale Atlas Britain*

Original edition printed 1990.

Cartography: All cartography in this atlas edited, designed and produced by the Mapping Services Department of AA Publishing (A05696).

This atlas contains Ordnance Survey data © Crown copyright and database right 2019.

Contains public sector information licensed under the Open Government Licence v3.0

Distances and journey times contains data available from openstreetmap.org © under the Open Database License found at opendatacommons.org

Publisher's notes: Published by AA Publishing (a trading name of AA Media Limited, whose registered office is Fanum House, Basing View, Basingstoke, Hampshire, RG21 4EA, UK. Registered number 06112600).

ISBN: 978 0 7495 8187 9

A CIP catalogue record for this book is available from The British Library.

Disclaimer: The contents of this atlas are believed to be correct at the time of the latest revision, it will not contain any subsequent amended, new or temporary information including diversions and traffic control or enforcement systems. The publishers cannot be held responsible or liable for any loss or damage occasioned to any person acting or refraining from action as a result of any use or reliance on material in this atlas, nor for any errors, omissions or changes in such material. This does not affect your statutory rights.

The publishers would welcome information to correct any errors or omissions and to keep this atlas up to date. Please write to the Atlas Editor, AA Publishing, The Automobile Association, Fanum House, Basing View, Basingstoke, Hampshire RG21 4EA, UK.
E-mail: *roadatlasfeedback@theaa.com*

Acknowledgements: AA Publishing would like to thank the following for information used in the creation of this atlas:
Cadw, English Heritage, Forestry Commission, Historic Scotland, National Trust and National Trust for Scotland, RSPB, The Wildlife Trust, Scottish Natural Heritage, Natural England, The Countryside Council for Wales. Award winning beaches from 'Blue Flag' and 'Keep Scotland Beautiful' (summer 2018 data): for latest information visit *www.blueflag.org* and *www.keepscotlandbeautiful.org*

Printer: Elcograf S.p.A, Italy

Scale 1:160,000
or 2.52 miles to 1 inch

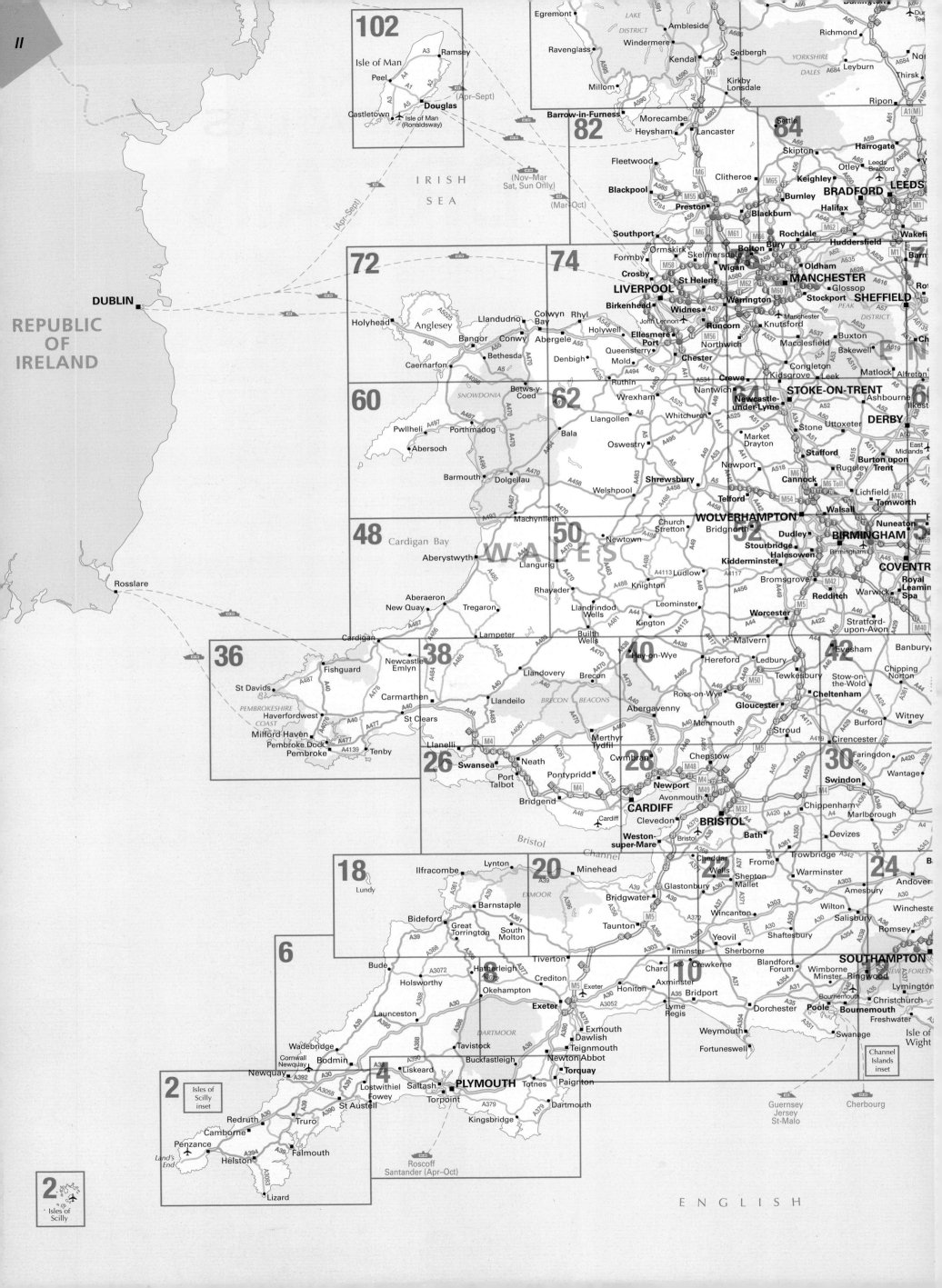

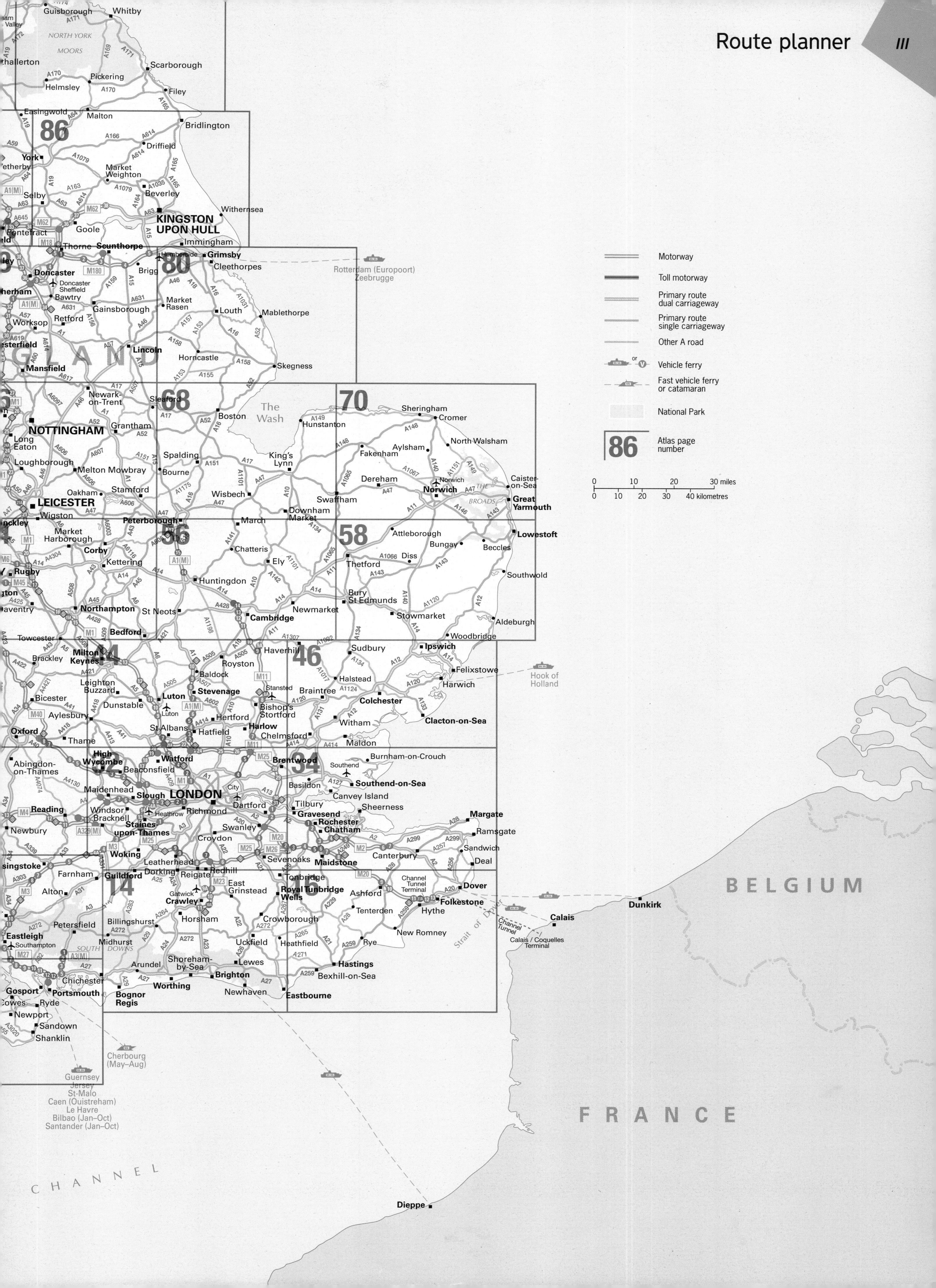

Motorway
Toll motorway
Primary route
dual carriageway
Primary route
single carriageway
Other A road
Vehicle ferry
Fast vehicle ferry
or catamaran
National Park

86 Atlas page
number

0   10   20   30 miles
0   10   20   30   40 kilometres

86

Guisborough · Whitby
NORTH YORK MOORS
halterton · A171 · Scarborough
Helmsley · Pickering · Filey
Easingwold · Malton · Bridlington
York · Driffield
etherby · Market Weighton · Beverley
Selby
KINGSTON UPON HULL · Withernsea
Thorne · Scunthorpe · Immingham
80 · Grimsby · Cleethorpes
Doncaster · Humberside
Bawtry · Market Rasen · Louth · Mablethorpe
Gainsborough · Skegness
Worksop · Retford · Horncastle
Mansfield · Lincoln

Rotterdam (Europoort) Zeebrugge

68 · **70** · Sheringham · Cromer
NOTTINGHAM · Boston · The Wash · Hunstanton · North Walsham
Grantham · Sleaford · King's Lynn · Aylsham
Loughborough · Spalding · Fakenham · A140
Melton Mowbray · Bourne · Dereham · Norwich
LEICESTER · Stamford · Wisbech · Swaffham · Great Yarmouth
Oakham · Peterborough · March · Downham Market · Caister-on-Sea
Wigston · **56** · **58** · Attleborough · Lowestoft
Corby · Kettering · Chatteris · Ely · Bungay · Beccles
Rugby · Huntingdon · Thetford · Diss · Southwold
Northampton · St Neots · Newmarket · Bury St Edmunds
Bedford · Cambridge · Stowmarket · Aldeburgh
Milton Keynes · Haverhill · **46** · Sudbury · Ipswich · Woodbridge
Royston · Stevenage · Braintree · Colchester · Felixstowe
Luton · Bishop's Stortford · Witham · Harwich · Hook of Holland
Oxford · St Albans · Hatfield · Harlow · Chelmsford · Clacton-on-Sea
32 · Watford · Brentwood · **34** · Maldon · Burnham-on-Crouch
High Wycombe · Slough · LONDON · Southend-on-Sea
Maidenhead · Dartford · Basildon · Canvey Island · Sheerness · Margate
Reading · Windsor · Richmond · Tilbury · Gravesend · Rochester · Ramsgate
Woking · Croydon · Swanley · Chatham · Sandwich · Deal
Guildford · **14** · Leatherhead · Sevenoaks · Maidstone · Canterbury
Dorking · Reigate · Tonbridge · M20 · Dover
Crawley · East Grinstead · Royal Tunbridge Wells · Ashford · Folkestone
Horsham · Crowborough · Tenterden · Hythe · Channel Tunnel Terminal
Petersfield · Midhurst · Uckfield · Heathfield · Rye · New Romney
Southampton · Arundel · Lewes · Hastings · Bexhill-on-Sea
Chichester · Worthing · Brighton · Newhaven · Eastbourne
Portsmouth · Bognor Regis · Shoreham-by-Sea
Gosport · Newport · Sandown · Shanklin

Cherbourg (May–Aug)
Guernsey
Jersey
St-Malo
Caen (Ouistreham)
Le Havre
Bilbao (Jan–Oct)
Santander (Jan–Oct)

CHANNEL

BELGIUM
FRANCE
Strait of Dover
Calais
Dunkirk
Calais / Coquelles Terminal
Channel Tunnel
Dieppe

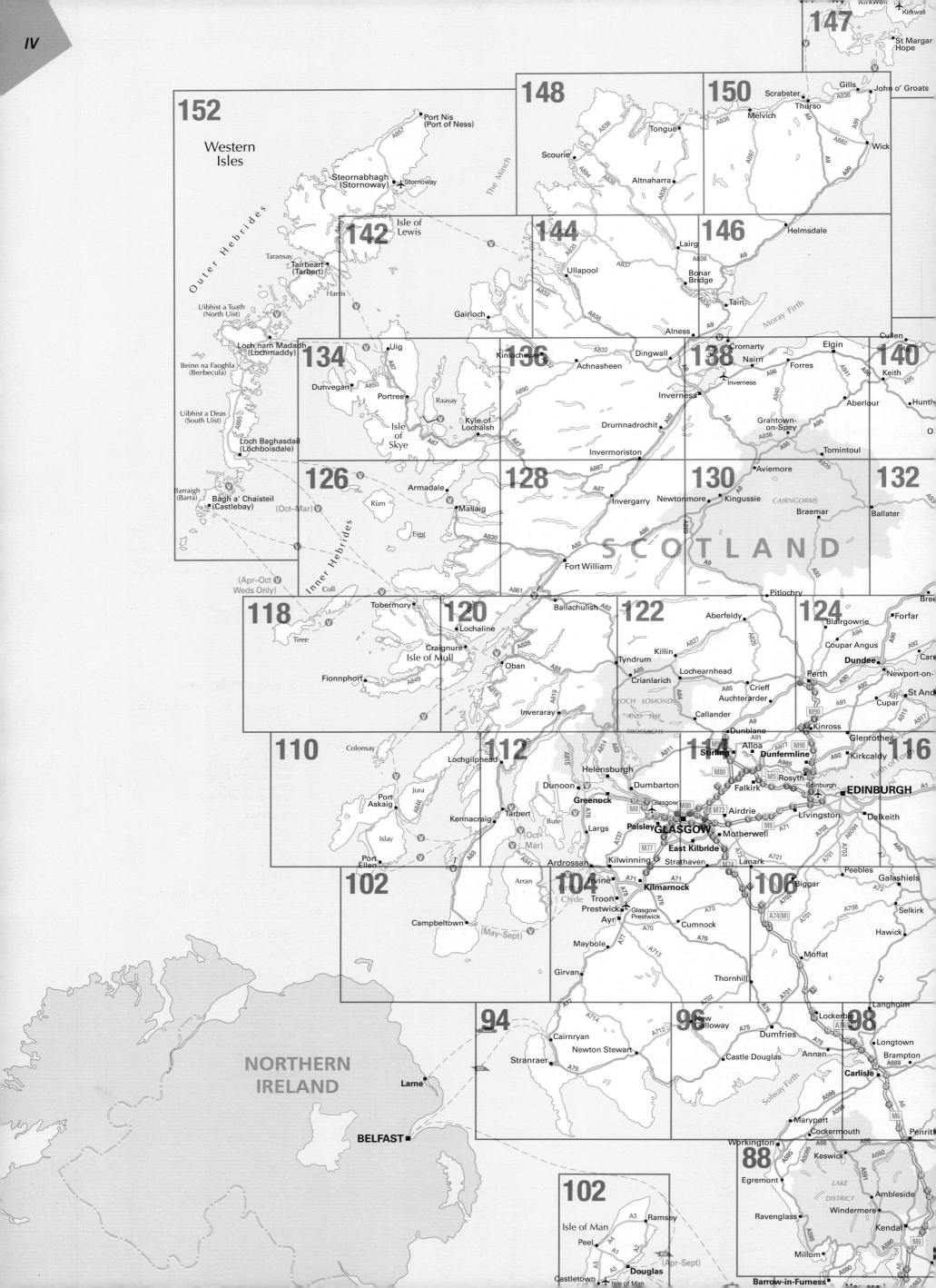

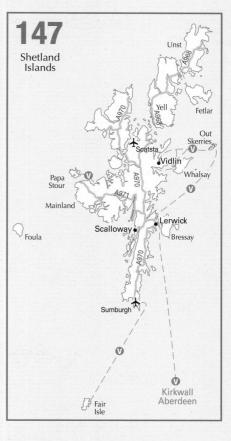

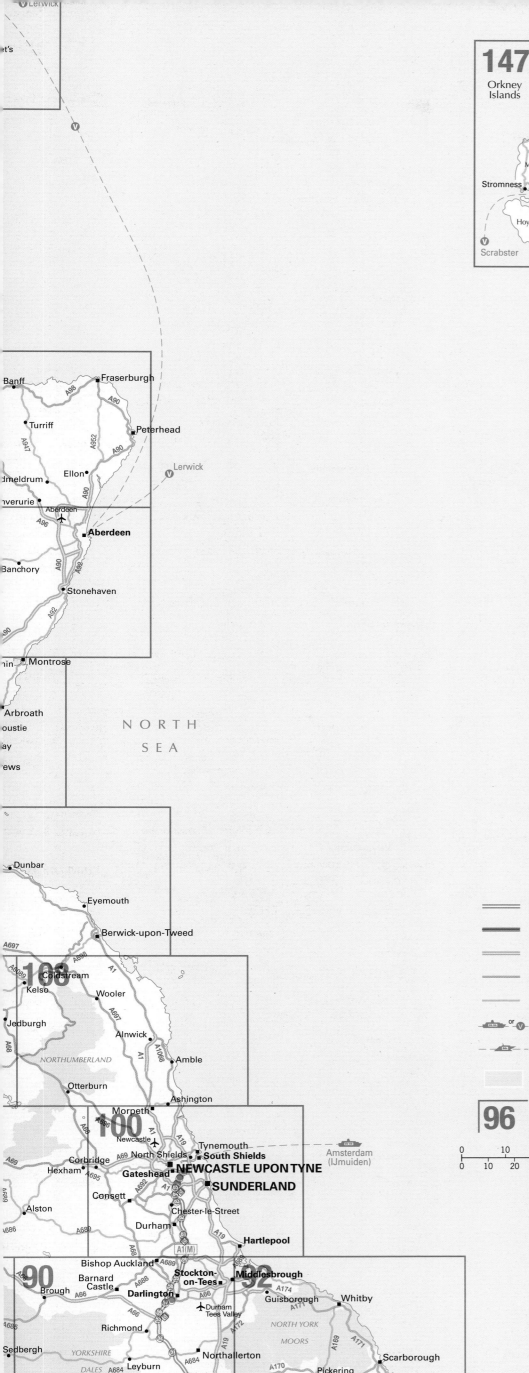

EMERGENCY DIVERSION ROUTES

In an emergency it may be necessary to close a section of motorway or other main road to traffic, so a temporary sign may advise drivers to follow a diversion route. To help drivers navigate the route, black symbols on yellow patches may be permanently displayed on existing direction signs, including motorway signs. Symbols may also be used on separate signs with yellow backgrounds.

For further information see *theaa.com/breakdown-cover/ advice/emergency-diversion-routes*

	Motorway
	Toll motorway
	Primary route dual carriageway
	Primary route single carriageway
	Other A road
or V	Vehicle ferry
	Fast vehicle ferry or catamaran
	National Park
96	Atlas page number

0   10   20   30 miles
0 10 20 30 40 kilometres

FERRY OPERATORS

Hebrides and west coast Scotland
calmac.co.uk
skyeferry.co.uk
western-ferries.co.uk

Orkney and Shetland
northlinkferries.co.uk
pentlandferries.co.uk
orkneyferries.co.uk
shetland.gov.uk/ferries

Isle of Man
steam-packet.com

Ireland
irishferries.com
poferries.com
stenaline.co.uk

North Sea (Scandinavia and Benelux)
dfdsseaways.co.uk
poferries.com

Isle of Wight
wightlink.co.uk
redfunnel.co.uk

Channel Islands
condorferries.co.uk

France and Belgium
brittany-ferries.co.uk
condorferries.co.uk
eurotunnel.com
dfdsseaways.co.uk
poferries.com

Northern Spain
brittany-ferries.co.uk

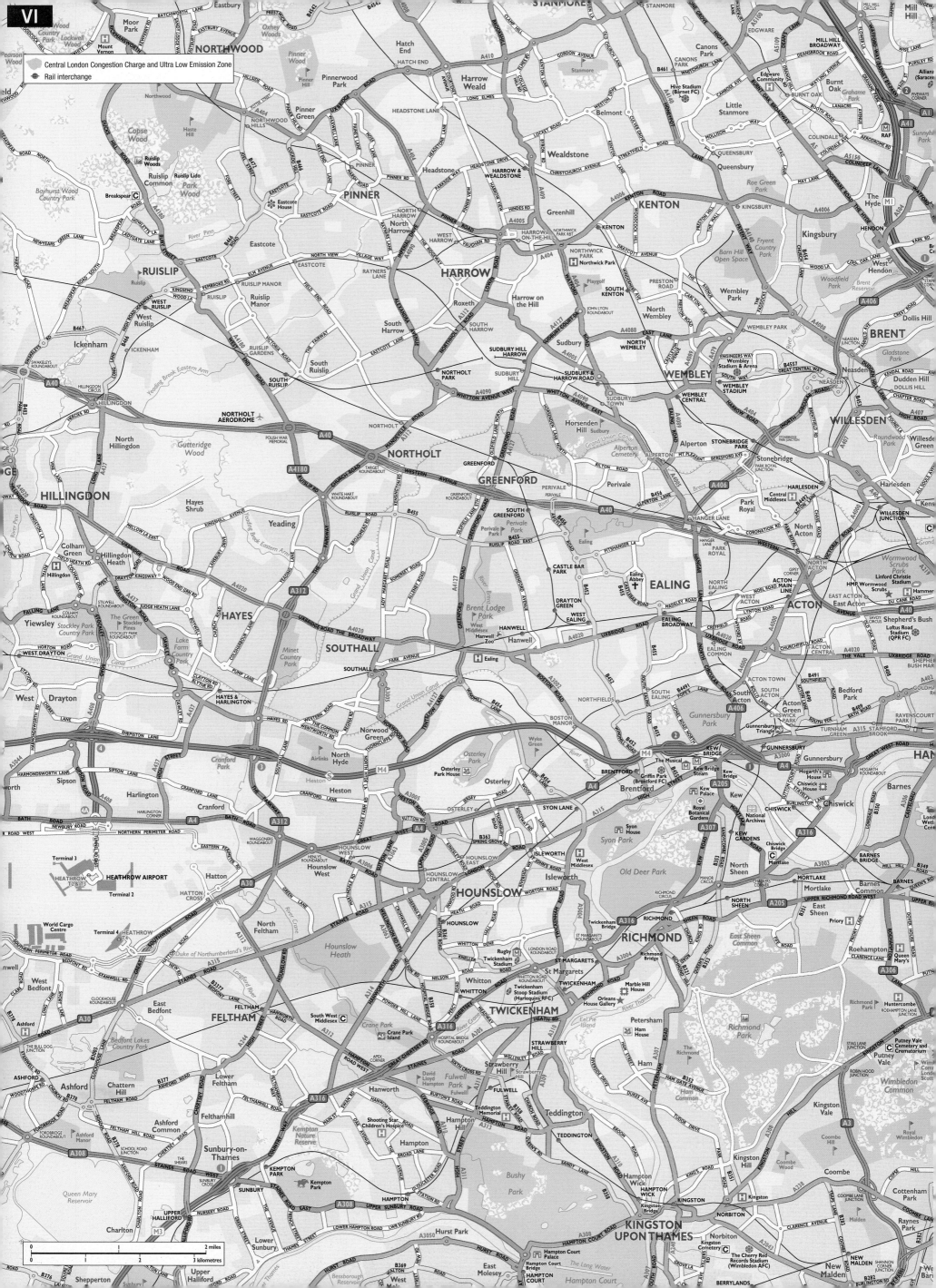

Smart motorways

Since Britain's first motorway (the Preston Bypass) opened in 1958, motorways have changed significantly. A vast increase in car journeys over the last 61 years has meant that motorways quickly filled to capacity. To combat this, the recent development of **smart motorways** uses technology to monitor and actively manage traffic flow and congestion.

How they work

Smart motorways utilise various active traffic management methods, monitored through a regional traffic control centre:

- Traffic flow is monitored using CCTV
- Speed limits are changed to smooth traffic flow and reduce stop-start driving
- Capacity of the motorway can be increased by either temporarily or permanently opening the hard shoulder to traffic
- Warning signs and messages alert drivers to hazards and traffic jams ahead
- Lanes can be closed in the case of an accident or emergency by displaying a red X sign

- Emergency refuge areas are located regularly along the motorway where there is no hard shoulder available

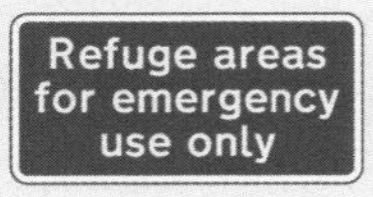

Refuge areas for emergency use only

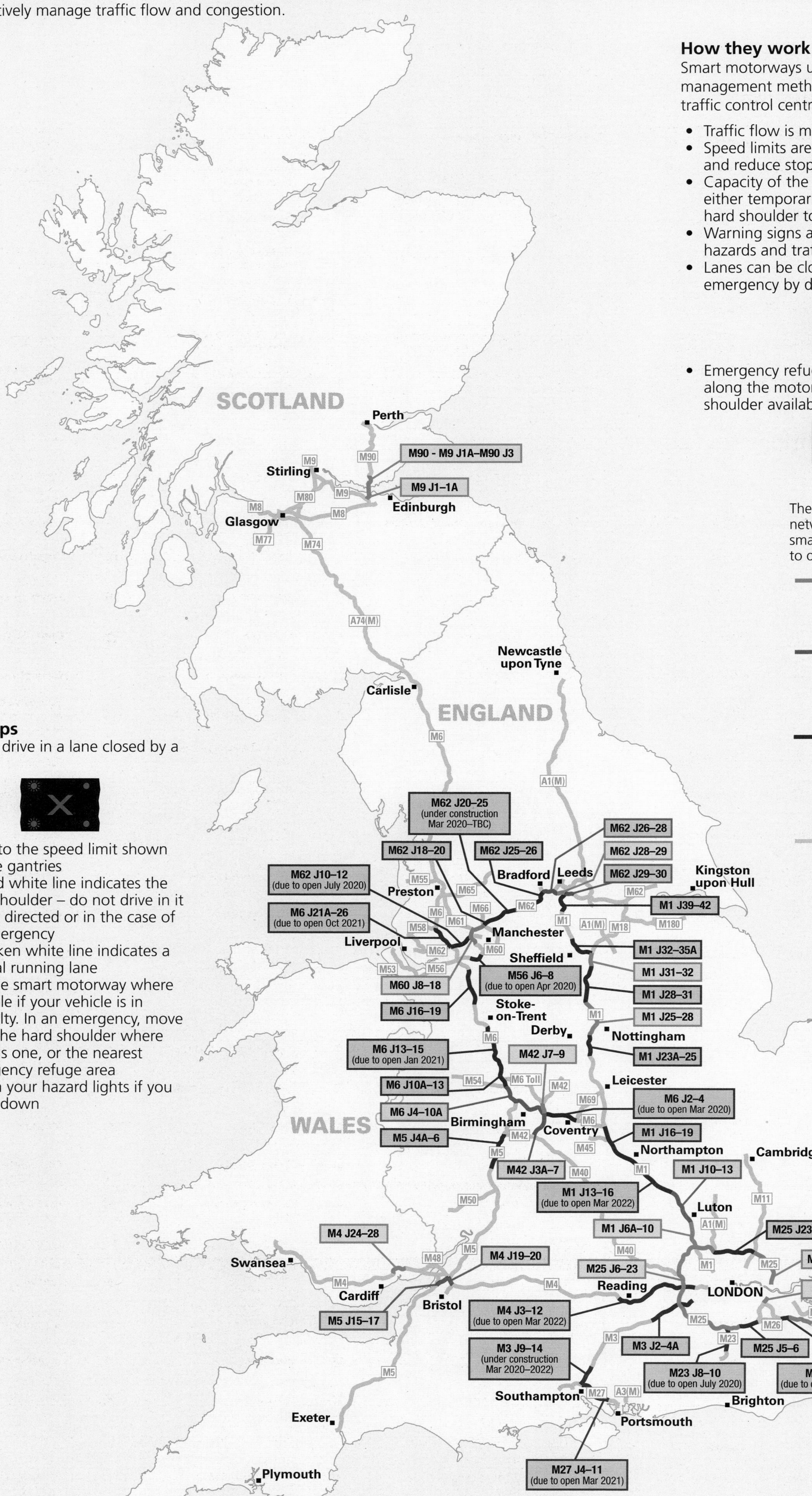

The map shows the main motorway network with the three different types of smart motorway in operation or planned to open over the next five years:

Controlled motorway
Variable speed limits without hard shoulder (the hard shoulder is used in emergencies only)

Hard shoulder running
Variable speed limits with part-time hard shoulder (the hard shoulder is open to traffic at busy times when signs permit)

All lane running
Variable speed limits with hard shoulder as permanent running lane (there is no hard shoulder); this is standard for all new motorway schemes since 2013

Standard motorway

Quick tips

- Never drive in a lane closed by a red X

- Keep to the speed limit shown on the gantries
- A solid white line indicates the hard shoulder – do not drive in it unless directed or in the case of an emergency
- A broken white line indicates a normal running lane
- Exit the smart motorway where possible if your vehicle is in difficulty. In an emergency, move onto the hard shoulder where there is one, or the nearest emergency refuge area
- Put on your hazard lights if you break down

Map labels

SCOTLAND

Perth

M90 - M9 J1A–M90 J3

Stirling

M9 J1–1A

Glasgow

Edinburgh

Newcastle upon Tyne

Carlisle

ENGLAND

M62 J20–25 (under construction Mar 2020–TBC)

M62 J18–20

M62 J25–26

M62 J26–28

M62 J28–29

M62 J29–30

Kingston upon Hull

M62 J10–12 (due to open July 2020)

Bradford

Leeds

Preston

M1 J39–42

M6 J21A–26 (due to open Oct 2021)

Manchester

Liverpool

M1 J32–35A

Sheffield

M56 J6–8 (due to open Apr 2020)

M1 J31–32

M60 J8–18

M1 J28–31

M6 J16–19

Stoke-on-Trent

M1 J25–28

Derby

Nottingham

M6 J13–15 (due to open Jan 2021)

M42 J7–9

M1 J23A–25

M6 J10A–13

Leicester

M6 J4–10A

M6 J2–4 (due to open Mar 2020)

WALES

Birmingham

Coventry

M1 J16–19

M5 J4A–6

Northampton

Cambridge

M42 J3A–7

M1 J10–13

M1 J13–16 (due to open Mar 2022)

Luton

M4 J24–28

M1 J6A–10

M25 J23–27

Swansea

M4 J19–20

M25 J27–30

M25 J6–23

M25 J2–3

Cardiff

Reading

LONDON

Bristol

M20 J4–7

M5 J15–17

M4 J3–12 (due to open Mar 2022)

M3 J2–4A

M25 J5–6

M3 J9–14 (under construction Mar 2020–2022)

M23 J8–10 (due to open July 2020)

M20 J3–5 (due to open May 2020)

Folkestone

Southampton

Brighton

Exeter

Portsmouth

Plymouth

M27 J4–11 (due to open Mar 2021)

Smart motorways (*Intelligent Transport Systems* in Scotland) are the responsibility of Highways England, Transport Scotland and Transport for Wales

Motoring information

M4	Motorway with number	Primary route junction with and without number	Roundabout
Toll / T4	Toll motorway with toll station	Restricted primary route junctions	Interchange/junction
6	Motorway junction with and without number	Primary route service area	Narrow primary/other A/B road with passing places (Scotland)
5	Restricted motorway junctions	BATH — Primary route destination	Road under construction
Fleet	Motorway service area, rest area	A1123 — Other A road single/dual carriageway	Road tunnel
	Motorway and junction under construction	B2070 — B road single/dual carriageway	Road toll, steep gradient (arrows point downhill)
A3	Primary route single/dual carriageway	Minor road more than 4 metres wide, less than 4 metres wide	Distance in miles between symbols

- Vehicle ferry (or V) — International freight terminal (F)
- Fast vehicle ferry or catamaran — 24-hour Accident & Emergency hospital (H)
- Railway line, in tunnel — Crematorium (C)
- Railway/tram station, level crossing — Park and Ride (at least 6 days per week) (P+R)
- Tourist railway — 628 / 637 Lecht Summit — Height in metres, mountain pass
- City, town, village or other built-up area — Snow gates (on main routes)
- Airport (major/minor), heliport — National boundary, County or administrative boundary

Touring information
To avoid disappointment, check opening times before visiting

Scenic route	Industrial interest	RSPB site	Cave or cavern	National Trust site
Tourist Information Centre	Aqueduct or viaduct	National Nature Reserve (England, Scotland, Wales)	Windmill, monument	National Trust for Scotland site
Tourist Information Centre (seasonal)	Garden	Wildlife Trust reserve	Beach (award winning)	English Heritage site
Visitor or heritage centre	Arboretum	Local nature reserve	Lighthouse	Historic Scotland site
Picnic site	Vineyard	Forest drive	Golf course	Cadw (Welsh heritage) site
Caravan site (AA inspected)	Brewery or distillery	National trail	Football stadium	Other place of interest
Camping site (AA inspected)	Country park	Waterfall	County cricket ground	Boxed symbols indicate attractions within urban areas
Caravan & camping site (AA inspected)	Agricultural showground	Viewpoint	Rugby Union national stadium	World Heritage Site (UNESCO)
Abbey, cathedral or priory	Theme park	Hill-fort	International athletics stadium	National Park and National Scenic Area (Scotland)
Ruined abbey, cathedral or priory	Farm or animal centre	Roman antiquity	Horse racing, show jumping	Forest Park
Castle	Zoological or wildlife collection	Prehistoric monument	Motor-racing circuit	Sandy beach
Historic house or building	Bird collection	1066 Battle site with year	Air show venue	Heritage coast
Museum or art gallery	Aquarium	Steam railway centre	Ski slope (natural, artificial)	Major shopping centre

Town plans

2 — Motorway and junction	Railway station	Toilet, with facilities for the less able	Tourist Information Centre	Abbey, chapel, church
4 — Primary road single/dual carriageway and numbered junction	Tramway	Building of interest	Visitor or heritage centre	Synagogue
37 — A road single/dual carriageway and numbered junction	London Underground station	Ruined building	Post Office	Mosque
B road single/dual carriageway	London Overground station	City wall	Public library	Golf course
Local road single/dual carriageway	Rail interchange	Cliff lift	Shopping centre	Racecourse
Other road single/dual carriageway, minor road	Docklands Light Railway (DLR) station	Escarpment	Shopmobility	Nature reserve
One-way, gated/closed road	Light rapid transit system station	River/canal, lake	Theatre or performing arts centre	Aquarium
Restricted access	Airport, heliport	Lock, weir	Cinema	World Heritage Site (UNESCO)
Pedestrian area	Railair terminal	Park/sports ground/open space	Museum	English Heritage site
Footpath	P+R — Park and Ride (at least 6 days per week)	Cemetery	Castle	Historic Scotland site
Road under construction	P P — Car park, with electric charging point	Woodland	Castle mound	Cadw (Welsh heritage) site
Road tunnel	Bus/coach station	Built-up area	Monument, statue	National Trust site
Level crossing	24-hour Accident & Emergency hospital, other hospital	Beach	Viewpoint	National Trust for Scotland site

Isles of Scilly

White Island

St Helen's
King Charles's Castle
BRYHER
Cromwell's Castle
Old Grimsby
ST MARTIN'S   St Martin's Head   38
Old Blockhouse   49
Higher Town
New Grimsby   Lizard Point
Pool
Isles of Scilly Heritage Coast   42
Great Ganilly
Tresco Abbey   TRESCO   Innisidgen Tomb   Eastern Isles
Bant's Carn Burial
Samson
Harry's Walls   ST MARY'S
Higher & Lower Moors
Hugh Town   Deep Point
Garrison Walls   Porth Hellick Down Tombs
Old Town   Isles of Scilly (St Mary's)
Peninnis Head
Middle Town   Penninis Head

North West Passage
Crow Bar
Crow Sound
A3110

Broad Sound
St Mary's Sound
Annet   Gugh
Smith Sound   ST AGNES
Horse Point
Western Rocks

0   1   2   3 miles
0   1   2   3   4   5 kilometres

a   b   c

Main map

St Agnes Heritage Coast
ST AGNES HEAD   St Agnes
Wheal Coates
Trevellas

Goonvrea
Porthtowan   Mount Hawke   Chiverton
South West Coast Path   St Agnes Mining District
Portreath   B3300   Cambrose   Menagissey   Mawla
Godrevy-Portreath Heritage Coast   Illogan   Wheal Peevor   Wheal Rose   North Country   A30   Mount Ambrose
Navax Point   Coombe   South Tehidy   Park Bottom   Paynter's Lane End   East Pool Mine   Redruth
Godrevy Point   B3301   Tehidy   Reskadinnick   Tuckingmill   C   Pool   Carn Brea   Carharrack
Gwealavellan   Treswithian   Camborne   Carn Brea   Trevarth   Lanner   A3
The Island or St Ives Head   Gwithian   Kehelland   Roseworthy   Penponds   Penhalurick   Penhal
Porthmeor   Carn Naun Point   St Ives Bay   Upton Towans   Connor Downs   Angarrack   Barripper   Carnhell Green   Troon   Bolenowe   Hendra   Four Lanes
Treveal   Hellesveor   St Ives   The Towans   Phillack   High Lanes   Realwa   Rosewarne   Praze-an-Beeble   Horsedown   Burras   Carnkie   Long
Zennor Head   Trendrine   Carbis Bay   Copperhouse   Gwinear   St Erth   Trenerth   Blackrock   Farm Common   Edgcombe
Gurnards Head   Zennor   Halsetown   Hayle   Praze   Crowan   Lezerea   Porkellis   Carnkie
South West Coast Path   Treen   Towednack   Cripplesease   Brunnion   P+R   Leedstown   Releath   Nancegollan   Trenwheal   Wendron   Trenear   Poldark
Pendeen Watch   B3306   Carn Galver Mine   Georgia   Nancledra   A30   St Erth   Kerthen Wood   Townshend   Godolphin House   Wendron Mining District   Manhay   Mine
Pendeen   Men-An-Tol   Chysauster Ancient Village   Canonstown   R Hayle   Godolphin Cross   Prospidnick   A394
Morvah   Mulfra Quoit   Bakers Pit   Whitecross   Fraddam   Relubbus   Trescowe   Carleen   Crowntown   Sithney Heritage Railway   Coverack Bridges
Lower Boscaswell   Geevor Tin Mine   Penwith Heritage Coast   Mulfra   New Mill   Castle Gate   Cockwells   St Hilary   Millpool   Balwest   Sithney Green   Lower Town   Brill
Levant Mine & Beam Engine   Pendeen Trewellard   Great Bosullow   Lanyon Quoit   Badger's Cross   Crowlas   Ludgvan   Goldsithney   Newtown   Germoe   Trew   Sithney   Manhay
Carnyorth   St Just Mining District   Boskednan   Boswarthan   Madron   Ludgvan   Longrock   Marazion   Perranuthnoe   Rosudgeon   Ashton   Breage   Helston
Botallack   B3318   Trengwainton Garden   Trevarrack   St Michael's Mount   Kenneggy   Rinsey Croft   Sithney Common   Gweek
Cape Cornwall   St Just   Tregeseal   Newbridge   Heamoor   Gulval   A30   Chyandour   Prussia Cove   Praa Sands   Rinsey   A394   Seal Sanctuary
Ballowall Barrow   Tremethick Cross   Penzance   Cudden Point   Rinsey Head   Trewavas   Helston   Mellangoose   Flambards   Mawgan
Bosavern   Grumbla   Sellan   Tereife   Newlyn   Trewavas Mining District   Trewavas Head   Porthleven   A3083   Garras   Trelowarren
Kelynack   Carn Euny Ancient Village   Sancreed   Drift   Tredavoe   St Michael's Mount   MOUNT'S BAY   Higher Pentire   Halliggye Fogou
Nanquidno   Brane   A30   Catchall   Kerris   Paul   Chyvarloe   Berepper   Gweek
Land's End   Crows-an-Wra   Sheffield   Mousehole   Gunwalloe   White Cross   Goon Down
Whitesand Bay   Trevorgans   St Buryan   Raginnis   Chyanvounder   Constantine
Sennen Cove   Escalls   Castallack   Cross Lanes   B3
Sennen   Bottoms   The Merry Maidens   Lamorna   Cury   Trewoon
LAND'S END   Land's End   B3283   Lamorna Cove   Angrouse   Mawgan   Gear
Trevescan   B3315   Trethewey   Boskenna   Poldhu Point   Mullion   Penhale
Polgigga   Treen   Merthen Point   Marconi Memorial
Porthcurno   B3315   Mullion Cove   Ruan Major   Kuggar
Roskestal   Telegraph   Mullion Island   Penhale
Porthgwarra   St Levan   Cribba Head   Predannack Head   Predannack Wollas   St Ruan   Ruan
Gwennap Head   Minack Open Air Theatre   South West Coast Path   Mount Hermon   Grade   Cam
Vellan Head   The Lizard   Church
The Lizard Heritage Coast
Lizard Head   Lizard   Bass Po
Kynance Cove   A3083
LIZARD POINT   Lizard Lighthouse & Heritage Centre   Devil

0   1   2   3   4   5 miles
0   1   2   3   4   5   6   7   8 kilometres

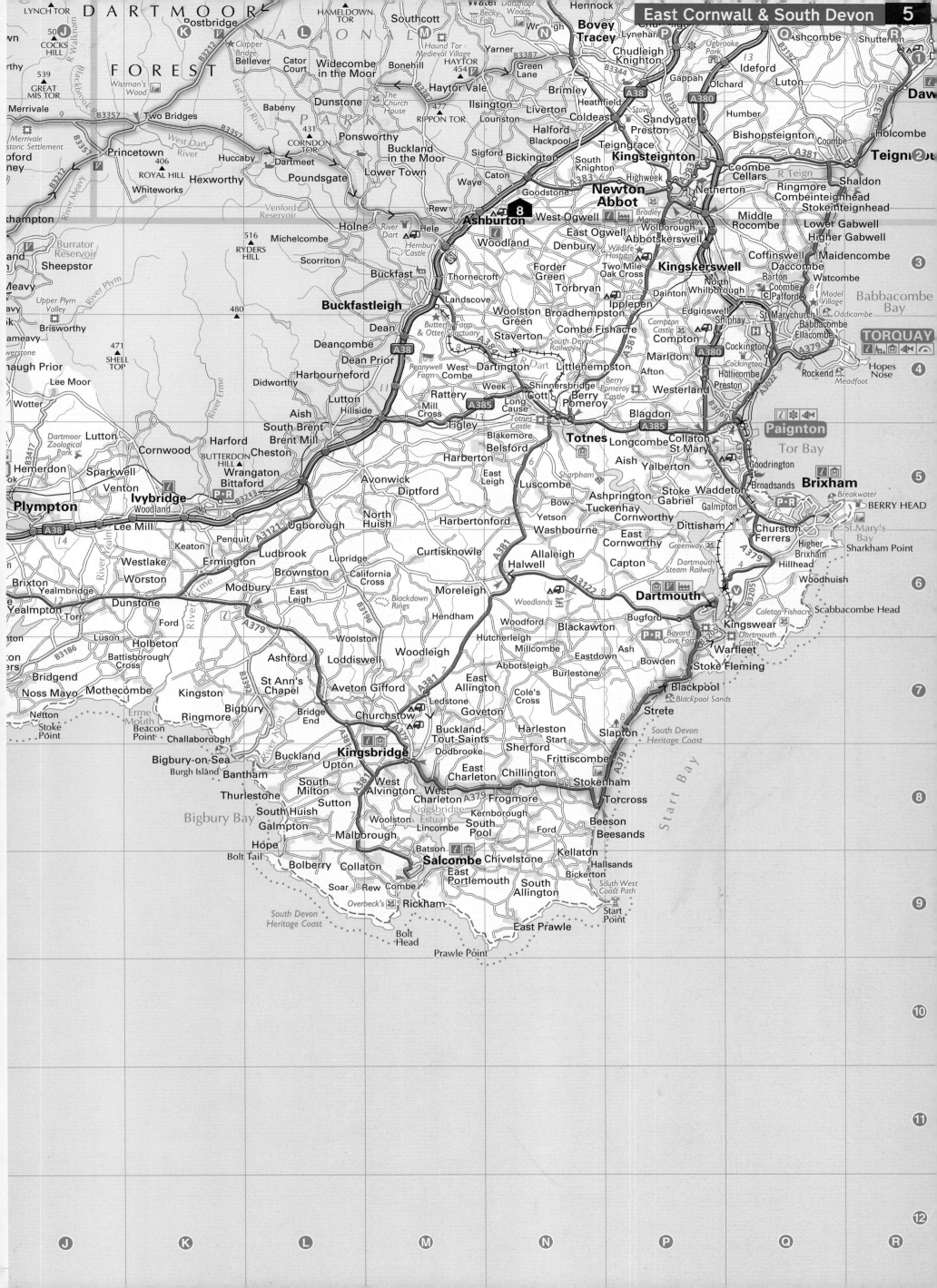

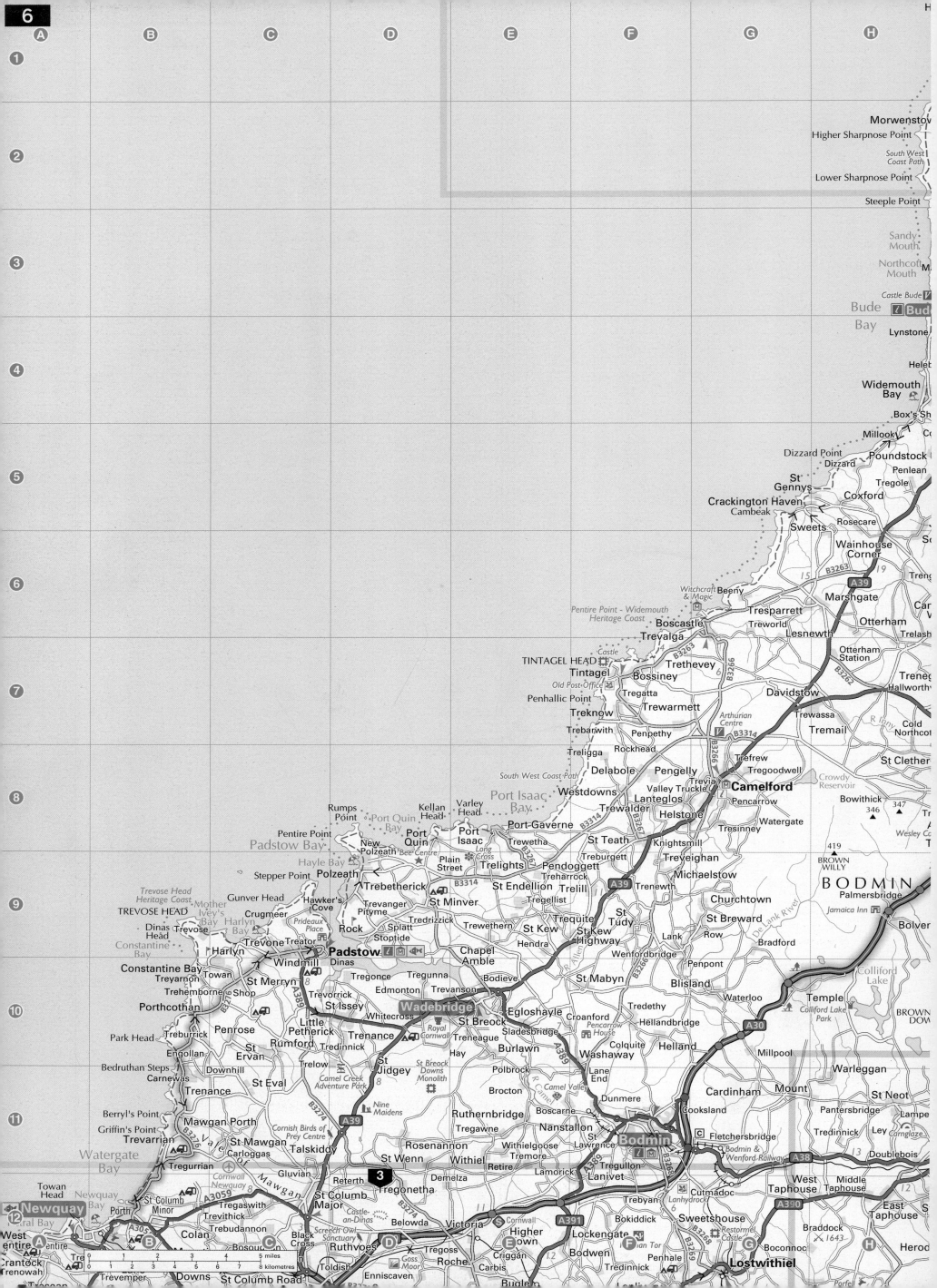

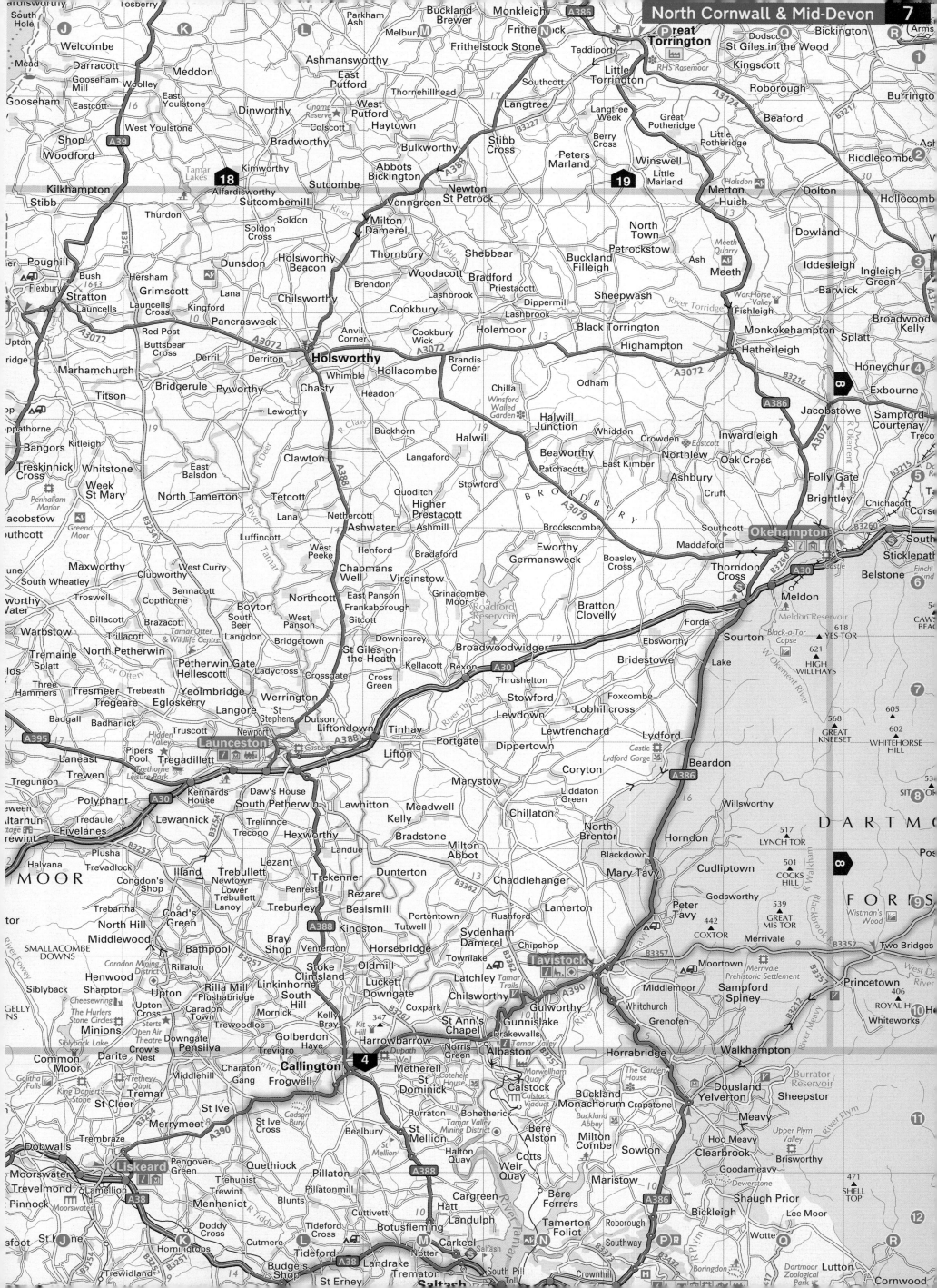

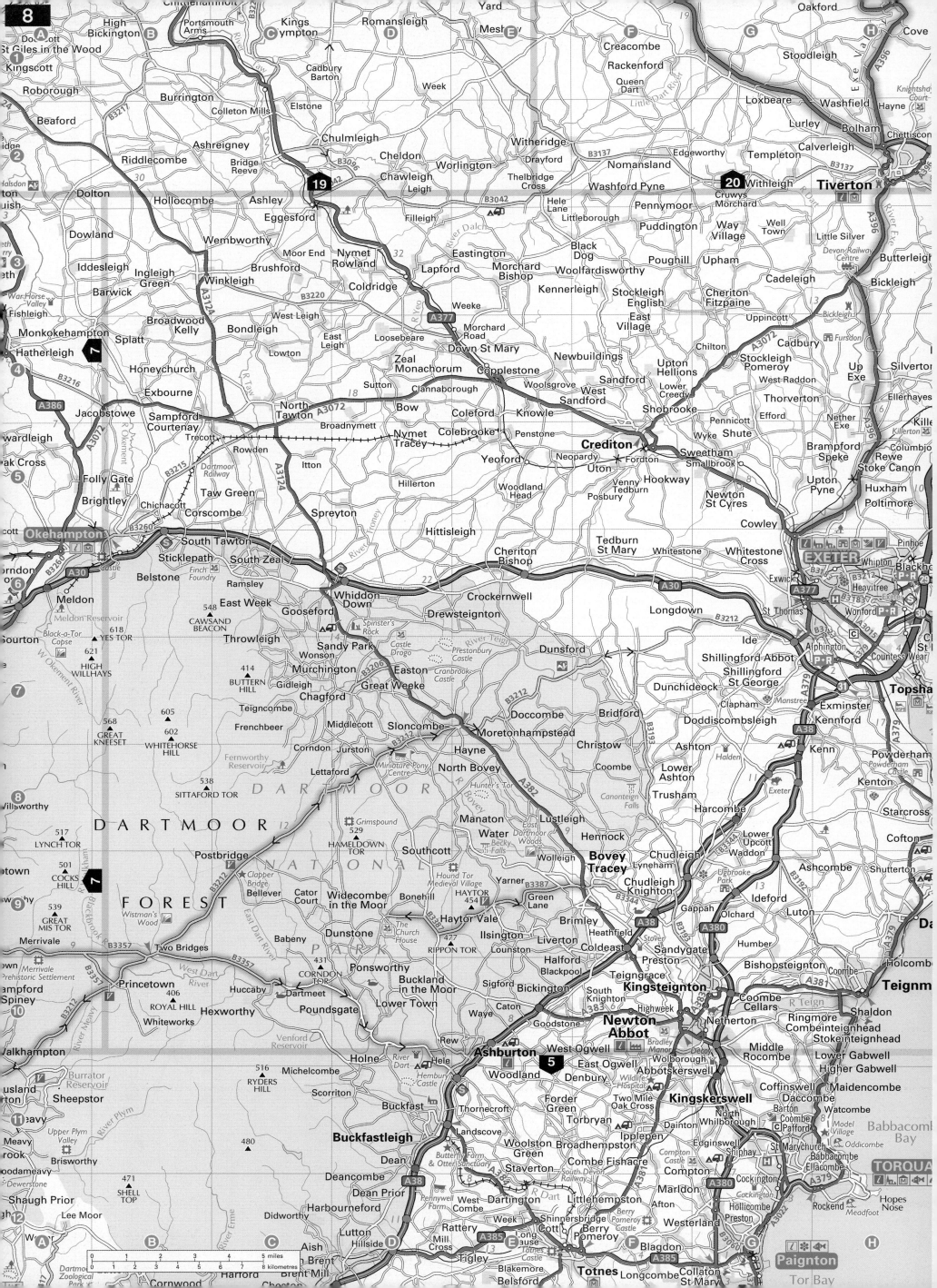

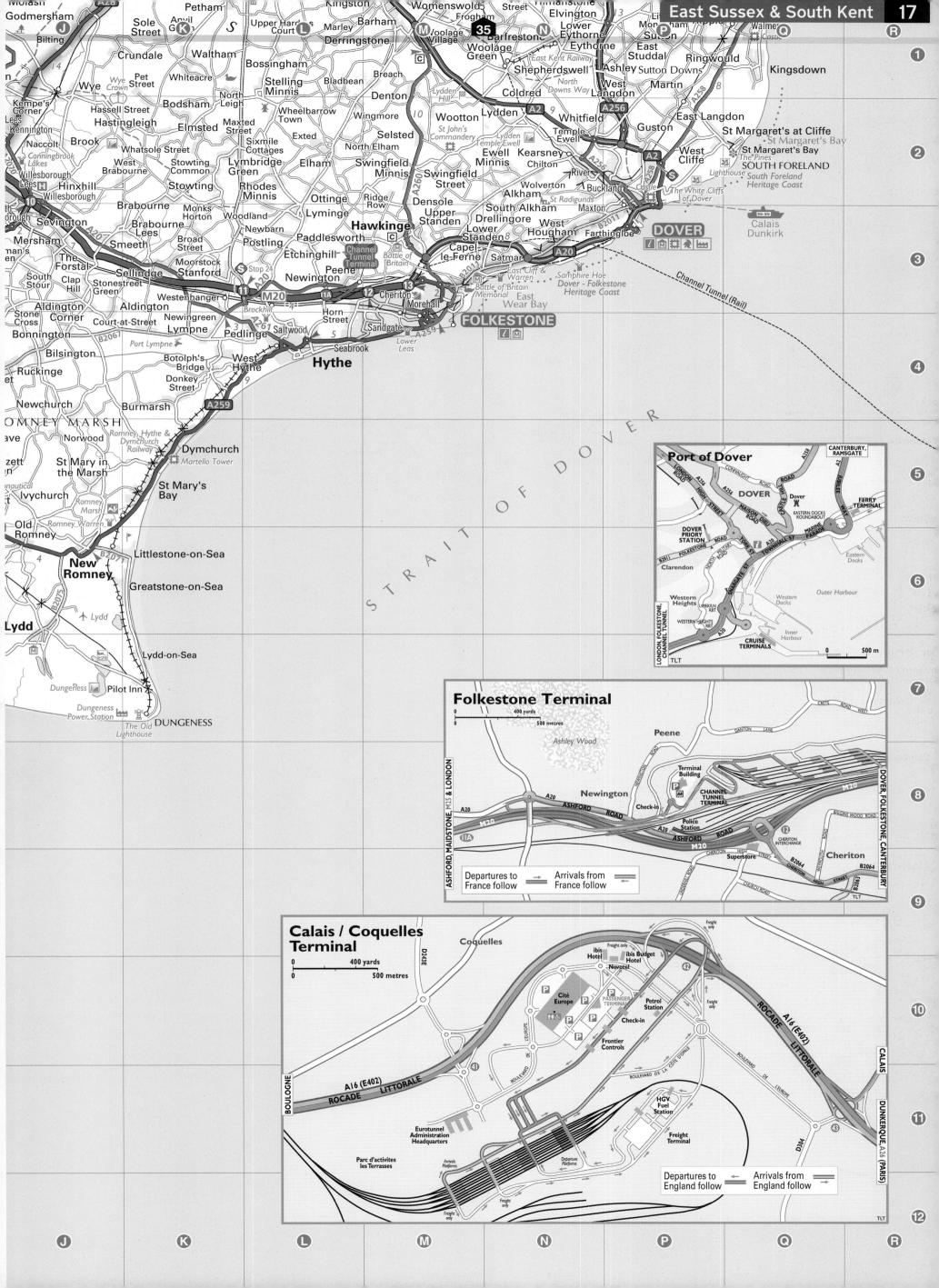

A B C D E F G H

NorthWest Point

Lundy Heritage Coast   LUNDY

▲142
Marine Reserve   Marisco
Shutter Point   Surf Point

Baggy Point   Putsborc
Croyde Bay   G
Croyde Bay

North Devon Heritage Coast

B A R N S T A P L E

Northam Burrows A
O R   Apl
B32
Westward Ho!

B I D E F O R D   B A Y

Abbotsham
Shipload Bay
HARTLAND POINT
Titchberry   Brownsham
Damehole Point   Hartland Abbey & Gardens   Clovelly   Hartland Heritage Coast   Ford Cross   Yeo Vale   Bi
Stoke   Velly   Buck's Mills   Fairy Cross
Hartland Quay   B3248   4   Higher Clovelly   Horns Cross   Woodtown   Littleha
Hartland   B3231   Buck's Cross   A39   Goldworthy   Salt
Speke's Mill Mouth   Milford   Milky Way   10
Docton Mill   Philham   Woolfardisworthy   Cranford   Parkham   Cabbacott   Buckland Brewer   Monk
Elmscott   Edistone   Parkham Ash   Fri
Hardisworthy   Tosberry   Melbury   Frithelstock St
South Hole   Ashmansworthy
Welcombe   East Putford   Thornehillhead   17
Mead   Darracott   Meddon   Lar
Gooseham Mill   Woolley   East Youlstone   Dinworthy   Gnome Reserve ★   West Putford   Haytown
Morwenstow   Eastcott   16   Colscott
Higher Sharpnose Point   West Youlstone   Bradworthy   Bulkworthy   Stibb Cross
South West Coast Path   Shop   A39   Kimworthy   Abbots Bickington   A388
Woodford   Tamar Lakes   Sutcombe   Newton St Petrock
Lower Sharpnose Point   Kilkhampton   ◆7   Alfardisworthy   Venngreen   Milton Damerel
Steeple Point   Stibb   Sutcombemill   River
Thurdon   Soldon   Thornbury   Shebbear
Sandy Mouth   B3254   Soldon Cross   Holsworthy Beacon   Woodacott   Bradford   Priesta
Northcott Mouth   Dunsdon   Brendon   Lashbrook
Maer   Poughill   Bush   Hersham   Lana   Chilsworthy   Cookbury
Castle Bude   1643   Grimscott   Kingford   Anvil Corner   Cookbury Wick   Holemoo
Flexbury   Stratton   Launcells   Pancrasweek   A3072   Chilla
Bude   Launcells Cross   10
Bude Bay   Lynstone   Red Post
Upton   Marhamchurch   Buttsbear Cross   Derri   Derriton   Holsworthy   Hollacombe   Brandis Corner
Helebridge   Whimble   Headon
Widemouth Bay   Bridgerule   Pyworthy   Chasty

A B C D E F G H

0 1 2 3 4 5 miles
0 1 2 3 4 5 6 7 8 kilometres

Congresbury · Littleton · Hawkfield · Belluton · Publow · Compton Dando · St Loe · Whiteway · Prior Park · Claverton · Monkton Combe

East Rolstone · Brinsea · Redhill · Regil · Chew Magna · Stanton Drew · Pensford · Stanton Prior · Englishcombe · Combe Down · Bradford-on-Avon

Wrington · Stock · Lye Cross · Cowslip Green · Butcombe · Chew Stoke · Stanton Wick · Chelwood · Hunstrete · Wilmington · Inglesbatch · Priston · South Stoke · Limpley Stoke · Winsley

Sandford · Blackmoor · Langford · Churchill · Lower Langford · Rickford · West Town · Nempnett Thrubwell · Bishop Sutton · Marksbury · Farmborough · Tunley · Dunkerton · Combe Hay · Freshford · Westwood

A368 · Upper Langford · Burrington · Rowberrow · Blagdon · Chew Valley Lake · Stowey · Clutton · Clutton Hill · Timsbury · Meadgate · Camerton · Carlingcott · Hinton Charterhouse · Wellow

Star · Sidcot · Shipham · Ubley · West Harptree · Temple Cloud · High Littleton · Withy Mills · White Ox Mead · Twinhoe · Hinton Charterhouse

Winscombe · Compton Bishop · Charterhouse · Cheddar Gorge & Caves · Compton Martin · Hallatrow · Paulton · Peasedown St John · Shoscombe · Norton St Philip · Farleigh Hungerford

Cross · Axbridge · Cheddar · Cheddar Complex · Ridge · East Harptree · Coley · Farrington Gurney · Midsomer Norton · Radstock · Writhlington · Faulkland · Woolverton · Tellisford

Weare · Hythe · Draycott · Priddy · Green Down · Chewton Mendip · Ston Easton · Clapton · Westfield · Charlton · Hemington · Laverton · Lullington

Wedmore · Rodney Stoke · Westbury-sub-Mendip · Green Ore · Emborough · Gurney Slade · Downside · Holcombe · Highbury · Upper Vobster · Hardington · Buckland Dinham · Oldford · Beckington

MENDIP HILLS · Ebbor Gorge · Wookey Hole · Binegar · Nettlebridge · Ashwick · Oakhill · Stoke St Michael · Leigh upon Mendip · Vobster · Little Green · Berkley

Mudgley · Bleadney · Yarley · Coxley Wick · Wells · Croscombe · Shepton Mallet · Doulting · East Cranmore · Whatley · Chantry · Lower Whatley · Nunney · Frome

Glastonbury · Street · Butleigh · Baltonsborough · Pylle · Evercreech · Bruton · Wincanton · Gillingham

Somerton · Langport · Charlton Adam · Castle Cary · Galhampton · Shepton Montague · Bayford · Stoke Trister

Martock · Ilchester · Yeovilton · Sparkford · South Cadbury · Compton Pauncefoot · Horsington · Templecombe

Crewkerne · Yeovil · Sherborne · Milborne Port · Henstridge · Stalbridge · Sturminster Newton

Montacute · Odcombe · Preston Plucknett · Bradford Abbas · North Wootton · Stourton Caundle · Lydlinch

Misterton · South Perrott · Halstock · Yetminster · Leigh · Pulham · Fifehead Neville · Okeford Fitzpaine

Drimpton · Chedington · Corscombe · Melbury Osmond · Hermitage · Middlemarsh · Buckland Newton · Mappowder · Woolland

Broadwindsor · Benville · Uphall · Holywell · Minterne Magna · Alton Pancras · Winterborne Houghton

A303 · A37 · A359 · A371 · A303 · A30

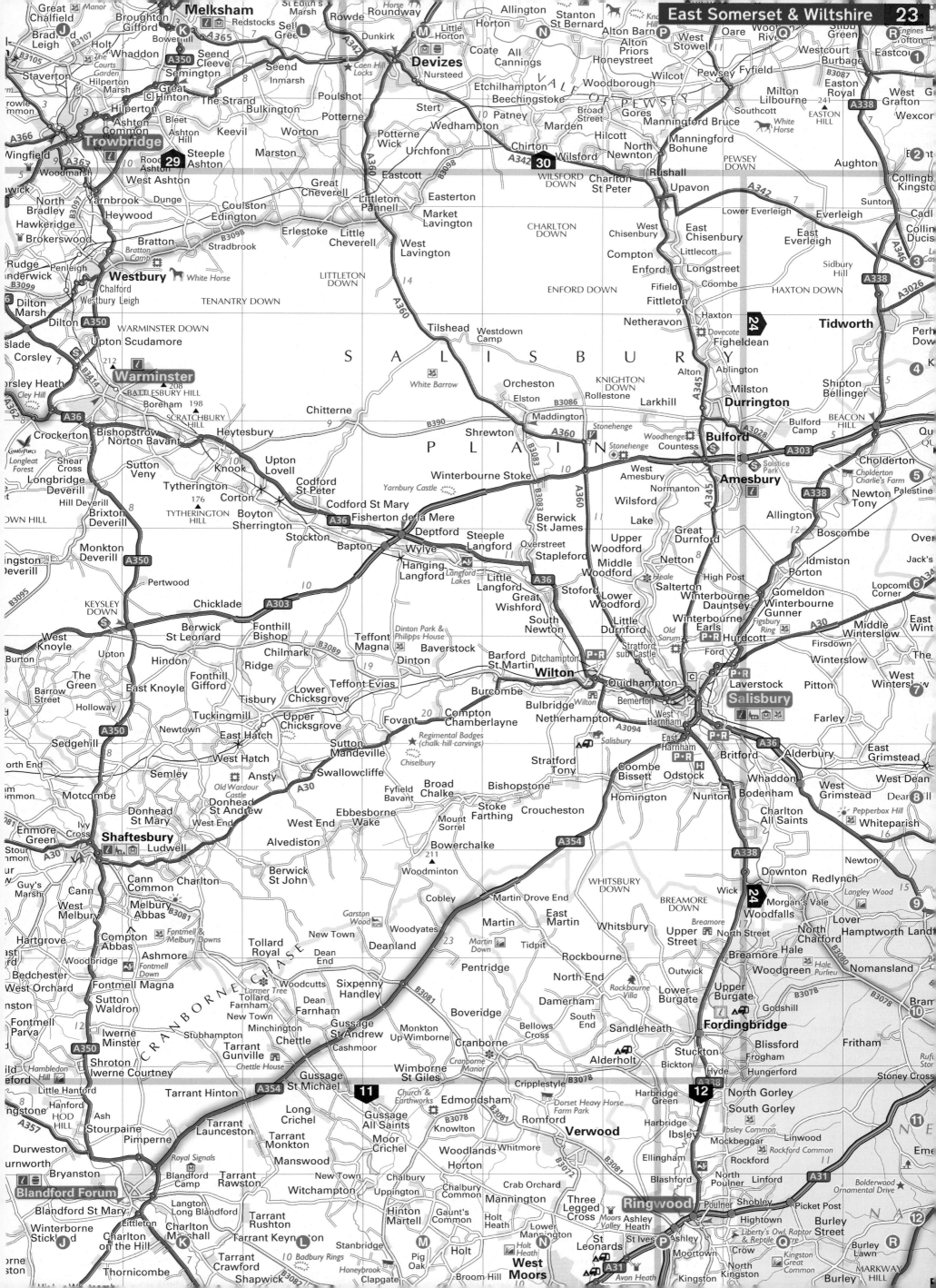

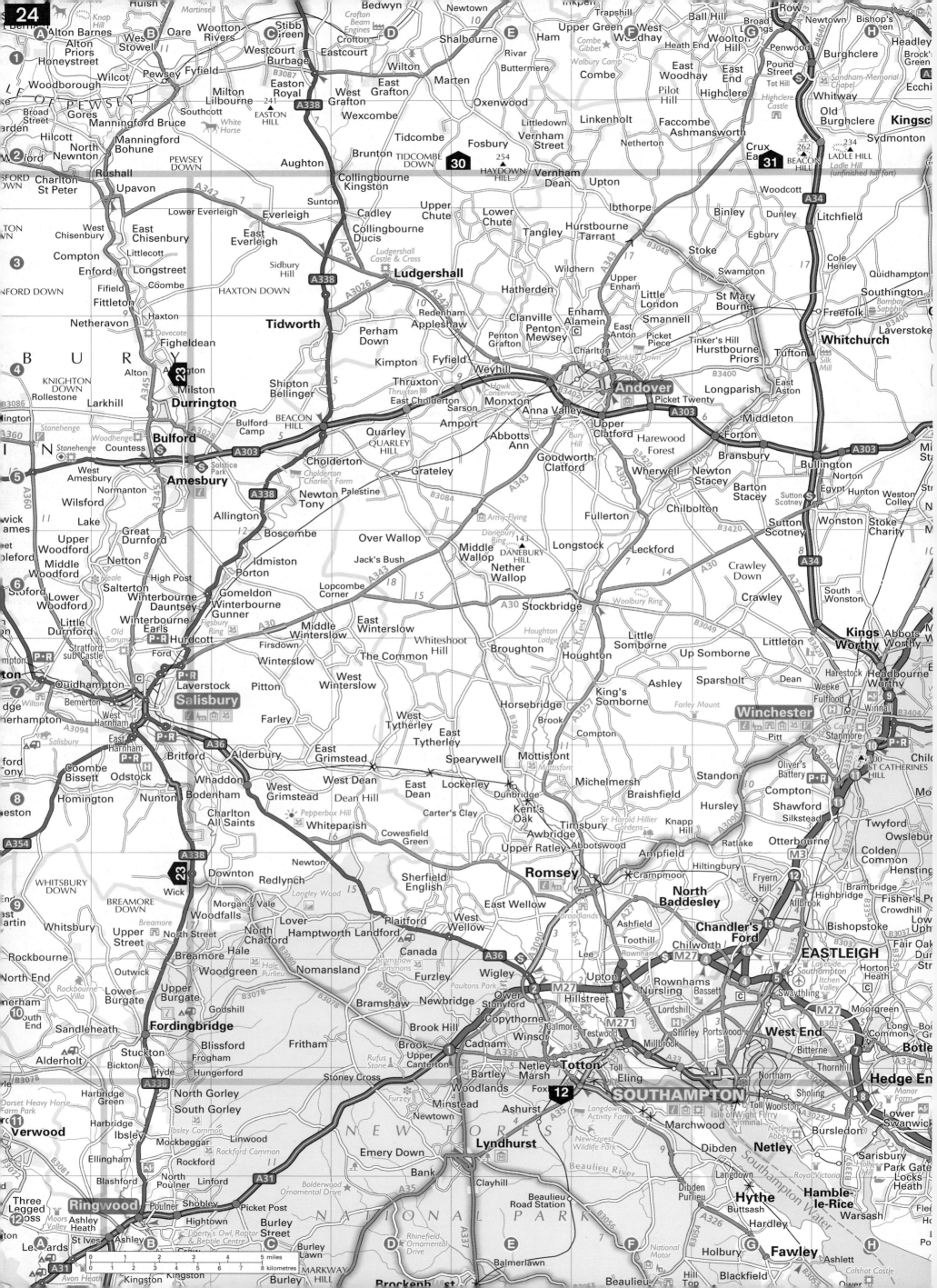

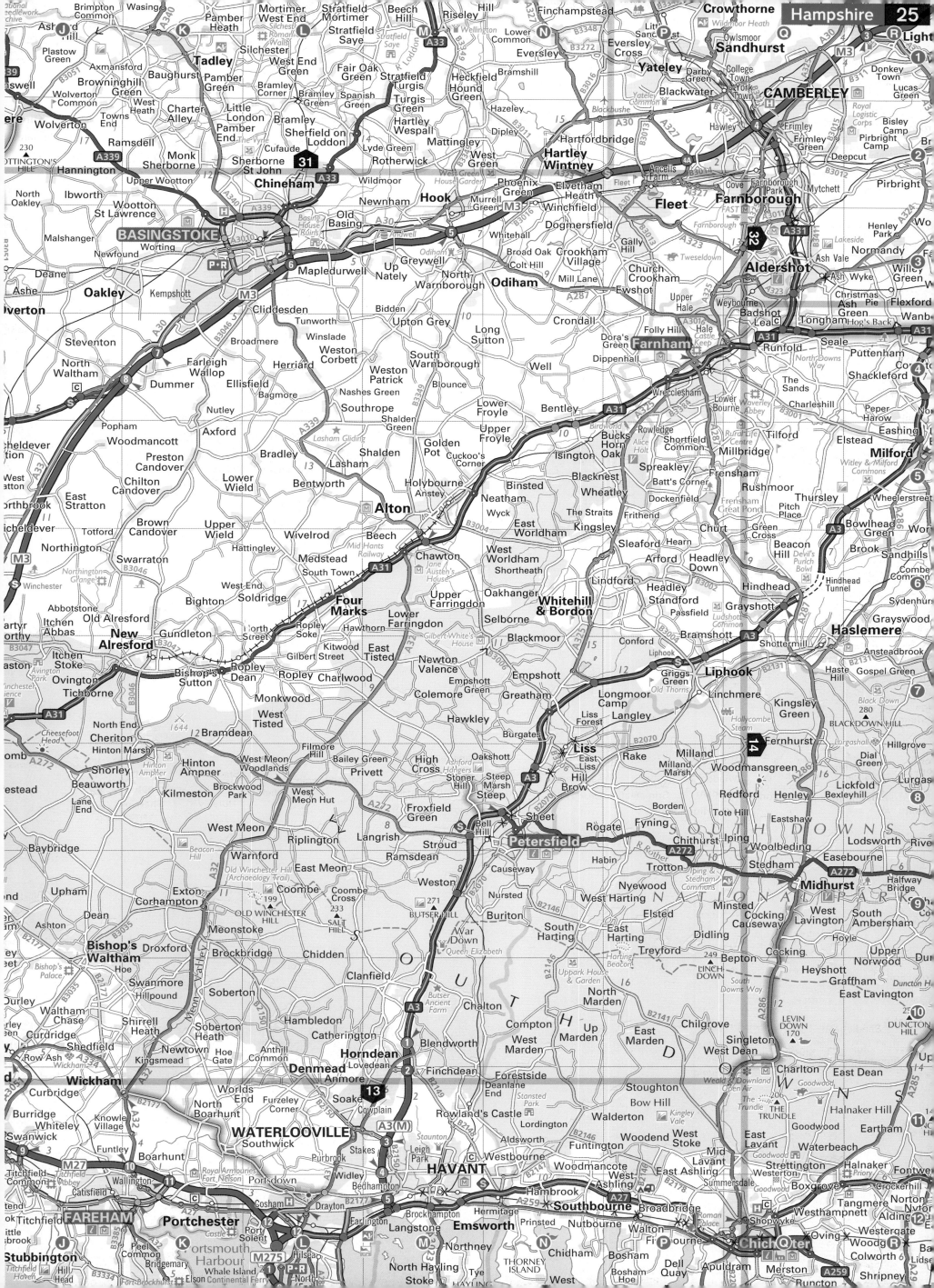

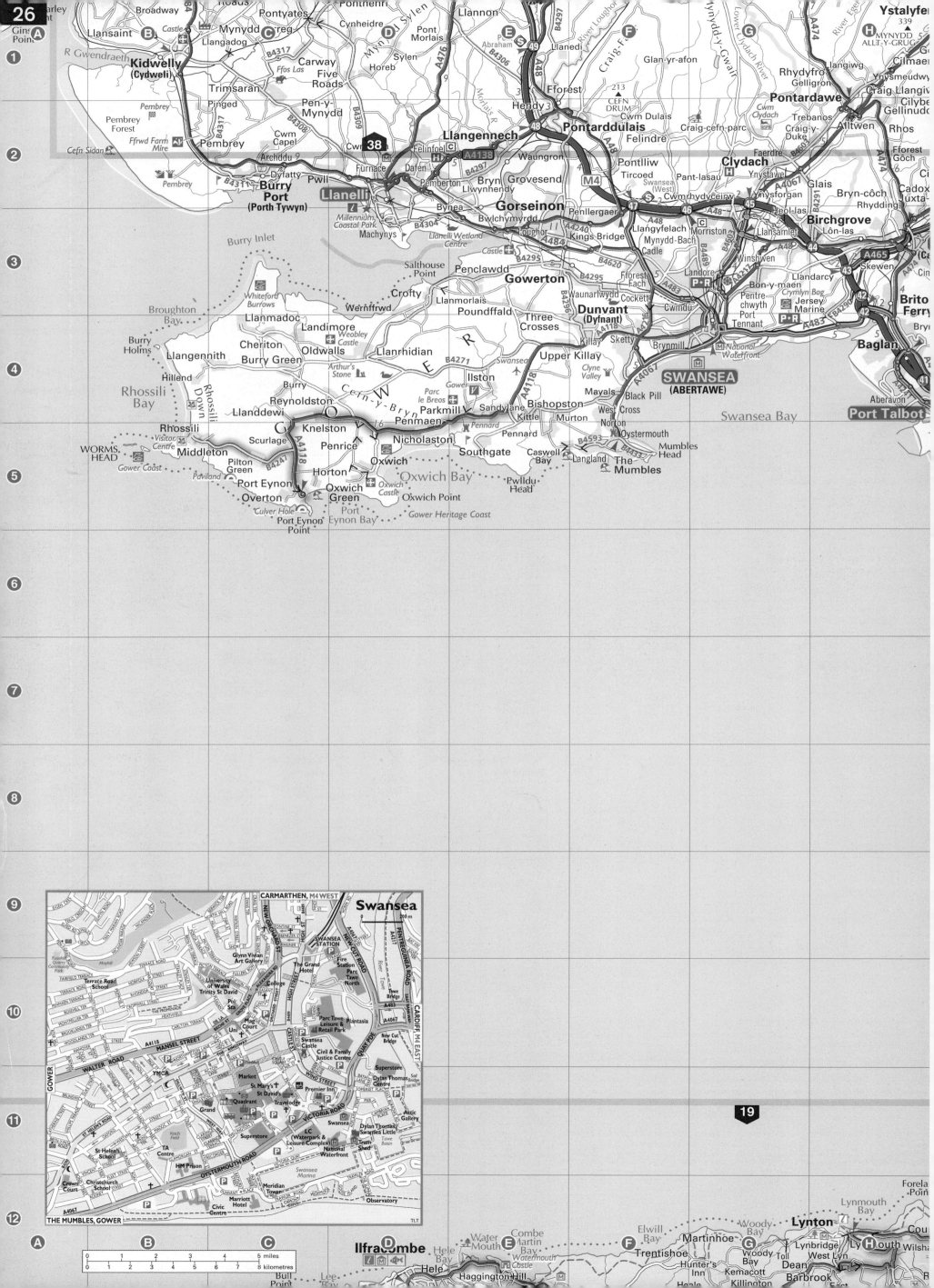

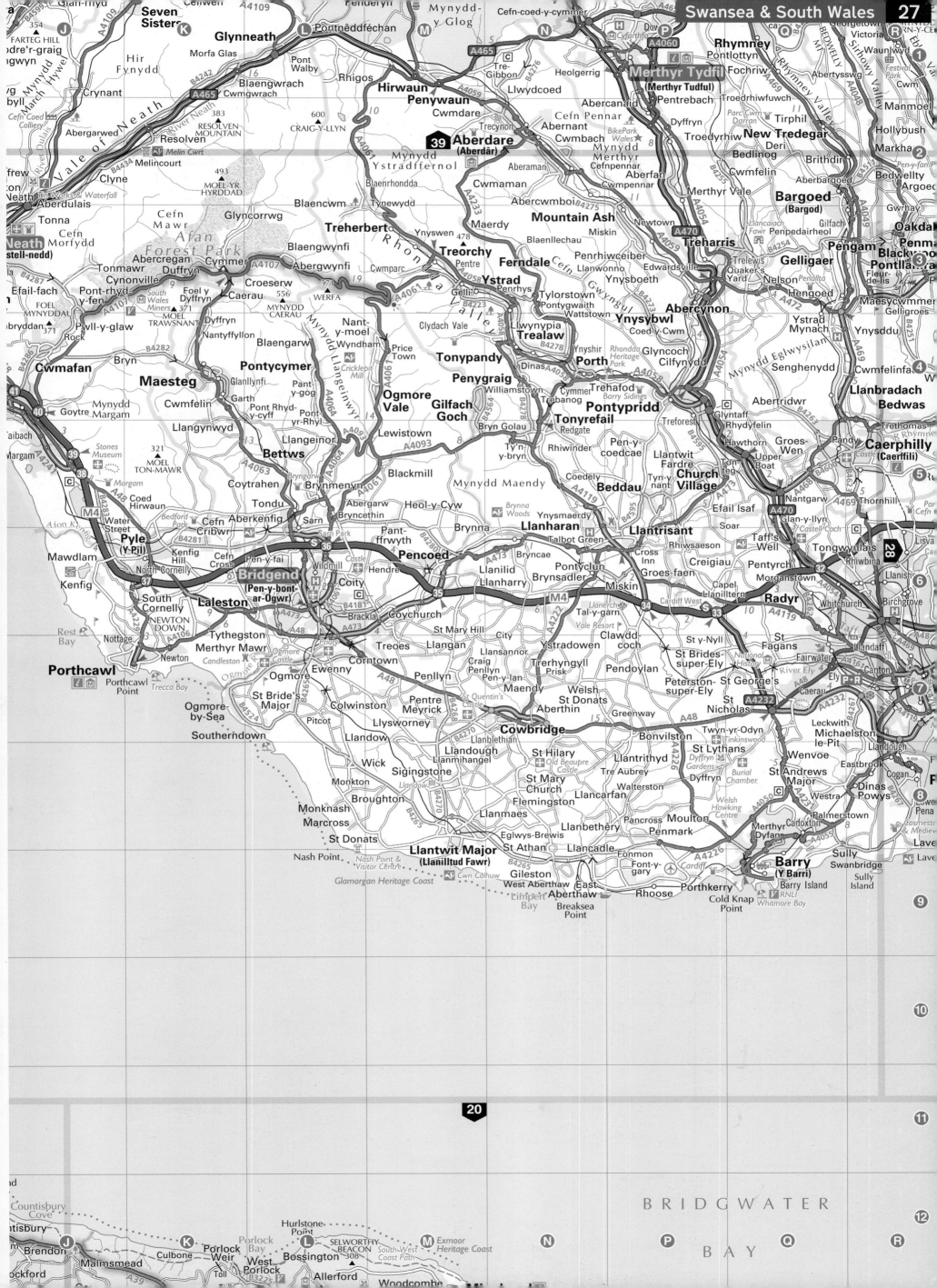

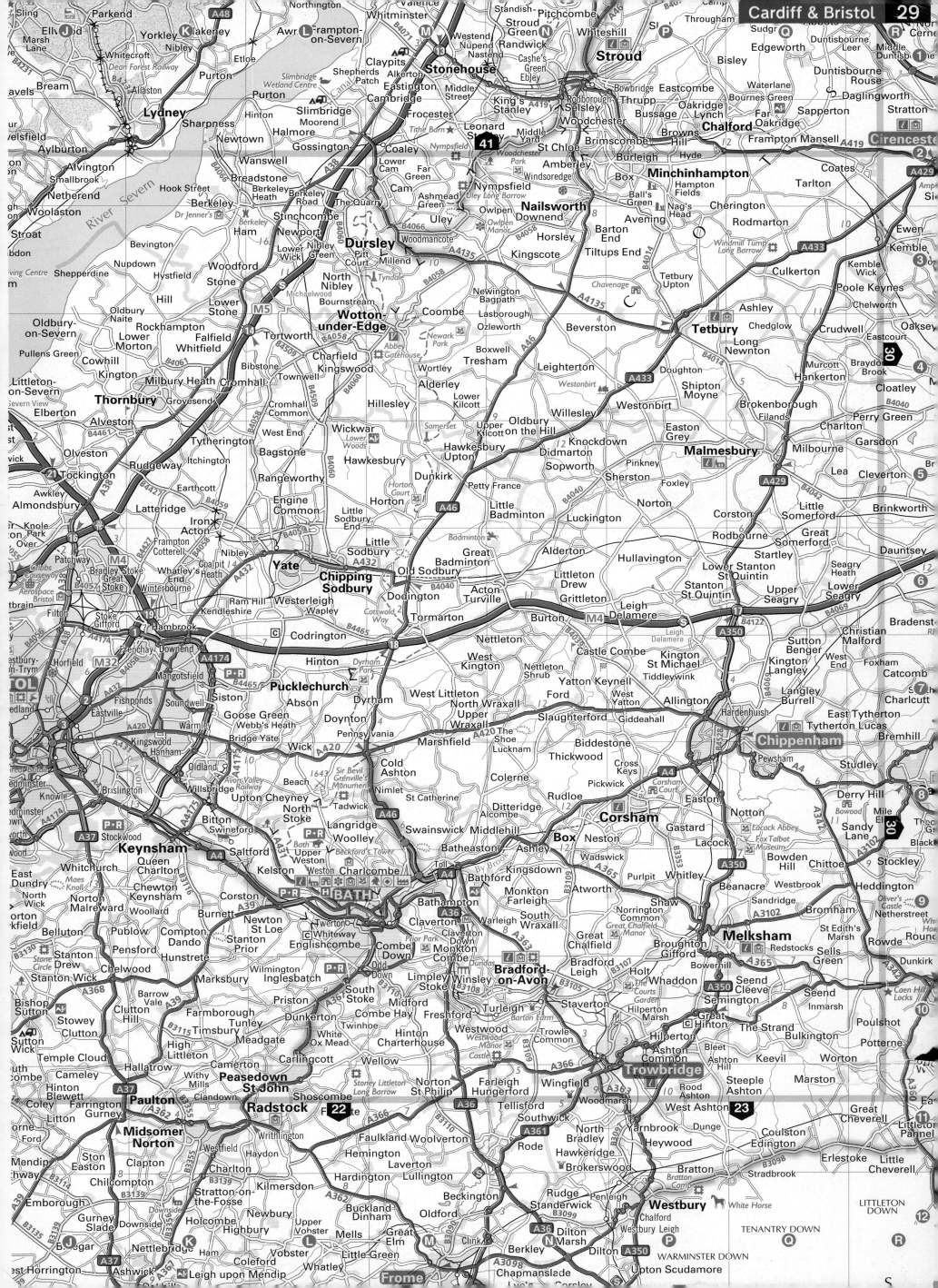

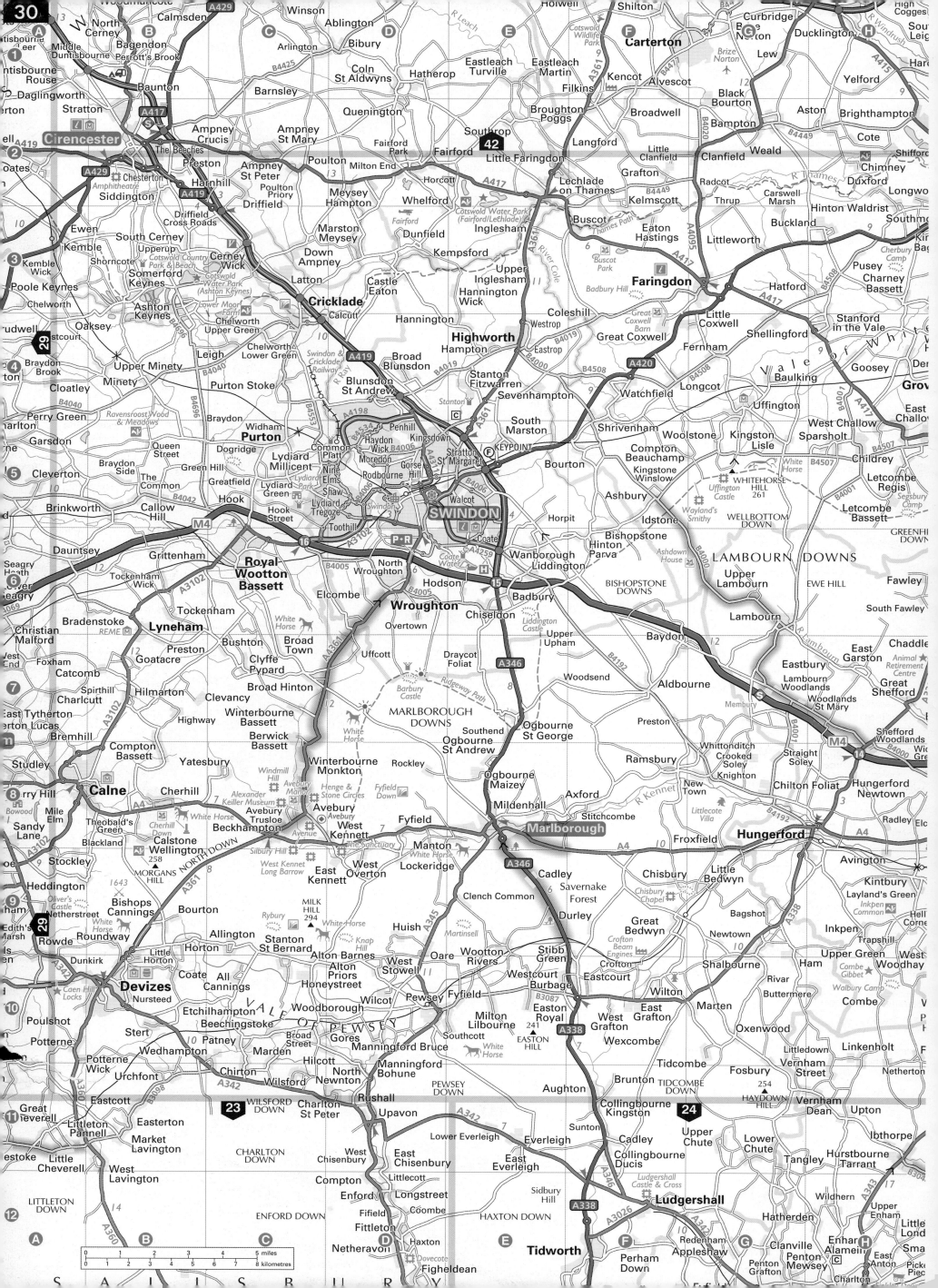

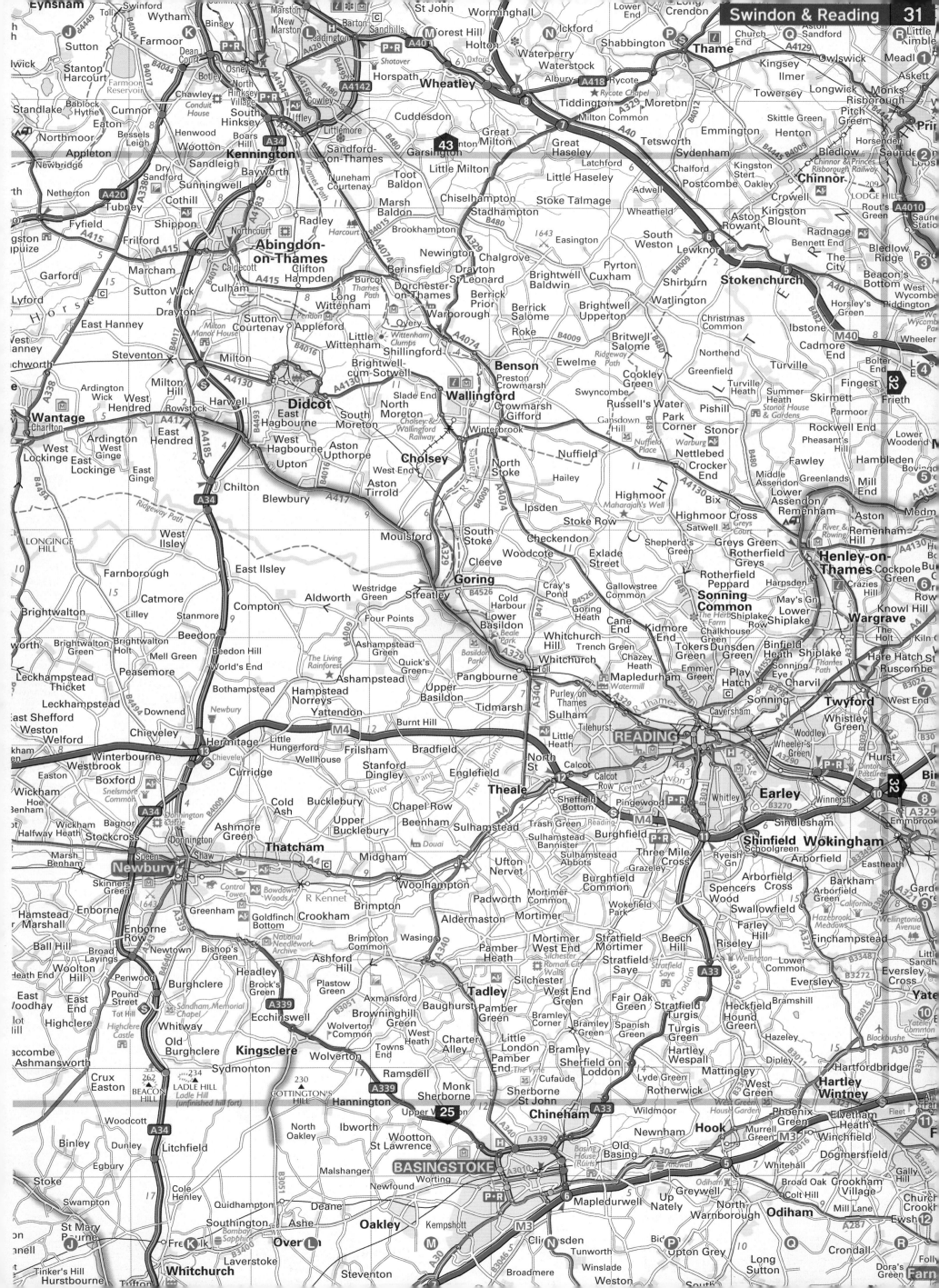

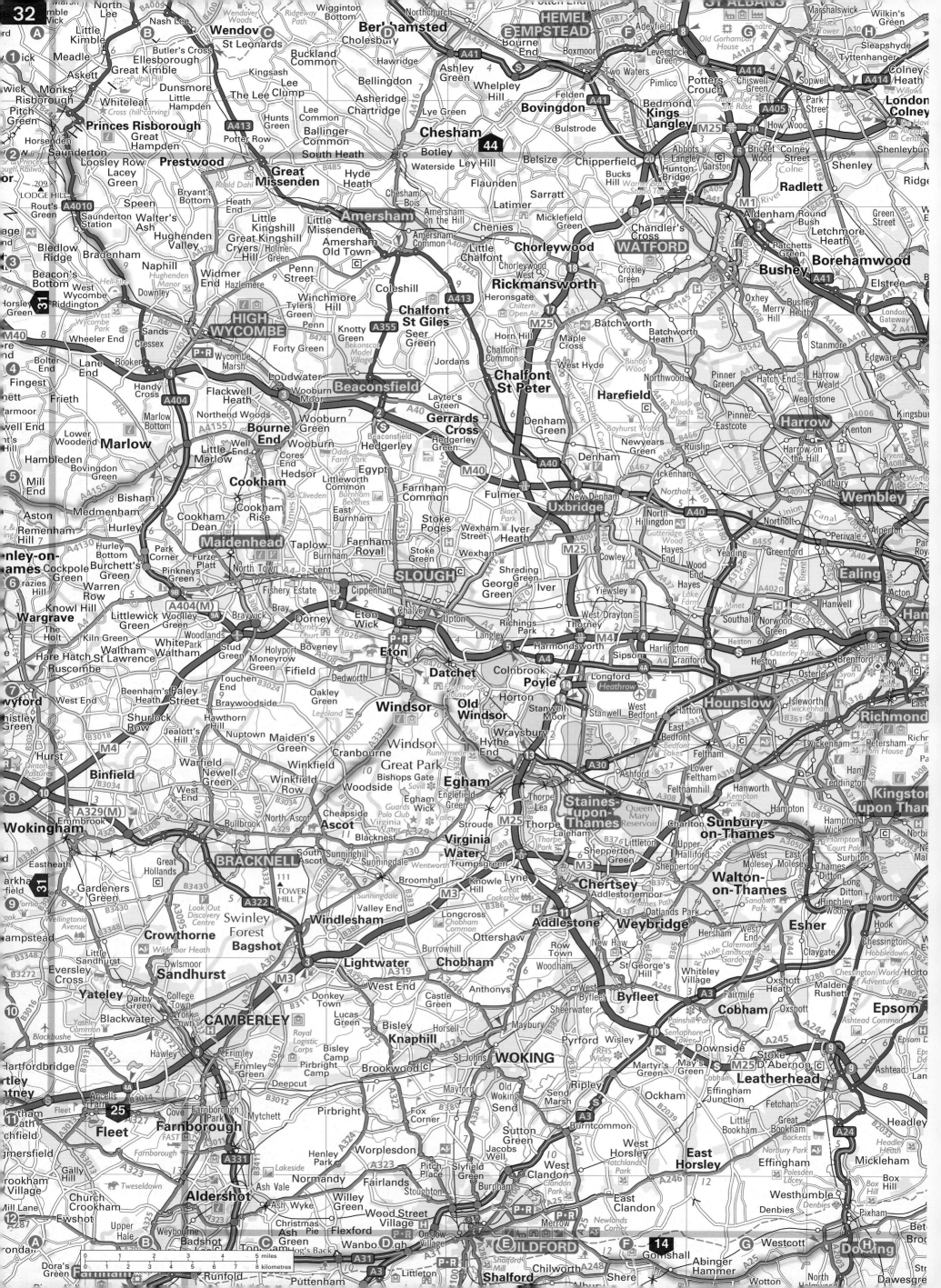

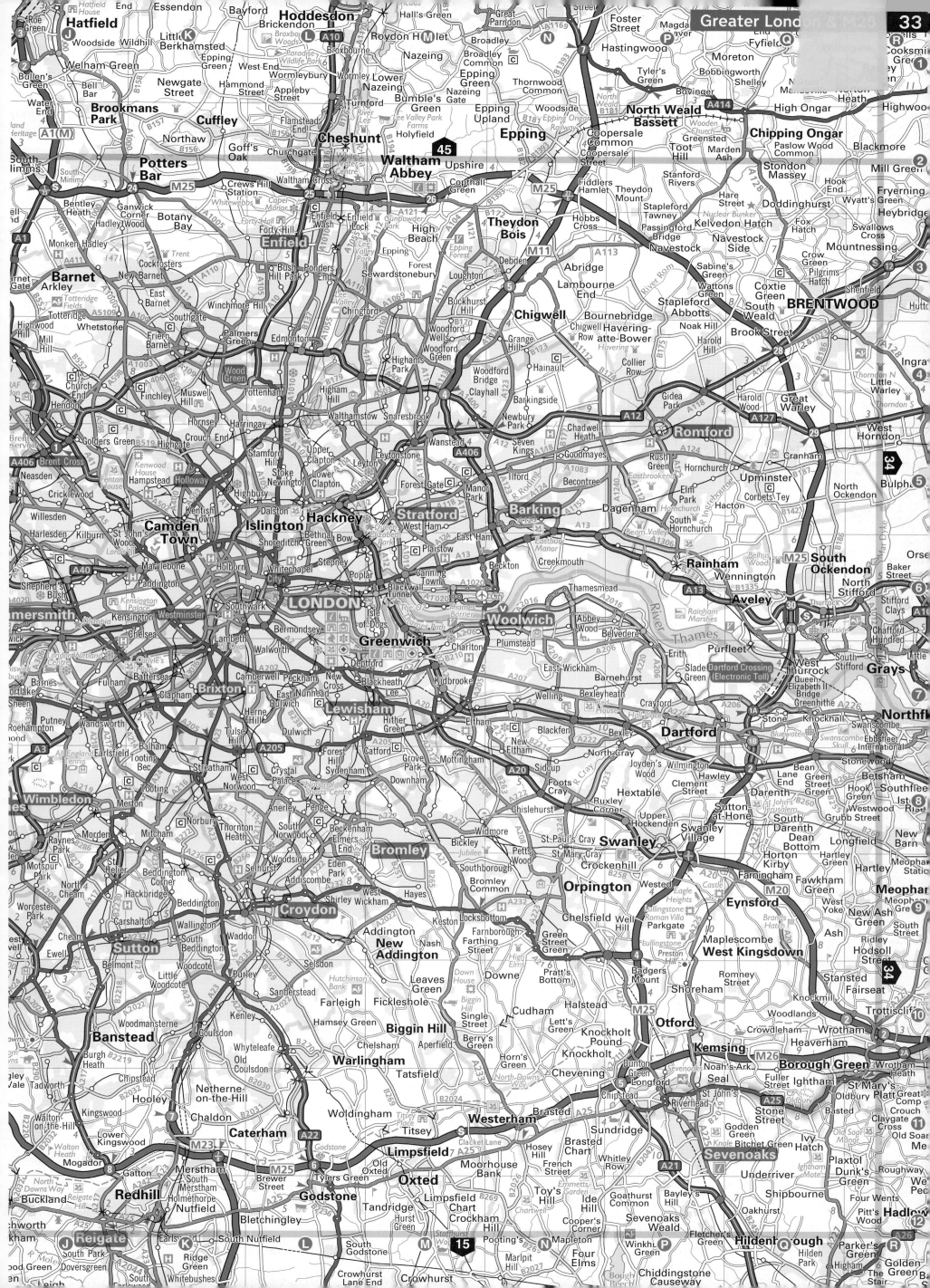

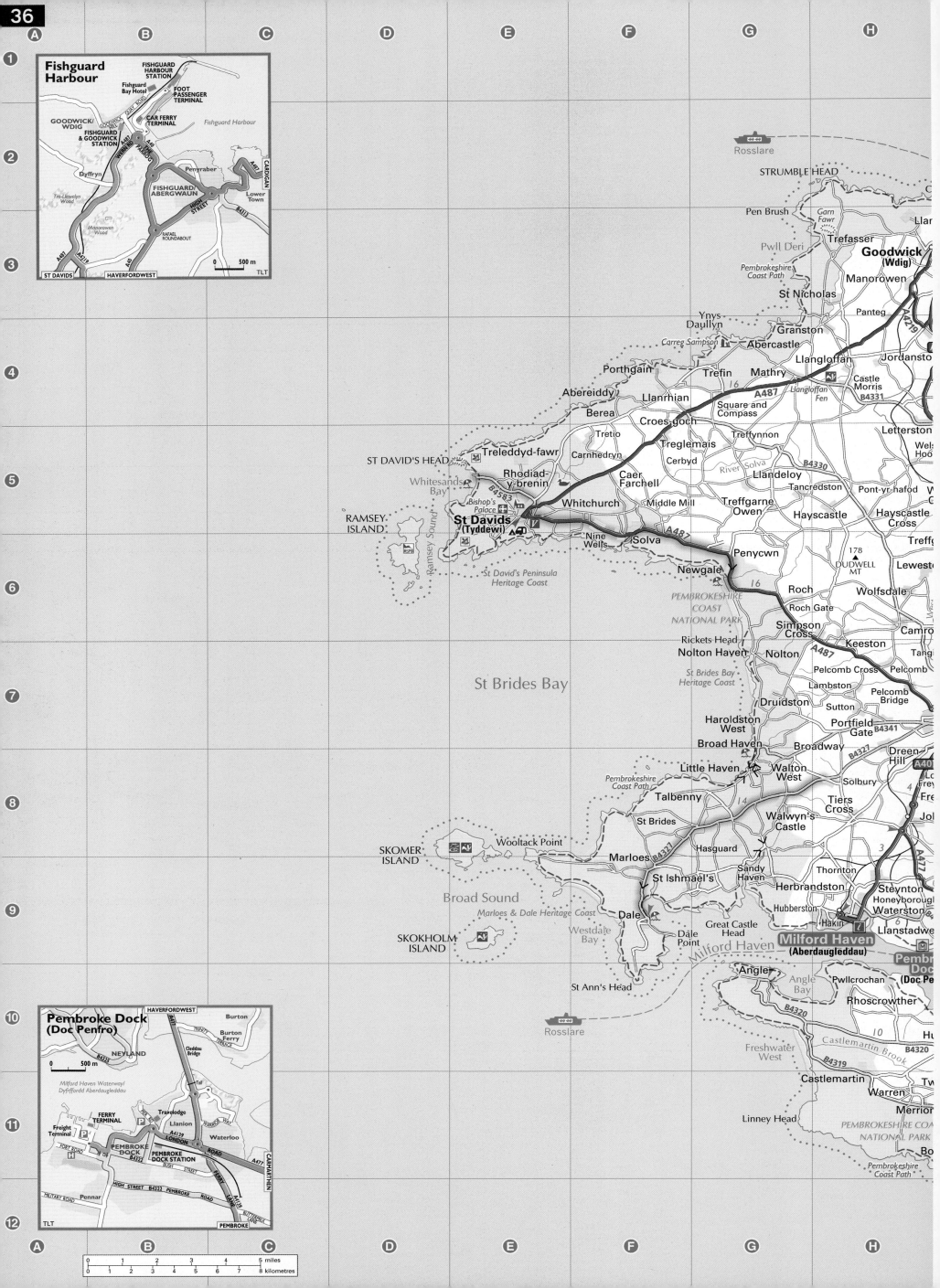

Fishguard Harbour

GOODWICK/WDIG
FISHGUARD & GOODWICK STATION
FISHGUARD HARBOUR STATION
Fishguard Bay Hotel
FOOT PASSENGER TERMINAL
CAR FERRY TERMINAL
Fishguard Harbour
Penyraber
Dyffryn
Tre-Llewelyn Wood
Manorowen Wood
FISHGUARD/ABERGWAUN
HIGH STREET
Lower Town
RAFAEL ROUNDABOUT
ST DAVIDS
HAVERFORDWEST
CARDIGAN
500 m
TLT

Rosslare
STRUMBLE HEAD
Pen Brush
Garn Fawr
Pwll Deri
Trefasser
Goodwick (Wdig)
Pembrokeshire Coast Path
Manorowen
St Nicholas
Panteg
Ynys Daullyn
Granston
Llangloffan
Jordansto
Carreg Sampson
Abercastle
Porthgain
Trefin
Mathry
Castle Morris
Llangloffan Fen
Llar
Abereiddy
Llanrhian
Square and Compass
Letterston
Wels Hoo
Berea
Croes-goch
Treffynnon
B4330
Tretio
Treglemais
Cerbyd
Llandeloy
River Solva
St DAVID'S HEAD
Treleddyd-fawr
Carnhedryn
Caer Farchell
Tancredston
Pont-yr-hafod
Whitesands Bay
Rhodiad-y-brenin
Treffgarne Owen
Hayscastle
Hayscastle Cross
Bishop's Palace
Whitchurch
Middle Mill
RAMSEY ISLAND
St Davids (Tyddewi)
Treff
Ramsey Sound
Nine Wells
Solva
Penycwn
178
Leweste
St David's Peninsula Heritage Coast
Newgale
DUDWELL MT
16
Roch
Wolfsdale
PEMBROKESHIRE COAST NATIONAL PARK
Roch Gate
Simpson Cross
Keeston
Camro
Rickets Head
Nolton Haven
Nolton
A487
Pelcomb Cross
Pelcomb
St Brides Bay
St Brides Bay Heritage Coast
Lambston
Pelcomb Bridge
St Brides Bay
Haroldston West
Sutton
Portfield Gate
B4341
Broad Haven
Broadway
Dreen Hill
B4327
A40
Little Haven
Walton West
Solbury
Lo Frey
Talbenny
Tiers Cross
Fre
Pembrokeshire Coast Path
St Brides
14
Walwyn's Castle
Jol
SKOMER ISLAND
Wooltack Point
Hasguard
Thornton
Marloes
B4327
Sandy Haven
Herbrandston
Steynton
St Ishmael's
Honeyborough
Waterston
A47
Broad Sound
Hubberston
6
Marloes & Dale Heritage Coast
Dale
Hakin
Llanstadwe
SKOKHOLM ISLAND
Westdale Bay
Dale Point
Great Castle Head
Milford Haven (Aberdaugleddau)
Pembr Doc
St Ann's Head
Milford Haven
Angle
Angle Bay
Pwllcrochan
(Doc Pe
Rosslare
Rhoscrowther
Freshwater West
Castlemartin Brook
B4320
10
Hu
B4319
Castlemartin
Tw
Linney Head
PEMBROKESHIRE COA NATIONAL PARK
Warren
Merrior
Pembrokeshire Coast Path
Bo

Pembroke Dock (Doc Penfro)

HAVERFORDWEST
Burton
NEYLAND
TRINITY
Burton Ferry
Burton Terrace
Cleddau Bridge
Toll
500 m
Milford Haven Waterway/ Dyfrffordd Aberdaugleddau
Travelodge
FERRY TERMINAL
Llanion
BARROW WAY
Freight Terminal
A4139 LONDON
Waterloo
PEMBROKE DOCK
B4322
PEMBROKE DOCK STATION
LONDON ROAD
A477
High Street
B4322
PEMBROKE ROAD
FERRY ROAD
A4139
Pennar
CARMARTHEN
MILITARY ROAD
TLT
PEMBROKE

A B C D E F G H

0 1 2 3 4 5 miles
0 1 2 3 4 5 6 7 8 kilometres

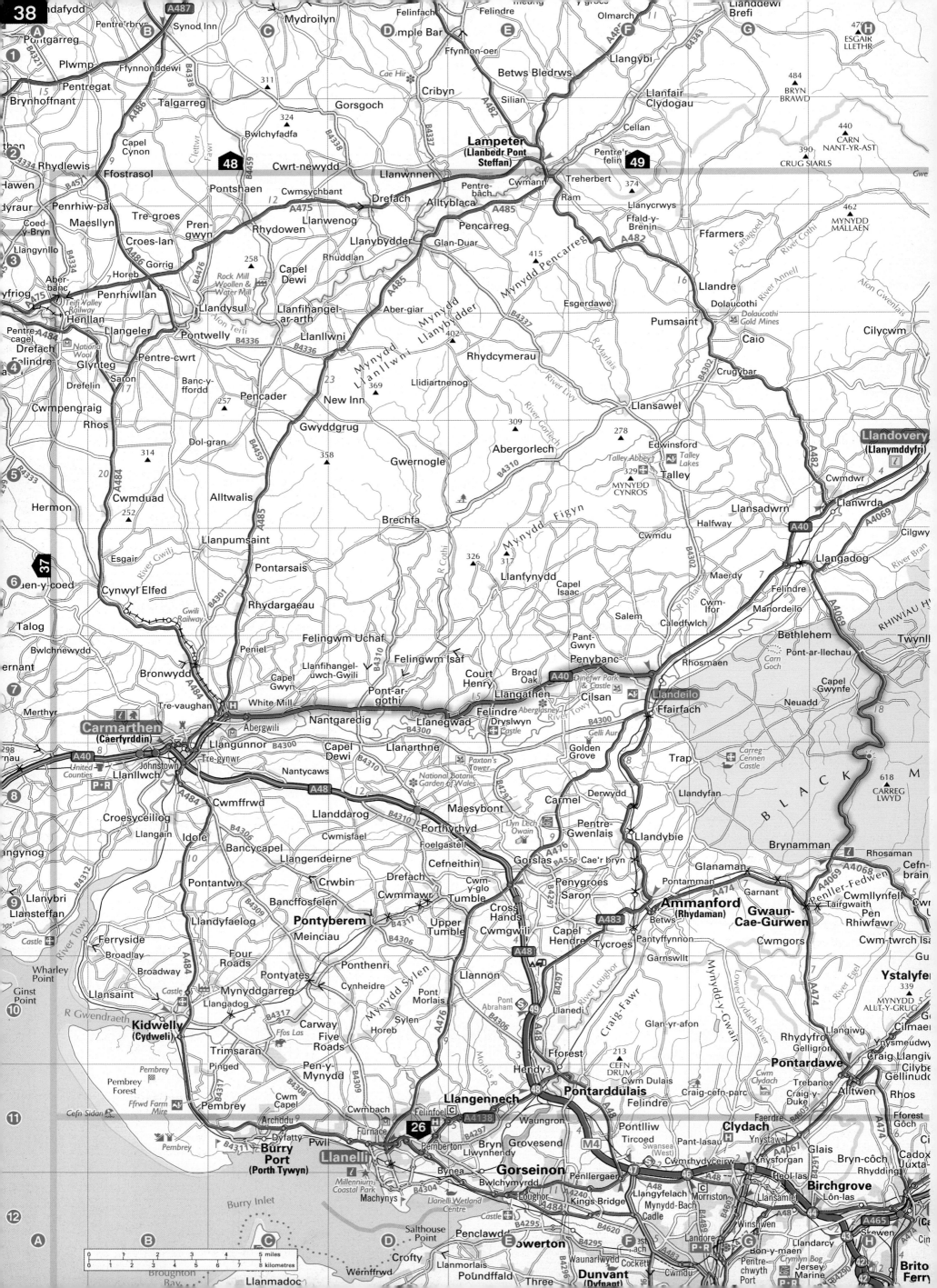

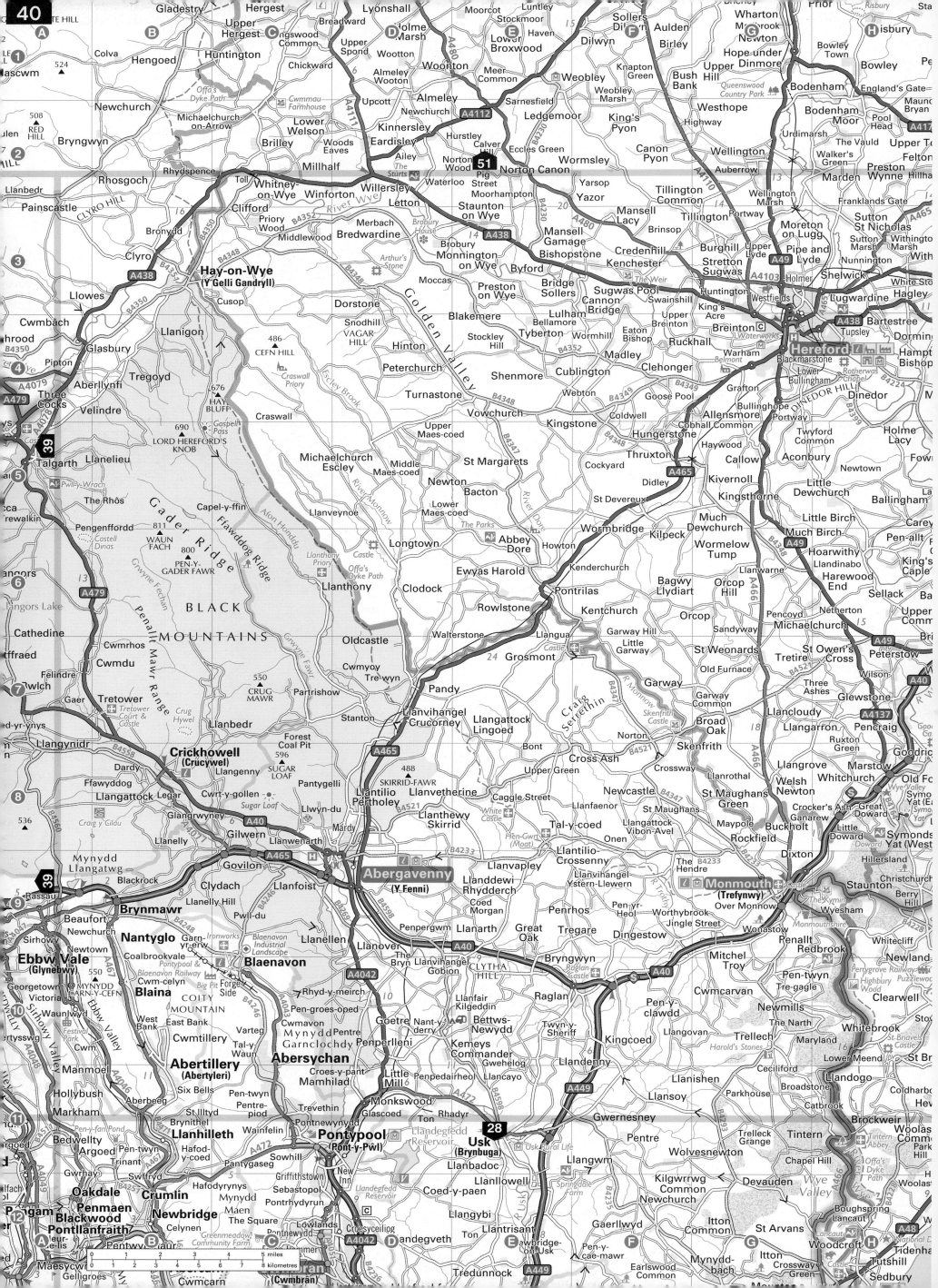

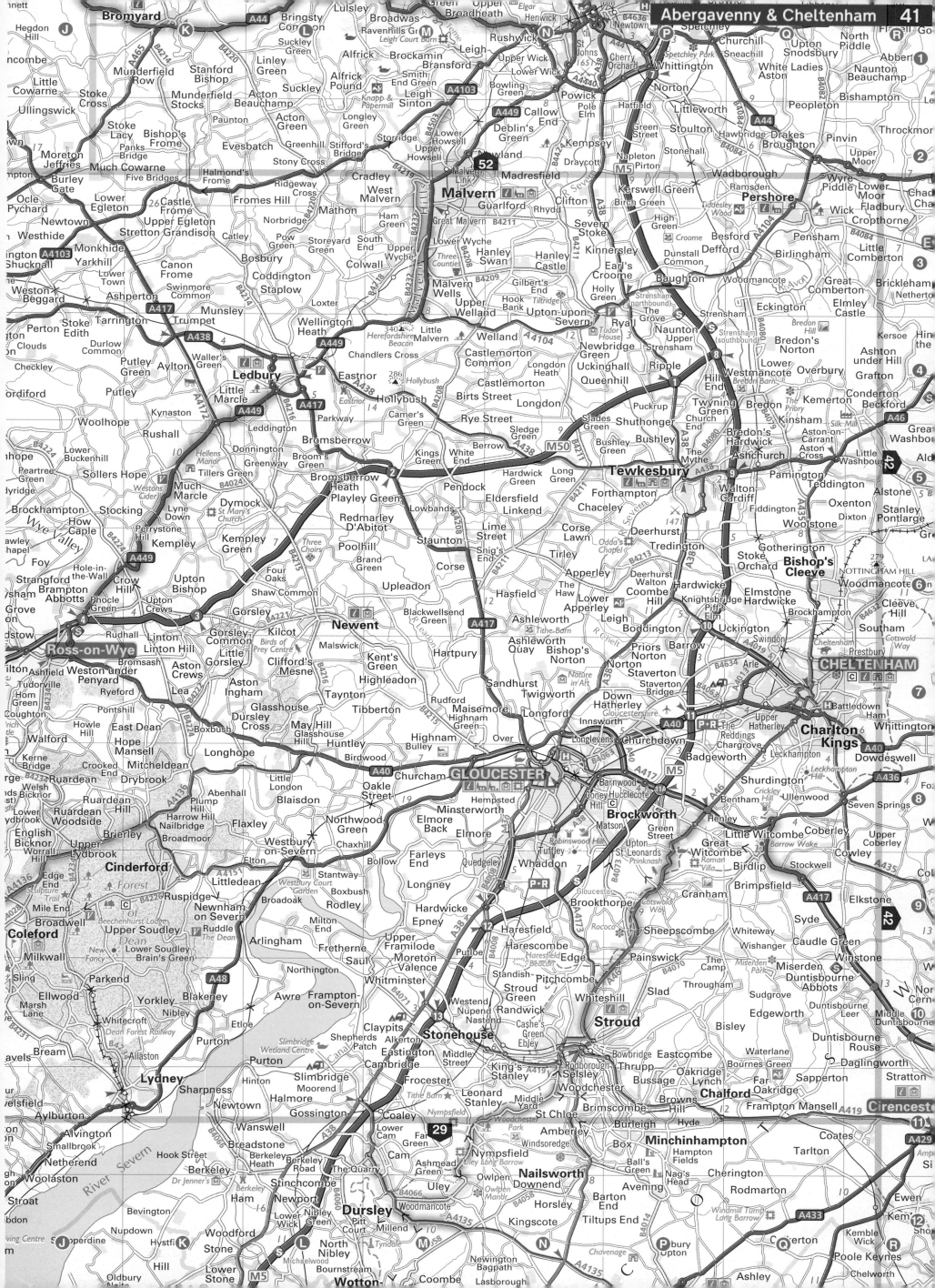

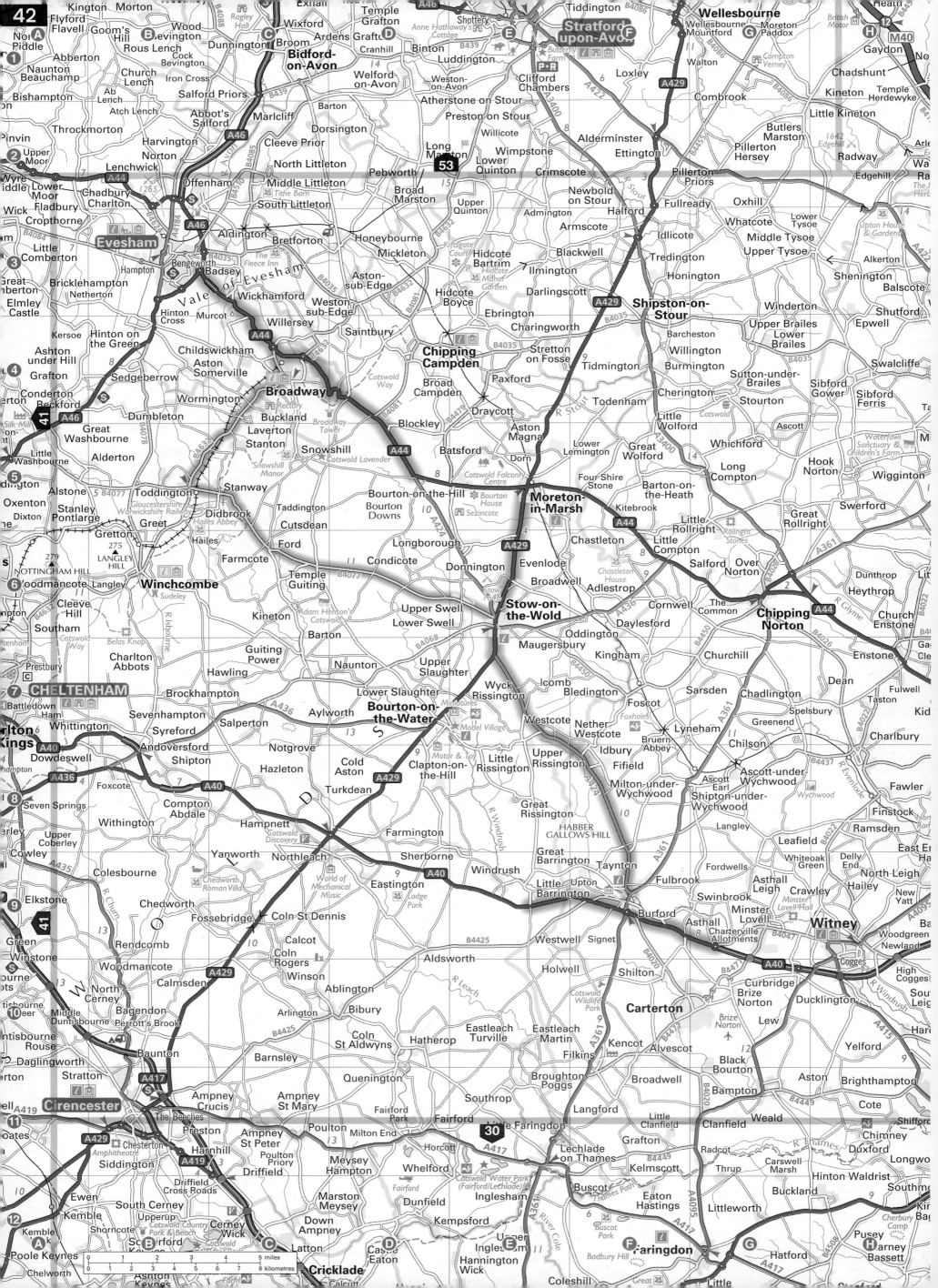

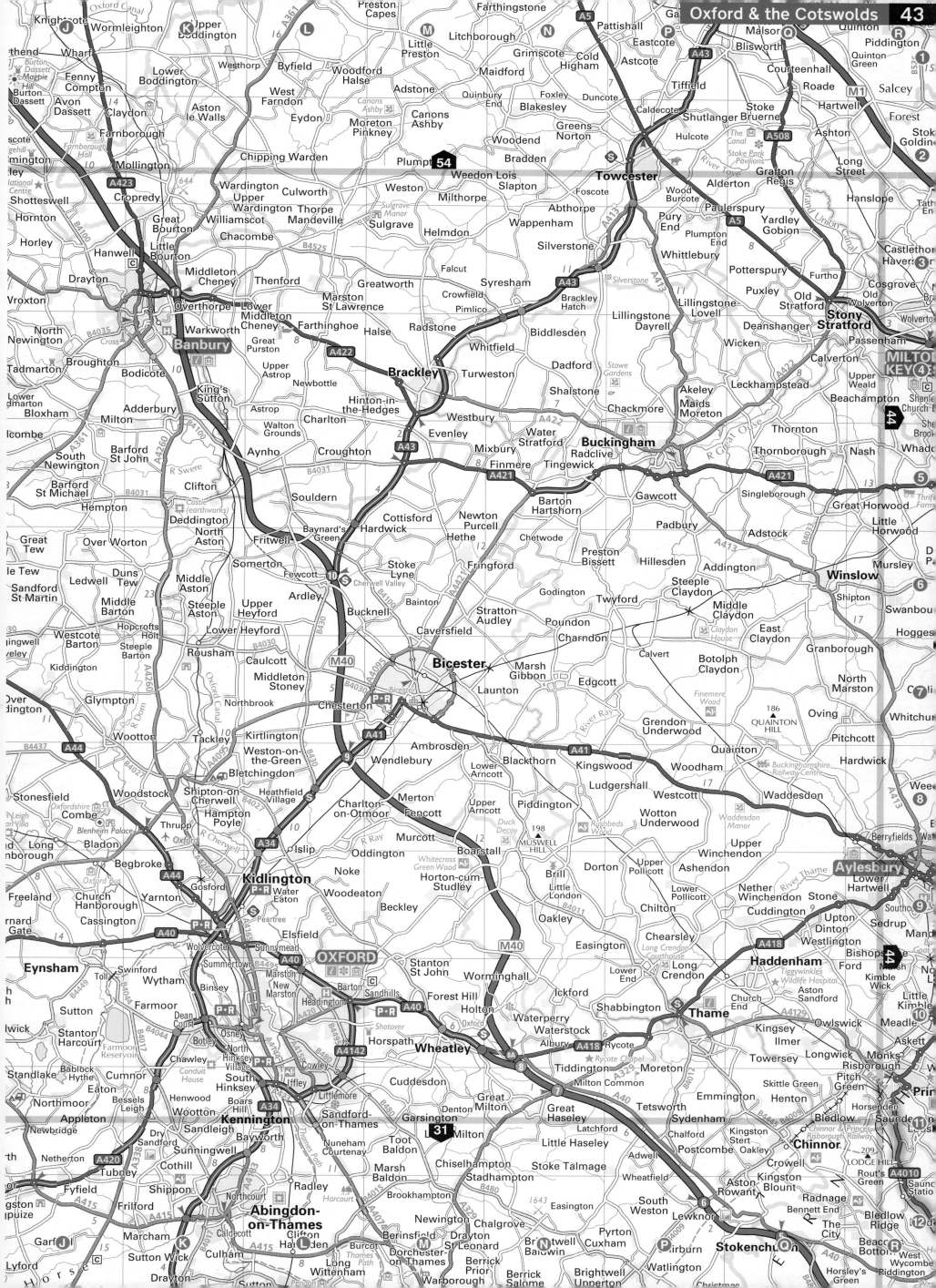

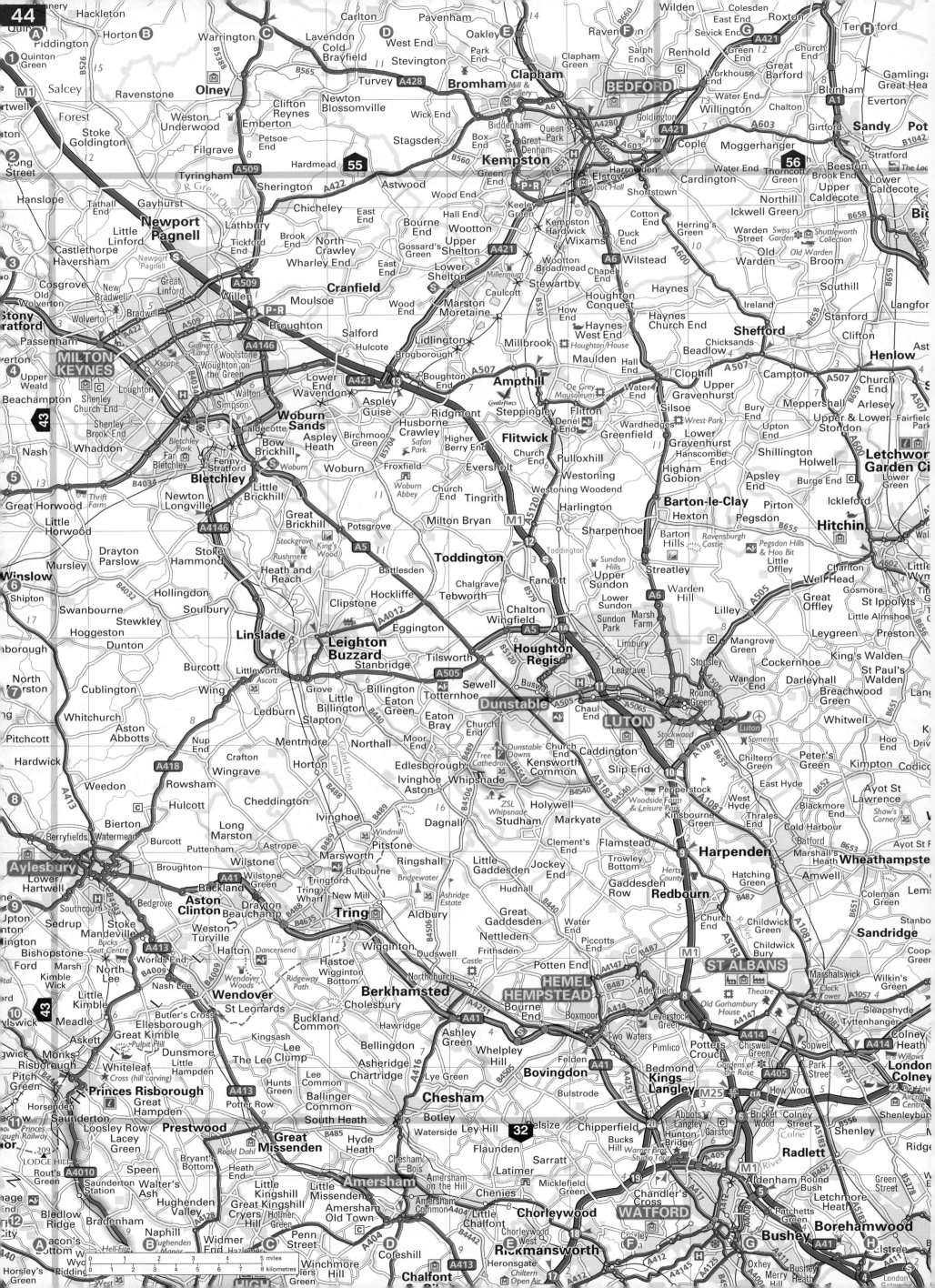

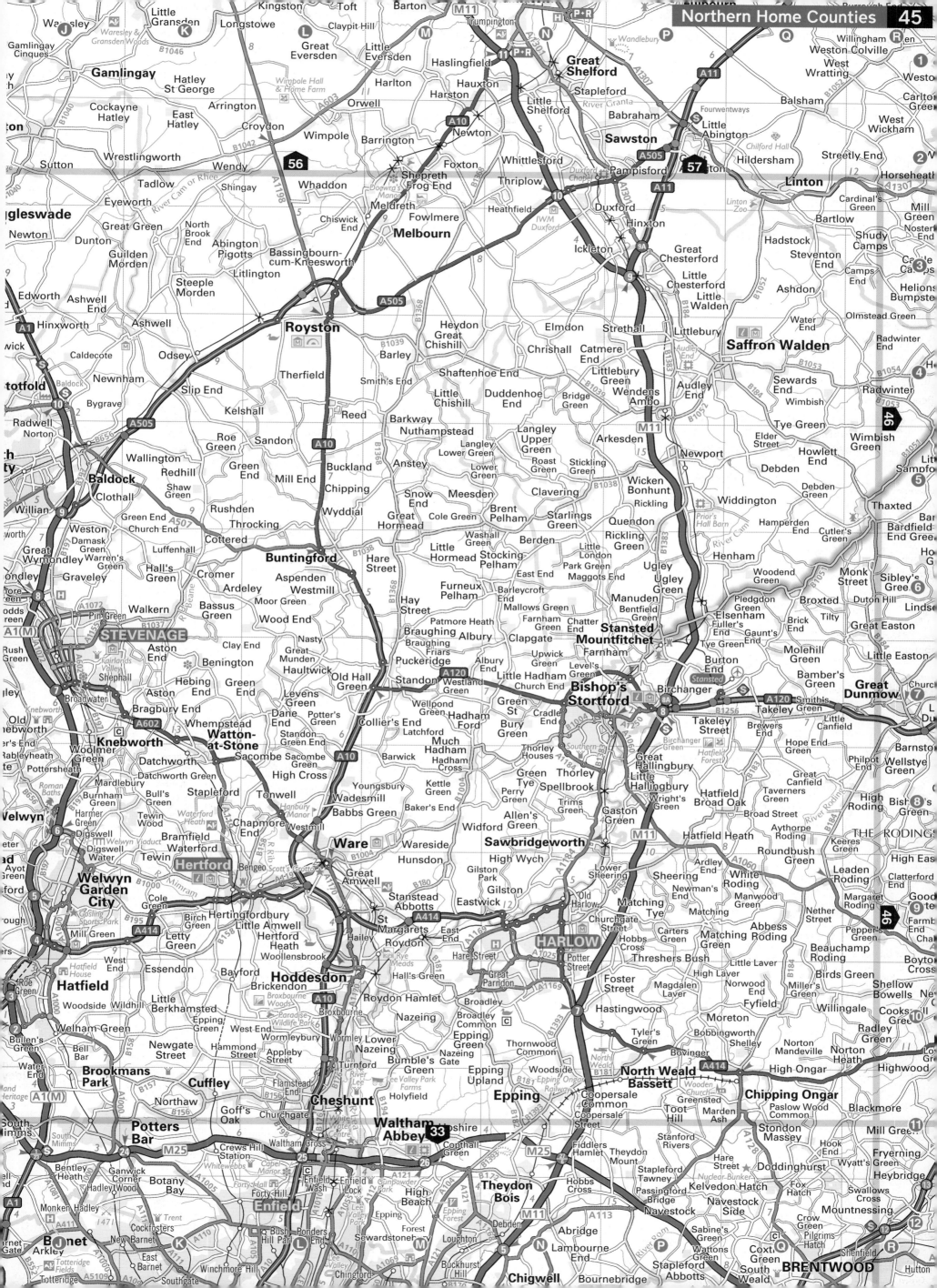

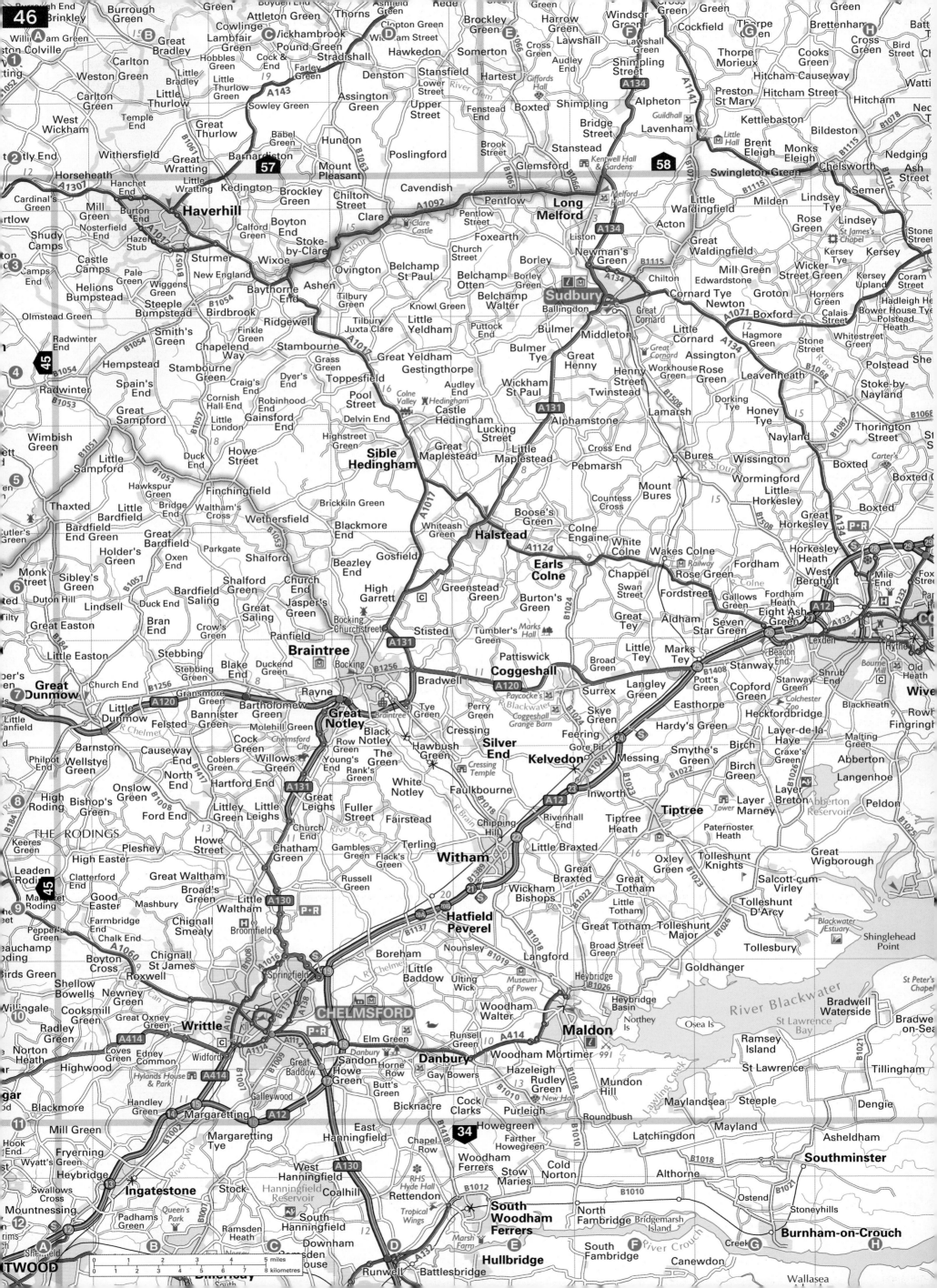

Harwich International Port

Ipswich

A B C D E F G H

Aberystwyth

0   200 m

CARDIGAN BAY

Cardigan Bay

Penglais Woods

Bandstand
St Paul Methodist
Aberystwyth North Beach
St David URC
Capel Morfa
The Morlan Centre
Ceredigion
Royal Pier
Bethel
Coastguard Station
CAB
University (Old College)
Clock Tower
Market Hall
Salvation Army
Monument
St Michael's
Aberystwyth Castle (ruins)
Castle
Eglwys y Santes Fair
Holy Trinity
St Padarn's Primary School
University (School of Art)
ABERYSTWYTH STATION
Superstores
Ystwyth Retail Park
Rheidol
Vale of Rheidol Steam Railway Station
Recreation Ground
Trefechan Bridge
Slipway
Justice Centre
Ro-fawr
Marina
Park Avenue (Aberystwyth Town FC)
Plascrug CP School
Fire Station
Police Station
TA Centre
Lifeboat Station
CARDIGAN
TLT

MACHYNLLETH, LLANGURIG
National Library of Wales

CARDIGAN BAY

Aberarth
Aberaeron
Pennant

New Quay (Ceinewydd)
Henfynyw
Foss-y-ffin
Llyswen
Mona
Llwyncelyn
A482
New
Ceredigion Heritage Coast
Maen-y-groes
Gilfachrheda
Llanina
Llanarth
Ciliau Aeron
Cwmtydu
Cross Inn
Oakford
B4339
Nanternis
B4342
Dihewyd
Ystrad Aero
Ynys-Lochtyn
Caerwedros
A487
Mydroilyn
Pendinas Lochtyn
Llwyndafydd
Pentre'rbryn
Synod Inn
Tem
Llangrannog
Pontgarreg
Plwmp
Ffynnonddewi
Cae Hir
Morfa
B4334
Ceredigion Heritage Coast
Penbryn
B4321
Pentregat
B4338
Cardigan Island
Mwnt Beach
Parcllyn
Sarnau
Brynhoffnant
Talgarreg
Gorsgoch
Cardigan Island Coastal Farm
Tresaith
15
311
Y Ferwig
Aberporth
324
Bwlchyfadfa
B4338
Gwbert on Sea
Blaenannerch
Tan-y-groes
Capel Cynon
Poppit Sands
A487
Glynarthen
Cwrt-newydd
Pembrokeshire Coast Path
Penparc
Tremain
Blaenporth
Rhydlewis
Ffostrasol
38
Llanw
Ceibwr Bay
Abbey & Coach House
St Dogmaels
Cardigan (Aberteifi)
Bettws Ifan
Hawen
ontshaen
Cwmsychbant
Drefa
Moylegrove
Bridgend
Llangoedmor
B4570
Beulah
Troedyraur
Penrhiw-pal
Tre-groes
Prengwyn
Rhydowen
Llanwenog
Monington
Pen-y-bryn
Teifi Marshes
Welsh Wildlife Centre
37
Ponthirwaun
Brongest
Coed-y-Bryn
Maesllyn
Croes-lan
A475
Llanybydde
Glanrhyd
Llantood
Bridell
Castle
Llandygwydd
Llangynllo
Gorrig
B4476
258
Capel Dewi
Rhuddlan
Pontgarreg
Cilgerran
IVY SIDE
Cwm-cou
Adpar
Llandyfriog
Aber-banc
Horeb
Rock Mill Woollen & Water Mill
Llandisul
Llanfihangel-ar-arth
Neverr
Felindre Farchog
B4582
Pengelli
Rhosi
Pen-rhiw
Abercych
Cenarth
National Coracle Centre
Newcastle Emlyn (Castell Newydd Emlyn)
Aber-arad
Pentre-cagel
Henllar
Llangeler
Teifi Valley Railway
Pontwelly
Drefach
Eglwyswrw
Pen-rher
Penrherber
Drefach
Castell Henllys
B4332
Afon Teifi
Afon Teifi
B4336
B4336

0   5 miles
0 1 2 3 4 5 6 7 8 kilometres

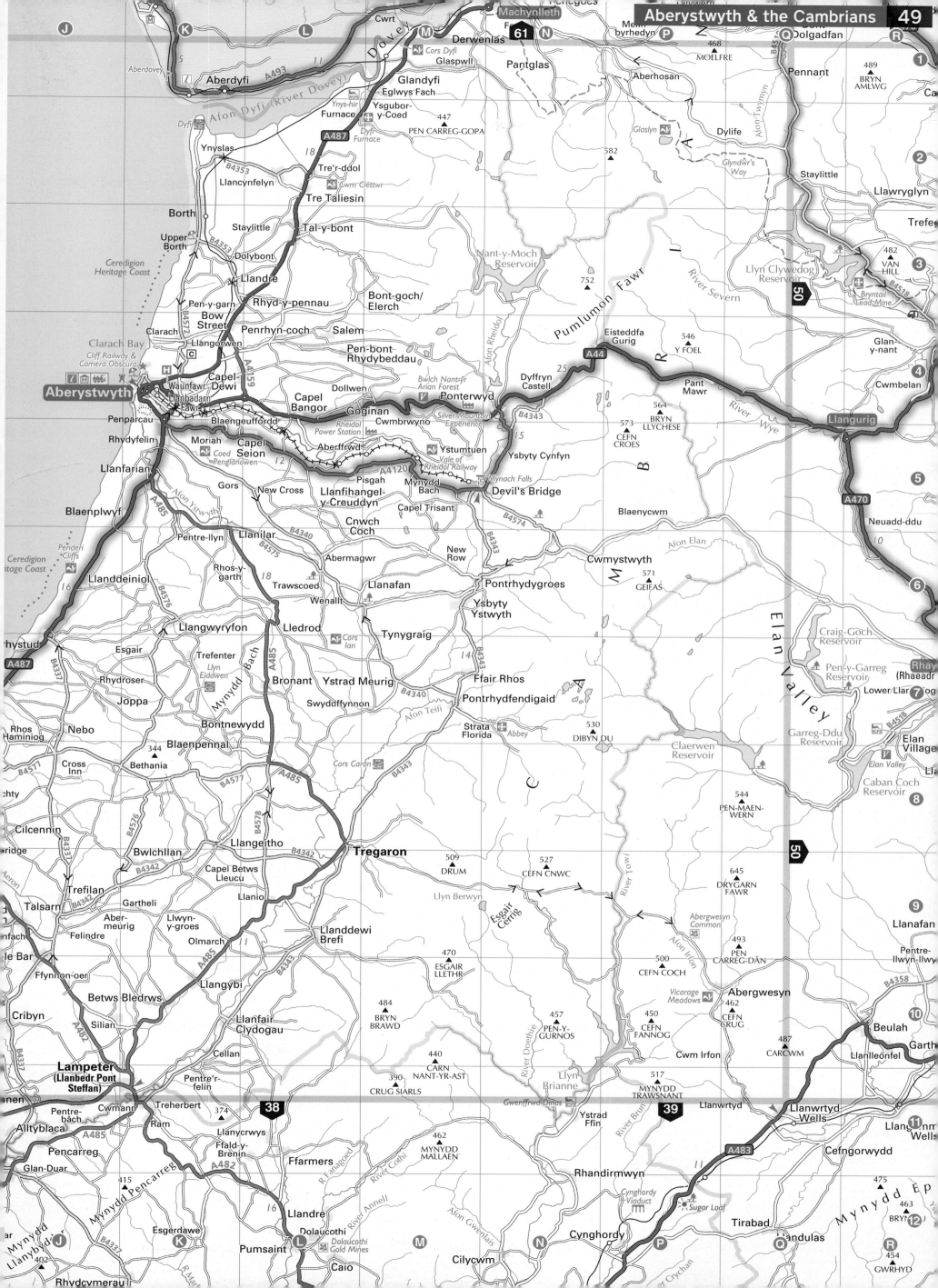

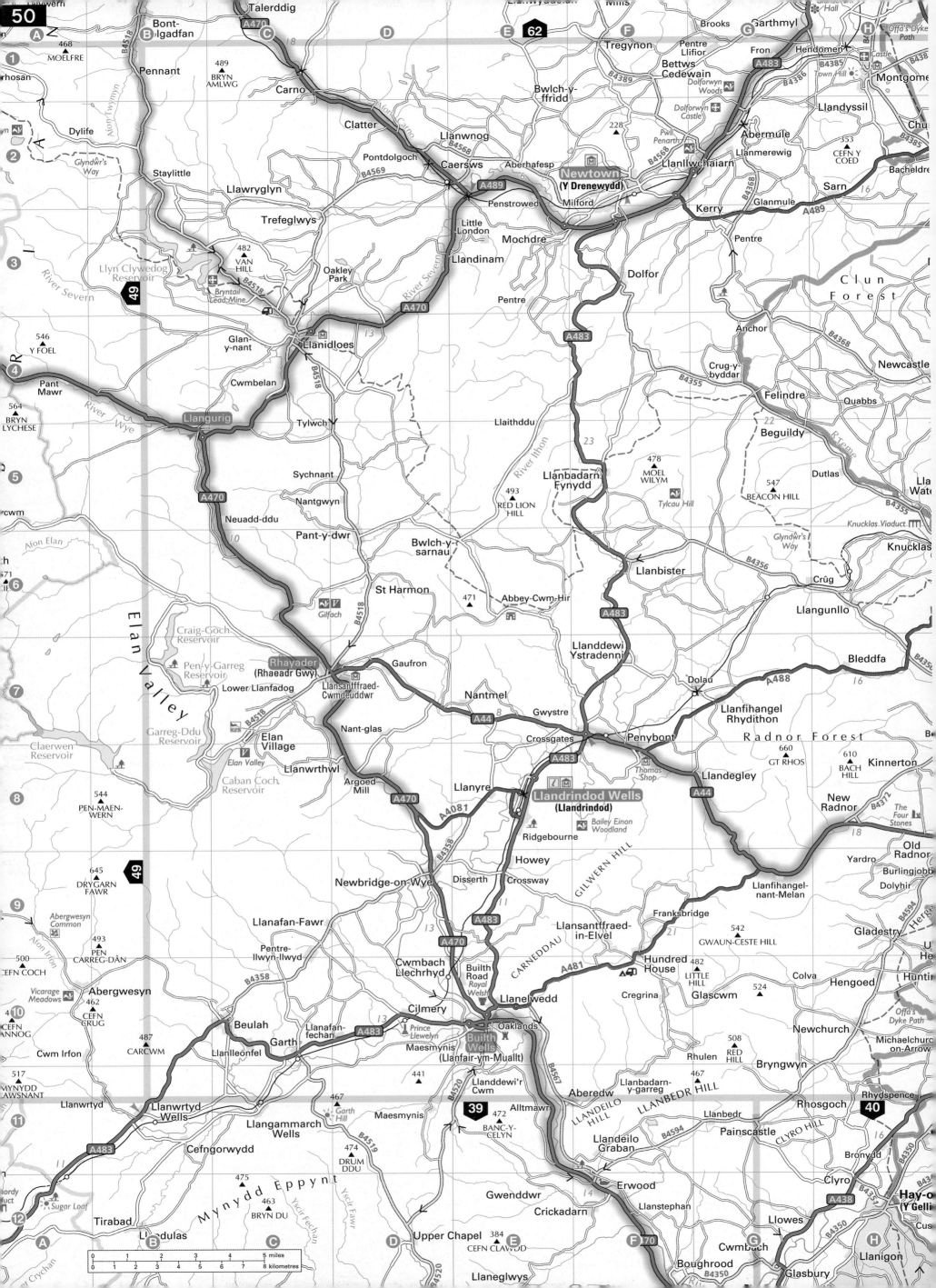

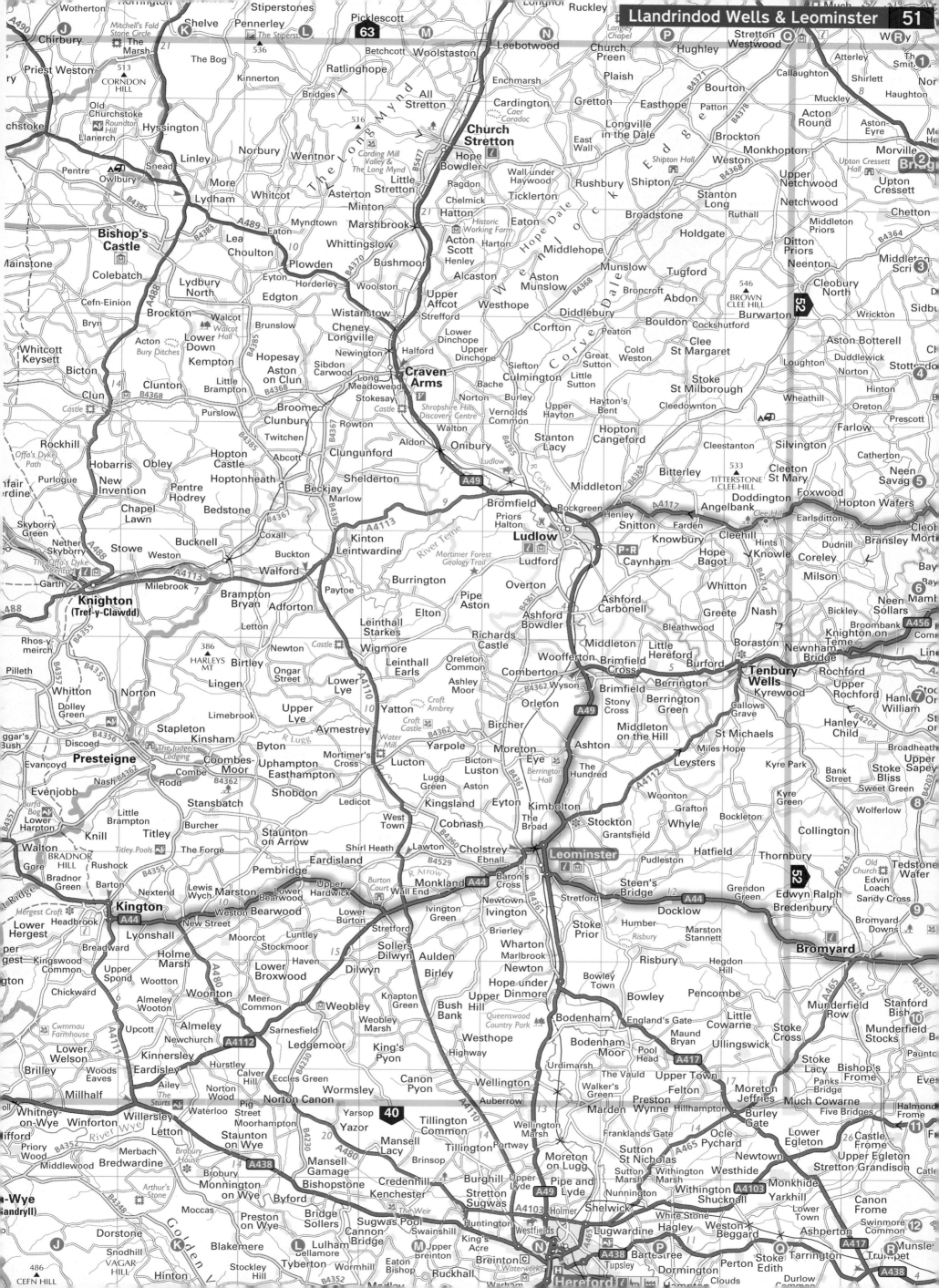

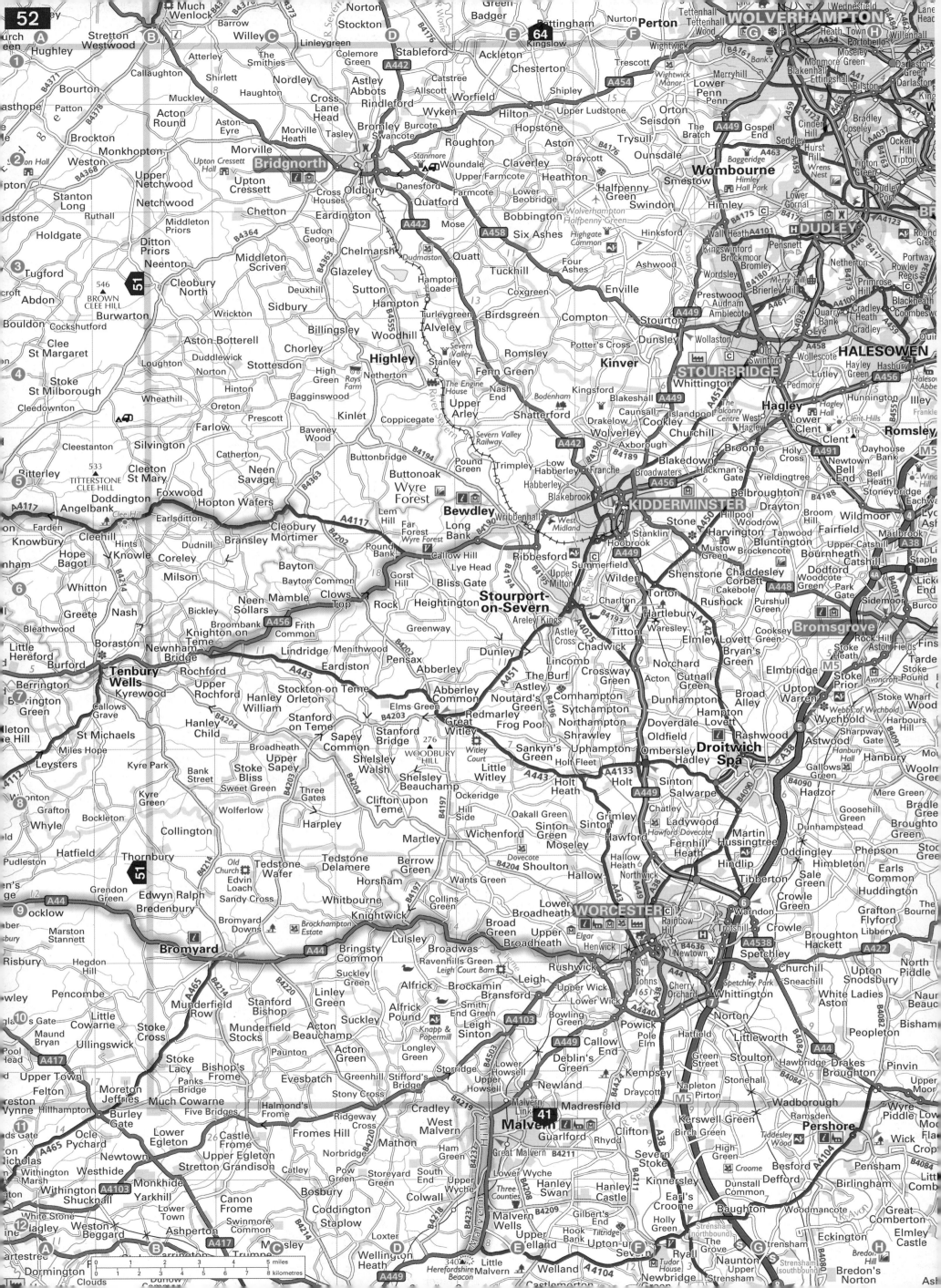

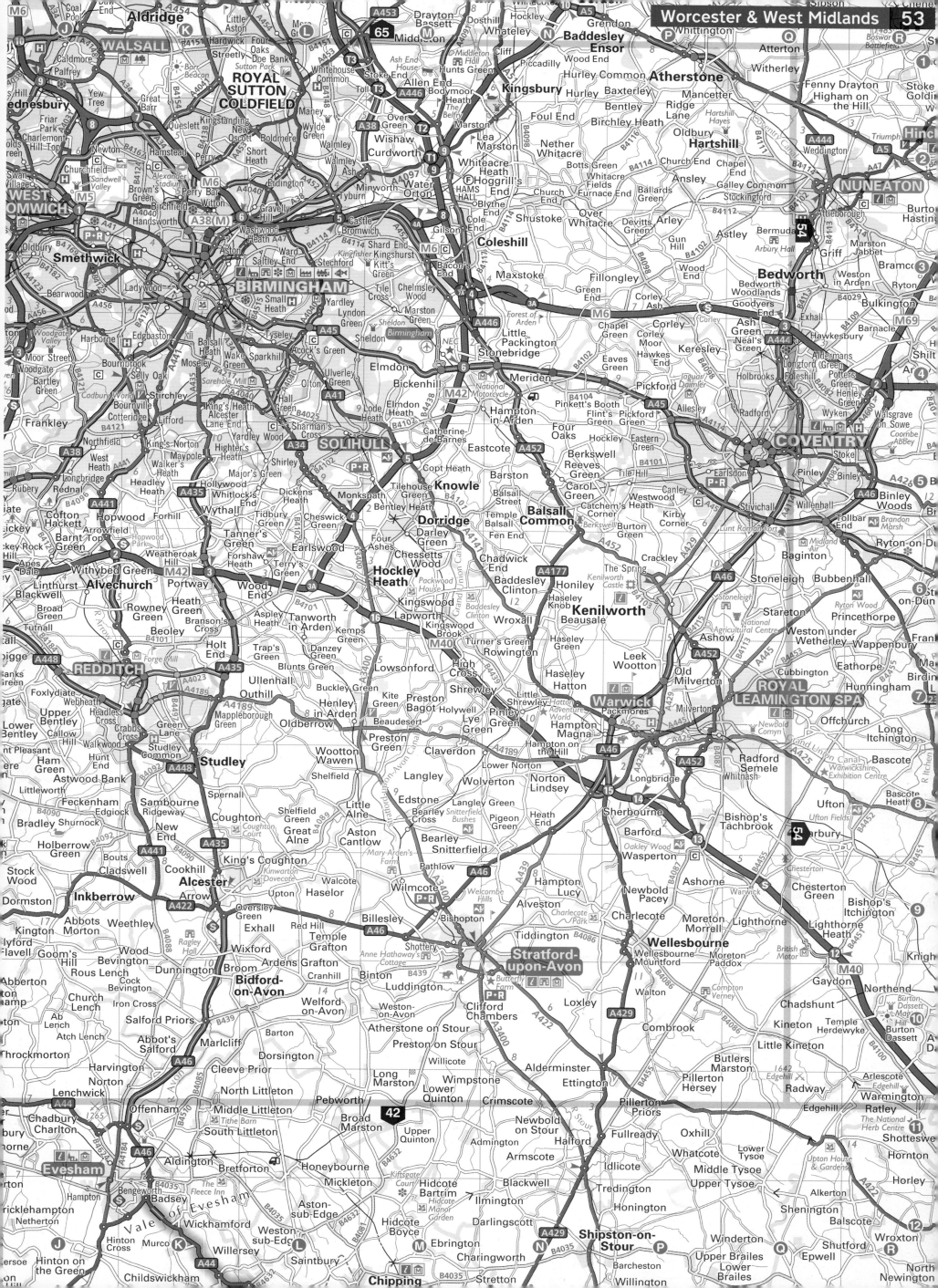

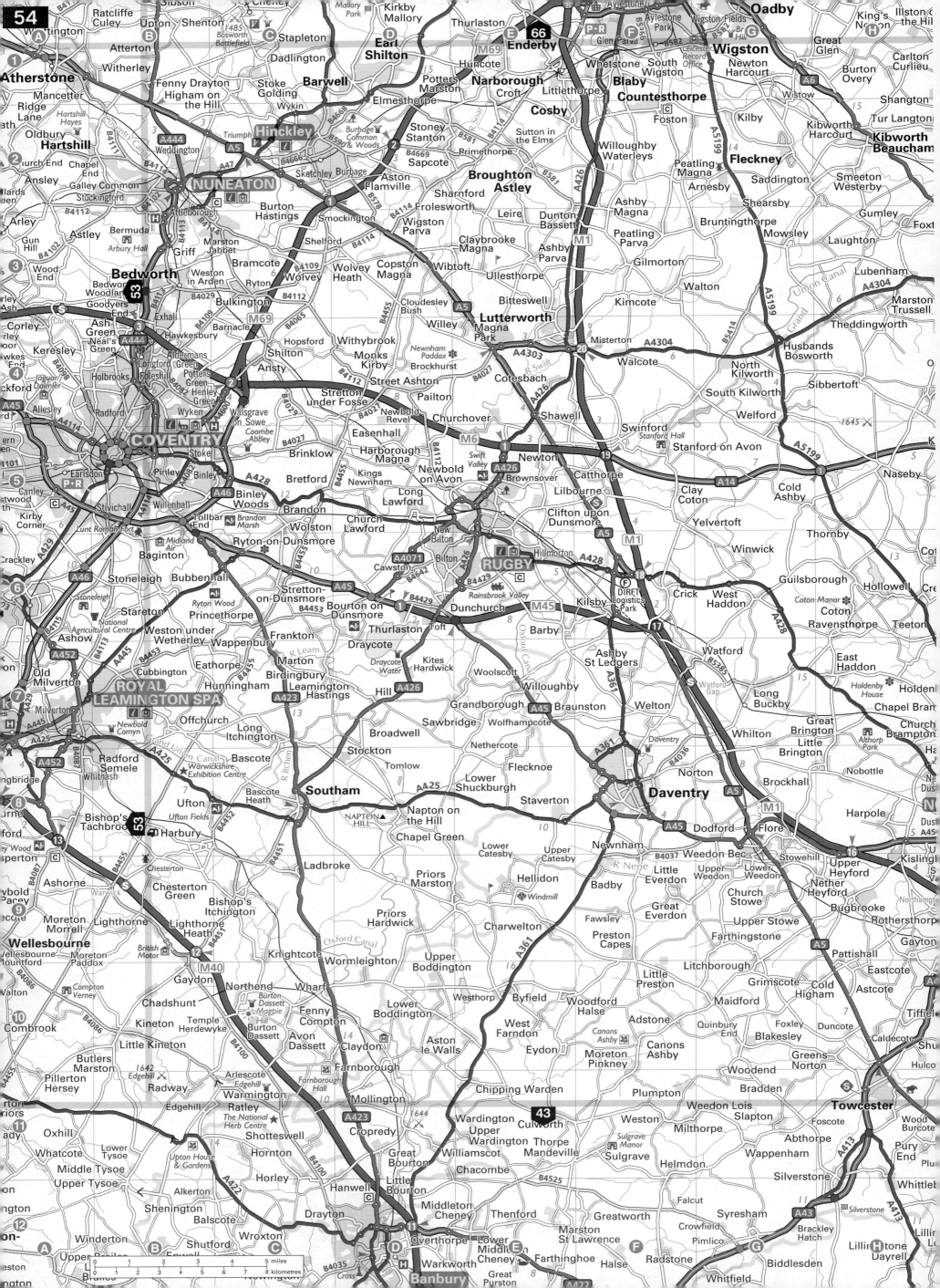

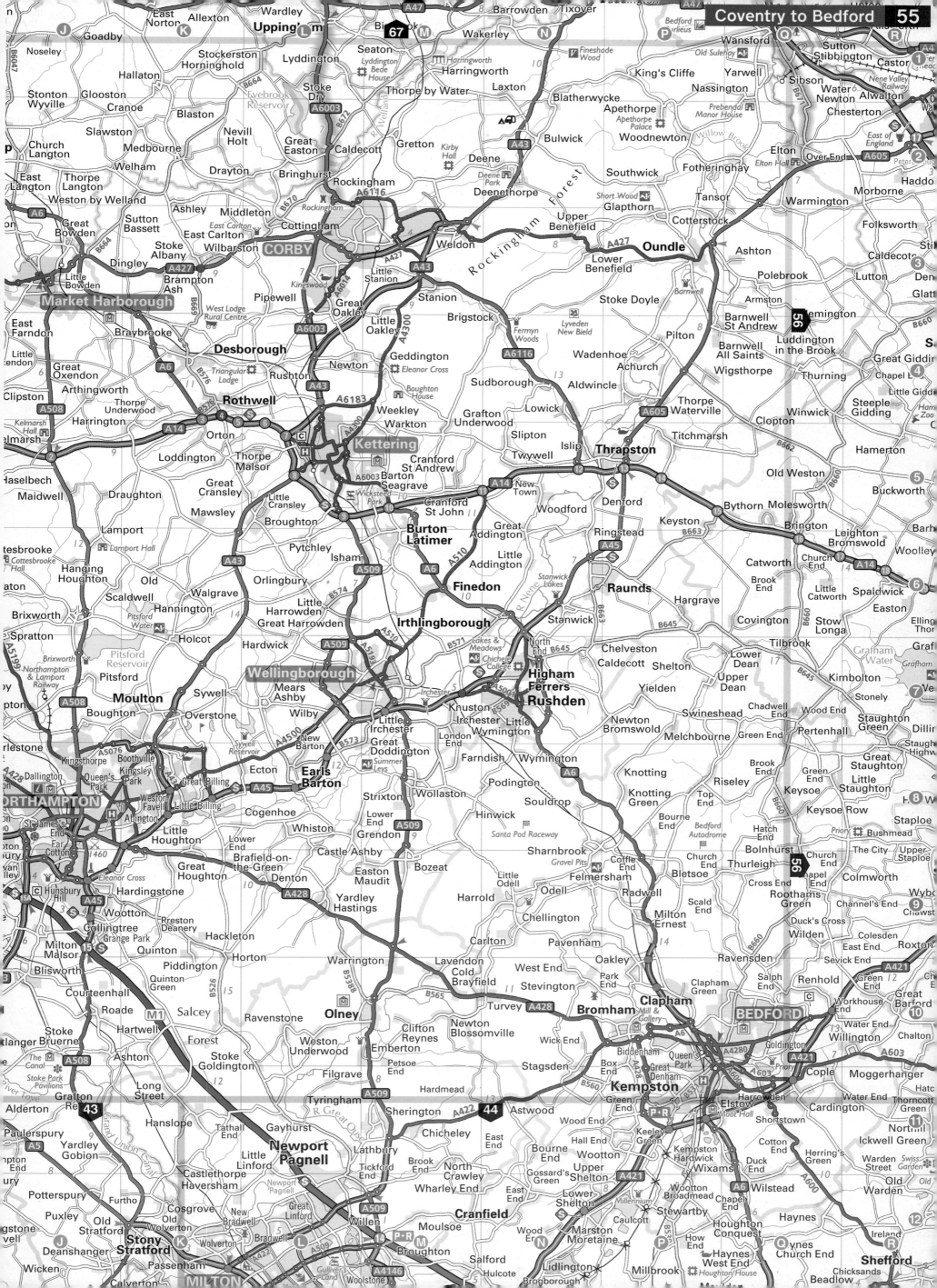

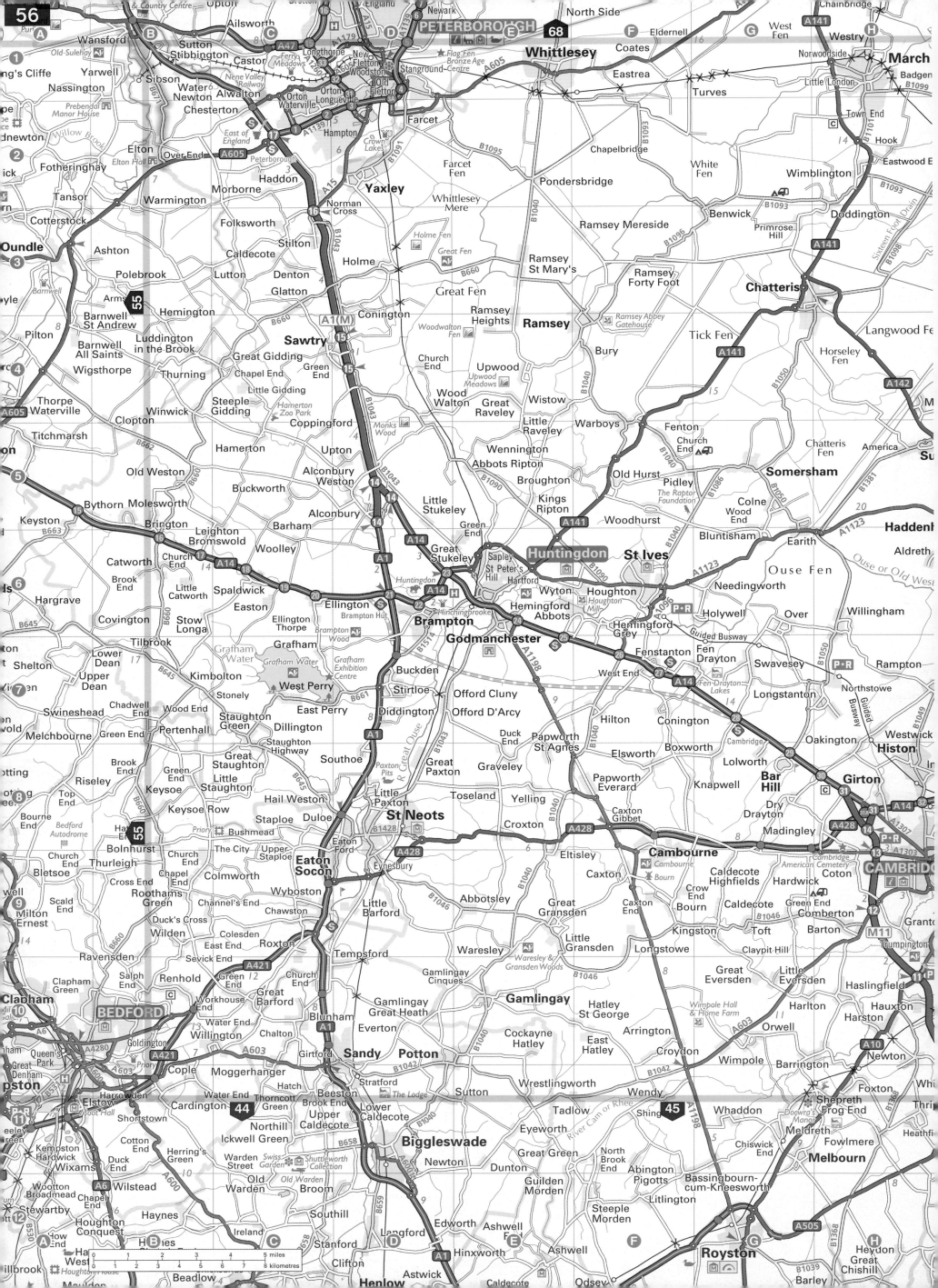

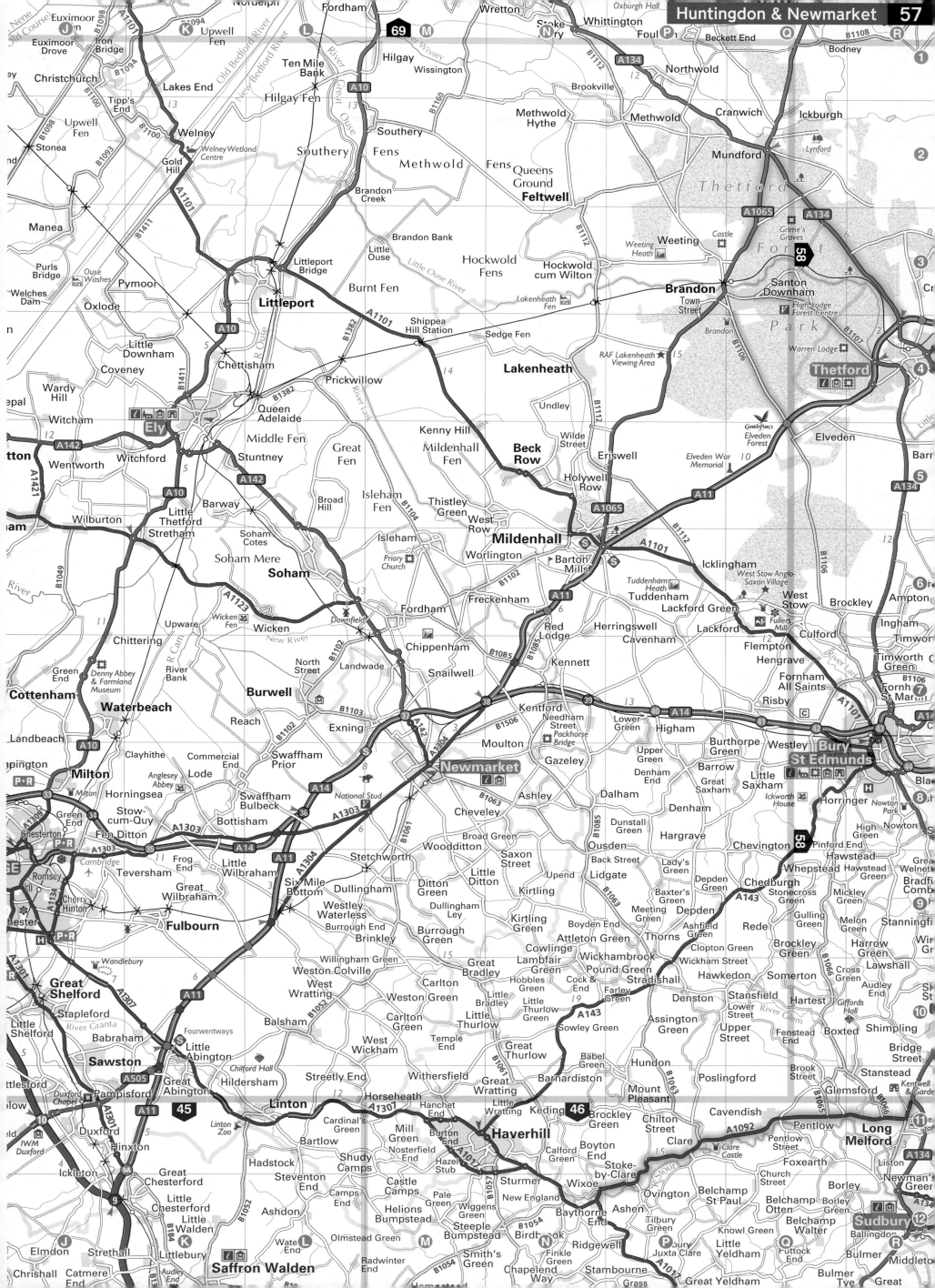

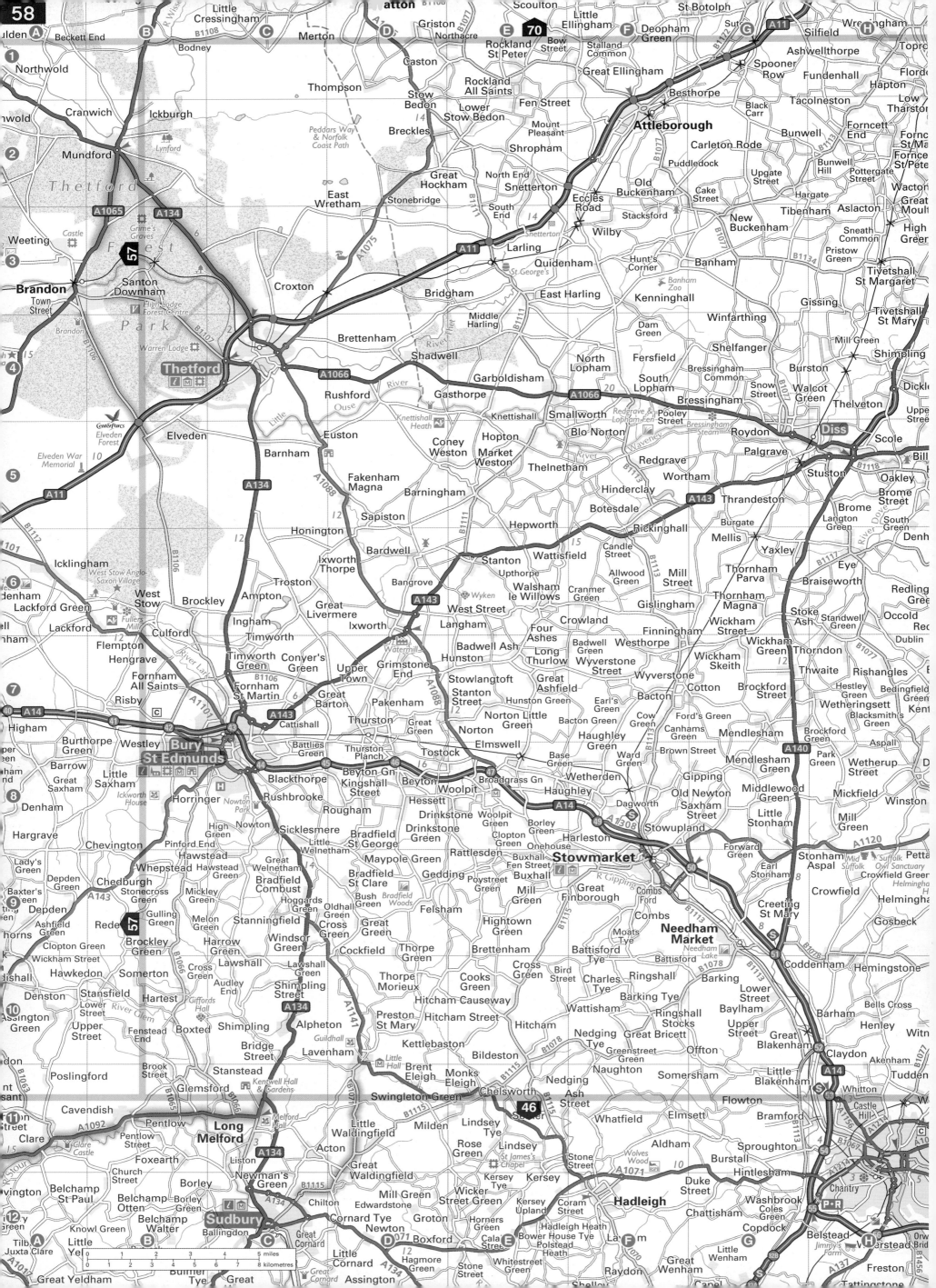

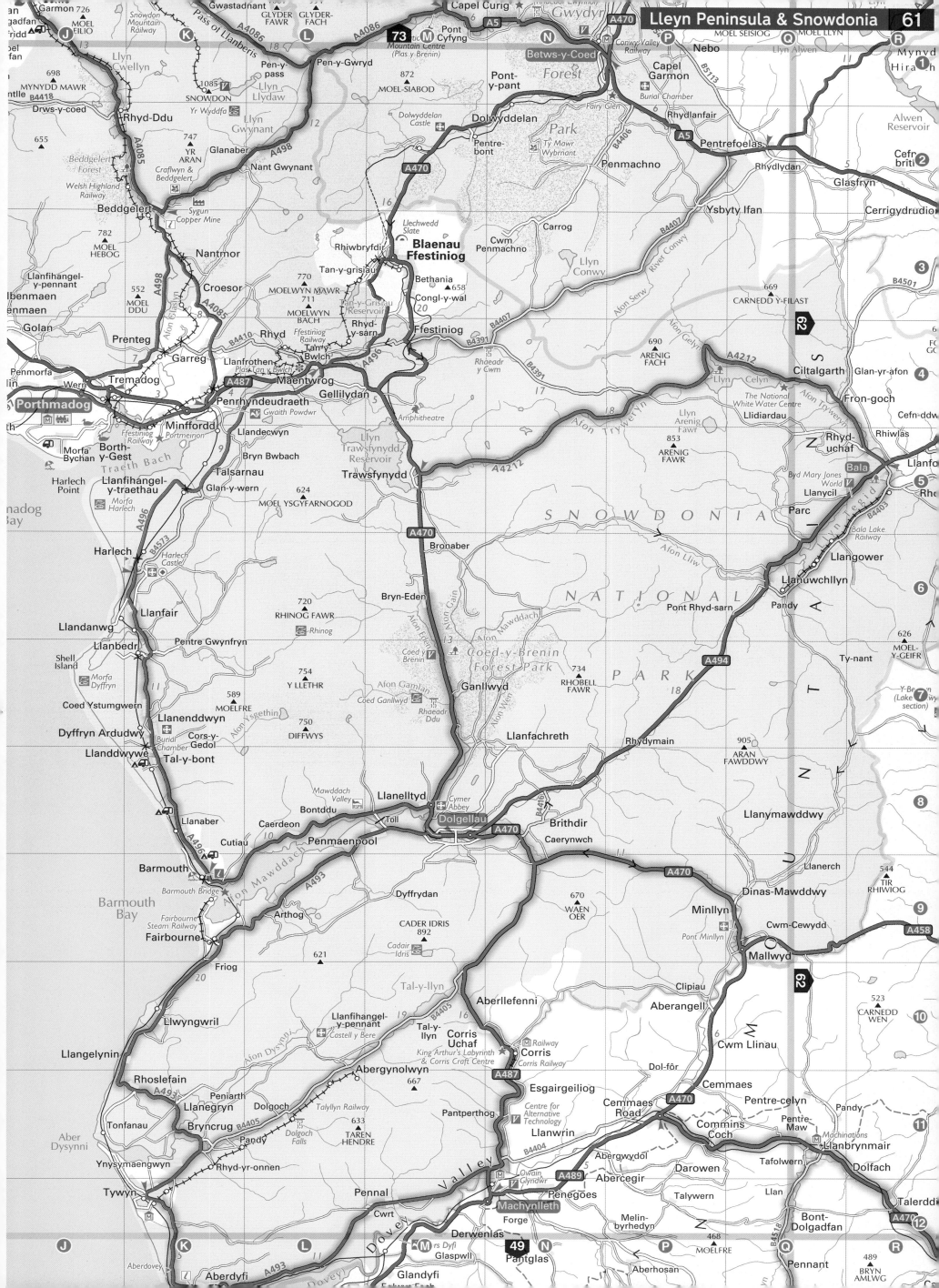

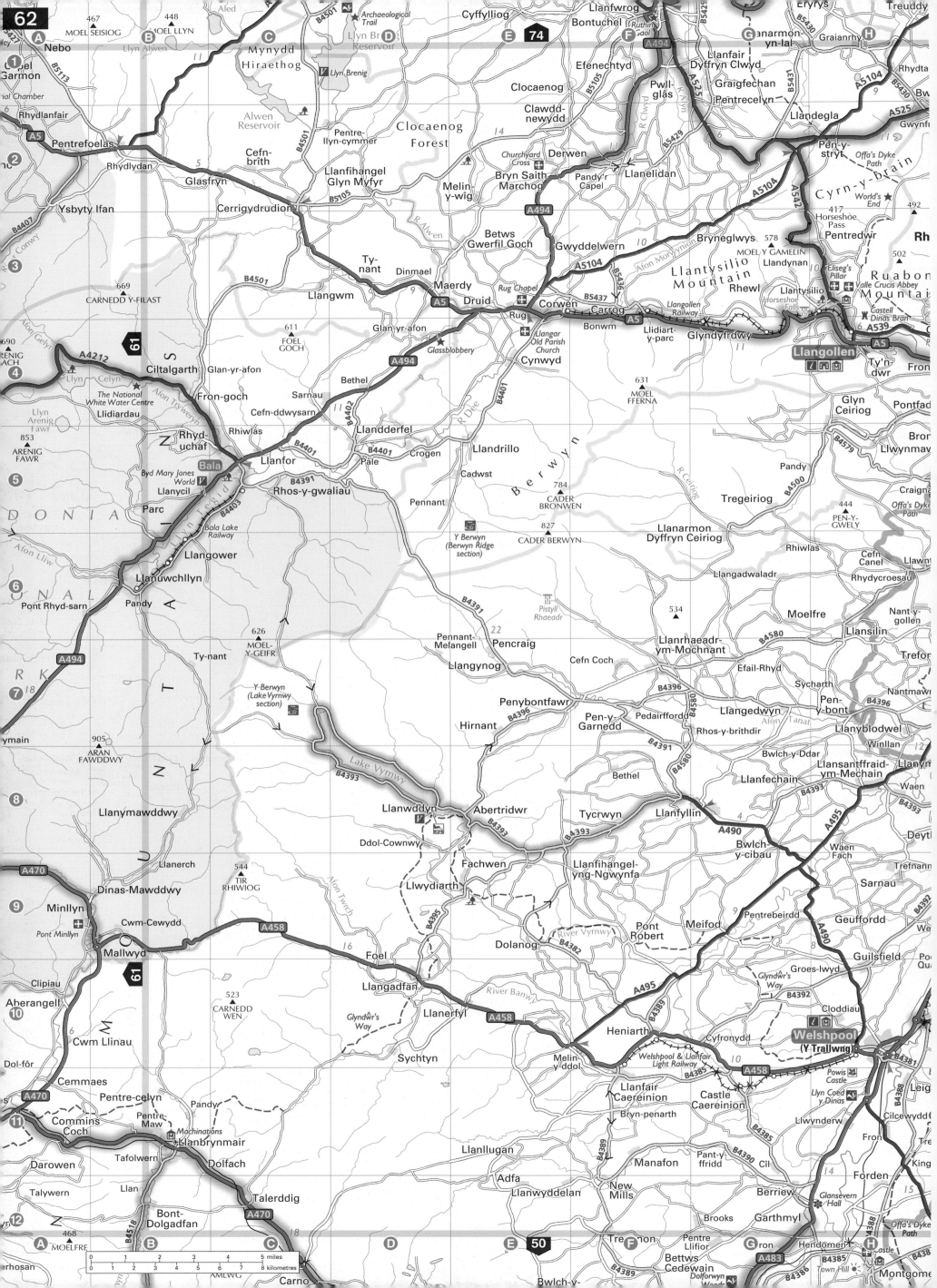

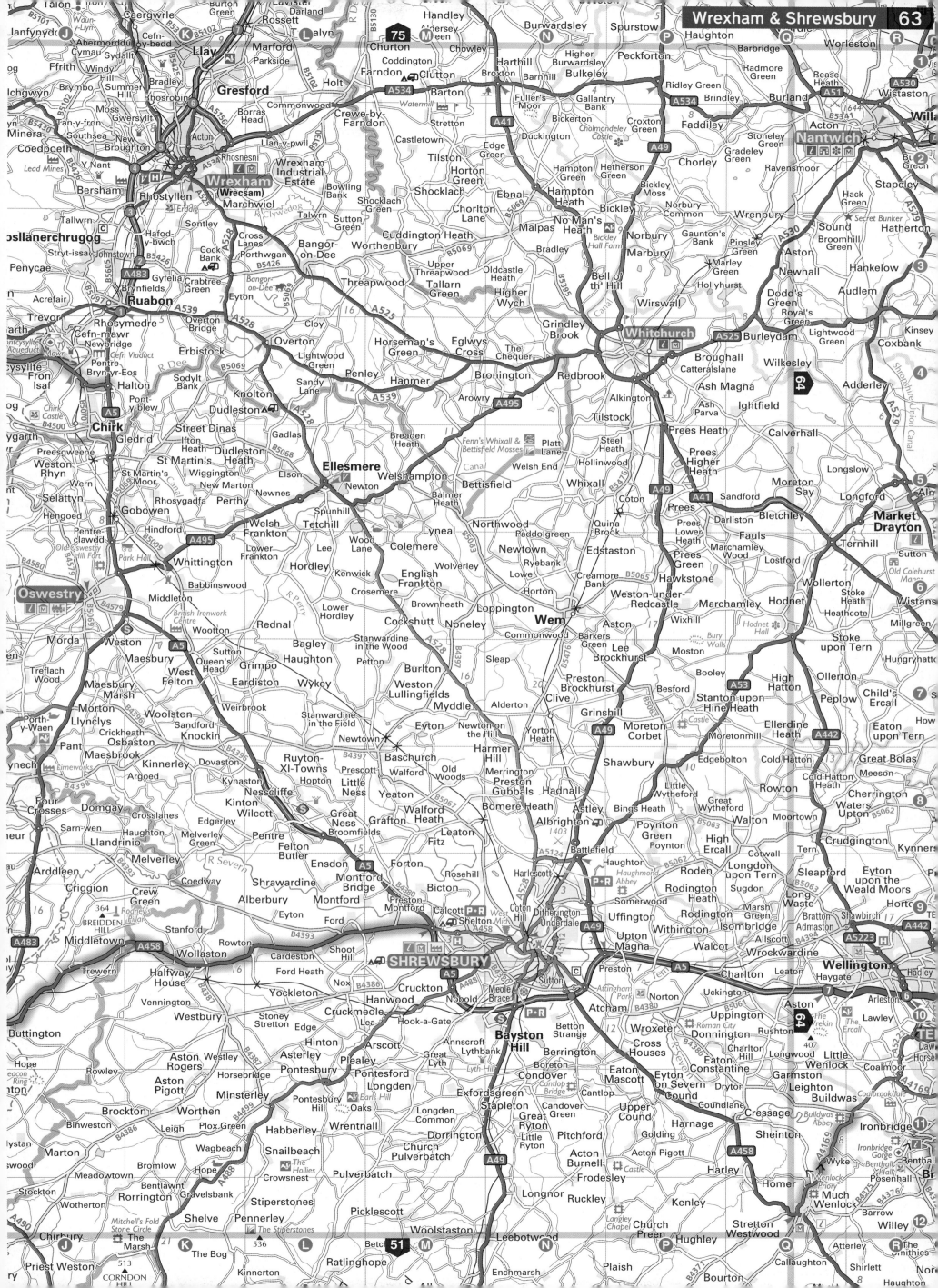

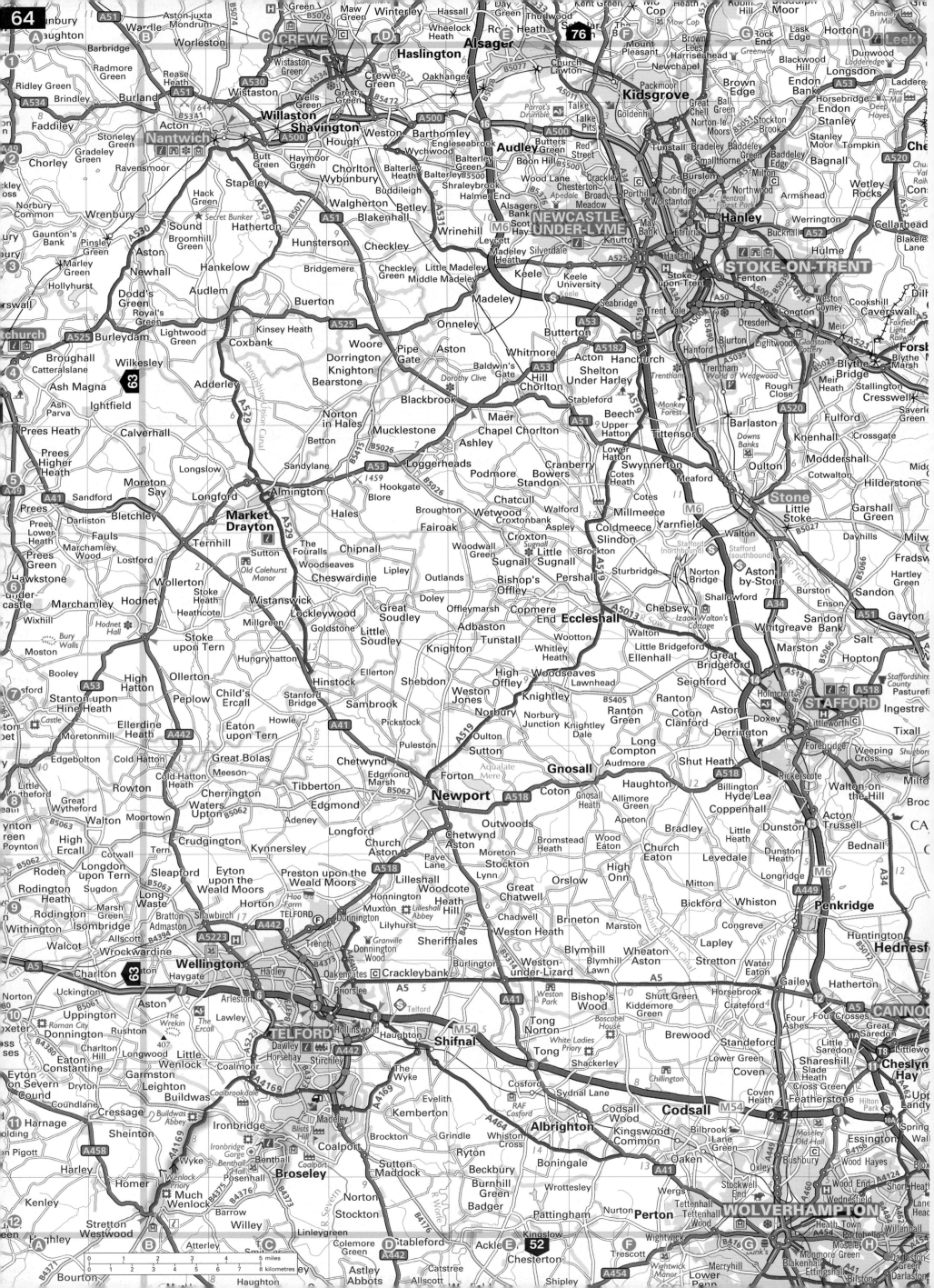

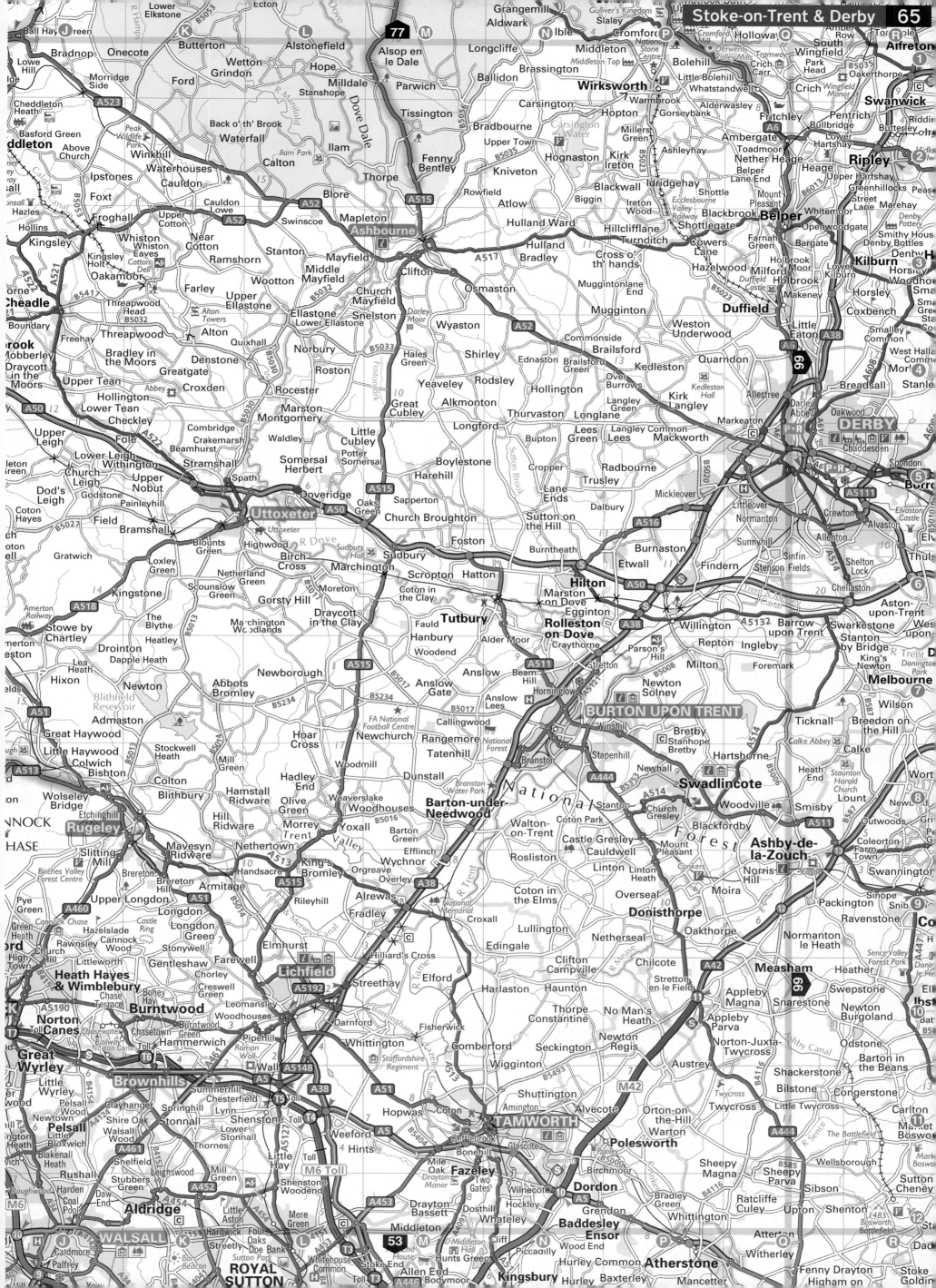

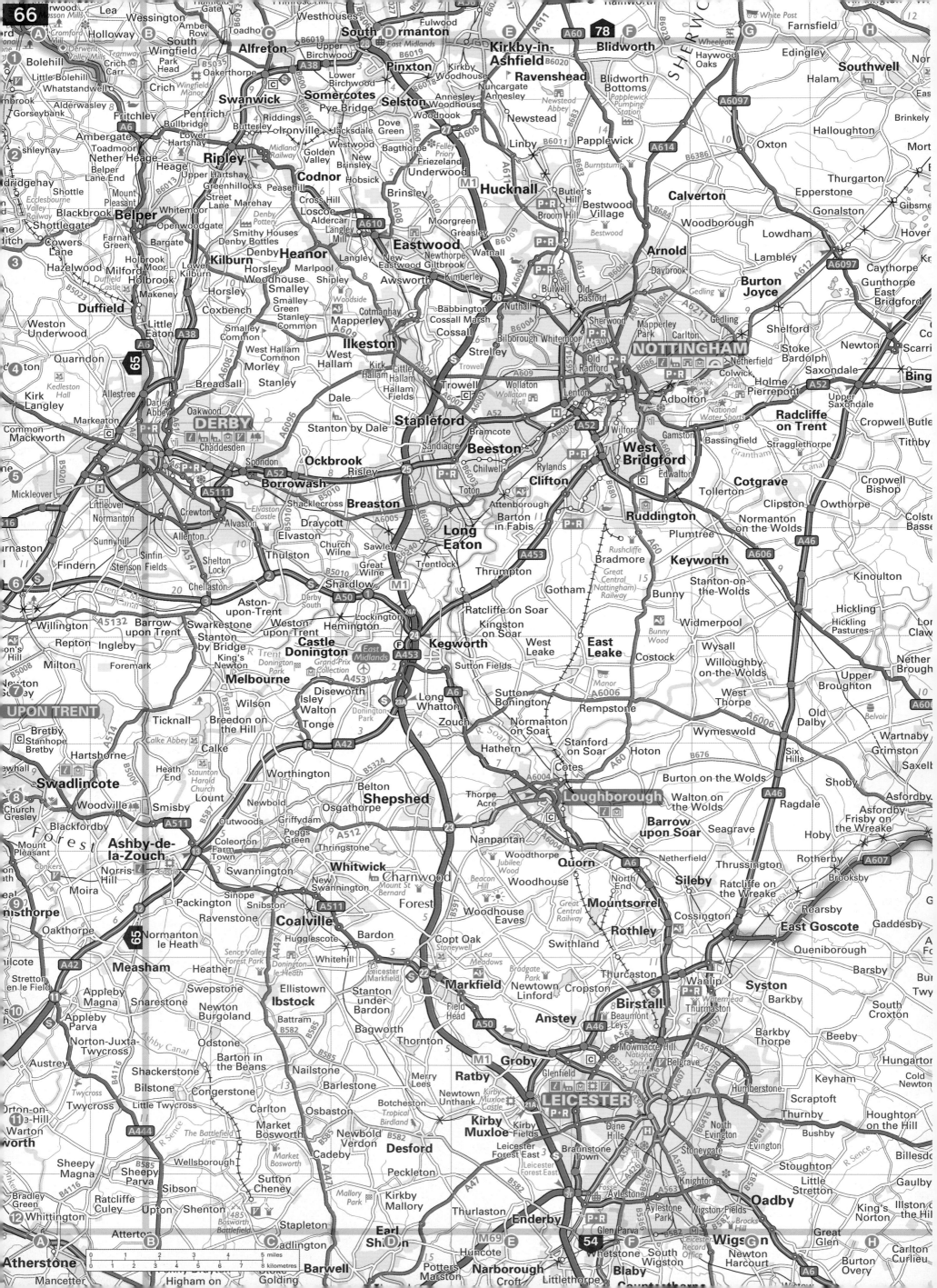

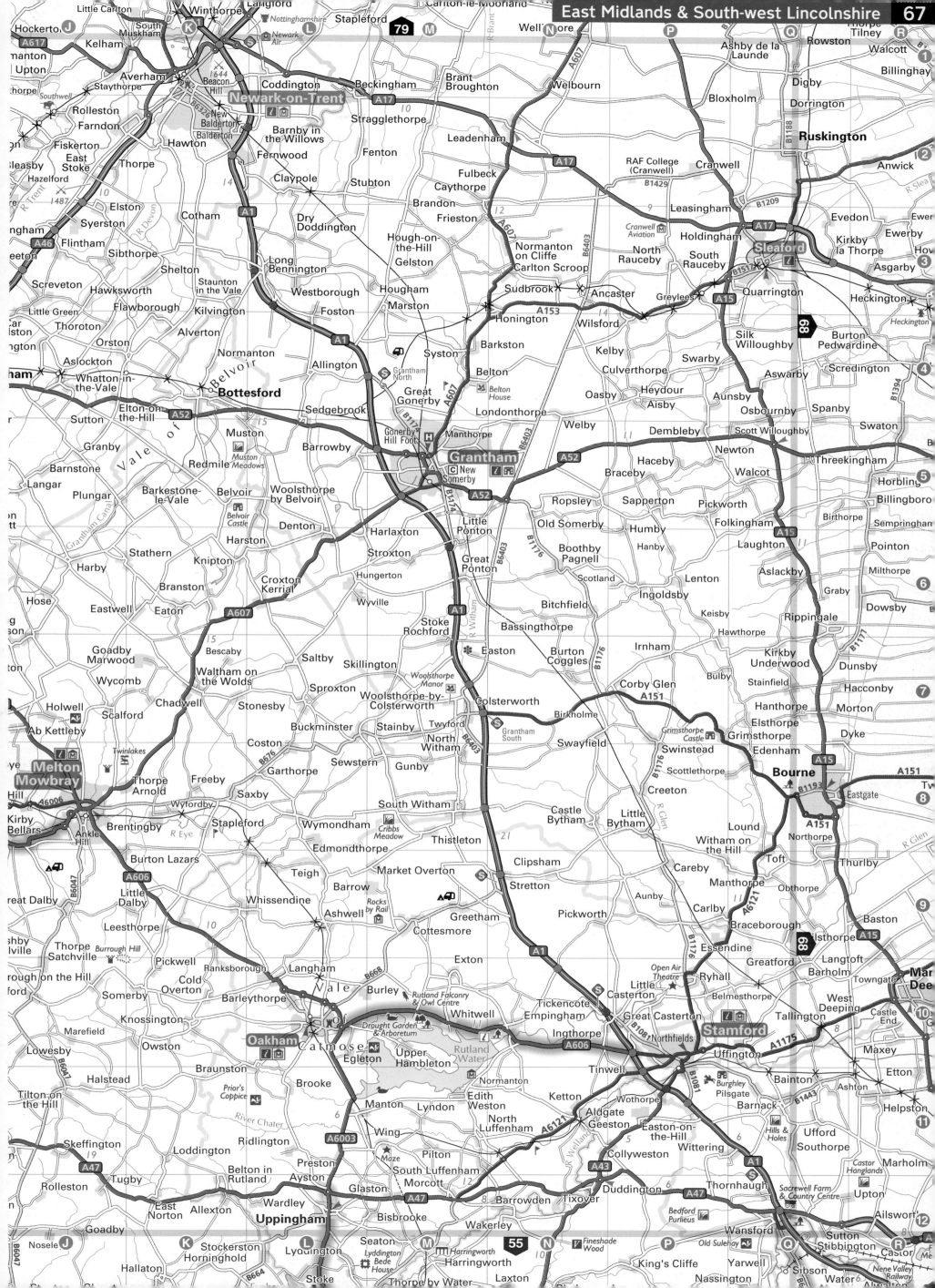

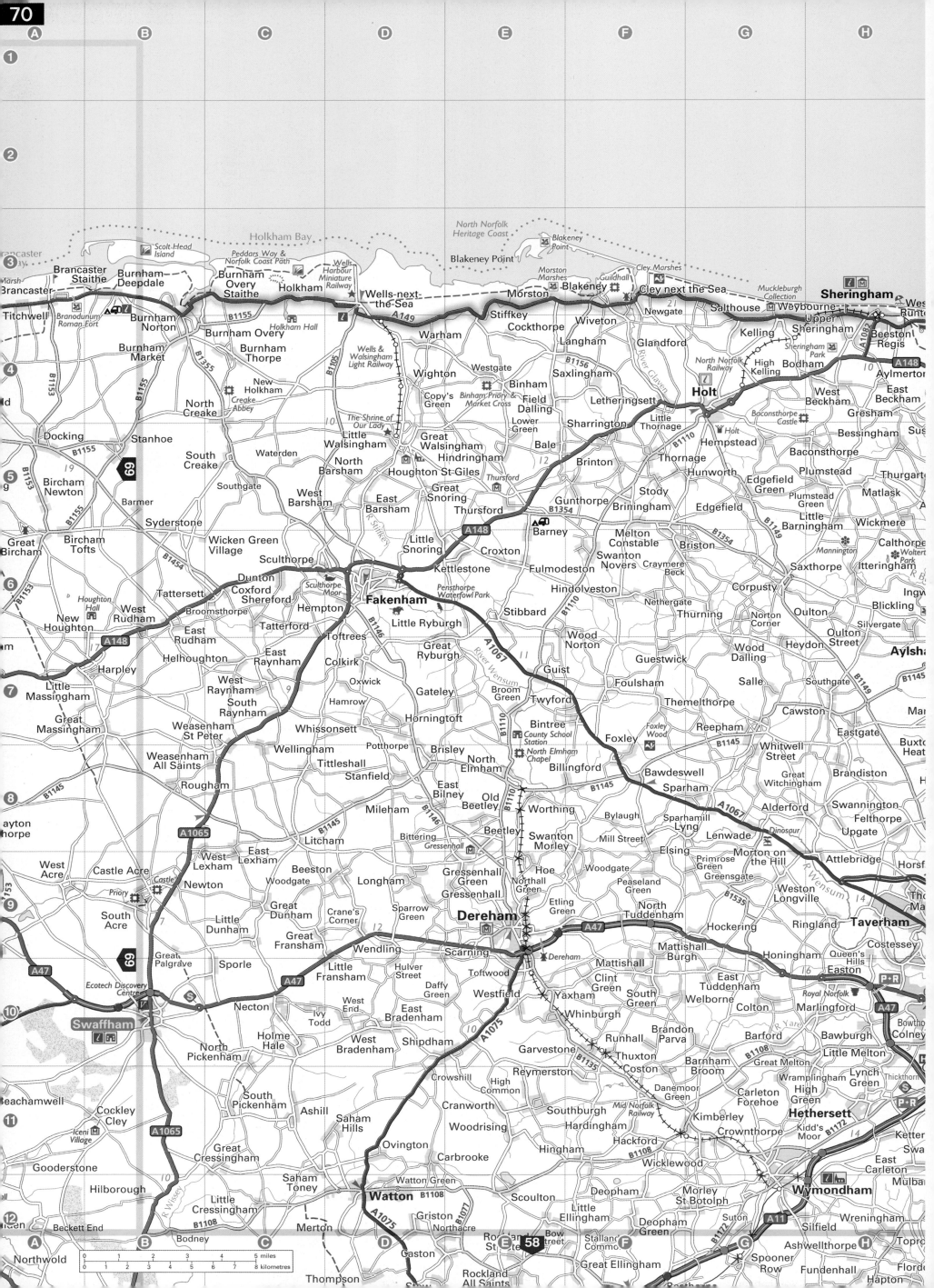

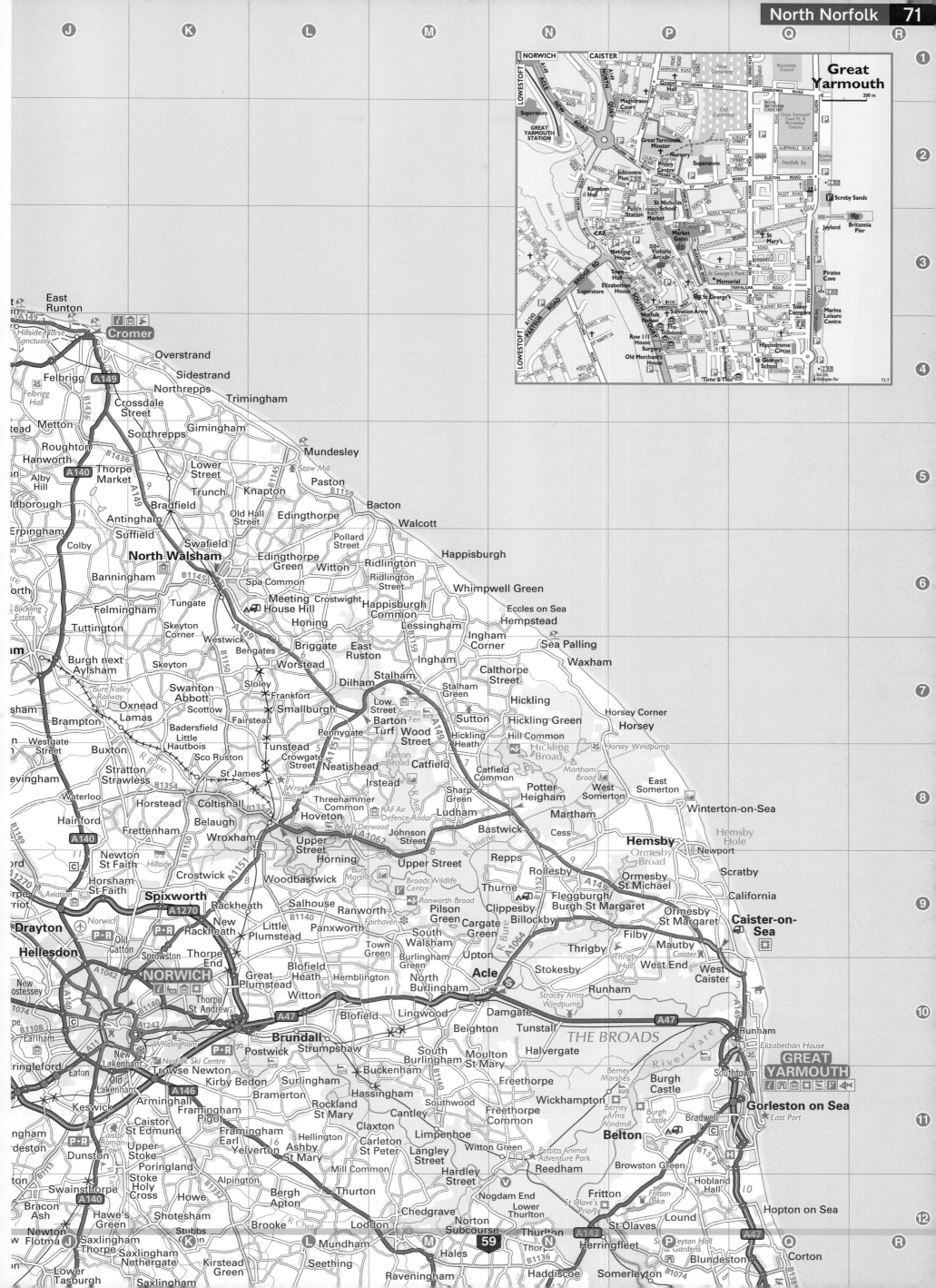

North Norfolk

J   K   L   M   N   P   Q   R

Great Yarmouth inset:

NORWICH · CAISTER
LOWESTOFT
Great Yarmouth Station
River Yare
Market Gates
Victoria Arcade
Town Hall
St Nicholas
St George's Park
Elizabethan House
Norfolk Nelson
The Tolhouse
Row III House Surgery
Old Merchant's House
Time & Tide
Great Yarmouth Minster
Nursery
Priory Centre
Norfolk Sq
Royal Britannia Crescent
Old Cemetery
New Cemetery
St Mary's
Joyland
Britannia Pier
Pirates Cove
Marina Leisure Centre
Hippodrome Circus
St George's School
Wellington Pier

East Runton
Cromer
Overstrand
Sidestrand
Northrepps
Trimingham
Felbrigg
Felbrigg Hall
Crossdale Street
Gimingham
Mundesley
Metton
Southrepps
Lower Street
Paston
Stow Mill
Roughton
Hanworth
Thorpe Market
Trunch
Knapton
Bacton
Alby Hill
Bradfield
Old Hall Street
Walcott
Antingham
Suffield
Swafield
Edingthorpe
Colby
Happisburgh
North Walsham
Edingthorpe Green
Witton
Ridlington
Whimpwell Green
Banningham
Spa Common
Ridlington Street
Eccles on Sea
Felmingham
Meeting House Hill
Crostwight
Happisburgh Common
Hempstead
Tungate
Honing
Lessingham
Ingham Corner
Sea Palling
Skeyton Corner
Westwick
Briggate
East Ruston
Ingham
Waxham
Tuttington
Bengates
Worstead
Calthorpe Street
Skeyton
Swanton Abbott
Sloley
Dilham
Stalham
Hickling
Horsey Corner
Oxnead
Scottow
Frankfort
Low Street
Stalham Green
Hickling Green
Horsey
Lamas
Smallburgh
Barton Turf
Sutton
Badersfield
Fairstead
Wood Street
Hickling Heath
Hill Common
Horsey Windpump
Little Hautbois
Tunstead
Crowgate Street
Neatishead
Catfield
Hickling Broad
Buxton
Sco Ruston
Pennygate
Barton Broad
Catfield Common
Martham Broad
Stratton Strawless
St James
Irstead
Sharp Green
Potter Heigham
West Somerton
East Somerton
Waterloo
Threehammer Common
Ludham
Martham
Winterton-on-Sea
Horstead
Coltishall
Wroxham Barns
RAF Air Defence Radar
Bastwick
Cess
Hemsby Hole
Hainford
Belaugh
Hoveton
Johnson Street
Hemsby
Newport
Frettenham
Wroxham
BeWILDerwood
Thurne
Repps
Ormesby Broad
Scratby
Newton St Faith
Upper Street
Horning
Upper Street
Rollesby
Ormesby St Michael
California
Horsham St Faith
Crostwick
Woodbastwick
Broads Wildlife Centre
Thurne
Fleggburgh
Ormesby St Margaret
Spixworth
Rackheath
Salhouse
Ranworth
Clippesby
Burgh St Margaret
Caister-on-Sea
Drayton
Old Catton
New Rackheath
Little Plumstead
Ranworth Broad
Fairhaven
Pilson Green
Billockby
Filby
Hellesdon
Sprowston
Thorpe End
Panxworth
South Walsham
Cargate Green
Mautby
West End
West Caister
NORWICH
Great Plumstead
Blofield Heath
Town Green
Burlingham Green
Upton
Thrigby
Thrigby Hall
Caister
Thorpe St Andrew
Witton
Hemblington
North Burlingham
Stokesby
Runham
Blofield
Lingwood
Acle
Damgate
Runham
Brundall
Postwick
Strumpshaw
Beighton
Tunstall
THE BROADS
River Yare
GREAT YARMOUTH
New Hostessey
Whitlingham
Norfolk Ski Centre
South Burlingham
Moulton St Mary
Halvergate
Stracey Arms Windpump
Southtown
Trowse Newton
Buckenham
Freethorpe
Berney Marshes
Gorleston on Sea
New Lakenham
Kirby Bedon
Surlingham
Southwood
Freethorpe Common
Berney Arms Windmill
Burgh Castle
East Port
Eaton
Old Lakenham
Bramerton
Hassingham
Cantley
Wickhampton
Burgh Castle
Bradwell
Keswick
Arminghall
Framingham Pigot
Rockland St Mary
Claxton
Limpenhoe
Witton Green
Belton
Caistor St Edmund
Framingham Earl Yelverton
Ashby St Mary
Carleton St Peter
Langley Street
Reedham
Pettitts Animal Adventure Park
Dunston
Upper Stoke
Hellington
Mill Common
Hardley Street
Browston Green
Poringland
Alpington
Bergh Apton
Thurton
Nogdam End
Fritton
Hobland Hall
Swainsthorpe
Stoke Holy Cross
Howe
Hawe's Green
Shotesham
Chedgrave
Lower Thurlton
Fritton Lake
St Olaves
Hopton on Sea
Bracon Ash
Brooke
Loddon
Norton Subcourse
Thurlton
St Olave's Priory
Somerleyton
Newton Flotman
Saxlingham Thorpe
Stubbs
Herringfleet
Corton
Lower Tasburgh
Saxlingham Nethergate
Saxlingham Green
Mundham
Hales
Haddiscoe
Blundeston
Kirstead Green
Seething
Raveningham
Somerleyton
Leyton Hall

A149 · A140 · B1436 · B1145 · B1150 · B1354 · B1159 · A1151 · A1062 · A1270 · B1140 · A47 · A146 · A143 · B1074 · B1136 · B1532 · A1042 · A1242 · A11 · A1074 · B1108 · B1332 · B1113

Holyhead Harbour

CAERNARFON

Llandudno

0   200 m

TABOR HILL · Great Orme Tramway · HILL TERRACE · Llandudno Pier · The Grand Hotel

Great Orme Tramway

Victoria · North Shore Beach

The Old Bank Gallery · War Memorial

Travelodge

GLODDAETH · Town Hall · St John's · Our Lady Star of the Sea · Victoria · Holy Trinity · Medical Centre · THE PARADE · The Promenade

DEGANWY · Conwy Archive Service · LLANDUDNO STATION · Mostyn Gallery · Parc Llandudno Retail Park · Swimming Pool · Venue Cymru · St Paul's · MOSTYN AVE

Police Station · Magistrates Court · Mostyn Champneys Retail Park · MOSTYN BROADWAY

Ysgol Tudno · CYLCH · TUDUR · Fire & Ambulance Station · CLARENCE CRESCENT · CLARENCE DRIVE

Ysgol Ffordd Dyffryn · Superstore · Ysgol Craig Y Don

Coach · Ysgol Morfa Rhianedd · Ysgol John Bright · CONWAY ROAD

Llandudno FC

TLT · A55, BETWS-Y-COED

Seawatch Centre

Moelfre

llgo

n-glas

Benllech

Red Wharf Bay

Red Wharf Bay · Glan-yr-afon · Penmon Priory · Toll · Caim · Penmon · Black Point · Puffin Island

Llanddona · Llangoed · B5109

Pentraeth

Hafoty Medieval House · Llanfaes · Gaol · Beaumaris Castle

Great Orme Heritage Coast · GREAT ORME'S HEAD · Great Orme Tramway · Toll · Little Ormes Head · Penrhyn Bay

Conwy Bay

Llandudno · Penrhyn-side · Llandrillo-yn-Rhos · Rhôs-on-Sea · Abergele Ro

Deganwy · Llanrhos · Pydew · Colwyn Bay (Bae Colwyn) · Abergele

Beaumaris · Courthouse

Llansadwrn · Llandegfan

Dwygyfylchi · Conwy · Tywyn · Llandudno Junction · Mochdre · Old Colwyn · Llanddulas · A55

Penmaenan · **Penmaenmawr** · Conwy Castle · Llansanffraid Glan Conwy · Llanelian-yn-Rhos · Bryn-y-Maen · Llysfaen · Rhyd-y-foel · **Aberge**

A5109 · **Llanfairfechan** · Capelulo · Henryd

Menai Bridge (Porthaethwy) · Penrhyn Castle · Spinnies Abergowen · Gorddinog · Nant-y-pandy · SNOWDONIA · Rowen · Dolwen · Dawn · Trofarth · Betws-yn-Rhos

llgwyngyll · **Bangor** · Glasinfryn · Abergwyngregyn · 610 TAL-Y-FAN · Ty'n-y-Groes · Bodnant · Eglwysbach · Graig · Tal-y-Cafn · **Llanfair Talhaiarn**

Britannia Bridge garnedd · Penrhos · Plas Newydd · Llandygai · Coedydd Aber · Caerhun · Pentre'r Felin · River Elwy

Capel-y-graig · Waen-wen · Rhyd-y-groes · Tal-y-bont · NATIONAL · Castell · Tal-y-Bont · Afon Anafon · **Llangernyw**

Seion · Pentir · Rachub · Llanllechid · MOEL WINION · Llanbedr-y-Cennin · Dolgarrog · Hafodunos · B5113

Llanddeiniolen · Sling · Waen-pentir · Gerlan · 580 · PARK · Pont Dolgarrog · Maenan

Saron · Rhiwlas · Mynydd Llandygai · 757 · 942 · Afon Dulyn · Surf Snowdonia · Llanddoged

Penisarwaun · Zip World · Ogwen Bank · Y DROSGL · FOEL-FRAS · A548 · Pandy Tudur

Cwm-y-glo · Brynrefail · Clwt-y-bont · Gallt-y-foel · **Bethesda** · Afon Caseg · Llyn Eigiau · Trefriw · Pentre-tafarn-y-fedw

Llanrug · Rhiwen · Deiniolen · 1062 · CARNEDD LLEWELYN · Llanrhychwyn · Woollen Mills · **Llanrwst** · Gwytherin

Groeslon · Dinorwic · 923 · A5 · 1044 · CARNEDD DAFYDD · Llyn Cowlyd · Cors Bodgynydd · Melin-y-coed · B5384

Llanberis · Padarn · National Slate · Dolbadarn Castle · Afon Ddu · Gwydir Uchaf Chapel · Pandy Tudur

Llanberis Lake Railway · 442 · Electric Mountain · Llyn Padarn · Llyn Peris · Pont Pen-y-benglog · 946 · Y GARN · Llyn Ogwen · Llyn Crafnant · Llyn Geirionydd · Gwydir · Llyn Aled

Waunfawr · Betws Garmon · 726 · MOEL EILIO · Snowdon Mountain Railway · Pass of Llanberis · Nant Peris · Gwastadnant · 1001 · GLYDER FAWR · 994 · Y TRYFAN · 917 · GLYDER FACH · The Ugly House (Ty Hyll) · Swallow Falls (Rhaeadr Ewynnol) · **Capel Curig** · Conwy Valley Railway · 467 · MOEL SEISIOG · 448 · MOEL LLYN

698 · MYNYDD MAWR · Llyn Cwellyn · 1085 · A4086 · Pen-y-pass · Pen-y-Gwryd · National Mountain Centre (Plas y B) · 61 · 872 · MOEL-SIABOD · **Pont-y-pant** · Nebo · Capel Garmon · Llyn Alwen · Llyn Aled · A543

Forest · Be-y-Coed · Burial Chamber · Mynyd Hiraeth · A544

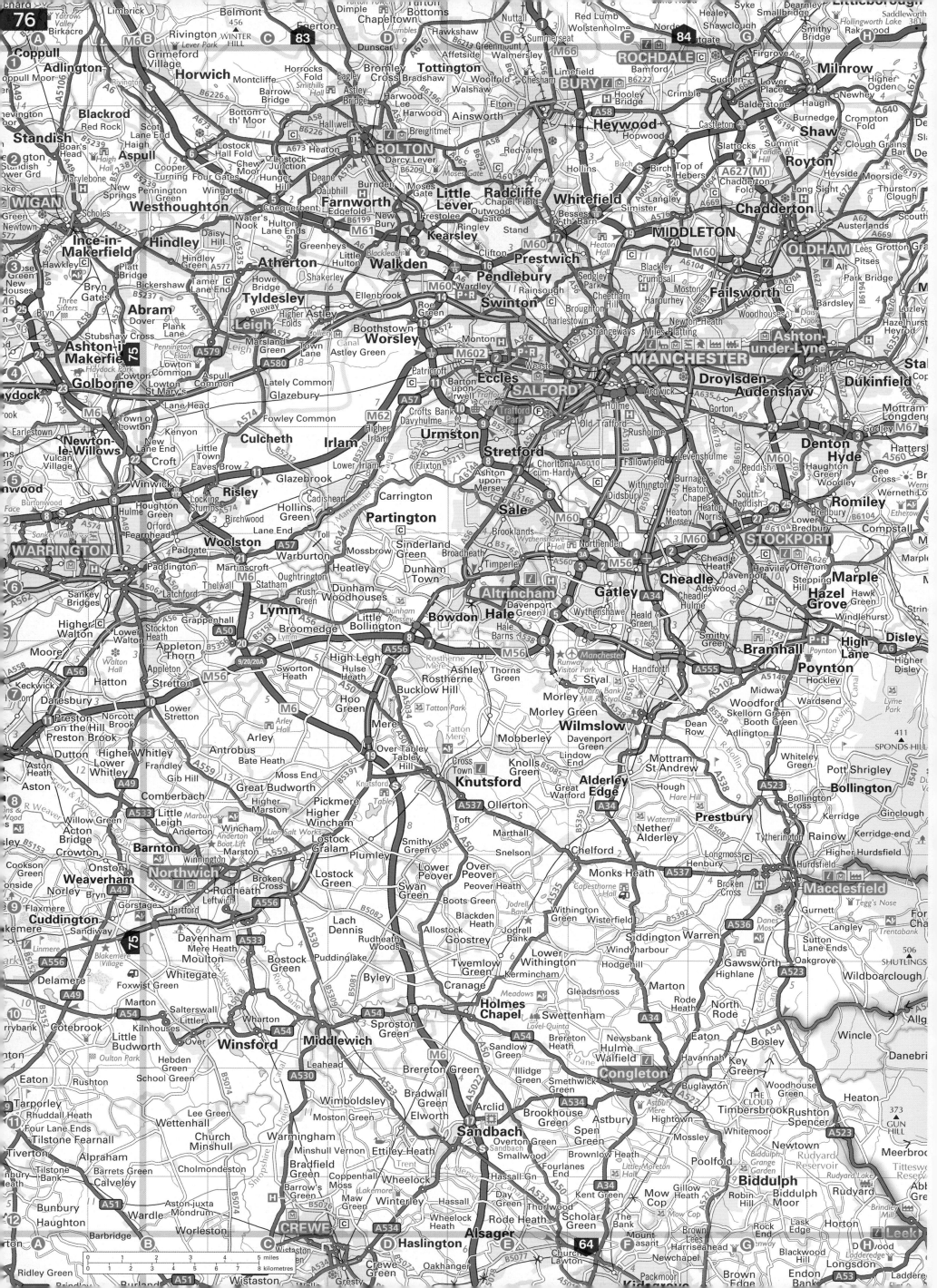

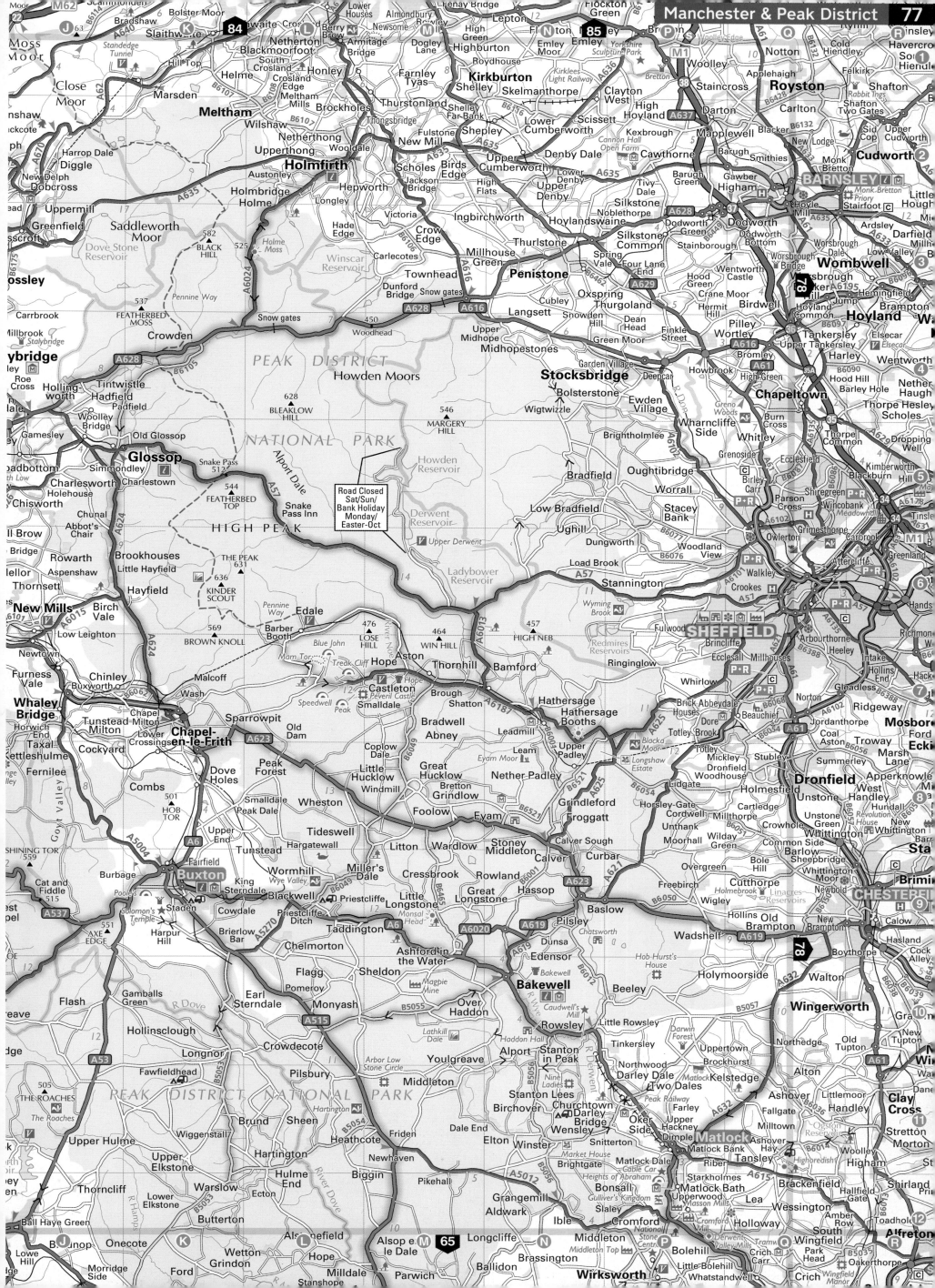

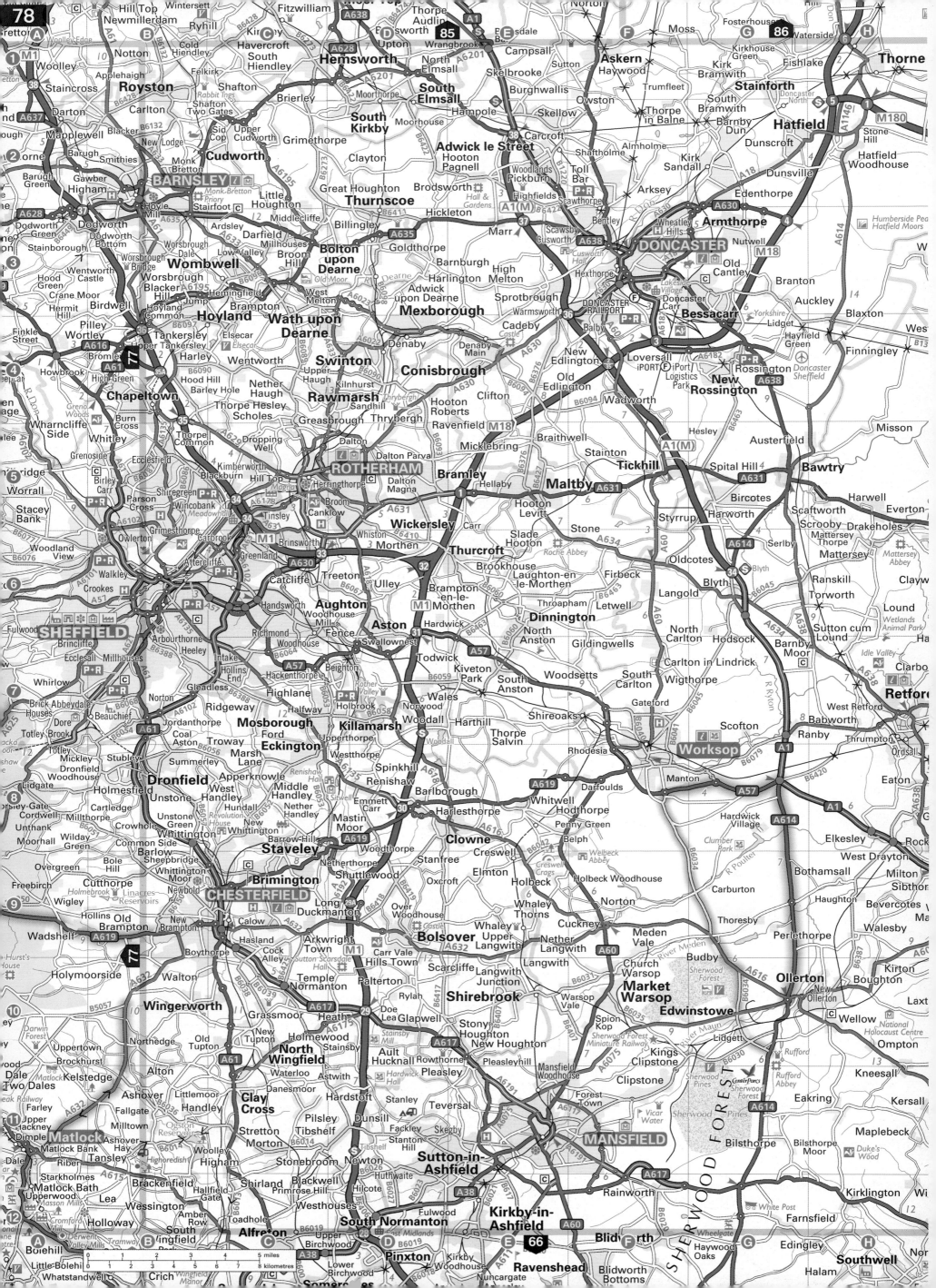

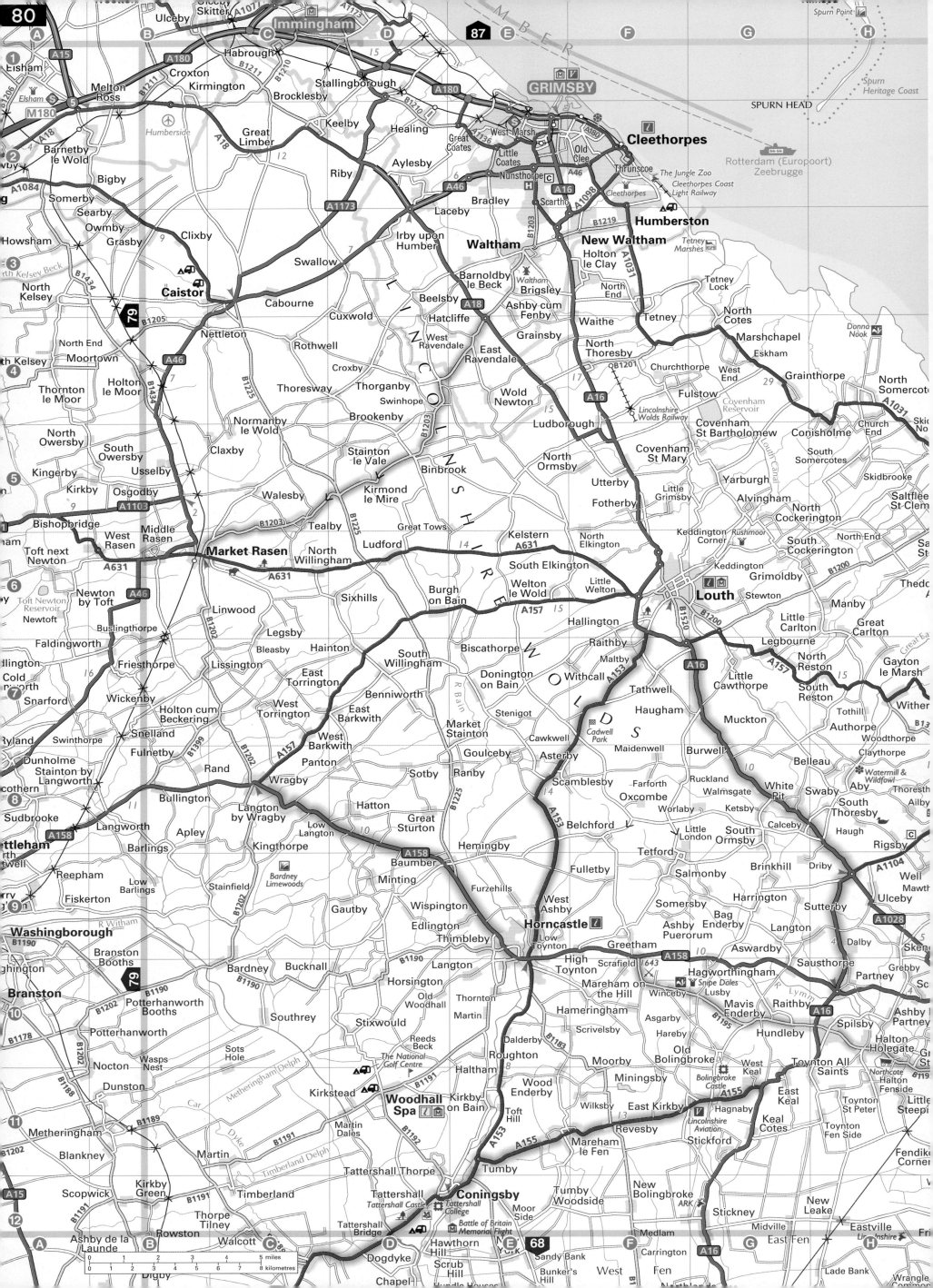

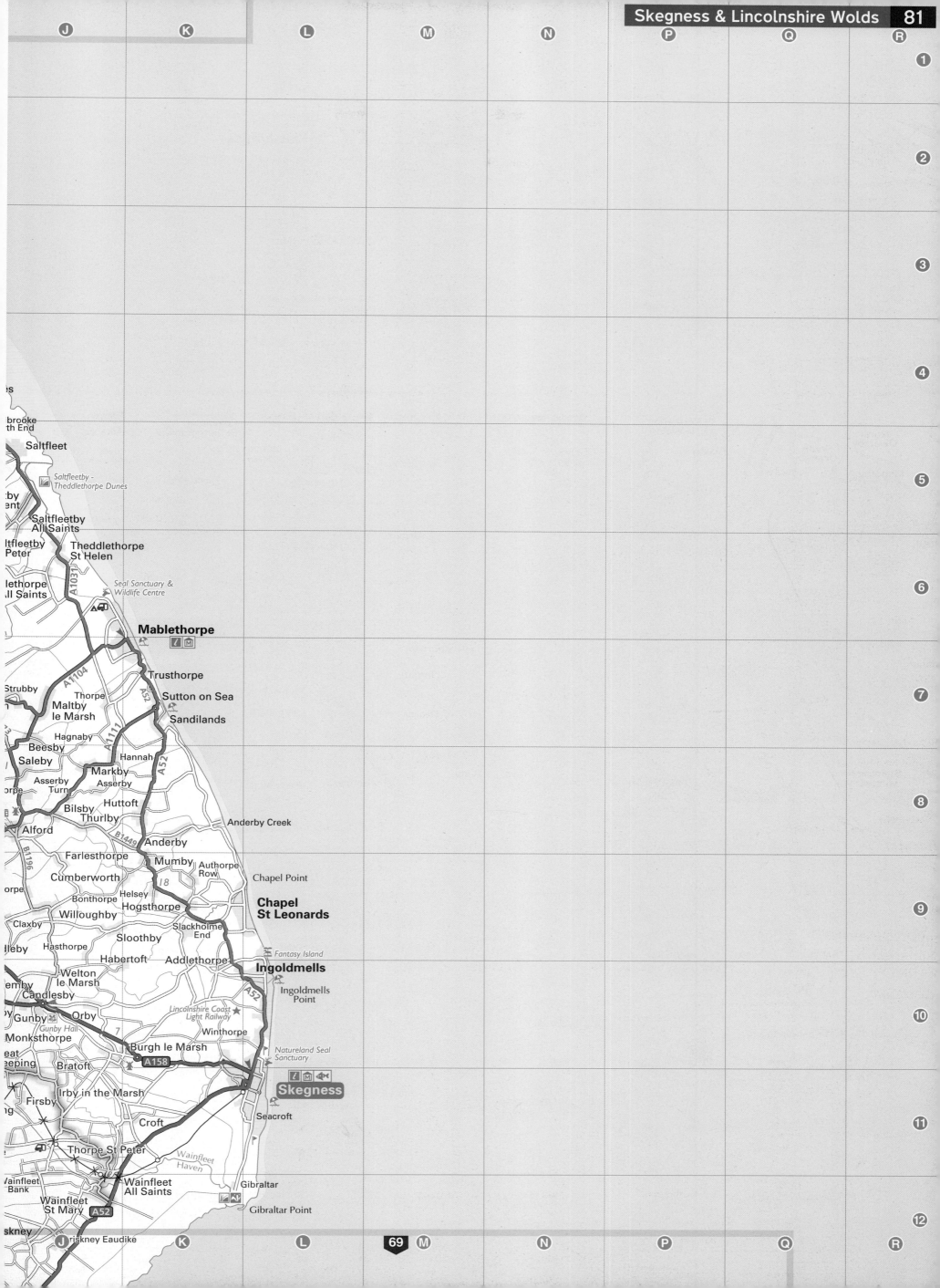

J   K   L   M   N   P   Q   R

1
2
3
4

Saltfleet

Saltfleetby -
Theddlethorpe Dunes

Saltfleetby
All Saints

Theddlethorpe
St Helen

Seal Sanctuary &
Wildlife Centre

Mablethorpe

Trusthorpe

Strubby

Thorpe
Maltby
le Marsh

Sutton on Sea

Sandilands

Hagnaby

Beesby

Saleby

Hannah

Markby

Asserby

Asserby
Turn

Bilsby

Thurlby

Huttoft

Alford

Anderby Creek

Anderby

Farlesthorpe

Mumby

Authorpe
Row

Cumberworth

Chapel Point

Helsey

Bonthorpe

Hogsthorpe

**Chapel
St Leonards**

Willoughby

Claxby

Sloothby

Slackholme
End

lleby

Hasthorpe

Habertoft

Addlethorpe

Fantasy Island

Ingoldmells

Welton
le Marsh

Ingoldmells
Point

emby

Candlesby

Orby

Lincolnshire Coast
Light Railway ★

Gunby

Gunby Hall

7

Winthorpe

Monksthorpe

Burgh le Marsh

Natureland Seal
Sanctuary

eeping

Bratoft

`A158`

Skegness

Irby in the Marsh

Firsby

Seacroft

Croft

Wainfleet
Haven

Thorpe St Peter

Gibraltar

Wainfleet
Bank

**Wainfleet
All Saints**

`A52`

Gibraltar Point

Wainfleet
St Mary

skney

J   **Friskney Eaudike**   K   L   `69` M   N   P   Q   R

5
6
7
8
9
10
11
12

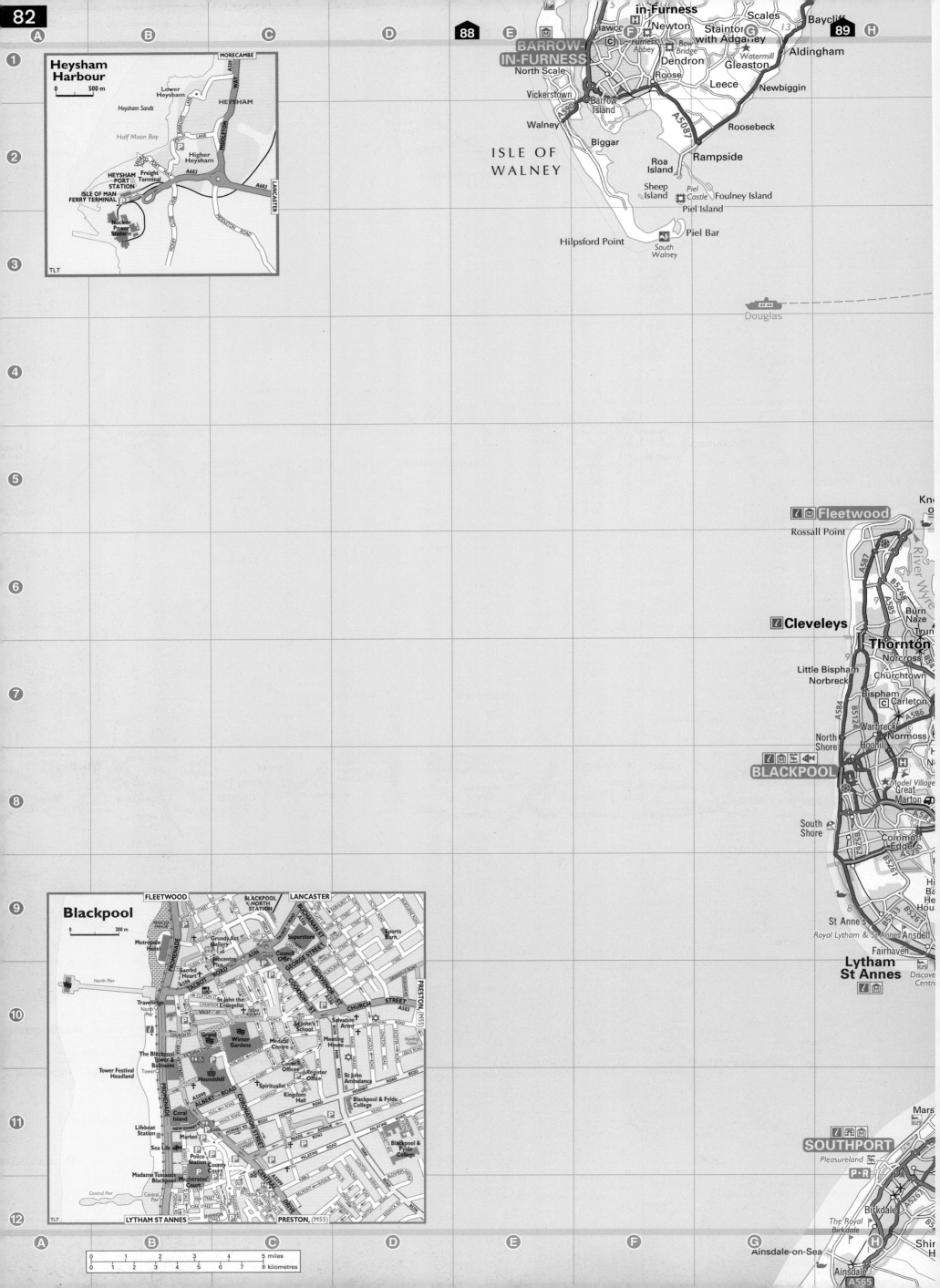

Heysham Harbour

0   500 m

MORECAMBE

Lower
Heysham

Heysham Sands

HEYSHAM

Half Moon Bay

Higher
Heysham

A683

HEYSHAM
PORT
STATION

ISLE OF MAN
FERRY TERMINAL

Freight
Terminal

LANCASTER

A683

Nuclear
Power
Stations

TLT

**BARROW
IN-FURNESS**

in-Furness

Scales   13   Baycliff

Hawcoat   Newton   Stainton
with Adgarley

Furness
Abbey   Bow
Bridge   Watermill   Aldingham

North Scale   Dendron   Gleaston

Vickerstown   Roose   Leece   Newbiggin

A590   Barrow
Island   A5087

Walney   Roosebeck

Biggar   Roa
Island   Rampside

**ISLE OF
WALNEY**   Sheep
Island   Piel
Castle   Foulney Island

Piel Island

Hilpsford Point   Piel Bar

South
Walney

Douglas

Blackpool

0   200 m

FLEETWOOD   BLACKPOOL
NORTH
STATION   LANCASTER

Metropole
Hotel   Grundy Art
Gallery   Sports
Barn

PROMENADE   Sacred
Heart   Jobcentre
Plus   Superstore

TALBOT ROAD   A586   Council
Offices   GEORGE STREET

North
Pier   CLIFTON ST   St John the
Evangelist   BUCHANAN ST   ABINGDON ST   CHURCH STREET

Travelodge   CHEAPSIDE   Cedar Square   COOKSON ST   DICKSON ROAD

Grand   St John's School   Salvation
Army   CHURCH   STREET   PRESTON, (M55)

Winter
Gardens   Medical
Centre   Meeting
House   A583

The Blackpool
Tower & Ballroom   Council
Offices   Spiritualist   St John
Ambulance   LEEDS ROAD

Tower Festival
Headland   Houndshill   Kingdom
Hall   B5261

ALBERT ROAD   A5099   Register
Office   Blackpool & Fylde
College

Coral Island   CORONATION STREET   HORNBY RD   Blackpool & Fylde
College

Lifeboat
Station   Market   HULL   VANCE RD   PALATINE   AVENUE   PALATINE ROAD

Sea Life   NEW BONNY'S   Police
Station   County
Court

Madame Tussauds
Blackpool   Magistrates
Court   CENTRAL DRIVE   CHAPEL STREET

Central Pier   YORK STREET

TLT   LYTHAM ST ANNES   PRESTON, (M55)

Fleetwood

Knc
O

Rossall Point   A587

River Wyre

B5268   A585

Cleveleys   Thornton   Burn
Naze   Trun

Little Bispham   Norcross

Norbreck   Churchtown

Bispham   Carleton

A584   B5124   Warbreck

North Shore   Normoss

Hoohill

BLACKPOOL   Model Village
Great
Marton

A583

South
Shore   B5262   Common
Edge

B5261

St Anne's   B5261
Royal Lytham & St Annes   Ansdell

Fairhaven

Lytham
St Annes   Discover
Centre

SOUTHPORT

Pleasureland

P·R

Mars

Birkdale

The Royal
Birkdale

Ainsdale-on-Sea   Ainsdale   A565   Shir

---

0   1   2   3   4   5 miles
0   1   2   3   4   5   6   7   8 kilometres

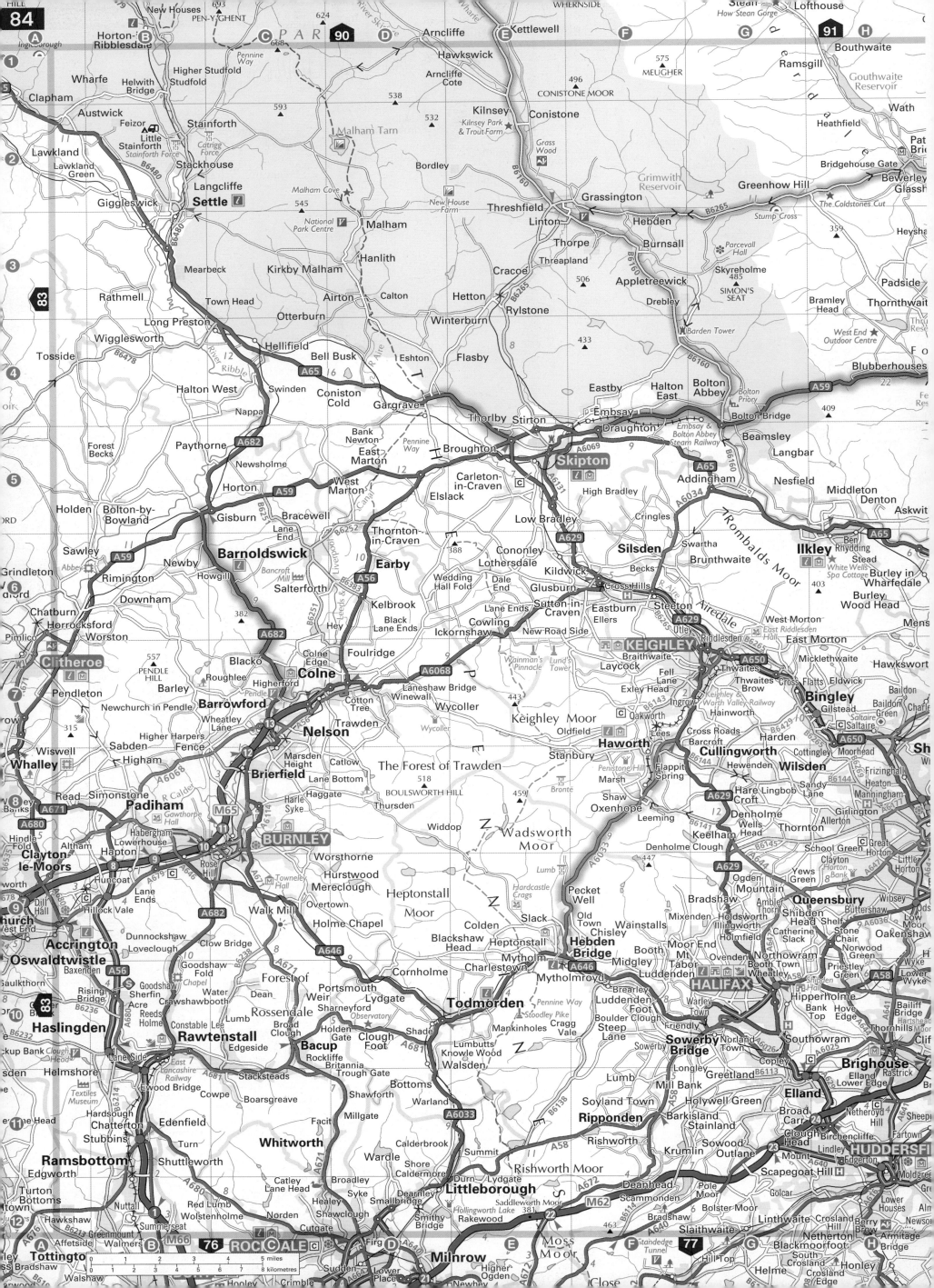

Port of Hull

0 ———— 1 km

TLT

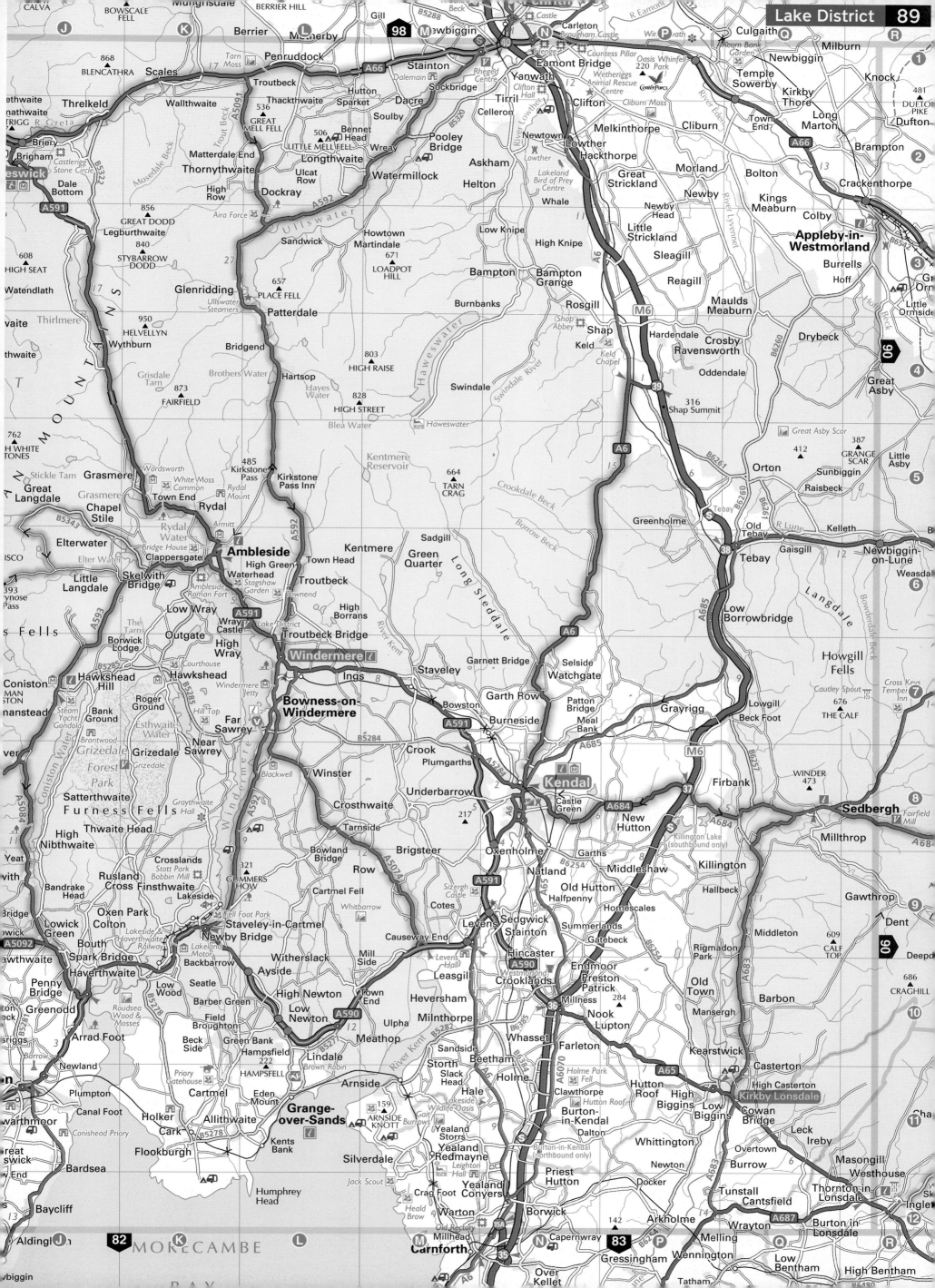

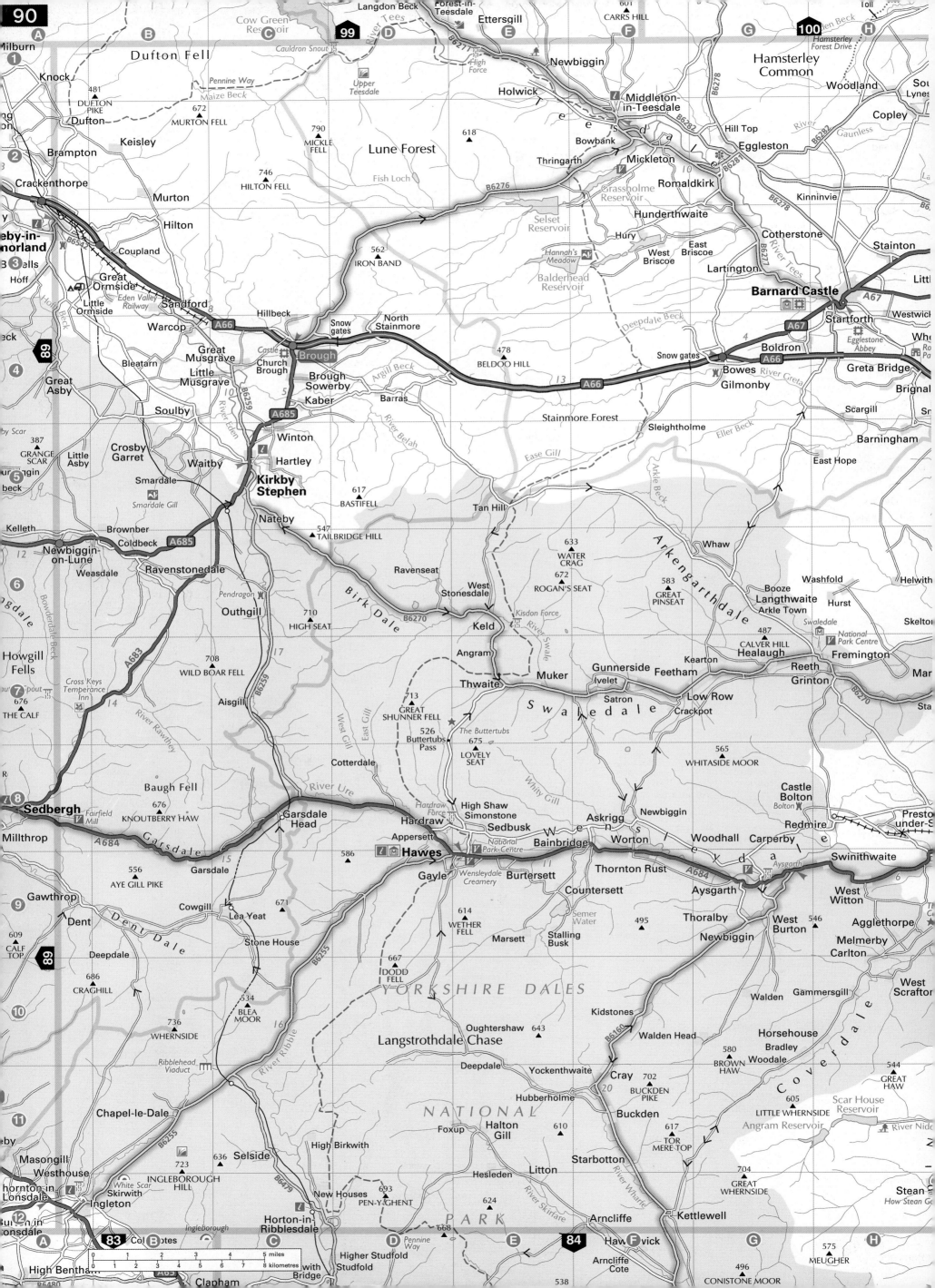

Middlesbrough

TRANSPORTER BRIDGE

MIDDLESBROUGH COLLEGE

MIDDLESBROUGH STATION

STOCKTON

TEESPORT

STOKESLEY

Whitby

Saltwick Bay
Abbey
Stainsacre
High Hawsker
Ness Point or North Cheek
Low Hawsker
Raw
Robin Hood's Bay
Fylingthorpe
Robin Hood's Bay
Old Peak or South Cheek
Ravenscar

Staintondale
Shire Horse Centre
Hayburn Wyke
Cloughton Newlands
Cloughton Wyke
Cloughton
Cromer Point

Harwood Dale
Bickley
Broxa
Silpho
Burniston
Langdale End
Hackness
Suffield
Newby
North Bay Railway
Cleveland Way
Wrench Green
Everley
Scalby
Castle
Forest Park
Sea Cut
Falsgrave
Scarborough
Oliver's Mount

Sawdon
West Ayton
East Ayton
Forge Valley Wood
Eastfield
Osgodby
Cayton Bay

Ruston
Hutton Buscel
Irton Seamer
Crossgates
High Killerby
The Wyke
Snainton
Wykeham
Cayton
Lebberston
Filey Brigg
Brompton-by-Sawdon
Gristhorpe
Willerby
Folkton
Muston
Filey
Flixton
West Flotmanby
Filey Bay
Staxton
Ganton
Sherburn
Hunmanby
Flamborough Head Heritage Coast
East Heslerton
Potter Brompton
Fordon
Reighton
Speeton
Bempton Cliffs
Thornwick Bay
Foxholes
Wold Newton
Burton Fleming
Buckton
North Landing
Bempton
Butterwick
Grindale
Flamborough Cliffs
Helperthorpe
Weaverthorpe
Thwing
Octon
Flamborough
Marton
FLAMBOROUGH HEAD
Sewerby

WHITBY

Alexandra Gardens
Peasholm Park
Bowls Centre
North Sands
North Bay
Cricket Ground
Royal Albert Park
Castle Hill
Scarborough Castle (Ruins)
Coastguard Station
Fire Sta
St Mary's
YMCA
Friarage School
Luna Park
Balmoral Centre
Lifeboat Station
Old Harbour
Town Hall
West Pier
Courts
Police Stn
Brunswick
Olympia Leisure
Grand Hotel
East Pier
Stephen Joseph
SCARBOROUGH STATION
Vincent's Pier
Rotunda Art Gallery
South Sands
South Bay
Superstore
Woodend Creative Workspace
Scarborough

PICKERING, MALTON

FILEY

TLT

A171 **A165** **A170** **A64** **A1039** **B1249** **B1261** **B1229** **B1255** **B1259**

A77

B734

River Stinchar

Colmonell

B734

Bennane Head

Ballantrae

Heronsford

Water of Tig

Currarie Port

Belfast

BENERAIRD 437

321 CARLOCK HILL

Larne

Milleur Point

Glen App

387 ALTIMEG HILL

Corsewall Point

Lady Bay

Glenwhilly

Laggang Standing S

Barnhills

Portencalzie

Main Water of Luce

Cross Water of Luce

B738

Kirkcolm

A718

Cairnryan

A77

Penwhirn Reservoir

Braid Fell

Loch Connell

Ervie

Low Barbeth

6

Beoch Burn

New Luce

B738

B738

Leswalt

Low Salchrie

Loch Ryan

Innermessan

A751

Black Loch

Castle Kennedy

White Loch

164 CRAIG FELL

Knocknain

B7043

Castle of St John

A77

Chlenry

Balgracie

Stranraer

Aird

Castle Kennedy

A75

10

Glenluce Abb

Auchnotteroch

H

Glenwhan

Dunragit

Glenluc

Portslogan

B738

Broadsea Bay

Lochans

Kildrochet House

Piltanton Burn

Whitecrook

Black Head

Dunskey

181 CAIRN PAT

8

14

B7077

B7084

Ringdoo Point

Milto

Portpatrick

A77

Stoneykirk

A716

19

Luce Sands

Stairhave

North Milmain

18

B7084

Au

Mull of Si

Cairngarroch

Kirkmadrine Stones

B7042

Sandhead

Money Head

High Ardwell

Ardwell Bay

Ardwell

Chapel Rossan

L U C E

Drumbreddon

Balgowan

Logan

Port Logan Bay

Port Logan

B7065

A716

Garrochtrie

Clanyard Bay

Kilstay

Laggantalluch Head

Kirkmaiden

Drummore

Barncorkrie

High Drummore

Cailiness Point

Damnaglaur

Maryport

B7041

Cardryne

Cardrain

West Cairngaan

MULL OF GALLOWAY

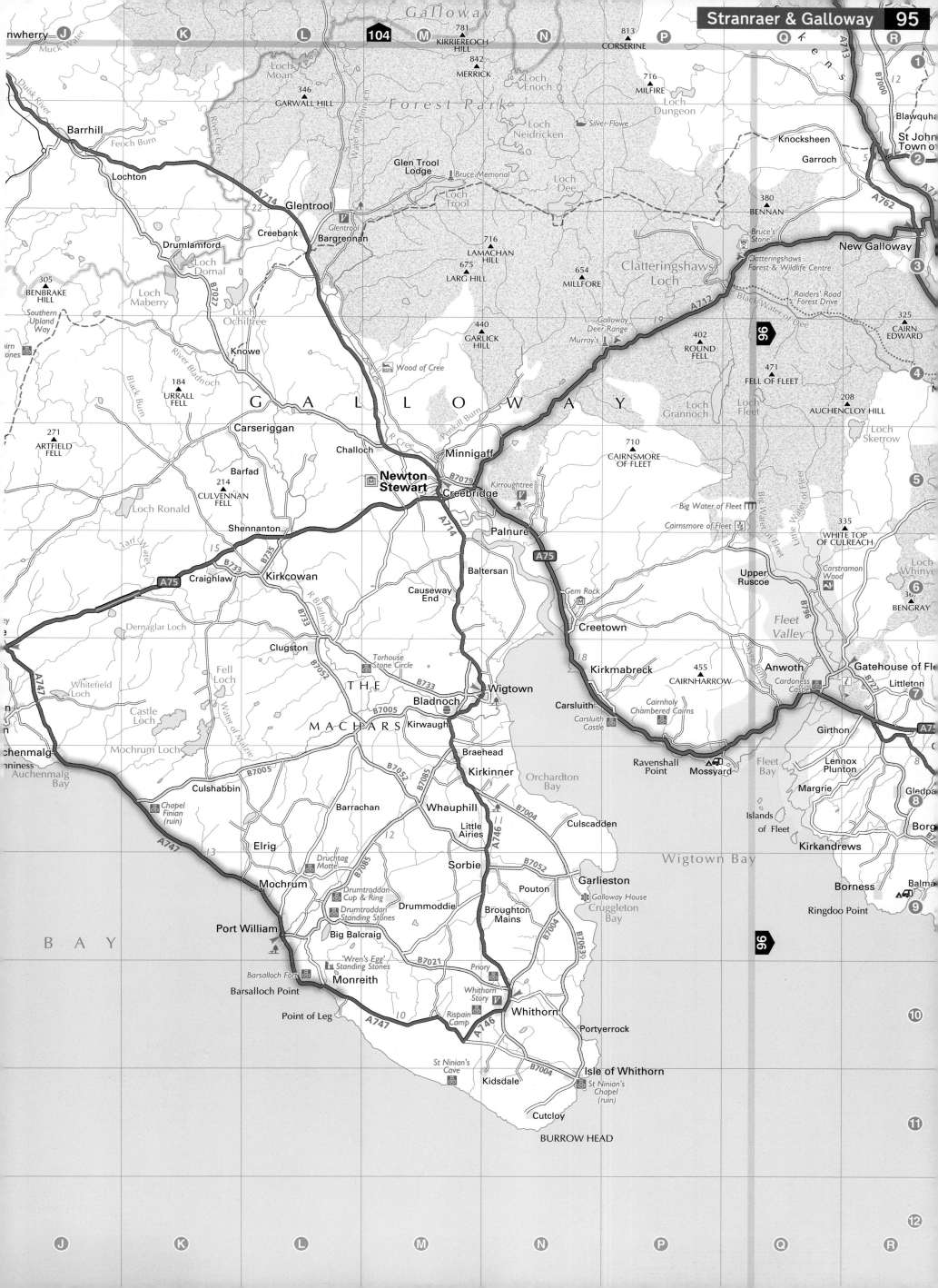

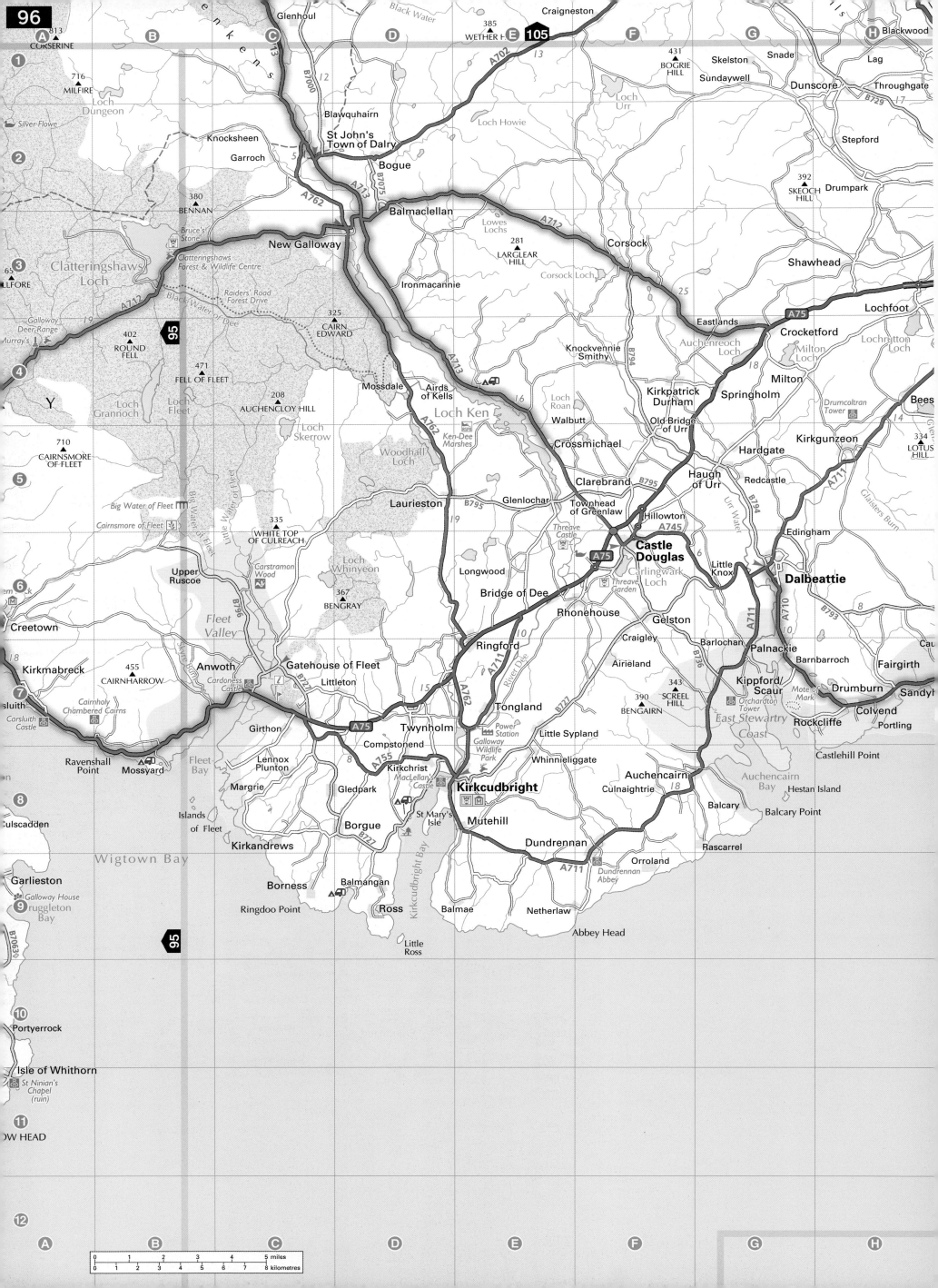

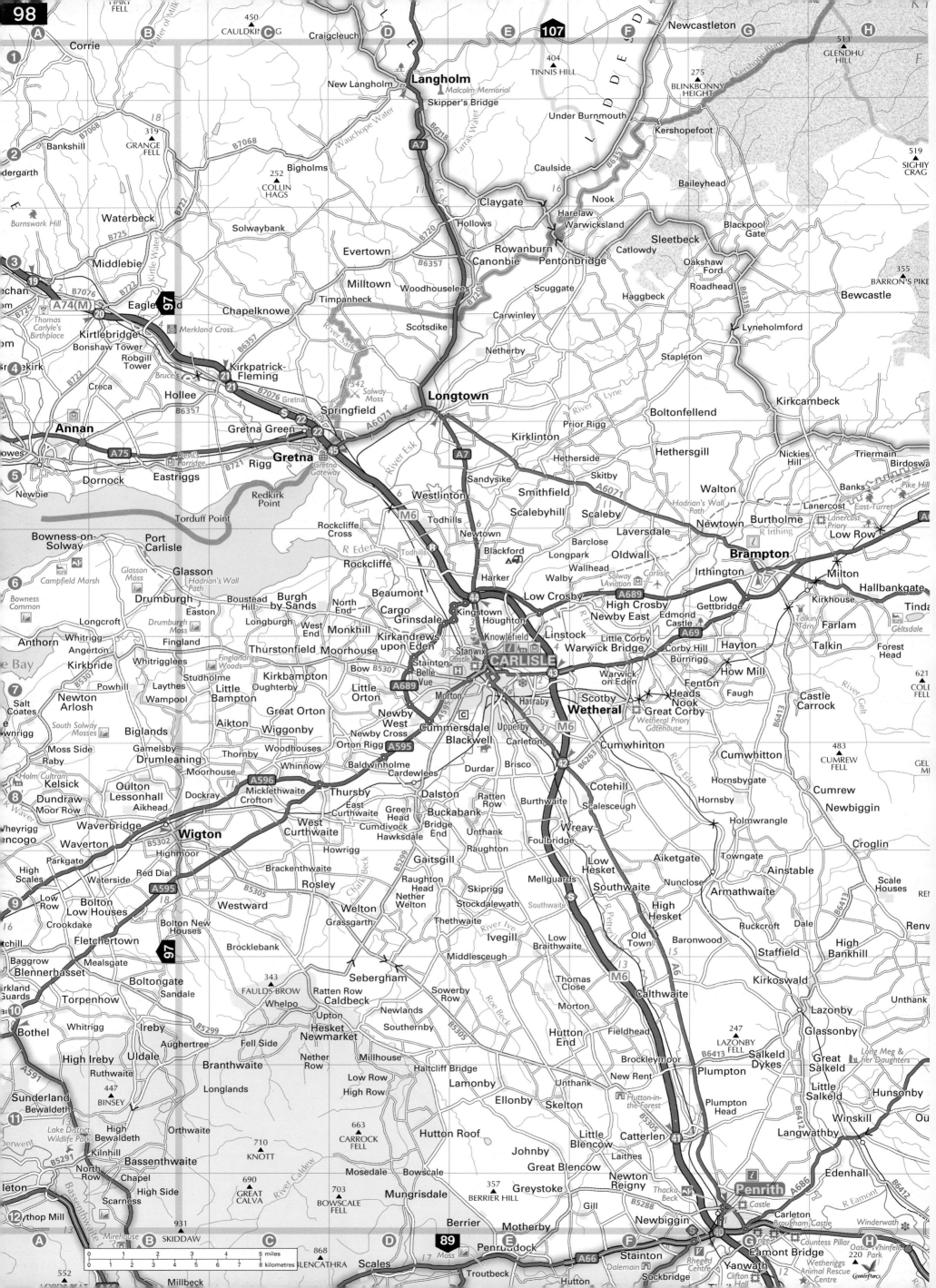

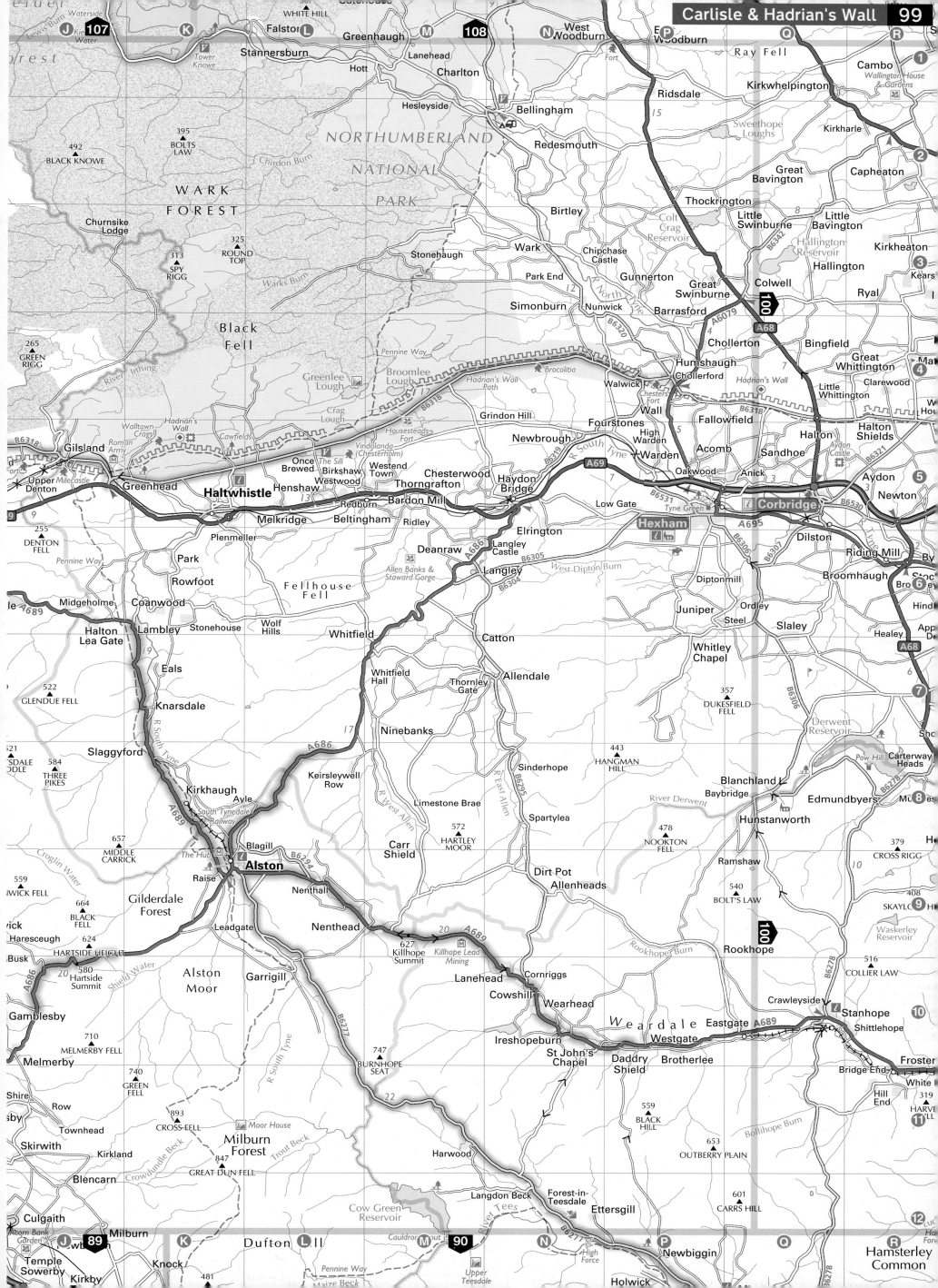

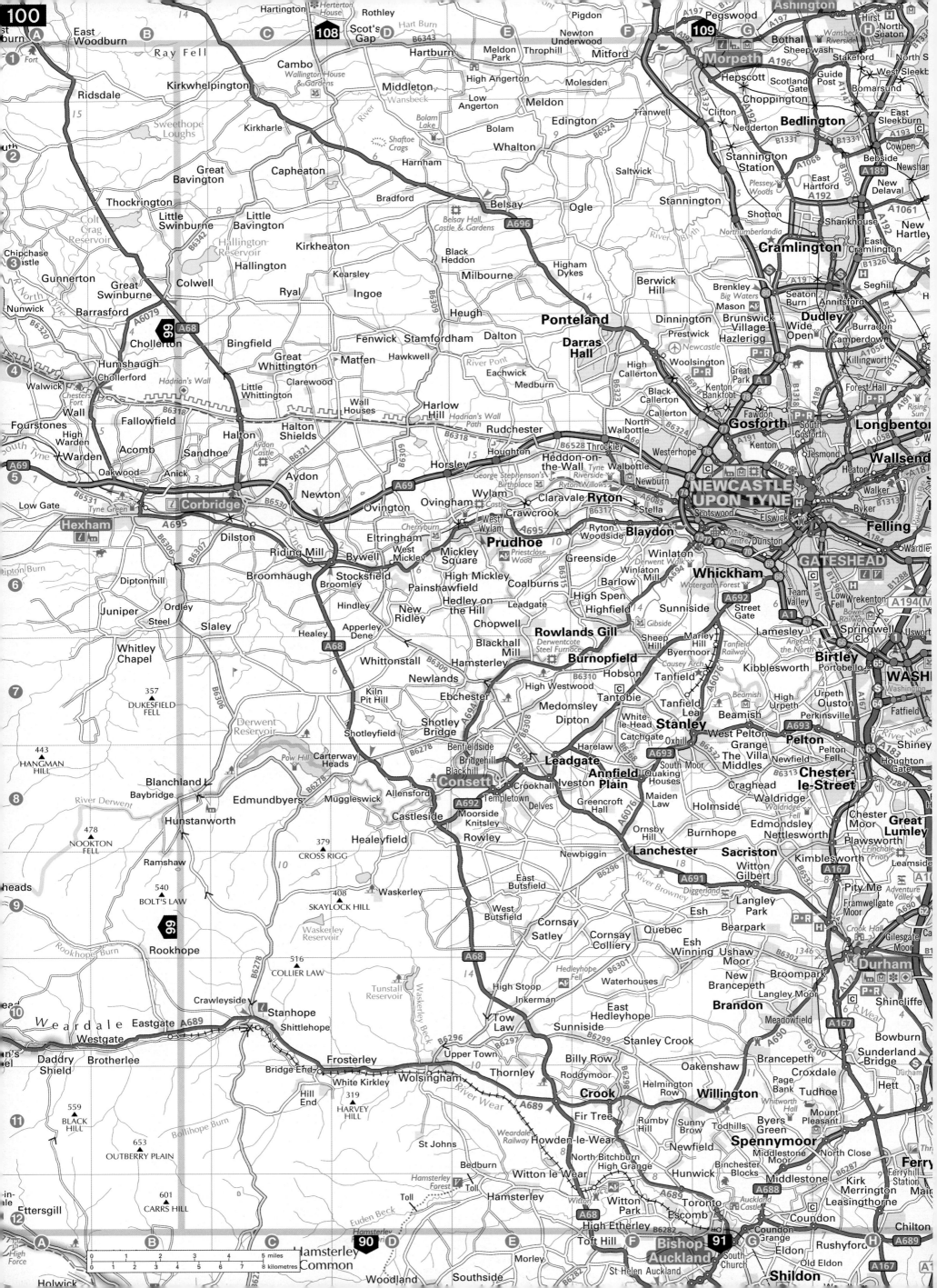

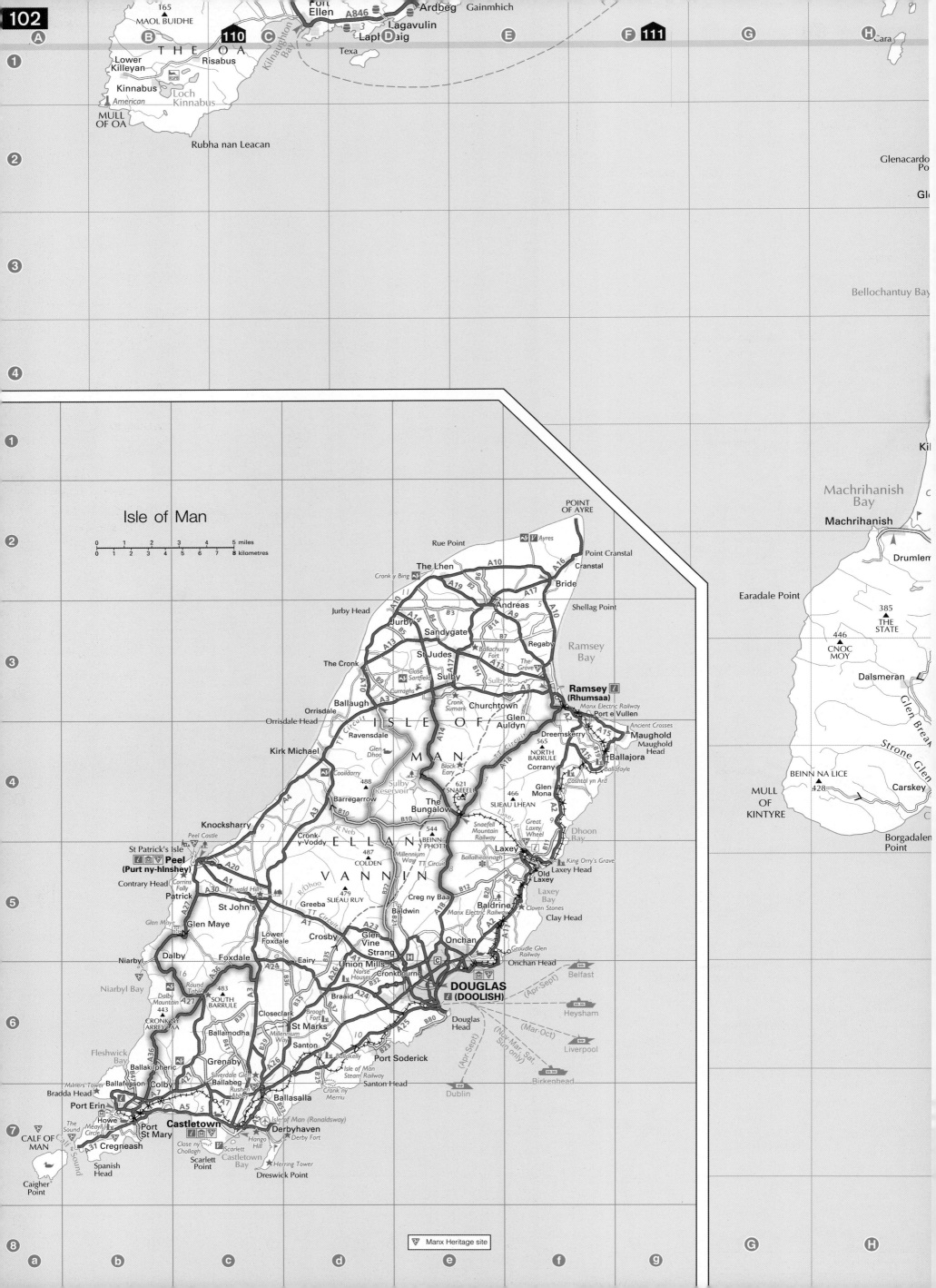

Isle of Man

0 1 2 3 4   5 miles
0 1 2 3 4 5 6 7   8 kilometres

Manx Heritage site

A R R A N

KILBRANNAN SOUND

Kintyre (west side)

Grogport
Barmollack
Pirnmill
Penrioch
North Arran
CAISTEAL ABHAIL
Corrie

354
CRUACH NAN GABHAR
Muasdale
Whitefarland
715
BEINN BHARRAIN
874
GOATFELL
Merkland Point

Belloch
Imachar
792
BEINN NUIS
Glen Rosa
Brodick Castle, Garden & Country Park

Clan MacAlister
Balliekine
Glen Iorsa
Iorsa Water
Brodick Bay

Bellochantuy
454
BEINN AN TUIRC
Torrisdale
Carradale
Bridgend
Dippen
Waterfoot
Carradale House
Port Righ
Carradale Point
ARRAN
Brodick
Strathwhillan
Corriegills

319
Cleongart
408
BÒRD MÓR
Saddell
Auchagallon Stone Circle
Machrie
Machrie Bay
Tormore
Machrie Moor Stone Circles
512
A'CHRUACH
Clauchlands Point
Margnaheglish
Lamlash
Holy Island

396
SGREADÀN HILL
Ugadale
Saddell Bay
Moss Farm Road Stone Circle
503
BEINN BHREAC
Balmichael
Torbeg
Shiskine
Drumadoon Point
Blackwaterfoot
Kilpatrick
Kilpatrick Dun
Lamlash Bay
Cordon
Auchencairn
Kingscross
Knockenkelly
Whiting Bay

Lussa Loch
Tangy Loch
Glen Lussa
Peninver
Ardnacross Bay
Drumadoon Bay
Brown Head
Glen Scorrodale
Carn Ban
Glenashdale
Largymore
Whiting Bay

Kilmichael
Campbeltown
Campbeltown Loch
Island Davaar
Corriecravie
Sliddery
Torr a' Chaisteal Fort
Kilmory Water
Dippin
Largybeg
Dippin Head

Stewarton
Kilkerran
Kildalloig
352
BEINN GHUILEAN
Achinhoan
Lagg
Torrylin Cairn
Kilmory
Bennan
Kildonan
(May–Sept, Sat only)
Campbeltown–Ardrossan (May–Sept)

Conie Glen
Glen Kerran
Ru Stafnish
Bennan Head
Pladda

Cattadale
Polliwilline Bay
Macharioch
Southend
Dunaverty
Sound of Sanda
Sheep Island
Sanda Island

Ailsa Craig
340
RSPB

0   1   2   3   4   5 miles
0 1 2 3 4 5 6 7 8 kilometres

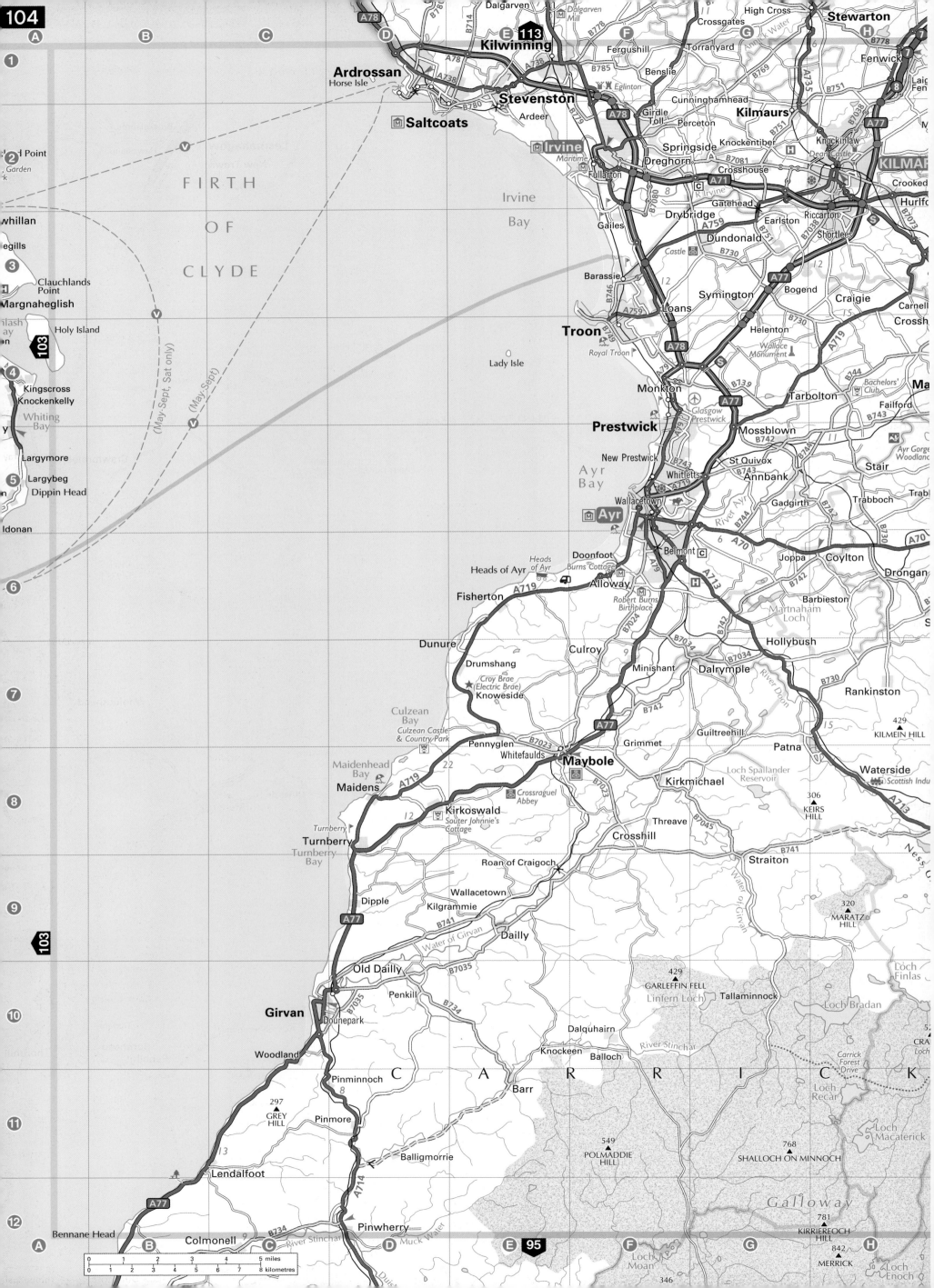

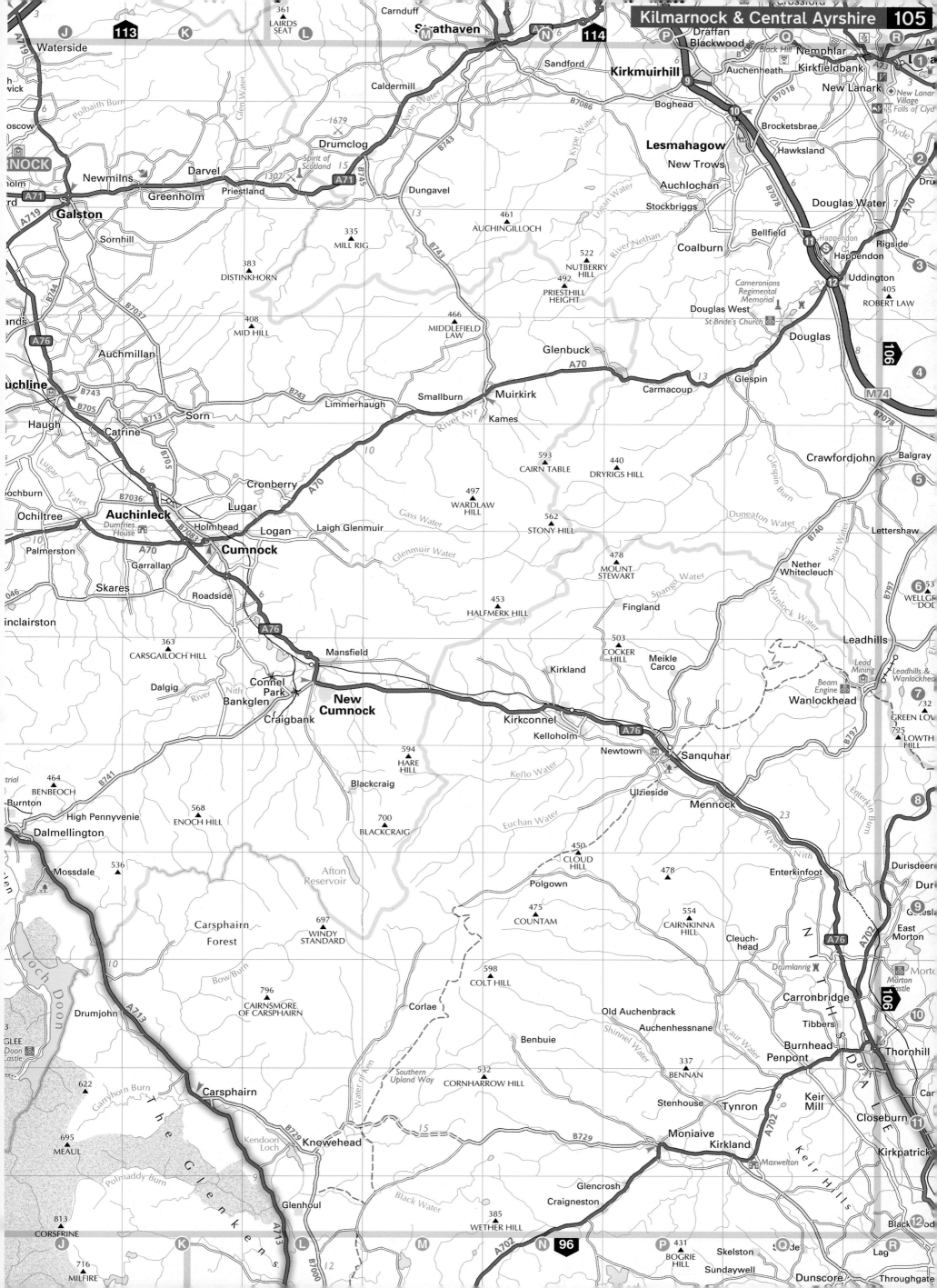

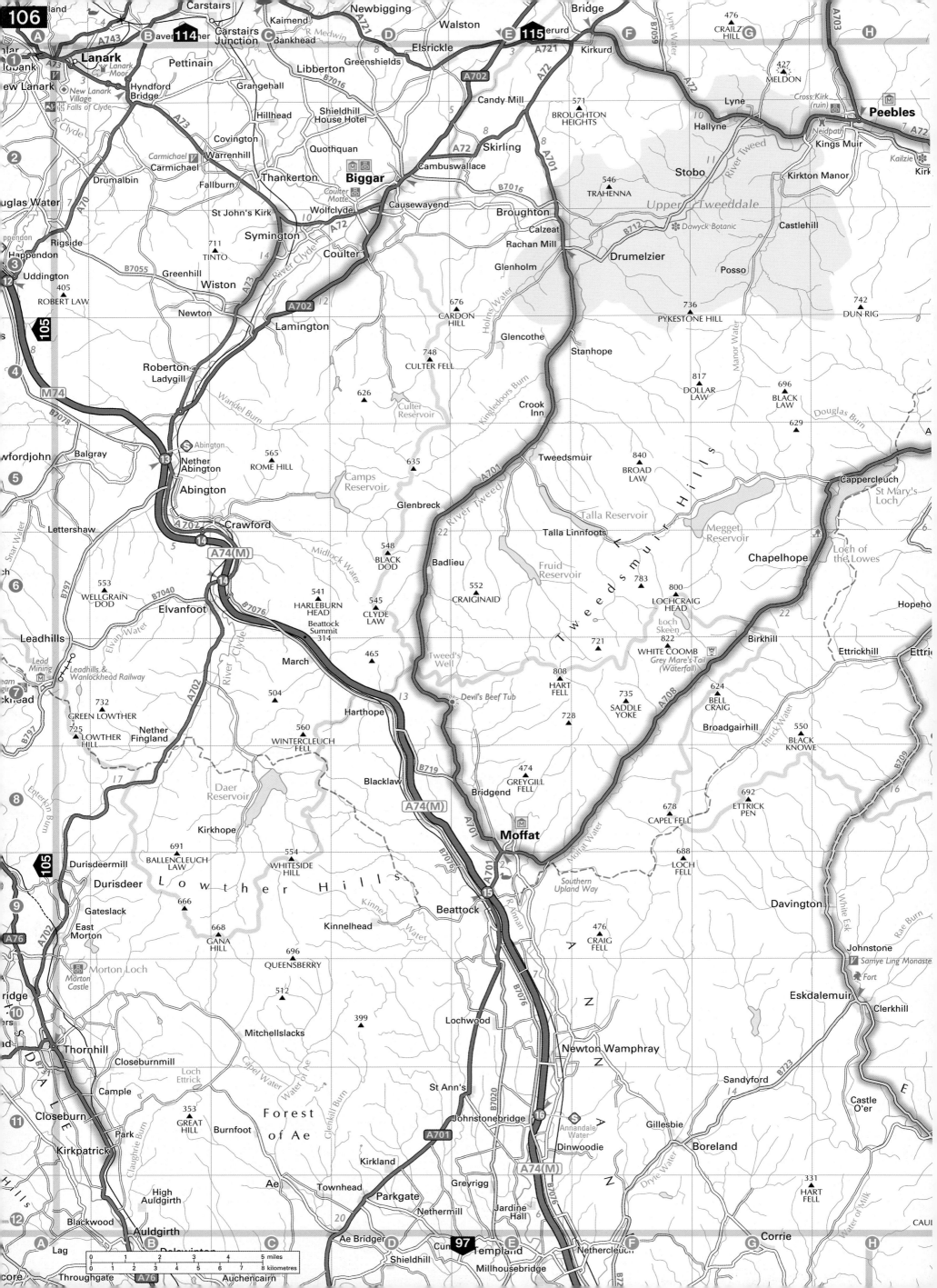

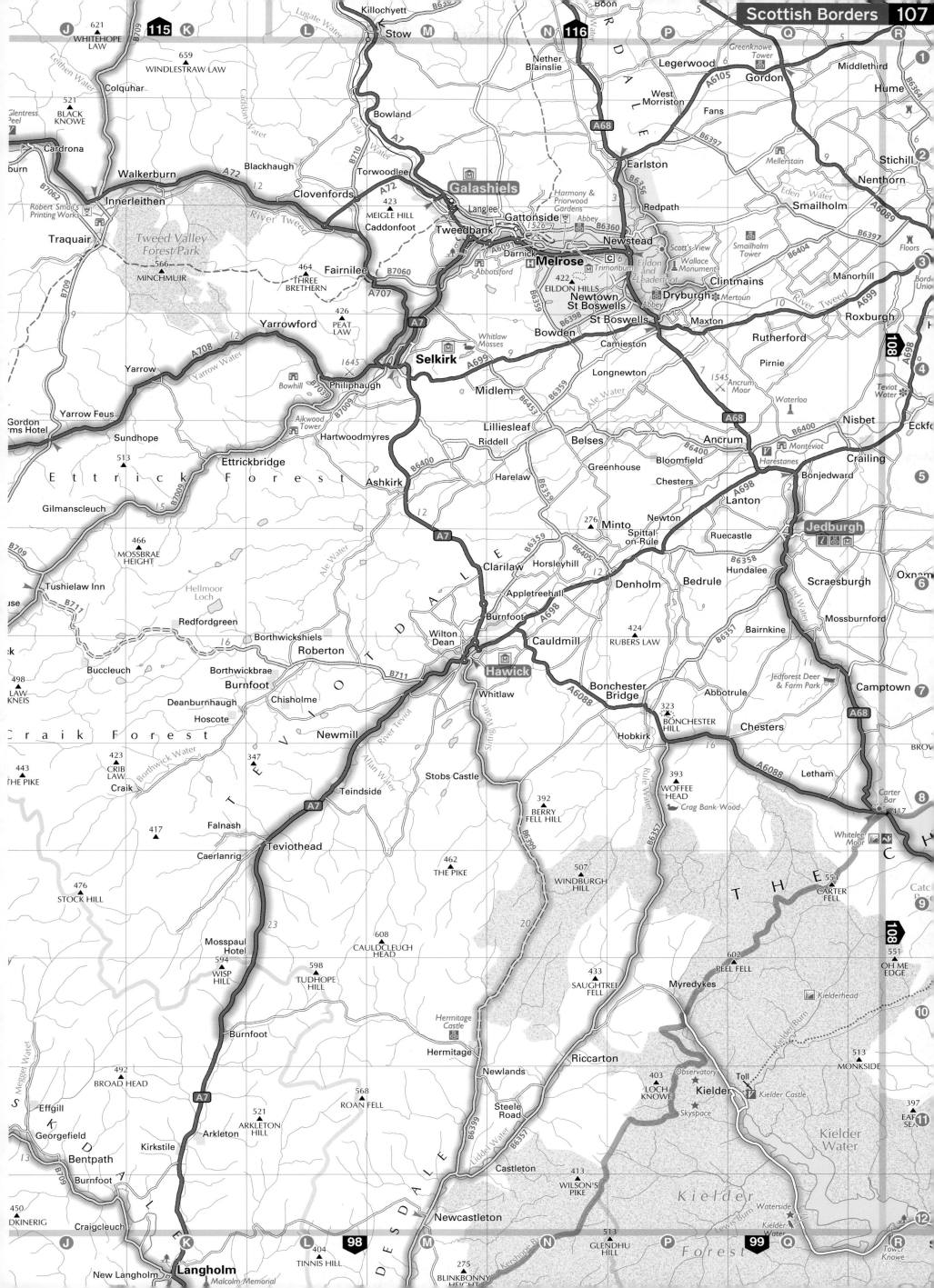

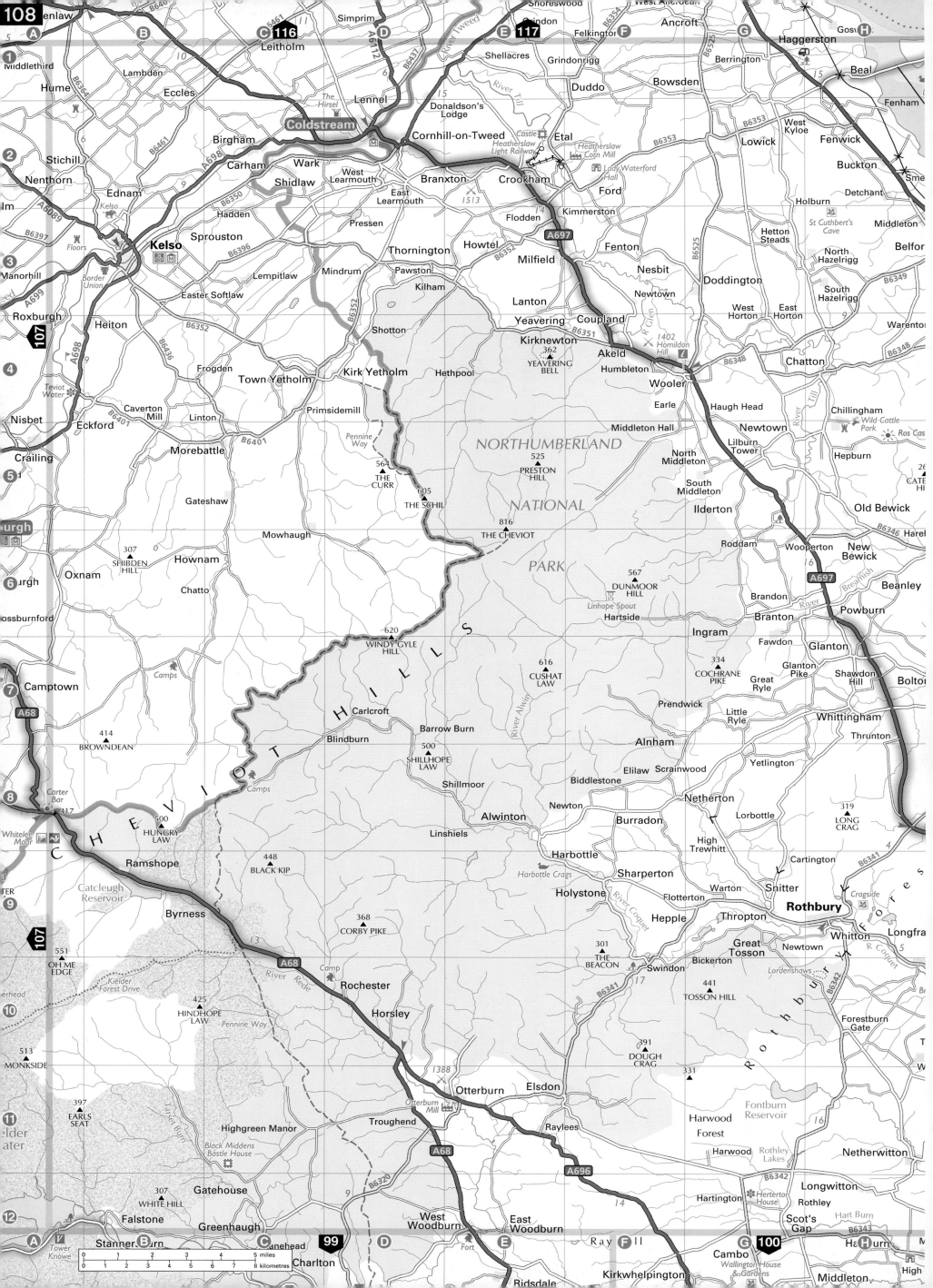

J **117** K L M N P Q R

1

HOLY ISLAND
Holy
Island
Lindisfarne
Priory
Castle Point
Guile Point
Causeway
flooded at
high tide

Longstone
FARNE
ISLANDS
Staple
Sound
Inner
Sound
North Northumberland
Heritage Coast

field Elwick
Ross

Low
Middleton
Easington
Waren
Mill
Outchester
Spindlestone

Bradford

Bellshill

Adderstone

Warenford

Budle
Bay
Budle
Bamburgh

New
Shoreston

Seahouses

Elford
North Sunderland

Beadnell

Newham
Swinhoe
Beadnell
Bay

Lucker

Newstead
Chathill
Tughall

Ellingham
Preston

North
Charlton
Fallodon

South
Charlton

West
Ditchburn

Eglingham

Brownieside

Doxford
Brunton
Christon
Bank

Newton-by-the-Sea
Embleton &
Newton Links

Embleton

Embleton
Bay

Dunstan
Steads
Dunstanburgh
Castle

Rock
Rennington

Dunstan

Stamford

Craster

Howick
Hall
Howick

Cullernose Point

Broxfield

Littlehoughton

Longhoughton

Boulmer

East
Bolton

Abberwick

River Aln

Broome
Park

Alnwick

Denwick

Hawkhill

Lesbury

Seaton Point

Aln Valley
Railway
Bilton

Hipsburn
Alnmouth

Alnmouth
Bay

Castle

Edlingham

Bilton
Banks

Shilbottle

High
Buston

Low
Buston

Birling

Warkworth Castle
& Hermitage
Warkworth

GLANTLEES
HILL
Newton-on-
the-Moor

Amble

Coquet Island

Swarland

Old
Swarland

North End

Guyzance

North
Togston

Gloster Hill

High
Hauxley

Felton

Acklington

Togston

Radcliffe

East
Thirston

Broomhill

Pauperhaugh

Weldon
Bridge

West
Thirston

South
Broomhill

Hadston

Eshott

Red Row

Druridge Bay

West
Chevington

Druridge

Druridge
Bay

Helm

Stobswood

Widdrington

North Northumberland
Heritage Coast

Longhorsley

Causey
Park

Causey Park
Bridge

Earsdon

Widdrington
Station

Cresswell

gates

Fenrother

Tritlington

Ulgham

Linton
Ellington

Lynemouth

Stanton

Hebron

Longhirst

Woodhorn
Beacon Point

Woodhorn Demesne

Pigdon

Newton
Underwood

Pegswood

Ashington

Hirst
North
Seaton

Newbiggin-by-
the-Sea

eldon
Park

Mitford

Morpeth

Bothal

Stakeford

North Seaton Colliery

N **101** P Q R

Hepscott

Molesden

Scotland
Gate

Guide
Post

West Sleekburn

Bomarsund

COLONSAY

Kilchattar

Garvard

Oronsay

Dubh Eilean
ORONSAY

Nave Island
Ardnave
Point
Gortantaoid
Point

Tòn Mhòr

Eilean Mòr
Sanaigmore
Kilnave

Rubha Lamanais
Loch
Gòrr
Loch Gruinart
Lecht Gruinart

Saligo Bay
B8018
B8017
Gleann Mòr
Eir

Coul Point
Loch
Gorm
Gruinart

Machir
Bay
Sunderland
B8018
Kilchoman
A847
Bridgend
Gartacho

Bruichladdich
Loch
Indaal

Kilchiaran Bay
Bowmore

Port
Charlotte
15
M

231
BEINN TART A'MHILL
RHINNS
River Laggan
IS

Lossit Bay
OF
Nerabus
Laggan
Point
Duich R.
A846
B8016

Rubha na
Faing
ISLAY
A847
Glenegedale

Portnahaven
11

Port Wemyss
Laggan
Islay

Orsay
RHINNS
POINT
Bay

Rubha Mòr
Kintra

165
MAOL BUIDHE
PE

THE OA

Killeyan
Lov
Risabus
G
H

Kinnabus
Loch

0 1 2 3 4 5 miles
0 1 2 3 4 5 6 7 8 kilometres

J K 119 L M N 120 P Q R

Gulf of Corryvreckan

1

Eilean Dubh
Kiloran Bay
143 CARNAN EOIN
Kiloran
Rubh' a' Geodha
Oban

Glengarrisdale Bay
295 CRUACH NA SEILCHEIG

Aird
Loch Craignish
Craignish Point
Island Macaskin
Temple Stone

2

Scalasaig
Machrins
B8085

Glendebadel Bay

364 BEN GARRISDALE

Loch Crinan
Crinan
Kilmahumaig
Bellanoch

3

Rubha Bàn

Corpach Bay

J U R A

466 BEINN BHREAC
Lussa River
Glen Grundale
Lealt Burn

112
Knapdale

Eilean Ghaoideamal

Shian Bay
453 RAINBERG MÒR

Ardlussa
Lussa Point
Lussagiven

Carsaig Bay
Tayvallich

Achnam
Kilmich
Taynish

4

Colonsay–Port Askaig

Loch Righ Mòr

A846

K N A P D A L E
B8025

Rubh' an t-Sàilein

Loch Tarbert

Keills Chapel
Loch na Cille

466 CRUACH LUSACH

5

Rubha a' Mhàil

506 SCRINADLE

398 BEINN TARSUINN

Danna Island
Castle Sween
Kilbride
Lochhead
Achal

6

Rubha Bholsa
363 SGARBH BREAC

Jura Forest
784 BEINN AN OIR
734
Paps of Jura

St Cormac's Chapel
Kilmory Knap Chapel
Kilmory
Kilmory Bay
Point of Knap
Ellary

Bunnahabhain
316 GUIR-BHEINN

Loch a' Chnuic Bhric

S O U N D   O F   J U R A

Loch Caolisport
Ormsary

7

Jura
24
Knockrome
Ardfernal

Druimdrishaig
Loch nan Torran
48 DUBH CHREAG

Port Askaig
Keills
Finlaggan
Loch Laggan
Feolin Ferry
560 GLAS BHEINN
Keils

Cretshengan
Coulaghailtro

8

Ballygrant
8
A846
Loch Ballygrant
Loch Lossit

529 DUBH BHEINN
Craighouse
Small Isles

Kilberry Sculptured Stones
Kilberry

266 BEINNE DUBH

342 BRAT BHEINN
Cabrach
Rubha na Caillich

213 CRUACH AIRDE
Kilberry Head
Keppoch Point
Tiretigan

Loch Stornoway
Torin

9

ssan
429 SGÒRR NAM FAOILEANN
471
Kilennan Burn

Am Fraoch Eilean
Brosdale Island
Rubha na Tràille

Port Askaig – Kennacraig

Ardpatrick
112
Portachoillan
Clachan

I S L A Y

490 BEINN BHEIGEIR

McArthur's Head

Ronachan Point
Ronachan

10

454 BEINN URARAIDH
Loch Uraraidh

Rubha Liath
Ardtalla
Claggain Bay

Kinerarach
Tarbert
GIGHA

Loch Ciaran
Loch Garasdale

346 BEINN SHOLUM

Kintour
Kildalton Cross
Ardmore Point

Port Ellen – Kennacraig

Rhunahaorine Point
Ardminish
Achamore

247 CRUACH MHIC GOUGAIN
CNOC A' SAMHLA

11

Port Ellen
A846
3
Lagavulin
Laphroaig
Texa

Ardbeg
Rubha na Gainmhich
Eilean a' Chùirn

Cara

Rhunahaorine
38
Tayinloan
Sound of Gigha

354

12

J K L 102 M N P 103 Q R

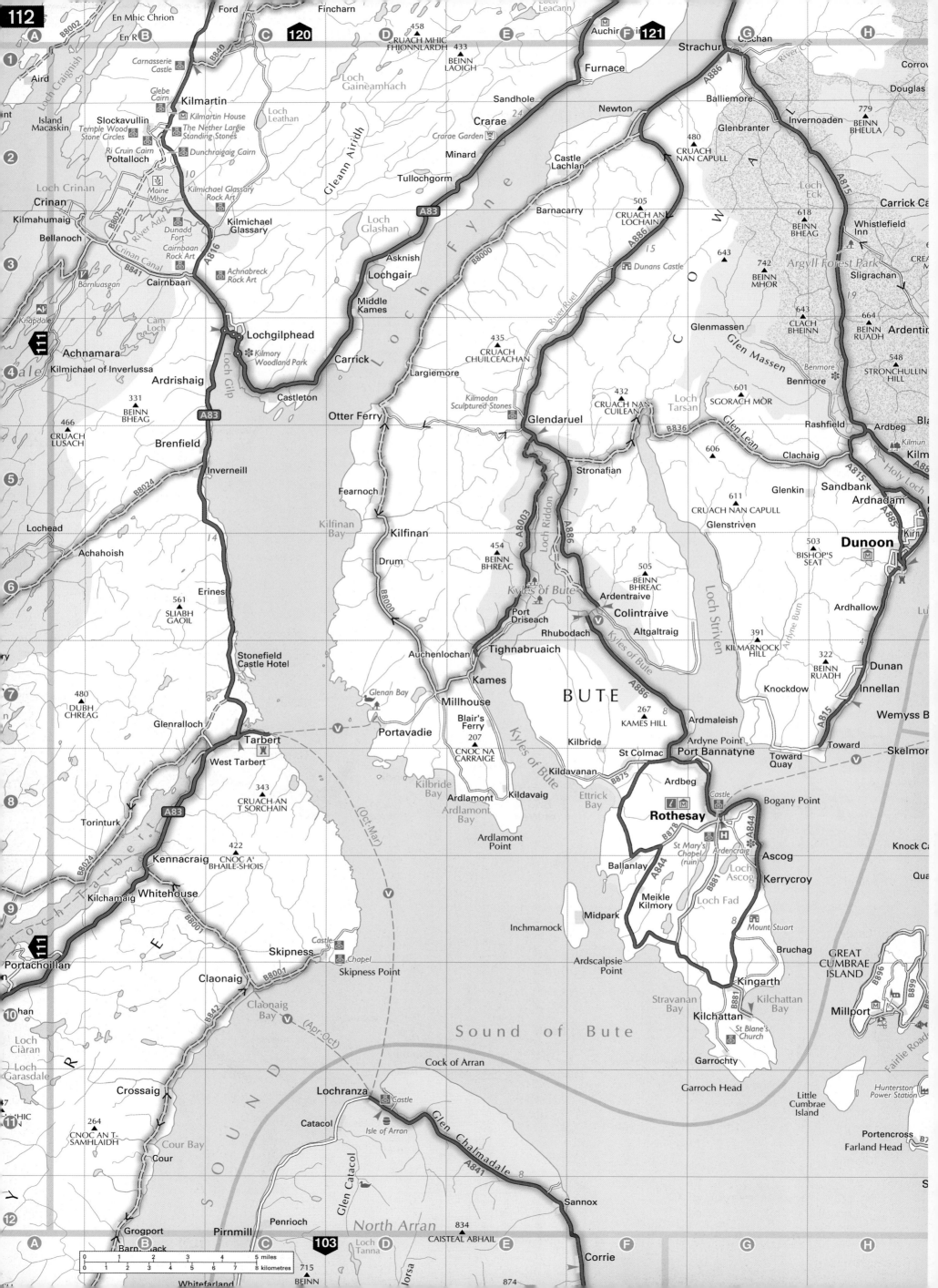

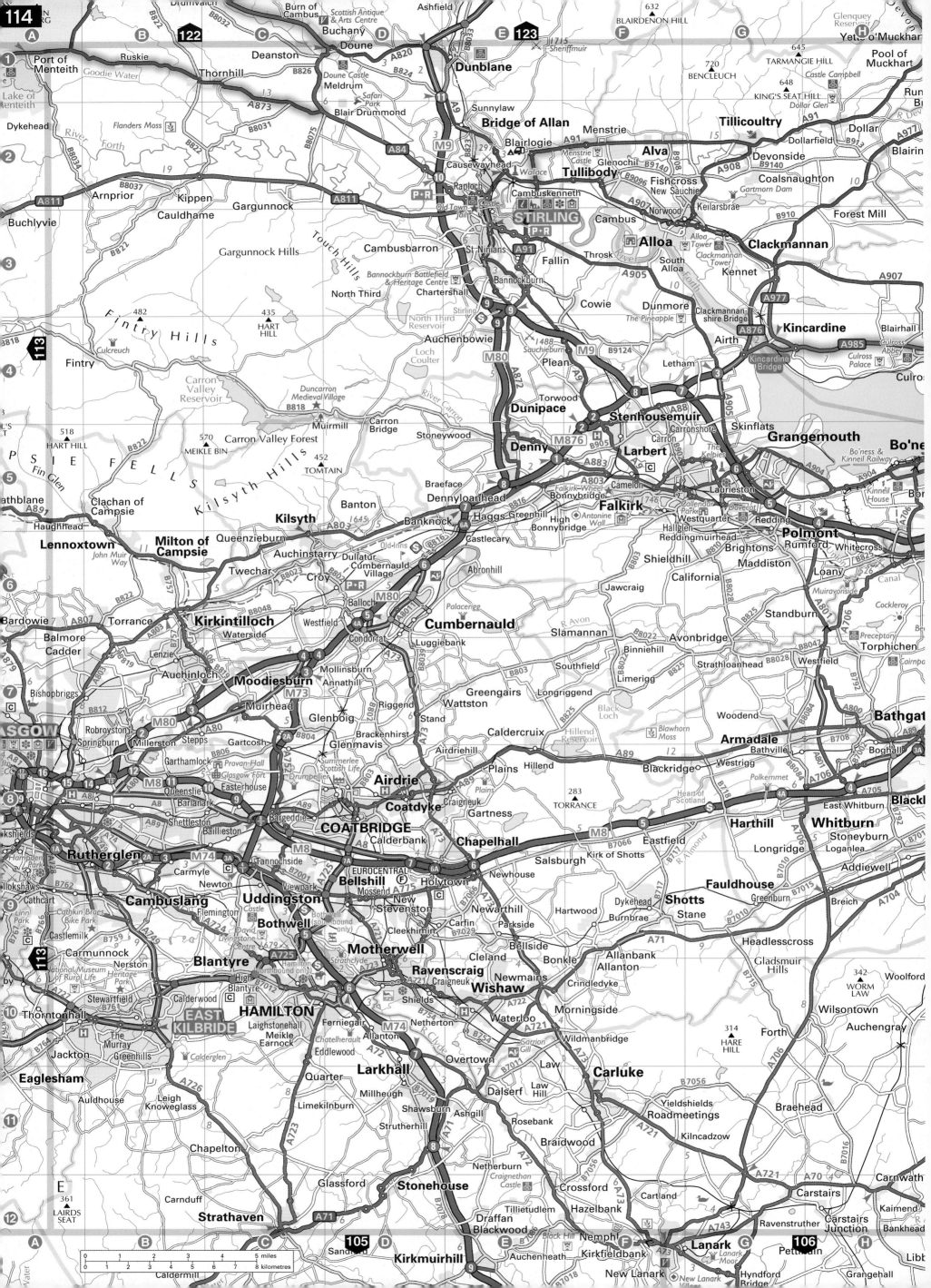

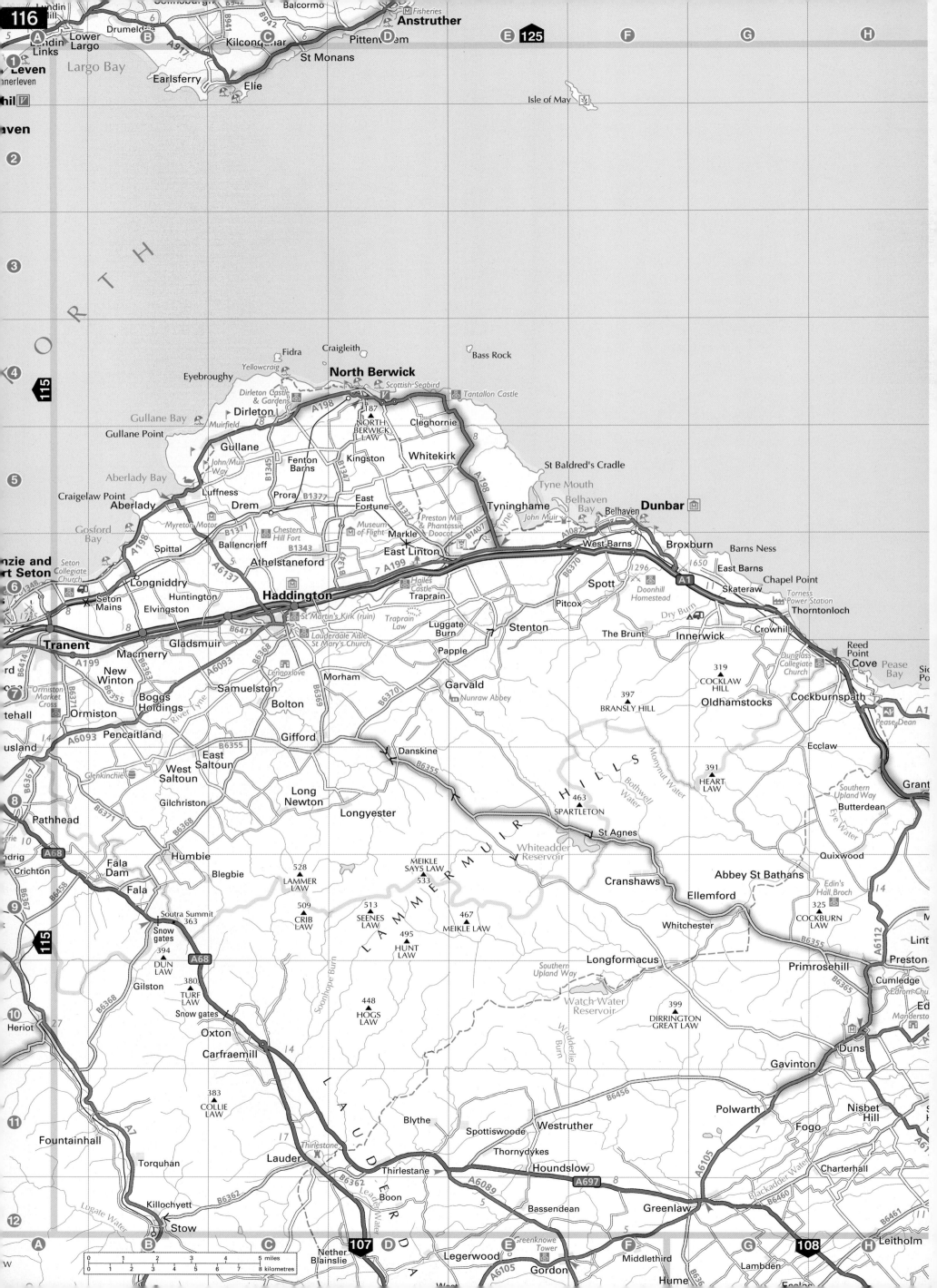

J   K   L   M   N   P   Q   R

1
2
3
4
5
6
7
8
9
10
11
12

Fast Castle Head

ST ABB'S HEAD

196
BROWN
RIG

Coldingham
Loch

St Abbs

Coldingham
Bay

shouse

Coldingham

Houndwood

A1107   22

Eyemouth

Heugh
Head

Cairncross

262
HORSELEY HILL

Reston

A1

Ayton

Burnmouth

Auchencrow

arygold

Lamberton

aw

Chirnside

Marshall Meadows Bay

Foulden

North Northumberland
Heritage Coast

Chirnsidebridge

15

Foulden
Tithe Barn

1333

Broadhaugh

Edington

Whiteadder Water

A6105

Allanton

Hutton

Berwick-upon-Tweed

Paxton

Castle

Barracks &
Main Guard

Town
Ramparts

Blackadder

B6460

Tweedmouth

Paxton

Whitsome

Hilton

Loanend

East
Ord

Spittal

13

Huds
Head

Horndean

Horncliffe

Scremerston

Ladykirk

Castle

Murton

Unthank

A1

Swinton

Norham

Thornton

Upsettlington

Shoreswood

West Allerdean

Cheswick

Simprim

Grindon

Ancroft

Goswick

Felkington

Causeway
flooded at
high tide

River Tweed

Haggerston

ellacres

Grindonrigg

Berrington

Beal

Holy
Island

Duddo

Bowsden

Lindisfarne
Castle

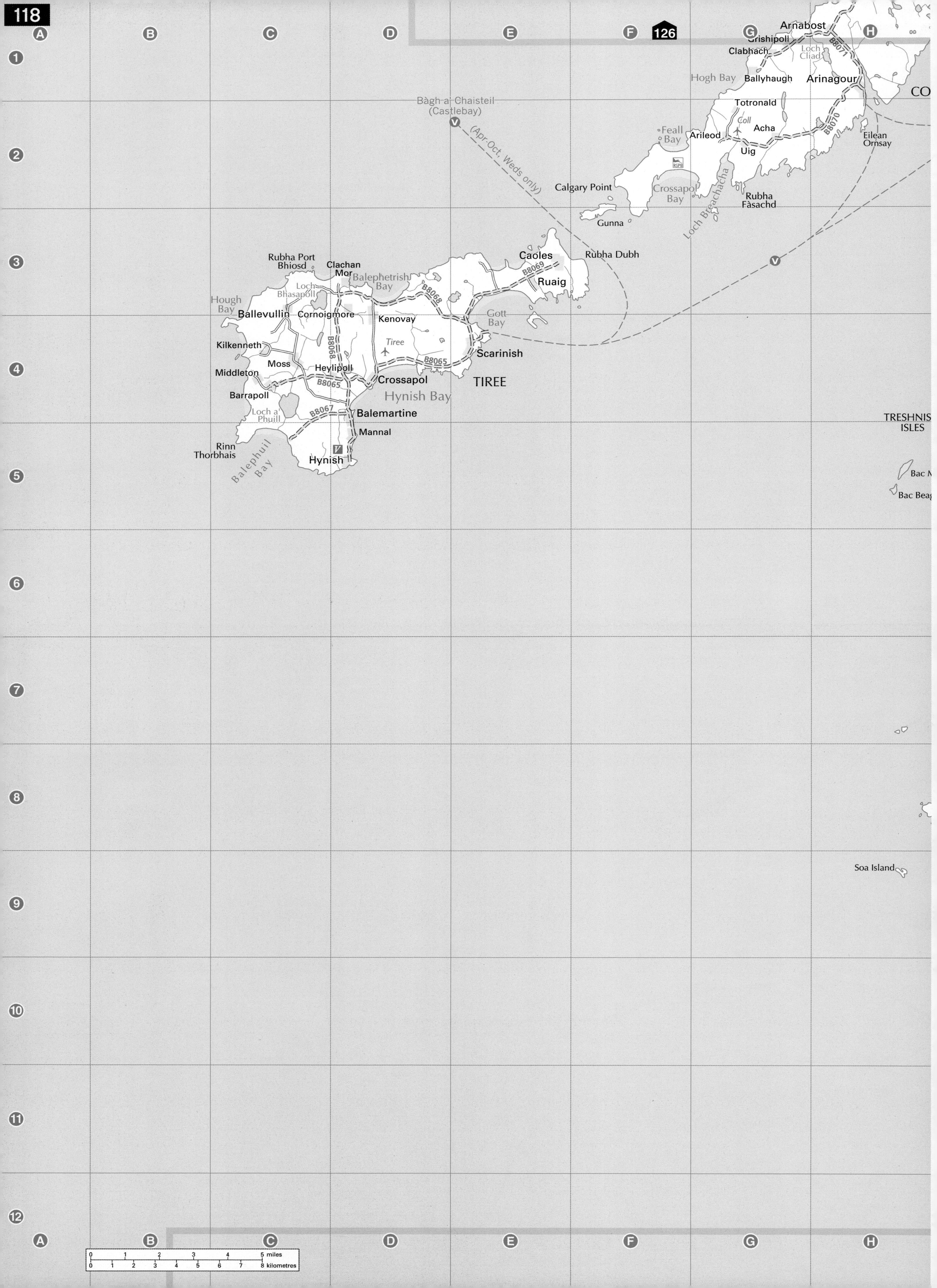

Arnabost
Grishipoll
Clabhach
Loch Cliad
B8071
Hogh Bay
Ballyhaugh
Arinagour
CO
Totronald
Coll
Acha
Bàgh a' Chaisteil
(Castlebay)
Arileod
Uig
Eilean
Ornsay
(Apr-Oct. Weds only)
Feall
Bay
Rubha
Fàsachd
Calgary Point
Crossapol
Bay
Loch Breachacha
Gunna

Rubha Port
Bhiosd
Clachan
Mor
Balephetrish
Bay
B8068
Caoles
Rubha Dubh
B8069
Ruaig
Hough
Bay
Loch
Bhasapoll
Ballevullin
Cornoigmore
Kenovay
Gott
Bay
Kilkenneth
B8068
Tiree
Scarinish
Moss
Heylipoll
B8065
Middleton
B8065
Crossapol
TIREE
TRESHNIS
ISLES
Barrapoll
Hynish Bay
Loch a'
Phuill
B8067
Balemartine
Bac N
Rinn
Thorbhais
Mannal
Bac Beag
Balephuil
Bay
Hynish

Soa Island

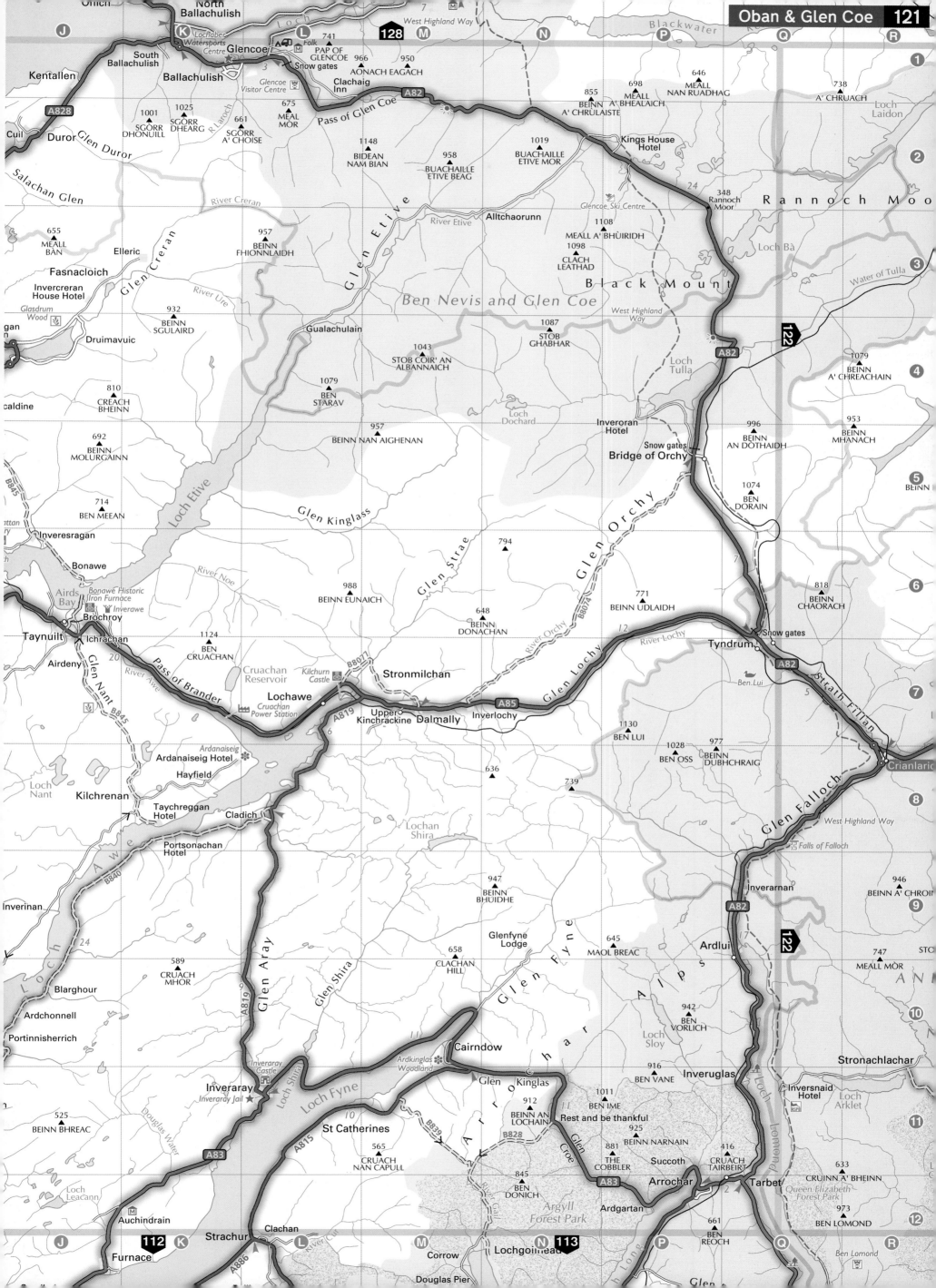

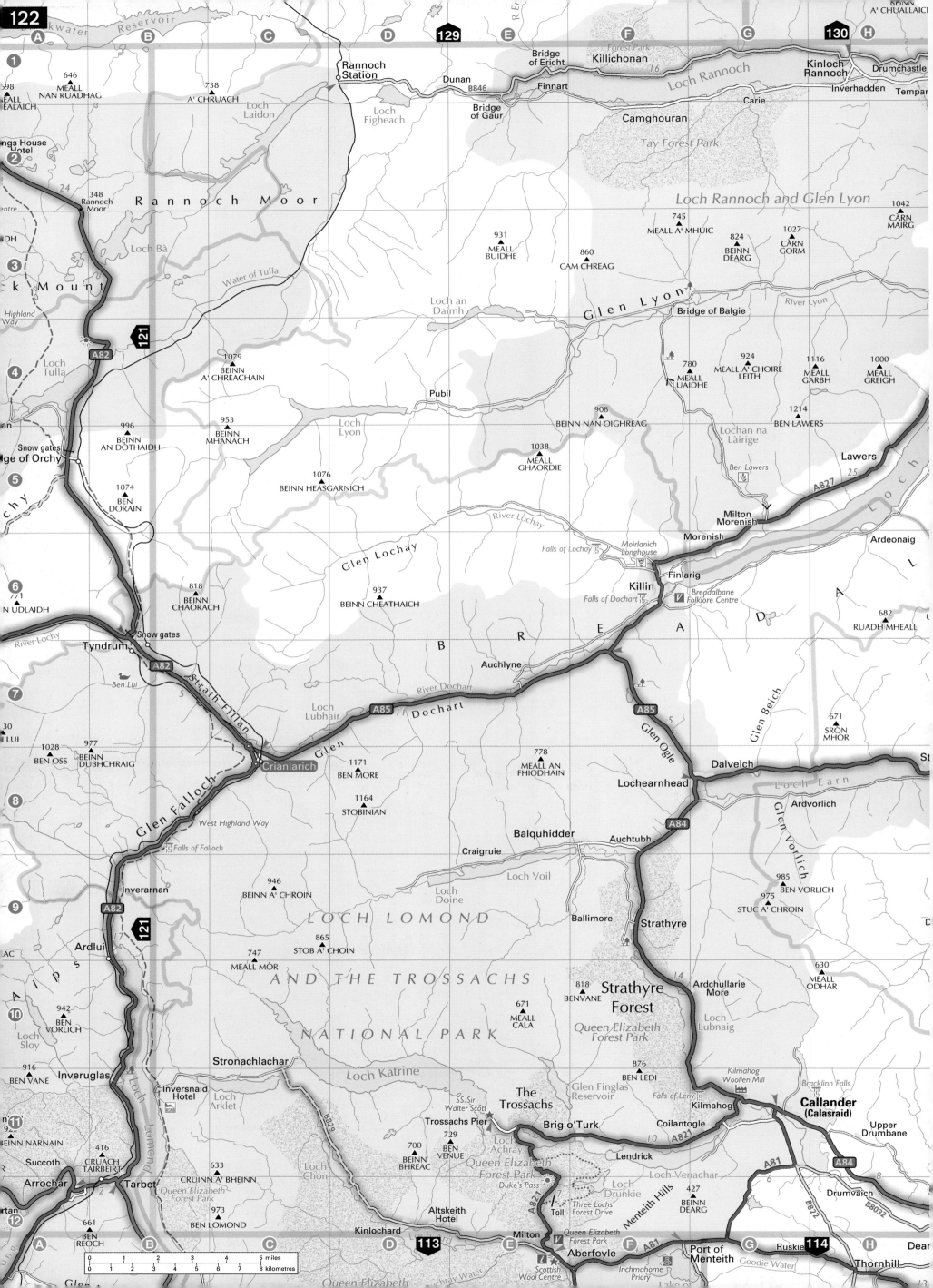

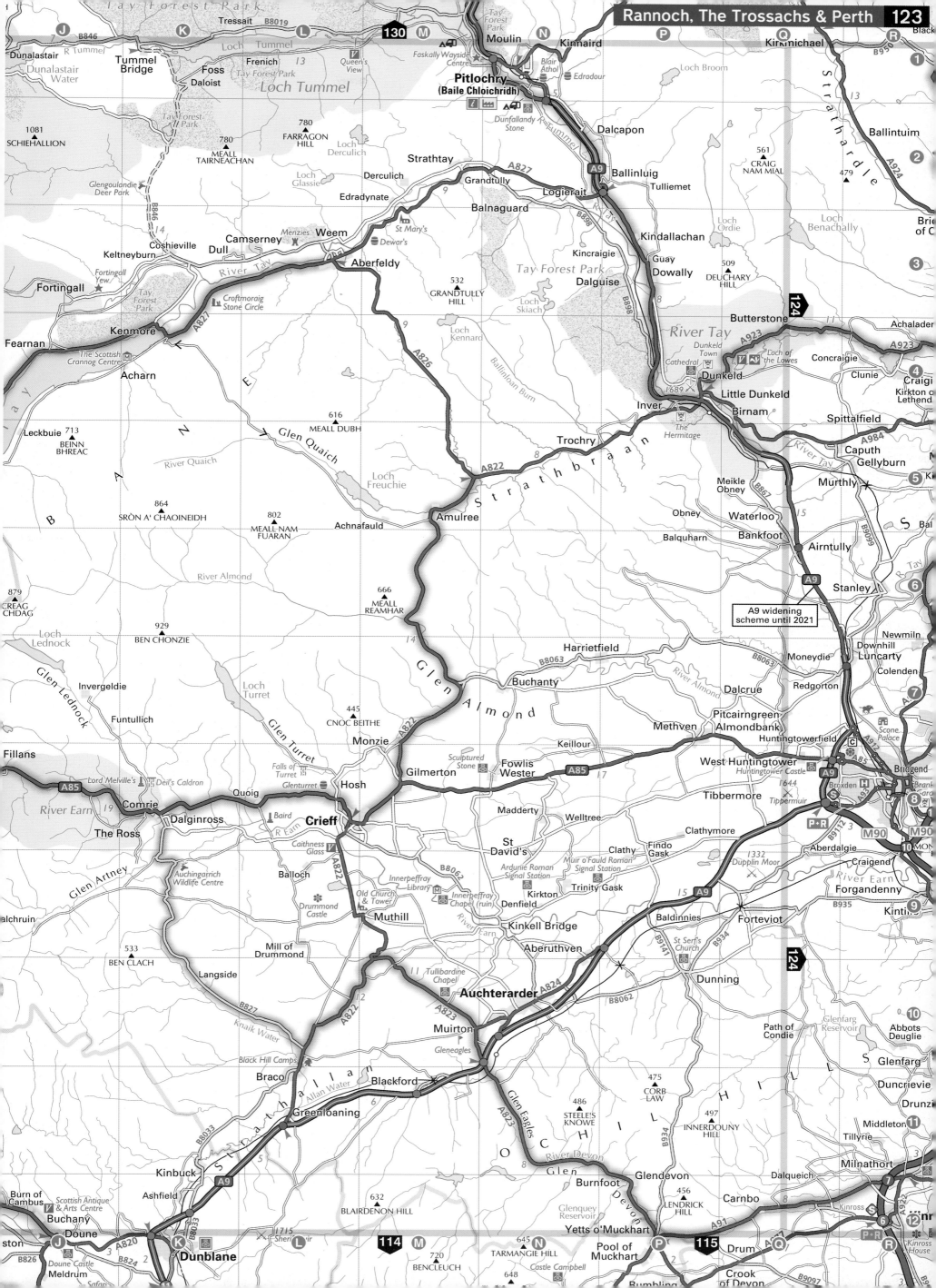

Tay Forest Park
Tressait B8019
B846
J
K
Dunalastair
Tummel Bridge
R Tummel
Dunalastair Water
Loch Tummel
Frenich
13
Foss
Daloist
Queen's View
Tay Forest Park
L
130
M
Moulin
N
Kinnaird
Faskally Wayside Centre
Blair Athol
Edradour
P
Kirkmichael
Q
B950
R
Black
Strathardle
13
1
1081
SCHIEHALLION
Pitlochry (Baile Chloichridh)
Dunfallandy Stone
5
Dalcapon
Ballintuim
A924
2
780
FARRAGON HILL
780
MEALL TAIRNEACHAN
Loch Derculich
Strathtay
Grandtully
Logierait
A827
Ballinluig
Tulliemet
561
CRAIG NAM MIAL
479
Glengoulandie Deer Park
B846
14
Derculich
Edradynate
Balnaguard
A9
Kincraigie
Kindallachan
Loch Ordie
Loch Benachally
Bri of C
3
Camserney
Weem
St Mary's
Menzies
Dewar's
Guay
Dowally
509
DEUCHARY HILL
Fortingall Yew
Fortingall
Coshieville
Dull
Aberfeldy
Tay Forest Park
Dalguise
B898
8
124
Keltneyburn
River Tay
Croftmoraig Stone Circle
532
GRANDTULLY HILL
Loch Skiach
River Tay
Butterstone
Achalader
A923
4
Fearnan
A827
Kenmore
The Scottish Crannog Centre
Loch Glassie
Loch Kennard
Dunkeld Town
Cathedral
Loch of the Lowes
Concraigie
Clunie
Craig
Kirkton Lethend
Acharn
1689
Dunkeld
Little Dunkeld
Inver
Birnam
Spittalfield
A984
Leckbuie
713
BEINN BHREAC
616
MEALL DUBH
Glen Quaich
The Hermitage
Trochry
Strathbraan
River Tay
Caputh
Gellyburn
5
A822
8
Meikle Obney
Murthly
B
864
SRÒN A' CHAOINEIDH
802
MEALL NAM FUARAN
Achnafauld
Amulree
Obney
Waterloo
Balquharn
Bankfoot
Airntully
B9099
S
Bal
River Quaich
Loch Freuchie
879
CREAG CHDAG
929
BEN CHONZIE
666
MEALL REAMHAR
14
Harrietfield
B8063
River Almond
B8063
Moneydie
Stanley
A9
A9 widening scheme until 2021
6
Loch Lednock
Invergeldie
Loch Turret
445
CNOC BEITHE
Glen Almond
Buchanty
Dalcrue
Pitcairngreen
Methven
Almondbank
Huntingtowerfield
Newmiln
Luncarty
Colenden
A7
Glen-Lednock
Funtullich
Glen Turret
Monzie
Keillour
Fowlis Wester
A85
17
West Huntingtower
Huntingtower Castle
A9
Broxden
Scone Palace
C
A93
Bridgend
Brank
Car
8
Fillans
A85
Lord Melville's
Deil's Caldron
Falls of Turret
Glenturret
Hosh
Gilmerton
Sculptured Stone
1644
Tippermuir
Tibbermore
H
River Earn
19
Comrie
Quoig
Crieff
Madderty
Welltree
Clathymore
P+R
B9112
3
M90
10
M90
Dalginross
Baird
R Earn
Caithness Glass
St David's
Clathy
Findo Gask
Aberdalgie
Craigend
River Earn
9
The Ross
Glen Artney
Auchingarrich Wildlife Centre
Balloch
Drummond Castle
Old Church & Tower
Innerpeffray Library
Innerpeffray Chapel (ruin)
B8062
Ardunie Roman Signal Station
Muir o'Fauld Roman Signal Station
Trinity Gask
Denfield
Kirkton
1332
Dupplin Moor
15
A9
Forgandenny
B935
Kintil
alchruin
Ben CLACH
533
Mill of Drummond
Muthill
River Earn
Kinkell Bridge
Aberuthven
St Serf's Church
B9141
Baldinnies
Fortevoit
124
Langside
B827
A822
Tullibardine Chapel
Dunning
Glenfarg Reservoir
10
Abbots Deuglie
Knaik Water
A824
Auchterarder
B8062
Path of Condie
Glenfarg
Duncrievie
Muirton
Gleneagles
A823
475
CORB LAW
Drunzi
11
Black Hill Camps
Braco
Blackford
Glen Eagles
486
STEELE'S KNOWE
497
INNERDOUNY HILL
Middleton
Tillyrie
Greenloaning
6
River Devon
Glendevon
Lendrick Hill
456
Carnbo
Milnathort
11
Kinbuck
A9
Burnfoot
Glenquey Reservoir
Dalqueich
6
Ashfield
Scottish Antique & Arts Centre
632
BLAIRDENON HILL
Glen Devon
Kinross
P+R
12
Buchany
Doune
B826
Doune Castle
Burn of Cambus
1715
SHERI
114
K
L
M
645
720
BENCLEUCH
TARMANGIE HILL
N
Pool of Muckhart
P
115
Q
R
ston
Meldrum
Dunblane
A820
B824
2
B033
648
Castle Campbell
Yetts o'Muckhart
A91
Drum
A9
P+R
6
Safari
Crook of Devon
B9097

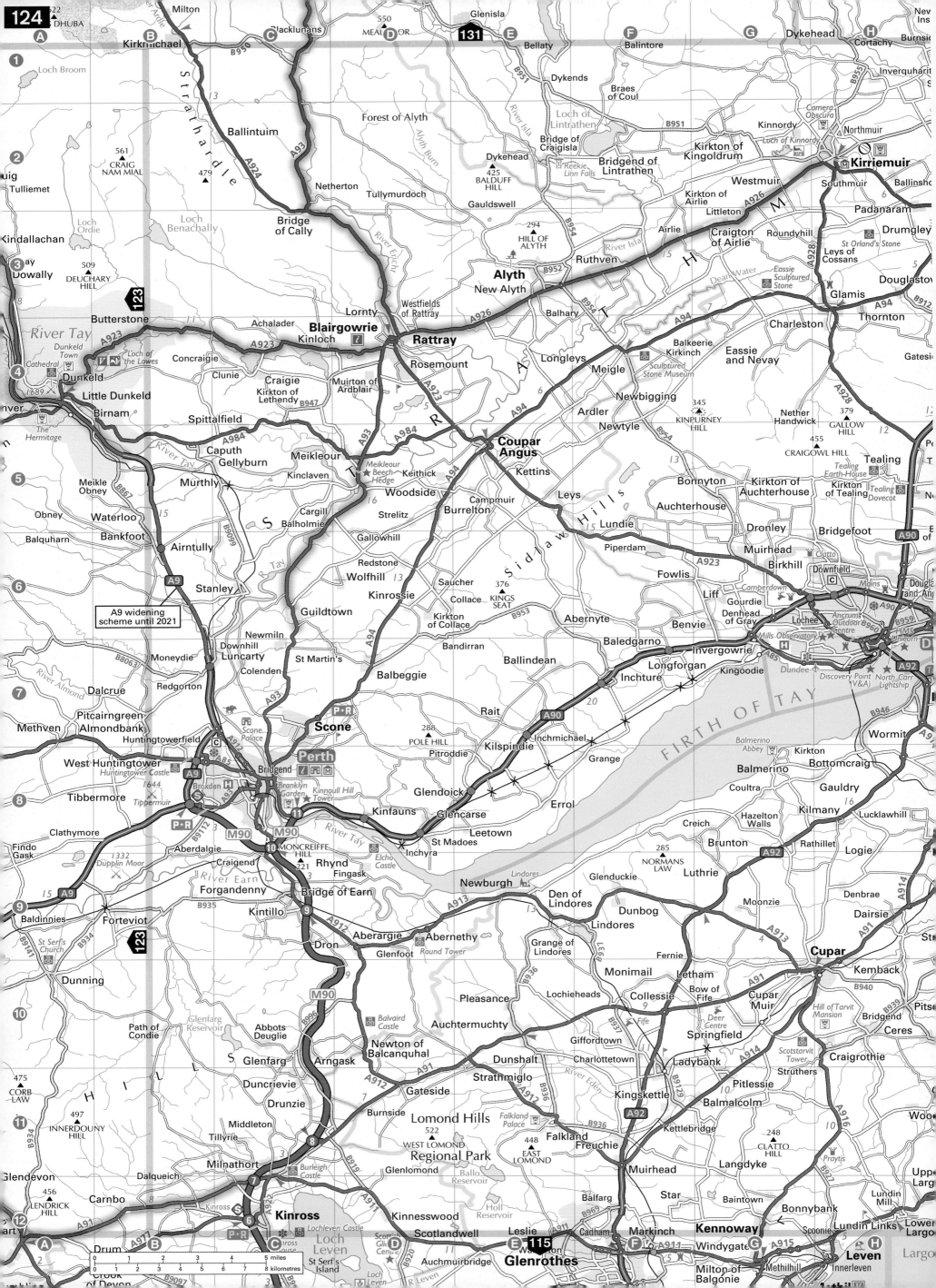

134

Loch Brit

GARS
BHEANN

225
CEANN NA BEINNE

Rubha an Dùnain

Soay Sound

139
BEINN
BHREAC

Mol-chlach

SOAY

Rubh'
Aonghais

CUILLIN SOUN

Loch Baghasdail
(Lochboisdale)

CANNA

210
CÀRN A' GHAILL

Garrisdale Point

A'Chill

Canna
Harbour

Kilmory
Bay

Rubha
Shamhnan
Insir

Sanday

Sound of Canna

302
MULLACH
MÒR

Rubha
na Roinne

A' Bhrideanach

570
ORVAL

Kinloch

Loch Scresort

Oigh-sgeir

RÙM

810
ASKIVAL

Harris
Bay

763
SGÙRR NAN
GILLEAN

All vehicles must have
the relevant island
permit prior to travel
to The Small Isles.
Services are seasonal,
day & weather dependent.

The Small Isles

Rubha nam
Meirleach

Sound of Rùm

Bay of
Laig

Rubha an
Fhasaidh

Laig

CRU

EIGG

393
AN SGÙRR

Sound of Eigg

Eilean
nan Each

MUCK

Port Mòr

Sanna Point

Sanna
Bay

Sanna

Portuairk

Achnaha

Ardnamurchan
Point

Achosnich

B8002

Bàgh a' Chaisteil
(Castlebay)
Loch Baghasdail
(Lochboisdale)
(Oct-Mar)

Eilean Mòr

Rubha
Mòr

Rubha
Sgor-innis

342
BEINN
NA SEILG

Ormsaigmore

Bousd

Sorisdale

Cliad
Bay

B8071

Arnabost

B8070

Grishipoll

Clab   h

Coll . Oban

Ardmore
Point

Sorne
Point

118

119

gh

Arinagour

Quinish Point

Glengorm Castle

COLL

0 1 2 3 4 5 miles
0 1 2 3 4 5 6 7 8 kilometres

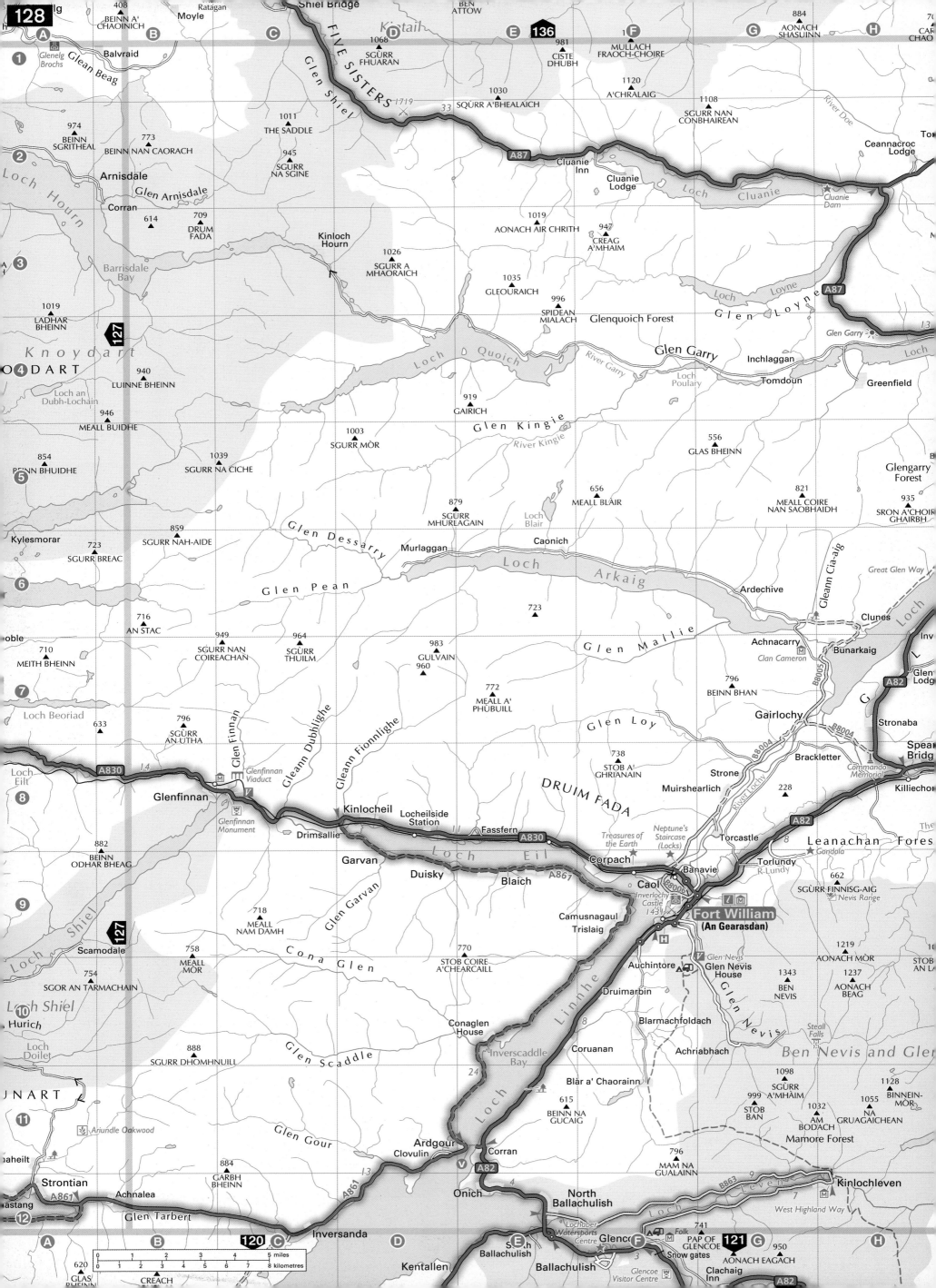

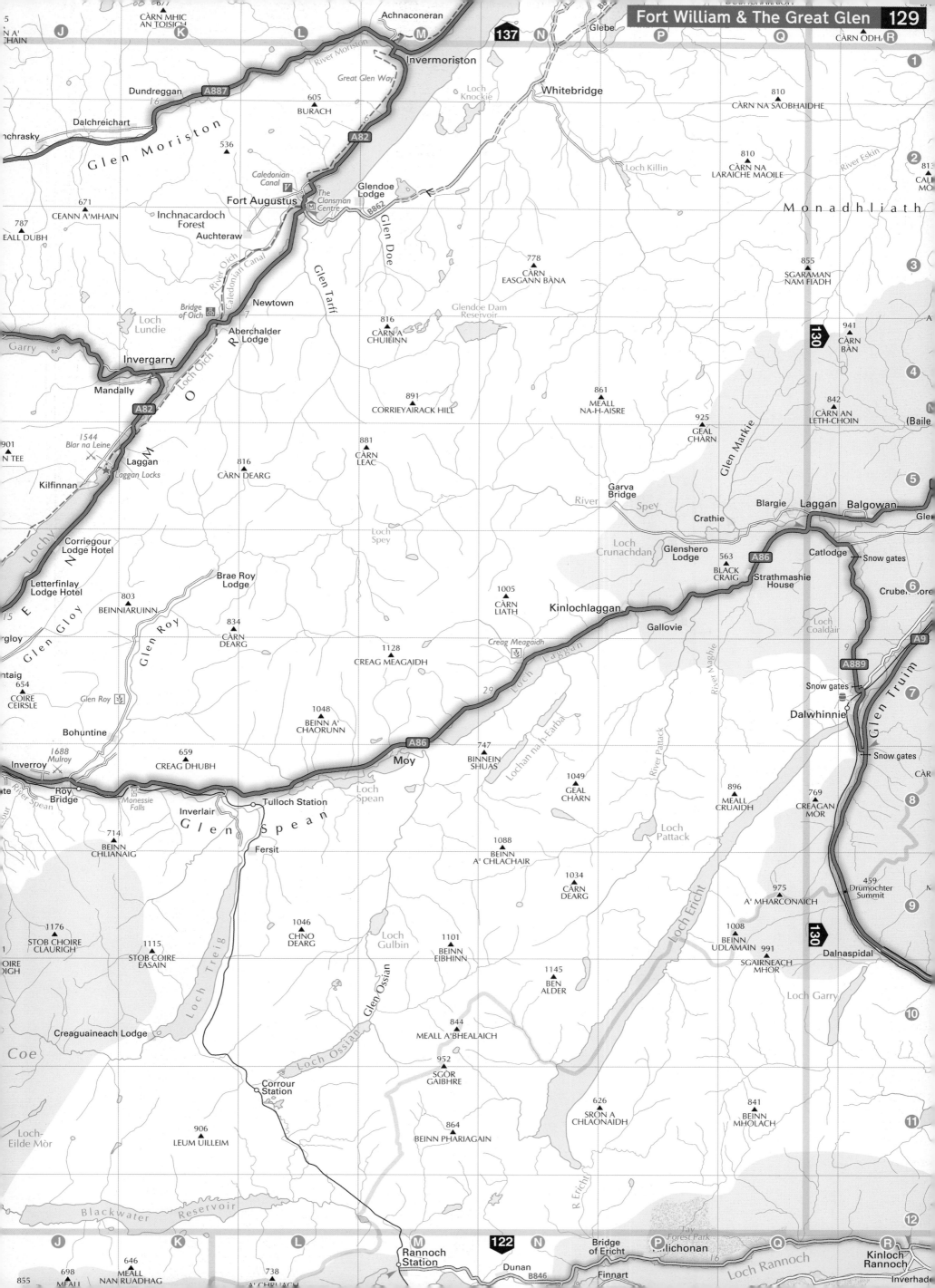

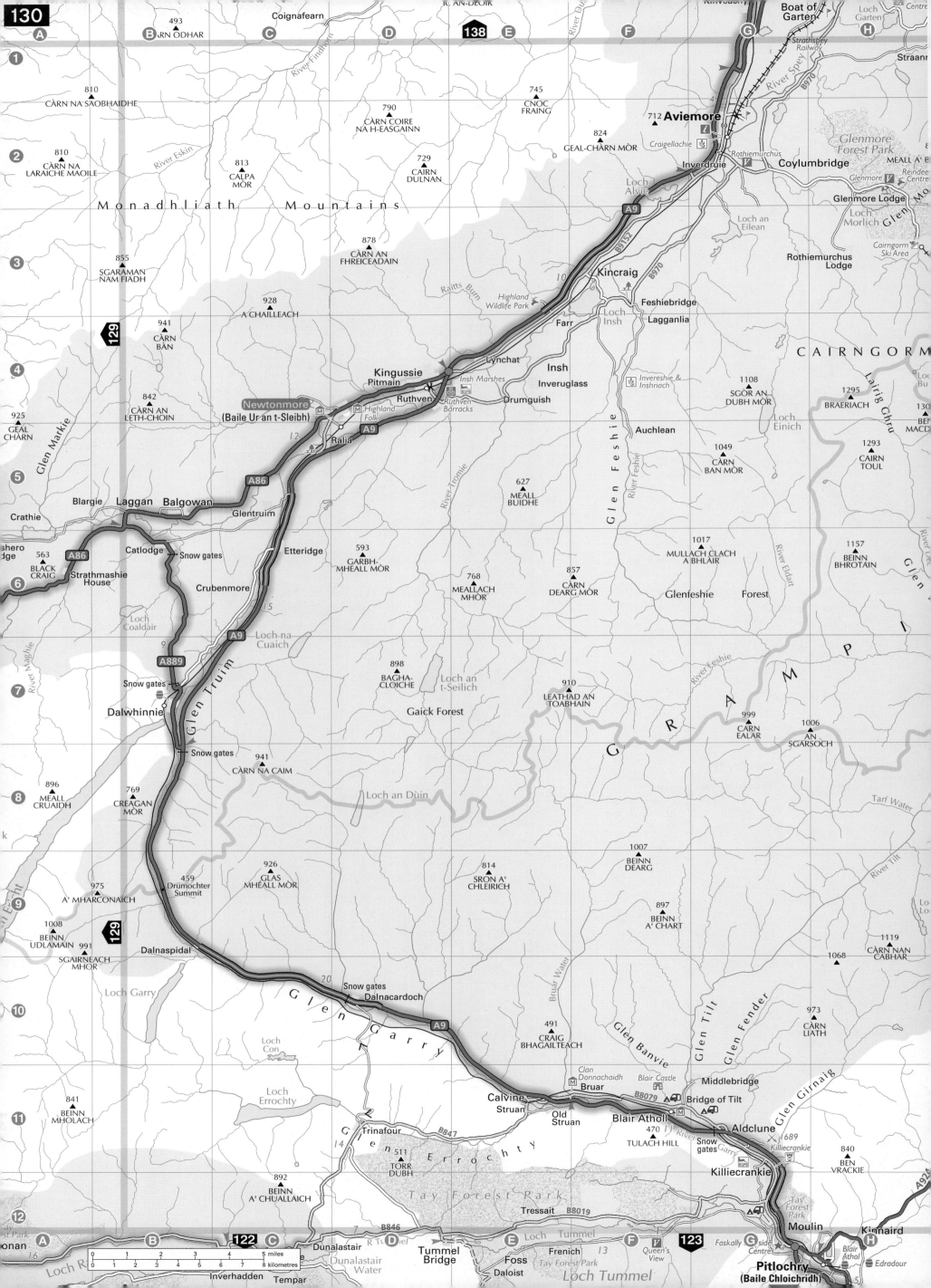

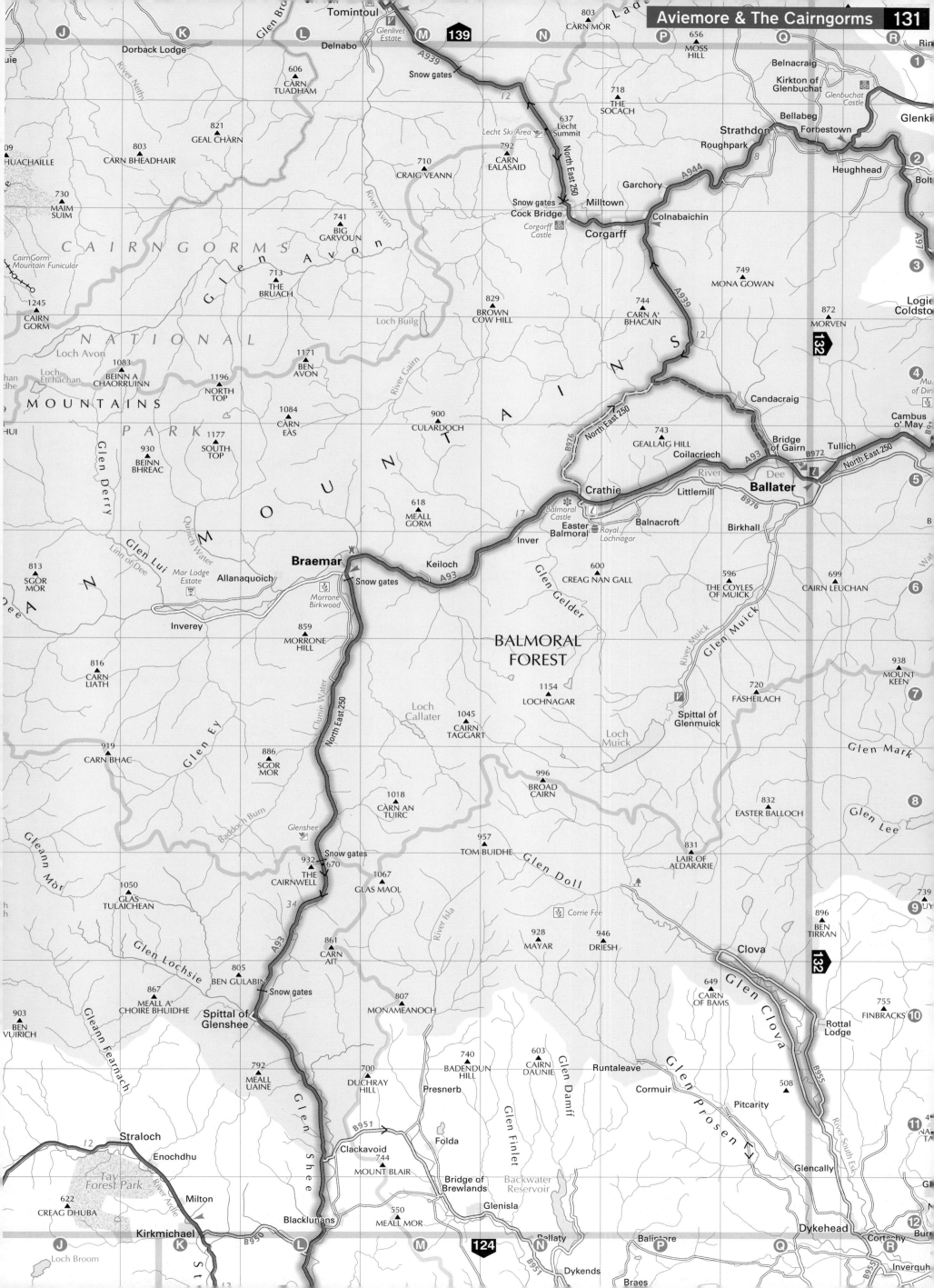

J K L M 139 N P Q R

Tomintoul
Dorback Lodge
Delnabo
Glenlivet Estate
803 CÀRN MÒR
MOSS HILL 656
Belnacraig
Kirkton of Glenbuchat
Glenbuchat Castle
Snow gates
606 CÀRN TUADHAM
718 THE SOCACH
Strathdon
Roughpark
Bellabeg
Forbestown
Glenki
821 GEAL CHÀRN
803 CARN BHEADHAIR
637 Lecht Summit
Lecht Ski Area
792 CARN EALASAID
Garchory
Heughhead
Bolt
730 MAIM SUIM
710 CRAIG VEANN
Snow gates
Cock Bridge
Corgarff Castle
Milltown
Colnabaichin
Corgarff
A944
A97
CAIRNGORMS
Glen Avon
River Avon
749 MONA GOWAN
CairnGorm Mountain Funicular
741 BIG GARVOUN
713 THE BRUACH
744 CARN A' BHACAIN
872 MORVEN
Logie Coldsto
1245 CAIRN GORM
NATIONAL
829 BROWN COW HILL
132
Loch Builg
1083 BEINN A CHAORRUINN
1171 BEN AVON
Candacraig
Mu of Dir
MOUNTAINS
1196 NORTH TOP
743 GEALLAIG HILL
B976
Coilacriech
Bridge of Gairn
Cambus o' May
1084 CÀRN EÀS
900 CULARDOCH
Tullich
1177 SOUTH TOP
North East 250
B972
North East 250
930 BEINN BHREAC
Crathie
Dee
Littlemill
Ballater
Glen Derry
618 MEALL GORM
Balmoral Castle
Easter Balmoral
Royal Lochnagar
Balnacroft
B976
Birkhall
Quoich Water
17
Inver
813 SGOR MÒR
Braemar
Keiloch
A93
600 CREAG NAN GALL
596 THE COYLES OF MUICK
699 CAIRN LEUCHAN
Glen Lui
Linn of Dee
Mar Lodge Estate
Allanaquoich
Snow gates
Glen Gelder
Inverey
Morrone Birkwood
859 MORRONE HILL
BALMORAL FOREST
1154 LOCHNAGAR
720 FASHEILACH
938 MOUNT KEEN
816 CARN LIATH
North East 250
Loch Callater
1045 CAIRN TAGGART
V Spittal of Glenmuick
Glen Muick
River Muick
Loch Muick
Glen Mark
919 CARN BHAC
886 SGOR MÒR
1018 CÀRN AN TUIRC
996 BROAD CAIRN
832 EASTER BALLOCH
Glen Lee
Clunie Water
Baddoch Burn
Glenshee
957 TOM BUIDHE
Glen Doll
831 LAIR OF ALDARARIE
Glen Clova
8
1050 GLAS TULAICHEAN
Snow gates
932 THE CAIRNWELL
670
1067 GLAS MAOL
Corrie Fee
Gleann Mòr
34
861 CARN AIT
928 MAYAR
946 DRIESH
Clova
896 BEN TIRRAN
132
739 UY
805 BEN GULABIN
649 CAIRN OF BAMS
755 FINBRACKS
10
867 MEALL A' CHOIRE BHUIDHE
Snow gates
807 MONAMEANOCH
A93
903 BEN VUIRICH
Spittal of Glenshee
Rottal Lodge
Glen Fearnach
Glen Lochsie
Glen Shee
792 MEALL UAINE
700 DUCHRAY HILL
740 BADENDUN HILL
603 CAIRN DAUNIE
Runtaleave
Cormuir
Pitcarity
508
B955
11
Presnerb
Glen Damf
Glen Prosen
NA TA
Straloch
Enochdhu
Glen Finlet
Glencally
Tay Forest Park
River Ardle
Clackavoid
B951
Folda
Backwater Reservoir
River South Esk
Milton
744 MOUNT BLAIR
Bridge of Brewlands
Dykehead
Cortachy
622 CREAG DHUBA
Kirkmichael
B950
Blacklunans
550 MEALL MOR
Glenisla
Ballaty
Balintore
Burr
12
Loch Broom
J K L M 124 N P Q R
Dykends
Braes
Inverqu

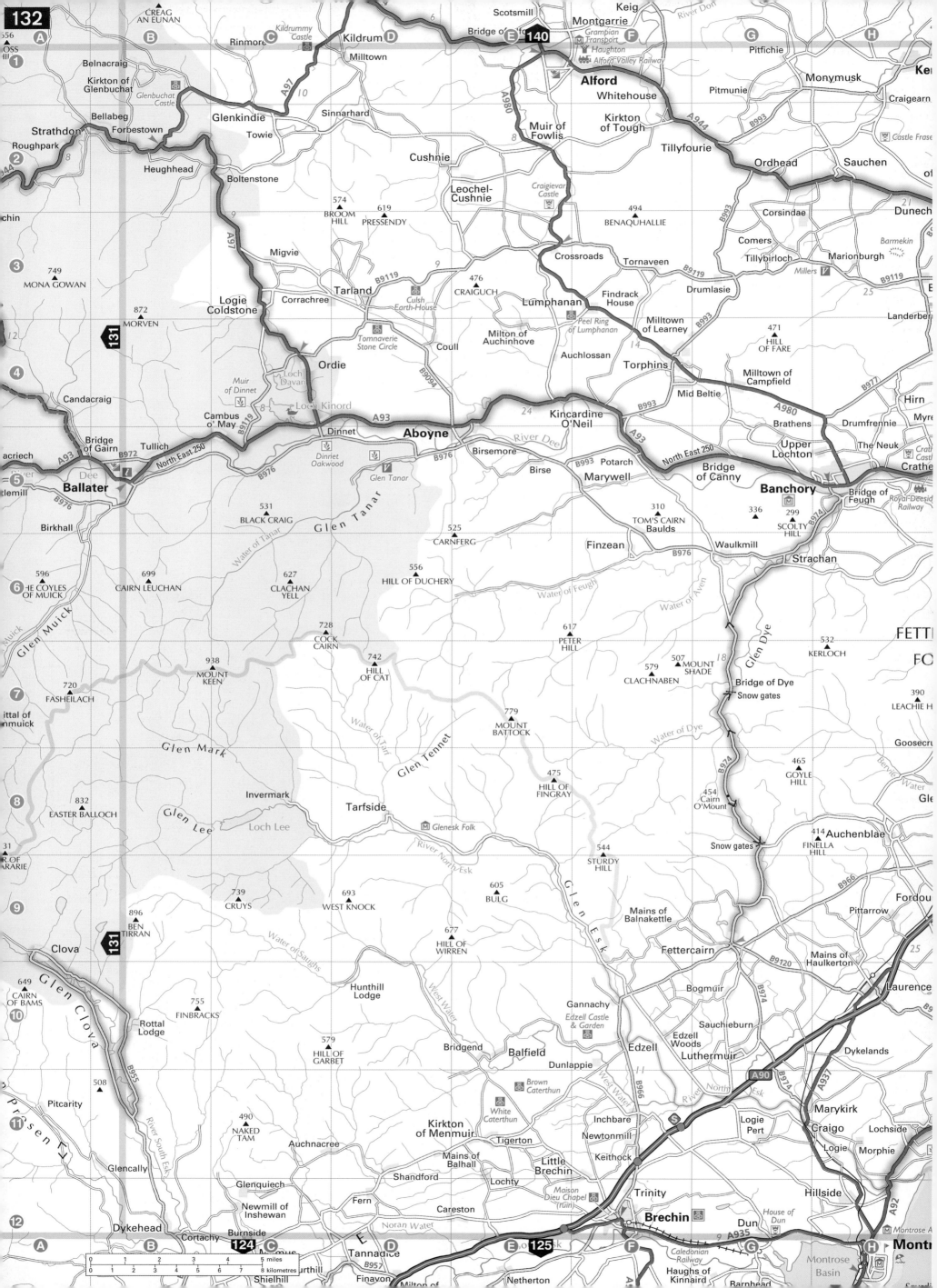

Thainstone
Kinkell Church
Newmachar
Kingseat
Balmedie

Kintore
Hatton of Fintray
Whitecairns
B979
141
Belhelvie
Balmedie
A90

Cottown
B994
Kinmundy
Cothal
Belhelvie

Leylodge
B971
R. Don
18

Lyne Skene
Blackburn
A90
Overton
Dyce Symbol Stones
A90
Potterton
A90

Skene House
B9126
Clinterty
A96
Stoneywood
A92
Blackdog

Millbuie
B979
Elrick Hill
Bankhead
A92
P+R
Bridge of Don

Kirkton of Skene
Westhill
Kingswells
Buxburn
Kittybrewster
Old Aberdeen

Garlogie
Carnie
Elrick
A944
Northfield
Kirkwall Lerwick

Cullerlie Stone Circle
Kingsford
P+R
ABERDEEN
Ruthrieston
Torry
Nigg Bay

Redhill
B9119
Easter Ord
Blacktop
Mannofield
Kincorth

Benthoul
A90
Cults
Nigg
Loirston

Craigton
A93
Bieldside
Banchory-Devenick
A92
Altens Haven

Hardgate
Milton of Murtle
Milltimber
B9077
Kingcausie
Charlestown
Cove Bay

West Park
Drum Castle
Peterculter
Kirkton of Maryculter
The Den & The Glen
Marywell

River Dee
Hillside
Auchlee
Findon
Portlethen
Old Portlethen

Durris
Denside
A90
Cammachmore
Downies
Cammachmore Bay

Woodlands
Cookney
Chapelton
Newtonhill
Skateraw

Crossroads
A957
Netherley
A92
Muchalls

Bridge of Muchalls
Doonie Point

HILL OF TRUSTA
320

Garron Point
Stonehaven Bay

Kirktown of Fetteresso
Stonehaven

Elfhill
Dunnottar

Tannachie
New Mill
Temple of Fiddes
A90

Drumlithie
Fowlsheugh
10

Mondynes
Crawton

Redmyre
Arbuthnott
Grassic Gibbon Centre
Catterline

B967
Kinneff

Inverbervie
Todhead Point

Bervie Bay

Gourdon

Benholm
Johnshaven

Milton Ness
St Cyrus

ELGIN
PETERHEAD
ABERDEEN
WESTBURN ROAD
HUTCHEON STREET
KING STREET
BEACH BOULEVARD
Footee
North Pier
SKENE
UNION STREET
FERRY TERMINAL
ABERDEEN STATION
Albert Basin
River Dee
WILLOWBANK ROAD
Ferryhill
Torry
RIVERSIDE DRIVE
DUNDEE

Aberdeen
ELGIN
PETERHEAD
Royal Cornhill Hospital
Causeway End Primary School
City
ALFORD
WESTBURN ROAD
A944
HUTCHEON STREET
NELSON ST
KING STREET
Skene Square School
Aberdeen College Gallowgate Centre
RGU
Woolmanhill
Robert Gordon's College
City Council (Marischal College)
Arts Centre
St Andrew Cathedral
Police HQ
Aberdeen Grammar School
Gilcomston School
Kingdom Hall
His Majesty's
Art Gallery
RGU
St Nicholas
Provost Skene's House
ibis Hotel
YMCA
HMRC
St Mary's Cathedral
Music Hall
Union Bridge
Maritime Museum
Merchant Quay
Harbour Office
Terminal Building
Harlaw Academy
St Margaret's School
Jurys Inn Hotel
Trinity Centre
UnionSquare
Northlink Ferries
Coastguard
ABERDEEN STATION
Fish Market
GREAT WESTERN ROAD
WILLOWBANK ROAD
Ferryhill School
Pavilion
Victoria Bridge
BANCHORY
DUNDEE, PERTH
FORFAR
River Dee

A B C D E F G H

1

Duntulm
Kilmaluag
Lùb Score
Skye Museum of Island Life
Borneskitaig
Flodigarry
Kilmuir
Heribusta
2
Balgown
Kilvaxter
542
MEAL NA SUIREAMACH
Digg
Brogaig
Stenscholl

Tairbeart (Tarbert)
142
464
BIODA BUIDHE

Loch nam Madadh (Lochmaddy)
Linicro
Totscore

3
Rubha Bhatairnis
Ascrib Islands
Idrigill
611
BEINN EDRA
Maligar
Marishader

Uig (Uige)
Fairy Glen

Uig Bay
Earlish

The Little Minch
283
BEN GEARY
Geary
Loch Snizort
Peinlich
608
CREAG A' LAIN

4
Trumpan
Gillen
River Hinnisdal
451
BEINN A' SGA

Ardmore Point
Hallin
Kingsburgh
Romesdal
River Romesdal

Isay
Mingay
Stein
Lusta
Eyre
Kensaleyre
River Haultin

5
DUNVEGAN HEAD
214
BEN DIUBAIG
Greshornish
Flashader
Treaslane

Loch Bay
Claigan
Upperglen
Edinbane
Bernisdale

Boreraig
327
BEINN BHREAC
Bay
Tote
Carbost
Borve

6
Uig
Skeabost

Feriniquarrie
Totaig
Dunvegan
Uigshader
Drumuie

Glendale
Glasphein
Colbost
Giant Angus MacAskill
265
BEN AKETIL
271
CRUACHAN BEINN A' CHEARCAILL

Milovaig
Lephin
Kilmuir
Glengrasco

Waterstein
Colbost Croft
Lonmore
Roskhill
Portree

Neist Point
Skinidin
Aros
417
BEINN NA GREINE

7
Hoe Rape
Ramasaig
469
HEALAVAL MORE
Orbost
Roag
Vatten
Glen Ose
Glenmore
Glenvarragill

Duirnish
Harlosh
Mugeary

Hoe Point
488
HEALAVAL BHEAG
Ose
Dun Beag
Bracadale
Loch Duagrich

8
368
BEINN NA BOINEID
Harlosh Island
Colbost Point
Struan
Coillore
439
ROINEVAL

Tarner Island
Idrigill Point
Ullinish Lodge Hotel
Wiay

Loch Bracadale
Oronsay
Portnalong

9
Rubha nan Clach
Fiskavaig
Fernilea
Talisker

369
ARNAVAL
Carbost
Drynoch

Talisker Bay
Merkadale
Sligachan

10
Talisker
447
BEINN BHREAC
Glen Grula
Glen Brittle
369
BEINN BHREAC

Minginish
Forest
Fairy Pools
965
SGURR NAN GILLEA

11
434
AN CRUACHIN
Glenbrittle
Cuillin Hills

Bualintur
974
SGURR A' GHEADAIDH
1009
SGURR ALASDAIR

12
225
CEANN NA BEINNE
894
GARS BHEINN

A B 126 E F G H

Rubha an Dùnain
Soay Sound
139
BEINN BHREAC

0 1 2 3 4 5 miles
0 1 2 3 4 5 6 7 8 kilometres

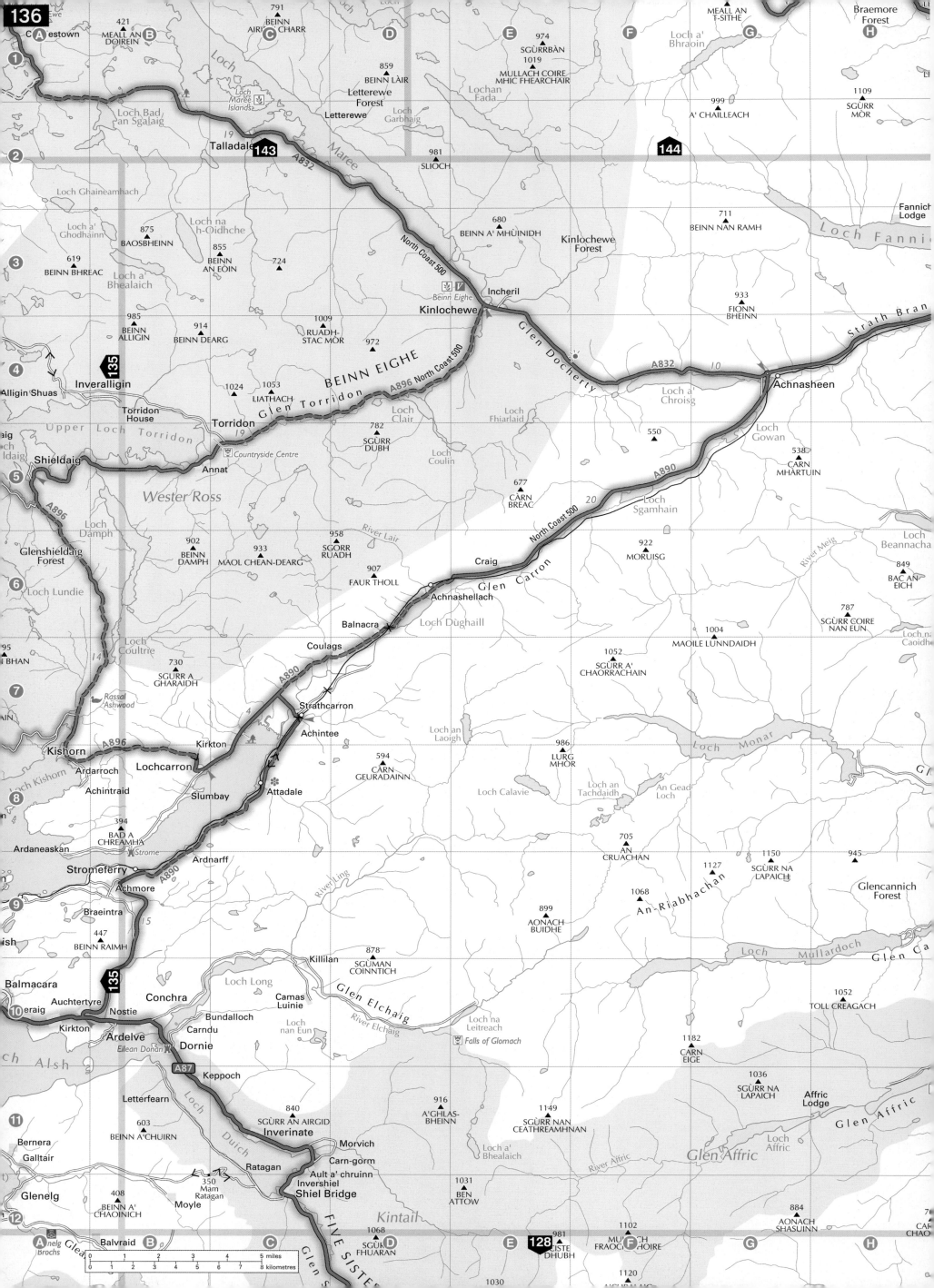

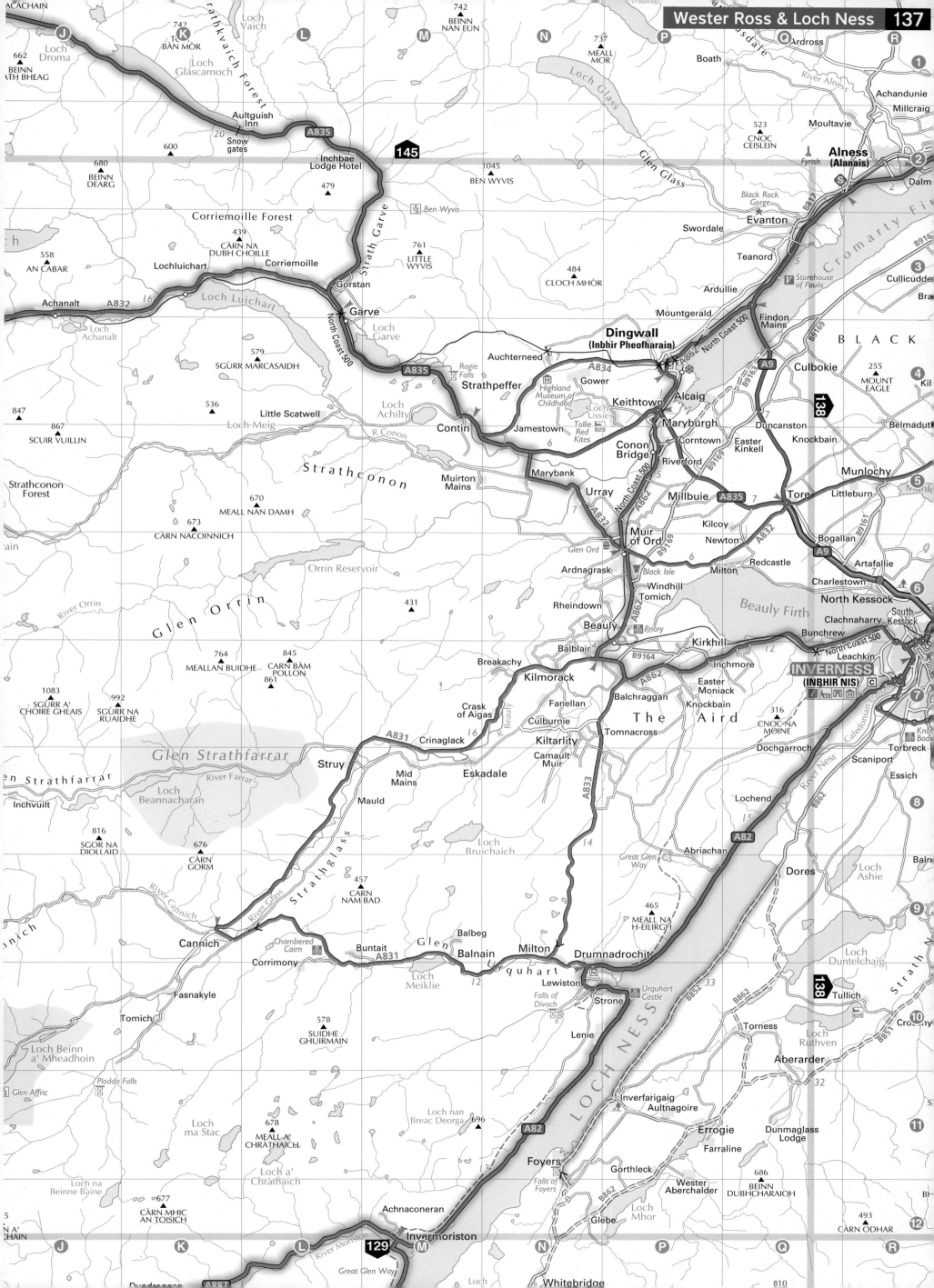

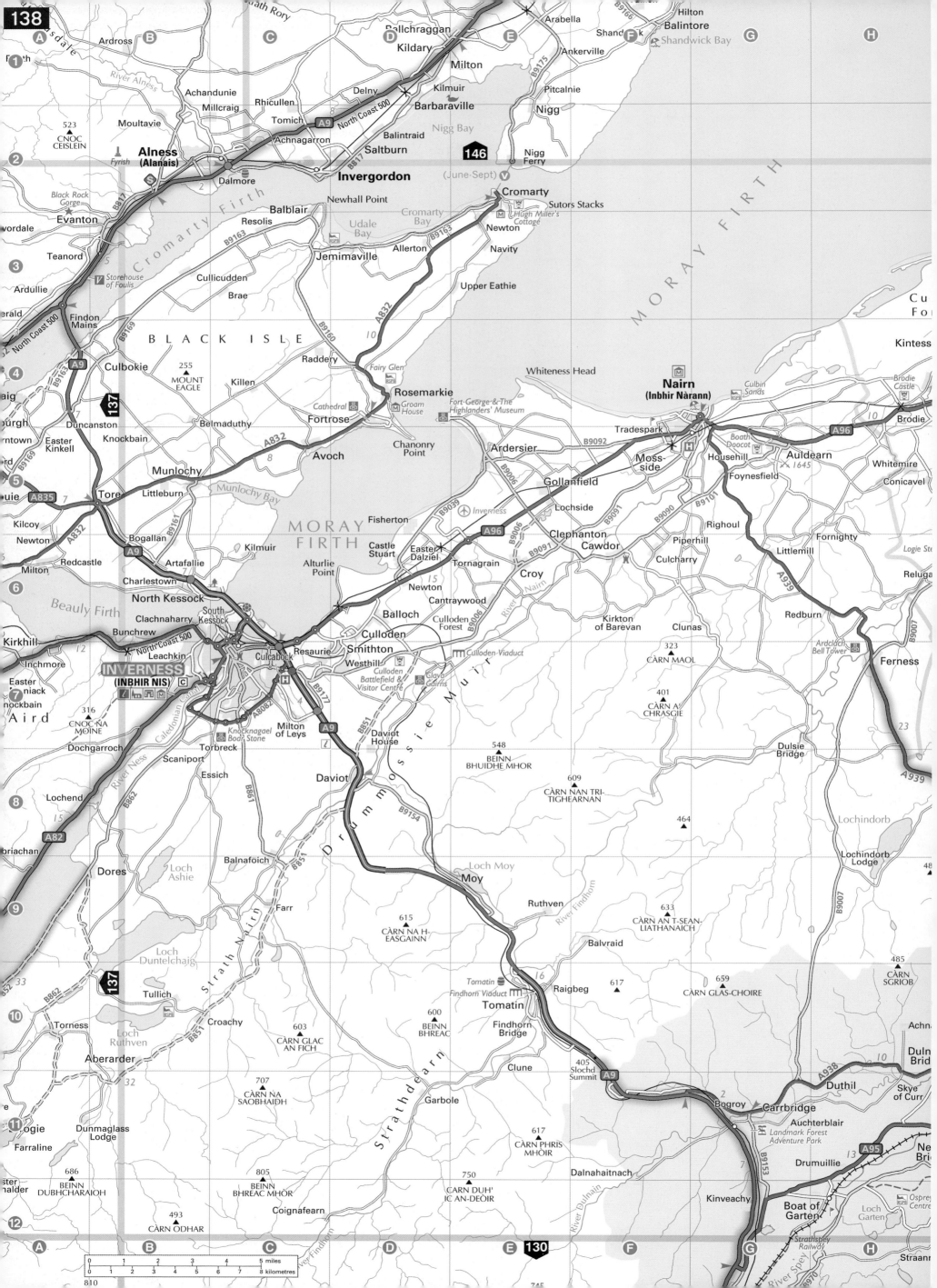

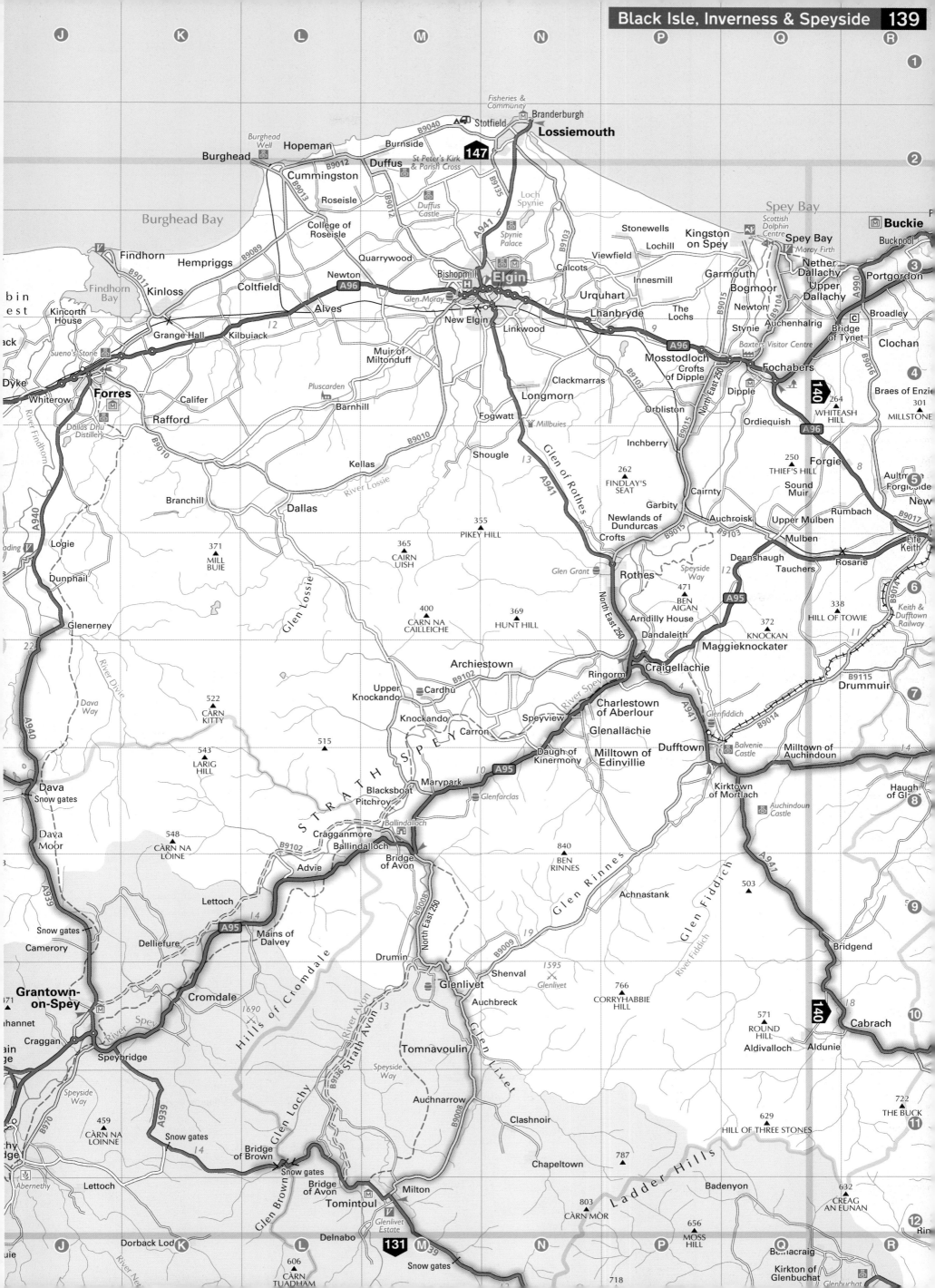

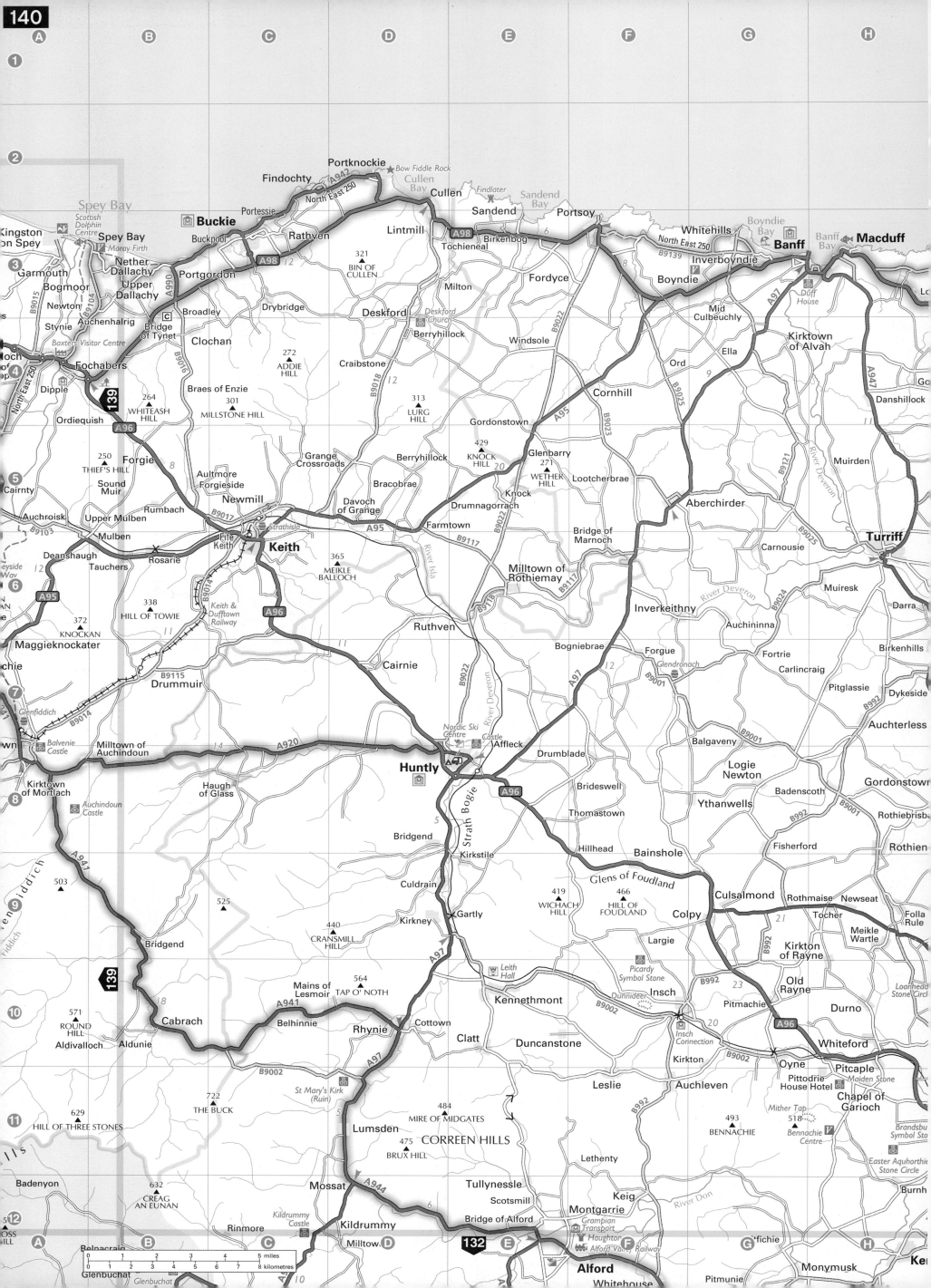

J K L M N P Q R
1
2
3
4
5
6
7
8
9
10
11
12

Troup Head
Cullykhan Bay
Gamrie Bay
Crovie
Gardenstown
Silverford
Dubford
ngmanhill
Clenerty
Minnonie
Netherbrae
rrachie
Crudie
B9105
Fintry
Garmond
B9027
New Byth
Balthangie
Cuminestown
13
B9170
Howe of Teuchar
Gourdas
North Millbrex
A947
Lethenty
Fyvie Castle
17
Fyvie
Woodhead
Haddo
ne
Cross of Jackston
Tulloch
St Katherines
Barthol Chapel
Earlsford
B9170
14
Tarves
orman
Craigdam
Daviot
A920
Oldmeldrum
Glen Garioch
Carnbrogie
B9001
Kirkton of Bourtie
Whiterashes
A947
Inverurie
Port Elphinstone
rvie
B993
Thainstone
Kinkell Church
B993
nnay
Kintore
B994
Cottown
A90
133

Pennan
Protstonhill
Gamrie
Glasslaw
221
BRACKLAMORE HILL
New Aberdour
Aberdour Bay
B9031
North East 250
Roseherty
Craigiefold
Coburby
Boyndlie
Tyrie
New Pitsligo
B9093
5
A981
A950
B9028
A948
B9170
B9029
Maud
New Deer
Slacks of Cairnbanno
Drymuir
Knaven
Cairnorrie
Brownhill
Inkhorn
B9005
Methlick
R Ythan
Woodhead
Haddo House
14
Wedderlairs
B9005
Ythanbank
Auchedly
Altar-Tomb of William Forbes
Kinharrachie
Ythsie
Esslemont
Tolquhon Castle
Pitmedden Garden
B999
A920
Pitmedden
Logierieve
Housieside
B9000
Udny Green
B999
Woodland
Pettymuk
Udny Station
Tillygreig
Cultercullen
Stralloch
Reisque
Kinmuck
Newmachar
B979
Causeyend
Hatton of Fintray
B977
Kinmundy
B977
Cothal
Dyce Symbol Stones
Potterton
A90

Pittulie
B9031
Pitsligo
Peathill
Percyhorner
Mid Ardlaw
B9032
Memsie
Memsie Cairn
Newburgh
234
WAUGHTON HILL
Strichen
12
New Leeds
B9093
Denhead
Fetterangus
Deer Abbey
6
B9106
Dunshillock
Old Deer
Railway
Blackhill of Clackriach
B9029
Aberdeenshire Farming
Aden
Stuartfield
Bulwark
Nethermuir
B9030
Kinnadie
Auchnagatt
12
Coldwells
Arthrath
Muirtack
A948
Toll of Birness
Birness
Artrochie
Ellon
P+R
B9005
Kirkton of Logie Buchan
Forvie
B9000
A90
Newburgh
Foveran
A975
Delfrigs
Balmedie
Balmedie
Whitecairns
Belhelvie
M
N

Sandhaven
Kinnaird Head
Castle, Lighthouse & Museum
Fraserburgh
Fraserburgh Bay
Kirktown
A90
Maggie's Hoosie
Cairnbulg
Inverallochy
Whitelinks Bay
Pitblae
Rathen
B9033
St Combs
Lonmay
Crofts of Savoch
Crimond
Blackhill
North East 250
18
A952
Leys
Backfolds
Kirktown
St Fergus
Scotstown Head
Rora
A90
Mintlaw
Longside
Inverugie
Buchanhaven
Peterhead
A950
Peterhead
Peterhead Bay
Inverquhomery
9
Invernettie
Millbreck
Nether Kinmundy
Hillhead of Cocklaw
Clola
Boddam
Blackhill
Stirling
Lendrum Terrace
Buchan Ness
Kinknockie
Ardallie
Longhaven
Hatton
A90
Auchiries
Bullers of Buchan
North Haven
14
Slains
Cruden Bay
Bogbrae
Chapel Hill
A975
Bay of Cruden
North East 250
20
21
Whinnyfold
The Skares
Kirkton of Slains
Collieston

River Ugie
Loch of Strathbeg
Rattray Head
Loch of Strathbeg

15
21
10
12
B9081
B9032
A981
B9093
10

A B C D E F G H

1

2

Loch Erisort
Baile Ailein
(Balalla)
Lacasaig
(Laxay)
Cromor
Gearraidh Bhaird
(Garyvard)
Marbhig
(Marvig)
Cearsiadar
(Kershader)
n a Bhruaich
(Aribruach)

B8060
Grabhair
(Gravir)
Loch Ouirn
A' Chabag

401
MÒR
MHONADH
152

PARK
Eishken
(Eisgein)
Leumrabhagh
(Lemreway)

571
BEINN MHOR
Loch Shell
Loch Brollum
Loch Claidh

Reinigeadal
(Rhenigidale)

SOUND OF SHIANT

as Scalpaigh
(les Scalpay)

SHIANT
ISLANDS

Sgalpaigh
(Scalpay)

THE

SCALPAY
152

THE LITTLE MINCH

Fladda-chùain

Eilean Trodday

Rubha Hunish

Duntulm
Kilmaluag
A855
Tairbeart
(Tarbert)
Lùb Score
Skye Museum
of Island Life
Flodigarry
Poldorais
Eilean Flodigarry
Borneskitaig
Heribusta
17
Kilmuir
Kilvaxter
542
MEAL NA
SUIREAMACH
Digg
Staffin
Bay
Staffin Island
Balgown
134
Brogaig
135
Stenscholl
Staffin
Linicro
tairnis
Totscore
464
BIODA
BUIDHE
Trotternish
Ellishader
River Rha
Maligar
Ascrib
Islands
Marishader
Valtos
Idrigill
River Conon
BEINN
EDRA
Garros
Rubha nam Brathai
283
BEN
(Uige)
Fairy
Glen
Culnaknock
Uig Bay

0   1   2   3   4   5 miles
0 1 2 3 4 5 6 7 8 kilometres

A B C D E F G H

148

J K L M N P Q R

Inverkirkaig

Rubha
Còigeach

Eilean Mòr

Enard Bay

Rubha Mòr
Reiff

Achnahaird

Altandhu

144

Loch
Osgaig

Loch Bad
a' Ghaill

Eilean Mullagrach

Polbain

Badentarbet

Isle Ristol

Badentarbet
Bay

Achiltibuie

Glas-leac Mòr

SUMMER ISLES

Polglass

Ben M
Coigea

Tanera
Beg

V
Steornabhagh
(Stornoway)

Tanera
Mòr

Horse
Island

Horse
Sound

Achduart

Glas-leac Beag

Culnacraig

Eilean Dubh

Priest
Island

Leac Dhonn

Isle
Martin

Cailleach Head

Scoraig

*Annat
Bay*

Ruigh'riabhach

635
BEINN GHOBHLACH

Greenstone
Point

Rubha Beag

Stattic Point

Mellon
Udrigle

GRUINARD
ISLAND

*Gruinard
Bay*

Badluarach

Little Loch Broom

Badrallach

Foura

Laide

A832

Badcaul

Rubha Rèidh

Rubha
nan Sasan

Cove

Mellon
Charles

Ormiscaig

North Coast 500

Gruinard

Ardessie

Camus

32

296
AN
CUAIDH

Aultbea

Loch a'
Bhaid-luachraich

Little Gruinard River

764
SAIL
MHOR

Dundonne

Melvaig

ISLE
OF EWE

Gruinard River

Lochan
Gaineamhaich

Aultgrishin

Loch Ewe

347
CREAG-
MHEAL BEAG

Strathnasheallag Forest

B8021

Inverasdale

Loch
Fada

1062
AN TEALLACH

293
CNOC
BREAC

Naast

Inverewe
Garden

681
BEINN A'
CHAISGEIN BEAG

Loch na
Sealga

8

North Erradale

Poolewe

Londubh

250
MEALL NA MEINE

144
Fisherfield Forest

906
BEINN DEARG MHOR

Fronn

Wester Ross

9

Big Sand

Strath
Heritage

A832

Dubh
Loch

Longa
Island

Smithstown

Lonemore

Auchtercairn

791
BEINN
AIRIDH CHARR

974
SGÙRRBÀN

Loch
Gairloch

Gairloch

V
Gairloch
& Loch Ewe

Charlestown

421
MEALL AN
DOIREIN

1019
MULLACH COIRE
MHIC FHEARCHAIR

10

Port
Henderson

Eilean
Horrisdale

B8056

859
BEINN LÀIR

Badachro

Opinan

Letterewe
Forest

Lochan
Fada

South Erradale

Loch
Maree
Islands

Letterewe

Loch
Garbhaig

Redpoint

135

Talladale

19

A832

981
SLIOCH

Maree

11

Red
Point

North Coast 500

136

Loch Ghaineamhach

680
BEINN A' MHÙINIDH

Kinlochew
Forest

Rubha
na Fearn

Loch
Torridon

Lower

875
BAOSBHEINN

Loch na
h-Oidhche

855
BEINN
AN EÒIN

724

Beinn Eighe

Incheril

619
BEINN BHREAC

Loch a'
Bhealaich

985

Kinlochewe

J K L M N P Q R

1
7

2

3

4

5

6

7

8

9

10

11

12

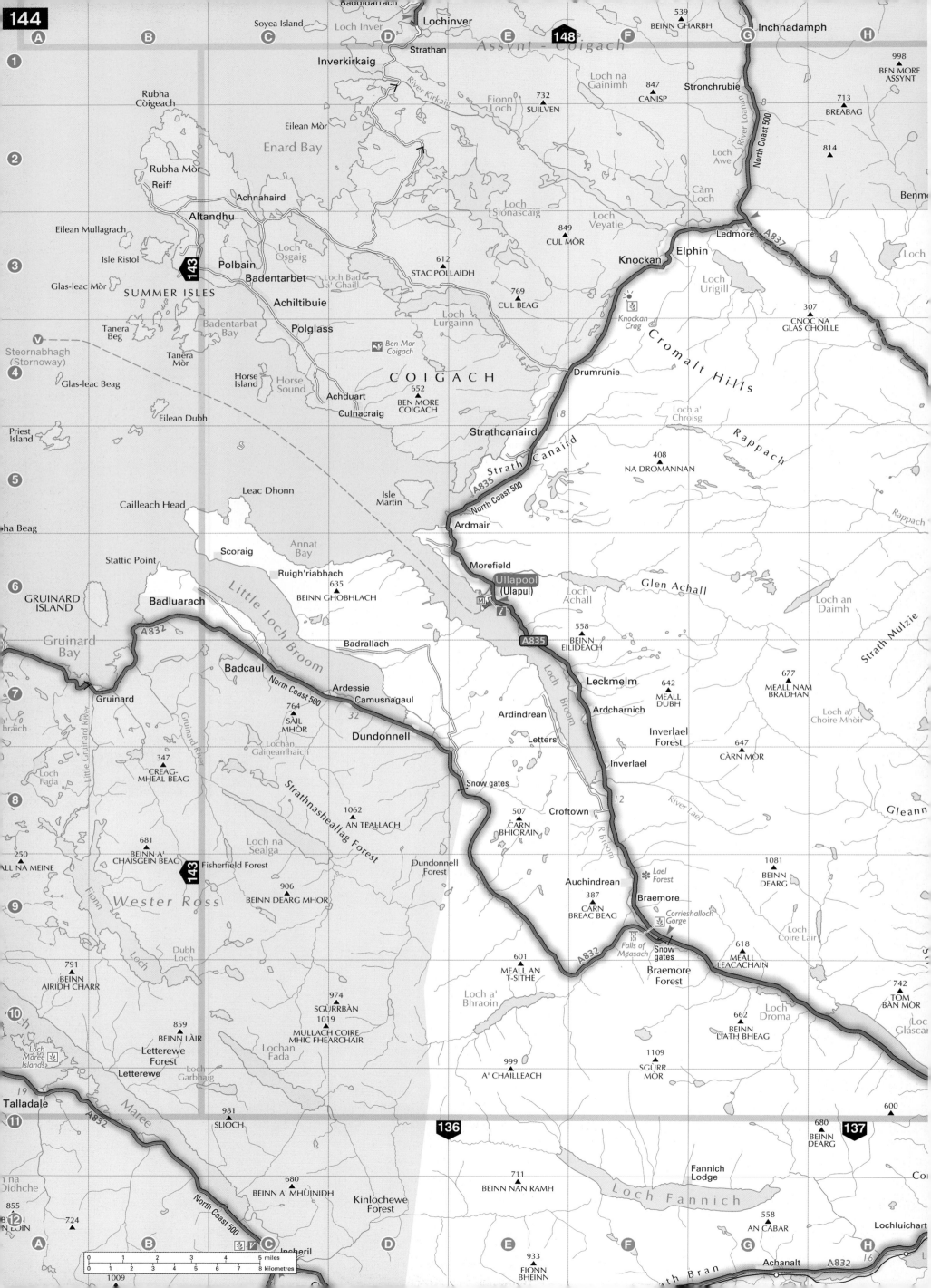

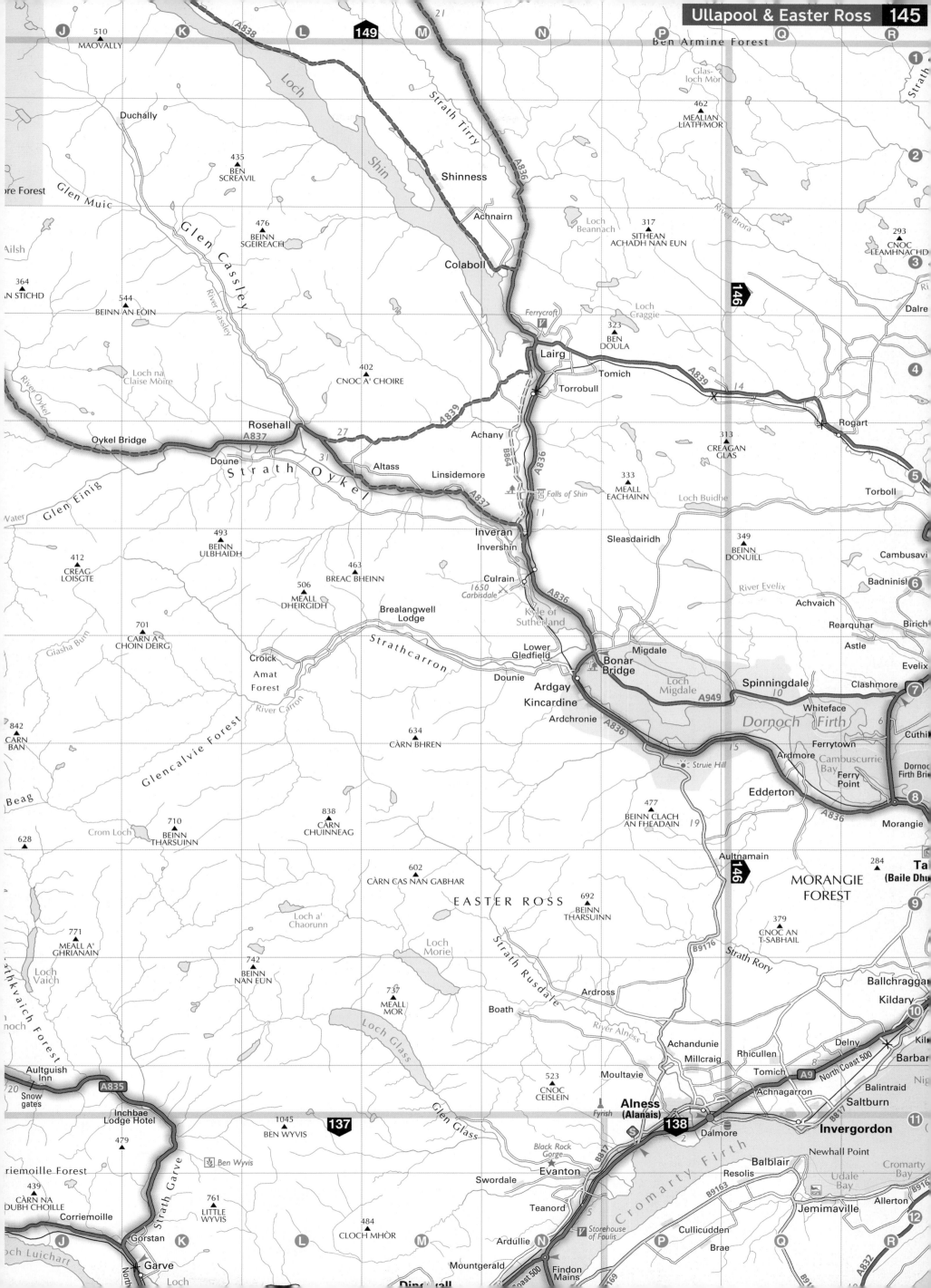

Orkney Islands

Shetland Islands

Faraid
Head

Sango
Bay

Whiten
Head

keil

Durness
Sango
bay
Smoo *Smoo*

Eilean Hoan

Eilean
Nan Ròn

Ardmore
Point

Kirtomy Point

St

ale

Sangomore

Neave or
Coomb Island

Farr Point

Armadale

Armadale Bay

Sangobeg
Ceannabeinne

408
BEN HUTIG

Strathan

Rabbit
Islands

Skerray

Torrisdale Farr
Bay   Bay

Kirtomy

15

Loch
Meadaidh

Talmine

Tongue
Bay

Achtoty

Farr

Swordly

4

423
MEALL
MEADHONACH

Melness
Midtown

Scullomie

Torrisdale

Bettyhill

Bettyhill

Achina

39

Laid

230
BEN
ARNABOLL

A838

North Coast 500

Coldbackie

Invernaver

Loch
Meadie

ALL
CRÀ

262
DRUIM
NAN CLIAR

Kyle of Tongue

Borgie

13

A836

228
BEINN
NAM BÒ

5

Loch Eriboll

Tongue

310
MEALL LEATHAD
NA CRAOIBHE

River Borgie

Skelpick

Loch Mòr
na Caoraçh

A838

31

Strath Beag

520
AN LEAN-CHÀRN

Kinloch

318
CNOC
CRAGGIE

Loch
Craggie

Strath Naver

Skelpick Burn

Loch
nan Clach

6

Loch Hope

Loch na
Seilg

Kyle of Tongue

17

598
MEALLAN
LIATH

12

Loch Strathy

335
MEALL BAD
NA CUAICHE

7

927
BEN
HOPE

763
BEN
LOYAL

527
BEINN
STUMANADH

213
CNOC
MALPELLY

B871

150

River Hope

Loch an
Deerie

A836

Loch
Loyal

345
CNOC NAM
TRI-CHLACH

Strath More

463
FEINNE-BHEINN MHÒR

557
CNOC NAN
CUILEAN

Loch Loyal
Lodge

Loch
Syre

Syre

River Naver

Loch

8

Dun Dórnaigil
Broch

Glen Golly

656
CNOC AN
DÀIMH MÒR

294
POLE
HILL

259
BEINN
ROSAIL

B871

404
BEINN
MHADADH

EAG

Loch
Meadie

16

590
BEN GRIA
MOR

757
CARN AN
TIONAIL

Strath Naver

12

B873

9

RG

N

Loch Coire na
Saidhe Duibhe

230
MEALL A'
BHROLLAICH

Loch Naver

270
BEADAIG

River Mallart

Loch
Rimsdale

Loch
nan Clàr

Altnaharra

Loch
Badanlòch

873
BEN
HEE

680
MEALL AN
LIATH MOR

Loch a'
Ghorm-choire

Loch an
Altan Fhèarna

Badanloc

10

CH

472
MEALL AN
FHUARAIN

959
BEN
KLIBRECK

Loch Choire Forest

Loch
Truderscaig

A836

Strath Vagastie

Loch a'
Bhealaich

Loch
Choire

694
CREAG N-
IOLAIRE

434
CNOC AN LIATH-
BHAID MHÒR

11

Loch
erkland

372
CNOC A'
GHRIAMA

Loch
Fiag

713
CREAG
MHOR

Borrobol Forest

Glen Fiag

37

Overscaig

A838

Crask Inn

346
CNOC A'
GHIUBHAIS

21

Gorm-loch
Mòr

364
CNOC NA
BREUN-CHOILLE

12

ALLY

Loch

J   K   145   L   M   N   P   Q   R

Ben Armine Forest

Glas-
loch Mòr

Strath Skinsdale

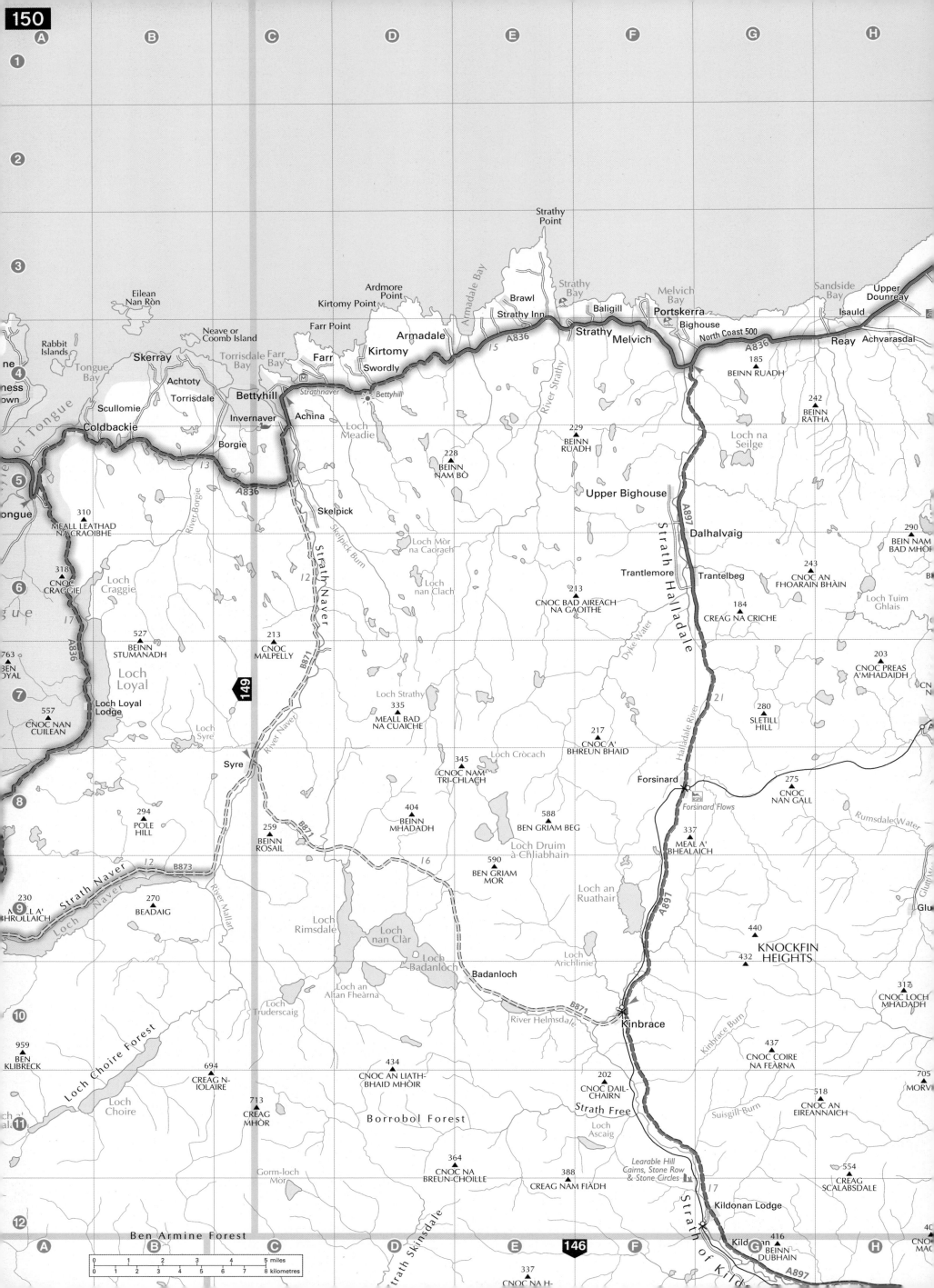

A B C D E F G H

1
2
3

Strathy
Point

Eilean
Nan Ròn

Rabbit
Islands

Neave or
Coomb Island

Ardmore
Point

Kirtomy Point

Farr Point

Armadale Bay

Brawl
Strathy
Bay

Strathy Inn
Baligill

Melvich
Bay

Portskerra
Bighouse

Sandside
Bay

Upper
Dounreay

Isauld

4

Tongue
Bay

Skerray

Achtoty

Torrisdale

Torrisdale Farr
Bay Bay

Farr

Kirtomy
Swordly

Armadale

Strathy
Melvich

North Coast 500

A836

Reay

Achvarasdal

185
▲ BEINN RUADH

242
▲ BEINN RATHA

Scullomie

Coldbackie

Bettyhill

Invernaver

Borgie

Strathnaver

Achina

Bettyhill

Loch
Meadie

River Strathy

228
▲ BEINN NAM BÒ

229
▲ BEINN RUADH

Loch na
Seilge

5

of Tongue

Tongue

A836

13

River Borgie

Skelpick

A836

Strath Naver

12

Loch Mòr
na Caoraeh

Loch
nan Clach

Upper Bighouse

Strath Halladale

Dalhalvaig

Trantlemore

Trantelbeg

290
▲ BEIN NAM
BAD MHÒR

310
▲ MEALL LEATHAD
NA CRAOIBHE

6

763
▲ BEN
OYAL

318
▲ CNOC
CRAGGIE

A836

17

ue

Loch
Craggie

Skelpick Burn

527
▲ BEINN
STUMANADH

213
▲ CNOC
MALPELLY

Loch Strathy

213
▲ CNOC BAD AIREACH
NA GAOITHE

243
▲ CNOC AN
FHOARAIN BHÀIN

184
▲ CREAG NA CRICHE

Loch Tuim
Ghlais

203
▲ CNOC PREAS
A'MHADAIDH

CN

7

Loch
Loyal

149

B871

River Naver

Loch
Syre

335
▲ MEALL BAD
NA CUAICHE

217
▲ CNOC A'
BHREUN BHAID

21

280
▲ SLETILL
HILL

557
▲ CNOC NAN
CUILEAN

Loch Loyal
Lodge

Syre

345
▲ CNOC NAM
TRI-CHLACH

Loch Cròcach

Forsinard

Halladale River

275
▲ CNOC
NAN GALL

8

294
▲ POLE
HILL

B871

259
▲ BEINN
ROSAIL

404
▲ BEINN
MHADADH

588
▲ BEN GRIAM BEG

Loch Druim
à Chliabhain

Forsinard Flows

337
▲ MEAL A'
BHEALAICH

Rumsdale Water

9

230
▲ M LL A'
HROLLAICH

270
▲ BEADAIG

B873

Strath Naver

12

Loch Naver

River Mallart

16

590
▲ BEN GRIAM
MOR

Loch an
Ruathair

A897

440
▲

KNOCKFIN
HEIGHTS

432
▲

313
▲ CNOC LOCH
MHADADH

Glu

10

959
▲ BEN
KLIBRECK

Loch Choire Forest

Loch
Rimsdale

Loch
nan Clàr

Loch
Badanlòch

Loch an
Altan Fheàrna

Badanloch

Loch
Arichlinie

B871

River Helmsdale

Kinbrace

Kinbrace Burn

437
▲ CNOC COIRE
NA FEÀRNA

11

Loch
Truderscaig

694
▲ CREAG N-
IOLAIRE

434
▲ CNOC AN LIATH-
BHAID MHÒIR

202
▲ CNOC DAIL-
CHAIRN

Strath Free

Loch
Ascaig

Suisgill Burn

518
▲ CNOC AN
EIREANNAICH

705
▲ MORVI

713
▲ CREAG
MHÒR

Loch
Choire

al

364
▲ CNOC NA
BREUN-CHOILLE

388
▲ CREAG NAM FIÀDH

Learable Hill
Cairns, Stone Row
& Stone Circles

17

554
▲ CREAG
SCALABSDALE

Strath of Kil

12

Ben Armine Forest

Gorm-loch
Mòr

Strath Skinsdale

Borrobol Forest

146

Kildonan Lodge

Strath of Kild

A897

337
CNOC NA H-

416
▲ BEINN
DUBHAIN

Kild

4

CNO

A B C D E F G H

P Langaton
   Point
   Nethertown   ISLAND OF
                     STROMA
   Mell   Uppertown
   Head
                              St-Margaret's-Hope
                              V

DUNCANSBY
HEAD

PENTLAND FIRTH

DUNNET HEAD ▲127
Briga Head   Dunnet
              Head
                              St John's Point
                    Scarfskerry   Inner Sound
         121   Castle
    DUNNET HILL   of-Mey   Huna
         Brough   St John's   Rattar Mey Gills Kirkstyle   John o' Groats
Stromness   Loch
V   Mey 15   Canisbay   Muckle Stack

Brims Ness   Holborn   Clarden   West Dunnet   Barrock   Skirza
              Head   Head   Skirza
St Mary's   Scrabster   Dunnet   Dunnet   Inkstack   Brabstermire   Head
Chapel (ruin)   Bay   Freswick
Crosskirk   Thurso   Slickly   Freswick Bay
         A836 A9 Bay   Thurso   Ness
Forss   Murkle Castlehill   Greenland   Gill Burn   Head
Skiall Achreamie   Thurso 5   Castletown   Caithness Broch
Lythmore   Glengolly   A836   Tain   Lyth   Auckengill
Shebster Westfield   Weydale   Olrig   Bowermadden   Sortat   Nybster
Cnoc Freiceadain   Hilliclay House   Brough Head
Long Cairns   B874   Sordale   B876   Bower Howe   Keiss
                     Roadside Knockdee Loch   Mireland
Broubster   B870   Scarmclate Halcro Kirk   North Coast 500
Shurrery   Loch   Halkirk   Clayock   Gillock   Loch
Loch Calder   Georgemas B874   of Wester   Sinclair's Bay
Shurrery   Dorrery Scotscalder   Junction   A882   Kirk Burn
Lodge   Station   Station 21   Killimster B876
IGH FÉITH 132   Olgrinmore Harpsdale 176   Reiss   Castle Girnigoe
HEMIGAL DRUIM A'   SPITTAL Loch Watten   Winless & Sinclair   Noss
160 CHRACAIRNIE   Westerdale HILL   Watten   Sibster   Head
Loch   Spittal   B870   Bilbster A882
Shurrery   23   Mybster   Loch of   Haster   Milton   Janetstown
                            Toftingall   A99   Wick
Loch   John o' Groats
luim   Loch More   River Thurso   Badlipster   Staxigoe
      Loch Ruard   Strath Beg   Janetstown Papigoe
                                                                     Wick H
00 BEUL   Loch   A9   145   Newton Wick Bay
FAIRE   Sand   136   Loch   BALLHARN   Old Wick   South Head
     BEINN CHÀITEAG Stemster   HILL   Grey Cairns Castle of Old Wick
Loch an   248   of Camster   Whiterow
Thulachan Loch   Achavanich STEMSTER HILL 212 Loch of   Loch
348   Sand   226   HILL OF Yarrows   Hempriggs
BEN   Dalnawillan   Loch   COIRE   YARROWS   Thrumster
ALISKY Lodge   Rangag   NA BEINN   Cairn o'Get A99
Lodge   Sarclet
264   287   Roster   Ulbster
CNOCAN   BEN-A-   Hill o'Many   Whaligoe
CONACHREAG   CHIELT   Stanes   Whaligoe Steps
                   Houstry   Upper   Mid Clyth   Bruan
                            Lybster Swiney
Smerral Land-   Occumster Halberry Head
         hallow   Forse Invershore Lybster Clyth Ness
Latheronwheel   Clan Lybster Lybster
Dunbeath Water Gunn Harbour Bay
         A9   Janetstown Latheron
Berriedale Water   Laidhay Croft
484 MAIDEN   Dunbeath   Snow gates
     PAP   Knockally   Dunbeath
626 SCARABEN   Ramscraigs   Bay
Langwell Forest   Borgue 20
         Newport
Langwell North Coast 500
House Berriedale
404
CREAG

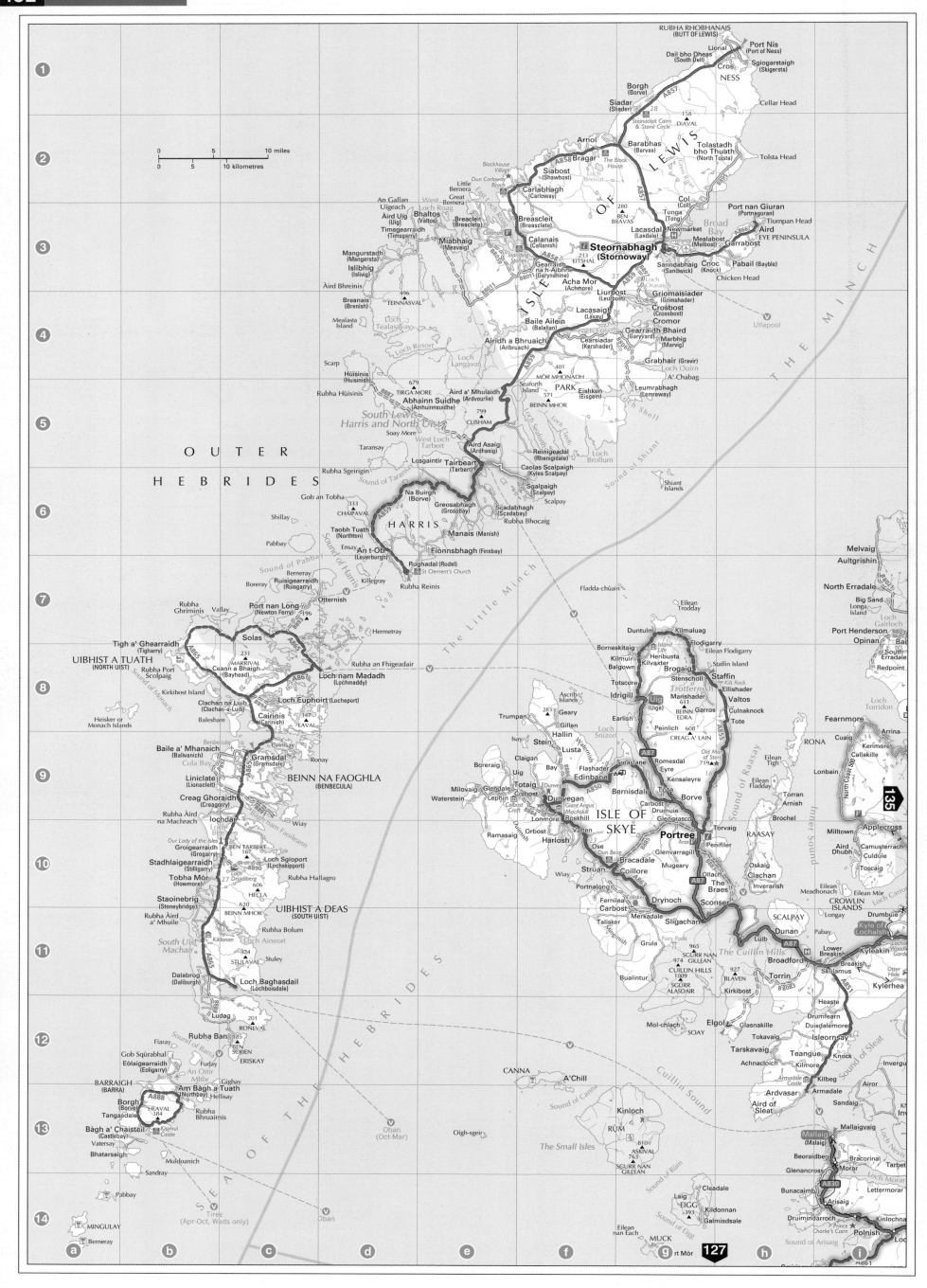

Motorway and primary route junctions which have access or exit restrictions are shown on the map pages thus:

M1 London - Leeds

Junction	Northbound	Southbound
2	Access only from A1 (northbound)	Exit only to A1 (southbound)
4	Access only from A41 (northbound)	Exit only to A41 (southbound)
6A	Access only from M25 (no link from A405)	Exit only to M25 (no link from A405)
7	Access only from A414	Exit only to A414
17	Exit only to M45	Access only from M45
19	Exit only to M6 (northbound)	Exit only to A14 (southbound)
21A	Exit only, no access	Access only, no exit
24A	Access only, no exit	Access only from A50 (eastbound)
35A	Exit only, no access	Access only, no exit
43	Exit only to M621	Access only from M621
48	Exit only to A1(M) (northbound)	Access only from A1(M) (southbound)

M2 Rochester - Faversham

Junction	Westbound	Eastbound
1	No exit to A2 (eastbound)	No access from A2 (westbound)

M3 Sunbury - Southampton

Junction	Northeastbound	Southwestbound
8	Access only from A303, no exit	Exit only to A303, no access
10	Exit only, no access	Access only, no exit
14	Access from M27 only, no exit	No access to M27 (westbound)

M4 London - South Wales

Junction	Westbound	Eastbound
1	Access only from A4 (westbound)	Exit only to A4 (eastbound)
2	Access only from A4 (westbound)	Access only from A4 (eastbound)
21	Exit only to M48	Access only from M48
23	Access only from M48	Exit only to M48
25	Exit only, no access	Access only, no exit
25A	Exit only, no access	Access only, no exit
29	Exit only to A48(M)	Access only from A48(M)
38	Exit only, no access	No restriction
39	Access only, no exit	No access or exit
42	Exit only to A483	Access only from A483

M5 Birmingham - Exeter

Junction	Northeastbound	Southwestbound
10	Access only, no exit	Exit only, no access
11A	Access only from A417 (westbound)	Exit only to A417 (eastbound)
18A	Exit only to M49	Access only from M49
18	Exit only, no access	Access only, no exit

M6 Toll Motorway

Junction	Northwestbound	Southeastbound
T1	Access only, no exit	No access or exit
T2	No access or exit	Exit only, no access
T5	Access only, no exit	Exit only to A5148 (northbound), no access
T7	Exit only, no access	Access only, no exit
T8	Exit only, no access	Access only, no exit

M6 Rugby - Carlisle

Junction	Northbound	Southbound
3A	Exit only to M6 Toll	Access only from M6 Toll
4	Exit only to M42 (southbound) & A446	Exit only to A446
4A	Access only from M42 (southbound)	Exit only to M42
5	Exit only, no access	Access only, no exit
10A	Exit only to M54	Access only from M54
11A	Access only from M6 Toll	Exit only to M6 Toll
with M56 (jct 20A)	No restriction	Access only from M56 (eastbound)
20	Exit only to M56 (westbound)	Access only from M56 (eastbound)
24	Access only, no exit	Exit only, no access
25	Exit only, no access	Access only, no exit
30	Access only from M61	Exit only to M61
31A	Exit only, no access	Access only, no exit
45	Exit only, no access	Access only, no exit

M8 Edinburgh - Bishopton

Junction	Westbound	Eastbound
6	Exit only, no access	Access only, no exit
6A	Access only, no exit	Exit only, no access
7	Access only, no exit	Exit only, no access
7A	Exit only, no access	Access only from A725 (northbound), no exit
8	No access from M73 (southbound) or from A8 (eastbound) & A89	No exit to M73 (northbound) or to A8 (westbound) & A89
9	Access only, no exit	Exit only, no access
13	Access only from M80 (southbound)	Exit only to M80 (northbound)
14	Access only, no exit	Exit only, no access
16	Exit only to A804	Access only from A879
17	Exit only to A82	No restriction
18	Access only from A82 (eastbound)	Exit only to A814
19	No access from A814 (westbound)	Exit only to A814 (westbound)
20	Exit only, no access	Access only, no exit
21	Access only, no exit	Exit only to A8
22	Exit only to M77 (southbound)	Access only from M77 (northbound)
23	Exit only to B768	Access only from B768
25	No access or exit from or to A8	No access or exit from or to A8
25A	Exit only, no access	Access only, no exit
28	Exit only, no access	Access only, no exit
28A	Exit only to A737	Access only from A737
29A	Exit only to A8	Access only, no exit

M9 Edinburgh - Dunblane

Junction	Northwestbound	Southeastbound
2	Access only, no exit	Exit only, no access
3	Exit only, no access	Access only, no exit
6	Access only, no exit	Exit only to A905
8	Exit only to M876 (southwestbound)	Access only from M876 (northeastbound)

M11 London - Cambridge

Junction	Northbound	Southbound
4	Access only from A406 (eastbound)	Exit only to A406
5	Exit only, no access	Access only, no exit
8A	Exit only, no access	No direct access, use jct 8
9	Exit only to A11	Access only from A11
13	Exit only, no access	Access only, no exit
14	Exit only, no access	Access only, no exit

M20 Swanley - Folkestone

Junction	Northwestbound	Southeastbound
2	Staggered junction; follow signs - access only	Staggered junction; follow signs - exit only
3	Exit only to M26 (westbound)	Access only from M26 (eastbound)
5	Access only from A20	For access follow signs - exit only to A20
6	No restriction	For exit follow signs
11A	Access only, no exit	Exit only, no access

M23 Hooley - Crawley

Junction	Northbound	Southbound
7	Exit only to A23 (northbound)	Access only from A23 (southbound)
10A	Access only, no exit	Exit only, no access

M25 London Orbital Motorway

Junction	Clockwise	Anticlockwise
1B	No direct access, use slip road to jct 2 Exit only	Access only, no exit
5	No exit to M26 (eastbound)	No access from M26
19	Exit only, no access	Access only, no exit
21	Access only from M1 (southbound) Exit only to M1 (northbound)	Access only from M1 (southbound) Exit only to M1 (northbound)
31	No exit (use slip road via jct 30), access only	No access (use slip road via jct 30), exit only

M26 Sevenoaks - Wrotham

Junction	Westbound	Eastbound
with M25 (jct 5)	Exit only to clockwise M25 (westbound)	Access only from anticlockwise M25 (eastbound)
with M20 (jct 3)	Access only from M20 (northwestbound)	Exit only to M20 (southeastbound)

M27 Cadnam - Portsmouth

Junction	Westbound	Eastbound
4	Staggered junction; follow signs - access only from M3 (southbound). Exit only to M3 (northbound)	Staggered junction; follow signs - access only from M3 (southbound). Exit only to M3 (northbound)
10	Exit only, no access	Access only, no exit
12	Staggered junction; follow signs - exit only to M275 (southbound)	Staggered junction; follow signs - access only from M275 (northbound)

M40 London - Birmingham

Junction	Northwestbound	Southeastbound
3	Exit only, no access	Access only, no exit
7	Exit only, no access	Access only, no exit
8	Exit only to M40/A40	Access only from M40/A40
13	Exit only, no access	Access only, no exit
14	Access only, no exit	Exit only, no access
16	Access only, no exit	Exit only, no access

M42 Bromsgrove - Measham

Junction	Northeastbound	Southwestbound
1	Access only, no exit	Exit only, no access
7	Exit only to M6 (northwestbound)	Access only from M6 (northwestbound)
7A	Exit only to M6 (southeastbound)	No access or exit
8	Access only from M6 (southeastbound)	Exit only to M6 (northwestbound)

M45 Coventry - M1

Junction	Westbound	Eastbound
Dunchurch (unnumbered)	Access only from A45	Exit only, no access
with M1 (jct 17)	Access only from M1 (northbound)	Exit only to M1 (southbound)

M48 Chepstow

Junction	Westbound	Eastbound
21	Access only from M4 (westbound)	Exit only to M4 (eastbound)
23	No exit to M4 (eastbound)	No access from M4 (westbound)

M53 Mersey Tunnel - Chester

Junction	Northbound	Southbound
11	Access only from M56 (westbound) Exit only to M56 (eastbound)	Access only from M56 (westbound) Exit only to M56 (eastbound)

M54 Telford - Birmingham

Junction	Westbound	Eastbound
with M6 (jct 10A)	Access only from M6 (northbound)	Exit only to M6 (southbound)

M56 Chester - Manchester

Junction	Westbound	Eastbound
1	Access only from M60 (westbound)	Exit only to M60 (eastbound) & A34 (northbound)
2	Exit only, no access	Access only, no exit
3	Access only, no exit	Exit only, no access
4	Exit only, no access	Access only, no exit
7	Exit only, no access	No restriction
8	Access only, no exit	No access or exit
9	No exit to M6 (southbound)	No access from M6 (northbound)
15	Exit only to M53	Access only from M53
16	No access or exit	No restriction

M57 Liverpool Outer Ring Road

Junction	Northwestbound	Southeastbound
3	Access only, no exit	Exit only, no access
5	Access only from A580 (westbound)	Exit only, no access

M58 Liverpool - Wigan

Junction	Westbound	Eastbound
1	Exit only, no access	Access only, no exit

M60 Manchester Orbital

Junction	Clockwise	Anticlockwise
2	Access only, no exit	Exit only, no access
3	No access from M56	Access only from A34 (northbound)
4	Access only from A34 (northbound). Exit only to M56	Access only from M56 (eastbound). Exit only to A34 (southbound)
5	Access and exit only from and to A5103 (northbound)	Access and exit only from and to A5103 (southbound)
7	No direct access, use slip road to jct 8. Exit only to A56	Access only from A56. No exit, use jct 8
14	Access from A580 (eastbound)	Exit only to A580 (westbound)
16	Access only, no exit	Exit only, no access
20	Exit only, no access	Access only, no exit
22	No restriction	Exit only, no access
25	Exit only, no access	No restriction
26	No restriction	Exit only, no access
27	Access only, no exit	Exit only, no access

M61 Manchester - Preston

Junction	Northwestbound	Southeastbound
3	No access or exit	Exit only, no access
with M6 (jct 30)	Exit only to M6 (northbound)	Access only from M6 (southbound)

M62 Liverpool - Kingston upon Hull

Junction	Westbound	Eastbound
23	Access only, no exit	Exit only, no access
32A	No access to A1(M) (southbound)	No restriction

M65 Preston - Colne

Junction	Northeastbound	Southwestbound
9	Exit only, no access	Access only, no exit
11	Access only, no exit	Exit only, no access

M66 Bury

Junction	Northbound	Southbound
with A56	Exit only to A56 (northbound)	Access only from A56 (southbound)
1	Exit only, no access	Access only, no exit

M67 Hyde Bypass

Junction	Westbound	Eastbound
1	Access only, no exit	Exit only, no access
2	Exit only, no access	Access only, no exit
3	Exit only, no access	No restriction

M69 Coventry - Leicester

Junction	Northbound	Southbound
2	Access only, no exit	Exit only, no access

M73 East of Glasgow

Junction	Northbound	Southbound
1	No exit to A74 & A721	No exit to A74 & A721
2	No access from or exit to A89. No access from (eastbound)	No access from or exit to A89. No exit to M8 (westbound)

M74 and A74(M) Glasgow - Gretna

Junction	Northbound	Southbound
3	Exit only, no access	Access only, no exit
3A	Access only, no exit	Exit only, no access
4	No access from A74 & A721	Access only, no exit to A74 & A721
7	Access only, no exit	Exit only, no access
9	No access or exit	Exit only, no access
10	No restriction	Access only, no exit
11	Access only, no exit	Exit only, no access
12	Exit only, no access	Access only, no exit
18	Exit only, no access	Access only, no exit

M77 Glasgow - Kilmarnock

Junction	Northbound	Southbound
with M8 (jct 22)	No exit to M8 (westbound)	No access from M8 (eastbound)
4	Access only, no exit	Exit only, no access
6	Access only, no exit	Exit only, no access
7	Access only, no exit	No restriction
8	Exit only, no access	Exit only, no access

M80 Glasgow - Stirling

Junction	Northbound	Southbound
4A	Exit only, no access	Access only, no exit
6A	Access only, no exit	Exit only, no access
8	Exit only to M876 (northeastbound)	Access only from M876 (southwestbound)

M90 Edinburgh - Perth

Junction	Northbound	Southbound
1	No exit, access only	Exit only to A90 (eastbound)
2A	Exit only to A92 (eastbound)	Access only from A92 (westbound)
7	Access only, no exit	Exit only, no access
8	Exit only, no access	Access only, no exit
10	No access from A912. No exit to A912 (southbound)	No access from A912 (northbound) No exit to A912

M180 Doncaster - Grimsby

Junction	Westbound	Eastbound
1	Access only, no exit	Exit only, no access

M606 Bradford Spur

Junction	Northbound	Southbound
2	Exit only, no access	No restriction

M621 Leeds - M1

Junction	Clockwise	Anticlockwise
2A	Access only, no exit	Exit only, no access
4	No exit or access	No restriction
5	Access only, no exit	Exit only, no access
6	Exit only, no access	Access only, no exit
with M1 (jct 43)	Exit only to M1 (southbound)	Access only from M1 (northbound)

M876 Bonnybridge - Kincardine Bridge

Junction	Northeastbound	Southwestbound
with M80 (jct 5)	Access only from M80 (northeastbound)	Exit only to M80 (southwestbound)
with M9 (jct 8)	Exit only to M9 (eastbound)	Access only from M9 (westbound)

A1(M) South Mimms - Baldock

Junction	Northbound	Southbound
2	Exit only, no access	Access only, no exit
3	No restriction	Exit only, no access
5	Access only, no exit	No access or exit

A1(M) Pontefract - Bedale

Junction	Northbound	Southbound
41	No access to M62 (eastbound)	No restriction
43	Access only from M1 (northbound)	Exit only to M1 (southbound)

A1(M) Scotch Corner - Newcastle upon Tyne

Junction	Northbound	Southbound
57	Exit only to A66(M) (eastbound)	Access only from A66(M) (westbound)
65	No access Exit only to A194(M) & A1 (northbound)	No exit Access only from A194(M) & A1 (southbound)

A3(M) Horndean - Havant

Junction	Northbound	Southbound
1	Access only from A3	Exit only to A3
4	Exit only, no access	Access only, no exit

A38(M) Birmingham, Victoria Road (Park Circus)

Junction	Northbound	Southbound
with B4132	No exit	No access

A48(M) Cardiff Spur

Junction	Westbound	Eastbound
29	Access only from M4 (westbound)	Exit only to M4 (eastbound)
29A	Exit only to A48 (westbound)	Access only from A48 (eastbound)

A57(M) Manchester, Brook Street (A34)

Junction	Westbound	Eastbound
with A34	No exit	No access

A58(M) Leeds, Park Lane and Westgate

Junction	Northbound	Southbound
with A58	No restriction	No access

A64(M) Leeds, Clay Pit Lane (A58)

Junction	Westbound	Eastbound
with A58	No exit (to Clay Pit Lane)	No access (from Clay Pit Lane)

A66(M) Darlington Spur

Junction	Westbound	Eastbound
with A1(M) (jct 57)	Exit only to A1(M) (southbound)	Access only from A1(M) (northbound)

A74(M) Gretna - Abington

Junction	Northbound	Southbound
18	Exit only, no access	No exit

A194(M) Newcastle upon Tyne

Junction	Northbound	Southbound
with A1(M) (jct 65)	Access only from A1(M) (northbound)	Exit only to A1(M) (southbound)

A12 M25 - Ipswich

Junction	Northeastbound	Southwestbound
13	Access only, no exit	No restriction
14	Exit only, no access	Access only, no exit
20A	Exit only, no access	Access only, no exit
20B	Access only, no exit	Exit only, no access
21	No restriction	Access only, no exit
23	Exit only, no access	Access only, no exit
24	Access only, no exit	Exit only, no access
27	Exit only, no access	Access only, no exit
Dedham & Stratford St Mary (unnumbered)	Exit only	Access only

A14 M1 - Felixstowe

Junction	Westbound	Eastbound
with M1/M6 (jct19)	Exit only to M6 and M1 (northbound)	Access only from M6 and M1 (southbound)
4	Exit only, no access	Access only, no exit
31	Exit only to M11 (for London)	Access only, no exit
31A	Exit only to A14 (northbound)	Access only, no exit
34	Access only, no exit	Exit only, no access
36	Exit only to A11, access only from A1303	Access only from A11
38	Access only from A11	Exit only to A11
39	Exit only, no access	Access only, no exit
61	Access only, no exit	Exit only, no access

A55 Holyhead - Chester

Junction	Westbound	Eastbound
8A	Exit only, no access	Access only, no exit
23A	Access only, no exit	Exit only, no access
24A	Exit only, no access	No access or exit
27A	No restriction	No access or exit
33A	Exit only, no access	No access or exit
33B	Exit only, no access	Access only, no exit
36A	Exit only to A5104	Access only from A5104

Index to place names

This index lists places appearing in the main map section of the atlas in alphabetical order. The reference following each name gives the atlas page number and grid reference of the square in which the place appears. The map shows counties, unitary authorities and administrative areas, together with a list of the abbreviated name forms used in the index.

The top 100 places of tourist interest are indexed in **red**, World Heritage sites in **green**, motorway service areas in **blue**, airports in blue *italic* and National Parks in green *italic.*

Scotland

Abers	Aberdeenshire
Ag & B	Argyll and Bute
Angus	Angus
Border	Scottish Borders
C Aber	City of Aberdeen
C Dund	City of Dundee
C Edin	City of Edinburgh
C Glas	City of Glasgow
Clacks	Clackmannanshire (1)
D & G	Dumfries & Galloway
E Ayrs	East Ayrshire
E Duns	East Dunbartonshire (2)
E Loth	East Lothian
E Rens	East Renfrewshire (3)
Falk	Falkirk
Fife	Fife
Highld	Highland
Inver	Inverclyde (4)
Mdloth	Midlothian (5)
Moray	Moray
N Ayrs	North Ayrshire
N Lans	North Lanarkshire (6)
Ork	Orkney Islands
P & K	Perth & Kinross
Rens	Renfrewshire (7)
S Ayrs	South Ayrshire
S Lans	South Lanarkshire
Shet	Shetland Islands
Stirlg	Stirling
W Duns	West Dunbartonshire (8)
W Isls	Western Isles (Na h-Eileanan an Iar)
W Loth	West Lothian

Wales

Blae G	Blaenau Gwent (9)
Brdgnd	Bridgend (10)
Caerph	Caerphilly (11)
Cardif	Cardiff
Carmth	Carmarthenshire
Cerdgn	Ceredigion
Conwy	Conwy
Denbgs	Denbighshire
Flints	Flintshire
Gwynd	Gwynedd
IoA	Isle of Anglesey
Mons	Monmouthshire
Myr Td	Merthyr Tydfil (12)
Neath	Neath Port Talbot (13)
Newpt	Newport (14)
Pembks	Pembrokeshire
Powys	Powys
Rhondd	Rhondda Cynon Taf (15)
Swans	Swansea
Torfn	Torfaen (16)
V Glam	Vale of Glamorgan (17)
Wrexhm	Wrexham

England

BaNES	Bath & N E Somerset (18)
Barns	Barnsley (19)
BCP	Bournemouth, Christchurch and Poole (20)
Bed	Bedford
Birm	Birmingham
Bl w D	Blackburn with Darwen (21)
Bolton	Bolton (22)
Bpool	Blackpool
Br & H	Brighton & Hove (23)
Br For	Bracknell Forest (24)
Bristl	City of Bristol
Bucks	Buckinghamshire
Bury	Bury (25)
C Beds	Central Bedfordshire
C Brad	City of Bradford
C Derb	City of Derby
C KuH	City of Kingston upon Hull
C Leic	City of Leicester
C Nott	City of Nottingham
C Pete	City of Peterborough
C Plym	City of Plymouth
C Port	City of Portsmouth
C Sotn	City of Southampton
C Stke	City of Stoke-on-Trent
C York	City of York
Calder	Calderdale (26)
Cambs	Cambridgeshire
Ches E	Cheshire East
Ches W	Cheshire West and Chester
Cnwll	Cornwall
Covtry	Coventry
Cumb	Cumbria
Darltn	Darlington (27)
Derbys	Derbyshire
Devon	Devon
Donc	Doncaster (28)
Dorset	Dorset
Dudley	Dudley (29)
Dur	Durham
E R Yk	East Riding of Yorkshire
E Susx	East Sussex
Essex	Essex
Gatesd	Gateshead (30)
Gloucs	Gloucestershire
Gt Lon	Greater London
Halton	Halton (31)
Hants	Hampshire
Hartpl	Hartlepool (32)
Herefs	Herefordshire
Herts	Hertfordshire
IoS	Isles of Scilly
IoW	Isle of Wight
Kent	Kent
Kirk	Kirklees (33)
Knows	Knowsley (34)
Lancs	Lancashire
Leeds	Leeds
Leics	Leicestershire
Lincs	Lincolnshire
Lpool	Liverpool
Luton	Luton
M Keyn	Milton Keynes
Manch	Manchester
Medway	Medway
Middsb	Middlesbrough
N Linc	North Lincolnshire
N Som	North Somerset
N Tyne	North Tyneside (35)
N u Ty	Newcastle upon Tyne
N York	North Yorkshire
NE Lin	North East Lincolnshire
Nhants	Northamptonshire
Norfk	Norfolk
Notts	Nottinghamshire
Nthumb	Northumberland
Oldham	Oldham (36)
Oxon	Oxfordshire
R & Cl	Redcar & Cleveland
Readg	Reading
Rochdl	Rochdale (37)
Rothm	Rotherham (38)
Rutlnd	Rutland
S Glos	South Gloucestershire (39)
S on T	Stockton-on-Tees (40)
S Tyne	South Tyneside (41)
Salfd	Salford (42)
Sandw	Sandwell (43)
Sefton	Sefton (44)
Sheff	Sheffield
Shrops	Shropshire
Slough	Slough (45)
Solhll	Solihull (46)
Somset	Somerset
St Hel	St Helens (47)
Staffs	Staffordshire
Sthend	Southend-on-Sea
Stockp	Stockport (48)
Suffk	Suffolk
Sundld	Sunderland
Surrey	Surrey
Swindn	Swindon
Tamesd	Tameside (49)
Thurr	Thurrock (50)
Torbay	Torbay
Traffd	Trafford (51)
W & M	Windsor & Maidenhead (52)
W Berk	West Berkshire
W Susx	West Sussex
Wakefd	Wakefield (53)
Warrtn	Warrington (54)
Warwks	Warwickshire
Wigan	Wigan (55)
Wilts	Wiltshire
Wirral	Wirral (56)
Wokham	Wokingham (57)
Wolves	Wolverhampton (58)
Worcs	Worcestershire
Wrekin	Telford & Wrekin (59)
Wsall	Walsall (60)

Channel Islands & Isle of Man

Guern	Guernsey
Jersey	Jersey
IoM	Isle of Man

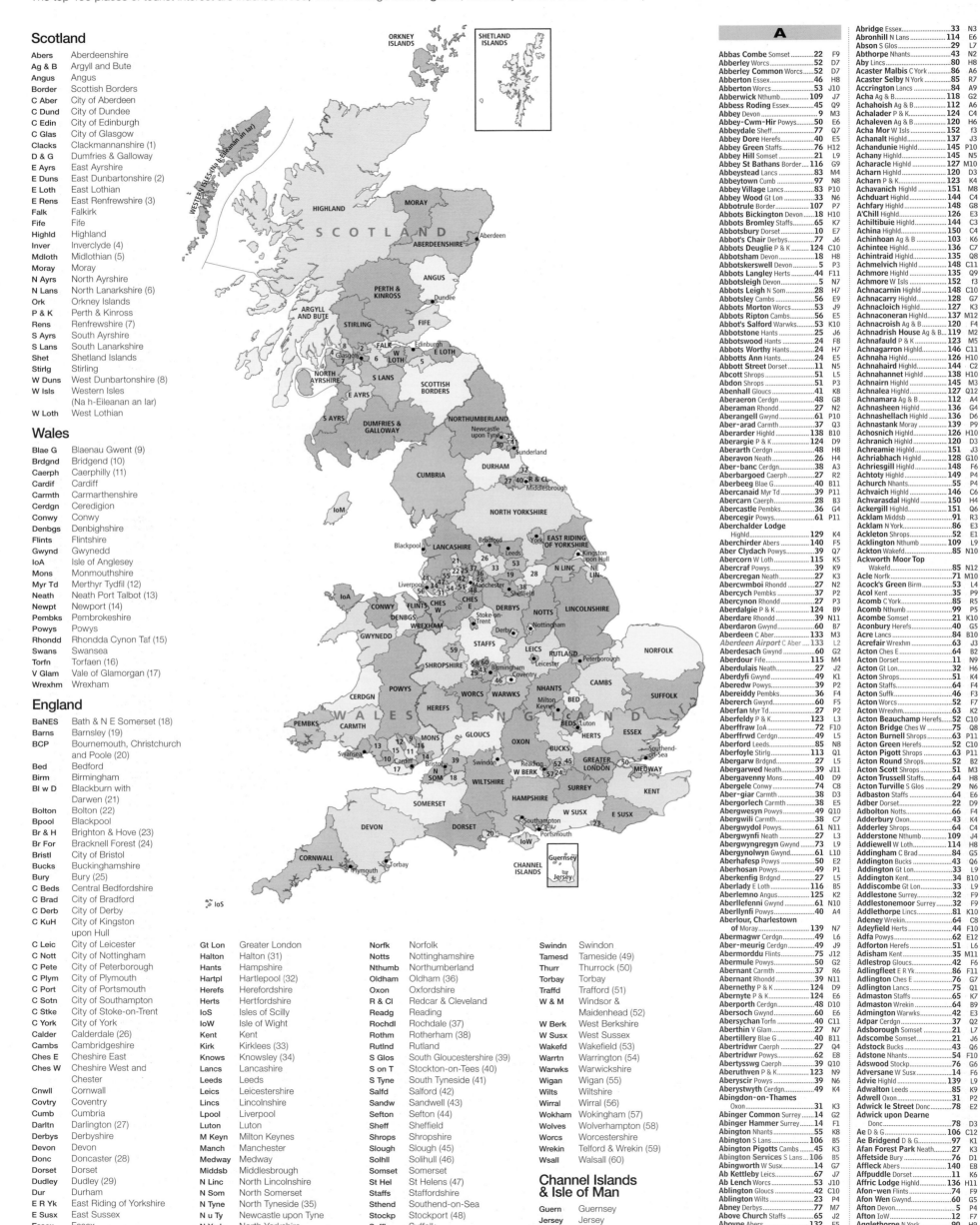

A

Abbas Combe Somset 22 F9
Abberley Worcs 52 D7
Abberley Common Worcs 52 D7
Abberton Essex 46 H8
Abberton Worcs 53 J10
Abberwick Nthumb 109 J7
Abbess Roding Essex 45 Q9
Abbey Devon 9 M3
Abbey-Cwm-Hir Powys 50 E6
Abbeydale Sheff 77 Q7
Abbey Dore Herefs 40 E5
Abbey Green Staffs 76 H12
Abbey Hill Somset 21 L9
Abbey St Bathans Border 116 G9
Abbeystead Lancs 83 M4
Abbeytown Cumb 97 N8
Abbey Village Lancs 83 P10
Abbey Wood Gt Lon 33 N6
Abbotrule Border 107 P7
Abbots Bickington Devon 18 H10
Abbots Bromley Staffs 65 K7
Abbotsbury Dorset 10 E7
Abbot's Chair Derbys 77 J6
Abbots Deuglie P & K 124 C10
Abbotsham Devon 18 H8
Abbotskerswell Devon 5 P3
Abbots Langley Herts 44 F11
Abbotsleigh Devon 5 N7
Abbots Leigh N Som 28 H7
Abbotsley Cambs 56 E9
Abbots Morton Worcs 53 J9
Abbots Ripton Cambs 56 E5
Abbot's Salford Warwks 53 K10
Abbotstone Hants 25 J6
Abbotswood Hants 24 F8
Abbots Worthy Hants 24 H7
Abbotts Ann Hants 24 E5
Abbott Street Dorset 11 N5
Abcott Shrops 51 L5
Abdon Shrops 51 P3
Abenhall Gloucs 41 K8
Aberaeron Cerdgn 48 G8
Aberaman Rhondd 27 N2
Aberangell Gwynd 61 P10
Aber-arad Carmth 37 Q3
Aberarder Highld 138 B10
Aberargie P & K 124 D9
Aberarth Cerdgn 48 H8
Aberavon Neath 26 H4
Aber-banc Cerdgn 38 A3
Aberbargoed Caerph 27 R2
Aberbeeg Blae G 40 B11
Abercanaid Myr Td 39 P11
Abercarn Caerph 28 B3
Abercastle Pembks 36 G4
Abercegir Powys 61 P11
Aberchalder Lodge Highld 129 K4
Aberchirder Abers 140 F5
Aber Clydach Powys 39 Q7
Abercorn W Loth 115 K5
Abercraf Powys 39 K9
Abercregan Neath 27 K3
Abercwmboi Rhondd 27 N2
Abercych Pembks 37 P2
Abercynon Rhondd 27 P3
Aberdalgie P & K 124 B9
Aberdare Rhondd 39 N11
Aberdaron Gwynd 60 B7
Aberdeen C Aber 133 M3
Aberdeen Airport C Aber 133 L2
Aberdesach Gwynd 60 G2
Aberdour Fife 115 M4
Aberdulais Neath 27 J2
Aberdyfi Gwynd 49 K1
Aberedw Powys 39 P2
Abereiddy Pembks 36 F4
Abererch Gwynd 60 F5
Aberfan Myr Td 27 P2
Aberfeldy P & K 123 L3
Aberffraw IoA 72 F10
Aberffrwd Cerdgn 49 L5
Aberford Leeds 85 N8
Aberfoyle Stirlg 113 Q1
Abergarw Brdgnd 27 L5
Abergarwed Neath 39 J11
Abergavenny Mons 40 D9
Abergele Conwy 74 C8
Aber-giar Carmth 38 D3
Abergorlech Carmth 38 E5
Abergwesyn Powys 49 Q10
Abergwili Carmth 38 C7
Abergwydol Powys 61 N11
Abergwynfi Neath 27 L3
Abergwyngregyn Gwynd 73 L9
Abergynolwyn Gwynd 61 L10
Aberhafesp Powys 50 E2
Aberhosan Powys 49 P1
Aberkenfig Brdgnd 27 L5
Aberlady E Loth 116 B5
Aberlemno Angus 125 K2
Aberllefenni Gwynd 61 N10
Aberllynfi Powys 40 A4
Aberlour, Charlestown of Moray 139 N7
Abermagwr Cerdgn 49 L6
Aber-meurig Cerdgn 49 J9
Abermorddu Flints 75 J12
Abermule Powys 50 G2
Abernant Carmth 37 R6
Abernant Rhondd 39 N11
Abernethy P & K 124 D9
Abernyte P & K 124 E6
Aberporth Cerdgn 48 D10
Abersoch Gwynd 60 E6
Abersychan Torfn 40 C11
Aberthin V Glam 27 N7
Abertillery Blae G 40 B11
Abertridwr Caerph 27 Q4
Abertridwr Powys 62 E8
Abertysswg Caerph 39 Q10
Aberuthven P & K 123 N9
Aberyscir Powys 39 N6
Aberystwyth Cerdgn 49 K4
Abingdon-on-Thames Oxon 31 K3
Abinger Common Surrey 14 G2
Abinger Hammer Surrey 14 F1
Abington Nhants 55 K8
Abington S Lans 106 B5
Abington Pigotts Cambs 45 K3
Abington Services S Lans 106 B5
Abingworth W Susx 14 G7
Ab Kettleby Leics 67 J7
Ab Lench Worcs 53 J10
Ablington Gloucs 42 C10
Ablington Wilts 23 P4
Abney Derbys 77 M7
Above Church Staffs 65 J2
Aboyne Abers 132 E5
Abhainn Suidhe W Isls 152 d5
Abram Wigan 75 Q3
Abriachan Highld 137 P9
Abridge Essex 33 N3
Abronhill N Lans 114 E6
Abson S Glos 29 L7
Abthorpe Nhants 43 N2
Aby Lincs 80 H8
Acaster Malbis C York 86 A6
Acaster Selby N York 85 R7
Accrington Lancs 84 A9
Acha Ag & B 118 G2
Achahoish Ag & B 112 A6
Achalader P & K 124 C4
Achaleven Ag & B 120 H6
Acha Mor W Isls 152 f3
Achanalt Highld 137 J3
Achandunie Highld 145 P10
Achany Highld 145 N5
Acharacle Highld 127 M10
Acharn Highld 120 D3
Acharn P & K 123 K4
Achavanich Highld 151 M8
Achduart Highld 144 C4
Achfary Highld 148 G8
A'Chill Highld 126 E3
Achiltibuie Highld 144 C3
Achina Highld 150 C4
Achinhoan Ag & B 103 K6
Achintee Highld 136 C7
Achintraid Highld 135 Q8
Achmelvich Highld 148 C11
Achmore Highld 135 Q9
Achmore W Isls 152 f3
Achnacarnin Highld 148 C10
Achnacarry Highld 128 G7
Achnacloich Highld 127 K3
Achnaconeran Highld 137 M12
Achnacroish Ag & B 120 F4
Achnadrish House Ag & B 119 M2
Achnafauld P & K 123 M5
Achnagarron Highld 146 C11
Achnaha Highld 126 H10
Achnahaird Highld 144 C2
Achnahannet Highld 138 H10
Achnairn Highld 145 M3
Achnalea Highld 127 Q12
Achnamara Ag & B 112 A4
Achnasheen Highld 136 G4
Achnashellach Highld 136 D6
Achnastank Moray 139 P9
Achosnich Highld 126 H10
Achranich Highld 120 D3
Achreamie Highld 151 J3
Achriabhach Highld 128 G10
Achriesgill Highld 148 F6
Achtoty Highld 149 P4
Achurch Nhants 55 P4
Achvaich Highld 146 C6
Achvarasdal Highld 150 H4
Ackergill Highld 151 Q6
Acklam Middsb 91 R3
Acklam N York 86 E3
Ackleton Shrops 52 E1
Acklington Nthumb 109 L9
Ackton Wakefd 85 N10
Ackworth Moor Top Wakefd 85 N12
Acle Norfk 71 M10
Acock's Green Birm 53 L4
Acol Kent 35 P9
Acomb C York 85 R5
Acomb Nthumb 99 P5
Acombe Somset 21 K10
Aconbury Herefs 40 G5
Acre Lancs 84 B10
Acrefair Wrexhm 63 J3
Acton Ches E 64 B2
Acton Dorset 11 N9
Acton Gt Lon 32 H6
Acton Shrops 51 K4
Acton Staffs 64 F4
Acton Suffk 46 F3
Acton Worcs 52 F7
Acton Wrexhm 63 K2
Acton Beauchamp Herefs 52 C10
Acton Bridge Ches W 75 Q8
Acton Burnell Shrops 63 P11
Acton Green Herefs 52 C10
Acton Pigott Shrops 63 P11
Acton Round Shrops 52 B2
Acton Scott Shrops 51 M3
Acton Trussell Staffs 64 H8
Acton Turville S Glos 29 N6
Adbaston Staffs 64 E6
Adber Dorset 22 D9
Adbolton Notts 66 F4
Adderbury Oxon 43 K4
Adderley Shrops 64 C4
Adderstone Nthumb 109 J4
Addiewell W Loth 114 H8
Addingham C Brad 84 G5
Addington Bucks 43 Q6
Addington Gt Lon 33 L9
Addington Kent 34 B10
Addiscombe Gt Lon 33 L9
Addlestone Surrey 32 F9
Addlestonemoor Surrey 32 F9
Addlethorpe Lincs 81 K10
Adeney Wrekin 64 C8
Adeyfield Herts 44 F10
Adfa Powys 62 E12
Adforton Herefs 51 L6
Adisham Kent 35 M11
Adlestrop Gloucs 42 F6
Adlingfleet E R Yk 86 F11
Adlington Ches E 76 G7
Adlington Lancs 75 Q1
Admaston Staffs 65 K7
Admaston Wrekin 64 B9
Admington Warwks 42 E3
Adpar Cerdgn 37 Q2
Adsborough Somset 21 L7
Adscombe Somset 21 J6
Adstock Bucks 43 Q6
Adstone Nhants 54 F10
Adswood Stockp 76 G6
Adversane W Susx 14 F6
Advie Highld 139 L9
Adwalton Leeds 85 K9
Adwell Oxon 31 P2
Adwick le Street Donc 78 E2
Adwick upon Dearne Donc 78 D3
Ae D & G 106 C12
Ae Bridgend D & G 97 K1
Afan Forest Park Neath 27 K3
Affetside Bury 76 D1
Affleck Abers 140 E8
Affpuddle Dorset 11 K6
Affric Lodge Highld 136 H11
Afon-wen Flints 74 F9
Afon Wen Gwynd 60 G5
Afton Devon 5 P4
Afton IoW 12 F7
Agglethorpe N York 90 H9
Aigburth Lpool 75 L6
Aike E R Yk 87 K6
Aiketgate Cumb 98 F9

Aikhead – Babbs Green 155

Aikhead Cumb 97 P8
Aikton Cumb 98 C7
Ailby Lincs 80 H8
Ailey Herefs 51 K11
Ailsworth C Pete 68 C12
Ainderby Quernhow N York 91 N10
Ainderby Steeple N York 91 N8
Aingers Green Essex 47 K7
Ainsdale Sefton 75 K1
Ainsdale-on-Sea Sefton 75 J1
Ainstable Cumb 98 G9
Ainsworth Bury 76 E2
Ainthorpe N York 92 E5
Aintree Sefton 75 L4
Ainville W Loth 115 K8
Aird Ag & B 111 R1
Aird D & G 94 F6
Aird W Isls 152 h3
Àird a' Mhulaidh W Isls 152 e5
Aird Asaig W Isls 152 e5
Aird Dhubh Highld 135 N8
Airdeny Ag & B 121 J7
Aird of Kinloch Ag & B 119 N7
Aird of Sleat Highld 127 K4
Airdrie N Lans 114 D8
Airdriehill N Lans 114 E8
Airds of Kells D & G 96 D4
Àird Uig W Isls 152 d3
Airidh a bhruaich W Isls 152 f4
Airieland D & G 96 F7
Airlie Angus 124 F3
Airmyn E R Yk 86 D10
Airntully P & K 124 C6
Airor Highld 127 N3
Airth Falk 114 G4
Airton N York 84 D3
Aisby Lincs 67 P4
Aisby Lincs 79 L5
Aisgill Cumb 90 C7
Aish Devon 5 L4
Aish Devon 5 P5
Aisholt Somset 21 K6
Aiskew N York 91 M9
Aislaby N York 92 F9
Aislaby N York 92 H5
Aislaby S on T 91 P4
Aisthorpe Lincs 79 N7
Aith Shet 147 i6
Akeld Nthumb 108 F4
Akeley Bucks 43 P4
Akenham Suffk 58 H11
Albaston Cnwll 7 M10
Alberbury Shrops 63 K9
Albourne W Susx 15 J7
Albourne Green W Susx 15 J7
Albrighton Shrops 63 N8
Albrighton Shrops 64 E11
Alburgh Norfk 59 K3
Albury Herts 45 N7
Albury Oxon 43 N10
Albury Surrey 14 F1
Albury End Herts 45 M7
Albury Heath Surrey 14 F2
Alby Hill Norfk 71 J5
Alcaig Highld 137 P4
Alcaston Shrops 51 M3
Alcester Warwks 53 K9
Alcester Lane End Birm 53 K4
Alciston E Susx 15 P9
Alcombe Somset 20 F4
Alcombe Wilts 29 N8
Alconbury Cambs 56 D5
Alconbury Weston Cambs 56 D5
Aldborough N York 85 N2
Aldborough Norfk 71 J5
Aldbourne Wilts 30 F7
Aldbrough E R Yk 87 N7
Aldbrough St John N York 91 K4
Aldbury Herts 44 D9
Aldcliffe Lancs 83 L3
Aldclune P & K 130 G11
Aldeburgh Suffk 59 P9
Aldeby Norfk 59 N2
Aldenham Herts 32 G3
Alderbury Wilts 24 C8
Aldercar Derbys 66 D3
Alderford Norfk 70 H8
Alderholt Dorset 23 P10
Alderley Gloucs 29 M4
Alderley Edge Ches E 76 F8
Aldermans Green Covtry 54 B4
Aldermaston W Berk 31 M9
Alderminster Warwks 53 N11
Alder Moor Staffs 65 N7
Aldersey Green Ches W 75 M12
Aldershot Hants 25 Q3
Alderton Gloucs 42 B5
Alderton Nhants 43 Q2
Alderton Shrops 63 N7
Alderton Suffk 47 P3
Alderton Wilts 29 N6
Alderwasley Derbys 65 P1
Aldfield N York 85 K1
Aldford Ches W 75 M11
Aldgate Rutlnd 67 N11
Aldham Essex 46 G6
Aldham Suffk 47 J3
Aldingbourne W Susx 14 C9
Aldingham Cumb 82 G1
Aldington Kent 17 J3
Aldington Worcs 42 C3
Aldington Corner Kent 17 J3
Aldivalloch Moray 139 Q10
Aldochlay Ag & B 113 M3
Aldon Shrops 51 M5
Aldoth Cumb 97 N8
Aldreth Cambs 56 H6
Aldridge Wsall 65 K12
Aldringham Suffk 59 N8
Aldro N York 86 E3
Aldsworth Gloucs 42 D9
Aldsworth W Susx 13 N3
Aldunie Moray 139 Q10
Aldwark Derbys 77 N12
Aldwark N York 85 P3
Aldwick W Susx 14 C11
Aldwincle Nhants 55 P4
Aldworth W Berk 31 L6
Alexandria W Duns 113 M5
Aley Somset 21 J6
Alfardisworthy Devon 7 K2
Alfington Devon 9 L5
Alfold Surrey 14 E4
Alfold Bars W Susx 14 E4
Alfold Crossways Surrey 14 E4
Alford Abers 132 F1
Alford Lincs 81 J8
Alford Somset 22 E7
Alfreton Derbys 66 C1
Alfrick Worcs 52 D10
Alfrick Pound Worcs 52 D10
Alfriston E Susx 15 P10
Algarkirk Lincs 68 F5
Alhampton Somset 22 E6
Alkborough N Linc 86 G11
Alkerton Gloucs 41 M10
Alkerton Oxon 42 H3
Alkham Kent 17 N2
Alkington Shrops 63 P4
Alkmonton Derbys 65 M4
Allaleigh Devon 5 N6
Allanaquoich Abers 131 L6
Allanbank N Lans 114 F9
Allanton Border 117 J10
Allanton N Lans 114 F10
Allanton S Lans 114 D10
Allaston Gloucs 41 K10
Allbrook Hants 24 G9
All Cannings Wilts 30 C10
Allendale Nthumb 99 N7
Allen End Warwks 53 M1
Allenheads Nthumb 99 N9
Allensford Dur 100 D8
Allen's Green Herts 45 N8
Allensmore Herefs 40 G4
Allenton C Derb 66 B6
Aller Devon 19 P8
Aller Somset 21 N7
Allerby Cumb 97 M10
Allercombe Devon 9 K6
Aller Cross Devon 19 N8
Allerford Somset 20 D4
Allerston N York 92 H10
Allerthorpe E R Yk 86 E6
Allerton C Brad 84 H8
Allerton Highld 138 D3
Allerton Lpool 75 L6
Allerton Bywater Leeds 85 N9
Allerton Mauleverer N York 85 N4
Allesley Covtry 53 P4
Allestree C Derb 65 Q4
Allet Common Cnwll 3 K5
Allexton Leics 67 K12
Allgreave Ches E 76 H10
Allhallows Medway 34 E7
Allhallows-on-Sea Medway 34 E6
Alligin Shuas Highld 135 Q4
Allimore Green Staffs 64 F8
Allington Dorset 10 C6
Allington Kent 34 D10
Allington Lincs 67 L4
Allington Wilts 24 C5
Allington Wilts 29 P7
Allington Wilts 30 C9
Allithwaite Cumb 89 K11
Alloa Clacks 114 F3
Allonby Cumb 97 M9
Allostock Ches W 76 D9
Alloway S Ayrs 104 F6
Allowenshay Somset 21 N10
All Saints South Elmham Suffk 59 L4
Allscott Shrops 52 D1
Allscott Wrekin 63 Q9
All Stretton Shrops 51 M2
Alltami Flints 75 J10
Alltchaorunn Highld 121 M3
Alltmawr Powys 39 P2
Alltwalis Carmth 38 C5
Alltwen Neath 38 H11
Alltyblaca Cerdgn 38 D3
Allweston Dorset 22 F10
Allwood Green Suffk 58 F6
Almeley Herefs 51 K10
Almeley Wooton Herefs 51 K10
Almer Dorset 11 L5
Almholme Donc 78 F2
Almington Staffs 64 C5
Almodington W Susx 13 P5
Almondbank P & K 123 Q7
Almondbury Kirk 85 J12
Almondsbury S Glos 29 J5
Alne N York 85 P2
Alness Highld 145 P11
Alnham Nthumb 108 F7
Alnmouth Nthumb 109 L7
Alnwick Nthumb 109 K7
Alperton Gt Lon 32 H5
Alphamstone Essex 46 F4
Alpheton Suffk 58 C10
Alphington Devon 8 H7
Alpington Norfk 71 L12
Alport Derbys 77 N10
Alpraham Ches E 75 P11
Alresford Essex 47 J7
Alrewas Staffs 65 M9
Alsager Ches E 64 E1
Alsagers Bank Staffs 64 E3
Alsop en le Dale Derbys 65 M1
Alston Cumb 99 K9
Alston Devon 9 P4
Alstone Gloucs 41 R5
Alstone Somset 21 M4
Alstonefield Staffs 65 L1
Alston Sutton Somset 21 P3
Alswear Devon 19 P9
Alt Oldham 76 H3
Altandhu Highld 143 P3
Altarnun Cnwll 7 J8
Altass Highld 145 M5
Altcreich Ag & B 120 C5
Altgaltraig Ag & B 112 F6
Altham Lancs 84 A8
Althorne Essex 34 G3
Althorpe N Linc 79 L2
Altnabreac Station Highld 150 H7
Altnaharra Highld 149 M9
Altofts Wakefd 85 M10
Alton Derbys 78 B10
Alton Hants 25 M5
Alton Staffs 65 K4
Alton Wilts 23 P4
Alton Barnes Wilts 30 C10
Alton Pancras Dorset 10 H4
Alton Priors Wilts 30 C10
Alton Towers Staffs 65 K4
Altrincham Traffd 76 E6
Altskeith Hotel Stirlg 122 D12
Alva Clacks 114 F2
Alvanley Ches W 75 N9
Alvaston C Derb 66 C5
Alvechurch Worcs 53 J6
Alvecote Warwks 65 N11
Alvediston Wilts 23 L8
Alveley Shrops 52 D4
Alverdiscott Devon 19 K8
Alverstoke Hants 13 K5
Alverstone IoW 13 K7
Alverthorpe Wakefd 85 L11
Alverton Notts 67 K4
Alves Moray 139 L3
Alvescot Oxon 42 F10
Alveston S Glos 29 K5
Alveston Warwks 53 N9
Alvingham Lincs 80 G5
Alvington Gloucs 29 J2
Alwalton C Pete 56 C1
Alwinton Nthumb 108 E8
Alwoodley Leeds 85 L7
Alwoodley Gates Leeds 85 L7
Alyth P & K 124 E3
Am Bàgh a Tuath W Isls 152 b13
Ambergate Derbys 65 Q2
Amber Hill Lincs 68 E3
Amberley Gloucs 29 N2
Amberley W Susx 14 E8
Amber Row Derbys 78 C12
Amberstone E Susx 15 Q8
Amble Nthumb 109 L9
Amblecote Dudley 52 G3
Ambler Thorn C Brad 84 G9
Ambleside Cumb 89 K6
Ambleston Pembks 37 K5
Ambrosden Oxon 43 M8
Amcotts N Linc 86 F12
America Cambs 56 H5
Amersham Bucks 32 D3
Amersham Common Bucks 32 D3
Amersham Old Town Bucks 32 D3
Amersham on the Hill Bucks 32 D3
Amerton Staffs 65 J7
Amesbury Wilts 23 P5
Amhuinnsuidhe W Isls 152 d5
Amington Staffs 65 N11
Amisfield D & G 97 K2
Amlwch IoA 72 G5
Ammanford Carmth 38 F9
Amotherby N York 92 F12
Ampfield Hants 24 F8
Ampleforth N York 92 C11
Ampney Crucis Gloucs 42 C11
Ampney St Mary Gloucs 42 C11
Ampney St Peter Gloucs 30 C2
Amport Hants 24 E4
Ampthill C Beds 44 E4
Ampton Suffk 58 C6
Amroth Pembks 37 M9
Amulree P & K 123 M5
Amwell Herts 44 H9
Anaheilt Highld 127 P11
Ancaster Lincs 67 N3
Ancells Farm Hants 25 P2
Anchor Shrops 50 G4
Ancroft Nthumb 117 M12
Ancrum Border 107 Q5
Ancton W Susx 14 D10
Anderby Lincs 81 K8
Anderby Creek Lincs 81 K8
Andersea Somset 21 M6
Andersfield Somset 21 L6
Anderson Dorset 11 L5
Anderton Ches W 76 B8
Anderton Cnwll 4 F6
Andover Hants 24 F4
Andoversford Gloucs 42 B8
Andreas IoM 102 e3
Anelog Gwynd 60 B6
Anerley Gt Lon 33 L8
Anfield Lpool 75 L5
Angarrack Cnwll 2 F7
Angarrick Cnwll 3 K7
Angelbank Shrops 51 P5
Angersleigh Somset 21 K9
Angerton Cumb 97 P7
Angle Pembks 36 G10
Anglesey IoA 72 G7
Anglesey Abbey Cambs 57 K8
Angmering W Susx 14 F10
Angram N York 85 Q5
Angram N York 90 E7
Angrouse Cnwll 2 G10
Anick Nthumb 99 Q5
Ankerville Highld 146 E10
Ankle Hill Leics 67 J8
Anlaby E R Yk 87 J9
Anmer Norfk 69 P6
Anmore Hants 13 L2
Annan D & G 97 P5
Annandale Water Services D & G 106 E11
Annaside Cumb 88 E9
Annat Highld 136 B5
Annathill N Lans 114 D7
Anna Valley Hants 24 F4
Annbank S Ayrs 104 G5
Anne Hathaway's Cottage Warwks 53 M9
Annesley Notts 66 E1
Annesley Woodhouse Notts 66 E2
Annfield Plain Dur 100 F8
Anniesland C Glas 113 Q7
Annitsford N Tyne 100 H3
Annscroft Shrops 63 M10
Ansdell Lancs 82 H9
Ansford Somset 22 E7
Ansley Warwks 53 P2
Anslow Staffs 65 N7
Anslow Gate Staffs 65 M7
Anslow Lees Staffs 65 M7
Ansteadbrook Surrey 14 D4
Anstey Hants 25 M5
Anstey Herts 45 M5
Anstey Leics 66 F10
Anstruther Fife 125 L12
Ansty W Susx 15 K6
Ansty Warwks 54 C4
Ansty Wilts 23 L8
Ansty Cross Dorset 11 J4
Anthill Common Hants 25 L11
Anthonys Surrey 32 E10
Anthorn Cumb 97 P6
Antingham Norfk 71 K5
An t-Ob W Isls 152 d6
Antonine Wall 114 F5
Anton's Gowt Lincs 68 F3
Antony Cnwll 4 F6
Antrobus Ches W 76 B8
Anvil Corner Devon 7 M4
Anvil Green Kent 35 K12
Anwick Lincs 68 C2
Anwoth D & G 96 C7
Aperfield Gt Lon 33 M10
Apes Dale Worcs 53 J6
Apethorpe Nhants 55 P2
Apeton Staffs 64 F8
Apley Lincs 80 B8
Apperknowle Derbys 78 C8
Apperley Gloucs 41 P6
Apperley Bridge C Brad 85 J7
Apperley Dene Nthumb 100 D6
Appersett N York 90 D8
Appin Ag & B 120 H4
Appleby N Linc 86 H12
Appleby-in-Westmorland Cumb 90 A3
Appleby Magna Leics 65 P10
Appleby Parva Leics 65 P10
Appleby Street Herts 45 L10
Applecross Highld 135 N7
Appledore Devon 19 J7
Appledore Devon 20 G10
Appledore Kent 16 G5
Appledore Heath Kent 16 G5
Appleford Oxon 31 L4
Applegarth Town D & G 97 M1
Applehaigh Wakefd 78 B1
Appleshaw Hants 24 E4
Applethwaite Cumb 88 H2
Appleton Halton 75 N6
Appleton Oxon 31 J2
Appleton Warrtn 76 B7
Appleton-le-Moors N York 92 E9
Appleton-le-Street N York 92 E12
Appleton Roebuck N York 85 Q7
Appleton Thorn Warrtn 76 B7
Appleton Wiske N York 91 P6
Appletreehall Border 107 N6
Appletreewick N York 84 F3
Appley Somset 20 G9
Appley Bridge Lancs 75 N2
Apse Heath IoW 13 J8
Apsley End C Beds 44 G5
Apuldram W Susx 13 P4
Arabella Highld 146 E10
Arbirlot Angus 125 M5
Arborfield Wokham 31 Q9
Arborfield Cross Wokham 31 Q9
Arborfield Green Wokham 31 Q9
Arbourthorne Sheff 78 B6
Arbroath Angus 125 M5
Arbuthnott Abers 133 J9
Arcadia Kent 16 F3
Archddu Carmth 26 C2
Archdeacon Newton Darltn 91 L3
Archencarroch W Duns 113 N5
Archiestown Moray 139 N7
Archirondel Jersey 13 d2
Arclid Ches E 76 E11
Ardallie Abers 141 N8
Ardanaiseig Hotel Ag & B 121 K8
Ardaneaskan Highld 135 Q9
Ardarroch Highld 135 Q8
Ardbeg Ag & B 111 J12
Ardbeg Ag & B 112 G8
Ardbeg Ag & B 112 H5
Ardcharnich Highld 144 F7
Ardchiavaig Ag & B 119 L9
Ardchonnell Ag & B 121 J10
Ardchronie Highld 145 N7
Ardchullarie More Stirlg 122 F10
Arddarroch Ag & B 113 J2
Arddleen Powys 63 J9
Ard Dorch Highld 135 K10
Ardechive Highld 128 G6
Ardeer N Ayrs 104 E2
Ardeley Herts 45 K6
Ardelve Highld 136 B10
Arden Ag & B 113 M4
Ardens Grafton Warwks 53 L9
Ardentallen Ag & B 120 F8
Ardentinny Ag & B 113 J4
Ardentraive Ag & B 112 F6
Ardeonaig Stirlg 122 H6
Ardersier Highld 138 E5
Ardessie Highld 144 D7
Ardfern Ag & B 120 E12
Ardfernal Ag & B 111 M7
Ardgartan Ag & B 121 P12
Ardgay Highld 145 N7
Ardgour Highld 128 E11
Ardgowan Inver 113 J6
Ardhallow Ag & B 112 H6
Ardhasig W Isls 152 e5
Ardheslaig Highld 135 P5
Ardindrean Highld 144 E7
Ardingly W Susx 15 L5
Ardington Oxon 31 J5
Ardington Wick Oxon 31 J4
Ardlamont Ag & B 112 E8
Ardleigh Essex 47 J6
Ardleigh Heath Essex 47 J5
Ardler P & K 124 F4
Ardley Oxon 43 L6
Ardley End Essex 45 P9
Ardlui Ag & B 121 Q9
Ardlussa Ag & B 111 N4
Ardmair Highld 144 D5
Ardmaleish Ag & B 112 F7
Ardminish Ag & B 111 P11
Ardmolich Highld 127 N10
Ardmore Ag & B 113 L5
Ardmore Highld 146 C8
Ardnadam Ag & B 112 H5
Ardnagrask Highld 137 P6
Ardnamurchan Highld 127 K10
Ardnarff Highld 136 B8
Ardnastang Highld 127 P12
Ardpatrick Ag & B 111 Q9
Ardrishaig Ag & B 112 C4
Ardross Highld 145 P10
Ardrossan N Ayrs 104 D1
Ardsley Barns 78 C3
Ardsley East Leeds 85 L10
Ardslignish Highld 127 K12
Ardtalla Ag & B 111 K10
Ardtoe Highld 127 L10
Arduaine Ag & B 120 E10
Ardullie Highld 137 Q3
Ardvasar Highld 127 L4
Ardvorlich P & K 122 G8
Ardvourlie W Isls 152 e5
Ardwell D & G 94 G9
Ardwick Manch 76 F4
Areley Kings Worcs 52 E6
Arevegaig Highld 127 M10
Arford Hants 25 P6
Arglam E R Yk 86 E8
Argoed Caerph 28 A2
Argoed Shrops 63 K8
Argoed Mill Powys 50 D8
Argos Hill E Susx 15 Q5
Argyll Forest Park Ag & B 121 N12
Aribruach W Isls 152 f4
Aridhglas Ag & B 119 K8
Arileod Ag & B 118 G2
Arinagour Ag & B 118 H1
Ariogan Ag & B 120 G7
Arisaig Highld 127 M7
Arisaig House Highld 127 M7
Arkendale N York 85 M3
Arkesden Essex 45 N5
Arkholme Lancs 89 P12
Arkleby Cumb 97 N10
Arkleton D & G 107 K11
Arkle Town N York 90 G6
Arkley Gt Lon 33 J3
Arksey Donc 78 F2
Arkwright Town Derbys 78 C9
Arle Gloucs 41 Q7
Arlecdon Cumb 88 D3
Arlescote Warwks 54 C11
Arlesey C Beds 44 H4
Arleston Wrekin 64 C10
Arley Ches E 76 C7
Arley Warwks 53 P3
Arlingham Gloucs 41 L9
Arlington Devon 19 M5
Arlington E Susx 15 P9
Arlington Gloucs 42 C10
Arlington Beccott Devon 19 M5
Armadale Highld 127 L4
Armadale Highld 150 D4
Armadale W Loth 114 G7
Armaside Cumb 88 F1
Armathwaite Cumb 98 G9
Arminghall Norfk 71 K11
Armitage Staffs 65 K9
Armitage Bridge Kirk 77 L1
Armley Leeds 85 L8
Armscote Warwks 42 F3
Armshead Staffs 64 H2
Armston Nhants 55 Q3
Armthorpe Donc 78 G3
Arnabost Ag & B 126 D12
Arnaby Cumb 88 G10
Arncliffe N York 90 F12
Arncliffe Cote N York 84 E1
Arncroach Fife 125 K11
Arndilly House Moray 139 P6
Arne Dorset 11 N7
Arnesby Leics 54 G2
Arngask P & K 124 C10
Arnisdale Highld 127 Q2
Arnish Highld 135 K6
Arniston Mdloth 115 Q9
Arnol W Isls 152 f2
Arnold E R Yk 87 L7
Arnold Notts 66 F3
Arnprior Stirlg 114 B2
Arnside Cumb 89 M11
Aros Ag & B 119 P4
Arowry Wrexhm 63 M4
Arrad Foot Cumb 89 J10
Arram E R Yk 87 K6
Arran N Ayrs 103 P3
Arrathorne N York 91 K8
Arreton IoW 13 J7
Arrina Highld 135 N4
Arrington Cambs 56 F10
Arrochar Ag & B 121 P12
Arrow Warwks 53 K9
Arrowfield Top Worcs 53 J6
Arscott Shrops 63 M10
Artafallie Highld 138 B6
Arthington Leeds 85 K6
Arthingworth Nhants 55 J4
Arthog Gwynd 61 L9
Arthrath Abers 141 M8
Arthursdale Leeds 85 M7
Artrochie Abers 141 N9
Arundel W Susx 14 E9
Asby Cumb 88 E3
Ascog Ag & B 112 G8
Ascot W & M 32 D8
Ascott Warwks 42 G5
Ascott Earl Oxon 42 G8
Ascott-under-Wychwood Oxon 42 G8
Asenby N York 91 P11
Asfordby Leics 66 H8
Asfordby Hill Leics 67 J8
Asgarby Lincs 68 C3
Asgarby Lincs 80 F10
Ash Devon 5 P7
Ash Devon 7 P3
Ash Dorset 11 L3
Ash Kent 33 R9
Ash Kent 35 N10
Ash Somset 21 L9
Ash Somset 21 Q9
Ash Surrey 32 C12
Ashampstead W Berk 31 M7
Ashampstead Green W Berk 31 M7
Ashbocking Suffk 59 J9
Ashbourne Derbys 65 M3
Ashbrittle Somset 20 G9
Ashburnham Place E Susx 16 C8
Ashburton Devon 5 M3
Ashbury Devon 7 P5
Ashbury Oxon 30 F5
Ashby N Linc 79 M2
Ashby by Partney Lincs 80 H10
Ashby cum Fenby NE Lin 80 E3
Ashby de la Launde Lincs 67 P1
Ashby-de-la-Zouch Leics 66 B9
Ashby Folville Leics 66 H9
Ashby Magna Leics 54 F3
Ashby Parva Leics 54 E3
Ashby Puerorum Lincs 80 F9
Ashby St Ledgers Nhants 54 F7
Ashby St Mary Norfk 71 L11
Ashchurch Gloucs 41 Q5
Ashcombe Devon 8 G9
Ashcombe N Som 28 D10
Ashcott Somset 21 P6
Ashdon Essex 45 Q3
Ashdown Forest E Susx 15 N5
Ashe Hants 25 J3
Asheldham Essex 34 H2
Ashen Essex 46 D3
Ashendon Bucks 43 P9
Asheridge Bucks 44 D10
Ashfield Hants 24 F9
Ashfield Herefs 41 J7
Ashfield Stirlg 123 K12
Ashfield cum Thorpe Suffk 59 J8
Ashfield Green Suffk 57 P9
Ashfield Green Suffk 59 K6
Ashfold Crossways W Susx 15 J5
Ashford Devon 5 L7
Ashford Devon 19 K6
Ashford Kent 16 H2
Ashford Surrey 32 F8
Ashford Bowdler Shrops 51 N6
Ashford Carbonell Shrops 51 N6
Ashford Hill Hants 31 L10
Ashford in the Water Derbys 77 M9
Ashgill S Lans 114 E11
Ash Green Surrey 14 C1
Ash Green Warwks 53 Q4
Ashill Devon 9 L2
Ashill Norfk 70 C11
Ashill Somset 21 M10
Ashingdon Essex 34 F4
Ashington BCP 11 N5
Ashington Nthumb 109 L12
Ashington Somset 22 D9
Ashington W Susx 14 G7
Ashkirk Border 107 M5
Ashlett Hants 12 H4
Ashleworth Gloucs 41 N6
Ashleworth Quay Gloucs 41 N6
Ashley Cambs 57 N8
Ashley Ches E 76 E7
Ashley Devon 8 C2
Ashley Dorset 11 Q4
Ashley Gloucs 29 Q3
Ashley Hants 12 D6
Ashley Hants 24 F7
Ashley Kent 17 P1
Ashley Nhants 55 K2
Ashley Staffs 64 E5
Ashley Wilts 29 N8
Ashley Green Bucks 44 D10
Ashleyhay Derbys 65 P2
Ashley Heath Dorset 11 Q4
Ashley Moor Herefs 51 N7
Ash Magna Shrops 63 P4
Ashmansworth Hants 31 J11
Ashmansworthy Devon 18 G9
Ashmead Green Gloucs 29 M2
Ashmill Devon 7 M6
Ash Mill Devon 19 Q8
Ashmore Dorset 23 K10
Ashmore Green W Berk 31 L8
Ashorne Warwks 53 P9
Ashover Derbys 77 Q11
Ashover Hay Derbys 77 Q11
Ashow Warwks 53 P6
Ash Parva Shrops 63 P4
Ashperton Herefs 41 K3
Ashprington Devon 5 N5
Ash Priors Somset 21 J7
Ashreigney Devon 19 M10
Ash Street Suffk 46 H2
Ashtead Surrey 32 H10
Ash Thomas Devon 9 J3
Ashton C Pete 68 B11
Ashton Ches W 75 N10
Ashton Cnwll 2 F9
Ashton Devon 8 F8
Ashton Hants 25 J9
Ashton Herefs 51 N8
Ashton Inver 113 J6
Ashton Nhants 55 J10
Ashton Nhants 55 Q3
Ashton Somset 21 N3
Ashton Common Wilts 29 P10
Ashton Hill Wilts 29 P10
Ashton-in-Makerfield Wigan 75 P4
Ashton Keynes Wilts 30 B3
Ashton under Hill Worcs 42 A4
Ashton-under-Lyne Tamesd 76 H4
Ashton upon Mersey Traffd 76 E5
Ashton Vale Bristl 28 H8
Ashurst Hants 12 E3
Ashurst Kent 15 P3
Ashurst Lancs 75 N2
Ashurst W Susx 14 H7
Ashurstwood W Susx 15 M3
Ash Vale Surrey 32 C12
Ashwater Devon 7 M6
Ashwell Herts 45 K4
Ashwell Rutlnd 67 L9
Ashwell Somset 21 N10
Ashwell End Herts 45 J4
Ashwellthorpe Norfk 58 H1
Ashwick Somset 22 E4
Ashwicken Norfk 69 N8
Ashwood Staffs 52 F3
Askam in Furness Cumb 88 G11
Askern Donc 78 F1
Askerswell Dorset 10 E6
Askett Bucks 44 B10
Askham Cumb 89 N2
Askham Notts 79 J8
Askham Bryan C York 85 Q5
Askham Richard C York 85 Q5
Asknish Ag & B 112 D3
Askrigg N York 90 F8
Askwith N York 85 J5
Aslackby Lincs 68 B6
Aslacton Norfk 58 H2
Aslockton Notts 67 J4
Asney Somset 21 P6
Aspall Suffk 58 H7
Aspatria Cumb 97 N10
Aspenden Herts 45 L6
Aspenshaw Derbys 77 J6
Asperton Lincs 68 E5
Aspley Staffs 64 F5
Aspley Guise C Beds 44 D4
Aspley Heath C Beds 44 D5
Aspley Heath Warwks 53 L6
Aspull Wigan 75 Q2
Aspull Common Wigan 76 B4
Asselby E R Yk 86 D9
Asserby Lincs 81 J8
Asserby Turn Lincs 81 J8
Assington Suffk 46 G4
Assington Green Suffk 57 P10
Astbury Ches E 76 F11
Astcote Nhants 54 H10
Asterby Lincs 80 E8
Asterley Shrops 63 L10
Asterton Shrops 51 L2
Asthall Oxon 42 G9
Asthall Leigh Oxon 42 G9
Astle Highld 146 D7
Astley Shrops 63 N8
Astley Warwks 53 P3
Astley Wigan 76 C3
Astley Worcs 52 E7
Astley Abbots Shrops 52 D1
Astley Bridge Bolton 76 D1
Astley Cross Worcs 52 E7
Astley Green Wigan 76 D4
Aston Birm 53 K3
Aston Ches E 63 Q3
Aston Ches W 75 P8
Aston Derbys 77 M7
Aston Flints 75 J10
Aston Herefs 51 M8
Aston Herts 45 K7
Aston Oxon 42 H11
Aston Rothm 78 D6
Aston Shrops 52 E2
Aston Shrops 63 N6
Aston Staffs 64 D4
Aston Staffs 64 G7
Aston Wokham 31 Q5
Aston Wrekin 63 Q10
Aston Abbotts Bucks 44 B7
Aston Botterell Shrops 52 B4
Aston-by-Stone Staffs 64 G6
Aston Cantlow Warwks 53 L8
Aston Clinton Bucks 44 C9
Aston Crews Herefs 41 K7
Aston Cross Gloucs 41 Q5
Aston End Herts 45 K7
Aston-Eyre Shrops 52 C2
Aston Fields Worcs 52 H7
Aston Flamville Leics 54 D2
Aston Heath Ches W 75 P8
Aston Ingham Herefs 41 K7
Aston juxta Mondrum Ches E 76 C12
Aston le Walls Nhants 54 E10
Aston Magna Gloucs 42 E4
Aston Munslow Shrops 51 N3
Aston-on-Carrant Gloucs 41 Q5
Aston on Clun Shrops 51 L4
Aston Pigott Shrops 63 K11
Aston Rogers Shrops 63 K11
Aston Rowant Oxon 31 P3
Aston Sandford Bucks 43 Q10
Aston Somerville Worcs 42 B4
Aston-sub-Edge Gloucs 42 D3
Aston Tirrold Oxon 31 L5
Aston-upon-Trent Derbys 66 C6
Aston Upthorpe Oxon 31 L5
Astrop Nhants 43 L4
Astrope Herts 44 C8
Astwick C Beds 45 J4
Astwith Derbys 78 D11
Astwood M Keyn 44 D2
Astwood Worcs 52 H7
Astwood Bank Worcs 53 K8
Aswarby Lincs 67 Q4
Aswardby Lincs 80 G9
Atcham Shrops 63 P10
Atch Lench Worcs 53 J10
Athelhampton Dorset 11 J6
Athelington Suffk 59 J6
Athelney Somset 21 M7
Athelstaneford E Loth 116 C6
Atherfield Green IoW 12 H9
Atherington Devon 19 L9
Atherington W Susx 14 E10
Atherstone Somset 21 N10
Atherstone Warwks 53 P1
Atherstone on Stour Warwks 53 M10
Atherton Wigan 76 C3
Atley Hill N York 91 M6
Atlow Derbys 65 N2
Attadale Highld 136 C8
Attenborough Notts 66 E5
Atterby Lincs 79 N5
Attercliffe Sheff 78 B6
Atterley Shrops 52 B1
Atterton Leics 54 B1
Attingham Park Shrops 63 P10
Attleborough Norfk 58 F2
Attleborough Warwks 54 B2
Attlebridge Norfk 70 H9
Attleton Green Suffk 57 P9
Atwick E R Yk 87 M5
Atworth Wilts 29 P9
Auberrow Herefs 40 G2
Aubourn Lincs 79 M11
Auchbreck Moray 139 M10
Auchedly Abers 141 L9
Auchenblae Abers 132 H8
Auchenbowie Stirlg 114 E4
Auchencairn D & G 96 G8
Auchencairn D & G 97 K1
Auchencairn N Ayrs 103 Q4
Auchencrow Border 117 J9
Auchendinny Mdloth 115 N9
Auchengray S Lans 114 H10
Auchenhalrig Moray 140 B3
Auchenheath S Lans 105 Q1
Auchenhessnane D & G 105 P10
Auchenlochan Ag & B 112 E7
Auchenmade N Ayrs 113 L11
Auchenmalg D & G 95 J8
Auchentiber N Ayrs 113 M11
Auchindrain Ag & B 121 K12
Auchindrean Highld 144 F9
Auchininna Abers 140 G6
Auchinleck E Ayrs 105 K5
Auchinloch N Lans 114 B7
Auchinstarry N Lans 114 C6
Auchintore Highld 128 F10
Auchiries Abers 141 P8
Auchlean Highld 130 F5
Auchlee Abers 133 L5
Auchleven Abers 140 F11
Auchlochan S Lans 105 P2
Auchlossan Abers 132 E4
Auchlyne Stirlg 122 E7
Auchmillan E Ayrs 105 J4
Auchmithie Angus 125 N4
Auchmuirbridge Fife 115 M1
Auchnacree Angus 132 D11
Auchnagatt Abers 141 M7
Auchnarrow Moray 139 M11
Auchnotteroch D & G 94 E6
Auchroisk Moray 139 Q5
Auchterarder P & K 123 N10
Auchteraw Highld 129 L3
Auchterblair Highld 138 G11
Auchtercairn Highld 143 L9
Auchterderran Fife 115 M2
Auchterhouse Angus 124 G5
Auchterless Abers 140 H7
Auchtermuchty Fife 124 E10
Auchterneed Highld 137 N4
Auchtertool Fife 115 M3
Auchtertyre Highld 135 Q10
Auchtubh Stirlg 122 F8
Auckengill Highld 151 Q4
Auckley Donc 78 G3
Audenshaw Tamesd 76 G4
Audlem Ches E 64 C3
Audley Staffs 64 E2
Audley End Essex 45 P4
Audley End Essex 46 E4
Audley End Suffk 58 C10
Audley End House & Gardens Essex 45 P4
Audmore Staffs 64 F8
Audnam Dudley 52 G3
Aughertree Cumb 97 Q10
Aughton E R Yk 86 D7
Aughton Lancs 75 L3
Aughton Lancs 83 M2
Aughton Rothm 78 D6
Aughton Wilts 30 F11
Aughton Park Lancs 75 L2
Auldearn Highld 138 G5
Aulden Herefs 51 M9
Auldgirth D & G 106 B12
Auldhouse S Lans 114 B11
Ault a' chruinn Highld 136 C11
Aultbea Highld 143 M7
Aultgrishin Highld 143 K8
Aultguish Inn Highld 145 J11
Ault Hucknall Derbys 78 D10
Aultmore Moray 140 B5
Aultnagoire Highld 137 P11
Aultnamain Highld 145 P9
Aunby Lincs 67 P9
Aunk Devon 9 K5
Aunsby Lincs 67 P4
Aust S Glos 28 H4
Austendike Lincs 68 F8
Austerfield Donc 78 H5
Austerlands Oldham 76 H3
Austhorpe Leeds 85 M8
Austonley Kirk 77 L2
Austrey Warwks 65 P11
Austwick N York 84 A2
Authorpe Lincs 80 H7
Authorpe Row Lincs 81 K9
Avebury Wilts 30 C8
Avebury Wilts 30 C8
Avebury Trusloe Wilts 30 C8
Aveley Thurr 33 Q6
Avening Gloucs 29 P3
Averham Notts 67 J1
Aveton Gifford Devon 5 L7
Aviemore Highld 130 G2
Avington W Berk 30 H9
Avoch Highld 138 C5
Avon Hants 12 B5
Avonbridge Falk 114 G7
Avon Dassett Warwks 54 C10
Avonmouth Bristl 28 G7
Avonwick Devon 5 L5
Awbridge Hants 24 E8
Awkley S Glos 29 J5
Awliscombe Devon 9 L4
Awre Gloucs 41 L10
Awsworth Notts 66 D3
Axborough Worcs 52 F5
Axbridge Somset 21 P2
Axford Hants 25 K5
Axford Wilts 30 F8
Axmansford Hants 31 M10
Axminster Devon 9 P5
Axmouth Devon 9 P6
Axton Flints 74 F7
Aycliffe Dur 91 M2
Aydon Nthumb 100 C5
Aylburton Gloucs 41 J11
Ayle Nthumb 99 K8
Aylesbeare Devon 9 K6
Aylesbury Bucks 44 B9
Aylesby NE Lin 80 D2
Aylesford Kent 34 C10
Aylesham Kent 35 M11
Aylestone C Leic 66 F12
Aylestone Park C Leic 66 F12
Aylmerton Norfk 71 J4
Aylsham Norfk 71 J7
Aylton Herefs 41 K4
Aylworth Gloucs 42 C7
Aymestrey Herefs 51 M7
Aynho Nhants 43 L5
Ayot Green Herts 45 J9
Ayot St Lawrence Herts 44 H8
Ayot St Peter Herts 45 J8
Ayr S Ayrs 104 F5
Aysgarth N York 90 G9
Ayshford Devon 20 G10
Ayside Cumb 89 L10
Ayston Rutlnd 67 L12
Aythorpe Roding Essex 45 Q8
Ayton Border 117 K9
Azerley N York 91 L11

B

Babbacombe Torbay 5 Q4
Babbington Notts 66 E3
Babbinswood Shrops 63 K6
Babbs Green Herts 45 M8

Babcary Somset 22 D7
Babel Carmth 39 K4
Babel Green Suffk 57 P11
Babell Flints 74 G9
Babeny Devon 8 C9
Bablock Hythe Oxon 43 J11
Babraham Cambs 57 K10
Babworth Notts 78 H7
Bachau IoA 72 G7
Bache Shrops 51 M4
Bacheldre Powys 50 F2
Backaland Ork 147 d3
Backbarrow Cumb 89 K10
Backe Carmth 37 P7
Backfolds Abers 141 N5
Backford Ches W 75 L9
Backford Cross Ches W 75 L9
Backies Highld 146 E5
Back of Keppoch Highld 127 M7
Back o' th' Brook Staffs 65 K2
Back Street Suffk 57 P9
Backwell N Som 28 G8
Backworth N Tyne 100 H4
Bacon's End Solhll 53 M3
Baconsthorpe Norfk 70 H5
Bacton Herefs 40 E5
Bacton Norfk 71 L5
Bacton Suffk 58 F7
Bacton Green Suffk 58 F7
Bacup Lancs 84 C10
Badachro Highld 143 L10
Badanloch Highld 150 E6
Badbury Swindn 30 E6
Badby Nhants 54 F9
Badcall Highld 148 F5
Badcaul Highld 144 C7
Baddeley Edge C Stke 64 G2
Baddeley Green C Stke 64 G2
Baddesley Clinton
  Warwks 53 N6
Baddesley Ensor Warwks 53 P1
Baddidarroch Highld 148 C12
Baddinsgill Border 115 L10
Badenscoth Abers 140 H8
Badentarbet Highld 144 C3
Badenyon Abers 139 Q12
Badersfield Norfk 71 K7
Badgall Cnwll 7 J7
Badgeney Cambs 56 H1
Badger Shrops 64 E12
Badger's Cross Cnwll 2 D8
Badgers Mount Kent 33 P10
Badgeworth Gloucs 41 P8
Badgworth Somset 21 N3
Badharlick Cnwll 7 K7
Badicaul Highld 135 N10
Badingham Suffk 59 L7
Badlesmere Kent 34 H11
Badlieu Border 106 D6
Badlipster Highld 151 N7
Badluarach Highld 144 B6
Badninish Highld 146 D6
Badrallach Highld 144 C3
Badsey Worcs 42 C3
Badshot Lea Surrey 14 B1
Badsworth Wakefd 85 P12
Badwell Ash Suffk 58 E7
Badwell Green Suffk 58 E7
Bagber Dorset 22 G10
Bagby N York 91 Q10
Bag Enderby Lincs 80 F9
Bagendon Gloucs 42 B10
Bagginswood Shrops 52 C4
Baggrow Cumb 97 N10
Bàgh a' Chaisteil W Isls 152 b13
Bagham Kent 35 J11
Bagillt Flints 74 H8
Baginton Warwks 53 Q6
Baglan Neath 26 H4
Bagley Leeds 85 K8
Bagley Shrops 63 L7
Bagley Somset 21 P4
Bagmore Hants 25 L4
Bagnall Staffs 64 H2
Bagnor W Berk 31 K8
Bagshot Surrey 32 C9
Bagshot Wilts 30 G9
Bagstone S Glos 29 L5
Bagthorpe Notts 66 D2
Bagworth Leics 66 D10
Bagwy Llydiart Herefs 40 F7
Baildon C Brad 84 H7
Baildon Green C Brad 84 H7
Baile Ailein W Isls 152 f4
Baile a' Mhanaich W Isls 152 c9
Baile Mòr Ag & B 119 J8
Bailey Green Hants 25 L8
Baileyhead Cumb 98 H10
Bailiff Bridge Calder 84 H10
Baillieston C Glas 114 C8
Bailrigg Lancs 83 L4
Bainbridge N York 90 F8
Bainshole Abers 140 F9
Bainton C Pete 68 B11
Bainton E R Yk 86 H5
Bainton Oxon 43 M6
Baintown Fife 124 G12
Bairnkine Border 107 Q6
Baker's End Herts 45 M8
Baker Street Thurr 34 B6
Bakewell Derbys 77 N10
Bala Gwynd 62 C5
Balallan W Isls 152 f4
Balbeg Highld 137 M9
Balbeggie P & K 124 D11
Balblair Highld 137 N7
Balblair Highld 138 C3
Balby Donc 78 F3
Balcary D & G 96 G6
Balchraggan Highld 137 P7
Balchreick Highld 148 E5
Balcombe W Susx 15 K5
Balcombe Lane W Susx 15 K4
Balcomie Links Fife 125 N11
Baldersby N York 91 N11
Baldersby St James
  N York 91 N11
Balderstone Lancs 83 P8
Balderstone Rochdl 76 G2
Balderton Notts 67 K2
Baldhu Cnwll 3 J6
Baldinnie Fife 124 H10
Baldinnies P & K 123 P9
Baldock Herts 45 J5
Baldock Services Herts 45 J4
Baldovie C Dund 125 J6
Baldrine IoM 102 f5
Baldslow E Susx 16 E8
Baldwin IoM 102 d5
Baldwinholme Cumb 98 D7
Baldwin's Gate Staffs 64 E4
Baldwin's Hill W Susx 15 M3
Bale Norfk 70 E5
Baledgarno P & K 124 F7
Balemartine Ag & B 118 b2
Balerno C Edin 115 L8
Balfarg Fife 124 F12
Balfield Angus 132 E10
Balfour Ork 147 c4
Balfron Stirlg 113 Q3
Balgaveny Abers 140 G7
Balgonar Fife 115 J3
Balgowan D & G 94 G9
Balgowan Highld 130 B5
Balgown Highld 134 G2

Balgracie D & G 94 E6
Balgray S Lans 106 A5
Balham Gt Lon 33 K7
Balhary P & K 124 E5
Balholmie P & K 124 C5
Baligill Highld 150 H3
Balintore Angus 124 F1
Balintore Highld 146 F10
Balintraid Highld 146 D11
Balivanich W Isls 152 c9
Balkeerie Angus 124 E4
Balkholme E R Yk 86 E9
Ballabeg IoM 102 c7
Ballachulish Highld 121 K1
Balladoole IoM 102 c8
Ballafesson IoM 102 b7
Ballajora IoM 102 f4
Ballakilpheric IoM 102 b6
Ballamodha IoM 102 c6
Ballanlay Ag & B 112 F9
Ballantrae S Ayrs 94 F2
Ballards Gore Essex 34 F4
Ballasalla IoM 102 c7
Ballater Abers 132 B5
Ballaugh IoM 102 d3
Ballchraggan Highld 146 D10
Ballencrieff E Loth 116 C6
Ballentoul P & K 131 J4
Ball Green C Stke 64 G2
Ball Haye Green Staffs 77 J12
Ball Hill Hants 31 J9
Ballidon Derbys 65 M1
Balliekine N Ayrs 103 M2
Balliemore Ag & B 112 G1
Balligmorrie S Ayrs 104 D11
Ballimore Stirlg 122 F9
Ballindalloch Moray 139 M8
Ballindean P & K 124 E7
Ballingdon Suffk 46 E4
Ballinger Common Bucks 44 C11
Ballingham Herefs 41 J5
Ballingry Fife 115 M2
Ballinluig P & K 123 N2
Ballinshoe Angus 124 H2
Ballintuim P & K 124 C1
Balloch Highld 138 C6
Balloch N Lans 114 D6
Balloch P & K 123 L9
Balloch S Ayrs 104 F10
Balloch W Duns 113 M5
Balls Cross W Susx 14 E5
Balls Green E Susx 15 P3
Ball's Green Gloucs 29 P7
Ballygown Ag & B 119 M4
Ballygrant Ag & B 111 J8
Ballyhaugh Ag & B 118 G1
Balmacara Highld 135 P10
Balmaclellan D & G 96 D2
Balmae D & G 96 E8
Balmaha Stirlg 113 N3
Balmalcolm Fife 124 G11
Balmangan D & G 96 D8
Balmedie Abers 141 M12
Balmer Heath Shrops 63 M5
Balmerino Fife 124 G8
Balmerlawn Hants 12 E4
Balmichael N Ayrs 103 N3
Balmore E Duns 114 A6
Balmuchy Highld 146 F9
Balmule Fife 115 M4
Balmullo Fife 124 H8
Balnacoil Highld 146 E3
Balnacra Highld 136 D6
Balnacroft Abers 131 P5
Balnafoich Highld 138 C9
Balnaguard P & K 123 N2
Balnahard Ag & B 119 M6
Balnain Highld 137 M9
Balnakeil Highld 149 J3
Balne N York 86 B11
Balquharn P & K 123 P5
Balquhidder Stirlg 122 F8
Balsall Common Solhll 53 N5
Balsall Heath Birm 53 K4
Balsall Street Solhll 53 N5
Balscote Oxon 42 H3
Balsham Cambs 57 L10
Baltasound Shet 147 k2
Balterley Staffs 64 E2
Balterley Green Staffs 64 E2
Balterley Heath Staffs 64 E2
Baltersan D & G 95 M6
Balthangie Abers 141 K5
Baltonsborough Somset 22 C6
Balvicar Ag & B 120 E4
Balvraid Highld 127 Q1
Balvraid Highld 138 F9
Balwest Cnwll 2 F8

Barber Green Cumb 89 L10
Barbieston S Ayrs 104 H6
Barbon Cumb 89 Q10
Barbridge Ches E 75 Q12
Barbrook Devon 19 N4
Barby Nhants 54 E6
Barcaldine Ag & B 120 H4
Barcheston Warwks 42 H4
Barclose Cumb 98 F6
Barcombe E Susx 15 M8
Barcombe Cross E Susx 15 M8
Barcroft C Brad 84 F7
Barden N York 91 J8
Barden Park Kent 15 Q2
Bardfield End Green
  Essex 46 A5
Bardfield Saling Essex 46 B6
Bardney Lincs 80 C10
Bardon Leics 66 D9
Bardon Mill Nthumb 99 M5
Bardowie E Duns 113 Q6
Bardown E Susx 16 B5
Bardrainney Inver 113 L6
Bardsea Cumb 89 J11
Bardsey Leeds 85 M6
Bardsey Island Gwynd 60 A8
Bardsley Oldham 76 H3
Bardwell Suffk 58 D6
Bare Lancs 83 K2
Bareppa Cnwll 3 J8
Barfad D & G 95 L5
Barford Norfk 70 G10
Barford Warwks 53 P8
Barford St John Oxon 43 K5
Barford St Martin Wilts 23 N7
Barford St Michael Oxon 43 K5
Barfrestone Kent 35 N12
Bargate Derbys 66 B3
Bargeddie N Lans 114 C8
Bargoed Caerph 27 Q2
Bargrennan D & G 95 L3
Barham Cambs 56 C5
Barham Kent 35 M12
Barham Suffk 58 H10
Bar Hill Cambs 56 G8
Barholm Lincs 68 B10
Barkby Leics 66 G10
Barkby Thorpe Leics 66 G10
Barkers Green Shrops 63 N6
Barkestone-le-Vale Leics 67 K5
Barkham Wokham 31 M9
Barking Gt Lon 33 N5
Barking Suffk 58 G10
Barkingside Gt Lon 33 N4
Barking Tye Suffk 58 F10
Barkisland Calder 84 G11
Barkla Shop Cnwll 3 J4
Barkston Lincs 67 M4
Barkston Ash N York 85 P8
Barkway Herts 45 M4
Barlanark C Glas 114 B8
Barlaston Staffs 64 G4
Barlavington W Susx 14 E7
Barlborough Derbys 78 D8
Barlby N York 86 B8
Barlestone Leics 66 C11
Barley Herts 45 M4
Barley Lancs 84 B7
Barleycroft End Herts 45 N6
Barley Hole Rothm 78 B4
Barleythorpe RutInd 67 L10
Barling Essex 34 G4
Barlings Lincs 79 Q8
Barlochan D & G 96 G7
Barlow Derbys 77 Q9
Barlow Gatesd 100 F6
Barlow N York 86 B9
Barmby Moor E R Yk 86 E5
Barmby on the Marsh
  E R Yk 86 E5
Barmer Norfk 69 Q5
Barming Heath Kent 34 C11
Barmollack Ag & B 103 L1
Barmouth Gwynd 61 K9
Barmpton Darltn 91 N3
Barmston E R Yk 87 M3
Barnaby Green Suffk 59 P5
Barnacarry Ag & B 112 G2
Barnack C Pete 67 Q11
Barnacle Warwks 54 C4
Barnard Castle Dur 90 H3
Barnard Gate Oxon 43 J9
Barnardiston Suffk 57 N11
Barnbarroch D & G 96 G7
Barnburgh Donc 78 D3
Barnby Suffk 59 P3
Barnby Dun Donc 78 G2
Barnby in the Willows
  Notts 67 L2
Barnby Moor Notts 78 H7
Barncorkrie D & G 94 F11
Barnehurst Gt Lon 33 P7
Barnes Gt Lon 33 J7
Barnes Street Kent 16 B1
Barnet Gt Lon 33 J3
Barnetby le Wold N Linc 79 Q2
Barnet Gate Gt Lon 33 J3
Barney Norfk 70 E6
Barnham Suffk 58 C5
Barnham W Susx 14 D10
Barnham Broom Norfk 70 G10
Barnhead Angus 125 N1
Barnhill C Dund 125 J6
Barnhill Ches W 63 M1
Barnhill Moray 139 L4
Barnhills D & G 94 E4
Barningham Dur 90 H5
Barningham Suffk 58 E5
Barnoldby le Beck NE Lin 80 E2
Barnoldswick Lancs 84 C6
Barns Green W Susx 14 G5
Barnsley Barns 77 Q2
Barnsley Gloucs 42 C10
Barnsole Kent 35 N11
Barnstaple Devon 19 L7
Barnston Essex 46 B8
Barnston Wirral 75 J7
Barnstone Notts 67 J5
Barnt Green Worcs 53 J6
Barnton C Edin 115 M6
Barnton Ches W 76 B8
Barnwell All Saints
  Nhants 55 P4
Barnwell St Andrew
  Nhants 55 P4
Barnwood Gloucs 41 P8
Baron's Cross Herefs 51 N9
Baronwood Cumb 98 G9
Barr S Ayrs 104 E11
Barra W Isls 152 b13
Barra Airport W Isls 152 b12
Barrachan D & G 95 K8
Barraigh W Isls 152 b13
Barrananaoil Ag & B 120 F11
Barrapoll Ag & B 118 C4
Barras Cumb 90 E4
Barrasford Nthumb 99 N4
Barregarrow IoM 102 d4
Barrets Green Ches E 75 P11
Barrhead E Rens 113 P9
Barrhill S Ayrs 94 H3
Barrington Cambs 56 G10
Barrington Somset 21 M9
Barripper Cnwll 2 G7
Barrmill N Ayrs 113 M11
Barrock Highld 151 N2

Barrock Highld 151 N2
Barrow Gloucs 41 P7
Barrow Lancs 83 Q7
Barrow Rutlnd 67 M9
Barrow Shrops 64 C12
Barrow Somset 22 G7
Barrow Suffk 57 P8
Barroway Drove Norfk 69 L11
Barrow Bridge Bolton 76 C1
Barrowby Lincs 67 L5
Barrowcliff N York 93 L8
Barrowden RutInd 67 N12
Barrowford Lancs 84 C7
Barrow Gurney N Som 28 H8
Barrow Haven N Linc 87 K10
Barrow Hill Derbys 78 C8
Barrow-in-Furness Cumb 82 F1
Barrow Island Cumb 82 F2
Barrow Nook Lancs 75 M3
Barrow's Green Ches E 76 C12
Barrow Street Wilts 22 H6
Barrow-upon-Humber
  N Linc 87 K11
Barrow upon Soar Leics 66 F8
Barrow upon Trent
  Derbys 66 B6
Barry Angus 125 K6
Barry V Glam 27 Q8
Barry Island V Glam 27 Q8
Barsby Leics 66 H10
Barsham Suffk 59 M3
Barston Solhll 53 N5
Bartestree Herefs 40 H4
Barthol Chapel Abers 141 K9
Bartholomew Green
  Essex 46 C7
Barthomley Ches E 64 E2
Bartley Hants 24 E10
Bartley Green Birm 53 J4
Bartlow Cambs 45 Q3
Barton Cambs 56 H9
Barton Ches W 63 M1
Barton Gloucs 42 C6
Barton Herefs 51 J9
Barton Lancs 75 L4
Barton Lancs 83 L8
Barton N York 91 L6
Barton Oxon 43 L10
Barton Torbay 5 Q5
Barton Warwks 53 L10
Barton Bendish Norfk 69 N11
Barton End Gloucs 29 L3
Barton Green Staffs 65 M8
Barton Hartshorn Bucks 43 N5
Barton Hill N York 86 D2
Barton in Fabis Notts 66 E6
Barton in the Beans Leics 66 C11
Barton-le-Clay C Beds 44 F5
Barton-le-Street N York 92 E12
Barton-le-Willows N York 86 D3
Barton Mills Suffk 57 N6
Barton-on-Sea Hants 12 C6
Barton-on-the-Heath
  Warwks 42 F5
Barton Park Services
  N York 91 L5
Barton St David Somset 22 C7
Barton Seagrave Nhants 55 M5
Barton Stacey Hants 24 G5
Barton Town Devon 19 N5
Barton Turf Norfk 71 M7
Barton-under-
  Needwood Staffs 65 M8
Barton-upon-Humber
  N Linc 87 J11
Barton upon Irwell Salfd 76 D4
Barton Waterside N Linc 87 J10
Barugh Barns 77 P2
Barugh Green Barns 77 P2
Barvas W Isls 152 g2
Barway Cambs 57 K6
Barwell Leics 54 D1
Barwick Devon 8 H4
Barwick Herts 45 M8
Barwick Somset 22 D2
Barwick in Elmet Leeds 85 N7
Baschurch Shrops 63 M8
Bascote Warwks 54 C8
Bascote Heath Warwks 54 C8
Base Green Suffk 58 F8
Basford Green Staffs 64 H2
Bashall Eaves Lancs 83 Q6
Bashall Town Lancs 83 Q6
Bashley Hants 12 D5
Basildon Essex 34 C4
Basingstoke Hants 25 L3
Baslow Derbys 77 N9
Bason Bridge Somset 21 M4
Bassaleg Newpt 28 C5
Bassendean Border 116 E12
Bassenthwaite Cumb 97 P11
Bassett C Sotn 24 G10
Bassingbourn-cum-
  Kneesworth Cambs 45 L3
Bassingfield Notts 66 G5
Bassingham Lincs 79 M11
Bassingthorpe Lincs 67 N6
Bassus Green Herts 45 L6
Basted Kent 33 Q11
Baston Lincs 68 B10
Bastwick Norfk 71 N8
Batch Somset 28 C10
Batchworth Herts 32 F3
Batchworth Heath Herts 32 F3
Batcombe Dorset 10 F4
Batcombe Somset 22 F5
Bate Heath Ches E 76 C8
Batford Herts 44 H8
Bath BaNES 29 M9
Bath BaNES 29 M9
Bathampton BaNES 29 M9
Bathealton Somset 20 H9
Batheaston BaNES 29 M9
Bathford BaNES 29 M9
Bathgate W Loth 114 H7
Bathley Notts 79 K12
Bathpool Cnwll 7 K9
Bathpool Somset 21 J8
Bath Side Essex 47 P6
Bathville W Loth 114 G8
Bathway Somset 22 C2
Batley Kirk 85 K10
Batsford Gloucs 42 F6
Batson Devon 5 M9
Battersby N York 92 C6
Battersea Gt Lon 33 K7
Battisborough Cross
  Devon 5 J7
Battisford Suffk 58 F10
Battisford Tye Suffk 58 F10
Battle E Susx 16 C7
Battle Powys 39 N5
Battledown Gloucs 41 Q7
Battlefield Shrops 63 N8
Battlesbridge Essex 34 D3
Battlesden C Beds 44 D6
Battleton Somset 20 E8
Battlies Green Suffk 58 C8
Battramsley Cross Hants 12 E5
Batt's Corner Hants 25 N4
Baughton Worcs 41 P3
Baughurst Hants 31 M10

Baulds Abers 132 F5
Baulking Oxon 30 G4
Baumber Lincs 80 D9
Baunton Gloucs 42 B10
Baveney Wood Shrops 52 C5
Baverstock Wilts 23 M7
Bawburgh Norfk 70 H10
Bawdeswell Norfk 70 F8
Bawdrip Somset 21 M5
Bawdsey Suffk 47 P4
Bawsey Norfk 69 M8
Bawtry Donc 78 G5
Baxenden Lancs 84 B10
Baxterley Warwks 53 P1
Baxter's Green Suffk 57 P9
Bay Highld 134 E5
Bayble W Isls 152 h3
Baybridge Hants 25 J8
Baybridge Nthumb 99 Q8
Baycliff Cumb 89 J12
Baydon Wilts 30 G7
Bayford Herts 45 K10
Bayford Somset 22 G7
Bayhead W Isls 152 b8
Bay Horse Lancs 83 L5
Bayley's Hill Kent 33 P11
Baylham Suffk 58 G10
Baynard's Green Oxon 43 L6
Baysdale Abbey N York 92 C5
Baysham Herefs 40 H6
Bayston Hill Shrops 63 N10
Baythorne End Essex 46 C3
Bayton Worcs 52 C6
Bayton Common Worcs 52 C6
Bayworth Oxon 31 K2
Beach S Glos 29 L8
Beachampton Bucks 43 Q4
Beachamwell Norfk 69 P11
Beachley Gloucs 28 H4
Beachy Head E Susx 15 Q11
Beacon Devon 9 M4
Beacon End Essex 46 G7
Beacon Hill Kent 16 E4
Beacon Hill Notts 67 K1
Beacon Hill Surrey 14 C3
Beacon's Bottom Bucks 31 R3
Beaconsfield Bucks 32 D4
Beaconsfield Services
  Bucks 32 D4
Beadlam N York 92 D10
Beadlow C Beds 44 G4
Beadnell Nthumb 109 L4
Beaford Devon 19 L10
Beal N York 86 C10
Beal Nthumb 108 H1
Bealbury Cnwll 4 H6
Bealsmill Cnwll 7 N7
Beam Hill Staffs 65 N7
Beamhurst Staffs 65 K5
Beaminster Dorset 10 D4
Beamish Dur 100 G7
Beamish Museum Dur 100 G7
Beamsley N York 84 G5
Bean Kent 33 Q8
Beanacre Wilts 29 P9
Beanley Nthumb 108 H6
Beardon Devon 7 P9
Beardwood Bl w D 83 P9
Beare Devon 9 M4
Beare Green Surrey 14 H2
Bearley Warwks 53 M8
Bearley Cross Warwks 53 M8
Bearpark Dur 100 G9
Bearsden E Duns 113 Q7
Bearsted Kent 34 E11
Bearstone Shrops 64 D4
Bearwood BCP 11 P5
Bearwood Birm 53 J4
Bearwood Herefs 51 L9
Beattock D & G 106 E9
Beauchamp Roding
  Essex 45 Q9
Beauchief Sheff 77 Q8
Beaudesert Warwks 53 M7
Beaufort Blae G 40 A9
Beaulieu Hants 12 E4
Beaulieu Road Station
  Hants 12 F3
Beauly Highld 137 P6
Beaumaris IoA 73 K8
Beaumaris Castle IoA 73 K8
Beaumont Cumb 98 D6
Beaumont Essex 47 L7
Beaumont Jersey 13 b2
Beaumont Hill Darltn 91 M3
Beaumont Leys C Leic 66 F10
Beausale Warwks 53 N6
Beauworth Hants 25 J8
Beaworthy Devon 7 N5
Beazley End Essex 46 C6
Bebington Wirral 75 K7
Bebside Nthumb 100 H2
Beccles Suffk 59 N3
Becconsall Lancs 83 K10
Beckbury Shrops 64 D11
Beckenham Gt Lon 33 L8
Beckermet Cumb 88 D5
Beckett End Norfk 69 P12
Beckfoot Cumb 88 G6
Beckfoot Cumb 88 H7
Beckfoot Cumb 97 M8
Beckford Worcs 41 R4
Beckhampton Wilts 30 C8
Beck Hole N York 92 G6
Beckingham Lincs 67 L1
Beckingham Notts 79 K5
Beckington Somset 22 H3
Beckjay Shrops 51 L5
Beckley E Susx 16 E6
Beckley Hants 12 C5
Beckley Oxon 43 M9
Beck Row Suffk 57 N5
Becks C Brad 84 F6
Beck Side Cumb 88 H10
Beck Side Cumb 89 K10
Beckton Gt Lon 33 N6
Beckwithshaw N York 85 K4
Becontree Gt Lon 33 N5
Becquet Vincent Jersey 13 c1
Bedale N York 91 M9
Bedburn Dur 100 E12
Bedchester Dorset 22 H10
Beddau Rhondd 27 P5
Beddgelert Gwynd 61 K3
Beddingham E Susx 15 N9
Beddington Gt Lon 33 K9
Beddington Corner
  Gt Lon 33 K9
Bedfield Suffk 59 J7
Bedford Bed 55 P10
Bedgebury Cross Kent 16 C4
Bedgrove Bucks 44 B9
Bedham W Susx 14 F6
Bedhampton Hants 13 L3
Bedingfield Suffk 59 J7
Bedingfield Green Suffk 59 J7
Bedlam N York 85 L3
Bedlington Nthumb 100 H2
Bedlinog Myr Td 39 Q10
Bedminster Bristl 28 H7
Bedminster Down Bristl 28 H7
Bedmond Herts 44 G11
Bednall Staffs 64 H8

Bedrule Border 107 P6
Bedstone Shrops 51 L5
Bedwas Caerph 28 A4
Bedwellty Caerph 27 R2
Bedworth Warwks 54 B3
Bedworth Woodlands
  Warwks 53 Q3
Beeby Leics 66 H10
Beech Hants 25 L5
Beech Staffs 64 F5
Beech Hill W Berk 31 P9
Beechingstoke Wilts 30 C10
Beedon W Berk 31 K7
Beedon Hill W Berk 31 K7
Beeford E R Yk 87 L4
Beeley Derbys 77 P10
Beelsby NE Lin 80 D3
Beenham W Berk 31 M8
Beenham's Heath W & M 32 B7
Beeny Cnwll 6 G6
Beer Devon 9 N7
Beer Somset 21 N7
Beercrocombe Somset 21 M8
Beer Hackett Dorset 10 E2
Beesands Devon 5 N9
Beesby Lincs 81 J7
Beeson Devon 5 N8
Beeston C Beds 56 D11
Beeston Ches W 75 P12
Beeston Leeds 85 L9
Beeston Norfk 70 D9
Beeston Notts 66 E5
Beeston Regis Norfk 70 H4
Beeswing D & G 96 H4
Beetham Cumb 89 M11
Beetham Somset 21 L11
Beetley Norfk 70 E9
Began Cardif 28 B6
Begbroke Oxon 43 K9
Begdale Cambs 69 J11
Begelly Pembks 37 M9
Beggarington Hill Leeds 85 L10
Beggar's Bush Powys 51 J8
Beguildy Powys 50 G5
Beighton Norfk 71 M10
Beighton Sheff 78 D7
Beinn Na Faoghla W Isls 152 c9
Beith N Ayrs 113 L10
Bekesbourne Kent 35 M11
Bekesbourne Hill Kent 35 L11
Belaugh Norfk 71 K8
Belbroughton Worcs 52 G6
Belchalwell Dorset 11 J3
Belchalwell Street Dorset 11 J3
Belchamp Otten Essex 46 E3
Belchamp St Paul Essex 46 D3
Belchamp Walter Essex 46 E3
Belchford Lincs 80 F8
Belford Nthumb 109 J3
Belgrave C Leic 66 F10
Belhaven E Loth 116 F5
Belhelvie Abers 141 M12
Belhinnie Abers 140 C10
Bellabeg Abers 131 Q12
Bellamore Herefs 40 E4
Bellanoch Ag & B 112 B3
Bellasize E R Yk 86 F9
Bellaty Angus 124 E1
Bell Bar Herts 45 J10
Bell Busk N York 84 D4
Belleau Lincs 80 H8
Bell End Worcs 52 H5
Bellerby N York 91 J8
Bellever Devon 8 C9
Belle Vue Cumb 98 D7
Belle Vue Wakefd 85 M11
Bellfield S Lans 105 Q3
Bell Heath Worcs 52 H5
Bell Hill Hants 25 M8
Bellingdon Bucks 44 D10
Bellingham Nthumb 99 N2
Belloch Ag & B 103 J2
Bellochantuy Ag & B 103 J3
Bell o' th' Hill Ches W 63 N3
Bellows Cross Dorset 23 N10
Bellshill N Lans 114 D9
Bellshill Nthumb 109 J4
Bellside N Lans 114 E9
Bellsquarry W Loth 115 J8
Bells Yew Green E Susx 15 R4
Belluton BaNES 29 J9
Belmaduthy Highld 138 B4
Belmesthorpe RutInd 67 P10
Belmont Bl w D 83 P12
Belmont Gt Lon 33 K9
Belmont S Ayrs 104 F5
Belmont Shet 147 j3
Belnacraig Abers 132 B1
Belowda Cnwll 3 N3
Belper Derbys 66 B3
Belper Lane End Derbys 65 Q2
Belph Derbys 78 E8
Belsay Nthumb 100 E3
Belses Border 107 P5
Belsford Devon 5 M6
Belsize Herts 44 F11
Belstead Suffk 47 K3
Belstone Devon 8 B5
Belstone Corner Devon 8 B5
Belthorn Bl w D 83 Q10
Beltinge Kent 35 L9
Beltingham Nthumb 99 M6
Beltoft N Linc 79 L2
Belton Leics 66 D8
Belton Lincs 67 M4
Belton N Linc 79 K2
Belton Norfk 71 P11
Belton in Rutland RutInd 67 L11
Belton House Lincs 67 M4
Beltring Kent 16 B1
Belvedere Gt Lon 33 P7
Belvoir Leics 67 L5
Bembridge IoW 13 J8
Bemerton Wilts 23 N7
Bempton E R Yk 93 P12
Benacre Suffk 59 Q4
Benbecula W Isls 152 c9
Benbecula Airport W Isls 152 c9
Benbuie D & G 105 Q10
Benderloch Ag & B 120 G5
Benenden Kent 16 D4
Benfieldside Dur 100 D7
Bengates Norfk 71 L7
Bengeo Herts 45 L8
Bengeworth Worcs 42 B3
Benhall Green Suffk 59 M8
Benhall Street Suffk 59 M8
Benholm Abers 133 K10
Beningbrough N York 85 Q4
Benington Herts 45 K6
Benington Lincs 68 H2
Benington Sea End Lincs 68 H2
Benllech IoA 72 H6
Benmore Ag & B 112 H4
Bennacott Cnwll 7 K6
Bennan N Ayrs 103 N5
Bennet Head Cumb 89 N2
Bennett End Bucks 31 R3
Benniworth Lincs 80 D7
Benover Kent 16 C1
Ben Rhydding C Brad 84 H6
Benslie N Ayrs 104 F2
Benson Oxon 31 N3
Bentfield Green Essex 45 P6

Benthall Shrops 64 C11
Bentham Gloucs 41 P8
Benthoul C Aber 133 J4
Bentlawnt Shrops 63 K12
Bentley Donc 78 F3
Bentley E R Yk 87 J8
Bentley Hants 25 M4
Bentley Suffk 47 K4
Bentley Warwks 53 P2
Bentley Heath Herts 33 J3
Bentley Heath Solhll 53 M5
Benton Devon 19 M6
Bentpath D & G 107 J11
Bentwichen Devon 19 P6
Bentworth Hants 25 L5
Benvie Angus 124 G6
Benville Dorset 10 D4
Benwick Cambs 56 G3
Beoley Worcs 53 K7
Beoraidbeg Highld 127 M6
Bepton W Susx 25 Q9
Berden Essex 45 N5
Berea Pembks 36 F4
Bere Alston Devon 4 G3
Bere Ferrers Devon 4 G4
Bere Regis Dorset 11 K6
Bergh Apton Norfk 71 L12
Berhill Somset 21 P6
Berinsfield Oxon 31 M3
Berkeley Gloucs 29 K2
Berkeley Heath Gloucs 29 L2
Berkeley Road Gloucs 29 L2
Berkhamsted Herts 44 E10
Berkley Somset 22 H3
Berkswell Solhll 53 N5
Bermondsey Gt Lon 33 L6
Bermuda Warwks 54 B3
Bernera Highld 135 P11
Bernisdale Highld 134 G6
Berrick Prior Oxon 31 N3
Berrick Salome Oxon 31 N3
Berriedale Highld 151 K12
Berrier Cumb 98 G12
Berriew Powys 62 G12
Berrington Nthumb 108 G3
Berrington Shrops 63 N10
Berrington Worcs 51 P7
Berrington Green Worcs 51 P7
Berrow Somset 21 L2
Berrow Worcs 41 M5
Berrow Green Worcs 52 D9
Berry Brow Kirk 77 H1
Berry Cross Devon 19 J10
Berry Down Devon 19 L5
Berryfields Bucks 43 R8
Berry Hill Gloucs 40 H9
Berry Hill Pembks 37 L2
Berryhillock Moray 140 D4
Berryhillock Moray 140 D5
Berrynarbor Devon 19 L4
Berry Pomeroy Devon 5 P4
Berry's Green Gt Lon 33 N10
Bersham Wrexm 63 J2
Berthengam Flints 74 F8
Berwick E Susx 15 P9
Berwick Bassett Wilts 30 C7
Berwick Hill Nthumb 100 F3
Berwick St James Wilts 23 M7
Berwick St John Wilts 23 J9
Berwick St Leonard Wilts 23 J7
Berwick Station E Susx 15 P9
Berwick-upon-Tweed
  Nthumb 117 K10
Bescaby Leics 67 K7
Bescar Lancs 75 L1
Besford Shrops 63 P7
Besford Worcs 41 P3
Bessacarr Donc 78 G4
Bessels Leigh Oxon 43 K11
Besses o' th' Barn Bury 76 E3
Bessingby E R Yk 87 M2
Bessingham Norfk 70 H5
Besthorpe Norfk 58 G2
Besthorpe Notts 79 K10
Bestwood Village Notts 66 F3
Beswick E R Yk 87 J5
Betchcott Shrops 51 M1
Betchworth Surrey 33 J12
Bethania Cerdgn 49 J8
Bethania Gwynd 61 J2
Bethania Gwynd 62 D4
Bethel Gwynd 62 D4
Bethel Gwynd 73 J10
Bethel IoA 72 F8
Bethel Powys 62 D4
Bethersden Kent 16 G3
Bethesda Gwynd 73 K10
Bethesda Pembks 37 L7
Bethlehem Carmth 38 H8
Bethnal Green Gt Lon 33 L6
Betley Staffs 64 E3
Betsham Kent 33 Q8
Betteshanger Kent 35 P11
Bettiscombe Dorset 10 B5
Bettisfield Wrexm 63 M5
Betton Shrops 64 C5
Betton Strange Shrops 63 N10
Bettws Brdgnd 27 L5
Bettws Newport 28 B5
Bettws Cedewain Powys 50 F1
Bettws Ifan Cerdgn 48 E10
Bettws-Newydd Mons 40 E10
Bettyhill Highld 150 C4
Betws Carmth 38 H9
Betws Bledrws Cerdgn 49 K10
Betws Garmon Gwynd 73 J12
Betws Gwerfil Goch
  Denbgs 62 E3
Betws-y-Coed Conwy 61 N1
Betws-yn-Rhos Conwy 74 B9
Beulah Cerdgn 48 D11
Beulah Powys 50 C4
Bevendean Br & H 15 L9
Bevercotes Notts 78 H9
Beverley E R Yk 87 J7
Beverstone Gloucs 29 P3
Bevington Gloucs 29 K3
Bewaldeth Cumb 97 P11
Bewcastle Cumb 98 H3
Bewdley Worcs 52 E5
Bewerley N York 84 H3
Bewholme E R Yk 87 M5
Bewlbridge Kent 16 B4
Bexhill-on-Sea E Susx 16 C9
Bexley Gt Lon 33 P7
Bexleyheath Gt Lon 33 N7
Bexleyhill W Susx 14 C6
Bexon Kent 34 F10
Bexwell Norfk 69 M11
Beyton Suffk 58 D8
Beyton Green Suffk 58 D8
Bhaltos W Isls 152 e3
Bhatarsaigh W Isls 152 b13
Bibury Gloucs 42 D10
Bicester Oxon 43 M7
Bickenhill Solhll 53 M4
Bicker Lincs 68 E4
Bicker Bar Lincs 68 E4
Bicker Gauntlet Lincs 68 E4
Bickershaw Wigan 76 B3
Bickerstaffe Lancs 75 M2
Bickerton Ches W 63 N2
Bickerton Devon 5 N10

Bickerton – Braeintra 157

Bickerton N York 85 P5
Bickerton Nthumb 108 G9
Bickford Staffs 64 G9
Bickington Devon 8 E10
Bickington Devon 19 K7
Bickleigh Devon 4 H4
Bickleigh Devon 8 H3
Bickleton Devon 19 K7
Bickley Ches W 63 P2
Bickley Gt Lon 33 M8
Bickley N York 93 J8
Bickley Worcs 52 B6
Bickley Moss Ches W 63 P2
Bicknacre Essex 46 D11
Bicknoller Somset 20 H5
Bicknor Kent 34 F10
Bickton Hants 23 P11
Bicton Herefs 51 M8
Bicton Shrops 51 J4
Bicton Shrops 63 M9
Bidborough Kent 15 Q2
Bidden Hants 25 M3
Biddenden Kent 16 E3
Biddenden Green Kent 16 F2
Biddenham Bed 55 P10
Biddestone Wilts 29 P7
Biddisham Somset 21 N3
Biddlesden Bucks 43 N4
Biddlestone Nthumb 108 F8
Biddulph Staffs 76 G12
Biddulph Moor Staffs 76 G12
Bideford Devon 19 J8
Bidford-on-Avon Warwks 53 L10
Bidston Wirral 75 J6
Bielby E R Yk 86 E6
Bieldside C Aber 133 L4
Bierley IoW 12 H9
Bierton Bucks 44 B8
Big Balcraig D & G 95 M9
Bigbury Devon 5 L7
Bigbury-on-Sea Devon 5 K8
Bigby Lincs 79 Q2
Biggar Cumb 82 F2
Biggar S Lans 106 D2
Biggin Derbys 65 N2
Biggin Derbys 77 M11
Biggin N York 85 Q8
Biggin Hill Gt Lon 33 M10
Biggleswade C Beds 44 H3
Bigholms D & G 98 C2
Bighouse Highld 150 F4
Bighton Hants 25 K6
Biglands Cumb 97 Q7
Bignor W Susx 14 D8
Bigrigg Cumb 88 D4
Big Sand Highld 143 K9
Bigton Shet 147 i9
Bilborough C Nott 66 E4
Bilbrook Somset 20 G5
Bilbrook Staffs 64 G11
Bilbrough N York 85 Q6
Bilbster Highld 151 N6
Bildershaw Dur 91 K2
Bildeston Suffk 58 E10
Billacott Cnwll 7 K6
Billericay Essex 34 B3
Billesdon Leics 67 J11
Billesley Warwks 53 L9
Billingborough Lincs 68 C5
Billinge St Hel 75 N4
Billingford Norfk 58 H5
Billingford Norfk 70 F8
Billingham S on T 91 Q2
Billinghay Lincs 68 C1
Billingley Barns 78 D3
Billingshurst W Susx 14 F6
Billingsley Shrops 52 D4
Billington C Beds 44 D7
Billington Lancs 83 Q8
Billington Staffs 64 G8
Billockby Norfk 71 N9
Billy Row Dur 100 F10
Bilsborrow Lancs 83 L7
Bilsby Lincs 81 J8
Bilsham W Susx 14 D10
Bilsington Kent 17 J4
Bilsthorpe Notts 78 G11
Bilsthorpe Moor Notts 78 G11
Bilston Mdloth 115 N8
Bilston Wolves 52 H1
Bilstone Leics 66 B11
Bilting Kent 17 J1
Bilton E R Yk 87 M8
Bilton N York 85 L4
Bilton Nthumb 109 L7
Bilton Warwks 54 D6
Bilton Banks Nthumb 109 K8
Bilton-in-Ainsty N York 85 P5
Binbrook Lincs 80 D5
Binchester Blocks Dur 100 G11
Bincombe Dorset 10 G8
Binegar Somset 22 E3
Bines Green W Susx 14 H7
Binfield Br For 32 B8
Binfield Heath Oxon 31 Q7
Bingfield Nthumb 100 C4
Bingham Notts 66 H4
Bingham's Melcombe Dorset 11 J4
Bingley C Brad 84 G7
Bings Heath Shrops 63 P8
Binham Norfk 70 E4
Binley Covtry 54 C5
Binley Hants 24 G3
Binley Woods Warwks 54 C5
Binnegar Dorset 11 L7
Binniehill Falk 114 F7
Binscombe Surrey 14 D2
Binsey Oxon 43 K10
Binstead IoW 13 K6
Binsted Hants 25 N5
Binsted W Susx 14 D9
Binton Warwks 53 L10
Bintree Norfk 70 F7
Binweston Shrops 63 J11
Birch Essex 46 G8
Birch Rochdl 76 F2
Bircham Newton Norfk 69 P5
Bircham Tofts Norfk 69 P5
Birchanger Essex 45 P7
Birchanger Green Services Essex 45 P7
Birch Cross Staffs 65 L6
Birchencliffe Kirk 84 H11
Bircher Herefs 51 N7
Birchett's Green E Susx 16 B4
Birchfield Birm 53 K2
Birch Green Essex 46 G8
Birch Green Herts 45 K9
Birch Green Worcs 41 P3
Birchgrove Cardif 28 A6
Birchgrove Swans 26 H3
Birchgrove W Susx 15 M5
Birch Heath Ches W 75 P11
Birch Hill Ches W 75 N9
Birchington Kent 35 N8
Birchington-on-Sea Kent 35 N8
Birchley Heath Warwks 53 P2
Birchmoor Warwks 65 N11
Birchmoor Green C Beds 44 D5
Birchover Derbys 77 N11
Birch Services Rochdl 76 F2
Birch Vale Derbys 77 J6
Birchwood Lincs 79 M10
Birch Wood Somset 21 K10
Birchwood Warrtn 76 C5
Bircotes Notts 78 G5
Birdbrook Essex 46 C3
Birdforth N York 91 R11
Birdham W Susx 13 P5
Birdingbury Warwks 54 C7
Birdlip Gloucs 41 Q9
Birdoswald Cumb 99 J5
Birdsall N York 86 F2
Birds Edge Kirk 77 M2
Birds Green Essex 45 Q10
Birdsgreen Shrops 52 E4
Birdsmoorgate Dorset 10 B4
Bird Street Suffk 58 E10
Birdwell Barns 77 Q3
Birdwood Gloucs 41 L8
Birgham Border 108 C2
Birichin Highld 146 D6
Birkacre Lancs 83 M12
Birkby N York 91 N6
Birkdale Sefton 82 H12
Birkenbog Abers 140 E3
Birkenhead Wirral 75 K6
Birkenhead (Queensway) Tunnel Lpool 75 K6
Birkenhills Abers 140 H7
Birkenshaw Kirk 85 J9
Birkhall Abers 131 Q5
Birkhill Angus 124 G6
Birkhill D & G 106 G6
Birkholme Lincs 67 N7
Birkin N York 85 Q10
Birks Leeds 85 K10
Birkshaw Nthumb 99 L5
Birley Herefs 51 M10
Birley Carr Sheff 77 Q5
Birling Kent 34 B10
Birling Nthumb 109 L8
Birling Gap E Susx 15 Q11
Birlingham Worcs 41 Q3
Birmingham Birm 53 K3
Birmingham Airport Solhll 53 M4
Birnam P & K 123 Q4
Birness Abers 141 N9
Birse Abers 132 E5
Birsemore Abers 132 E5
Birstall Kirk 85 K10
Birstall Leics 66 F10
Birstwith N York 85 K3
Birthorpe Lincs 68 B5
Birtley Gatesd 100 H7
Birtley Herefs 51 L7
Birtley Nthumb 99 N3
Birts Street Worcs 41 M4
Bisbrooke Rutlnd 67 M12
Biscathorpe Lincs 80 E7
Biscovey Cnwll 3 P4
Bisham W & M 32 B5
Bishampton Worcs 53 J10
Bish Mill Devon 19 P8
Bishop Auckland Dur 91 L1
Bishopbridge Lincs 79 P5
Bishopbriggs E Duns 114 A7
Bishop Burton E R Yk 87 J7
Bishop Middleham Dur 101 J12
Bishopmill Moray 139 N3
Bishop Monkton N York 85 M3
Bishop Norton Lincs 79 N5
Bishopsbourne Kent 35 L11
Bishops Cannings Wilts 30 B9
Bishop's Castle Shrops 51 K3
Bishop's Caundle Dorset 22 F10
Bishop's Cleeve Gloucs 41 Q6
Bishop's Frome Herefs 52 C11
Bishops Gate Surrey 32 D8
Bishop's Green Essex 46 A8
Bishop's Green Hants 31 K9
Bishop's Hull Somset 21 K8
Bishop's Itchington Warwks 54 C9
Bishops Lydeard Somset 21 J7
Bishop's Norton Gloucs 41 N7
Bishop's Nympton Devon 19 P8
Bishop's Offley Staffs 64 E6
Bishop's Stortford Herts 45 N7
Bishop's Sutton Hants 25 K7
Bishop's Tachbrook Warwks 53 P8
Bishop's Tawton Devon 19 L7
Bishopsteignton Devon 8 G10
Bishopstoke Hants 24 H9
Bishopston Swans 26 E4
Bishopstone Bucks 44 A9
Bishopstone E Susx 15 N10
Bishopstone Herefs 40 F3
Bishopstone Kent 35 M8
Bishopstone Swindn 30 F5
Bishopstone Wilts 23 N8
Bishopstrow Wilts 23 K5
Bishop Sutton BaNES 29 J10
Bishop's Waltham Hants 25 J10
Bishopswood Somset 21 L10
Bishop's Wood Staffs 64 F10
Bishopsworth Bristl 28 H8
Bishop Thornton N York 85 K3
Bishopthorpe C York 86 B6
Bishopton Darltn 91 N2
Bishopton Rens 113 N7
Bishopton Warwks 53 M9
Bishop Wilton E R Yk 86 E4
Bishton Newpt 28 E5
Bishton Staffs 65 J8
Bisley Gloucs 41 P10
Bisley Surrey 32 D10
Bisley Camp Surrey 32 D10
Bispham Bpool 82 H7
Bispham Green Lancs 75 N1
Bissoe Cnwll 3 K6
Bisterne Hants 12 B4
Bitchet Green Kent 33 Q11
Bitchfield Lincs 67 N6
Bittadon Devon 19 K5
Bittaford Devon 5 L5
Bittering Norfk 70 D8
Bitterley Shrops 51 P5
Bitterne C Sotn 24 G10
Bitteswell Leics 54 E3
Bitton S Glos 29 K8
Bix Oxon 31 P5
Bixter Shet 147 i6
Blaby Leics 54 F1
Blackadder Border 117 J10
Blackawton Devon 5 N6
Blackbeck Cumb 88 D5
Blackborough Devon 9 L3
Blackborough End Norfk 69 M9
Black Bourton Oxon 42 G10
Blackboys E Susx 15 P6
Blackbrook Derbys 65 Q3
Blackbrook St Hel 75 P5
Blackbrook Staffs 64 E4
Blackbrook Surrey 14 H1
Blackburn Abers 133 K2
Blackburn Bl w D 83 P9
Blackburn Rothm 78 C5
Blackburn W Loth 114 H8
Blackburn with Darwen Services Bl w D 83 Q10
Black Callerton N u Ty 100 F4
Black Carr Norfk 58 G2
Black Corner W Susx 15 K3
Blackcraig E Ayrs 105 L8
Black Crofts Ag & B 120 H6
Black Cross Cnwll 3 M2
Blackden Heath Ches E 76 E9
Blackdog Abers 133 M1
Black Dog Devon 8 E3
Blackdown Devon 7 P9
Blackdown Dorset 10 B4
Blackdyke Cumb 97 N8
Blacker Barns 77 Q2
Blacker Hill Barns 78 B3
Blackfen Gt Lon 33 N7
Blackfield Hants 12 G4
Blackford Cumb 98 E6
Blackford P & K 123 M11
Blackford Somset 21 N4
Blackford Somset 22 F8
Blackfordby Leics 65 Q8
Blackgang IoW 12 H9
Blackhall C Edin 115 M6
Blackhall Colliery Dur 101 L10
Blackhall Mill Gatesd 100 E7
Blackhall Rocks Dur 101 L10
Blackhaugh Border 107 L2
Blackheath Essex 46 H7
Blackheath Gt Lon 33 M7
Blackheath Sandw 52 H3
Blackheath Suffk 59 N6
Blackheath Surrey 14 E2
Black Heddon Nthumb 100 D3
Blackhill Abers 141 P5
Blackhill Abers 141 Q7
Blackhill Dur 100 E8
Blackhill of Clackriach Abers 141 M6
Blackhorse Devon 9 J6
Blackjack Lincs 68 E4
Blackland Wilts 30 B8
Black Lane Ends Lancs 84 D6
Blacklaw D & G 106 D8
Blackley Manch 76 F3
Blacklunans P & K 131 L12
Blackmarstone Herefs 40 G4
Blackmill Brdgnd 27 M5
Blackmoor Hants 25 N7
Black Moor Leeds 85 L7
Blackmoor N Som 28 G10
Blackmoorfoot Kirk 77 L1
Blackmoor Gate Devon 19 M5
Blackmore Essex 45 R11
Blackmore End Essex 46 C5
Blackmore End Herts 44 H8
Black Mountains 40 C6
Blackness Falk 115 J5
Blacknest Hants 25 P5
Blacknest W & M 32 D8
Black Notley Essex 46 D7
Blacko Lancs 84 C6
Black Pill Swans 26 F4
Blackpool Bpool 82 H8
Blackpool Devon 5 P7
Blackpool Devon 8 F10
Blackpool Gate Cumb 98 G3
Blackpool Zoo Bpool 82 H8
Blackridge W Loth 114 G8
Blackrock Cnwll 2 G7
Blackrock Mons 40 B9
Blackrod Bolton 75 Q2
Blacksboat Moray 139 M8
Blackshaw D & G 97 L5
Blackshaw Head Calder 84 E9
Blacksmith's Green Suffk 58 H7
Blacksnape Bl w D 83 Q11
Blackstone W Susx 15 J7
Black Street Suffk 59 P3
Black Tar Pembks 37 J8
Blackthorn Oxon 43 N8
Blackthorpe Suffk 58 D8
Blacktoft E R Yk 86 F10
Blacktop C Aber 133 L3
Black Torrington Devon 7 N4
Blackwall Derbys 65 N2
Blackwall Tunnel Gt Lon 33 M6
Blackwater Cnwll 3 J5
Blackwater Hants 32 B10
Blackwater IoW 12 H7
Blackwater Somset 21 L10
Blackwaterfoot N Ayrs 103 N4
Blackwell Cumb 98 E7
Blackwell Darltn 91 M4
Blackwell Derbys 77 L9
Blackwell Derbys 78 D12
Blackwell Warwks 42 F3
Blackwell Worcs 53 J6
Blackwellsend Green Gloucs 41 M6
Blackwood Caerph 28 A3
Blackwood D & G 106 B12
Blackwood S Lans 105 P1
Blackwood Hill Staffs 64 H1
Blacon Ches W 75 L10
Bladbean Kent 17 L1
Bladnoch D & G 95 M7
Bladon Oxon 43 K8
Bladon Somset 21 P9
Blaenannerch Cerdgn 48 D11
Blaenau Ffestiniog Gwynd 61 M3
Blaenavon Torfn 40 C10
Blaenavon Industrial Landscape Torfn 40 C10
Blaencwm Rhondd 27 L3
Blaen Dyryn Powys 39 M4
Blaenffos Pembks 37 N3
Blaengarw Brdgnd 27 L4
Blaengeuffordd Cerdgn 49 L4
Blaengwrach Neath 39 K10
Blaengwynfi Neath 27 L3
Blaenllechau Rhondd 27 N3
Blaenpennal Cerdgn 49 K8
Blaenplwyf Cerdgn 49 K5
Blaenporth Cerdgn 48 D11
Blaenrhondda Rhondd 27 M2
Blaenwaun Carmth 37 P5
Blaen-y-coed Carmth 37 R5
Blaen-y-cwm Blae G 39 Q9
Blaenycwm Cerdgn 49 P5
Blagdon N Som 28 G10
Blagdon Somset 21 K9
Blagdon Torbay 5 P4
Blagdon Hill Somset 21 K10
Blagill Cumb 99 L9
Blaguegate Lancs 75 M2
Blaich Highld 128 F9
Blain Highld 127 M10
Blaina Blae G 40 B10
Blair Atholl P & K 130 F11
Blair Drummond Stirlg 114 D2
Blairgowrie P & K 124 D4
Blairhall Fife 114 H4
Blairingone P & K 114 H2
Blairlogie Stirlg 114 E2
Blairmore Ag & B 113 J5
Blairmore Highld 148 E5
Blair's Ferry Ag & B 112 E7
Blaisdon Gloucs 41 L8
Blakebrook Worcs 52 F5
Blakedown Worcs 52 G5
Blake End Essex 46 C7
Blakeley Lane Staffs 65 J3
Blakemere Ches W 75 P9
Blakemere Herefs 40 E3
Blakemore Devon 5 M5
Blakenall Heath Wsall 65 J11
Blakeney Gloucs 41 K10
Blakeney Norfk 70 F3
Blakenhall Ches E 64 D3
Blakenhall Wolves 52 G1
Blakeshall Worcs 52 F4
Blakesley Nhants 54 G10
Blanchland Nthumb 100 B8
Blandford Camp Dorset 11 M3
Blandford Forum Dorset 11 L3
Blandford St Mary Dorset 11 L4
Bland Hill N York 85 J4
Blanefield Stirlg 113 Q5
Blankney Lincs 79 Q11
Blantyre S Lans 114 C9
Blàr a' Chaorainn Highld 128 F11
Blarghour Ag & B 121 J10
Blargie Highld 129 Q5
Blarmachfoldach Highld 128 F10
Blashford Hants 12 B3
Blaston Leics 55 K2
Blatherwycke Nhants 55 N2
Blawith Cumb 89 J9
Blawquhairn D & G 96 C2
Blaxhall Suffk 59 M9
Blaxton Donc 78 H4
Blaydon Gatesd 100 F5
Bleadney Somset 22 B4
Bleadon N Som 28 D11
Bleak Street Somset 22 G7
Blean Kent 35 K10
Bleasby Lincs 80 C7
Bleasby Notts 66 H2
Bleasdale Lancs 83 N6
Bleatarn Cumb 90 B4
Bleathwood Herefs 51 P6
Blebocraigs Fife 124 H10
Bleddfa Powys 50 H7
Bledington Gloucs 42 F7
Bledlow Bucks 43 Q11
Bledlow Ridge Bucks 31 R3
Bleet Wilts 29 P10
Blegbie E Loth 116 C9
Blencarn Cumb 99 J12
Blencogo Cumb 97 P8
Blendworth Hants 25 M10
Blenheim Palace Oxon 43 J8
Blennerhasset Cumb 97 N10
Bletchingdon Oxon 43 L8
Bletchingley Surrey 33 L12
Bletchley M Keyn 44 B5
Bletchley Shrops 64 B5
Bletchley Park Museum M Keyn 44 B5
Bletherston Pembks 37 L6
Bletsoe Bed 55 P9
Blewbury Oxon 31 L5
Blickling Norfk 70 H6
Blidworth Notts 66 F1
Blidworth Bottoms Notts 66 F1
Blindburn Nthumb 108 C7
Blindcrake Cumb 97 N11
Blindley Heath Surrey 15 L2
Blisland Cnwll 6 G10
Blissford Hants 24 B10
Bliss Gate Worcs 52 D6
Blisworth Nhants 55 J10
Blithbury Staffs 65 K8
Blitterlees Cumb 97 M8
Blockley Gloucs 42 D5
Blofield Norfk 71 L10
Blofield Heath Norfk 71 L10
Blo Norton Norfk 58 F5
Bloomfield Border 107 P5
Blore Staffs 64 D5
Blore Staffs 65 L2
Blounce Hants 25 M4
Blounts Green Staffs 65 K6
Blowick Sefton 83 J12
Bloxham Oxon 43 J4
Bloxholm Lincs 67 Q1
Bloxwich Wsall 65 J11
Bloxworth Dorset 11 L6
Blubberhouses N York 85 J4
Blue Anchor Cnwll 3 M3
Blue Anchor Somset 20 G5
Blue Bell Hill Kent 34 D10
Blue John Cavern Derbys 77 L7
Blundellsands Sefton 75 J4
Blundeston Suffk 59 Q1
Blunham C Beds 56 C10
Blunsdon St Andrew Swindn 30 D4
Bluntington Worcs 52 G6
Bluntisham Cambs 56 G6
Blunts Cnwll 4 E4
Blunts Green Warwks 53 L7
Blurton C Stke 64 G4
Blyborough Lincs 79 M5
Blyford Suffk 59 N5
Blymhill Staffs 64 F10
Blymhill Lawn Staffs 64 F10
Blyth Notts 78 G6
Blyth Nthumb 101 J2
Blyth Bridge Border 115 L12
Blythburgh Suffk 59 N5
Blythe Border 116 D11
Blythe Bridge Staffs 64 H4
Blythe End Warwks 53 N2
Blythe Marsh Staffs 64 H4
Blyth Services Notts 78 G6
Blyton Lincs 79 L5
Boarhills Fife 125 L10
Boarhunt Hants 13 K3
Boarley Kent 34 D10
Boarsgreave Lancs 84 C11
Boarshead E Susx 15 P4
Boar's Head Wigan 75 P2
Boars Hill Oxon 43 K11
Boarstall Bucks 43 N9
Boasley Cross Devon 7 P6
Boath Highld 145 N10
Boat of Garten Highld 138 H12
Bobbing Kent 34 F9
Bobbington Staffs 52 E2
Bobbingworth Essex 45 Q10
Bocaddon Cnwll 4 B5
Bocking Essex 46 D7
Bocking Churchstreet Essex 46 D6
Bockleton Worcs 51 Q8
Boconnoc Cnwll 4 A4
Boddam Abers 141 R7
Boddam Shet 147 i9
Boddington Gloucs 41 P6
Bodedern IoA 72 E7
Bodelwyddan Denbgs 74 D8
Bodenham Herefs 51 P10
Bodenham Wilts 23 Q8
Bodenham Moor Herefs 51 P10
Bodewryd IoA 72 G5
Bodfari Denbgs 74 F9
Bodffordd IoA 72 G8
Bodham Norfk 70 H4
Bodiam E Susx 16 D5
Bodicote Oxon 43 K4
Bodieve Cnwll 6 E10
Bodinnick Cnwll 3 R4
Bodle Street Green E Susx 16 B8
Bodmin Cnwll 6 F11
Bodmin Moor Cnwll 6 H9
Bodney Norfk 70 B12
Bodorgan IoA 72 F10
Bodsham Kent 17 K2
Boduan Gwynd 60 E4
Bodwen Cnwll 3 P2
Bodymoor Heath Warwks 53 M1
Bogallan Highld 138 B6
Bogbrae Abers 141 P8
Bogend S Ayrs 104 G3
Boggs Holdings E Loth 116 B7
Boghall Mdloth 115 N8
Boghall W Loth 114 H7
Boghead S Lans 105 P1
Bogmoor Moray 139 Q3
Bogmuir Abers 132 G10
Bogniebrae Abers 140 F7
Bognor Regis W Susx 14 D11
Bogroy Highld 138 G11
Bogue D & G 96 D2
Bohetherick Cnwll 4 F3
Bohortha Cnwll 3 L8
Bohuntine Highld 129 J7
Bojewyan Cnwll 2 C7
Bokiddick Cnwll 3 P2
Bolam Dur 91 K2
Bolam Nthumb 100 E2
Bolberry Devon 5 L9
Bold Heath St Hel 75 P6
Boldmere Birm 53 L2
Boldon Colliery S Tyne 101 J6
Boldre Hants 12 E5
Boldron Dur 90 G4
Bole Notts 79 K6
Bolehill Derbys 65 P1
Bole Hill Derbys 77 Q9
Bolenowe Cnwll 2 G7
Bolham Devon 20 E10
Bolham Water Devon 21 J10
Bolingey Cnwll 3 J4
Bollington Ches E 76 H8
Bollington Cross Ches E 76 G8
Bollow Gloucs 41 M9
Bolney W Susx 15 J6
Bolnhurst Bed 56 B8
Bolnore W Susx 15 L6
Bolshan Angus 125 M2
Bolsover Derbys 78 D9
Bolster Moor Kirk 84 G12
Bolsterstone Sheff 77 P4
Boltby N York 91 R9
Boltenstone Abers 132 C2
Bolter End Bucks 31 R4
Bolton Bolton 76 D2
Bolton Cumb 89 Q2
Bolton E Loth 116 C7
Bolton E R Yk 86 E5
Bolton Nthumb 109 J7
Bolton Abbey N York 84 G4
Bolton Bridge N York 84 G4
Bolton-by-Bowland Lancs 84 B5
Boltonfellend Cumb 98 F4
Boltongate Cumb 97 P10
Bolton-le-Sands Lancs 83 L2
Bolton Low Houses Cumb 97 P10
Bolton New Houses Cumb 97 Q9
Bolton-on-Swale N York 91 L7
Bolton Percy N York 85 Q7
Bolton Town End Lancs 83 L2
Bolton upon Dearne Barns 78 D3
Bolventor Cnwll 6 H9
Bomarsund Nthumb 100 H1
Bomere Heath Shrops 63 M8
Bonar Bridge Highld 145 N7
Bonawe Ag & B 121 J6
Bonby N Linc 87 J12
Boncath Pembks 37 N3
Bonchester Bridge Border 107 P7
Bonchurch IoW 13 K9
Bondleigh Devon 8 C4
Bonds Lancs 83 L6
Bonehill Devon 8 D9
Bonehill Staffs 65 M11
Bo'ness Falk 114 H5
Boney Hay Staffs 65 K10
Bonhill W Duns 113 M5
Boningale Shrops 64 F11
Bonjedward Border 107 Q5
Bonkle N Lans 114 F10
Bonnington Angus 125 L5
Bonnington Kent 17 J4
Bonnybank Fife 124 G12
Bonnybridge Falk 114 E5
Bonnykelly Abers 141 L5
Bonnyrigg Mdloth 115 P8
Bonnyton Angus 124 G5
Bonsall Derbys 77 P12
Bonshaw Tower D & G 97 P4
Bont Mons 40 E8
Bontddu Gwynd 61 L8
Bont-Dolgadfan Powys 62 B12
Bont-goch Cerdgn 49 L3
Bonthorpe Lincs 81 J9
Bontnewydd Cerdgn 49 K7
Bontnewydd Gwynd 72 H11
Bontuchel Denbgs 74 F12
Bonvilston V Glam 27 P7
Bonwm Denbgs 62 F4
Bon-y-maen Swans 26 G3
Boode Devon 19 K6
Booker Bucks 32 B4
Booley Shrops 63 P7
Boon Border 116 D12
Boon Hill Staffs 64 E2
Boorley Green Hants 24 H10
Boosbeck R & Cl 92 D3
Boose's Green Essex 46 E5
Boot Cumb 88 G6
Booth Calder 84 F9
Boothby Graffoe Lincs 79 N11
Boothby Pagnell Lincs 67 N6
Boothferry E R Yk 86 D10
Booth Green Ches E 76 G7
Boothstown Salfd 76 D3
Booth Town Calder 84 G10
Boothville Nhants 55 K8
Bootle Cumb 88 E9
Bootle Sefton 75 K5
Boots Green Ches W 76 D9
Boot Street Suffk 59 J11
Booze N York 90 G6
Boraston Shrops 51 Q6
Bordeaux Guern 12 d1
Borden Kent 34 F9
Borden W Susx 25 P8
Border Cumb 97 N7
Bordley N York 84 E2
Bordon Hants 25 N6
Boreham Essex 46 D9
Boreham Wilts 23 K4
Boreham Street E Susx 16 B8
Borehamwood Herts 32 H3
Boreland D & G 106 F11
Boreraig Highld 134 C5
Boreton Shrops 63 N10
Borgh W Isls 152 b13
Borgh W Isls 152 g1
Borgie Highld 149 P5
Borgue D & G 96 D8
Borgue Highld 151 L11
Borley Essex 46 E3
Borley Green Essex 46 E3
Borley Green Suffk 58 E8
Borneskitaig Highld 142 D11
Borness D & G 96 C9
Boroughbridge N York 85 N2
Borough Green Kent 33 R11
Borras Head Wrexhm 63 L2
Borrowash Derbys 66 C5
Borrowby N York 91 P9
Borrowby N York 92 F4
Borrowdale Cumb 88 H3
Borrowstoun Falk 114 H5
Borstal Medway 34 C9
Borth Cerdgn 49 K3
Borthwick Mdloth 115 Q9
Borthwickbrae Border 107 L7
Borthwickshiels Border 107 L6
Borth-y-Gest Gwynd 61 J5
Borve Highld 134 H6
Borve W Isls 152 b13
Borve W Isls 152 d6
Borve W Isls 152 g1
Borwick Lancs 89 N12
Borwick Lodge Cumb 89 K7
Borwick Rails Cumb 88 G10
Bosavern Cnwll 2 B8
Bosbury Herefs 41 L3
Boscarne Cnwll 6 F11
Boscastle Cnwll 6 G6
Boscombe BCP 11 Q6
Boscombe Wilts 24 C5
Boscoppa Cnwll 3 P4
Bosham W Susx 13 P4
Bosham Hoe W Susx 13 P4
Bosherston Pembks 37 J11
Boskednan Cnwll 2 C7
Boskenna Cnwll 2 C9
Bosley Ches E 76 G10
Bosoughan Cnwll 3 L2
Bossall N York 86 D3
Bossiney Cnwll 6 F7
Bossingham Kent 17 L1
Bossington Somset 20 D4
Bostock Green Ches W 76 C10
Boston Lincs 68 F3
Boston Spa Leeds 85 N6
Boswarthan Cnwll 2 C8
Boswinger Cnwll 3 N6
Botallack Cnwll 2 B8
Botany Bay Gt Lon 33 K3
Botcheston Leics 66 D11
Botesdale Suffk 58 F5
Bothal Nthumb 100 G1
Bothampstead W Berk 31 L7
Bothamsall Notts 78 H9
Bothel Cumb 97 N10
Bothenhampton Dorset 10 D6
Bothwell S Lans 114 C9
Bothwell Services S Lans 114 C9
Botley Bucks 44 D11
Botley Hants 24 H10
Botley Oxon 43 K10
Botolph Claydon Bucks 43 Q7
Botolphs W Susx 14 H9
Botolph's Bridge Kent 17 K4
Bottesford Leics 67 K4
Bottesford N Linc 79 M2
Bottisham Cambs 57 K8
Bottomcraig Fife 124 G8
Bottom of Hutton Lancs 83 L9
Bottom o' th' Moor Bolton 76 C1
Bottoms Calder 84 D11
Bottoms Cnwll 2 B9
Botts Green Warwks 53 N2
Botusfleming Cnwll 4 F4
Botwnnog Gwynd 60 D6
Bough Beech Kent 15 P1
Boughrood Powys 39 Q4
Boughspring Gloucs 28 H3
Boughton Nhants 55 J7
Boughton Norfk 69 N11
Boughton Notts 78 H10
Boughton Aluph Kent 17 J1
Boughton End C Beds 44 E4
Boughton Green Kent 34 D12
Boughton Malherbe Kent 34 F12
Boughton Monchelsea Kent 34 D12
Boughton Street Kent 35 J10
Boulby R & Cl 92 F3
Boulder Clough Calder 84 F10
Bouldnor IoW 12 F7
Bouldon Shrops 51 P4
Boulmer Nthumb 109 L7
Boulston Pembks 37 J8
Boultham Lincs 79 N10
Boundary Staffs 64 H4
Bourn Cambs 56 F9
Bournbrook Birm 53 K4
Bourne Lincs 68 B8
Bournebridge Essex 33 P3
Bourne End Bed 55 P8
Bourne End Bucks 32 C5
Bourne End C Beds 44 D3
Bourne End Herts 44 E10
Bournemouth BCP 11 Q6
Bournemouth Airport BCP 11 Q5
Bournes Green Gloucs 41 Q10
Bournes Green Sthend 34 F5
Bournheath Worcs 52 H6
Bournmoor Dur 100 H8
Bournstream Gloucs 29 M3
Bournville Birm 53 K4
Bourton Dorset 22 G7
Bourton N Som 28 E9
Bourton Oxon 30 F5
Bourton Shrops 51 Q1
Bourton Wilts 30 B9
Bourton on Dunsmore Warwks 54 D6
Bourton-on-the-Hill Gloucs 42 E5
Bourton-on-the-Water Gloucs 42 E7
Bousd Ag & B 126 D11
Boustead Hill Cumb 98 C6
Bouth Cumb 89 J9
Bouthwaite N York 84 H1
Bouts Worcs 53 J9
Boveney Bucks 32 D7
Boveridge Dorset 23 N10
Bovey Tracey Devon 8 F9
Bovingdon Herts 44 E11
Bovingdon Green Bucks 32 B5
Bovinger Essex 45 P10
Bovington Dorset 11 K7
Bovington Camp Dorset 11 K7
Bow Cumb 98 D7
Bow Devon 5 N5
Bow Devon 8 D4
Bow Gt Lon 33 L6
Bow Ork 147 c6
Bowbank Dur 90 F2
Bow Brickhill M Keyn 44 C5
Bowbridge Gloucs 41 P10
Bowburn Dur 100 H10
Bowcombe IoW 12 H7
Bowd Devon 9 L7
Bowden Border 107 N4
Bowden Devon 5 P7
Bowden Hill Wilts 29 Q9
Bowdon Traffd 76 E6
Bower Highld 151 N4
Bowerchalke Wilts 23 M8
Bowerhill Wilts 29 Q10
Bower Hinton Somset 21 P10
Bower House Tye Suffk 46 H3
Bowermadden Highld 151 N4
Bowers Staffs 64 F5
Bowers Gifford Essex 34 D5
Bowershall Fife 115 K3
Bower's Row Leeds 85 N9
Bowgreave Lancs 83 L6
Bowhouse D & G 97 L5
Bowithick Cnwll 6 H8
Bowker's Green Lancs 75 L3
Bowland Border 107 M2
Bowland Bridge Cumb 89 L9
Bowley Herefs 51 P10
Bowley Town Herefs 51 P10
Bowlhead Green Surrey 14 C3
Bowling C Brad 85 J9
Bowling W Duns 113 N6
Bowling Bank Wrexhm 63 L2
Bowling Green Worcs 52 F10
Bowmanstead Cumb 89 J7
Bowmore Ag & B 110 G9
Bowness-on-Solway Cumb 97 P6
Bowness-on-Windermere Cumb 89 L7
Bow of Fife Fife 124 G10
Bowriefauld Angus 125 K3
Bowscale Cumb 98 D12
Bowsden Nthumb 108 G1
Bowston Cumb 89 M7
Bow Street Cerdgn 49 K4
Bow Street Norfk 58 F1
Bowthorpe Norfk 70 H10
Box Gloucs 29 P2
Box Wilts 29 N8
Boxbush Gloucs 41 K7
Boxbush Gloucs 41 M9
Box End Bed 55 P10
Boxford Suffk 46 G4
Boxford W Berk 31 J8
Boxgrove W Susx 14 C9
Box Hill Surrey 32 H12
Boxley Kent 34 D10
Boxmoor Herts 44 F10
Box's Shop Cnwll 7 J4
Boxted Essex 46 H5
Boxted Essex 46 H5
Boxted Suffk 58 B10
Boxted Cross Essex 46 H5
Boxwell Gloucs 29 N4
Boxworth Cambs 56 G8
Boyden End Suffk 57 P9
Boyden Gate Kent 35 M9
Boylestone Derbys 65 M5
Boyndie Abers 140 G3
Boyndlie Abers 141 L3
Boynton E R Yk 87 L2
Boysack Angus 125 M3
Boys Hill Dorset 10 G3
Boythorpe Derbys 78 C9
Boyton Cnwll 7 L6
Boyton Suffk 47 Q2
Boyton Wilts 23 L5
Boyton Cross Essex 46 B10
Boyton End Suffk 46 C3
Bozeat Nhants 55 M9
Braaid IoM 102 d6
Brabling Green Suffk 59 L7
Brabourne Kent 17 K2
Brabourne Lees Kent 17 K3
Brabstermire Highld 151 P3
Bracadale Highld 134 F8
Braceborough Lincs 67 Q9
Bracebridge Heath Lincs 79 N10
Bracebridge Low Fields Lincs 79 N10
Braceby Lincs 67 P5
Bracewell Lancs 84 C5
Brackenfield Derbys 78 B12
Brackenhirst N Lans 114 D7
Brackenthwaite Cumb 98 C9
Brackenthwaite N York 85 L5
Brackla Brdgnd 27 L6
Bracklesham W Susx 13 P5
Brackletter Highld 128 H8
Brackley Nhants 43 M4
Brackley Hatch Nhants 43 N3
Bracknell Br For 32 B8
Braco P & K 123 L11
Bracobrae Moray 140 D5
Bracon Ash Norfk 71 J12
Bracora Highld 127 N6
Bracorina Highld 127 N6
Bradaford Devon 7 M6
Bradbourne Derbys 65 M2
Bradbury Dur 91 N1
Bradden Nhants 54 G11
Braddock Cnwll 4 B4
Bradeley C Stke 64 G2
Bradenham Bucks 32 B3
Bradenstoke Wilts 30 B6
Bradfield Devon 9 K3
Bradfield Essex 47 L5
Bradfield Norfk 71 K5
Bradfield Sheff 77 P5
Bradfield W Berk 31 M8
Bradfield Combust Suffk 58 C9
Bradfield Green Ches E 76 C11
Bradfield Heath Essex 47 L6
Bradfield St Clare Suffk 58 D9
Bradfield St George Suffk 58 D8
Bradford C Brad 84 H8
Bradford Cnwll 6 G9
Bradford Devon 7 M3
Bradford Nthumb 100 D2
Bradford Nthumb 109 J3
Bradford Abbas Dorset 22 D10
Bradford Leigh Wilts 29 N10
Bradford-on-Avon Wilts 29 N10
Bradford-on-Tone Somset 21 J9
Bradford Peverell Dorset 10 G6
Bradiford Devon 19 L6
Brading IoW 13 K7
Bradley Ches W 63 N3
Bradley Derbys 65 N3
Bradley Hants 25 L5
Bradley Kirk 85 J11
Bradley N York 90 G10
Bradley NE Lin 80 E2
Bradley Staffs 64 G8
Bradley Wolves 52 H2
Bradley Worcs 53 J8
Bradley Wrexhm 63 K1
Bradley Green Somset 21 L6
Bradley Green Warwks 65 P12
Bradley Green Worcs 53 J8
Bradley in the Moors Staffs 65 K4
Bradley Stoke S Glos 29 J6
Bradmore Notts 66 F6
Bradney Somset 21 M5
Bradninch Devon 9 J4
Bradninch Devon 19 M7
Bradnop Staffs 65 J1
Bradpole Dorset 10 D6
Bradshaw Bolton 76 D1
Bradshaw Calder 84 G9
Bradshaw Kirk 84 G12
Bradstone Devon 7 M8
Bradwall Green Ches E 76 E11
Bradwell Derbys 77 M7
Bradwell Devon 19 K5
Bradwell Essex 46 E7
Bradwell M Keyn 44 B3
Bradwell Norfk 71 P11
Bradwell-on-Sea Essex 46 H10
Bradwell Waterside Essex 46 H10
Bradworthy Devon 18 F10
Brae Highld 138 C3
Brae Shet 147 i5
Braeface Falk 114 E5
Braehead Angus 125 N2
Braehead D & G 95 M8
Braehead S Lans 114 H11
Braeintra Highld 136 B9

Braemar Abers ... 131 L6
Braemore Highld ... 144 F9
Braemore Highld ... 151 K10
Brae Roy Lodge Highld ... 129 K6
Braeside Inver ... 113 J5
Braes of Coul Angus ... 124 F1
Braes of Enzie Moray ... 140 B4
Braeswick Ork ... 147 e2
Braevallich Ag & B ... 120 H11
Braewick Shet ... 147 h4
Brafferton Darltn ... 91 M2
Brafferton N York ... 85 N1
Brafield-on-the-Green Nhants ... 55 K9
Bragar W Isls ... 152 f2
Bragbury End Herts ... 45 K7
Braidwood S Lans ... 114 F11
Brailsford Derbys ... 65 N4
Brailsford Green Derbys ... 65 N4
Brain's Green Gloucs ... 41 K10
Braintree Essex ... 46 D7
Braiseworth Suffk ... 58 H6
Braishfield Hants ... 24 F8
Braithwaite C Brad ... 84 F7
Braithwaite Cumb ... 88 H2
Braithwell Donc ... 78 E5
Braken Hill Wakefd ... 85 N12
Bramber W Susx ... 14 H8
Brambridge Hants ... 24 H9
Bramcote Notts ... 66 E5
Bramcote Warwks ... 54 C3
Bramdean Hants ... 25 K8
Bramerton Norfk ... 71 L11
Bramfield Herts ... 45 K8
Bramfield Suffk ... 59 M6
Bramford Suffk ... 47 K2
Bramhall Stockp ... 76 G7
Bramham Leeds ... 85 N6
Bramhope Leeds ... 85 K6
Bramley Hants ... 31 N10
Bramley Leeds ... 85 K8
Bramley Rothm ... 78 D5
Bramley Surrey ... 14 E2
Bramley Corner Hants ... 31 N10
Bramley Green Hants ... 31 N10
Bramley Head N York ... 84 H4
Bramling Kent ... 35 M11
Brampford Speke Devon ... 8 H5
Brampton Cambs ... 56 D6
Brampton Cumb ... 89 R2
Brampton Cumb ... 89 Q8
Brampton Lincs ... 79 L8
Brampton Norfk ... 71 J7
Brampton Rothm ... 78 C3
Brampton Suffk ... 59 N5
Brampton Abbotts Herefs ... 41 J6
Brampton Ash Nhants ... 55 K3
Brampton Bryan Herefs ... 51 L6
Brampton-en-le-Morthen Rothm ... 78 D6
Bramshall Staffs ... 65 K5
Bramshaw Hants ... 24 D10
Bramshill Hants ... 31 Q10
Bramshott Hants ... 25 P7
Bramwell Somset ... 21 M7
Branault Highld ... 127 J10
Brancaster Norfk ... 69 P3
Brancaster Staithe Norfk ... 69 Q3
Brancepeth Dur ... 100 G10
Branchill Moray ... 139 K5
Brand End Lincs ... 68 G3
Branderburgh Moray ... 147 N11
Brandesburton E R Yk ... 87 L6
Brandeston Suffk ... 59 L6
Brand Green Gloucs ... 41 L6
Brandis Corner Devon ... 7 N4
Brandiston Norfk ... 70 H8
Brandon Dur ... 100 G10
Brandon Lincs ... 67 M3
Brandon Nthumb ... 108 H5
Brandon Suffk ... 57 Q3
Brandon Warwks ... 54 B5
Brandon Bank Norfk ... 57 M3
Brandon Creek Norfk ... 57 L2
Brandon Parva Norfk ... 70 G10
Brandsby N York ... 92 C12
Brandy Wharf Lincs ... 79 P4
Brane Cnwll ... 2 C9
Branksome BCP ... 11 P6
Branksome Park BCP ... 11 P6
Bransbury Hants ... 24 G5
Bransby Lincs ... 79 M8
Branscombe Devon ... 9 M7
Bransford Worcs ... 52 E10
Bransgore Hants ... 12 C5
Bransholme C KuH ... 87 L8
Branson's Cross Worcs ... 53 C5
Branston Leics ... 67 K6
Branston Lincs ... 79 P10
Branston Staffs ... 65 N8
Branston Booths Lincs ... 79 Q10
Branstone IoW ... 13 H8
Brant Broughton Lincs ... 67 M1
Brantham Suffk ... 47 K5
Branthwaite Cumb ... 88 E2
Branthwaite Cumb ... 98 C10
Brantingham E R Yk ... 86 H9
Branton Donc ... 78 G4
Branton Nthumb ... 108 H5
Branton Green N York ... 85 N3
Branxton Nthumb ... 108 E2
Brassey Green Ches W ... 75 N11
Brassington Derbys ... 65 N2
Brasted Kent ... 33 N11
Brasted Chart Kent ... 33 N11
Brathens Abers ... 132 G5
Bratoft Lincs ... 81 J10
Brattleby Lincs ... 79 N7
Bratton Somset ... 20 E4
Bratton Wilts ... 23 J3
Bratton Wrekin ... 64 B9
Bratton Clovelly Devon ... 7 N6
Bratton Fleming Devon ... 19 N6
Bratton Seymour Somset ... 22 F7
Braughing Herts ... 45 M6
Braughing Friars Herts ... 45 M7
Braunston Nhants ... 54 E7
Braunston Rutlnd ... 67 K10
Braunstone Town Leics ... 66 F12
Braunton Devon ... 19 J5
Brawby N York ... 92 E11
Brawl Highld ... 150 G3
Braworth N York ... 92 A5
Bray W & M ... 32 D6
Braybrooke Nhants ... 55 J4
Braydon Wilts ... 30 B5
Braydon Brook Wilts ... 30 A4
Braydon Side Wilts ... 30 B5
Brayford Devon ... 19 N6
Bray's Hill E Susx ... 113 J4
Bray Shop Cnwll ... 7 L10
Braystones Cumb ... 88 D4
Braythorn N York ... 85 K5
Brayton N York ... 86 B7
Braywick W & M ... 32 C6
Braywoodside W & M ... 32 C7
Brazacott Cnwll ... 7 K6
Breach Herefs ... 41 M7
Breach Kent ... 34 F9
Breachwood Green Herts ... 44 G7
Breacleit W Isls ... 152 d3
Breaclete W Isls ... 152 d3
Breaden Heath Shrops ... 63 M5
Breadsall Derbys ... 66 B4

Breadstone Gloucs ... 29 L2
Breadward Herefs ... 51 J9
Breage Cnwll ... 2 F9
Breakachy Highld ... 137 N7
Breakish Highld ... 135 M11
Brealangwell Lodge Highld ... 145 M6
Bream Gloucs ... 41 J10
Breamore Hants ... 23 P9
Brean Somset ... 28 D11
Breanais W Isls ... 152 d4
Brearley Calder ... 84 F10
Brearton N York ... 85 L3
Breascleit W Isls ... 152 f3
Breasclete W Isls ... 152 f3
Breaston Derbys ... 66 D5
Brechfa Carmth ... 38 D6
Brechin Angus ... 132 F12
Breckles Norfk ... 58 D2
Brecon Powys ... 39 P6
Brecon Beacons National Park ... 39 N7
Bredbury Stockp ... 76 G5
Brede E Susx ... 16 E7
Bredenbury Herefs ... 51 Q9
Bredfield Suffk ... 59 K10
Bredgar Kent ... 34 F10
Bredhurst Kent ... 34 D10
Bredon's Hardwick Worcs ... 41 Q4
Bredon's Norton Worcs ... 41 P5
Bredwardine Herefs ... 40 G4
Breedon on the Hill Leics ... 66 C7
Breich W Loth ... 114 H9
Breightmet Bolton ... 76 D2
Breighton E R Yk ... 86 D8
Breinton Herefs ... 40 G4
Bremhill Wilts ... 29 R8
Bremridge Devon ... 19 N7
Brenchley Kent ... 16 B2
Brendon Devon ... 7 L3
Brendon Devon ... 19 P4
Brendon Hill Somset ... 20 G6
Brenfield Ag & B ... 112 B5
Brenish W Isls ... 152 d4
Brenkley N u Ty ... 100 G3
Brent Cross Gt Lon ... 33 J5
Brent Eleigh Suffk ... 58 D11
Brentford Gt Lon ... 32 H7
Brentingby Leics ... 67 K8
Brent Knoll Somset ... 21 M4
Brent Mill Devon ... 5 L5
Brent Pelham Herts ... 45 N5
Brentwood Essex ... 33 Q4
Brenzett Kent ... 16 H5
Brenzett Green Kent ... 16 H5
Brereton Staffs ... 65 K9
Brereton Green Ches E ... 76 E10
Brereton Heath Ches E ... 76 E10
Brereton Hill Staffs ... 65 K9
Bressay Shet ... 147 j5
Bressingham Norfk ... 58 G4
Bressingham Common Norfk ... 58 G4
Bretby Derbys ... 65 P7
Bretford Warwks ... 54 C5
Bretforton Worcs ... 42 C3
Bretherton Lancs ... 83 L11
Brettabister Shet ... 147 j4
Brettenham Norfk ... 58 D4
Brettenham Suffk ... 58 E10
Bretton C Pete ... 68 C12
Bretton Derbys ... 77 M8
Bretton Flints ... 75 K11
Brewers End Essex ... 45 Q7
Brewer Street Surrey ... 33 L12
Brewood Staffs ... 64 G10
Briantspuddle Dorset ... 11 L6
Brick End Essex ... 45 Q6
Brickendon Herts ... 45 L10
Bricket Wood Herts ... 44 G11
Brick Houses Sheff ... 77 P7
Brickkiln Green Essex ... 46 C5
Bricklehampton Worcs ... 41 R3
Bride IoM ... 102 f2
Bridekirk Cumb ... 97 H11
Bridell Pembks ... 37 N2
Bridestowe Devon ... 7 P7
Brideswell Abers ... 140 F8
Bridford Devon ... 8 F7
Bridge Kent ... 35 L11
Bridge End Cumb ... 88 G10
Bridge End Cumb ... 98 D8
Bridge End Devon ... 5 L7
Bridge End Dur ... 100 C11
Bridge End Essex ... 46 B5
Bridge End Lincs ... 68 C5
Bridgefoot Angus ... 124 H6
Bridgefoot Cumb ... 97 L12
Bridge Green Essex ... 45 N4
Bridgehampton Somset ... 22 D8
Bridge Hewick N York ... 85 M1
Bridgehill Dur ... 100 E6
Bridgehouse Gate N York ... 84 H2
Bridgemary Hants ... 13 K4
Bridgemere Ches E ... 64 D3
Bridgend Abers ... 140 D8
Bridgend Ag & B ... 103 L2
Bridgend Ag & B ... 110 H9
Bridgend Angus ... 132 E10
Bridgend Brdgnd ... 27 L6
Bridgend Cerdgn ... 48 B11
Bridgend Cumb ... 89 L4
Bridgend D & G ... 106 E8
Bridgend Devon ... 5 J7
Bridgend Fife ... 124 H10
Bridgend Moray ... 140 B9
Bridgend P & K ... 124 C8
Bridgend W Loth ... 115 J3
Bridgend of Lintrathen Angus ... 124 F2
Bridge of Alford Abers ... 140 E12
Bridge of Allan Stirlg ... 114 C12
Bridge of Avon Moray ... 139 L12
Bridge of Avon Moray ... 139 M8
Bridge of Balgie P & K ... 122 F7
Bridge of Brewlands Angus ... 131 M12
Bridge of Brown Highld ... 139 L11
Bridge of Cally P & K ... 124 C2
Bridge of Canny Abers ... 132 G5
Bridge of Craigisla Angus ... 124 E2
Bridge of Dee D & G ... 96 E6
Bridge of Don C Aber ... 133 M2
Bridge of Dye Abers ... 132 G7
Bridge of Earn P & K ... 124 E1
Bridge of Ericht P & K ... 122 E5
Bridge of Feugh Abers ... 132 H5
Bridge of Gairn Abers ... 131 Q5
Bridge of Gaur P & K ... 122 E5
Bridge of Marnoch Abers ... 140 F6
Bridge of Muchalls Abers ... 133 L5
Bridge of Orchy Ag & B ... 121 P5
Bridge of Tilt P & K ... 130 H1
Bridge of Tynet Moray ... 140 B4
Bridge of Walls Shet ... 147 h6
Bridge of Weir Rens ... 113 M8
Bridge Reeve Devon ... 7 K4
Bridges Shrops ... 63 J4
Bridge Sollers Herefs ... 40 G4
Bridge Street Suffk ... 58 C10
Bridgetown Cnwll ... 7 J7
Bridgetown Somset ... 20 E7
Bridge Trafford Ches W ... 75 M9
Bridge Yate S Glos ... 29 K8

Bridgham Norfk ... 58 E3
Bridgnorth Shrops ... 52 D2
Bridgwater Somset ... 21 L6
Bridgwater Services Somset ... 21 M6
Bridlington E R Yk ... 87 M2
Bridport Dorset ... 10 D6
Bridstow Herefs ... 41 J7
Brierfield Lancs ... 84 C8
Brierley Barns ... 78 C2
Brierley Gloucs ... 41 J8
Brierley Herefs ... 51 N9
Brierley Hill Dudley ... 52 G3
Brierlow Bar Derbys ... 77 K9
Brierton Hartpl ... 101 L12
Briery Cumb ... 89 J2
Brigg N Linc ... 79 P2
Briggate Norfk ... 71 L7
Briggswath N York ... 92 H5
Brigham Cumb ... 89 J2
Brigham Cumb ... 97 M12
Brigham E R Yk ... 87 K4
Brighouse Calder ... 84 H10
Brighstone IoW ... 12 G8
Brightgate Derbys ... 77 P11
Brighthampton Oxon ... 42 H11
Brightholmlee Sheff ... 77 P5
Brightley Devon ... 8 B5
Brightling E Susx ... 16 B6
Brightlingsea Essex ... 47 K8
Brighton Br & H ... 15 K10
Brighton Cnwll ... 3 M4
Brighton City Airport W Susx ... 14 H9
Brighton le Sands Sefton ... 75 K4
Brightons Falk ... 114 G6
Brightwalton W Berk ... 31 J6
Brightwalton Green W Berk ... 31 J6
Brightwalton Holt W Berk ... 31 J7
Brightwell Suffk ... 47 N3
Brightwell Baldwin Oxon ... 31 N4
Brightwell-cum-Sotwell Oxon ... 31 M4
Brightwell Upperton Oxon ... 31 N3
Brignall Dur ... 90 H4
Brig o'Turk Stirlg ... 122 F11
Brigsley NE Lin ... 80 E3
Brigsteer Cumb ... 89 M9
Brigstock Nhants ... 55 N4
Brill Bucks ... 43 N9
Brill Cnwll ... 2 H8
Brilley Herefs ... 51 J11
Brimfield Herefs ... 51 N7
Brimfield Cross Herefs ... 51 P7
Brimington Derbys ... 78 C9
Brimley Devon ... 8 E9
Brimpsfield Gloucs ... 41 Q9
Brimpton W Berk ... 31 L9
Brimscombe Gloucs ... 41 P11
Brimstage Wirral ... 75 J7
Brincliffe Sheff ... 77 Q7
Brind E R Yk ... 86 D9
Brindham Somset ... 22 C5
Brindister Shet ... 147 h6
Brindle Lancs ... 83 N10
Brindley Ches E ... 63 Q2
Brineton Staffs ... 64 E9
Bringhurst Leics ... 55 K2
Brington Cambs ... 56 C5
Bringsty Common Herefs ... 52 C9
Brinian Ork ... 147 c3
Briningham Norfk ... 70 F5
Brinkely Notts ... 66 H2
Brinkhill Lincs ... 80 G9
Brinkley Cambs ... 57 M9
Brinklow Warwks ... 54 D5
Brinkworth Wilts ... 30 B5
Brinscall Lancs ... 83 N11
Brinscombe Somset ... 21 P3
Brinsea N Som ... 28 F10
Brinsley Notts ... 66 D2
Brinsop Herefs ... 40 F3
Brinsworth Rothm ... 78 C6
Brinton Norfk ... 70 F5
Brinyan Ork ... 147 c3
Brisco Cumb ... 98 E8
Brisley Norfk ... 70 D8
Brislington Bristl ... 29 J8
Brissenden Green Kent ... 16 G3
Bristol Bristl ... 29 J8
Bristol Airport N Som ... 28 G9
Bristol Zoo Gardens Bristl ... 28 H7
Briston Norfk ... 70 F6
Brisworthy Devon ... 5 J4
Britannia Lancs ... 84 C11
Britford Wilts ... 23 P8
Brithdir Caerph ... 39 Q11
Brithdir Gwynd ... 61 N8
British Legion Village Kent ... 34 C10
Briton Ferry Neath ... 26 H1
Britwell Salome Oxon ... 31 N4
Brixham Torbay ... 5 Q6
Brixton Devon ... 5 J6
Brixton Gt Lon ... 33 K7
Brixton Deverill Wilts ... 23 J6
Brixworth Nhants ... 55 J6
Brize Norton Oxon ... 42 G10
Brize Norton Airport Oxon ... 42 G10
Broad Alley Worcs ... 52 G7
Broad Blunsdon Swindn ... 30 D4
Broadbottom Tamesd ... 77 J5
Broadbridge W Susx ... 13 P4
Broadbridge Heath W Susx ... 14 G4
Broad Campden Gloucs ... 42 C4
Broad Carr Calder ... 84 G11
Broad Chalke Wilts ... 23 M8
Broad Clough Lancs ... 84 C10
Broadclyst Devon ... 9 J5
Broadfield Pembks ... 37 M9
Broadford Highld ... 135 L11
Broad Ford Kent ... 16 C3
Broadford Bridge W Susx ... 14 G6
Broadgairhill Border ... 106 G7
Broadgrass Green Suffk ... 58 E8
Broad Green Cambs ... 57 N8
Broad Green Essex ... 46 F6
Broad Green Worcs ... 52 E9
Broad Green Worcs ... 53 J4
Broadhaugh Border ... 117 J10
Broad Haven Pembks ... 36 G8
Broadheath Traffd ... 76 E6
Broadheath Worcs ... 52 C8
Broadhembury Devon ... 9 L4
Broadhempston Devon ... 5 N5
Broad Hill Cambs ... 57 L5
Broad Hinton Wilts ... 30 D6
Broadholme Lincs ... 79 M9
Broadland Row E Susx ... 16 E7
Broadlay Carmth ... 38 B10
Broad Laying Hants ... 31 J10
Broadley Lancs ... 84 C12
Broadley Moray ... 140 B3
Broadley Common Essex ... 45 M10
Broad Marston Worcs ... 42 C3
Broadmayne Dorset ... 10 H7
Broadmere Hants ... 25 K4

Broadmoor Gloucs ... 41 K8
Broadmoor Pembks ... 37 L9
Broadnymett Devon ... 8 D4
Broad Oak Carmth ... 38 E7
Broad Oak Cumb ... 88 F6
Broadoak Dorset ... 10 C5
Broad Oak E Susx ... 15 R6
Broad Oak E Susx ... 16 E7
Broadoak Gloucs ... 41 L9
Broad Oak Hants ... 25 N3
Broad Oak Herefs ... 40 G7
Broad Oak Kent ... 35 L10
Broad Oak St Hel ... 75 P5
Broadoak Wrexhm ... 75 L12
Broad Road Suffk ... 59 K5
Broads Green Essex ... 46 C9
Broadsands Torbay ... 5 Q7
Broadstairs Kent ... 35 Q9
Broadstone BCP ... 11 N6
Broadstone Mons ... 40 G11
Broadstone Shrops ... 51 P3
Broad Street E Susx ... 16 E7
Broad Street Essex ... 45 Q8
Broad Street Kent ... 17 K3
Broad Street Kent ... 34 E11
Broad Street Medway ... 34 D8
Broad Street Wilts ... 30 C10
Broad Street Green Essex ... 46 F9
Broad Town Wilts ... 30 C7
Broadwas Worcs ... 52 D9
Broadwater Herts ... 45 J7
Broadwater W Susx ... 14 G10
Broadwaters Worcs ... 52 F5
Broadway Carmth ... 37 Q8
Broadway Carmth ... 38 B10
Broadway Pembks ... 36 G8
Broadway Somset ... 21 M10
Broadway Suffk ... 59 M5
Broadway Worcs ... 42 C4
Broadwell Gloucs ... 41 J9
Broadwell Gloucs ... 42 G6
Broadwell Oxon ... 42 F10
Broadwell Warwks ... 54 D7
Broadwey Dorset ... 10 G8
Broadwindsor Dorset ... 10 C4
Broadwood Kelly Devon ... 8 B4
Broadwoodwidger Devon ... 7 M7
Brobury Herefs ... 40 G3
Brochel Highld ... 135 K9
Brochroy Ag & B ... 121 J6
Brock Lancs ... 83 L7
Brockamin Worcs ... 52 E10
Brockbridge Hants ... 25 K9
Brockdish Norfk ... 59 J5
Brockencote Worcs ... 52 G6
Brockenhurst Hants ... 12 F4
Brocketsbrae S Lans ... 105 Q2
Brockford Green Suffk ... 58 G7
Brockford Street Suffk ... 58 G7
Brockhall Nhants ... 54 G8
Brockham Surrey ... 14 H1
Brockhampton Gloucs ... 41 R7
Brockhampton Gloucs ... 42 B7
Brockhampton Hants ... 13 M3
Brockhampton Herefs ... 41 J5
Brockhampton Green Dorset ... 10 H3
Brockholes Kirk ... 77 M2
Brockhurst Derbys ... 77 Q10
Brockhurst Warwks ... 54 D4
Brocklebank Cumb ... 98 C9
Brocklesby Lincs ... 80 C1
Brockley N Som ... 28 G9
Brockley Suffk ... 58 B6
Brockley Green Suffk ... 46 C2
Brockley Green Suffk ... 58 B9
Brockleymoor Cumb ... 98 F11
Brockmoor Dudley ... 52 G3
Brockscombe Devon ... 7 N6
Brock's Green Hants ... 31 K10
Brockton Shrops ... 51 P2
Brockton Shrops ... 51 P3
Brockton Shrops ... 63 K11
Brockton Shrops ... 64 E2
Brockton Staffs ... 64 F6
Brockweir Gloucs ... 28 H2
Brockwood Park Hants ... 25 K8
Brockworth Gloucs ... 41 P8
Brocton Cnwll ... 3 M2
Brocton Staffs ... 64 H8
Brodick N Ayrs ... 103 Q3
Brodie Moray ... 138 H4
Brodsworth Donc ... 78 E3
Brogaig Highld ... 134 H2
Brogborough C Beds ... 44 D4
Brokenborough Wilts ... 29 Q4
Broken Cross Ches E ... 76 G9
Broken Cross Ches W ... 76 C9
Brokerswood Wilts ... 23 J3
Bromborough Wirral ... 75 K7
Brome Suffk ... 58 H5
Brome Street Suffk ... 58 H5
Bromeswell Suffk ... 59 L10
Bromfield Cumb ... 97 M9
Bromfield Shrops ... 51 N5
Bromham Bed ... 55 P10
Bromham Wilts ... 29 Q9
Bromley Barns ... 77 Q4
Bromley Dudley ... 52 G3
Bromley Gt Lon ... 33 M8
Bromley Shrops ... 52 D2
Bromley Common Gt Lon ... 33 M8
Bromley Cross Bolton ... 76 D1
Bromley Cross Essex ... 47 J6
Bromley Green Kent ... 16 H3
Bromlow Shrops ... 63 K11
Brompton Medway ... 34 D8
Brompton N York ... 91 P7
Brompton-by-Sawdon N York ... 93 J10
Brompton-on-Swale N York ... 91 L7
Brompton Ralph Somset ... 20 H7
Brompton Regis Somset ... 20 E7
Bromsash Herefs ... 41 K7
Bromsberrow Gloucs ... 41 L5
Bromsberrow Heath Gloucs ... 41 L5
Bromsgrove Worcs ... 52 H6
Bromstead Heath Staffs ... 64 E8
Bromyard Herefs ... 52 C9
Bromyard Downs Herefs ... 52 C9
Bronaber Gwynd ... 61 N6
Bronant Cerdgn ... 49 L2
Broncroft Shrops ... 51 P3
Brongest Cerdgn ... 48 E11
Bronington Wrexhm ... 63 N4
Bronllys Powys ... 39 Q4
Bronwydd Carmth ... 38 B7
Bronydd Powys ... 40 D3
Bronygarth Shrops ... 63 J5
Brook Carmth ... 37 P8
Brook Hants ... 24 D10
Brook Hants ... 24 E7
Brook IoW ... 12 F7
Brook Kent ... 17 J2
Brook Surrey ... 14 D3
Brook Surrey ... 14 F2
Brooke Norfk ... 71 L12
Brooke Rutlnd ... 67 K11
Brookenby Lincs ... 80 D5
Brook End Bed ... 56 C11
Brook End C Beds ... 56 C11
Brook End Cambs ... 56 Q6
Brook End M Keyn ... 44 C4

Brookfield Rens ... 113 N8
Brookhampton Oxon ... 31 M3
Brookhampton Somset ... 22 E8
Brook Hill Hants ... 24 D10
Brook House Denbgs ... 74 G10
Brookhouse Lancs ... 83 M2
Brookhouse Rothm ... 78 E6
Brookhouse Green Ches E ... 76 E11
Brookhouses Derbys ... 77 J6
Brookland Kent ... 16 H5
Brooklands Traffd ... 76 E5
Brookmans Park Herts ... 45 J11
Brooks Powys ... 62 G12
Brooksby Leics ... 66 H9
Brooks End Kent ... 35 N9
Brooks Green W Susx ... 14 G6
Brook Street Essex ... 33 Q4
Brook Street Kent ... 16 G4
Brook Street Kent ... 58 B11
Brook Street W Susx ... 15 K5
Brookthorpe Gloucs ... 41 N9
Brookville Norfk ... 57 P1
Brookwood Surrey ... 32 D11
Broom C Beds ... 44 H3
Broom Rothm ... 78 D5
Broom Warwks ... 53 K10
Broombank Worcs ... 52 C6
Broome Norfk ... 59 M2
Broome Shrops ... 51 M4
Broome Worcs ... 52 G5
Broomedge Warrtn ... 76 D6
Broome Park Nthumb ... 109 J7
Broomer's Corner W Susx ... 14 G6
Broomershill W Susx ... 14 F7
Broomfield Kent ... 34 E11
Broomfield Kent ... 35 M9
Broomfield Somset ... 21 K7
Broomfields Shrops ... 63 M8
Broomfleet E R Yk ... 86 G9
Broom Green Norfk ... 70 E7
Broomhall W & M ... 32 D9
Broomhaugh Nthumb ... 100 C6
Broom Hill Barns ... 78 C3
Broom Hill Dorset ... 11 P4
Broom Hill Notts ... 66 E3
Broomhill Nthumb ... 109 L9
Broom Hill Worcs ... 52 G5
Broomhill Green Ches E ... 64 B3
Broomley Nthumb ... 100 D6
Broompark Dur ... 100 G10
Broom's Green Gloucs ... 41 L5
Broomsthorpe Norfk ... 70 C6
Broom Street Kent ... 35 J10
Brora Highld ... 146 G4
Broseley Shrops ... 64 C11
Brotherhouse Bar Lincs ... 68 G11
Brotherlee Dur ... 99 P10
Brothertoft Lincs ... 68 G3
Brotherton N York ... 85 P9
Brotton R & Cl ... 92 E3
Broubster Highld ... 151 K4
Brough Cumb ... 90 C4
Brough Derbys ... 77 M7
Brough E R Yk ... 86 H10
Brough Highld ... 151 M2
Brough Notts ... 79 L12
Brough Shrops ... 63 P4
Brough Sowerby Cumb ... 90 C4
Broughall Shrops ... 63 P4
Brougham Cumb ... 89 Q3
Broughton Border ... 106 E3
Broughton Bucks ... 44 B9
Broughton Cambs ... 56 F5
Broughton Flints ... 75 K11
Broughton Hants ... 24 E7
Broughton Lancs ... 83 M8
Broughton M Keyn ... 44 C4
Broughton N Linc ... 79 P2
Broughton N York ... 84 F5
Broughton N York ... 92 F11
Broughton Nhants ... 55 K5
Broughton Oxon ... 43 J4
Broughton Salfd ... 76 F3
Broughton Staffs ... 64 F6
Broughton V Glam ... 27 K7
Broughton Astley Leics ... 54 E2
Broughton Beck Cumb ... 89 J10
Broughton Gifford Wilts ... 29 P9
Broughton Green Worcs ... 52 H8
Broughton Hackett Worcs ... 52 H9
Broughton-in-Furness Cumb ... 88 G9
Broughton Mains D & G ... 95 N9
Broughton Mills Cumb ... 88 H8
Broughton Moor Cumb ... 97 L11
Broughton Poggs Oxon ... 42 F11
Broughton Tower Cumb ... 88 G9
Broughty Ferry C Dund ... 125 J7
Brough with St Giles N York ... 91 L7
Brow End Cumb ... 88 H11
Browhouses D & G ... 97 P5
Brown Candover Hants ... 25 K5
Brown Edge Lancs ... 83 J12
Brown Edge Staffs ... 64 G1
Brown Heath Ches W ... 75 M10
Brownheath Shrops ... 63 M6
Brownhill Abers ... 141 K8
Brownhills Fife ... 125 K9
Brownhills Wsall ... 65 K11
Brownieside Nthumb ... 109 K5
Browninghill Green Hants ... 31 M10
Brown Lees Staffs ... 64 G11
Brownlow Heath Ches E ... 76 F11
Brownrigg Cumb ... 88 D3
Brownrigg Cumb ... 97 M9
Brownsea Island Dorset ... 11 N7
Brown's Green Birm ... 53 K2
Brownsham Devon ... 18 F8
Browns Hill Gloucs ... 41 P11
Brownsover Warwks ... 54 E5
Brownston Devon ... 5 L6
Brown Street Suffk ... 58 F8
Brow-of-the-Hill Norfk ... 69 M8
Browston Green Norfk ... 71 P11
Broxa N York ... 93 J8
Broxbourne Herts ... 45 L10
Broxburn E Loth ... 116 F6
Broxburn W Loth ... 115 J7
Broxfield Nthumb ... 109 K6
Broxted Essex ... 45 Q5
Broxton Ches W ... 63 N2
Broyle Side E Susx ... 15 N8
Bruan Highld ... 151 N8
Bruar P & K ... 130 H1
Bruchag Ag & B ... 112 D9
Bruera Ches W ... 75 M11
Bruern Abbey Oxon ... 42 F7
Bruichladdich Ag & B ... 110 G9
Bruisyard Suffk ... 59 L7
Bruisyard Street Suffk ... 59 L7
Brumby N Linc ... 79 M2
Brund Staffs ... 77 L11
Brundall Norfk ... 71 L10
Brundish Suffk ... 59 K7
Brundish Street Suffk ... 59 K6
Brunery Highld ... 127 N10
Brunnion Cnwll ... 2 E7
Brunslow Shrops ... 51 L4
Brunswick Village N u Ty ... 100 G4
Bruntcliffe Leeds ... 85 K10
Bruntingthorpe Leics ... 54 F2
Brunthwaite C Brad ... 84 F6
Bruntland Abers ... 140 C11
Brunton Fife ... 124 H11
Brunton Nthumb ... 109 K4

Brunton Fife ... 124 G8
Brunton Nthumb ... 109 K5
Brunton Wilts ... 30 F11
Brushford Devon ... 8 C3
Brushford Somset ... 20 E8
Bruton Somset ... 22 F6
Bryan's Green Worcs ... 52 G7
Bryanston Dorset ... 11 L3
Bryant's Bottom Bucks ... 32 B2
Brydekirk D & G ... 97 N4
Brymbo Wrexhm ... 63 J1
Brympton Somset ... 22 C10
Bryn Carmth ... 26 E2
Bryn Ches W ... 75 Q9
Bryn Neath ... 27 J4
Bryn Wigan ... 75 P3
Brynamman Carmth ... 38 H9
Brynberian Pembks ... 37 L3
Bryn-côch Neath ... 26 H2
Bryncae Rhondd ... 27 K6
Bryncethin Brdgnd ... 27 L5
Bryncir Gwynd ... 60 H3
Bryncroes Gwynd ... 60 C6
Bryncrug Gwynd ... 61 K11
Bryn Du IoA ... 72 G9
Bryn-Eden Gwynd ... 61 M6
Bryneglwys Denbgs ... 62 G3
Brynfields Wrexhm ... 63 K3
Brynford Flints ... 74 G9
Bryn Gates Wigan ... 75 Q3
Bryn Golau Rhondd ... 27 L5
Bryngwran IoA ... 72 F8
Bryngwyn Mons ... 40 E10
Bryngwyn Powys ... 50 G4
Bryn-Henllan Pembks ... 37 K3
Brynhoffnant Cerdgn ... 48 E10
Bryning Lancs ... 83 J9
Brynithel Blae G ... 40 B8
Bryn-mawr Gwynd ... 60 D5
Brynmawr Blae G ... 40 B9
Brynmenyn Brdgnd ... 27 L5
Brynmill Swans ... 26 F4
Brynna Rhondd ... 27 N6
Bryn-penarth Powys ... 62 F11
Brynrefail Gwynd ... 73 J11
Brynrefail IoA ... 72 H6
Brynsadler Rhondd ... 27 N6
Bryn Saith Marchog Denbgs ... 62 G2
Brynsiencyn IoA ... 72 H10
Brynteg IoA ... 72 H7
Bryn-y-bal Flints ... 73 J10
Bryn-y-Maen Conwy ... 73 P8
Bryn-yr-Eos Wrexhm ... 63 J4
Bualintur Highld ... 134 G11
Buarth-draw Flints ... 74 G8
Bubbenhall Warwks ... 54 B6
Bubwith E R Yk ... 86 D8
Buccleuch Border ... 107 J7
Buchanan Smithy Stirlg ... 113 N3
Buchanhaven Abers ... 141 Q6
Buchanty P & K ... 123 N7
Buchany Stirlg ... 123 J12
Buchlyvie Stirlg ... 113 J9
Buckabank Cumb ... 98 D9
Buckden Cambs ... 56 D7
Buckden N York ... 90 F11
Buckenham Norfk ... 71 M11
Buckerell Devon ... 9 L5
Buckfast Devon ... 5 M3
Buckfastleigh Devon ... 5 M3
Buckhaven Fife ... 115 Q2
Buckholt Mons ... 40 H8
Buckhorn Devon ... 7 M5
Buckhorn Weston Dorset ... 22 G9
Buckhurst Hill Essex ... 33 M3
Buckie Moray ... 140 C3
Buckingham Bucks ... 43 P5
Buckland Bucks ... 44 C9
Buckland Devon ... 5 L8
Buckland Gloucs ... 42 C4
Buckland Herts ... 45 L5
Buckland Kent ... 17 P2
Buckland Oxon ... 30 H3
Buckland Surrey ... 33 J12
Buckland Brewer Devon ... 18 H9
Buckland Common Bucks ... 44 C10
Buckland Dinham Somset ... 22 G3
Buckland Filleigh Devon ... 7 P4
Buckland in the Moor Devon ... 8 D10
Buckland Monachorum Devon ... 4 H3
Buckland Newton Dorset ... 10 H3
Buckland Ripers Dorset ... 10 G8
Buckland St Mary Somset ... 21 K10
Buckland-Tout-Saints Devon ... 5 M8
Bucklebury W Berk ... 31 L8
Bucklers Hard Hants ... 12 G5
Bucklesham Suffk ... 47 M3
Buckley Flints ... 75 J11
Buckley Green Warwks ... 53 M7
Bucklow Hill Ches E ... 76 D7
Buckminster Leics ... 67 L7
Bucknall C Stke ... 64 G3
Bucknall Lincs ... 80 D10
Bucknell Oxon ... 43 M6
Bucknell Shrops ... 51 K6
Buckpool Moray ... 140 C3
Bucksburn C Aber ... 133 L2
Buck's Cross Devon ... 18 G8
Bucks Green W Susx ... 14 F4
Buckshaw Village Lancs ... 83 M11
Bucks Hill Herts ... 32 F2
Bucks Horn Oak Hants ... 25 P5
Buck's Mills Devon ... 18 G8
Buckton E R Yk ... 93 N12
Buckton Herefs ... 51 L6
Buckton Nthumb ... 108 H2
Buckworth Cambs ... 56 C5
Budby Notts ... 78 F10
Buddileigh Staffs ... 64 D2
Bude Cnwll ... 7 J4
Budge's Shop Cnwll ... 4 G5
Budlake Devon ... 9 J5
Budle Nthumb ... 109 J2
Budleigh Salterton Devon ... 9 K8
Budlett's Common E Susx ... 15 N6
Budock Water Cnwll ... 3 K6
Buerton Ches E ... 64 C4
Bugbrooke Nhants ... 54 G9
Bugford Devon ... 5 P6
Buglawton Ches E ... 76 G11
Bugle Cnwll ... 3 N4
Bugley Dorset ... 22 G9
Bugthorpe E R Yk ... 86 E4
Buildwas Shrops ... 64 B11
Builth Road Powys ... 50 E10
Builth Wells Powys ... 50 E10
Bulbourne Herts ... 44 D9
Bulbridge Wilts ... 23 N7
Bulby Lincs ... 67 Q7
Bulford Wilts ... 23 Q5
Bulford Camp Wilts ... 23 Q5
Bulkeley Ches E ... 63 P2
Bulkington Warwks ... 54 C3
Bulkington Wilts ... 29 Q10
Bulkworthy Devon ... 18 H9
Bullamoor N York ... 91 P8
Bullbridge Derbys ... 66 B2

Bullbridge Derbys ... 66 B2
Bullbrook Br For ... 32 C8
Bullen's Green Herts ... 45 J10
Bulley Gloucs ... 41 M8
Bullgill Cumb ... 97 M10
Bullinghope Herefs ... 40 G4
Bullington Hants ... 24 G5
Bullington Lincs ... 80 B8
Bullockstone Kent ... 35 L9
Bull's Green Herts ... 45 K8
Bull's Green Norfk ... 59 N2
Bulmer Essex ... 46 E4
Bulmer N York ... 86 C2
Bulmer Tye Essex ... 46 E4
Bulphan Thurr ... 34 B5
Bulstone Devon ... 9 L7
Bulstrode Herts ... 44 E11
Bulverhythe E Susx ... 16 D9
Bulwark Abers ... 141 M7
Bulwell C Nott ... 66 E3
Bulwick Nhants ... 55 N2
Bumble's Green Essex ... 45 M10
Bunacaimb Highld ... 127 N8
Bunarkaig Highld ... 128 E7
Bunbury Ches E ... 75 P12
Bunchrew Highld ... 138 B6
Buncton W Susx ... 14 G8
Bundalloch Highld ... 136 B10
Bunessan Ag & B ... 119 L8
Bungay Suffk ... 59 L3
Bunkers Hill Lincs ... 68 E1
Bunnahabhain Ag & B ... 111 J4
Bunny Notts ... 66 F6
Buntait Highld ... 137 N9
Buntingford Herts ... 45 L6
Bunwell Norfk ... 58 H2
Bunwell Hill Norfk ... 58 H2
Bupton Derbys ... 65 N5
Burbage Derbys ... 77 K9
Burbage Leics ... 54 D4
Burbage Wilts ... 30 F10
Burcher Herefs ... 51 K8
Burchett's Green W & M ... 32 B6
Burcombe Wilts ... 23 N7
Burcot Oxon ... 31 M3
Burcot Worcs ... 52 H6
Burcote Shrops ... 52 D2
Burcott Bucks ... 44 B8
Burcott Bucks ... 44 C7
Burdale N York ... 86 G3
Bures Essex ... 46 F5
Burford Oxon ... 42 F8
Burford Shrops ... 51 P7
Burg Ag & B ... 119 L4
Burgate Hants ... 23 P9
Burgates Hants ... 25 N7
Burge End Herts ... 44 G5
Burgess Hill W Susx ... 15 K7
Burgh Suffk ... 59 J10
Burgh by Sands Cumb ... 98 C6
Burgh Castle Norfk ... 71 P11
Burghclere Hants ... 31 K10
Burghead Moray ... 139 L2
Burghfield W Berk ... 31 N9
Burghfield Common W Berk ... 31 N9
Burgh Heath Surrey ... 33 J10
Burgh Hill E Susx ... 16 C5
Burghill Herefs ... 40 G3
Burgh Island Devon ... 5 K8
Burgh le Marsh Lincs ... 81 J10
Burgh next Aylsham Norfk ... 71 J7
Burgh on Bain Lincs ... 80 E6
Burgh St Margaret Norfk ... 71 N9
Burgh St Peter Norfk ... 59 P2
Burghwallis Donc ... 78 E1
Burham Kent ... 34 C10
Buriton Hants ... 25 M9
Burland Ches E ... 63 Q2
Burlawn Cnwll ... 6 E10
Burleigh Gloucs ... 41 P10
Burlescombe Devon ... 20 G10
Burleston Dorset ... 11 J5
Burlestone Devon ... 5 N7
Burley Hants ... 12 C4
Burley Rutlnd ... 67 L10
Burley Shrops ... 51 N4
Burleydam Ches E ... 64 B3
Burley Gate Herefs ... 41 J3
Burley in Wharfedale C Brad ... 84 H6
Burley Lawn Hants ... 12 C4
Burley Street Hants ... 12 C4
Burley Wood Head C Brad ... 84 H6
Burlingham Green Norfk ... 71 M10
Burlingjobb Powys ... 51 J9
Burlington Shrops ... 64 E10
Burlton Shrops ... 63 M7
Burmarsh Kent ... 17 K4
Burmington Warwks ... 42 F4
Burn N York ... 86 B9
Burnage Manch ... 76 F5
Burnaston Derbys ... 65 P6
Burnbanks Cumb ... 89 N3
Burnbrae N Lans ... 114 E9
Burn Bridge N York ... 85 L5
Burnby E R Yk ... 86 F6
Burn Cross Sheff ... 77 Q4
Burndell W Susx ... 14 E10
Burnden Bolton ... 76 D2
Burnedge Rochdl ... 76 G2
Burneside Cumb ... 89 N7
Burneston N York ... 91 M9
Burnett BaNES ... 29 K9
Burnfoot Border ... 107 L7
Burnfoot Border ... 107 N6
Burnfoot D & G ... 106 C11
Burnfoot D & G ... 107 J12
Burnfoot D & G ... 107 K10
Burnfoot P & K ... 123 P12
Burnham Bucks ... 32 D6
Burnham Deepdale Norfk ... 69 Q3
Burnham Green Herts ... 45 K8
Burnham Market Norfk ... 70 B4
Burnham Norton Norfk ... 70 B4
Burnham-on-Crouch Essex ... 34 G3
Burnham-on-Sea Somset ... 21 M4
Burnham Overy Norfk ... 70 C3
Burnham Overy Staithe Norfk ... 70 C3
Burnham Thorpe Norfk ... 70 C4
Burnhead D & G ... 105 Q10
Burnhervie Abers ... 140 H12
Burnhill Green Staffs ... 64 E12
Burnhope Dur ... 100 F8
Burnhouse N Ayrs ... 113 M11
Burniston N York ... 93 L9
Burnley Lancs ... 84 C9
Burnmouth Border ... 117 L9
Burn Naze Lancs ... 82 H6
Burn of Cambus Stirlg ... 123 J12
Burnopfield Dur ... 100 F7
Burnrigg Cumb ... 98 F6
Burnsall N York ... 84 H3
Burnside Angus ... 124 H2
Burnside Fife ... 124 E11
Burnside Moray ... 139 L4
Burnside W Loth ... 115 K6
Burnside of Duntrune Angus ... 125 J6

Burntcommon – Chargrove 159

Burntcommon Surrey 32 E11
Burntheath Derbys 65 N6
Burnt Heath Essex 47 J6
Burnt Hill W Berk 31 M7
Burnthouse Cnwll 3 J7
Burnt Houses Dur 91 J2
Burntisland Fife 115 N4
Burnt Oak E Susx 15 P5
Burnton E Ayrs 105 J8
Burntwood Flints 75 J10
Burntwood Staffs 65 K10
Burntwood Green Staffs 65 K10
Burnt Yates N York 85 K3
Burnworthy Somset 21 K10
Burpham Surrey 32 E12
Burpham W Susx 14 E9
Burradon N Tyne 100 H4
Burradon Nthumb 108 F8
Burrafirth Shet 147 k2
Burras Cnwll 2 H7
Burraton Cnwll 4 F3
Burravoe Shet 147 j4
Burrells Cumb 89 R3
Burrelton P & K 124 D5
Burridge Devon 9 Q3
Burridge Devon 19 L6
Burridge Hants 13 J3
Burrill N York 91 L9
Burringham N Linc 79 L2
Burrington Devon 19 M10
Burrington Herefs 51 M6
Burrington N Som 28 G10
Burrough End Cambs 57 M9
Burrough Green Cambs 57 M9
Burrough on the Hill Leics 67 J10
Burrow Lancs 89 Q11
Burrow Somset 20 E5
Burrow Bridge Somset 21 M7
Burrowhill Surrey 32 D9
Burrows Cross Surrey 14 F2
Burry Swans 26 C4
Burry Green Swans 26 C4
Burry Port Carmth 26 C2
Burscough Lancs 75 M1
Burscough Bridge Lancs 75 M1
Bursea E R Yk 86 E8
Burshill E R Yk 87 K5
Bursledon Hants 12 H3
Burslem C Stke 64 F2
Burstall Suffk 47 K3
Burstock Dorset 10 C4
Burston Norfk 58 H4
Burston Staffs 64 H6
Burstow Surrey 15 K3
Burstwick E R Yk 87 N9
Burtersett N York 90 E9
Burtholme Cumb 98 G5
Burthorpe Green Suffk 57 P8
Burthwaite Cumb 98 E8
Burthy Cnwll 3 M3
Burtle Hill Somset 21 N4
Burtoft Lincs 68 E5
Burton BCP 12 C6
Burton Ches W 75 K9
Burton Ches W 75 N11
Burton Dorset 10 G6
Burton Nthumb 109 K3
Burton Pembks 37 J9
Burton Somset 21 K4
Burton Somset 22 C10
Burton Wilts 22 H7
Burton Wilts 29 N6
Burton Agnes E R Yk 87 L3
Burton Bradstock Dorset 10 D7
Burton-by-Lincoln Lincs 79 N9
Burton Coggles Lincs 67 N7
Burton Dassett Warwks 54 C10
Burton End Essex 45 P7
Burton End Suffk 46 B3
Burton Fleming E R Yk 93 M12
Burton Green Warwks 53 P5
Burton Green Wrexhm 75 K12
Burton Hastings Warwks 54 C3
Burton-in-Kendal Cumb 89 N11
Burton-in-Kendal Services Cumb 89 N11
Burton in Lonsdale N York 89 Q12
Burton Joyce Notts 66 G3
Burton Latimer Nhants 55 M6
Burton Lazars Leics 67 J9
Burton Leonard N York 85 L2
Burton on the Wolds Leics 66 F8
Burton Overy Leics 54 H1
Burton Pedwardine Lincs 68 C4
Burton Pidsea E R Yk 87 N9
Burton Salmon N York 85 P9
Burton's Green Essex 46 E6
Burton upon Stather N Linc 86 G11
Burton upon Trent Staffs 65 N7
Burton Waters Lincs 79 M9
Burtonwood Warrtn 75 P5
Burtonwood Services Warrtn 75 P5
Burwardsley Ches W 75 N12
Burwarton Shrops 52 B4
Burwash E Susx 16 B6
Burwash Common E Susx 16 B6
Burwash Weald E Susx 16 B6
Burwell Cambs 57 L7
Burwell Lincs 80 G8
Burwen IoA 72 G5
Burwick Ork 147 c6
Bury Bury 76 E1
Bury Cambs 56 F4
Bury Somset 20 E8
Bury W Susx 14 E8
Bury End C Beds 44 G5
Bury Green Herts 45 N7
Bury St Edmunds Suffk 58 C8
Burythorpe N York 86 E2
Busby E Rens 113 Q10
Busby Stoop N York 91 P10
Buscot Oxon 30 F3
Bush Abers 133 J11
Bush Cnwll 7 J3
Bush Bank Herefs 51 M10
Bushbury Wolves 64 G11
Bushby Leics 66 G11
Bushey Herts 32 G3
Bushey Heath Herts 32 G3
Bush Green Norfk 59 J3
Bush Green Suffk 58 D9
Bush Hill Park Gt Lon 33 L3
Bushley Worcs 41 P5
Bushley Green Worcs 41 N5
Bushmead Bed 56 C8
Bushmoor Shrops 51 M3
Bushton Wilts 30 C7
Busk Cumb 98 H10
Buslingthorpe Lincs 79 Q6
Bussage Gloucs 41 P11
Bussex Somset 21 M6
Butcher's Cross E Susx 15 Q6
Butcombe N Som 28 G10
Bute Ag & B 112 F7
Butleigh Somset 22 C6
Butleigh Wootton Somset 22 C6
Butler's Cross Bucks 44 B10
Butler's Hill Notts 66 E3
Butlers Marston Warwks 53 Q10
Butley Suffk 59 M10
Butley High Corner Suffk 59 M10
Buttercrambe N York 86 D4
Butterdean Border 116 H8
Butterknowle Dur 91 J2
Butterleigh Devon 9 J3
Butterley Derbys 66 C2
Buttermere Cumb 88 G3
Buttermere Wilts 30 H10
Butters Green Staffs 64 E2
Buttershaw C Brad 84 H9
Butterstone P & K 123 Q4
Butterton Staffs 64 F4
Butterton Staffs 77 K12
Butterwick Dur 101 K12
Butterwick Lincs 68 G3
Butterwick N York 87 J1
Butterwick N York 92 E11
Butt Green Ches E 64 C2
Buttington Powys 62 H10
Buttonbridge Shrops 52 D5
Buttonoak Shrops 52 D5
Buttsash Hants 12 G3
Buttsbear Cross Cnwll 7 K4
Butt's Green Essex 46 D11
Buxhall Suffk 58 E9
Buxhall Fen Street Suffk 58 E9
Buxted E Susx 15 P6
Buxton Derbys 77 K9
Buxton Norfk 71 J8
Buxton Heath Norfk 71 J8
Buxworth Derbys 77 J7
Bwlch Powys 39 Q7
Bwlchgwyn Wrexhm 63 J2
Bwlchllan Cerdgn 49 K9
Bwlchnewydd Carmth 38 A7
Bwlchtocyn Gwynd 60 E7
Bwlch-y-cibau Powys 62 G8
Bwlch-y-Ddar Powys 62 G8
Bwlchyfadfa Cerdgn 48 G10
Bwlch-y-ffridd Powys 50 E2
Bwlch-y-groes Pembks 37 P3
Bwlchymyrdd Swans 26 E3
Bwlch-y-sarnau Powys 50 E6
Byermoor Gatesd 100 F7
Byers Green Dur 100 G11
Byfield Nhants 54 E10
Byfleet Surrey 32 F10
Byford Herefs 40 E3
Bygrave Herts 45 K4
Byker N u Ty 100 H5
Byland Abbey N York 92 B11
Bylaugh Norfk 70 F8
Bylchau Conwy 74 D11
Byley Ches W 76 D10
Bynea Carmth 26 E3
Byrness Nthumb 108 C9
Bystock Devon 9 J8
Bythorn Cambs 55 Q5
Byton Herefs 51 L8
Bywell Nthumb 100 D6
Byworth W Susx 14 E6

C

Cabbacott Devon 18 H9
Cabourne Lincs 80 C3
Cabrach Ag & B 111 L8
Cabrach Moray 140 B10
Cabus Lancs 83 L5
Cackle Street E Susx 15 N5
Cackle Street E Susx 16 C7
Cackle Street E Susx 16 E8
Cadbury Devon 8 G4
Cadbury Barton Devon 19 N10
Cadbury World Birm 53 K4
Cadder E Duns 114 B7
Caddington C Beds 44 F8
Caddonfoot Border 107 L3
Cadeby Donc 78 E4
Cadeby Leics 66 C11
Cadeleigh Devon 8 G3
Cade Street E Susx 15 R6
Cadgwith Cnwll 2 H11
Cadham Fife 124 F12
Cadishead Salfd 76 D5
Cadle Swans 26 F3
Cadley Lancs 83 M9
Cadley Wilts 30 F9
Cadley Wilts 30 E9
Cadmore End Bucks 31 R4
Cadnam Hants 24 E10
Cadney N Linc 79 P3
Cadole Flints 74 H11
Cadoxton V Glam 27 Q8
Cadoxton Juxta-Neath Neath 26 H3
Cadwst Denbgs 62 E5
Caeathro Gwynd 72 H11
Caehopkin Powys 39 K9
Caenby Lincs 79 P6
Caerau Brdgnd 27 K3
Caerau Cardif 27 Q7
Cae'r-bont Powys 39 J9
Cae'r bryn Carmth 38 F9
Caerdeon Gwynd 61 L8
Caer Farchell Pembks 36 E5
Caergeiliog IoA 72 E8
Caergwrle Flints 75 J12
Caerhun Conwy 73 N9
Caerlanrig Border 107 K9
Caerleon Newpt 28 D4
Caernarfon Gwynd 72 H11
Caernarfon Castle Gwynd 72 H11
Caerphilly Caerph 27 R5
Caersws Powys 50 E2
Caerwedros Cerdgn 48 F9
Caerwent Mons 28 G4
Caerwys Flints 74 G9
Caerynwch Gwynd 61 N8
Caggle Street Mons 40 E8
Caim IoA 73 K7
Caio Carmth 38 G4
Cairinis W Isls 152 c8
Cairnbaan Ag & B 112 B3
Cairnbulg Abers 141 P3
Cairncross Border 117 K8
Cairncurran Inver 113 L7
Cairndow Ag & B 121 M10
Cairneyhill Fife 115 J4
Cairngarroch D & G 94 F8
Cairngorms National Park 131 K4
Cairnie Abers 140 D7
Cairnorrie Abers 141 L7
Cairnryan D & G 94 F4
Cairnty Moray 139 P5
Caister-on-Sea Norfk 71 Q9
Caistor Lincs 80 C3
Caistor St Edmund Norfk 71 J11
Cakebole Worcs 52 G6
Cake Street Norfk 58 G2
Calais Street Suffk 46 H4
Calanais W Isls 152 f3
Calbourne IoW 12 G7
Calceby Lincs 80 G8
Calcoed Flints 74 G8
Calcot Gloucs 42 C9
Calcot W Berk 31 N8
Calcot Row W Berk 31 P8
Calcots Moray 139 N3
Calcott Kent 35 L9
Calcott Shrops 63 M9
Calcutt N York 85 M4
Calcutt Wilts 30 D4
Caldbeck Cumb 98 C10
Caldbergh N York 91 J9
Caldecote Cambs 56 C3
Caldecote Cambs 56 G9
Caldecote Herts 45 J4
Caldecote Nhants 54 H10
Caldecote Highfields Cambs 56 G9
Caldecott Nhants 55 N7
Caldecott Oxon 31 K3
Caldecott Rutlnd 55 L2
Caldecotte M Keyn 44 C5
Calder Cumb 88 D6
Calderbank N Lans 114 D8
Calder Bridge Cumb 88 D5
Calderbrook Rochdl 84 E11
Caldercruix N Lans 114 E7
Calder Grove Wakefd 85 L11
Caldermill S Lans 105 M1
Caldermore Rochdl 84 D12
Calder Vale Lancs 83 M6
Calderwood S Lans 114 B10
Caldey Island Pembks 37 M11
Caldicot Mons 28 G5
Caldmore Wsall 53 J1
Caldwell N York 91 K4
Caldy Wirral 74 H6
Caledfwlch Carmth 38 G6
Calenick Cnwll 3 J6
Calf of Man IoM 102 a7
Calford Green Suffk 46 C3
Calfsound Ork 147 d2
Calgary Ag & B 119 L2
Califer Moray 139 K4
California Falk 114 G6
California Norfk 71 P9
California Cross Devon 5 L6
Calke Derbys 66 B8
Calke Abbey Derbys 66 B8
Callakille Highld 135 M5
Callander Stirlg 122 G11
Callanish W Isls 152 f3
Callaughton Shrops 52 B1
Callerton N u Ty 100 F4
Callestick Cnwll 3 J4
Calligarry Highld 127 L4
Callington Cnwll 4 E3
Callingwood Staffs 65 M7
Callow Herefs 40 G5
Callow End Worcs 52 F10
Callow Hill Wilts 30 B5
Callow Hill Worcs 52 D6
Callow Hill Worcs 53 J7
Callows Grave Worcs 51 P7
Calmore Hants 24 E10
Calmsden Gloucs 42 B10
Calne Wilts 30 A8
Calow Derbys 78 C9
Calshot Hants 12 H4
Calstock Cnwll 4 G3
Calstone Wellington Wilts 30 B8
Calthorpe Norfk 71 J6
Calthorpe Street Norfk 71 M7
Calthwaite Cumb 98 F10
Calton N York 84 D3
Calton Staffs 65 L2
Calveley Ches E 75 Q12
Calver Derbys 77 N9
Calverhall Shrops 63 Q5
Calver Hill Herefs 51 L11
Calverleigh Devon 20 E10
Calverley Leeds 85 J8
Calver Sough Derbys 77 N8
Calvert Bucks 43 P7
Calverton M Keyn 43 R4
Calverton Notts 66 G2
Calvine P & K 130 E11
Calvo Cumb 97 N8
Calzeat Border 106 E3
Cam Gloucs 29 M2
Camasachoirce Highld 127 P12
Camasine Highld 127 N12
Camas Luinie Highld 136 C10
Camastianavaig Highld 135 J8
Camault Muir Highld 137 N8
Camber E Susx 16 G7
Camberley Surrey 32 C10
Camberwell Gt Lon 33 L7
Camblesforth N York 86 C10
Cambo Nthumb 100 C1
Cambois Nthumb 100 H2
Camborne Cnwll 2 G6
Camborne & Redruth Mining District Cnwll 2 G6
Cambourne Cambs 56 F8
Cambridge Cambs 57 J9
Cambridge Gloucs 41 M11
Cambridge Airport Cambs 57 J9
Cambrose Cnwll 2 H5
Cambus Clacks 114 F2
Cambusavie Highld 146 D6
Cambusbarron Stirlg 114 E3
Cambuskenneth Stirlg 114 E2
Cambuslang S Lans 114 B9
Cambus o' May Abers 132 C5
Cambuswallace S Lans 106 D2
Camden Town Gt Lon 33 K5
Cameley BaNES 29 J11
Camelford Cnwll 6 G8
Camelon Falk 114 F5
Camerory Highld 139 J9
Camer's Green Worcs 41 M5
Camerton BaNES 29 K11
Camerton Cumb 97 L12
Camghouran P & K 122 F2
Camieston Border 107 P4
Cammachmore Abers 133 L5
Cammeringham Lincs 79 N7
Camore Highld 146 D7
Campbeltown Ag & B 103 K6
Campbeltown Airport Ag & B 103 J5
Camperdown N Tyne 100 H4
Cample D & G 106 B11
Campmuir P & K 124 E5
Camps W Loth 115 K7
Campsall Donc 78 E1
Campsea Ash Suffk 59 L9
Camps End Cambs 45 R3
Campton C Beds 44 G4
Camptown Border 107 R7
Camrose Pembks 36 H6
Camserney P & K 123 L3
Camusnagaul Highld 128 F9
Camusnagaul Highld 144 D7
Camusteel Highld 135 N7
Camusterrach Highld 135 N7
Canada Hants 24 D9
Canal Foot Cumb 89 J11
Canaston Bridge Pembks 37 L7
Candacraig Abers 131 Q4
Candlesby Lincs 81 J10
Candle Street Suffk 58 F6
Candover Green Shrops 63 N11
Candy Mill Border 106 E1
Cane End Oxon 31 P6
Canewdon Essex 34 F4
Canford Bottom Dorset 11 P5
Canford Cliffs BCP 11 P7
Canford Heath BCP 11 P6
Canford Magna BCP 11 P5
Canhams Green Suffk 58 F7
Canisbay Highld 151 Q2
Canklow Rothm 78 C5
Canley Covtry 53 P5
Cann Dorset 23 J9
Canna Highld 126 D3
Cann Common Dorset 23 K9
Cannich Highld 137 K9
Cannington Somset 21 L5
Canning Town Gt Lon 33 M6
Cannock Staffs 64 H10
Cannock Chase Staffs 65 J8
Cannock Wood Staffs 65 K9
Cannon Bridge Herefs 40 F3
Canonbie D & G 98 E3
Canon Frome Herefs 41 K3
Canon Pyon Herefs 51 M11
Canons Ashby Nhants 54 F10
Canonstown Cnwll 2 E7
Canterbury Kent 35 L10
Canterbury Cathedral Kent 35 L10
Cantley Norfk 71 M11
Cantlop Shrops 63 N11
Canton Cardif 27 R7
Cantraywood Highld 138 E6
Cantsfield Lancs 89 Q12
Canvey Island Essex 34 D6
Canwick Lincs 79 N10
Canworthy Water Cnwll 7 J6
Caol Highld 128 F9
Caolas Scalpaigh W Isls 152 f6
Caoles Ag & B 118 E3
Caonich Highld 128 E6
Capel Kent 16 B2
Capel Surrey 14 H3
Capel Bangor Cerdgn 49 L4
Capel Betws Lleucu Cerdgn 49 K9
Capel Coch IoA 72 G7
Capel Curig Conwy 73 M12
Capel Cynon Cerdgn 48 F10
Capel Dewi Carmth 38 C7
Capel Dewi Cerdgn 38 C3
Capel-Dewi Cerdgn 49 K4
Capel Garmon Conwy 61 P1
Capel Green Suffk 59 M10
Capel Gwyn Carmth 38 C7
Capel Gwyn IoA 72 E8
Capel Gwynfe Carmth 38 H7
Capel Hendre Carmth 38 F9
Capel Isaac Carmth 38 E6
Capel Iwan Carmth 37 Q3
Capel-le-Ferne Kent 17 N3
Capelles Guern 12 c2
Capel Llanilltern Cardif 27 P6
Capel Mawr IoA 72 G9
Capel Parc IoA 72 G6
Capel St Andrew Suffk 59 M11
Capel St Mary Suffk 47 K4
Capel Seion Cerdgn 49 L5
Capel Trisant Cerdgn 49 M5
Capeluchaf Gwynd 60 G2
Capelulo Conwy 73 N8
Capel-y-ffin Powys 40 C5
Capel-y-graig Gwynd 73 J10
Capenhurst Ches W 75 L9
Capernwray Lancs 89 N12
Cape Wrath Highld 148 F2
Capheaton Nthumb 100 D2
Caplaw E Rens 113 N9
Capon's Green Suffk 59 K7
Cappercleuch Border 106 H5
Capstone Medway 34 D9
Capton Devon 5 P6
Capton Somset 20 H5
Caputh P & K 124 B5
Caradon Mining District Cnwll 7 K10
Caradon Town Cnwll 7 K10
Carbeth Inn Stirlg 113 Q5
Carbis Cnwll 3 L5
Carbis Bay Cnwll 2 E7
Carbost Highld 134 G6
Carbost Highld 134 G9
Carbrook Sheff 78 C6
Carbrooke Norfk 70 D11
Carburton Notts 78 G9
Carclaze Cnwll 3 P4
Car Colston Notts 67 J4
Carcroft Donc 78 E2
Cardenden Fife 115 M2
Cardeston Shrops 63 L9
Cardewlees Cumb 98 D8
Cardhu Moray 139 M7
Cardiff Cardif 28 A7
Cardiff Airport V Glam 27 P9
Cardiff Gate Services Cardif 28 B6
Cardiff West Services Cardif 27 P6
Cardigan Cerdgn 48 B11
Cardinal's Green Cambs 45 R2
Cardington Bed 56 B11
Cardington Shrops 51 N1
Cardinham Cnwll 6 G11
Cardrain D & G 94 G12
Cardrona Border 107 J2
Cardross Ag & B 113 L6
Cardryne D & G 94 G11
Cardurnock Cumb 97 P6
Careby Lincs 67 P9
Careston Angus 132 E12
Carew Pembks 37 K9
Carew Cheriton Pembks 37 K10
Carew Newton Pembks 37 K9
Carey Herefs 40 H5
Carfin N Lans 114 E9
Carfraemill Border 116 C10
Cargate Green Norfk 71 M9
Cargenbridge D & G 97 J3
Cargill P & K 124 C5
Cargo Cumb 98 D6
Cargreen Cnwll 4 F4
Cargurrel Cnwll 3 L7
Carham Nthumb 108 C2
Carhampton Somset 20 G5
Carharrack Cnwll 3 J6
Carie P & K 122 G1
Carinish W Isls 152 c8
Carisbrooke IoW 12 H7
Cark Cumb 89 K11
Carkeel Cnwll 4 F5
Càrlabhagh W Isls 152 e2
Carland Cross Cnwll 3 L4
Carlbury Darltn 91 L4
Carlby Lincs 67 P9
Carlcroft Nthumb 108 D7
Carlecotes Barns 77 M3
Carleen Cnwll 2 F8
Carlesmoor N York 91 L12
Carleton Cumb 88 D5
Carleton Cumb 98 E7
Carleton Cumb 98 G12
Carleton Lancs 82 H7
Carleton Wakefd 85 P11
Carleton Forehoe Norfk 70 G11
Carleton-in-Craven N York 84 E5
Carleton Rode Norfk 58 G2
Carleton St Peter Norfk 71 L11
Carlidnack Cnwll 3 J8
Carlincraig Abers 140 G7
Carlingcott BaNES 29 L10
Carlin How R & Cl 92 E3
Carlisle Cumb 98 E7
Carlisle Airport Cumb 98 F6
Carloggas Cnwll 6 C11
Carlops Border 115 L10
Carloway W Isls 152 e2
Carlton Barns 78 B2
Carlton Bed 55 N9
Carlton Cambs 57 M10
Carlton Leeds 85 M9
Carlton Leics 66 C11
Carlton N York 86 C10
Carlton N York 90 H10
Carlton N York 92 C9
Carlton Notts 66 G4
Carlton S on T 91 P2
Carlton Suffk 59 M8
Carlton Colville Suffk 59 P3
Carlton Curlieu Leics 54 H1
Carlton Green Cambs 57 M10
Carlton Husthwaite N York 92 A11
Carlton-in-Cleveland N York 92 A6
Carlton in Lindrick Notts 78 F7
Carlton-le-Moorland Lincs 79 M12
Carlton Miniott N York 91 P10
Carlton-on-Trent Notts 79 K11
Carlton Scroop Lincs 67 N3
Carluke S Lans 114 F11
Carlyon Bay Cnwll 3 P4
Carmacoup S Lans 105 P4
Carmarthen Carmth 38 B7
Carmel Carmth 38 E8
Carmel Flints 74 G8
Carmel Gwynd 60 H1
Carmichael S Lans 106 B2
Carmunnock C Glas 114 A9
Carmyle C Glas 114 B9
Carmyllie Angus 125 L4
Carnaby E R Yk 87 L2
Carnbee Fife 125 K11
Carnbo P & K 123 Q12
Carn Brea Cnwll 2 H6
Carnbrogie Abers 141 K10
Carndu Highld 136 B10
Carnduff S Lans 114 B12
Carne Cnwll 3 J9
Carne Cnwll 3 M7
Carne Cnwll 3 N3
Carnell E Ayrs 105 J3
Carnewas Cnwll 6 B11
Carnforth Lancs 83 L1
Carn-gorm Highld 136 C11
Carnhedryn Pembks 36 F5
Carnhell Green Cnwll 2 F7
Carnie Abers 133 K3
Carnkie Cnwll 2 H6
Carnkie Cnwll 2 H7
Carnkiet Cnwll 3 K4
Carno Powys 50 C1
Carnock Fife 115 J3
Carnon Downs Cnwll 3 K6
Carnousie Abers 140 G6
Carnoustie Angus 125 L6
Carnsmerry Cnwll 3 P3
Carnwath S Lans 114 H12
Carnyorth Cnwll 2 B8
Carol Green Solhll 53 N5
Carpalla Cnwll 3 N4
Carperby N York 90 G9
Carr Rothm 78 E6
Carradale Ag & B 103 L2
Carrbridge Highld 138 G11
Carrbrook Tamesd 77 J3
Carrefour Jersey 13 b1
Carreglefn IoA 72 F6
Carr Gate Wakefd 85 L10
Carrhouse N Linc 79 K2
Carrick Ag & B 112 D4
Carrick Castle Ag & B 113 J2
Carriden Falk 115 J5
Carrington Lincs 68 F1
Carrington Mdloth 115 P9
Carrington Traffd 76 D5
Carrog Conwy 61 N3
Carrog Denbgs 62 F3
Carron Falk 114 F5
Carron Moray 139 N7
Carronbridge D & G 105 R10
Carron Bridge Stirlg 114 D4
Carronshore Falk 114 G5
Carrow Hill Mons 28 F4
Carr Shield Nthumb 99 M8
Carrutherstown D & G 97 M4
Carruth House Inver 113 M8
Carr Vale Derbys 78 D9
Carrville Dur 100 H9
Carsaig Ag & B 119 P8
Carseriggan D & G 95 K5
Carsethorn D & G 97 K6
Carshalton Gt Lon 33 K9
Carsington Derbys 65 N2
Carskey Ag & B 103 J8
Carsluith D & G 95 N7
Carsphairn D & G 105 K11
Carstairs S Lans 114 G12
Carstairs Junction S Lans 114 H12
Carswell Marsh Oxon 30 G3
Carter's Clay Hants 24 E8
Carters Green Essex 45 P9
Carterton Oxon 42 G10
Carterway Heads Nthumb 100 D8
Carthew Cnwll 3 N3
Carthorpe N York 91 M10
Cartington Nthumb 108 G9
Cartland S Lans 114 F12
Cartledge Derbys 77 Q8
Cartmel Cumb 89 K11
Cartmel Fell Cumb 89 L9
Carway Carmth 38 C10
Carwinley Cumb 98 E4
Cashe's Green Gloucs 41 N10
Cashmoor Dorset 23 L10
Cassington Oxon 43 K9
Cassop Dur 101 J10
Castallack Cnwll 2 D9
Castel Guern 12 c2
Castell Conwy 73 N10
Castell-y-bwch Torfn 28 C4
Casterton Cumb 89 Q11
Castle Cnwll 3 Q3
Castle Acre Norfk 70 B9
Castle Ashby Nhants 55 L8
Castlebay W Isls 152 b13
Castle Bolton N York 90 G8
Castle Bromwich Solhll 53 L3
Castle Bytham Lincs 67 N8
Castlebythe Pembks 37 K5
Castle Caereinion Powys 62 G11
Castle Camps Cambs 46 A3
Castle Carrock Cumb 98 G7
Castlecary Falk 114 E6
Castle Cary Somset 22 E7
Castle Combe Wilts 29 N7
Castle Donington Leics 66 D7
Castle Douglas D & G 96 F6
Castle Eaton Swindn 30 D3
Castle Eden Dur 101 L10
Castle End C Pete 68 C10
Castleford Wakefd 85 N10
Castle Frome Herefs 41 K3
Castle Gate Cnwll 2 D7
Castle Green Cumb 89 N8
Castle Green Surrey 32 D10
Castle Gresley Derbys 65 P8
Castle Hedingham Essex 46 D4
Castlehill Border 106 G3
Castlehill Highld 151 M3
Castle Hill Kent 16 C2
Castle Hill Suffk 47 L2
Castlehill W Duns 113 M6
Castle Howard N York 86 D1
Castle Kennedy D & G 94 G6
Castle Lachlan Ag & B 112 E2
Castlemartin Pembks 36 H11
Castlemilk C Glas 114 A9
Castle Morris Pembks 36 H4
Castlemorton Worcs 41 M4
Castlemorton Common Worcs 41 M4
Castle O'er D & G 106 H11
Castle Rising Norfk 69 M7
Castleside Dur 100 D8
Castle Stuart Highld 138 D6
Castlethorpe M Keyn 44 A3
Castlethorpe N Linc 79 N2
Castleton Ag & B 112 C4
Castleton Border 107 N11
Castleton Derbys 77 M7
Castleton N York 92 E5
Castleton Newpt 28 C6
Castleton Rochdl 76 G2
Castletown Ches W 63 M2
Castletown Dorset 10 G10
Castletown Highld 151 M3
Castletown IoM 102 c7
Castletown Sundld 101 J6
Castley N York 85 K6
Caston Norfk 58 E1
Castor C Pete 56 C1
Caswell Bay Swans 26 E5
Catacol N Ayrs 112 D11
Cat and Fiddle Derbys 77 J9
Catbrain S Glos 28 H6
Catbrook Mons 40 G11
Catch Flints 74 H9
Catchall Cnwll 2 C9
Catchem's Corner Solhll 53 N5
Catchgate Dur 100 F8
Catcliffe Rothm 78 C6
Catcomb Wilts 30 B7
Catcott Somset 21 N5
Catcott Burtle Somset 21 N5
Caterham Surrey 33 L11
Catfield Norfk 71 M8
Catfield Common Norfk 71 M8
Catford Gt Lon 33 L8
Catforth Lancs 83 L8
Cathcart C Glas 113 R9
Cathedine Powys 39 Q6
Catherine-de-Barnes Solhll 53 M5
Catherine Slack C Brad 84 G9
Catherington Hants 25 M10
Catherston Leweston Dorset 10 B6
Catherton Shrops 52 C5
Catisfield Hants 13 J3
Catley Herefs 41 K3
Catley Lane Head Rochdl 84 C12
Catlodge Highld 130 B6
Catlow Lancs 84 C8
Catlowdy Cumb 98 F3
Catmere End Essex 45 P4
Catmore W Berk 31 K6
Caton Devon 8 E10
Caton Lancs 83 M2
Caton Green Lancs 83 M2
Cator Court Devon 8 C9
Catrine E Ayrs 105 K5
Cat's Ash Newpt 28 E4
Catsfield E Susx 16 C8
Catsfield Stream E Susx 16 C8
Catsgore Somset 22 C8
Catsham Somset 22 D6
Catshill Worcs 52 H6
Catstree Shrops 52 D1
Cattadale Ag & B 103 J7
Cattal N York 85 P4
Cattawade Suffk 47 K5
Catterall Lancs 83 L6
Catteralslane Shrops 63 P4
Catterick N York 91 L7
Catterick Bridge N York 91 L7
Catterick Garrison N York 91 K7
Catterlen Cumb 98 F11
Catterline Abers 133 L8
Catterton N York 85 Q6
Catteshall Surrey 14 D2
Catthorpe Leics 54 F5
Cattishall Suffk 58 C7
Cattistock Dorset 10 F5
Catton N York 91 N11
Catton Nthumb 99 M7
Catwick E R Yk 87 L6
Catworth Cambs 56 B6
Caudle Green Gloucs 41 Q9
Caulcott C Beds 44 E3
Caulcott Oxon 43 L7
Cauldcots Angus 125 N3
Cauldhame Stirlg 114 B2
Cauldmill Border 107 N6
Cauldon Staffs 65 K2
Cauldon Lowe Staffs 65 K3
Cauldwell Derbys 65 N9
Caulkerbush D & G 97 J7
Caulside D & G 98 F2
Caundle Marsh Dorset 22 F10
Caunsall Worcs 52 F4
Caunton Notts 79 J11
Causeway Hants 25 N9
Causeway End Cumb 89 M9
Causeway End D & G 95 M6
Causeway End Essex 46 B8
Causewayend S Lans 106 D2
Causewayhead Cumb 97 M7
Causewayhead Stirlg 114 E2
Causeyend Abers 141 M12
Causey Park Nthumb 109 K10
Causey Park Bridge Nthumb 109 K10
Cavendish Suffk 46 E2
Cavenham Suffk 57 P6
Caversfield Oxon 43 M6
Caversham Readg 31 P7
Caverswall Staffs 64 H4
Caverton Mill Border 108 B5
Cavil E R Yk 86 E9
Cawdor Highld 138 F6
Cawkwell Lincs 80 F7
Cawood N York 86 A8
Cawsand Cnwll 4 F6
Cawston Norfk 70 H7
Cawston Warwks 54 D6
Cawthorn N York 92 F9
Cawthorne Barns 77 P2
Cawton N York 92 D11
Caxton Cambs 56 F9
Caxton End Cambs 56 F9
Caxton Gibbet Cambs 56 E8
Caynham Shrops 51 P6
Caythorpe Lincs 67 M2
Caythorpe Notts 66 H3
Cayton N York 93 L10
Ceannabeinne Highld 149 K3
Ceann a Bhaigh W Isls 152 b8
Ceannacroc Lodge Highld 128 H2
Cearsiadar W Isls 152 f4
Ceciliford Mons 40 G11
Cefn Newpt 28 C5
Cefn Berain Conwy 74 D10
Cefn-brith Conwy 62 C2
Cefn-bryn-brain Carmth 38 H9
Cefn Byrle Powys 39 K9
Cefn Canel Powys 62 H6
Cefn Coch Powys 62 F7
Cefn-coed-y-cymmer Myr Td 39 N10
Cefn Cribwr Brdgnd 27 K6
Cefn Cross Brdgnd 27 K6
Cefn-ddwysarn Gwynd 62 C4
Cefn-Einion Shrops 51 J3
Cefneithin Carmth 38 E9
Cefngorwydd Powys 39 L3
Cefn-mawr Wrexhm 63 J4
Cefnpennar Rhondd 27 N2
Cefn-y-bedd Flints 63 K1
Cefn-y-pant Carmth 37 N5
Ceint IoA 72 H8
Cellan Cerdgn 49 K10
Cellardyke Fife 125 L12
Cellarhead Staffs 64 H3
Celleron Cumb 89 M2
Celynen Caerph 28 B3
Cemaes IoA 72 F5
Cemmaes Powys 61 P11
Cemmaes Road Powys 61 P11
Cenarth Cerdgn 37 P2
Cerbyd Pembks 36 F5
Ceres Fife 124 H10
Cerne Abbas Dorset 10 G4
Cerney Wick Gloucs 30 C3
Cerrigceinwen IoA 72 G9
Cerrigydrudion Conwy 62 C2
Cess Norfk 71 N8
Ceunant Gwynd 73 J11
Chaceley Gloucs 41 P5
Chacewater Cnwll 3 J5
Chackmore Bucks 43 P4
Chacombe Nhants 43 K3
Chadbury Worcs 42 B2
Chadderton Oldham 76 G3
Chadderton Fold Oldham 76 G2
Chaddesden C Derb 66 C5
Chaddesley Corbett Worcs 52 G6
Chaddlehanger Devon 7 N9
Chaddleworth W Berk 31 J7
Chadlington Oxon 42 G7
Chadshunt Warwks 53 Q10
Chadwell Leics 67 K7
Chadwell Shrops 64 E9
Chadwell End Bed 55 Q7
Chadwell Heath Gt Lon 33 N5
Chadwell St Mary Thurr 34 B6
Chadwick Worcs 52 F7
Chadwick End Solhll 53 N6
Chadwick Green St Hel 75 N4
Chaffcombe Somset 9 Q3
Chafford Hundred Thurr 33 R6
Chagford Devon 8 D7
Chailey E Susx 15 M7
Chainbridge Cambs 68 H12
Chainhurst Kent 16 C1
Chalbury Dorset 11 N3
Chalbury Common Dorset 11 P3
Chaldon Surrey 33 K11
Chaldon Herring Dorset 11 J8
Chale IoW 12 H9
Chale Green IoW 12 H9
Chalfont Common Bucks 32 E4
Chalfont St Giles Bucks 32 E4
Chalfont St Peter Bucks 32 E4
Chalford Gloucs 41 P11
Chalford Oxon 31 P2
Chalford Wilts 23 J3
Chalgrave C Beds 44 E6
Chalgrove Oxon 31 N3
Chalk Kent 34 B8
Chalk End Essex 46 A9
Chalkhouse Green Oxon 31 P6
Chalkway Somset 10 B3
Chalkwell Kent 34 F9
Challaborough Devon 5 K8
Challacombe Devon 19 N5
Challoch D & G 95 M5
Challock Kent 34 H12
Chalmington Dorset 10 F4
Chalton C Beds 44 E6
Chalton C Beds 56 C10
Chalton Hants 25 M10
Chalvey Slough 32 D6
Chalvington E Susx 15 P9
Chambers Green Kent 16 G2
Chandler's Cross Herts 32 F3
Chandlers Cross Worcs 41 M4
Chandler's Ford Hants 24 G9
Channel's End Bed 56 B9
Channel Tunnel Terminal Kent 17 L3
Chantry Somset 22 G4
Chantry Suffk 47 L3
Chapel Cumb 97 P12
Chapel Fife 115 N3
Chapel Allerton Leeds 85 L8
Chapel Allerton Somset 21 N3
Chapel Amble Cnwll 6 E9
Chapel Brampton Nhants 55 J7
Chapelbridge Cambs 56 F2
Chapel Chorlton Staffs 64 E5
Chapel Cross E Susx 15 R7
Chapel End Bed 56 B9
Chapel End C Beds 44 F3
Chapel End Cambs 56 C4
Chapel End Warwks 53 Q2
Chapelend Way Essex 46 C4
Chapel-en-le-Frith Derbys 77 K7
Chapel Field Bury 76 E2
Chapelgate Lincs 68 H7
Chapel Green Warwks 53 P4
Chapel Green Warwks 54 D8
Chapel Haddlesey N York 86 A10
Chapelhall N Lans 114 E8
Chapel Hill Abers 141 P9
Chapel Hill Lincs 68 D1
Chapel Hill Mons 28 H2
Chapel Hill N York 85 M6
Chapelhope Border 106 G6
Chapelknowe D & G 98 C4
Chapel Lawn Shrops 51 K6
Chapel-le-Dale N York 90 B11
Chapel Leigh Somset 20 H7
Chapel Milton Derbys 77 K7
Chapel of Garioch Abers 140 H11
Chapel Rossan D & G 94 G9
Chapel Row E Susx 16 B8
Chapel Row Essex 34 D2
Chapel Row W Berk 31 M8
Chapels Cumb 88 H10
Chapel St Leonards Lincs 81 L9
Chapel Stile Cumb 89 J6
Chapelton Abers 133 L6
Chapelton Angus 125 M3
Chapelton Devon 19 L8
Chapelton S Lans 114 C11
Chapeltown Bl w D 83 Q12
Chapel Town Cnwll 3 L3
Chapeltown Moray 139 N11
Chapeltown Sheff 78 B4
Chapmanslade Wilts 23 J4
Chapmans Well Devon 7 L6
Chapmore End Herts 45 L8
Chappel Essex 46 F6
Charaton Cnwll 4 D3
Chard Somset 9 Q3
Chard Junction Somset 9 Q4
Chardleigh Green Somset 9 Q3
Chardstock Devon 9 Q4
Charfield S Glos 29 L4
Chargrove Gloucs 41 Q8

Charing *Kent* 16 G1
Charing Heath *Kent* 16 G1
Charing Hill *Kent* 34 G12
Charingworth *Gloucs* 42 E4
Charlbury *Oxon* 42 H7
Charlcombe *BaNES* 29 M9
Charlcutt *Wilts* 30 A7
Charlecote *Warwks* 42 P9
Charlemont *Sandw* 53 J2
Charles *Devon* 7 N7
Charleshill *Surrey* 14 C2
Charleston *Angus* 124 H4
Charlestown *C Aber* 133 M4
Charlestown *C Brad* 84 E10
Charlestown *Calder* 84 E10
Charlestown *Cnwll* 3 P4
Charlestown *Cnwll* 3 P4
Charlestown *Derbys* 77 J5
Charlestown *Dorset* 10 G9
Charlestown *Fife* 115 J2
Charlestown *Highld* 138 B6
Charlestown *Highld* 143 L10
Charlestown *Salfd* 76 E4
Charlestown of
  Aberlour *Moray* 139 N7
Charles Tye *Suffk* 58 F11
Charlesworth *Derbys* 77 J5
Charlinch *Somset* 21 K6
Charlottetown *Fife* 124 F10
Charlton *Gt Lon* 33 M7
Charlton *Hants* 24 F4
Charlton *Herts* 44 H6
Charlton *Nhants* 43 L4
Charlton *Nthumb* 99 M1
Charlton *Oxon* 31 J5
Charlton *Somset* 21 L8
Charlton *Somset* 22 E5
Charlton *Somset* 22 F3
Charlton *Somset* 22 F3
Charlton *Surrey* 32 F8
Charlton *W Susx* 14 C8
Charlton *Wilts* 23 K9
Charlton *Wilts* 29 Q4
Charlton *Wilts* 42 B3
Charlton *Worcs* 52 F6
Charlton *Wrekin* 63 Q10
Charlton Abbots *Gloucs* 42 B7
Charlton Adam *Somset* 22 C7
Charlton All Saints *Wilts* 24 B8
Charlton Down *Dorset* 10 G6
Charlton Hill *Shrops* 63 P10
Charlton Horethorne
  Somset 22 F8
Charlton Kings *Gloucs* 41 Q7
Charlton Mackrell
  Somset 22 C7
Charlton Marshall *Dorset* 11 L4
Charlton Musgrove
  Somset 22 G7
Charlton-on-Otmoor
  Oxon 43 M8
Charlton on the Hill
  Dorset 11 L4
Charlton St Peter *Wilts* 30 D11
Charlwood *Hants* 25 L7
Charlwood *Surrey* 15 J3
Charminster *Dorset* 10 G6
Charmouth *Dorset* 10 B6
Charndon *Bucks* 43 P7
Charney Bassett *Oxon* 30 H3
Charnock Green *Lancs* 83 M11
Charnock Richard *Lancs* 83 M10
Charnock Richard
  Services *Lancs* 83 M12
Charsfield *Suffk* 59 K9
Chart Corner *Kent* 34 D12
Charter Alley *Hants* 31 M10
Charterhall *Border* 116 H11
Charterhouse *Somset* 22 C2
Chartershall *Stirlg* 114 E3
Charterville Allotments
  Oxon 42 G9
Chartham *Kent* 35 K11
Chartham Hatch *Kent* 35 K11
Chart Hill *Kent* 16 D1
Chartridge *Bucks* 44 D1
Chart Sutton *Kent* 16 E1
Charvil *Wokham* 31 Q7
Charwelton *Nhants* 54 E9
Chase Terrace *Staffs* 65 J10
Chasetown *Staffs* 65 K10
Chastleton *Oxon* 42 F6
Chasty *Devon* 7 L4
Chatburn *Lancs* 84 A6
Chatcull *Staffs* 64 E5
Chatham *Caerph* 28 B4
Chatham *Medway* 34 D9
Chatham Green *Essex* 46 C8
Chathill *Nthumb* 109 K4
Chatley *Worcs* 52 F8
Chatsworth House
  Derbys 77 N9
Chattenden *Medway* 34 D8
Chatter End *Essex* 45 N6
Chatteris *Cambs* 56 H3
Chatterton *Lancs* 84 B11
Chattisham *Suffk* 47 K3
Chatto *Border* 108 D5
Chatton *Nthumb* 108 H4
Chaul End *C Beds* 44 F7
Chawleigh *Devon* 19 N11
Chawley *Oxon* 43 K10
Chawston *Bed* 56 C9
Chawton *Hants* 25 M6
Chaxhill *Gloucs* 41 L9
Chazey Heath *Oxon* 31 P7
Cheadle *Staffs* 65 J4
Cheadle *Stockp* 76 G6
Cheadle Heath *Stockp* 76 G6
Cheadle Hulme *Stockp* 76 G6
Cheam *Gt Lon* 32 H9
Cheapside *W & M* 32 D8
Chearsley *Bucks* 43 P9
Chebsey *Staffs* 64 F6
Checkendon *Oxon* 31 N6
Checkley *Ches E* 64 D3
Checkley *Herefs* 41 J4
Checkley *Staffs* 65 J4
Checkley Green *Ches E* 64 D3
Chedburgh *Suffk* 57 Q9
Cheddar *Somset* 21 N3
Cheddington *Bucks* 44 D7
Cheddleton *Staffs* 64 H2
Cheddleton Heath *Staffs* 65 J2
Cheddon Fitzpaine
  Somset 21 K8
Chedglow *Wilts* 29 Q4
Chedgrave *Norfk* 71 M12
Chedington *Dorset* 10 D4
Chediston *Suffk* 59 M5
Chedworth *Gloucs* 42 B9
Chedzoy *Somset* 21 M6
Cheeseman's Green *Kent* 17 J3
Cheetham Hill *Manch* 76 F3
Cheldon *Devon* 19 P10
Chelford *Ches E* 76 F9
Chellaston *C Derb* 66 B6
Chellington *Bed* 55 M9
Chelmarsh *Shrops* 52 D4
Chelmick *Shrops* 51 M4
Chelmondiston *Suffk* 47 M4
Chelmorton *Derbys* 77 M9
Chelmsford *Essex* 46 C10
Chelmsley Wood *Solhll* 53 M3
Chelsea *Gt Lon* 33 K7

Chelsfield *Gt Lon* 33 N9
Chelsham *Surrey* 33 L10
Chelston *Somset* 21 J9
Chelsworth *Suffk* 58 E11
Cheltenham *Gloucs* 41 Q7
Chelveston *Nhants* 55 N7
Chelvey *N Som* 28 G8
Chelwood *BaNES* 29 K10
Chelwood Common
  E Susx 15 M5
Chelwood Gate *E Susx* 15 M5
Chelworth *Wilts* 29 R3
Chelworth Lower Green
  Wilts 30 C4
Chelworth Upper Green
  Wilts 30 C4
Cheney Longville *Shrops* 51 M4
Chenies *Bucks* 32 E3
Chepstow *Mons* 28 H4
Chequerbent *Bolton* 76 C2
Chequers Corner *Norfk* 69 J11
Cherhill *Wilts* 30 B8
Cherington *Gloucs* 29 P4
Cherington *Warwks* 42 G4
Cheriton *Devon* 19 P4
Cheriton *Hants* 25 K7
Cheriton *Kent* 17 M3
Cheriton *Pembks* 37 J11
Cheriton *Swans* 26 C4
Cheriton Bishop *Devon* 8 G3
Cheriton Fitzpaine *Devon* 8 G3
Cherrington *Wrekin* 64 C8
Cherry Burton *E R Yk* 87 J7
Cherry Hinton *Cambs* 57 J9
Cherry Orchard *Worcs* 52 F10
Cherry Willingham *Lincs* 79 P9
Chertsey *Surrey* 32 F9
Cherwell Valley Services
  Oxon 43 L6
Cheselbourne *Dorset* 11 J5
Chesham *Bucks* 44 D1
Chesham *Bury* 76 E1
Chesham Bois *Bucks* 32 D2
Cheshunt *Herts* 45 L11
Chesley *Kent* 34 E9
Cheslyn Hay *Staffs* 64 H10
Chessetts Wood *Warwks* 53 M6
Chessington *Gt Lon* 32 H9
Chessington World of
  Adventures *Gt Lon* 32 H10
Chester *Ches W* 75 L10
Chesterblade *Somset* 22 F5
Chesterfield *Derbys* 78 C9
Chesterfield *Staffs* 65 L11
Chesterhill *Mdloth* 115 Q8
Chester-le-Street *Dur* 100 H8
Chester Moor *Dur* 100 H8
Chesters *Border* 107 P5
Chesters *Border* 107 P5
Chester Services *Ches W* 75 M8
Chesterton *Cambs* 56 C2
Chesterton *Cambs* 56 J8
Chesterton *Gloucs* 30 B2
Chesterton *Oxon* 43 M7
Chesterton *Shrops* 52 E1
Chesterton *Staffs* 64 F2
Chesterton Green
  Warwks 54 B10
Chesterwood *Nthumb* 99 M5
Chester Zoo *Ches W* 75 L9
Chestfield *Kent* 35 K9
Chestnut Street *Kent* 34 E9
Cheston *Devon* 5 L5
Cheswardine *Shrops* 64 D6
Cheswick *Nthumb* 117 M12
Cheswick Green *Solhll* 53 L5
Chetnole *Dorset* 10 F3
Chettiscombe *Devon* 20 F10
Chettisham *Cambs* 57 K4
Chettle *Dorset* 23 L10
Chetton *Shrops* 52 C3
Chetwode *Bucks* 43 N6
Chetwynd *Wrekin* 64 D8
Chetwynd Aston *Wrekin* 64 D8
Cheveley *Cambs* 57 N8
Chevening *Kent* 33 N10
Cheverton *IoW* 12 G8
Chevington *Suffk* 57 Q9
Cheviot Hills 108 B8
Chevithorne *Devon* 20 F10
Chew Magna *BaNES* 29 J9
Chew Moor *Bolton* 76 C2
Chew Stoke *BaNES* 28 H10
Chewton Keynsham
  BaNES 29 K9
Chewton Mendip *Somset* 22 D3
Chicacott *Devon* 8 B5
Chicheley *M Keyn* 44 C2
Chichester *W Susx* 14 B10
Chickerell *Dorset* 10 G8
Chickering *Suffk* 59 J5
Chicklade *Wilts* 23 K6
Chicksands *C Beds* 44 F3
Chickward *Herefs* 45 J10
Chidden *Hants* 25 L10
Chiddingfold *Surrey* 14 D4
Chiddingly *E Susx* 15 P8
Chiddingstone *Kent* 15 P2
Chiddingstone
  Causeway *Kent* 15 P1
Chiddingstone Hoath
  Kent 15 P2
Chideock *Dorset* 10 C6
Chidham *W Susx* 13 N4
Chidswell *Kirk* 85 K10
Chieveley *W Berk* 31 K7
Chieveley Services
  W Berk 31 K8
Chignall St James *Essex* 46 B9
Chignall Smealy *Essex* 46 B9
Chigwell *Essex* 33 N3
Chigwell Row *Essex* 33 N4
Chilbolton *Hants* 24 F5
Chilcomb *Hants* 24 H7
Chilcombe *Dorset* 10 E6
Chilcompton *Somset* 22 E3
Chilcote *Leics* 65 P10
Childer Thornton *Ches W* 75 L8
Child Okeford *Dorset* 23 J10
Childrey *Oxon* 30 H5
Child's Ercall *Shrops* 64 C7
Childswickham *Worcs* 42 C4
Childwall *Lpool* 75 L6
Childwick Bury *Herts* 44 G9
Childwick Green *Herts* 44 G9
Chilfrome *Dorset* 10 F5
Chilgrove *W Susx* 13 N3
Chilham *Kent* 35 J11
Chilla *Devon* 7 N4
Chillaton *Devon* 7 N8
Chillenden *Kent* 35 N11
Chillerton *IoW* 12 H8
Chillesford *Suffk* 59 M10
Chillingham *Nthumb* 108 H4
Chillington *Devon* 5 Q7
Chillington *Somset* 10 C2
Chilmark *Wilts* 23 L7
Chilmington Green *Kent* 16 H3
Chilson *Oxon* 42 G8
Chilsworthy *Cnwll* 7 M10
Chilsworthy *Devon* 7 L4
Chiltern Green *C Beds* 44 G8
Chiltern Hills 31 Q3
Chilthorne Domer
  Somset 22 C9

Chilton *Bucks* 43 P9
Chilton *Devon* 8 G4
Chilton *Dur* 100 H12
Chilton *Kent* 17 N2
Chilton *Oxon* 31 K5
Chilton Candover *Hants* 25 K5
Chilton Cantelo *Somset* 22 D9
Chilton Foliat *Wilts* 30 G8
Chilton Polden *Somset* 21 N5
Chilton Street *Suffk* 46 D3
Chilton Trinity *Somset* 21 L5
Chilwell *Notts* 66 E5
Chilworth *Hants* 24 G9
Chilworth *Surrey* 14 F1
Chimney *Oxon* 30 H2
Chineham *Hants* 25 L2
Chingford *Gt Lon* 33 M3
Chinley *Derbys* 77 K7
Chinnor *Oxon* 31 Q2
Chipchase Castle *Nthumb* 99 M3
Chipnall *Shrops* 64 D6
Chippenham *Cambs* 57 M6
Chippenham *Wilts* 29 Q6
Chipperfield *Herts* 44 F11
Chipping *Herts* 45 L5
Chipping *Lancs* 83 N6
Chipping Campden
  Gloucs 42 D4
Chipping Hill *Essex* 46 D8
Chipping Norton *Oxon* 42 G6
Chipping Ongar *Essex* 45 Q11
Chipping Sodbury *S Glos* 29 L6
Chipping Warden *Nhants* 54 E3
Chipshop *Devon* 7 N9
Chipstable *Somset* 20 G8
Chipstead *Kent* 33 P11
Chipstead *Surrey* 33 K11
Chirbury *Shrops* 51 K3
Chirk *Wrexhm* 63 J5
Chirnside *Border* 117 J10
Chirnsidebridge *Border* 117 J10
Chirton *Wilts* 30 C11
Chisbury *Wilts* 30 F9
Chiselborough *Somset* 21 P10
Chiseldon *Swindn* 30 E6
Chiselhampton *Oxon* 31 M3
Chisholme *Border* 107 L7
Chislehurst *Gt Lon* 33 N8
Chislet *Kent* 35 N9
Chiswell Green *Herts* 44 G10
Chiswick *Gt Lon* 33 J7
Chiswick End *Cambs* 45 L3
Chisworth *Derbys* 77 J5
Chithurst *W Susx* 25 P8
Chittering *Cambs* 57 J7
Chitterne *Wilts* 23 L5
Chittlehamholt *Devon* 19 M9
Chittlehampton *Devon* 19 M8
Chittoe *Wilts* 29 Q9
Chivelstone *Devon* 5 P7
Chivenor *Devon* 19 K6
Chiverton Cross *Cnwll* 3 J4
Chlenry *D & G* 94 G6
Chobham *Surrey* 32 D10
Cholderton *Wilts* 24 C5
Cholesbury *Bucks* 44 D10
Chollerford *Nthumb* 99 P4
Chollerton *Nthumb* 99 P4
Cholmondeston *Ches E* 76 B11
Cholsey *Oxon* 31 M5
Cholstrey *Herefs* 51 M9
Chop Gate *N York* 92 B7
Choppington *Nthumb* 100 H2
Chopwell *Gatesd* 100 E6
Chorley *Ches E* 63 P2
Chorley *Lancs* 83 N11
Chorley *Shrops* 52 C5
Chorley *Staffs* 65 K10
Chorleywood *Herts* 32 E3
Chorleywood West *Herts* 32 E3
Chorlton *Ches E* 64 D2
Chorlton-cum-Hardy
  Manch 76 F4
Chorlton Lane *Ches W* 63 M3
Choulton *Shrops* 51 L3
Chowley *Ches W* 75 N12
Chrishall *Essex* 45 M4
Chrisswell *Inver* 113 J6
Christchurch *BCP* 12 B6
Christchurch *Cambs* 57 J1
Christchurch *Gloucs* 40 H9
Christchurch *Newpt* 28 D4
Christian Malford *Wilts* 29 Q5
Christleton *Ches W* 75 M10
Christmas Common *Oxon* 31 P4
Christmas Pie *Surrey* 32 C12
Christon *N Som* 28 E11
Christon Bank *Nthumb* 109 K5
Christow *Devon* 8 G7
Christ's Hospital *W Susx* 14 F5
Chuck Hatch *E Susx* 15 N4
Chudleigh *Devon* 8 J8
Chudleigh Knighton
  Devon 8 J9
Chulmleigh *Devon* 19 N10
Chunal *Derbys* 77 J5
Church *Lancs* 83 R9
Church Aston *Wrekin* 64 D8
Church Brampton *Nhants* 55 J7
Church Brough *Cumb* 90 C4
Church Broughton
  Derbys 65 M5
Church Cove *Cnwll* 2 H12
Church Crookham *Hants* 25 P3
Churchdown *Gloucs* 41 Q7
Church Eaton *Staffs* 64 F8
Church End *Bed* 55 P9
Church End *Bed* 55 M9
Church End *Bucks* 43 Q10
Church End *C Beds* 44 D5
Church End *C Beds* 44 E6
Church End *C Beds* 44 E8
Church End *Cambs* 56 C10
Church End *Cambs* 56 D4
Church End *Cambs* 56 H4
Churchend *Essex* 34 H4
Church End *Essex* 46 A6
Church End *Essex* 46 C6
Church End *Essex* 46 C7
Church End *Gloucs* 41 P4
Church End *Gt Lon* 33 J4
Church End *Hants* 44 G9
Church End *Herts* 45 J8
Church End *Herts* 45 L11
Church End *Lincs* 68 E4
Church End *Lincs* 80 E6
Church End *Warwks* 53 M2
Church End *Warwks* 53 N2
Church Enstone *Oxon* 42 H6
Church Fenton *N York* 85 Q10
Churchfield *Sandw* 53 J2
Churchgate Street *Essex* 45 N9
Church Green *Devon* 9 M5
Church Gresley *Derbys* 65 P9
Church Hanborough
  Oxon 43 J9
Church Hill *Staffs* 65 J10
Church Houses *N York* 92 D7

Churchill *Devon* 9 P4
Churchill *Devon* 19 L5
Churchill *N Som* 28 F10
Churchill *Oxon* 42 G7
Churchill *Worcs* 52 G10
Churchill *Worcs* 52 G5
Churchinford *Somset* 21 K11
Church Knowle *Dorset* 11 M8
Church Laneham *Notts* 79 J9
Church Langton *Leics* 55 J2
Church Lawford *Warwks* 54 C5
Church Lawton *Ches E* 64 F1
Church Leigh *Staffs* 65 J5
Church Lench *Worcs* 53 J10
Church Minshull *Ches E* 76 C11
Church Norton *W Susx* 14 B10
Churchover *Warwks* 54 E4
Church Preen *Shrops* 51 P3
Church Pulverbatch
  Shrops 63 M11
Churchstanton *Somset* 21 J2
Churchstow *Devon* 5 P6
Church Stowe *Nhants* 54 G9
Church Street *Essex* 46 D3
Church Street *Kent* 34 C7
Church Street *Suffk* 59 P4
Church Stretton *Shrops* 51 M2
Churchthorpe *Lincs* 80 F4
Churchtown *Bpool* 82 H7
Churchtown *Cnwll* 6 G9
Churchtown *Derbys* 77 P11
Churchtown *Devon* 19 M4
Churchtown *IoM* 102 f3
Churchtown *Lancs* 83 L6
Church Town *N Linc* 79 K2
Churchtown *Sefton* 83 J11
Church Village *Rhondd* 27 P5
Church Warsop *Notts* 78 F10
Church Wilne *Derbys* 66 D6
Churnside Lodge *Nthumb* 99 M2
Churston Ferrers *Torbay* 5 Q5
Churt *Surrey* 25 Q6
Churton *Ches W* 75 M12
Churwell *Leeds* 85 K9
Chwilog *Gwynd* 60 G4
Chyandour *Cnwll* 2 D8
Chyeowling *Cnwll* 3 K6
Chyvarloe *Cnwll* 2 G10
Cil *Powys* 62 G11
Cilcain *Flints* 74 F11
Cilcennin *Cerdgn* 49 J8
Cilcewydd *Powys* 62 H11
Cilfrew *Neath* 27 J4
Cilfynydd *Rhondd* 27 P4
Cilgerran *Pembks* 37 N2
Cilgwyn *Carmth* 38 H6
Cilgwyn *Gwynd* 60 H1
Ciliau-Aeron *Cerdgn* 48 H3
Cilmaengwyn *Neath* 38 H10
Cilmery *Powys* 50 D10
Cilsan *Carmth* 38 F7
Ciltalgarth *Gwynd* 62 B4
Cilycwm *Carmth* 38 H4
Cimla *Neath* 27 J3
Cinderford *Gloucs* 41 K9
Cinder Hill *Wolves* 52 H2
Cippenham *Slough* 32 D6
Cirencester *Gloucs* 30 B2
Citadilla *N York* 91 L7
City *Ches W* 75 J9
City *Gt Lon* 33 L6
City *V Glam* 27 N7
City Airport *Gt Lon* 33 M6
City Dulas *IoA* 72 H6
Clabhach *Ag & B* 118 G1
Clachaig *Ag & B* 112 G5
Clachaig Inn *Highld* 121 L1
Clachan *Ag & B* 111 Q10
Clachan *Ag & B* 120 E9
Clachan *Ag & B* 120 E9
Clachan *Highld* 135 K8
Clachan-a-Luib *W Isls* 152 c8
Clachan Mor *Ag & B* 118 D3
Clachan na Luib *W Isls* 152 c8
Clachan of Campsie
  E Duns 114 A5
Clachan-Seil *Ag & B* 120 C4
Clachnaharry *Highld* 138 B6
Clachtoll *Highld* 148 C11
Clackavoid *P & K* 131 L1
Clacket Lane Services
  Surrey 33 M11
Clackmannan *Clacks* 114 G3
Clackmannanshire
  Bridge *Fife* 114 G4
Clackmarras *Moray* 139 N4
Clacton-on-Sea *Essex* 47 L8
Cladich *Ag & B* 121 L8
Cladswell *Warwks* 53 K9
Claggan *Highld* 120 D3
Claigan *Highld* 134 D5
Clandown *BaNES* 22 F2
Clanfield *Hants* 25 M10
Clanfield *Oxon* 42 G11
Clannaborough *Devon* 8 D4
Clanville *Hants* 24 E4
Clanville *Somset* 22 E7
Claonaig *Ag & B* 112 C10
Clapgate *Dorset* 11 M4
Clapgate *Herts* 45 N7
Clapham *Bed* 55 P10
Clapham *Devon* 8 H5
Clapham *Gt Lon* 33 K7
Clapham *N York* 83 R1
Clapham *W Susx* 14 F9
Clapham Green *Bed* 55 P10
Clap Hill *Kent* 17 J3
Clappersgate *Cumb* 89 K6
Clapton *Somset* 10 C3
Clapton *Somset* 22 E3
Clapton-in-Gordano
  N Som 28 G7
Clapton-on-the-Hill
  Gloucs 42 D8
Clapworthy *Devon* 19 N8
Clarach *Cerdgn* 49 K4
Claravale *Gatesd* 100 F6
Clarbeston *Pembks* 37 K6
Clarbeston Road *Pembks* 37 K6
Clarborough *Notts* 78 H9
Clare *Suffk* 46 D3
Clarebrand *D & G* 96 F3
Clarencefield *D & G* 97 M4
Clarewood *Nthumb* 100 C4
Clarilaw *Border* 107 N6
Clark's Green *Surrey* 14 H3
Clarkston *E Rens* 113 H9
Clashmore *Highld* 146 D9
Clashmore *Highld* 148 B10
Clashnessie *Highld* 148 B10
Clashnoir *Moray* 139 N11
Clathy *P & K* 123 M9
Clathymore *P & K* 123 P8
Clatt *Abers* 140 E10
Clatter *Powys* 50 D2
Clatterford End *Essex* 46 A6
Clatworthy *Somset* 20 G7
Claughton *Lancs* 83 M7
Claughton *Lancs* 83 N3
Claughton *Wirral* 75 J6
Clavelshay *Somset* 21 L7
Claverdon *Warwks* 53 M7

Claverham *N Som* 28 F9
Clavering *Essex* 45 N5
Claverley *Shrops* 52 E2
Claverton *BaNES* 29 M9
Claverton Down *BaNES* 29 M9
Clawdd-coch *V Glam* 27 P7
Clawdd-newydd *Denbgs* 62 G2
Clawthorpe *Cumb* 89 N11
Clawton *Devon* 7 L5
Claxby *Lincs* 80 C5
Claxby *Lincs* 81 J9
Claxton *N York* 86 C3
Claxton *Norfk* 71 N11
Claybrooke Magna *Leics* 54 E3
Clay Coton *Nhants* 54 F5
Clay Cross *Derbys* 78 C11
Claydon *Oxon* 54 D10
Claydon *Suffk* 58 H10
Clay End *Herts* 45 J7
Claygate *D & G* 98 E2
Claygate *Kent* 16 C2
Claygate *Surrey* 32 H9
Claygate Cross *Kent* 33 K11
Clayhall *Gt Lon* 33 M4
Clayhanger *Devon* 20 G8
Clayhanger *Wsall* 65 K11
Clayhidon *Devon* 21 J10
Clayhill *E Susx* 16 E6
Clayhill *Hants* 12 E3
Clayhithe *Cambs* 57 J8
Clayock *Highld* 151 L5
Claypit Hill *Cambs* 56 G9
Claypits *Gloucs* 41 M10
Claypole *Lincs* 67 L2
Claythorpe *Lincs* 80 H8
Clayton *C Brad* 84 H9
Clayton *Donc* 78 D2
Clayton *W Susx* 15 K8
Clayton Green *Lancs* 83 M9
Clayton-le-Moors *Lancs* 83 R9
Clayton-le-Woods *Lancs* 83 M10
Clayton West *Kirk* 77 M2
Clayworth *Notts* 79 J6
Cleadale *Highld* 126 H6
Cleadon *S Tyne* 101 K6
Clearbrook *Devon* 4 H4
Clearwell *Gloucs* 40 H10
Cleasby *N York* 91 L4
Cleat *Ork* 147 c6
Cleatlam *Dur* 91 J3
Cleator *Cumb* 88 D4
Cleator Moor *Cumb* 88 D4
Cleckheaton *Kirk* 85 J10
Cleedownton *Shrops* 51 Q5
Cleehill *Shrops* 51 Q5
Cleekhimin *N Lans* 114 D9
Clee St Margaret *Shrops* 51 P4
Cleestanton *Shrops* 51 Q5
Cleethorpes *NE Lin* 80 F2
Cleeton St Mary *Shrops* 51 Q5
Cleeve *N Som* 28 F9
Cleeve *Oxon* 31 M6
Cleeve Hill *Gloucs* 41 R6
Cleeve Prior *Worcs* 53 K10
Cleghornie *E Loth* 116 D5
Clehonger *Herefs* 40 F4
Cleish *P & K* 115 K2
Cleland *N Lans* 114 D9
Clement's End *C Beds* 44 E8
Clement Street *Kent* 33 P8
Clenamacrie *Ag & B* 120 H7
Clench Common *Wilts* 30 D9
Clenchwarton *Norfk* 69 L8
Clenerty *Abers* 141 J4
Clent *Worcs* 52 H5
Cleobury Mortimer
  Shrops 52 C5
Cleobury North *Shrops* 52 B3
Cleongart *Ag & B* 103 J3
Clephanton *Highld* 138 E6
Clerkhill *D & G* 106 H10
Cleuch-head *Ag & B* 105 Q9
Clevancy *Wilts* 30 B7
Clevedon *N Som* 28 F8
Cleveley *Oxon* 42 H7
Cleveleys *Lancs* 82 H6
Cleverton *Wilts* 29 R5
Clewer *Somset* 21 P3
Cley next the Sea *Norfk* 70 F3
Cliburn *Cumb* 89 P2
Cliddesden *Hants* 25 K3
Cliff *Warwks* 53 N1
Cliffe *Medway* 34 C7
Cliffe *N York* 91 R1
Cliffe *N York* 86 C9
Cliffe End *E Susx* 16 F8
Cliffe Woods *Medway* 34 C7
Clifford *Herefs* 40 C3
Clifford *Leeds* 85 N6
Clifford Chambers
  Warwks 53 M10
Clifford's Mesne *Gloucs* 41 L7
Cliffsend *Kent* 35 P9
Clifton *Bristl* 28 H7
Clifton *C Beds* 44 H4
Clifton *C Nott* 66 E5
Clifton *C York* 86 B5
Clifton *Calder* 84 H10
Clifton *Cumb* 89 P2
Clifton *Derbys* 65 M3
Clifton *Donc* 78 E4
Clifton *Lancs* 83 J5
Clifton *Nthumb* 100 G2
Clifton *Oxon* 43 K5
Clifton *Salfd* 76 F2
Clifton *Worcs* 41 N2
Clifton Campville *Staffs* 65 N10
Clifton Hampden *Oxon* 31 L3
Clifton Reynes *M Keyn* 55 M9
Clifton upon Dunsmore
  Warwks 54 E5
Clifton upon Teme *Worcs* 52 D8
Cliftonville *Kent* 35 Q8
Climping *W Susx* 14 E9
Clink *Somset* 22 H4
Clint *N York* 85 K3
Clinterty *C Aber* 133 M2
Clintmains *Border* 107 P3
Clipiau *Gwynd* 61 P9
Clippesby *Norfk* 71 N9
Clipsham *Rutlnd* 67 N9
Clipston *Nhants* 54 H4
Clipstone *C Beds* 44 D6
Clipstone *Notts* 78 E11
Clitheroe *Lancs* 83 R7
Clive *Shrops* 63 N8
Clivocast *Shet* 147 m2
Clixby *Lincs* 80 D3
Cloatley *Wilts* 29 R4
Clocaenog *Denbgs* 62 F2
Clochan *Moray* 140 B4
Clochtow *Abers* 141 Q9
Clock Face *St Hel* 75 N5
Cloddiau *Powys* 62 H11
Clodock *Herefs* 40 D5
Cloford *Somset* 22 G5
Clophill *C Beds* 44 F4
Clopton *Nhants* 55 P5
Clopton *Suffk* 59 J10
Clopton Corner *Suffk* 59 J9
Codsall *Staffs* 64 F11

Codsall Wood *Staffs* 64 F11
Coedely *Rhondd* 27 N5
Coed Hirwaun *Neath* 27 K5
Coedkernew *Newpt* 28 C6
Coed Morgan *Mons* 40 E9
Coedpoeth *Wrexhm* 63 J2
Coed Talon *Flints* 75 J11
Coedway *Shrops* 63 K9
Coed-y-Bryn *Cerdgn* 48 F11
Coed-y-caerau *Newpt* 28 E4
Coed-y-Cwm *Rhondd* 27 P4
Coed-y-paen *Mons* 28 D3
Coed-yr-ynys *Powys* 39 P7
Coed Ystumgwern *Gwynd* 61 J9
Coelbren *Powys* 39 K9
Coffinswell *Devon* 5 Q4
Coffle End *Bed* 55 P9
Cofton *Devon* 5 R4
Cofton Hackett *Worcs* 53 J5
Cogan *V Glam* 28 A8
Cogenhoe *Nhants* 55 L8
Cogges *Oxon* 42 H9
Coggeshall *Essex* 46 E7
Coggin's Mill *E Susx* 15 Q5
Coignafearn *Highld* 138 C12
Coilacriech *Abers* 131 P5
Coilantogle *Stirlg* 122 G11
Coillore *Highld* 134 F8
Coity *Brdgnd* 27 L6
Col *W Isls* 152 g3
Colaboll *Highld* 145 N3
Colan *Cnwll* 3 L2
Colaton Raleigh *Devon* 9 K7
Colbost *Highld* 134 D6
Colburn *N York* 91 K7
Colby *Cumb* 89 Q3
Colby *IoM* 102 c7
Colby *Norfk* 71 J6
Colchester *Essex* 46 H6
Colchester Zoo *Essex* 46 G7
Cold Ash *W Berk* 31 L8
Cold Ashby *Nhants* 54 G5
Cold Ashton *S Glos* 29 M8
Cold Aston *Gloucs* 42 C8
Coldbackie *Highld* 149 M5
Cold Blow *Pembks* 37 M8
Cold Brayfield *M Keyn* 55 M10
Cold Cotes *N York* 83 Q1
Coldean *Br & H* 15 L9
Coldeast *Devon* 5 Q2
Colden *Calder* 84 E9
Colden Common *Hants* 24 H9
Coldfair Green *Suffk* 59 N8
Coldham *Cambs* 68 H11
Cold Hanworth *Lincs* 79 P7
Coldharbour *Cnwll* 3 J5
Coldharbour *Devon* 20 G11
Coldharbour *Gloucs* 40 H11
Coldharbour *Herts* 44 G8
Cold Harbour *Oxon* 31 N6
Coldharbour *Surrey* 14 G2
Cold Hatton *Wrekin* 64 B8
Cold Hatton Heath
  Wrekin 64 B8
Cold Hesledon *Dur* 101 K9
Cold Hiendley *Wakefd* 78 B3
Cold Higham *Nhants* 54 H10
Coldingham *Border* 117 K8
Cold Kirby *N York* 92 B10
Coldmeece *Staffs* 64 C10
Cold Newton *Leics* 66 H11
Cold Northcott *Cnwll* 7 J7
Cold Norton *Essex* 34 E2
Cold Overton *Leics* 67 K9
Coldred *Kent* 17 N1
Coldridge *Devon* 8 D3
Coldstream *Border* 108 D2
Coldwaltham *W Susx* 14 E7
Coldwell *Herefs* 40 F4
Coldwells *Abers* 141 M8
Cold Weston *Shrops* 51 P4
Cole *Somset* 22 F6
Colebatch *Shrops* 51 K3
Colebrook *C Plym* 4 J5
Colebrooke *Devon* 8 J3
Coleby *Lincs* 79 N11
Coleby *N Linc* 86 G11
Cole End *Warwks* 53 M3
Coleford *Devon* 8 E4
Coleford *Gloucs* 41 J9
Coleford *Somset* 22 F4
Coleford Water *Somset* 20 H6
Colegate End *Norfk* 59 J3
Cole Green *Herts* 45 K9
Cole Green *Herts* 45 M5
Cole Henley *Hants* 24 H3
Colehill *Dorset* 11 N4
Coleman Green *Herts* 44 H9
Coleman's Hatch *E Susx* 15 N4
Colemere *Shrops* 63 M6
Colemore *Hants* 25 M7
Colemore Green *Shrops* 52 D2
Colenden *P & K* 124 C7
Coleorton *Leics* 66 C9
Colerne *Wilts* 29 N7
Colesbourne *Gloucs* 42 A9
Cole's Cross *Devon* 5 N5
Coles Cross *Dorset* 10 C4
Colesden *Bed* 56 C9
Coles Green *Suffk* 47 J3
Coleshill *Bucks* 32 D2
Coleshill *Oxon* 30 F4
Coleshill *Warwks* 53 M3
Colestocks *Devon* 9 L5
Coley *BaNES* 22 B2
Colgate *W Susx* 15 J4
Colinsburgh *Fife* 125 J12
Colinton *C Edin* 115 M7
Colintraive *Ag & B* 112 F6
Colkirk *Norfk* 70 D7
Coll *W Isls* 118 H1
Coll *W Isls* 152 g3
Collace *P & K* 124 G7
Collafirth *Shet* 147 i6
Coll Airport *Ag & B* 118 G2
Collaton *Devon* 5 M9
Collaton St Mary *Torbay* 5 P5
College of Roseisle
  Moray 139 L3
College Town *Br For* 32 B10
Collessie *Fife* 124 F10
Colleton Mills *Devon* 19 N10
Collier Row *Gt Lon* 33 P4
Collier's End *Herts* 45 L7
Collier's Green *E Susx* 16 D4
Colliers Green *Kent* 16 D3
Collier Street *Kent* 16 C2
Colliery Row *Sundld* 101 J8
Collieston *Abers* 141 P10
Collin *D & G* 97 K3
Collingbourne Ducis
  Wilts 24 D3
Collingbourne Kingston
  Wilts 24 D2
Collingham *Leeds* 85 N6
Collingham *Notts* 79 L11
Collington *Herefs* 52 B8
Collingtree *Nhants* 55 J9
Collins Green *Warrtn* 75 P5
Collins Green *Worcs* 52 D9
Colliston *Angus* 125 L4
Colliton *Devon* 9 K4
Collyweston *Nhants* 67 N11
Colmonell *S Ayrs* 94 D8

Colmworth Bed...56 B9
Colnabaichin Abers...131 P3
Colnbrook Slough...32 E7
Colne Cambs...56 C5
Colne Lancs...84 D7
Colne Bridge Kirk...85 J11
Colne Edge Lancs...84 D7
Colne Engaine Essex...46 E5
Colney Norfk...70 H10
Colney Heath Herts...44 H10
Colney Street Herts...44 H11
Coln Rogers Gloucs...42 C9
Coln St Aldwyns Gloucs...42 D10
Coln St Dennis Gloucs...42 C9
Colonsay Ag & B...111 J2
Colonsay Airport Ag & B...110 H3
Colpy Abers...140 F9
Colquhar Border...107 J2
Colquite Cnwll...6 F10
Colscott Devon...18 G10
Colsterdale N York...91 J10
Colsterworth Lincs...67 M7
Colston Bassett Notts...66 H5
Coltfield Moray...139 L3
Colt Hill Hants...25 N3
Coltishall Norfk...71 K8
Colton Cumb...89 J9
Colton Leeds...85 M8
Colton N York...85 N6
Colton Norfk...70 G10
Colton Staffs...65 K8
Colt's Hill Kent...16 B2
Columbjohn Devon...8 H5
Colva Powys...50 H10
Colvend D & G...96 H7
Colwall Herefs...41 M3
Colwell Nthumb...99 Q3
Colwich Staffs...65 J8
Colwick Notts...66 G4
Colwinston V Glam...27 M7
Colworth W Susx...14 C10
Colwyn Bay Conwy...73 P8
Colyford Devon...9 N6
Colyton Devon...9 N6
Combe Devon...5 M9
Combe Herefs...51 K8
Combe Oxon...42 H8
Combe W Berk...30 H10
Combe Almer Dorset...11 M5
Combe Common Surrey...14 Q4
Combe Down BaNES...29 L10
Combe Fishacre Devon...5 P4
Combe Florey Somset...21 J6
Combe Hay BaNES...29 L10
Combeinteignhead Devon...8 G10
Combe Martin Devon...19 L4
Combe Raleigh Devon...9 M4
Comberbach Ches W...76 B8
Comberford Staffs...65 M10
Comberton Cambs...56 G9
Comberton Herefs...51 N7
Combe St Nicholas Somset...9 P6
Combpyne Devon...9 P6
Combridge Staffs...65 K5
Combrook Warwks...53 P10
Combs Derbys...77 K8
Combs Suffk...58 F9
Combs Ford Suffk...58 F9
Combwich Somset...21 L5
Comers Abers...132 G3
Comhampton Worcs...52 F7
Commercial End Cambs...57 K8
Commins Coch Powys...61 P11
Commondale N York...92 G6
Common Edge Bpool...82 H8
Common End Cumb...88 D7
Common Moor Cnwll...4 C3
Common Platt Wilts...30 B6
Commonside Ches W...75 P9
Commonside Derbys...65 N4
Common Side Derbys...77 Q8
Commonwood Wrexhm...63 L1
Compass Somset...21 L6
Compstall Stockp...76 H5
Compstonend D & G...96 D8
Compton Devon...5 P4
Compton Hants...24 H7
Compton Hants...24 H8
Compton Staffs...52 F4
Compton Surrey...14 D1
Compton W Berk...31 L6
Compton W Susx...25 N10
Compton Wilts...23 P3
Compton Abbas Dorset...23 J4
Compton Abdale Gloucs...42 C8
Compton Bassett Wilts...30 B8
Compton Beauchamp Oxon...30 G4
Compton Bishop Somset...21 N2
Compton Chamberlayne Wilts...23 M7
Compton Dando BaNES...28 H9
Compton Dundon Somset...22 C7
Compton Durville Somset...21 P10
Compton Greenfield S Glos...28 G6
Compton Martin BaNES...28 H11
Compton Pauncefoot Somset...22 E8
Compton Valence Dorset...10 E6
Comrie Fife...115 J3
Comrie P & K...123 K8
Conaglen House Highld...128 E9
Concraigie P & K...124 C4
Conder Green Lancs...83 N4
Conderton Worcs...42 A3
Condicote Gloucs...42 D6
Condorrat N Lans...114 D6
Condover Shrops...63 N11
Coney Hill Gloucs...41 N8
Coneyhurst Common W Susx...14 G6
Coneysthorpe N York...86 D9
Coneythorpe N York...85 N3
Coney Weston Suffk...58 E5
Congdon's Shop Cnwll...7 K9
Congerstone Leics...66 C11
Congham Norfk...69 N7
Congleton Ches E...76 E10
Congl-y-wal Gwynd...61 M3
Congresbury N Som...28 F9
Congreve Staffs...64 G9
Conheath D & G...97 K4
Conicavel Moray...138 H5
Coningsby Lincs...80 D12
Conington Cambs...56 D3
Conington Cambs...56 D5
Conisbrough Donc...78 E4
Conisholme Lincs...80 H4
Coniston Cumb...89 J7
Coniston E R Yk...87 M4
Coniston Cold N York...84 D4
Conistone N York...84 F2
Connah's Quay Flints...75 J10
Connel Ag & B...120 G6
Connel Park E Ayrs...105 L7
Connor Downs Cnwll...2 F6
Cononbridge Highld...137 P5
Cononley N York...84 C6
Cononsyth Angus...125 K3
Consall Staffs...64 H2
Consett Dur...100 E8

Constable Burton N York...91 K8
Constable Lee Lancs...84 B10
Constantine Cnwll...3 J8
Constantine Bay Cnwll...6 C10
Contin Highld...137 M4
Conwy Conwy...73 N8
Conwy Castle Conwy...73 N8
Conyer Kent...34 G9
Conyer's Green Suffk...58 C7
Cooden E Susx...16 C9
Cookbury Devon...7 M3
Cookbury Wick Devon...7 M4
Cookham W & M...32 C5
Cookham Dean W & M...32 B5
Cookham Rise W & M...32 C5
Cookhill Worcs...53 K9
Cookley Suffk...59 L5
Cookley Worcs...52 F5
Cookley Green Oxon...31 P4
Cookney Abers...133 L6
Cooksbridge E Susx...15 M8
Cooksey Green Worcs...52 G7
Cook's Green Essex...47 L8
Cooks Green Suffk...58 E10
Cooksland Cnwll...6 F11
Cookson Green Ches W...75 P9
Coolham W Susx...14 G6
Cooling Medway...34 D7
Cooling Street Medway...34 D7
Coombe Cnwll...2 F6
Coombe Cnwll...3 K6
Coombe Cnwll...3 M4
Coombe Devon...8 F8
Coombe Devon...8 H10
Coombe Devon...9 L6
Coombe Gloucs...29 M3
Coombe Hants...25 L9
Coombe Wilts...23 P3
Coombe Bissett Wilts...23 P8
Coombe Cellars Devon...8 G10
Coombe Cross Hants...25 L9
Coombe Hill Gloucs...41 P6
Coombe Keynes Dorset...11 K8
Coombes W Susx...14 G9
Coombes-Moor Herefs...51 L8
Coombe Street Somset...22 G7
Coombeswood Dudley...52 H3
Coopersale Common Essex...45 N11
Coopersale Street Essex...45 N11
Cooper's Corner Kent...33 P12
Coopers Green E Susx...15 N6
Coopers Green Herts...44 H9
Cooper Street Kent...35 P10
Cootham W Susx...14 F8
Copdock Suffk...47 K3
Copford Green Essex...46 G7
Copgrove N York...85 M3
Copister Shet...147 j4
Cople Bed...56 B11
Copley Calder...84 G10
Copley Dur...90 H3
Copley Tameside...76 H4
Coplow Dale Derbys...77 M9
Copmanthorpe C York...85 R6
Copmere End Staffs...64 E6
Copp Lancs...83 K7
Coppathorne Cnwll...7 J3
Coppenhall Staffs...64 G8
Coppenhall Moss Ches E...76 D12
Copperhouse Cnwll...2 F7
Coppicegate Shrops...52 D5
Coppingford Cambs...56 C5
Coppins Corner Kent...16 G1
Copplestone Devon...8 E4
Coppull Lancs...83 M12
Coppull Moor Lancs...75 P1
Copsale W Susx...14 H6
Copster Green Lancs...83 P8
Copston Magna Warwks...54 C3
Cop Street Kent...35 N10
Copthall Green Essex...33 M2
Copt Heath Solhll...53 M5
Copt Hewick N York...85 M1
Copthorne Cnwll...7 K6
Copthorne Surrey...15 K3
Copt Oak Leics...66 D9
Copy's Green Norfk...70 D4
Copythorne Hants...24 E10
Coram Street Suffk...46 H3
Corbets Tey Gt Lon...33 Q5
Corbière Jersey...13 a3
Corbridge Nthumb...100 C5
Corby Nhants...55 M3
Corby Glen Lincs...67 P7
Corby Hill Cumb...98 F7
Cordon N Ayrs...103 Q4
Cordwell Derbys...77 P8
Coreley Shrops...52 B6
Cores End Bucks...32 C5
Corfe Somset...21 K8
Corfe Castle Dorset...11 M8
Corfe Mullen Dorset...11 N5
Corfton Shrops...51 N4
Corgarff Abers...131 P3
Corhampton Hants...25 K9
Corks Pond Kent...16 B3
Corlae D & G...105 M10
Corley Warwks...53 P4
Corley Ash Warwks...53 P4
Corley Moor Warwks...53 P4
Corley Services Warwks...53 P3
Cormuir Angus...131 P11
Cornard Tye Suffk...46 F3
Corndon Devon...8 C7
Corner Row Lancs...83 K8
Corney Cumb...88 D8
Cornforth Dur...101 J11
Cornhill Abers...140 F4
Cornhill-on-Tweed Nthumb...108 D2
Cornholme Calder...84 D10
Cornish Hall End Essex...46 B4
Corniogmore Ag & B...118 C3
Cornriggs Dur...99 N10
Cornsay Dur...100 F9
Cornsay Colliery Dur...100 F9
Corntown Highld...137 P5
Corntown V Glam...27 L7
Cornwall Airport Newquay Cnwll...3 L2
Cornwell Oxon...42 F6
Cornwood Devon...5 K5
Cornworthy Devon...5 P5
Corpach Highld...128 F9
Corpusty Norfk...70 G6
Corrachree Abers...132 D3
Corran Highld...127 Q4
Corran Highld...128 E11
Corrany IoM...102 e4
Corrie D & G...97 P1
Corrie N Ayrs...103 Q3
Corriecravie N Ayrs...103 N5
Corriegills N Ayrs...103 Q3
Corriegour Lodge Hotel Highld...129 J6
Corriemoille Highld...137 L3
Corrimony Highld...137 L10
Corringham Lincs...79 P4
Corringham Thurr...34 C5
Corris Gwynd...61 M12
Corris Uchaf Gwynd...61 M10

Corrow Ag & B...113 J1
Corry Highld...135 L11
Corscombe Devon...8 D4
Corscombe Dorset...10 D4
Corse Gloucs...41 M6
Corse Lawn Gloucs...41 N5
Corsham Wilts...29 P8
Corsindae Abers...132 G3
Corsley Wilts...23 J4
Corsley Heath Wilts...22 H4
Corsock D & G...96 F3
Corston BaNES...29 L9
Corston Wilts...29 Q5
Corstorphine C Edin...115 M7
Cors-y-Gedol Gwynd...61 K7
Cortachy Angus...132 B12
Corton Suffk...59 Q1
Corton Wilts...23 M5
Corton Denham Somset...22 E9
Coruanan Highld...128 E10
Corwen Denbgs...62 E3
Coryates Dorset...10 F7
Coryton Devon...7 N8
Coryton Thurr...34 C6
Cosby Leics...54 F2
Coseley Dudley...52 H2
Cosford Shrops...64 E11
Cosgrove Nhants...43 M3
Cosham C Port...13 L4
Cosheston Pembks...37 K10
Coshieville P & K...123 K3
Cossall Notts...66 D4
Cossall Marsh Notts...66 D4
Cossington Leics...66 G9
Cossington Somset...21 M5
Costessey Norfk...70 H9
Costock Notts...66 F7
Coston Leics...67 L8
Coston Norfk...70 F11
Cote Oxon...42 H11
Cote Somset...21 L4
Cotebrook Ches W...75 P10
Cotehill Cumb...98 F8
Cotes Cumb...89 M9
Cotes Leics...66 F8
Cotes Staffs...64 F5
Cotesbach Leics...54 E4
Cotford St Luke Somset...21 J8
Cotgrave Notts...66 G5
Cothal Abers...133 L1
Cotham Notts...67 K3
Cothelstone Somset...21 J7
Cotherstone Dur...90 H3
Cothill Oxon...31 K2
Cotleigh Devon...9 N4
Cotmanhay Derbys...66 D4
Coton Cambs...56 H9
Coton Nhants...54 H6
Coton Shrops...63 P5
Coton Staffs...64 H6
Coton Staffs...64 H6
Coton Staffs...65 H11
Coton Clanford Staffs...64 F7
Coton Hayes Staffs...65 H5
Coton Hill Shrops...63 N9
Coton in the Clay Staffs...65 M6
Coton in the Elms Derbys...65 N9
Coton Park Derbys...65 P8
Cotswolds...42 A10
Cotswold Wildlife Park & Gardens Oxon...42 E10
Cott Devon...5 N4
Cottam E R Yk...87 J2
Cottam Lancs...83 L8
Cottam Notts...79 M8
Cottenham Cambs...57 J7
Cotterdale N York...90 D8
Cottered Herts...45 K6
Cotteridge Birm...53 J4
Cotterstock Nhants...55 P3
Cottesbrooke Nhants...54 H6
Cottesmore Rutlnd...67 M9
Cottingham E R Yk...87 K8
Cottingham Nhants...55 L3
Cottingley C Brad...84 H8
Cottisford Oxon...43 M5
Cotton Staffs...65 J3
Cotton End Bed...44 F3
Cotton Tree Lancs...84 D7
Cottown Abers...140 G10
Cottown Abers...140 D10
Cottown of Gight Abers...141 K8
Cotts Devon...4 H4
Cotwall Wrekin...63 Q8
Cotwalton Staffs...64 H5
Couch's Mill Cnwll...4 A5
Coughton Herefs...41 J7
Coughton Warwks...53 K8
Coulaghailtro Ag & B...111 Q8
Coulags Highld...136 D7
Coulderton Cumb...88 C5
Coull Abers...132 D4
Coulport Ag & B...113 J4
Coulsdon Gt Lon...33 K10
Coulston Wilts...23 J3
Coulter S Lans...106 D3
Coultershaw Bridge W Susx...14 C7
Coultings Somset...21 K5
Coulton N York...92 C12
Coultra Fife...124 G2
Cound Shrops...63 P11
Coundlane Shrops...63 P11
Coundon Dur...100 L1
Coundon Grange Dur...91 L1
Countersett N York...90 H9
Countess Wilts...23 P5
Countess Cross Essex...46 F5
Countess Wear Devon...8 H7
Countesthorpe Leics...54 F2
Countisbury Devon...19 N3
Coupar Angus P & K...124 E5
Coup Green Lancs...83 N9
Coupland Cumb...90 B3
Coupland Nthumb...108 F4
Cour Ag & B...112 B11
Court-at-Street Kent...17 K4
Courteachan Highld...127 N7
Courteenhall Nhants...55 J9
Court Henry Carmth...38 E7
Courtsend Essex...35 J4
Courtway Somset...21 K6
Cousland Mdloth...115 Q7
Cousley Wood E Susx...16 B4
Cove Ag & B...113 J5
Cove Border...116 H7
Cove Devon...20 E9
Cove Hants...25 Q2
Cove Highld...143 K7
Cove Bay C Aber...133 M4
Cove Bottom Suffk...59 Q5
Covehithe Suffk...59 Q4
Coven Staffs...64 G11
Coveney Cambs...57 J4
Covenham St Bartholomew Lincs...80 G5
Covenham St Mary Lincs...80 G4
Coven Heath Staffs...64 G11
Coventry Covtry...53 Q5
Coverack Cnwll...3 K9
Coverack Bridges Cnwll...2 G8
Coverham N York...91 J9
Covington Cambs...55 Q6
Covington S Lans...106 C2
Cowan Bridge Lancs...89 Q11

Cowbeech E Susx...16 A8
Cowbit Lincs...68 E8
Cowbridge V Glam...27 M7
Cowdale Derbys...77 K9
Cowden Kent...15 N3
Cowdenbeath Fife...115 L3
Cowden Pound Kent...15 N2
Cowden Station Kent...15 N2
Cowers Lane Derbys...65 P3
Cowes IoW...12 H5
Cowesby N York...91 Q9
Cowesfield Green Wilts...24 D8
Cowfold W Susx...15 J6
Cowgill Cumb...90 C9
Cow Green Suffk...58 F7
Cowhill S Glos...29 J4
Cowie Stirlg...114 F4
Cowlam E R Yk...86 H2
Cowley Devon...8 H5
Cowley Gloucs...41 Q8
Cowley Gt Lon...32 F6
Cowley Oxon...43 L11
Cowling Lancs...83 N11
Cowling N York...84 E6
Cowling N York...91 L9
Cowlinge Suffk...57 N10
Cowmes Kirk...85 J12
Cowpe Lancs...84 C11
Cowpen Nthumb...100 H2
Cowpen Bewley S on T...91 N2
Cowplain Hants...13 M3
Cowshill Dur...99 N10
Cowslip Green N Som...28 G10
Cowthorpe N York...85 N5
Coxall Herefs...51 L6
Coxbank Ches E...64 C4
Coxbench Derbys...66 B3
Coxbridge Somset...22 C6
Cox Common Suffk...59 M4
Coxford Cnwll...6 H5
Coxford Norfk...70 C6
Coxgreen Staffs...52 E3
Coxheath Kent...34 C12
Coxhoe Dur...101 J11
Coxley Somset...22 C5
Coxley Wakefd...85 K11
Coxley Wick Somset...22 C4
Coxpark Cnwll...7 M10
Coxtie Green Essex...33 Q3
Coxwold N York...92 B11
Coychurch Brdgnd...27 M6
Coylton S Ayrs...104 H6
Coylumbridge Highld...130 G2
Coytrahen Brdgnd...27 L5
Crabbs Cross Worcs...53 K7
Crab Orchard Dorset...11 Q3
Crabtree W Susx...15 J5
Crabtree Green Wrexhm...63 K3
Crackenthorpe Cumb...89 Q3
Crackington Haven Cnwll...6 G5
Crackley Staffs...64 F2
Crackley Warwks...53 P6
Crackleybank Shrops...64 D10
Crackpot N York...90 F7
Cracoe N York...84 D3
Craddock Devon...20 H11
Cradle End Herts...45 M7
Cradley Dudley...52 G4
Cradley Herefs...41 L2
Cradley Heath Sandw...52 H3
Cradoc Powys...39 N5
Crafthole Cnwll...4 E6
Crafton Bucks...44 C8
Crag Foot Lancs...89 M12
Craggan Highld...139 J10
Cragganmore Moray...139 M8
Cragg Hill Leeds...85 K7
Cragg Vale Calder...84 F10
Craghead Dur...100 G8
Crai Powys...39 J7
Craibstone Moray...140 D4
Craichie Angus...125 K3
Craig Angus...125 N3
Craig Highld...136 F6
Craigbank E Ayrs...105 L7
Craigburn Border...115 N9
Craig-cefn-parc Swans...38 G11
Craigcleuch D & G...107 K12
Craigdam Abers...141 K10
Craigdhu Ag & B...120 F11
Craigearn Abers...132 H2
Craigellachie Moray...139 P7
Craigend P & K...124 C9
Craigend Rens...113 N7
Craigendoran Ag & B...113 L5
Craigends Rens...113 N8
Craighlaw Ag & B...95 K6
Craighouse Ag & B...111 L8
Craigie P & K...124 C4
Craigie S Ayrs...104 H3
Craigiefold Abers...141 M3
Craigley D & G...96 F6
Craig Llangiwg Neath...38 H10
Craiglockhart C Edin...115 M7
Craigmillar C Edin...115 N7
Craignant Shrops...63 J5
Craigneston D & G...105 M10
Craigneuk N Lans...114 D10
Craigneuk N Lans...114 D8
Craignure Ag & B...120 D5
Craigo Angus...132 H12
Craig Penllyn V Glam...27 M7
Craigrothie Fife...124 H10
Craigruie Stirlg...122 E4
Craig's End Essex...46 C4
Craigton Angus...125 K5
Craigton C Aber...133 K4
Craigton E Rens...113 P9
Craigton of Airlie Angus...124 G3
Craig-y-Duke Neath...38 H11
Craig-y-nos Powys...39 K8
Craik Border...107 J7
Crail Fife...125 M11
Crailing Border...107 R5
Craiselound N Lincs...79 L4
Crakehall N York...91 L9
Crakehill N York...91 Q12
Crakemarsh Staffs...65 K5
Crambe N York...86 C2
Cramlington Nthumb...100 H4
Cramond C Edin...115 M6
Cramond Bridge C Edin...115 M6
Crampmoor Hants...24 F8
Cranage Ches E...76 D10
Cranberry Staffs...64 F5
Cranborne Dorset...23 N10
Cranbourne Br For...32 C8
Cranbrook Devon...8 H5
Cranbrook Kent...16 D4
Cranbrook Common Kent...16 D3
Crane Moor Barns...77 P3
Crane's Corner Norfk...70 D9
Cranfield C Beds...44 D4
Cranford Gt Lon...32 G7
Cranford St Andrew Nhants...55 M5
Cranford St John Nhants...55 M5
Cranham Gloucs...41 P9
Cranham Gt Lon...33 Q5
Cranhill Warwks...53 L10
Crank St Hel...75 N4
Cranleigh Surrey...14 F3
Cranmer Green Suffk...58 G6

Cranmore IoW...12 F7
Cranmore Somset...22 F5
Cranoe Leics...55 J2
Cransford Suffk...59 L7
Cranshaws Border...116 F7
Cranstal IoM...102 f2
Cranswick E R Yk...87 J5
Crantock Cnwll...3 K2
Cranwell Lincs...67 P2
Cranwich Norfk...57 P2
Cranworth Norfk...70 E11
Craobh Haven Ag & B...120 E11
Crapstone Devon...4 H3
Crarae Ag & B...112 C2
Crask Inn Highld...149 L11
Crask of Aigas Highld...137 N7
Craster Nthumb...109 L6
Craswall Herefs...40 C4
Cratfield Suffk...59 L5
Crathes Abers...133 J5
Crathie Abers...131 M5
Crathie Highld...129 Q5
Crathorne N York...91 Q5
Craven Arms Shrops...51 M4
Crawcrook Gatesd...100 E5
Crawford Lancs...75 N3
Crawford S Lans...106 C5
Crawfordjohn S Lans...106 A5
Crawley Hants...24 G6
Crawley Oxon...42 H9
Crawley W Susx...15 K3
Crawley Down W Susx...15 L3
Crawleyside Dur...100 C10
Crawshawbooth Lancs...84 B10
Crawton Abers...133 L8
Craxe's Green Essex...46 G8
Cray N York...90 F11
Crayford Gt Lon...33 P7
Crayke N York...85 R1
Craymere Beck Norfk...70 G5
Cray's Pond Oxon...31 N6
Craythorne Staffs...65 M7
Craze Lowman Devon...20 F10
Crazies Hill Wokham...31 R6
Creacombe Devon...20 C9
Creagan Inn Ag & B...121 J4
Creag Ghoraidh W Isls...152 c9
Creagorry W Isls...152 c9
Creaguaineach Lodge Highld...129 K10
Creamore Bank Shrops...63 N6
Creaton Nhants...54 H6
Creca D & G...97 P4
Credenhill Herefs...40 F3
Crediton Devon...8 E4
Creebank D & G...95 L3
Creebridge D & G...95 M5
Creech Dorset...11 M8
Creech Heathfield Somset...21 L8
Creech St Michael Somset...21 L8
Creed Cnwll...3 M3
Creekmoor BCP...11 N6
Creekmouth Gt Lon...33 N6
Creeksea Essex...34 G3
Creeting St Mary Suffk...58 G9
Creeton Lincs...67 N6
Creetown D & G...95 M6
Cregneash IoM...102 b7
Creg ny Baa IoM...102 e5
Creich Fife...124 G8
Creigiau Cardif...27 P6
Cremyll Cnwll...4 G6
Cressage Shrops...63 Q11
Cressbrook Derbys...77 M9
Cresselly Pembks...37 L9
Cressex Bucks...32 C4
Cressing Essex...46 E7
Cresswell Nthumb...109 M11
Cresswell Pembks...37 K9
Cresswell Staffs...64 H5
Creswell Derbys...78 E9
Creswell Green Staffs...65 K10
Cretingham Suffk...59 J8
Cretshengan Ag & B...111 Q8
Crewe Ches E...64 D1
Crewe-by-Farndon Ches W...63 M2
Crewe Green Ches E...64 D1
Crew Green Powys...63 K9
Crewkerne Somset...10 C3
Crews Hill Station Gt Lon...33 K2
Crewton C Derb...66 B6
Crianlarich Stirlg...122 C8
Cribyn Cerdgn...49 J10
Criccieth Gwynd...60 H4
Crich Derbys...65 Q1
Crich Carr Derbys...65 Q1
Crichton Mdloth...115 Q9
Crick Mons...28 H4
Crick Nhants...54 E6
Crickadarn Powys...39 P3
Cricket St Thomas Somset...10 B3
Crickheath Shrops...63 J7
Crickhowell Powys...40 B9
Cricklade Wilts...30 C4
Cricklewood Gt Lon...33 J5
Cridling Stubbs N York...85 Q11
Crieff P & K...123 L8
Criggan Cnwll...3 P2
Criggion Powys...63 J9
Crigglestone Wakefd...85 L12
Crimble Rochdl...76 F1
Crimond Abers...141 P4
Crimplesham Norfk...69 M11
Crimscote Warwks...42 H2
Crinaglack Highld...137 M8
Crinan Ag & B...112 A2
Crindledyke N Lans...114 E10
Cringleford Norfk...71 J11
Cringles C Brad...84 F5
Crinow Pembks...37 M7
Cripplesease Cnwll...2 E7
Cripplestyle Dorset...23 N11
Cripp's Corner E Susx...16 D6
Croachy Highld...138 B10
Croanford Cnwll...6 F10
Crockenhill Kent...33 P9
Crocker End Oxon...31 P6
Crockerhill W Susx...14 C9
Crockernwell Devon...8 D6
Crocker's Ash Herefs...40 H8
Crockerton Wilts...23 J5
Crocketford D & G...96 G4
Crockey Hill C York...86 B6
Crockham Hill Kent...33 N12
Crockhurst Street Kent...16 B2
Crockleford Heath Essex...47 J6
Crock Street Somset...21 M11
Croeserw Neath...27 K3
Croes-goch Pembks...36 F4
Croes-lan Cerdgn...38 D3
Croesor Gwynd...61 K3
Croesyceiliog Carmth...38 B8
Croesyceiliog Torfn...28 C3
Croes-y-mwyalch Torfn...28 C3
Croes-y-pant Mons...40 D11
Croft Leics...54 E2
Croft Lincs...81 K11
Croft Warrtn...76 B4
Croftamie Stirlg...113 N3

Croft Mitchell Cnwll...2 G7
Crofton Cumb...98 C8
Crofton Wakefd...85 K11
Crofton Wilts...30 F10
Croft-on-Tees N York...91 M5
Croftown Highld...144 F8
Crofts Moray...139 P6
Crofts Bank Traffd...76 E4
Crofts of Dipple Moray...139 P4
Crofts of Savoch Abers...141 P4
Crofty Swans...26 D3
Crogen Gwynd...62 D5
Croggan Ag & B...120 D7
Croglin Cumb...98 H9
Croick Highld...145 L7
Cromarty Highld...138 E2
Crombie Fife...115 J4
Cromdale Highld...139 K10
Cromer Herts...45 J6
Cromer Norfk...71 K4
Cromford Derbys...65 P1
Cromhall S Glos...29 J4
Cromhall Common S Glos...29 L4
Cromor W Isls...152 g4
Crompton Fold Oldham...76 H2
Cromwell Notts...79 K11
Cronberry E Ayrs...105 L5
Crondall Hants...25 N4
Cronkbourne IoM...102 e6
Cronk-y-Voddy IoM...102 d4
Cronton Knows...75 M6
Crook Cumb...89 M7
Crook Dur...100 F11
Crookdake Cumb...97 P9
Crooke Wigan...75 P2
Crooked End Gloucs...41 J8
Crookedholm E Ayrs...104 H2
Crooked Soley Wilts...30 G8
Crookes Sheff...77 Q6
Crookhall Dur...100 E8
Crookham Nthumb...108 E2
Crookham W Berk...31 L8
Crookham Village Hants...25 N4
Crook Inn Border...106 H4
Crooklands Cumb...89 N10
Crook of Devon P & K...115 J1
Cropper Derbys...65 M5
Cropredy Oxon...43 K2
Cropston Leics...66 F10
Cropthorne Worcs...42 A3
Cropton N York...92 F9
Cropwell Bishop Notts...66 H5
Cropwell Butler Notts...66 H5
Cros W Isls...152 h1
Crosbost W Isls...152 g4
Crosby Cumb...97 M10
Crosby IoM...102 d5
Crosby N Linc...79 M1
Crosby Sefton...75 K4
Crosby Garret Cumb...90 B5
Crosby Ravensworth Cumb...89 Q4
Crosby Villa Cumb...97 M10
Croscombe Somset...22 D5
Crosemere Shrops...63 M6
Crosland Edge Kirk...77 L1
Crosland Hill Kirk...84 H12
Cross Somset...21 N2
Crossaig Ag & B...112 B11
Crossapol Ag & B...118 C3
Cross Ash Mons...40 F7
Cross-at-Hand Kent...16 D1
Crossbost W Isls...152 g4
Crossbush W Susx...14 E9
Crosscanonby Cumb...97 L10
Cross Coombe Cnwll...2 H4
Cross End Beds...55 Q9
Cross End Essex...46 F5
Crossens Sefton...83 J11
Cross Flatts C Brad...84 H7
Crossford Fife...115 K4
Crossford S Lans...114 E12
Crossgate Cnwll...7 L7
Crossgate Lincs...68 E7
Crossgate Staffs...64 H5
Crossgatehall E Loth...115 Q7
Crossgates E Ayrs...113 M12
Crossgates Fife...115 K4
Crossgates N York...93 L10
Crossgates Powys...50 F7
Crossgill Lancs...83 M3
Cross Green Devon...7 M7
Cross Green Leeds...85 L8
Cross Green Staffs...64 G11
Cross Green Suffk...58 D10
Cross Green Suffk...58 C10
Crosshands Carmth...37 P9
Cross Hands Carmth...38 E9
Crosshands E Ayrs...105 J5
Cross Hands Pembks...37 L7
Cross Hill Derbys...66 C3
Crosshill Fife...115 L1
Crosshill S Ayrs...104 H8
Cross Hills N York...84 F6
Crosshouse E Ayrs...104 G2
Cross Houses Shrops...52 C2
Cross Houses Shrops...63 P10
Cross in Hand E Susx...15 P5
Cross Inn Cerdgn...48 F8
Cross Inn Cerdgn...49 J4
Cross Inn Pembks...37 J6
Cross Inn Rhondd...27 P6
Cross Keys Ag & B...113 L4
Crosskeys Caerph...28 B3
Cross Keys Wilts...29 P8
Crosskirk Highld...150 H2
Crosslands Cumb...89 K9
Cross Lane IoW...12 H7
Cross Lane Head Shrops...52 D2
Cross Lanes Cnwll...2 H10
Cross Lanes Cnwll...3 J5
Cross Lanes N York...85 N2
Cross Lanes N York...92 B12
Cross Lanes Wrexhm...63 K3
Crosslee Rens...113 N8
Crossley Kirk...85 J11
Crossmichael D & G...96 G6
Cross Oak Powys...39 P7
Cross of Jackston Abers...141 J9
Cross o' th' hands Derbys...65 P4
Crosspost W Susx...15 J5
Crossroads Abers...132 H4
Crossroads Abers...133 J5
Cross Roads C Brad...84 F7
Cross Street Suffk...59 J5
Crosston Angus...125 K2
Cross Town Ches E...76 D8
Crossway Mons...40 F7
Crossway Powys...50 F10
Crossway Green Worcs...52 F7
Crossways Dorset...11 J6
Crosswell Pembks...37 M3
Crosthwaite Cumb...89 M7
Croston Lancs...83 L11
Crostwick Norfk...71 K9
Crostwight Norfk...71 L6
Crouch Kent...34 A11
Croucheston Wilts...23 N7
Crouch End Gt Lon...33 K5
Crouch Hill Dorset...10 H2

Crough House Green Kent...15 N2
Croughton Nhants...43 L5
Crovie Abers...141 K3
Crow Hants...12 B4
Crowan Cnwll...2 G7
Crowborough E Susx...15 P4
Crowborough Warren E Susx...15 P5
Crowcombe Somset...21 J6
Crowdecote Derbys...77 L10
Crowden Derbys...77 K4
Crowden Devon...7 P5
Crowdhill Hants...24 H9
Crowdleham Kent...33 Q10
Crow Edge Barns...77 M3
Crowell Oxon...31 Q2
Crow End Cambs...56 F9
Crowfield Nhants...43 N3
Crowfield Suffk...58 H8
Crowfield Green Suffk...58 H8
Crowgate Street Norfk...71 L8
Crowhill E Loth...116 H6
Crow Hill Herefs...41 K6
Crowhole Derbys...77 Q8
Crowhurst E Susx...16 D8
Crowhurst Surrey...15 M1
Crowhurst Lane End Surrey...15 M1
Crowland Lincs...68 E10
Crowland Suffk...58 E6
Crowlas Cnwll...2 E8
Crowle Lincs...79 K1
Crowle Worcs...52 G9
Crowle Green Worcs...52 G9
Crown Corner Suffk...59 K6
Crownhill C Plym...4 G5
Crownpits Surrey...14 D2
Crownthorpe Norfk...70 G11
Crowntown Cnwll...2 G8
Crows-an-Wra Cnwll...2 C9
Crow's Green Essex...46 C6
Crowshill Norfk...70 D11
Crow's Nest Cnwll...4 C3
Crowsnest Shrops...63 L11
Crowthorne Wokham...32 C9
Crowton Ches W...75 P9
Croxall Staffs...65 M9
Croxby Lincs...80 D4
Croxdale Dur...100 H11
Croxden Staffs...65 K4
Croxley Green Herts...32 F3
Croxteth Lpool...75 L4
Croxton Cambs...56 E8
Croxton N Linc...80 B1
Croxton Norfk...58 C3
Croxton Norfk...70 E6
Croxton Staffs...64 E6
Croxtonbank Staffs...64 E6
Croxton Green Ches E...63 P2
Croxton Kerrial Leics...67 L6
Croy Highld...138 E6
Croy N Lans...114 C6
Croyde Devon...19 J5
Croyde Bay Devon...18 H5
Croydon Cambs...56 F10
Croydon Gt Lon...33 L9
Crubenmore Highld...130 C6
Cruckmeole Shrops...63 M10
Cruckton Shrops...63 M10
Cruden Bay Abers...141 Q8
Crudgington Wrekin...64 B8
Crudie Abers...141 J4
Crudwell Wilts...29 Q4
Cruft Devon...7 P5
Crûg Powys...50 G6
Crugmeer Cnwll...6 C9
Crug-y-byddar Powys...50 G4
Crumlin Caerph...28 B3
Crumplehorn Cnwll...4 B6
Crumpsall Manch...76 F3
Crundale Kent...17 J1
Crundale Pembks...37 J7
Crunwere Pembks...37 N8
Cruwys Morchard Devon...20 D11
Crux Easton Hants...24 H3
Cruxton Devon...10 D5
Crwbin Carmth...38 C5
Cryers Hill Bucks...32 C3
Crymych Pembks...37 N4
Crynant Neath...38 H11
Crystal Palace Gt Lon...33 L8
Cuaig Highld...135 N4
Cuan Ag & B...120 E10
Cubbington Warwks...53 Q7
Cubert Cnwll...3 J3
Cubley Barns...77 N3
Cublington Bucks...44 B7
Cublington Herefs...40 E4
Cuckfield W Susx...15 K6
Cucklington Somset...22 G8
Cuckney Notts...78 F9
Cuckoo Bridge Lincs...68 D8
Cuckoo's Corner Hants...25 M5
Cuckoo's Nest Ches W...75 L11
Cuddesdon Oxon...43 M11
Cuddington Bucks...43 Q9
Cuddington Ches W...75 Q9
Cuddington Heath Ches W...63 M3
Cuddy Hill Lancs...83 L7
Cudham Gt Lon...33 N10
Cudliptown Devon...7 P9
Cudnell BCP...11 P5
Cudworth Barns...78 C2
Cudworth Somset...10 C2
Cuerdley Cross Warrtn...75 P5
Cufaude Hants...31 N11
Cuffley Herts...45 K11
Cuil Highld...121 J2
Culbokie Highld...137 P4
Culbone Somset...20 C4
Culburnie Highld...137 N7
Culcabock Highld...138 C6
Culcharry Highld...138 F6
Culcheth Warrtn...76 C5
Culdrain Abers...140 D9
Culduie Highld...135 N8
Culford Suffk...58 C5
Culgaith Cumb...99 J12
Culham Oxon...31 L3
Culkein Highld...148 C9
Culkein Drumbeg Highld...148 D10
Culkerton Gloucs...29 Q3
Cullen Moray...140 D2
Cullercoats N Tyne...101 K4
Cullerlie Abers...133 J4
Cullicudden Highld...138 C3
Cuillin Hills Highld...134 H11
Cullingworth C Brad...84 G7
Cullipool Ag & B...120 D10
Cullivoe Shet...147 j2
Culloden Highld...138 D6
Cullompton Devon...9 J3
Cullompton Services Devon...9 J3
Culm Davy Devon...20 H10
Culmington Shrops...51 N3
Culmstock Devon...20 H10
Culnacraig Highld...144 D4
Culnaightrie D & G...96 F8
Culnaknock Highld...135 J3
Culpho Suffk...59 J10

Place	County	Page	Grid
Culrain	Highld	145	N6
Culross	Fife	114	H4
Culroy	S Ayrs	104	F7
Culsalmond	Abers	140	G9
Culscadden	D & G	95	N8
Culshabbin	D & G	95	K8
Culswick	Shet	147	h7
Cultercullen	Abers	141	M11
Cults	C Aber	133	L4
Culverstone Green	Kent	34	B9
Culverthorpe	Lincs	67	P4
Culworth	Nhants	43	L2
Culzean Castle & Country Park	S Ayrs	104	D8
Cumbernauld	N Lans	114	D6
Cumbernauld Village	N Lans	114	D6
Cumberworth	Lincs	81	K9
Cumdivock	Cumb	98	D8
Cuminestown	Abers	141	K6
Cumledge	Border	116	H10
Cummersdale	Cumb	98	D7
Cummertrees	D & G	97	N5
Cummingston	Moray	139	L2
Cumnock	E Ayrs	105	K6
Cumnor	Oxon	43	K11
Cumrew	Cumb	98	G8
Cumrue	D & G	97	L1
Cumwhinton	Cumb	98	F7
Cumwhitton	Cumb	98	G8
Cundall	N York	91	P12
Cunninghamhead	N Ayrs	104	G1
Cunningsburgh	Shet	147	i8
Cupar	Fife	124	G10
Cupar Muir	Fife	124	G10
Curbar	Derbys	77	N9
Curbridge	Hants	13	J2
Curbridge	Oxon	42	G10
Curdridge	Hants	25	J10
Curdworth	Warwks	53	M2
Curland	Somset	21	L10
Curridge	W Berk	31	K8
Currie	C Edin	115	M8
Curry Mallet	Somset	21	M9
Curry Rivel	Somset	21	N8
Curteis' Corner	Kent	16	E3
Curtisden Green	Kent	16	C3
Curtisknowle	Devon	5	M6
Cury	Cnwll	2	H10
Cushnie	Abers	132	D2
Cushuish	Somset	21	K7
Cusop	Herefs	40	C3
Cusworth	Donc	78	F3
Cutcloy	D & G	95	N11
Cutcombe	Somset	20	E5
Cutgate	Rochdl	84	C12
Cuthill	Highld	146	D7
Cutiau	Gwynd	61	L8
Cutler's Green	Essex	45	Q5
Cutmadoc	Cnwll	3	Q2
Cutmere	Cnwll	4	E4
Cutnall Green	Worcs	52	G7
Cutsdean	Gloucs	42	C6
Cutsyke	Wakefd	85	N10
Cutthorpe	Derbys	77	Q9
Cuttivett	Cnwll	4	N3
Cuxham	Oxon	31	N3
Cuxton	Medway	34	C9
Cuxwold	Lincs	80	D3
Cwm	Blae G	40	B10
Cwm	Denbgs	74	E8
Cwmafan	Neath	27	N2
Cwmaman	Rhondd	27	N2
Cwmann	Carmth	38	E2
Cwmavon	Torfn	40	C10
Cwmbach	Carmth	37	P5
Cwmbach	Carmth	38	D11
Cwmbach	Powys	40	A4
Cwmbach	Rhondd	39	N11
Cwmbach Llechrhyd	Powys	50	D10
Cwmbelan	Powys	50	C4
Cwmbran	Torfn	28	C3
Cwmbrwyno	Cerdgn	49	M4
Cwm Capel	Carmth	38	C11
Cwmcarn	Caerph	28	B4
Cwmcarvan	Mons	40	G10
Cwm-celyn	Blae G	40	B10
Cwm-Cewydd	Gwynd	61	Q9
Cwm-cou	Cerdgn	37	Q2
Cwm Crawnon	Powys	39	N11
Cwmdare	Rhondd	39	N11
Cwmdu	Carmth	38	F6
Cwmdu	Powys	40	A7
Cwmdu	Swans	26	F3
Cwmduad	Carmth	38	B5
Cwm Dulais	Swans	38	F11
Cwmdwr	Carmth	38	H5
Cwmfelin	Brdgnd	27	K4
Cwmfelin	Myr Td	27	P2
Cwmfelin Boeth	Carmth	37	N7
Cwmfelinfach	Caerph	28	B4
Cwmfelin Mynach	Carmth	37	P5
Cwmffrwd	Carmth	38	B8
Cwmgiedd	Powys	39	J9
Cwmgorse	Carmth	38	G9
Cwm Gwaun	Pembks	37	K4
Cwmgwili	Carmth	38	D9
Cwmgwrach	Neath	39	L10
Cwm-Ifor	Carmth	38	G6
Cwm Irfon	Powys	49	Q10
Cwmisfael	Carmth	38	D8
Cwm Llinau	Powys	61	P10
Cwmllynfell	Neath	38	H9
Cwmmawr	Carmth	38	D9
Cwm Morgan	Carmth	37	Q3
Cwmparc	Rhondd	27	M3
Cwmpengraig	Carmth	37	R3
Cwm Penmachno	Conwy	61	N3
Cwmpennar	Rhondd	27	N2
Cwmrhos	Powys	40	B7
Cwmrhydyceirw	Swans	26	G2
Cwmsychbant	Cerdgn	38	C2
Cwmtillery	Blae G	40	B10
Cwm-twrch Isaf	Powys	39	J9
Cwm-twrch Uchaf	Powys	38	H9
Cwm-y-glo	Carmth	38	E9
Cwm-y-glo	Gwynd	73	J11
Cwmyoy	Mons	40	D7
Cwmystwyth	Cerdgn	49	M12
Cwrt	Gwynd	61	L2
Cwrt-newydd	Cerdgn	48	H11
Cwrt-y-gollen	Powys	40	B8
Cyfarthfa Castle Museum	Myr Td	39	P10
Cyffylliog	Denbgs	74	E12
Cyfronydd	Powys	62	G10
Cylibebyll	Neath	38	H11
Cymau	Flints	63	J1
Cymmer	Neath	27	K3
Cymmer	Rhondd	27	M4
Cynghordy	Carmth	39	J4
Cynheidre	Carmth	38	D10
Cynonville	Neath	27	K3
Cynwyd	Denbgs	62	E4
Cynwyl Elfed	Carmth	38	B6

D

Place	County	Page	Grid
Daccombe	Devon	5	Q3
Dacre	Cumb	89	M1
Dacre	N York	85	J3
Dacre Banks	N York	85	J3
Daddry Shield	Dur	99	P10
Dadford	Bucks	43	N4
Dadlington	Leics	54	C1
Dafen	Carmth	26	D2
Daffy Green	Norfk	70	E10
Dagenham	Gt Lon	33	P5
Daglingworth	Gloucs	42	A10
Dagnall	Bucks	44	E8
Dagworth	Suffk	58	F8
Dail bho Dheas	W Isls	152	g1
Dailly	S Ayrs	104	E9
Dainton	Devon	5	P3
Dairsie	Fife	124	H9
Daisy Hill	Bolton	76	C3
Daisy Hill	Leeds	85	K9
Dalabrog	W Isls	152	b11
Dalavich	Ag & B	120	H10
Dalbury	Derbys	65	N5
Dalby	IoM	102	b6
Dalby	Lincs	86	B1
Dalby	N York	86	G1
Dalcapon	P & K	123	N2
Dalchalm	Highld	146	G4
Dalchreichart	Highld	129	J2
Dalchruin	P & K	123	J9
Dalcrue	P & K	123	Q7
Dalderby	Lincs	80	E10
Dalditch	Devon	9	K8
Dale	Derbys	66	C4
Dale	Pembks	36	F9
Dale Bottom	Cumb	89	J2
Dale End	Derbys	77	N11
Dale End	N York	84	E6
Dale Hill	E Susx	16	C5
Dalehouse	N York	92	F3
Dalelia	Highld	127	N10
Dalgarven	N Ayrs	113	K12
Dalgety Bay	Fife	115	L4
Dalginross	P & K	123	K8
Dalguise	P & K	123	P3
Dalhalvaig	Highld	150	F6
Dalham	Suffk	57	M8
Dalibburgh	W Isls	152	b11
Dalkeith	Mdloth	115	Q8
Dallas	Moray	139	L5
Dallinghoo	Suffk	59	K9
Dallington	E Susx	16	B7
Dallington	Nhants	55	J8
Dallow	N York	91	K12
Dalmally	Ag & B	121	M7
Dalmary	Stirlg	113	P2
Dalmellington	E Ayrs	105	J8
Dalmeny	C Edin	115	L6
Dalmore	Highld	138	C2
Dalmuir	W Duns	113	P7
Dalnabreck	Highld	127	M10
Dalnacardoch	P & K	130	D10
Dalnahaitnach	Highld	138	F11
Dalnaspidal	P & K	130	B9
Dalnawillan Lodge	Highld	151	J8
Daloist	P & K	123	K1
Dalqueich	P & K	124	B12
Dalquhairn	S Ayrs	104	F10
Dalreavoch	Highld	146	D3
Dalry	N Ayrs	113	K11
Dalrymple	E Ayrs	104	F7
Dalserf	S Lans	114	E11
Dalsmeran	Ag & B	102	H7
Dalston	Cumb	98	D8
Dalston	Gt Lon	33	L5
Dalswinton	D & G	97	J1
Dalton	Cumb	89	N11
Dalton	D & G	97	M3
Dalton	Lancs	75	N2
Dalton	N York	91	J5
Dalton	N York	91	Q11
Dalton	Nthumb	100	E4
Dalton	Rothm	78	D5
Dalton-in-Furness	Cumb	88	H12
Dalton Magna	Rothm	78	D5
Dalton-le-Dale	Dur	101	K8
Dalton-on-Tees	N York	91	M5
Dalton Parva	Rothm	78	D5
Dalton Piercy	Hartpl	101	L12
Dalveich	Stirlg	122	G8
Dalwhinnie	Highld	130	B7
Dalwood	Devon	10	N5
Damask Green	Herts	45	J6
Damerham	Hants	23	N10
Damgate	Norfk	71	M10
Dam Green	Norfk	58	F4
Damnaglaur	D & G	94	G11
Danaway	Kent	34	F9
Danbury	Essex	46	D10
Danby	N York	92	E5
Danby Bottom	N York	92	E6
Danby Wiske	N York	91	N7
Dandaleith	Highld	139	P6
Danderhall	Mdloth	115	P7
Danebridge	Ches E	76	H10
Dane End	Herts	45	J7
Danegate	E Susx	15	Q4
Danehill	E Susx	15	M5
Dane Hills	Leic	54	F11
Danemoor Green	Norfk	70	F11
Danesford	Shrops	52	D2
Danesmoor	Derbys	78	C11
Daniel's Water	Kent	16	G3
Danshillock	Abers	140	H4
Danskine	E Loth	116	D8
Danthorpe	E R Yk	87	N8
Danzey Green	Warwks	53	L7
Dapple Heath	Staffs	65	K7
Darby Green	Hants	32	B10
Darcy Lever	Bolton	76	B3
Dardy	Powys	40	B8
Darenth	Kent	33	Q8
Daresbury	Halton	75	P7
Darfield	Barns	78	C4
Darfoulds	Notts	78	F8
Dargate	Kent	35	K10
Dargavel	Rens	113	M7
Darite	Cnwll	4	C3
Darland	Medway	34	D9
Darland	Wrexhm	75	L12
Darlaston	Wsall	52	H1
Darlaston Green	Wsall	52	H1
Darley	N York	85	J3
Darley Abbey	C Derb	66	B4
Darley Bridge	Derbys	77	P11
Darley Dale	Derbys	77	P11
Darleyhall	Herts	44	G7
Darley Head	N York	85	J3
Darlingscott	Warwks	42	H3
Darlington	Darltn	91	M4
Darliston	Shrops	63	P5
Darlton	Notts	78	H9
Darnford	Staffs	65	L10
Darnick	Border	107	N3
Darowen	Powys	61	P11
Darra	Abers	140	H6
Darracott	Devon	18	G8
Darracott	Devon	19	J5
Darras Hall	Nthumb	100	F4
Darrington	Wakefd	85	P11
Darsham	Suffk	59	N6
Darshill	Somset	22	E4
Dartford	Kent	33	P7
Dartford Crossing	Kent	33	Q7
Dartington	Devon	5	N5
Dartmeet	Devon	8	C10
Dartmoor National Park	Devon	8	D9
Dartmouth	Devon	5	P6
Darton	Barns	77	P2
Darvel	E Ayrs	105	K2
Darwell Hole	E Susx	16	B7
Darwen	Bl w D	83	Q10
Datchet	W & M	32	E7
Datchworth	Herts	45	K8
Datchworth Green	Herts	45	K8
Daubhill	Bolton	76	B3
Daugh of Kinermony	Moray	139	N7
Dauntsey	Wilts	30	A6
Dava	Highld	139	J8
Davenham	Ches W	76	B10
Davenport	Stockp	76	G6
Davenport Green	Ches E	76	F8
Davenport Green	Traffd	76	E6
Daventry	Nhants	54	F8
Davidson's Mains	C Edin	115	M6
Davidstow	Cnwll	6	H5
David Street	Kent	34	B9
Davington	D & G	106	H9
Davington Hill	Kent	34	H10
Daviot	Abers	141	J10
Daviot	Highld	138	D8
Daviot House	Highld	138	D8
Davis's Town	E Susx	15	P7
Davoch of Grange	Moray	140	D5
Davyhulme	Traffd	76	D4
Daw End	Wsall	65	J12
Dawesgreen	Surrey	15	J1
Dawley	Wrekin	64	C10
Dawlish	Devon	9	H9
Dawlish Warren	Devon	9	J9
Dawn	Conwy	73	Q9
Daws Green	Somset	21	K9
Daws Heath	Essex	34	E4
Daw's House	Cnwll	7	L8
Daybrook	Notts	66	F3
Dayhills	Staffs	64	H5
Dayhouse Bank	Worcs	52	H5
Daylesford	Gloucs	42	F6
Ddol	Denbgs	74	D9
Ddol-Cownwy	Powys	62	D8
Deal	Kent	35	Q12
Dean	Cumb	88	D2
Dean	Devon	5	M4
Dean	Devon	19	M4
Dean	Dorset	23	L10
Dean	Hants	25	G7
Dean	Hants	25	J9
Dean	Lancs	84	C10
Dean	Oxon	42	H7
Dean Bottom	Kent	33	Q8
Deanburnhaugh	Border	107	K7
Deancombe	Devon	5	M7
Dean Court	Oxon	43	K10
Deane	Bolton	76	C2
Deane	Hants	25	G4
Dean End	Dorset	23	L10
Dean Head	Barns	77	P4
Deanhead	Kirk	84	F12
Deanland	Dorset	23	L9
Deanlane End	W Susx	25	N11
Dean Prior	Devon	5	M4
Dean Row	Ches E	76	G7
Deans	W Loth	115	J7
Deanscales	Cumb	88	E1
Deanshanger	Nhants	43	Q4
Deanshaugh	Moray	139	Q6
Deanston	Stirlg	114	C1
Dean Street	Kent	34	D11
Dearham	Cumb	97	M9
Dearnley	Rochdl	84	D12
Debach	Suffk	59	K10
Debden	Essex	33	N3
Debden	Essex	45	Q5
Debden Green	Essex	45	Q5
Deblin's Green	Worcs	52	E11
Dechmont	W Loth	115	J7
Dechmont Road	W Loth	115	J7
Deddington	Oxon	43	K5
Dedham	Essex	47	J5
Dedham Heath	Essex	47	J5
Dedworth	W & M	32	D7
Deene	Nhants	55	N2
Deenethorpe	Nhants	55	N2
Deepcar	Sheff	77	P4
Deepcut	Surrey	32	C11
Deepdale	Cumb	90	B9
Deepdale	N York	90	E5
Deeping Gate	C Pete	68	C10
Deeping St James	Lincs	68	C10
Deeping St Nicholas	Lincs	68	D9
Deerhurst	Gloucs	41	P6
Deerhurst Walton	Gloucs	41	P6
Deerton Street	Kent	34	H9
Defford	Worcs	41	Q3
Defynnog	Powys	39	L6
Deganwy	Conwy	73	N8
Degnish	Ag & B	120	E10
Deighton	C York	86	B5
Deighton	N York	91	P6
Deiniolen	Gwynd	73	K11
Delabole	Cnwll	6	F8
Delamere	Ches W	75	P10
Delfrigs	Abers	141	M11
Delley	Devon	19	K8
Dellifure	Highld	139	K9
Dell Quay	W Susx	13	P4
Delly End	Oxon	42	H9
Delnabo	Moray	139	L12
Delnashaugh	Moray	139	L10
Delny	Highld	146	D10
Delph	Oldham	77	J2
Delves	Dur	100	E8
Delvin End	Essex	46	D5
Dembleby	Lincs	67	P5
Demelza	Cnwll	3	L3
Denaby	Donc	78	D4
Denaby Main	Donc	78	E4
Denbies	Surrey	32	H12
Denbigh	Denbgs	74	E12
Denbrae	Fife	124	G9
Denbury	Devon	5	N3
Denby	Derbys	66	C3
Denby Bottles	Derbys	66	C3
Denby Dale	Kirk	77	N2
Denchworth	Oxon	30	H4
Dendron	Cumb	88	H11
Denel End	C Beds	44	E4
Denfield	P & K	123	N9
Denford	Nhants	55	N5
Dengie	Essex	46	H11
Denham	Bucks	32	F5
Denham	Suffk	57	J6
Denham	Suffk	59	J6
Denham End	Suffk	57	M6
Denham Green	Bucks	32	F5
Denham Street	Suffk	59	J6
Denhead	Abers	141	N5
Denhead	Fife	125	J10
Denhead of Gray	C Dund	124	G6
Denholm	Border	107	N5
Denholme	C Brad	84	G8
Denholme Clough	C Brad	84	G8
Denio	Gwynd	60	E5
Denmead	Hants	25	L11
Denmore	C Aber	133	M2
Denne Park	W Susx	14	H5
Dennington	Suffk	59	K7
Denny	Falk	114	E6
Dennyloanhead	Falk	114	E6
Denshaw	Oldham	76	H1
Denside	Abers	133	K5
Densole	Kent	17	M2
Denston	Suffk	57	P10
Denstone	Staffs	65	K4
Denstroude	Kent	35	K10
Dent	Cumb	90	B9
Denton	Cambs	56	C3
Denton	Darltn	91	L3
Denton	E Susx	15	N10
Denton	Kent	17	M1
Denton	Kent	34	B7
Denton	Lincs	67	L6
Denton	N York	85	J6
Denton	Norfk	59	L3
Denton	Oxon	43	M11
Denton	Tamesd	76	H4
Denver	Norfk	69	L11
Denwick	Nthumb	109	K7
Deopham	Norfk	70	F12
Deopham Green	Norfk	70	F12
Depden	Suffk	57	P9
Depden Green	Suffk	57	P9
Deptford	Gt Lon	33	L7
Deptford	Wilts	23	M2
Derby	C Derb	66	B5
Derbyhaven	IoM	102	c7
Derculich	P & K	123	M2
Dereham	Norfk	70	E9
Deri	Caerph	27	P2
Derril	Devon	7	K4
Derringstone	Kent	35	M12
Derrington	Staffs	64	G7
Derriton	Devon	7	L4
Derry Hill	Wilts	29	Q6
Derrythorpe	N Linc	79	N2
Dersingham	Norfk	69	N6
Dervaig	Ag & B	119	M2
Derwen	Denbgs	62	E2
Derwenlas	Powys	61	N12
Derwent Valley Mills	Derbys	65	P1
Derwent Water	Cumb	88	H3
Derwydd	Carmth	38	F8
Desborough	Nhants	55	K4
Desford	Leics	66	D11
Detchant	Nthumb	108	H2
Detling	Kent	34	D10
Deuxhill	Shrops	52	C3
Devauden	Mons	28	G8
Devil's Bridge	Cerdgn	49	M5
Devitts Green	Warwks	53	P3
Devizes	Wilts	30	B10
Devonport	C Plym	4	E5
Devonside	Clacks	114	G2
Devoran	Cnwll	3	K6
Devoran & Perran	Cnwll	3	K7
Dewarton	Mdloth	115	Q8
Dewlish	Dorset	11	J5
Dewsbury	Kirk	85	K11
Dewsbury Moor	Kirk	85	K10
Deytheur	Powys	62	H8
Dial	N Som	28	H9
Dial Green	W Susx	14	E6
Dial Post	W Susx	14	H7
Dibberford	Dorset	10	C4
Dibden	Hants	12	J3
Dibden Purlieu	Hants	12	G3
Dickens Heath	Solhll	53	L5
Dickleburgh	Norfk	58	H4
Didbrook	Gloucs	42	B5
Didcot	Oxon	31	L4
Diddington	Cambs	56	D7
Diddlebury	Shrops	51	N3
Didley	Herefs	40	G4
Didling	W Susx	25	P9
Didmarton	Gloucs	29	N5
Didsbury	Manch	76	F4
Didworthy	Devon	5	L5
Digby	Lincs	67	Q1
Digg	Highld	134	H2
Diggle	Oldham	77	J2
Digmoor	Lancs	75	N3
Digswell	Herts	45	J8
Digswell Water	Herts	45	J8
Dihewyd	Cerdgn	48	H9
Dilham	Norfk	71	L7
Dilhorne	Staffs	64	H3
Dill Hall	Lancs	83	R9
Dillarburn	S Lans	114	E12
Dillington	Cambs	56	C7
Dilston	Nthumb	100	C5
Dilton Marsh	Wilts	23	Q4
Dilwyn	Herefs	51	L9
Dimple	Bolton	83	Q12
Dimple	Derbys	77	P11
Dinas	Carmth	37	P4
Dinas	Cnwll	6	C10
Dinas	Gwynd	60	D5
Dinas	Gwynd	72	F3
Dinas	Rhondd	27	N4
Dinas Cross	Pembks	37	K3
Dinas Dinlle	Gwynd	72	G12
Dinas-Mawddwy	Gwynd	61	Q9
Dinas Powys	V Glam	27	R8
Dinder	Somset	22	C4
Dinedor	Herefs	40	H4
Dingestow	Mons	40	F9
Dingle	Lpool	75	L6
Dingleden	Kent	16	E5
Dingley	Nhants	55	K3
Dingwall	Highld	137	P4
Dinmael	Conwy	62	E3
Dinnet	Abers	132	C5
Dinnington	N u Ty	100	G4
Dinnington	Rothm	78	E6
Dinnington	Somset	21	N11
Dinorwic	Gwynd	73	K11
Dinton	Bucks	43	R9
Dinton	Wilts	23	M7
Dinwoodie	D & G	106	E11
Dinworthy	Devon	18	F10
Dipford	Somset	21	K8
Dipley	Hants	31	Q11
Dippen	Ag & B	103	L2
Dippenhall	Surrey	25	P4
Dippermill	Devon	7	N2
Dippertown	Devon	7	N8
Dippin	N Ayrs	103	Q5
Dipple	Moray	139	Q4
Dipple	S Ayrs	104	D9
Diptford	Devon	5	M5
Dipton	Dur	100	F7
Diptonmill	Nthumb	99	P6
Dirleton	E Loth	116	C4
Dirt Pot	Nthumb	99	N9
Discoed	Powys	51	J8
Diseworth	Leics	66	D7
Dishforth	N York	91	P11
Disley	Ches E	76	H7
Diss	Norfk	58	H5
Disserth	Powys	50	E9
Distington	Cumb	88	D3
Ditchampton	Wilts	23	N7
Ditcheat	Somset	22	E6
Ditchingham	Norfk	59	L2
Ditchling	E Susx	15	L8
Ditherington	Shrops	63	N9
Ditteridge	Wilts	29	N8
Dittisham	Devon	5	P6
Ditton	Kent	34	C10
Ditton Green	Cambs	57	M9
Ditton Priors	Shrops	51	Q3
Dixton	Gloucs	41	Q5
Dixton	Mons	40	G9
Dizzard	Cnwll	6	H3
Dobcross	Oldham	77	J2
Dobwalls	Cnwll	4	C4
Doccombe	Devon	8	E7
Dochgarroch	Highld	138	B2
Dockenfield	Surrey	25	P5
Docker	Lancs	89	N11
Docking	Norfk	69	P5
Docklow	Herefs	51	P9
Dockray	Cumb	89	L2
Dockray	Cumb	98	D6
Dodbrooke	Devon	5	M8
Doddinghurst	Essex	33	Q2
Doddington	Cambs	56	H3
Doddington	Kent	34	G11
Doddington	Lincs	79	M9
Doddington	Nthumb	108	G3
Doddington	Shrops	51	P6
Doddiscombsleigh	Devon	8	F7
Dodd's Green	Ches E	63	Q3
Doddshill	Norfk	69	N6
Doddy Cross	Cnwll	4	D4
Dodford	Nhants	54	G8
Dodford	Worcs	52	G6
Dodington	S Glos	29	M6
Dodington	Somset	21	J4
Dodleston	Ches W	75	K11
Dodscott	Devon	19	K9
Dodside	E Rens	113	P10
Dod's Leigh	Staffs	65	J5
Dodworth	Barns	77	P3
Dodworth Bottom	Barns	77	M7
Dodworth Green	Barns	77	P3
Doe Bank	Birm	53	L1
Doe Lea	Derbys	78	D10
Dogdyke	Lincs	68	D1
Dogley Lane	Kirk	85	J12
Dogmersfield	Hants	25	N3
Dogridge	Wilts	30	C5
Dogsthorpe	C Pete	68	C12
Dog Village	Devon	9	J5
Dolanog	Powys	62	E9
Dolau	Powys	50	G7
Dolaucothi	Carmth	38	G3
Dolbenmaen	Gwynd	60	H3
Doley	Staffs	64	D6
Dolfach	Powys	62	B11
Dolfor	Powys	50	F3
Dolgarrog	Conwy	73	N10
Dolgellau	Gwynd	61	L11
Dolgoch	Gwynd	61	L11
Dol-gran	Carmth	38	C5
Doll	Highld	146	F4
Dollar	Clacks	114	H2
Dollarfield	Clacks	114	H2
Dolley Green	Powys	51	J8
Dollwen	Cerdgn	49	M4
Dolphin	Flints	74	H9
Dolphinholme	Lancs	83	M4
Dolphinton	S Lans	115	K10
Dolton	Devon	19	L11
Dolwen	Conwy	73	Q9
Dolwyddelan	Conwy	61	M2
Dolybont	Cerdgn	49	K3
Dolyhir	Powys	50	H9
Domgay	Powys	63	J8
Donaldson's Lodge	Nthumb	108	D1
Doncaster	Donc	78	F3
Doncaster Carr	Donc	78	F3
Doncaster North Services	Donc	78	H2
Doncaster Sheffield Airport	Donc	78	G4
Donhead St Andrew	Wilts	23	K8
Donhead St Mary	Wilts	23	K8
Donibristle	Fife	115	L3
Doniford	Somset	20	F4
Donington	Lincs	68	D5
Donington on Bain	Lincs	80	E7
Donington Park Services	Leics	66	D7
Donington Southing	Lincs	68	D5
Donisthorpe	Leics	65	P9
Donkey Street	Kent	17	K4
Donkey Town	Surrey	32	D10
Donnington	Gloucs	42	E6
Donnington	Herefs	41	M5
Donnington	Shrops	63	P10
Donnington	W Berk	31	K8
Donnington	W Susx	13	Q4
Donnington	Wrekin	64	D9
Donnington Wood	Wrekin	64	D9
Donyatt	Somset	21	M10
Doomsday Green	W Susx	14	H5
Doonfoot	S Ayrs	104	F6
Dora's Green	Hants	25	P4
Dorback Lodge	Highld	131	K5
Dorchester	Dorset	10	H6
Dorchester-on-Thames	Oxon	31	M3
Dordon	Warwks	65	P11
Dore	Sheff	77	P7
Dores	Highld	137	Q9
Dorking	Surrey	14	H1
Dorking Tye	Suffk	46	H4
Dormans Park	Surrey	15	M2
Dormansland	Surrey	15	M2
Dormington	Herefs	41	J4
Dormston	Worcs	53	J9
Dorn	Gloucs	42	E5
Dornie	Highld	136	B10
Dornoch	Highld	146	E7
Dornock	D & G	97	R4
Dorrery	Highld	151	K6
Dorridge	Solhll	53	M6
Dorrington	Lincs	67	Q2
Dorrington	Shrops	63	N12
Dorsington	Warwks	53	L11
Dorstone	Herefs	40	E3
Dorton	Bucks	43	N9
Dosthill	Staffs	65	N12
Dothan	IoA	72	F9
Dottery	Dorset	10	C6
Doublebois	Cnwll	4	C4
Doughton	Gloucs	29	P4
Douglas	IoM	102	e6
Douglas	S Lans	105	Q4
Douglas and Angus	C Dund	124	H6
Douglas Pier	Ag & B	113	J1
Douglastown	Angus	124	H3
Douglas Water	S Lans	105	Q3
Douglas West	S Lans	105	Q3
Doulting	Somset	22	E6
Dounby	Ork	147	b4
Doune	Highld	145	L5
Doune	Stirlg	114	D1
Dounepark	S Ayrs	104	D10
Dounie	Highld	145	N7
Dousland	Devon	5	K4
Dovaston	Shrops	63	K8
Dove Dale	Derbys	65	L2
Dove Green	Notts	66	D2
Dove Holes	Derbys	77	K8
Dovenby	Cumb	97	M11
Dover	Kent	17	P2
Dover	Wigan	75	Q4
Dover Castle	Kent	17	P2
Dovercourt	Essex	47	N5
Doverdale	Worcs	52	F7
Doveridge	Derbys	65	L5
Doversgreen	Surrey	15	J1
Dowally	P & K	123	P3
Dowbridge	Lancs	83	K9
Dowdeswell	Gloucs	42	B7
Dowlais	Myr Td	39	P10
Dowland	Devon	7	Q3
Dowlish Ford	Somset	21	M10
Dowlish Wake	Somset	21	N10
Down Ampney	Gloucs	30	C5
Downderry	Cnwll	4	D6
Downe	Gt Lon	33	N10
Downend	Gloucs	29	N3
Downend	IoW	12	H8
Downend	S Glos	29	K7
Downend	W Berk	31	K7
Downfield	C Dund	124	H6
Downgate	Cnwll	7	L10
Downgate	Cnwll	7	L10
Downham	Essex	34	C2
Downham	Gt Lon	33	M8
Downham	Lancs	84	B6
Downham Market	Norfk	69	L11
Down Hatherley	Gloucs	41	P7
Downhead	Somset	22	D8
Downhead	Somset	22	F4
Downhill	Cnwll	6	B11
Downholland Cross	Lancs	75	L2
Downholme	N York	91	J7
Downicarey	Devon	7	M7
Downies	Abers	133	M5
Downing	Flints	74	G8
Downley	Bucks	32	B3
Down St Mary	Devon	8	D4
Downside	Somset	22	D4
Downside	Surrey	32	H10
Down Thomas	Devon	4	H7
Downton	Hants	12	B6
Downton	Wilts	24	C9
Dowsby	Lincs	68	C6
Dowsdale	Lincs	68	F10
Doxey	Staffs	64	G8
Doxford	Nthumb	109	K5
Doynton	S Glos	29	L7
Draethen	Caerph	28	B5
Draffan	S Lans	114	D12
Dragonby	N Linc	79	M1
Dragons Green	W Susx	14	H6
Drakeholes	Notts	78	H5
Drakelow	Worcs	52	F4
Drakemyre	N Ayrs	113	K11
Drakes Broughton	Worcs	52	H11
Drakewalls	Cnwll	7	N10
Draughton	Nhants	55	J5
Draughton	N York	84	F5
Drax	N York	86	C10
Drax Hales	N York	86	C10
Draycote	Warwks	54	D6
Draycot Foliat	Swindn	30	E7
Draycott	Derbys	66	D5
Draycott	Gloucs	42	E4
Draycott	Shrops	52	E2
Draycott	Somset	21	Q3
Draycott	Somset	22	D8
Draycott	Worcs	52	G5
Draycott in the Clay	Staffs	65	M6
Draycott in the Moors	Staffs	64	H4
Drayford	Devon	19	Q10
Drayton	C Port	13	L4
Drayton	Leics	55	L2
Drayton	Lincs	68	D5
Drayton	Norfk	71	J9
Drayton	Oxon	31	K3
Drayton	Oxon	43	K3
Drayton	Somset	21	N8
Drayton	Worcs	52	G5
Drayton Bassett	Staffs	65	M12
Drayton Beauchamp	Bucks	44	D8
Drayton Manor Park	Staffs	65	M12
Drayton Parslow	Bucks	44	B6
Drayton St Leonard	Oxon	31	M3
Drebley	N York	84	F4
Dreemskerry	IoM	102	e3
Dreen Hill	Pembks	36	H7
Drefach	Carmth	38	A4
Drefach	Carmth	38	D9
Drefach	Cerdgn	38	D2
Drefelin	Carmth	38	A4
Dreghorn	N Ayrs	104	F2
Drellingore	Kent	17	M3
Drem	E Loth	116	C5
Dresden	C Stke	64	G4
Drewsteignton	Devon	8	D6
Driby	Lincs	80	G9
Driffield	E R Yk	87	J4
Driffield	Gloucs	30	C4
Driffield Cross Roads	Gloucs	30	C4
Drift	Cnwll	2	C9
Drigg	Cumb	88	E7
Drighlington	Leeds	85	K9
Drimnin	Highld	119	P2
Drimpton	Dorset	10	C4
Drimsallie	Highld	128	C8
Dringhouses	C York	86	A5
Drinkstone	Suffk	58	E8
Drinkstone Green	Suffk	58	E8
Drive End	Dorset	10	E3
Driver's End	Herts	45	J7
Droitwich Spa	Worcs	52	G8
Dron	P & K	124	C7
Dronfield	Derbys	78	B8
Dronfield Woodhouse	Derbys	77	Q7
Drongan	E Ayrs	104	H6
Dronley	Angus	124	G6
Droop	Dorset	11	J4
Dropping Well	Rothm	77	Q5
Droxford	Hants	25	K9
Droylsden	Tamesd	76	G4
Druid	Denbgs	62	E3
Druidston	Pembks	36	G7
Druimarbin	Highld	128	F10
Druimavuic	Ag & B	121	K4
Druimdrishaig	Ag & B	111	R3
Druimindarroch	Highld	127	M9
Drum	Ag & B	112	D6
Drum	P & K	115	J1
Drumalbin	S Lans	106	B2
Drumbeg	Highld	148	D10
Drumblade	Abers	140	E7
Drumbreddon	D & G	94	F9
Drumburgh	Cumb	98	B6
Drumburn	D & G	96	H6
Drumchapel	C Glas	113	Q7
Drumchastle	P & K	122	H1
Drumclog	S Lans	105	M2
Drumelzier	Border	106	F3
Drumfearn	Highld	127	M1
Drumfrennie	Abers	132	H5
Drumgley	Angus	124	H3
Drumguish	Highld	130	H4
Drumin	Moray	139	M10
Drumjohn	D & G	105	J10
Drumlamford	S Ayrs	95	K3
Drumlasie	Abers	132	G3
Drumleaning	Cumb	98	B8
Drumlemble	Ag & B	103	J8
Drumlithie	Abers	133	J8
Drummoddie	D & G	95	M9
Drummore	D & G	94	G11
Drummuir	Moray	140	B7
Drumnadrochit	Highld	137	N2
Drumnagorrach	Moray	140	E5
Drumpark	D & G	96	H2
Drumrunie	Highld	144	F4
Drumshang	S Ayrs	104	D8
Drumuie	Highld	134	H6
Drumuillie	Highld	138	H11
Drumvaich	Stirlg	122	H12
Drunzie	P & K	124	C11
Druridge	Nthumb	109	M10
Drury	Flints	75	J10
Drws-y-coed	Gwynd	61	J1
Drybeck	Cumb	89	Q4
Drybridge	Moray	140	C3
Drybridge	N Ayrs	104	G2
Drybrook	Gloucs	41	K8
Dryburgh	Border	107	P3
Dry Doddington	Lincs	67	L3
Dry Drayton	Cambs	56	E8
Drymen	Stirlg	113	P3
Drymuir	Abers	141	L6
Drynoch	Highld	134	G9
Dry Sandford	Oxon	31	K2
Dryslwyn	Carmth	38	E7
Dry Street	Essex	34	C4
Dryton	Shrops	63	P11
Dubford	Abers	141	J3
Dublin	Suffk	58	H7
Duchally	Highld	145	J2
Duck End	Bed	44	F3
Duck End	Cambs	56	E8
Duck End	Essex	45	R5
Duck End	Essex	46	B6
Duckend Green	Essex	46	C7
Duckington	Ches W	63	N2
Ducklington	Oxon	42	H10
Duck's Cross	Bed	56	B9
Duddenhoe End	Essex	45	M4
Duddingston	C Edin	115	P7
Duddington	Nhants	67	N12
Duddleswick	Shrops	52	C4
Duddlewick	Shrops	52	C4
Duddo	Nthumb	108	E1
Duddon	Ches W	75	N10
Duddon Bridge	Cumb	88	H8
Duddon Common	Ches W	75	N10
Dudleston	Shrops	63	K5
Dudleston Heath	Shrops	63	L5
Dudley	Dudley	52	H2
Dudley	N Tyne	100	H3
Dudley Hill	C Brad	85	J9
Dudley Port	Sandw	52	H2
Dudnill	Shrops	51	Q6
Dudsbury	Dorset	11	P5
Dudswell	Herts	44	E9
Duffield	Derbys	65	Q4
Duffryn	Neath	27	J3
Dufftown	Moray	139	P8
Duffus	Moray	139	L2
Dufton	Cumb	89	Q2
Duggleby	N York	86	H2
Duirinish	Highld	135	P9
Duisdalemore	Highld	127	M2
Duisky	Highld	128	D8
Dukestown	Blae G	39	Q9
Duke Street	Suffk	47	J3
Dukinfield	Tamesd	76	H4
Dulas	IoA	72	H6
Dulcote	Somset	22	C4
Dulford	Devon	9	P3
Dull	P & K	123	K3
Dullatur	N Lans	114	D6
Dullingham	Cambs	57	M9
Dullingham Ley	Cambs	57	M9
Dulnain Bridge	Highld	139	J11
Duloe	Bed	56	C8
Duloe	Cnwll	4	C5
Dulsie Bridge	Highld	138	G8
Dulverton	Somset	20	E8
Dulwich	Gt Lon	33	L7
Dumbarton	W Duns	113	M6
Dumbleton	Gloucs	42	A4
Dumfries	D & G	97	K3
Dumgoyne	Stirlg	113	Q5
Dummer	Hants	25	K4
Dumpton	Kent	35	R9
Dun	Angus	132	G12
Dunalastair	P & K	123	J1
Dunan	Ag & B	112	H7
Dunan	Highld	135	K9
Dunan	P & K	122	C1
Dunaverty	Ag & B	103	J8
Dunball	Somset	21	M5
Dunbar	E Loth	116	F5
Dunbeath	Highld	151	L10
Dunbeg	Ag & B	120	G5
Dunblane	Stirlg	114	E1
Dunbog	Fife	124	F9
Dunbridge	Hants	24	E9
Duncanston	Highld	137	P4
Duncanstone	Abers	140	E10
Dunchideock	Devon	8	G7
Dunchurch	Warwks	54	D6
Duncote	Nhants	55	H10
Duncow	D & G	97	J2
Duncrievie	P & K	124	C11
Duncton	W Susx	14	D7
Dundee	C Dund	124	H6
Dundee Airport	C Dund	124	H7
Dundon	Somset	22	C7
Dundonald	S Ayrs	104	G2
Dundonnell	Highld	144	G7
Dundraw	Cumb	97	P8
Dundreggan	Highld	129	J3
Dundrennan	D & G	96	G8
Dundry	N Som	28	H8
Dunecht	Abers	133	J2
Dunfermline	Fife	115	K4
Dunfield	Gloucs	30	D3
Dunford Bridge	Barns	77	M3
Dungate	Kent	34	G10
Dungavel	S Lans	105	M2
Dunge	Wilts	23	Q4
Dungeness	Kent	17	K7
Dungworth	Sheff	77	P4
Dunham Massey	Traffd	76	D6
Dunham-on-the-Hill	Ches W	75	N9
Dunham-on-Trent	Notts	79	K9
Dunhampton	Worcs	52	F7
Dunham Town	Traffd	76	D6
Dunham Woodhouses	Traffd	76	D6
Dunholme	Lincs	79	P9
Dunino	Fife	125	K10
Dunipace	Falk	114	F5
Dunkeld	P & K	123	P4
Dunkerton	BaNES	29	L11
Dunkeswell	Devon	9	P3

Dunkeswick – Everingham 163

Dunkeswick N York 85 L6
Dunkirk Ches W 75 L9
Dunkirk Kent 35 J10
Dunkirk S Glos 29 M5
Dunkirk Wilts 30 A10
Dunk's Green Kent 33 R11
Dunlappie Angus 132 F10
Dunley Hants 24 G3
Dunley Worcs 52 E7
Dunlop E Ayrs 113 M11
Dunmaglass Highld 137 Q11
Dunmere Cnwll 6 F11
Dunmore Falk 114 G3
Dunnet Highld 151 M2
Dunnichen Angus 125 K3
Dunning P & K 123 P10
Dunnington C York 86 C5
Dunnington E R Yk 87 M5
Dunnington Warwks 53 K10
Dunnockshaw Lancs 84 B9
Dunn Street Kent 34 D10
Dunoon Ag & B 112 H6
Dunphail Moray 139 J6
Dunragit D & G 94 H7
Duns Border 116 H10
Dunsa Derbys 77 N9
Dunsby Lincs 68 B7
Dunscar Bolton 76 D1
Dunscore D & G 96 H1
Dunscroft Donc 78 G2
Dunsdale R & Cl 92 C3
Dunsden Green Oxon 31 Q7
Dunsdon Devon 7 K3
Dunsfold Surrey 14 E4
Dunsford Devon 8 F7
Dunshalt Fife 124 E10
Dunshillock Abers 141 N6
Dunsill Notts 78 D11
Dunsley N York 92 H4
Dunsley Staffs 52 F4
Dunsmore Bucks 44 B10
Dunsop Bridge Lancs 83 P5
Dunstable C Beds 44 E7
Dunstall Staffs 65 M8
Dunstall Common Worcs 41 P3
Dunstall Green Suffk 57 P8
Dunstan Nthumb 109 L6
Dunstan Steads Nthumb 109 L5
Dunster Somset 20 F5
Duns Tew Oxon 43 K6
Dunston Gatesd 100 G6
Dunston Lincs 79 Q11
Dunston Norfk 71 J11
Dunston Staffs 64 H8
Dunstone Devon 5 J6
Dunstone Devon 8 D9
Dunston Heath Staffs 64 G8
Dunsville Donc 78 G2
Dunswell E R Yk 87 K8
Dunsyre S Lans 115 K11
Dunterton Devon 7 M9
Dunthrop Oxon 42 H6
Duntisbourne Abbots Gloucs 41 R10
Duntisbourne Leer Gloucs 41 R10
Duntisbourne Rouse Gloucs 42 A10
Duntish Dorset 10 H3
Duntocher W Duns 113 P7
Dunton Bucks 44 B7
Dunton C Beds 45 J3
Dunton Norfk 70 C6
Dunton Bassett Leics 54 E3
Dunton Green Kent 33 P11
Dunton Wayletts Essex 34 B4
Duntulm Highld 142 D10
Dunure S Ayrs 104 E7
Dunvant Swans 26 F4
Dunvegan Highld 134 D6
Dunwich Suffk 59 P6
Dunwood Staffs 64 H1
Durdar Cumb 98 E8
Durgan Cnwll 3 J9
Durham Dur 100 H9
Durham Cathedral Dur 100 H10
Durham Services Dur 100 H11
Durham Tees Valley Airport S on T 91 P4
Durisdeer D & G 106 A9
Durisdeermill D & G 106 A9
Durkar Wakefd 85 L11
Durleigh Somset 21 L6
Durley Hants 24 J10
Durley Wilts 30 F9
Durley Street Hants 25 J10
Durlock Kent 35 N10
Durlock Kent 35 P9
Durlow Common Herefs 41 K4
Durn Rochdl 84 E12
Durness Highld 149 J3
Durno Abers 140 H10
Duror Highld 121 J2
Durran Ag & B 120 H11
Durrington W Susx 14 G9
Durrington Wilts 23 P4
Durris Abers 133 J5
Dursley Gloucs 29 M3
Dursley Cross Gloucs 41 L7
Durston Somset 21 L7
Durweston Dorset 11 L3
Duston Nhants 55 J8
Duthil Highld 138 H11
Dutlas Powys 50 H5
Duton Hill Essex 45 R6
Dutson Cnwll 7 L7
Dutton Ches W 75 P8
Duxford Cambs 45 N2
Duxford Oxon 30 H2
Duxford IWM Cambs 45 N2
Dwygyfylchi Conwy 73 M8
Dwyran IoA 72 G10
Dyce C Aber 133 L2
Dyer's End Essex 46 C4
Dyfatty Carmth 26 C2
Dyffrydan Gwynd 61 M9
Dyffryn Brdgnd 27 K3
Dyffryn Myr Td 39 P11
Dyffryn V Glam 27 P8
Dyffryn Ardudwy Gwynd 61 K7
Dyffryn Castell Cerdgn 49 N4
Dyffryn Cellwen Neath 39 K9
Dyke Lincs 68 B7
Dyke Moray 138 H4
Dykehead Angus 124 E2
Dykehead Angus 132 B12
Dykehead N Lans 114 F9
Dykehead Stirlg 114 A2
Dykelands Abers 132 H10
Dykends Angus 124 E1
Dykeside Abers 140 H7
Dylife Powys 49 Q2
Dymchurch Kent 17 K5
Dymock Gloucs 41 L5
Dyrham S Glos 29 L7
Dysart Fife 115 P3
Dyserth Denbgs 74 E8

E

Eachway Worcs 53 J5
Eachwick Nthumb 100 E4
Eagland Hill Lancs 83 K6
Eagle Lincs 79 L10
Eagle Barnsdale Lincs 79 L10
Eagle Moor Lincs 79 M10
Eaglescliffe S on T 91 P4
Eaglesfield Cumb 88 E1
Eaglesfield D & G 97 P3
Eaglesham E Rens 113 Q11
Eagley Bolton 76 D1
Eairy IoM 102 d6
Eakring Notts 78 H11
Ealand N Linc 79 K1
Ealing Gt Lon 32 H6
Eals Nthumb 99 K7
Eamont Bridge Cumb 89 N1
Earby Lancs 84 D6
Earcroft Bl w D 83 P10
Eardington Shrops 52 D2
Eardisland Herefs 51 L9
Eardisley Herefs 51 K11
Eardiston Shrops 63 L7
Eardiston Worcs 52 C7
Earith Cambs 56 G6
Earle Nthumb 108 F4
Earlestown St Hel 75 P5
Earley Wokham 31 Q8
Earlham Norfk 71 J10
Earlish Highld 134 G4
Earls Barton Nhants 55 L8
Earls Colne Essex 46 F6
Earls Common Worcs 52 H9
Earl's Croome Worcs 41 P3
Earlsditton Shrops 52 B5
Earlsdon Covtry 53 Q5
Earl's Down E Susx 16 B7
Earlsferry Fife 116 C1
Earlsfield Gt Lon 33 J8
Earlsford Abers 141 K9
Earl's Green Suffk 58 F7
Earlsheaton Kirk 85 K11
Earl Shilton Leics 54 D1
Earl Soham Suffk 59 J8
Earl Sterndale Derbys 77 K10
Earlston Border 107 P2
Earlston E Ayrs 104 H3
Earl Stonham Suffk 58 G9
Earlswood Surrey 15 K1
Earlswood Warwks 53 L6
Earlswood Common Mons 28 F3
Earnley W Susx 13 P5
Earnshaw Bridge Lancs 83 M10
Earsdon N Tyne 101 J4
Earsdon Nthumb 109 K11
Earsham Norfk 59 L3
Earswick C York 86 B4
Eartham W Susx 14 D9
Earthcott S Glos 29 K5
Easby N York 92 C5
Easdale Ag & B 120 D9
Easebourne W Susx 14 C6
Easenhall Warwks 54 D5
Eashing Surrey 14 D2
Easington Bucks 43 P9
Easington Dur 101 K9
Easington E R Yk 87 R11
Easington Nthumb 109 J3
Easington Oxon 31 N3
Easington R & Cl 92 F3
Easington Colliery Dur 101 L9
Easington Lane Sundld 101 K9
Easingwold N York 85 Q1
Easole Street Kent 35 N12
Eassie and Nevay Angus 124 G4
East Aberthaw V Glam 27 N9
East Allington Devon 5 N7
East Anstey Devon 20 D8
East Anton Hants 24 F4
East Appleton N York 91 L7
East Ashey IoW 13 K7
East Ashling W Susx 13 P3
East Aston Hants 24 G4
East Ayton N York 93 K9
East Balsdon Cnwll 7 K5
East Bank Blae G 40 B10
East Barkwith Lincs 80 D7
East Barming Kent 34 C11
East Barnby N York 92 G4
East Barnet Gt Lon 33 K3
East Barns E Loth 116 G6
East Barsham Norfk 70 D5
East Beckham Norfk 70 H4
East Bedfont Gt Lon 32 F7
East Bergholt Suffk 47 J5
East Bierley Kirk 85 J9
East Bilney Norfk 70 D8
East Blatchington E Susx 15 N10
East Bloxworth Dorset 11 L6
East Boldon S Tyne 101 K6
East Boldre Hants 12 F4
East Bolton Nthumb 109 J6
Eastbourne Darltn 91 M4
Eastbourne E Susx 16 A11
East Bower Somset 21 M6
East Bradenham Norfk 70 D10
East Brent Somset 21 M3
Eastbridge Suffk 59 N7
East Bridgford Notts 66 H3
East Briscoe Dur 90 F3
Eastbrook V Glam 27 R8
East Buckland Devon 19 N7
East Budleigh Devon 9 K8
Eastburn C Brad 84 F6
Eastburn E R Yk 87 J4
East Burnham Bucks 32 D5
East Burton Dorset 11 K7
Eastbury W Berk 30 H7
East Butsfield Dur 100 E9
East Butterwick N Linc 79 L2
Eastby N York 84 F4
East Calder W Loth 115 K7
East Carleton Norfk 70 H11
East Carlton Leeds 85 J6
East Carlton Nhants 55 L3
East Chaldon Dorset 11 J8
East Challow Oxon 30 H5
East Charleton Devon 5 M8
East Chelborough Dorset 10 E4
East Chiltington E Susx 15 L8
East Chinnock Somset 22 C10
East Chisenbury Wilts 23 P3
East Cholderton Hants 24 E4
Eastchurch Kent 34 H8
East Clandon Surrey 32 F12
East Claydon Bucks 43 Q6
East Clevedon N Som 28 F8
East Coker Somset 22 C11
Eastcombe Gloucs 41 P10
Eastcombe Somset 21 J7
East Compton Somset 22 E5
East Cornworthy Devon 5 P6
East Cote Cumb 97 M7
Eastcote Gt Lon 32 G5
Eastcote Nhants 54 H10
Eastcote Solhll 53 M5
Eastcott Cnwll 18 E10
Eastcott Wilts 23 M2
East Cottingwith E R Yk 86 D7
Eastcourt Wilts 29 R4
Eastcourt Wilts 30 F10
East Cowes IoW 12 H5
East Cowick E R Yk 86 C11
East Cowton N York 91 M6
East Cramlington Nthumb 100 H3
East Cranmore Somset 22 F5
East Creech Dorset 11 M8
East Curthwaite Cumb 98 D8
East Dean E Susx 15 Q11
East Dean Gloucs 41 K7
East Dean Hants 24 D8
East Dean W Susx 14 C8
Eastdown Devon 5 P7
East Down Devon 19 L5
East Drayton Notts 79 K8
East Dulwich Gt Lon 33 L7
East Dundry N Som 28 H9
East Ella C KuH 87 K9
East End Bed 56 B9
East End C Beds 44 D3
East End E R Yk 87 M9
East End E R Yk 87 P9
Eastend Essex 34 G4
East End Essex 45 M9
East End Hants 12 F5
East End Hants 31 J10
East End Herts 45 N6
East End Kent 16 E4
East End Kent 34 H7
East End M Keyn 44 D3
East End Oxon 43 J8
East End Somset 22 F4
East End Suffk 47 K5
Easter Balmoral Abers 131 N5
Easter Compton S Glos 28 H6
Easter Dalziel Highld 138 D6
Eastergate W Susx 14 D10
Easterhouse C Glas 114 C8
Easter Howgate Mdloth 115 N8
Easter Kinkell Highld 137 Q5
Easter Moniack Highld 137 P7
Eastern Green Covtry 53 P5
Easter Ord Abers 133 K3
Easter Pitkierie Fife 125 L11
Easter Skeld Shet 147 h7
Easter Softlaw Border 108 B3
Easterton Wilts 23 M2
Eastertown Somset 21 M2
East Everleigh Wilts 24 C3
East Farleigh Kent 34 C11
East Farndon Nhants 55 J4
East Ferry Lincs 79 K4
Eastfield N Lans 114 G8
Eastfield N York 93 L10
East Firsby Lincs 79 P6
East Fortune E Loth 116 D5
East Garforth Leeds 85 N8
East Garston W Berk 30 H7
Eastgate Dur 99 Q10
Eastgate Lincs 68 B8
Eastgate Norfk 70 H7
East Ginge Oxon 31 J5
East Goscote Leics 66 G9
East Grafton Wilts 30 F10
East Green Suffk 59 M7
East Grimstead Wilts 24 C8
East Grinstead W Susx 15 M3
East Guldeford E Susx 16 G6
East Haddon Nhants 54 H7
East Hagbourne Oxon 31 L5
East Halton N Linc 87 L11
East Ham Gt Lon 33 M5
Eastham Wirral 75 K7
Eastham Ferry Wirral 75 L7
Easthampton Herefs 51 L8
East Hanney Oxon 31 J4
East Hanningfield Essex 34 D2
East Hardwick Wakefd 85 P11
East Harling Norfk 58 E3
East Harlsey N York 91 P7
East Harnham Wilts 23 P7
East Harptree BaNES 28 H11
East Hartford Nthumb 100 H2
East Harting W Susx 25 P9
East Hatch Wilts 23 K7
East Hatley Cambs 56 F10
East Hauxwell N York 91 K8
East Haven Angus 125 L5
Eastheath Wokham 31 R9
East Heckington Lincs 68 D3
East Hedleyhope Dur 100 F10
East Helmsdale Highld 147 J2
East Hendred Oxon 31 K5
East Heslerton N York 93 J11
East Hewish N Som 28 E9
East Hoathly E Susx 15 P7
East Holme Dorset 11 L7
East Hope Dur 90 H5
Easthope Shrops 51 P1
Easthorpe Essex 46 G7
Easthorpe Notts 66 H1
East Horrington Somset 22 D4
East Horsley Surrey 32 F11
East Horton Nthumb 108 G4
East Howe BCP 11 P5
East Huntspill Somset 21 M4
East Hyde C Beds 44 G8
East Ilkerton Devon 19 P4
East Ilsley W Berk 31 K6
Eastington Devon 8 D3
Eastington Gloucs 41 M10
Eastington Gloucs 42 D9
East Keal Lincs 80 G11
East Kennett Wilts 30 D9
East Keswick Leeds 85 M6
East Kilbride S Lans 114 B10
East Kimber Devon 7 P5
East Kirkby Lincs 80 F11
East Knighton Dorset 11 K7
East Knowstone Devon 20 C8
East Knoyle Wilts 23 K7
East Lambrook Somset 21 P9
Eastlands D & G 96 G4
East Langdon Kent 17 P2
East Langton Leics 55 J2
East Lavant W Susx 13 Q3
East Lavington W Susx 14 D7
East Layton N York 91 K5
Eastleach Martin Gloucs 42 E10
Eastleach Turville Gloucs 42 E10
East Leake Notts 66 F7
East Learmouth Nthumb 108 D2
East Leigh Devon 5 L6
East Leigh Devon 5 M5
East Leigh Devon 8 D4
Eastleigh Devon 19 J8
Eastleigh Hants 24 G9
East Lexham Norfk 70 C8
Eastling Kent 34 G11
East Linton E Loth 116 D6
East Liss Hants 25 N8
East Lockinge Oxon 31 J5
East Lound N Linc 79 K4
East Lulworth Dorset 11 L8
East Lutton N York 86 H1
East Lydeard Somset 21 J7
East Lydford Somset 22 D7
East Malling Kent 34 C11
East Malling Heath Kent 34 C11
East Marden W Susx 25 P10
East Markham Notts 79 J9
East Martin Hants 23 N9
East Marton N York 84 D5
East Meon Hants 25 L9
East Mere Devon 20 F10
East Mersea Essex 47 J9
East Midlands Airport Leics 66 D7
East Molesey Surrey 32 G9
Eastmoor Norfk 69 P11
East Morden Dorset 11 M6
East Morton C Brad 84 G7
East Morton D & G 106 A9
East Ness N York 92 E11
East Newton E R Yk 87 P7
Eastney C Port 13 L5
Eastnor Herefs 41 L4
East Norton Leics 67 K12
Eastoft N Linc 86 E12
East Ogwell Devon 5 P3
Easton Cambs 56 C6
Easton Cumb 98 C6
Easton Devon 8 D7
Easton Dorset 10 H10
Easton Hants 24 H7
Easton Lincs 67 M7
Easton Norfk 70 H10
Easton Somset 22 C4
Easton Suffk 59 K9
Easton W Berk 31 J8
Easton Wilts 29 P8
Easton Grey Wilts 29 P5
Easton-in-Gordano N Som 28 G7
Easton Maudit Nhants 55 M9
Easton-on-the-Hill Nhants 67 P11
Easton Royal Wilts 30 E10
East Orchard Dorset 23 J10
East Ord Nthumb 117 L11
East Panson Devon 7 L6
East Parley BCP 11 Q5
East Peckham Kent 16 B1
East Pennard Somset 22 D6
East Perry Cambs 56 C7
East Portlemouth Devon 5 M9
East Prawle Devon 5 N9
East Preston W Susx 14 F10
East Pulham Dorset 10 H3
East Putford Devon 18 G10
East Quantoxhead Somset 21 J5
East Rainham Medway 34 E9
East Rainton Sundld 101 J8
East Ravendale NE Lin 80 E4
East Raynham Norfk 70 C7
Eastrea Cambs 56 F1
Eastriggs D & G 97 Q5
East Rigton Leeds 85 M6
Eastrington E R Yk 86 E9
East Rolstone N Som 28 E10
Eastrop Swindn 30 E4
East Rounton N York 91 P6
East Rudham Norfk 70 B6
East Runton Norfk 71 J4
East Ruston Norfk 71 L6
Eastry Kent 35 P11
East Saltoun E Loth 116 B8
Eastshaw W Susx 14 C6
East Sheen Gt Lon 32 H7
East Shefford W Berk 30 H7
East Sleekburn Nthumb 100 H2
East Somerton Norfk 71 P8
East Stockwith Lincs 79 K5
East Stoke Dorset 11 L7
East Stoke Notts 67 J2
East Stour Dorset 22 H9
East Stour Common Dorset 22 H8
East Stourmouth Kent 35 N10
East Stowford Devon 19 M8
East Stratton Hants 25 J5
East Studdal Kent 17 P1
East Sutton Kent 16 E1
East Taphouse Cnwll 4 B4
East-the-Water Devon 19 J8
East Thirston Nthumb 109 K9
East Tilbury Thurr 34 B6
East Tilbury Village Thurr 34 B7
East Tisted Hants 25 M7
East Torrington Lincs 80 C7
East Tuddenham Norfk 70 G10
East Tytherley Hants 24 E7
East Tytherton Wilts 29 Q7
East Village Devon 8 F4
Eastville Bristl 29 J7
Eastville Lincs 80 H12
East Wall Shrops 51 N2
East Walton Norfk 69 P8
East Water Somset 22 C3
East Week Devon 8 C6
Eastwell Leics 67 K6
East Wellow Hants 24 E9
East Wemyss Fife 115 Q2
East Whitburn W Loth 114 H8
Eastwick Herts 45 N9
East Wickham Gt Lon 33 N7
East Williamston Pembks 37 L9
East Winch Norfk 69 N9
East Winterslow Wilts 24 C7
East Wittering W Susx 13 N5
East Witton N York 91 J9
Eastwood Notts 66 D3
Eastwood Sthend 34 E5
East Woodburn Nthumb 99 P1
Eastwood End Cambs 56 H2
East Woodhay Hants 31 J10
East Woodlands Somset 22 H5
East Worldham Hants 25 N6
East Wretham Norfk 58 D3
East Youlstone Devon 18 E10
Eathorpe Warwks 54 C7
Eaton Ches E 76 G10
Eaton Ches W 75 P11
Eaton Leics 67 K6
Eaton Norfk 71 J11
Eaton Notts 78 H8
Eaton Oxon 43 J11
Eaton Shrops 51 L3
Eaton Shrops 51 N3
Eaton Bishop Herefs 40 F4
Eaton Bray C Beds 44 D7
Eaton Constantine Shrops 63 Q11
Eaton Ford Cambs 56 D8
Eaton Green C Beds 44 D7
Eaton Hastings Oxon 30 F3
Eaton Mascott Shrops 63 P11
Eaton Socon Cambs 56 D9
Eaton upon Tern Shrops 64 C7
Eaves Brow Warrtn 76 B5
Eaves Green Solhll 53 N4
Ebberston N York 92 H10
Ebbesborne Wake Wilts 23 L9
Ebbw Vale Blae G 39 R9
Ebchester Dur 100 E7
Ebdon N Som 28 E9
Ebford Devon 9 J7
Ebley Gloucs 41 N10
Ebnal Ches W 63 N3
Ebnall Herefs 51 M9
Ebrington Gloucs 42 E4
Ebsworthy Devon 7 P6
Ecchinswell Hants 31 K10
Ecclaw Border 116 G7
Ecclefechan D & G 97 P3
Eccles Border 108 B2
Eccles Kent 34 C10
Eccles Salfd 76 E4
Ecclesall Sheff 77 Q7
Ecclesfield Sheff 78 B5
Eccles Green Herefs 51 L11
Eccleshall Staffs 64 F6
Eccleshill C Brad 85 J8
Ecclesmachan W Loth 115 K6
Eccles on Sea Norfk 71 N6
Eccles Road Norfk 58 F2
Eccleston Ches W 75 L11
Eccleston Lancs 83 M11
Eccleston St Hel 75 N4
Eccleston Green Lancs 83 M12
Echt Abers 132 H3
Eckford Border 108 A4
Eckington Derbys 78 C8
Eckington Worcs 41 Q3
Ecton Nhants 55 L8
Ecton Staffs 77 L12
Edale Derbys 77 L6
Eday Ork 147 d3
Eday Airport Ork 147 d2
Edburton W Susx 15 J8
Edderside Cumb 97 M9
Edderton Highld 146 C8
Eddington Kent 35 L9
Eddleston Border 115 N11
Eddlewood S Lans 114 C10
Edenbridge Kent 15 N2
Edenfield Lancs 84 B11
Edenhall Cumb 98 H11
Edenham Lincs 67 Q8
Eden Mount Cumb 89 L11
Eden Park Gt Lon 33 L9
Eden Project Cnwll 3 P4
Edensor Derbys 77 N9
Edentaggart Ag & B 113 L3
Edenthorpe Donc 78 G3
Edern Gwynd 60 D4
Edgarley Somset 22 C6
Edgbaston Birm 53 K4
Edgcombe Cnwll 2 H8
Edgcott Bucks 43 P7
Edgcott Somset 20 C5
Edge Gloucs 41 N9
Edge Shrops 63 L10
Edgebolton Shrops 63 P8
Edge End Gloucs 41 J9
Edgefield Norfk 70 G5
Edgefield Green Norfk 70 G5
Edgefold Bolton 76 C3
Edge Green Ches W 63 N2
Edgehill Warwks 42 H2
Edgerley Shrops 63 K8
Edgerton Kirk 84 H11
Edgeside Lancs 84 C10
Edgeworth Gloucs 41 Q10
Edgeworthy Devon 20 C10
Edginswell Torbay 5 Q3
Edgiock Worcs 53 K8
Edgmond Wrekin 64 D8
Edgmond Marsh Wrekin 64 D8
Edgton Shrops 51 L3
Edgware Gt Lon 32 H4
Edgworth Bl w D 83 R11
Edinbane Highld 134 F6
Edinburgh C Edin 115 N6
Edinburgh Airport C Edin 115 L6
Edinburgh Castle C Edin 115 N6
Edinburgh Old & New Town C Edin 115 N6
Edinburgh Royal Botanic Gardens C Edin 115 N6
Edinburgh Zoo RZSS C Edin 115 M6
Edingale Staffs 65 N9
Edingham D & G 96 G6
Edingley Notts 66 H1
Edingthorpe Norfk 71 L6
Edingthorpe Green Norfk 71 L6
Edington Border 117 K10
Edington Nthumb 100 F2
Edington Somset 21 N5
Edington Wilts 23 L3
Edington Burtle Somset 21 N5
Edingworth Somset 21 N3
Edistone Devon 18 E9
Edithmead Somset 21 M3
Edith Weston Rutlnd 67 M11
Edlesborough Bucks 44 D8
Edlingham Nthumb 109 J8
Edlington Lincs 80 E9
Edmond Castle Cumb 98 G6
Edmondsham Dorset 11 P2
Edmondsley Dur 100 G8
Edmondthorpe Leics 67 L8
Edmonton Cnwll 6 D10
Edmonton Gt Lon 33 L4
Edmundbyers Dur 100 C8
Ednam Border 108 B2
Ednaston Derbys 65 N4
Edney Common Essex 46 B10
Edradynate P & K 123 M2
Edrom Border 117 J10
Edstaston Shrops 63 N6
Edstone Warwks 53 M8
Edvin Loach Herefs 52 C9
Edwalton Notts 66 F5
Edwardstone Suffk 46 G3
Edwardsville Myr Td 27 P3
Edwinsford Carmth 38 F5
Edwinstowe Notts 78 G10
Edworth C Beds 45 J3
Edwyn Ralph Herefs 52 B9
Edzell Angus 132 F10
Edzell Woods Abers 132 F10
Efail-fach Neath 27 J3
Efail Isaf Rhondd 27 P5
Efailnewydd Gwynd 60 F5
Efail-Rhyd Powys 62 G7
Efailwen Carmth 37 M5
Efenechtyd Denbgs 62 F1
Effgill D & G 107 J11
Effingham Surrey 32 G11
Effingham Junction Surrey 32 G11
Efflinch Staffs 65 M9
Efford Devon 8 G4
Egbury Hants 24 G3
Egdean W Susx 14 D6
Egerton Bolton 83 Q12
Egerton Kent 16 G1
Egerton Forstal Kent 16 F1
Eggborough N York 85 R10
Eggbuckland C Plym 4 H5
Eggesford Devon 8 C3
Eggington C Beds 44 D6
Egginton Derbys 65 P6
Egglescliffe S on T 91 P4
Eggleston Dur 90 G2
Egham Surrey 32 E8
Egham Wick Surrey 32 D8
Egleton Rutlnd 67 L10
Eglingham Nthumb 109 J6
Egloshayle Cnwll 6 E10
Egloskerry Cnwll 7 K7
Eglwysbach Conwy 73 P9
Eglwys-Brewis V Glam 27 N8
Eglwys Cross Wrexhm 63 M4
Eglwys Fach Cerdgn 49 M1
Eglwyswrw Pembks 37 M3
Egmanton Notts 79 J10
Egremont Cumb 88 D5
Egremont Wirral 75 K5
Egton N York 92 G5
Egton Bridge N York 92 G6
Egypt Bucks 32 D5
Egypt Hants 24 H5
Eigg Highld 126 H7
Eight Ash Green Essex 46 G6
Eilanreach Highld 135 P12
Eilean Donan Castle Highld 136 B10
Eisgein W Isls 152 f5
Eishken W Isls 152 f5
Eisteddfa Gurig Cerdgn 49 N4
Elan Valley Powys 50 B7
Elan Village Powys 50 C7
Elberton S Glos 29 J5
Elbridge W Susx 14 C10
Elburton C Plym 4 H6
Elcombe Swindn 30 D6
Elcot W Berk 31 J8
Eldernell Cambs 68 F12
Eldersfield Worcs 41 M5
Elderslie Rens 113 N8
Elder Street Essex 45 Q5
Eldon Dur 91 L1
Eldwick C Brad 84 H7
Elerch Cerdgn 49 L3
Elfhill Abers 133 J7
Elford Nthumb 109 K3
Elford Staffs 65 M10
Elgin Moray 139 N3
Elgol Highld 127 J2
Elham Kent 17 L2
Elie Fife 116 C1
Elilaw Nthumb 108 F8
Elim IoA 72 F7
Eling Hants 24 F11
Elkesley Notts 78 H8
Elkstone Gloucs 41 R9
Ella Abers 140 G4
Ellacombe Torbay 5 Q4
Elland Calder 84 H11
Elland Lower Edge Calder 84 H11
Ellary Ag & B 111 Q6
Ellastone Staffs 65 L3
Ellel Lancs 83 L4
Ellemford Border 116 G9
Ellenabeich Ag & B 120 D9
Ellenborough Cumb 97 L11
Ellenbrook Salfd 76 D3
Ellenhall Staffs 64 F7
Ellen's Green Surrey 14 G4
Ellerbeck N York 91 Q7
Ellerby N York 92 G4
Ellerdine Heath Wrekin 63 Q7
Ellerhayes Devon 9 J4
Elleric Ag & B 121 K3
Ellerker E R Yk 86 G9
Ellers N York 84 F6
Ellerton E R Yk 86 D7
Ellerton N York 91 L7
Ellerton Shrops 64 D7
Ellesborough Bucks 44 B10
Ellesmere Shrops 63 L5
Ellesmere Port Ches W 75 L8
Ellingham Hants 12 B3
Ellingham Norfk 59 M2
Ellingham Nthumb 109 K5
Ellingstring N York 91 K10
Ellington Cambs 56 C6
Ellington Nthumb 109 M11
Ellington Thorpe Cambs 56 C6
Elliots Green Somset 22 H4
Ellisfield Hants 25 L4
Ellishader Highld 135 J3
Ellistown Leics 66 C10
Ellon Abers 141 M9
Ellonby Cumb 98 E11
Ellough Suffk 59 N3
Elloughton E R Yk 86 H9
Ellwood Gloucs 41 J10
Elm Cambs 69 J10
Elmbridge Worcs 52 G7
Elmdon Essex 45 N4
Elmdon Solhll 53 M4
Elmdon Heath Solhll 53 M4
Elmer W Susx 14 E10
Elmers End Gt Lon 33 L8
Elmer's Green Lancs 75 N2
Elmesthorpe Leics 54 D1
Elm Green Essex 46 D10
Elmhurst Staffs 65 L9
Elmley Castle Worcs 41 R3
Elmley Lovett Worcs 52 G7
Elmore Gloucs 41 M8
Elmore Back Gloucs 41 M8
Elm Park Gt Lon 33 P5
Elmscott Devon 18 E9
Elmsett Suffk 47 J2
Elms Green Worcs 52 D7
Elmstead Heath Essex 47 J7
Elmstead Market Essex 47 J7
Elmstead Row Essex 47 J7
Elmsted Kent 17 K2
Elmstone Kent 35 N10
Elmstone Hardwicke Gloucs 41 Q6
Elmswell E R Yk 87 J3
Elmswell Suffk 58 E8
Elmton Derbys 78 E9
Elphin Highld 144 F3
Elphinstone E Loth 115 R7
Elrick Abers 133 K3
Elrig D & G 95 L8
Elrington Nthumb 99 N5
Elsdon Nthumb 108 E11
Elsecar Barns 78 C4
Elsenham Essex 45 P6
Elsfield Oxon 43 L9
Elsham N Linc 79 P1
Elsing Norfk 70 F9
Elslack N York 84 D5
Elson Hants 13 K4
Elson Shrops 63 L5
Elsrickle S Lans 106 D1
Elstead Surrey 14 C2
Elsted W Susx 25 P9
Elsthorpe Lincs 67 Q7
Elstob Dur 91 N2
Elston Lancs 83 N8
Elston Notts 67 J3
Elston Wilts 23 N4
Elstone Devon 19 N10
Elstow Bed 44 E2
Elstree Herts 32 H3
Elstronwick E R Yk 87 N9
Elswick Lancs 83 K7
Elswick N u Ty 100 G5
Elsworth Cambs 56 F8
Elterwater Cumb 89 J6
Eltham Gt Lon 33 M8
Eltisley Cambs 56 E8
Elton Bury 76 E1
Elton Cambs 56 B2
Elton Ches W 75 M8
Elton Derbys 77 N11
Elton Gloucs 41 L9
Elton Herefs 51 M6
Elton S on T 91 P3
Elton Green Ches W 75 M8
Elton-on-the-Hill Notts 67 J4
Eltringham Nthumb 100 D6
Elvanfoot S Lans 106 C6
Elvaston Derbys 66 C6
Elveden Suffk 58 B5
Elvetham Heath Hants 25 P2
Elvingston E Loth 116 B6
Elvington C York 86 C6
Elvington Kent 35 N12
Elwell Devon 19 M7
Elwick Hartpl 101 L11
Elwick Nthumb 109 J2
Elworth Ches E 76 D11
Elworthy Somset 20 H6
Ely Cambs 57 K4
Ely Cardif 27 Q7
Emberton M Keyn 55 M10
Embleton Cumb 97 N12
Embleton Dur 101 K12
Embleton Nthumb 109 L5
Embo Highld 146 E6
Emborough Somset 22 E3
Embo Street Highld 146 E7
Embsay N York 84 F4
Emery Down Hants 12 D3
Emley Kirk 77 N1
Emley Moor Kirk 77 N1
Emmbrook Wokham 32 A8
Emmer Green Readg 31 P7
Emmett Carr Derbys 78 D8
Emmington Oxon 43 Q11
Emneth Norfk 69 J10
Emneth Hungate Norfk 69 K10
Empingham Rutlnd 67 N10
Empshott Hants 25 N7
Empshott Green Hants 25 N7
Emsworth Hants 13 N3
Enborne W Berk 31 J9
Enborne Row W Berk 31 J9
Enchmarsh Shrops 51 N1
Enderby Leics 66 E12
Endmoor Cumb 89 N10
Endon Staffs 64 G2
Endon Bank Staffs 64 G1
Enfield Gt Lon 33 L3
Enfield Lock Gt Lon 33 L3
Enfield Wash Gt Lon 33 L3
Enford Wilts 23 P3
Engine Common S Glos 29 L5
England's Gate Herefs 51 P10
Englefield W Berk 31 N8
Englefield Green Surrey 32 E8
Engleseabrook Ches E 64 D2
English Bicknor Gloucs 41 J8
Englishcombe BaNES 29 L9
English Frankton Shrops 63 M6
Engollan Cnwll 6 B10
Enham Alamein Hants 24 F3
Enmore Somset 21 K6
Enmore Green Dorset 23 J8
Ennerdale Bridge Cumb 88 E3
Enniscaven Cnwll 3 N3
Enochdhu P & K 131 K11
Ensay Ag & B 119 K3
Ensbury BCP 11 Q5
Ensdon Shrops 63 L9
Ensis Devon 19 L8
Enson Staffs 64 H6
Enstone Oxon 42 H7
Enterkinfoot D & G 105 Q9
Enterpen N York 91 Q5
Enville Staffs 52 F3
Eòlaigearraidh W Isls 152 b12
Eoligarry W Isls 152 b12
Epney Gloucs 41 M9
Epperstone Notts 66 G2
Epping Essex 45 N11
Epping Green Essex 45 N10
Epping Green Herts 45 K10
Epping Upland Essex 45 N10
Eppleby N York 91 K4
Eppleworth E R Yk 87 J9
Epsom Surrey 33 J10
Epwell Oxon 42 H4
Epworth N Linc 79 K3
Epworth Turbary N Linc 79 J3
Erbistock Wrexhm 63 K4
Erdington Birm 53 L2
Eridge Green E Susx 15 Q4
Eridge Station E Susx 15 P4
Erines Ag & B 112 C6
Eriska Ag & B 120 G4
Eriswell Suffk 57 N5
Erith Gt Lon 33 P7
Erlestoke Wilts 23 L3
Ermington Devon 5 K6
Erpingham Norfk 71 J6
Erriottwood Kent 34 G10
Errogie Highld 137 P11
Errol P & K 124 E8
Erskine Rens 113 P7
Erskine Bridge Rens 113 N7
Ervie D & G 94 E5
Erwarton Suffk 47 M5
Erwood Powys 39 Q3
Eryholme N York 91 N5
Eryrys Denbgs 74 H12
Escalls Cnwll 2 B9
Escomb Dur 100 F12
Escott Somset 20 H6
Escrick N York 86 B6
Esgair Carmth 38 B6
Esgair Cerdgn 49 K7
Esgairgeiliog Powys 61 N11
Esgerdawe Carmth 38 F3
Esgyryn Conwy 73 P8
Esh Dur 100 F9
Esher Surrey 32 G9
Esholt C Brad 85 J7
Eshott Nthumb 109 K10
Eshton N York 84 D4
Esh Winning Dur 100 G10
Eskadale Highld 137 M8
Eskbank Mdloth 115 P8
Eskdale Green Cumb 88 F6
Eskdalemuir D & G 106 H10
Eske E R Yk 87 K6
Eskham Lincs 80 G4
Eskholme Donc 86 B11
Esperley Lane Ends Dur 91 J2
Esprick Lancs 83 K8
Essendine Rutlnd 67 P9
Essendon Herts 45 K10
Essich Highld 138 B8
Essington Staffs 64 H11
Esslemont Abers 141 M10
Eston R & Cl 92 B3
Etal Nthumb 108 E2
Etchilhampton Wilts 30 B10
Etchingham E Susx 16 C5
Etchinghill Kent 17 L3
Etchinghill Staffs 65 J8
Etchingwood E Susx 15 P6
Etling Green Norfk 70 F9
Etloe Gloucs 41 K10
Eton W & M 32 D7
Eton Wick W & M 32 D7
Etruria C Stke 64 F3
Etteridge Highld 130 C6
Ettersgill Dur 99 N12
Ettiley Heath Ches E 76 D11
Ettingshall Wolves 52 H1
Ettington Warwks 53 P11
Etton C Pete 68 C11
Etton E R Yk 86 H6
Ettrick Border 106 H7
Ettrickbridge Border 107 K5
Ettrickhill Border 106 H7
Etwall Derbys 65 P6
Eudon George Shrops 52 C3
Euston Suffk 58 C5
Euximoor Drove Cambs 57 J1
Euxton Lancs 83 M11
Evancoyd Powys 51 J8
Evanton Highld 137 Q3
Evedon Lincs 68 B3
Evelith Shrops 64 D11
Evelix Highld 146 D7
Evenjobb Powys 51 J8
Evenley Nhants 43 M5
Evenlode Gloucs 42 E6
Even Swindon Swindn 30 D5
Evenwood Dur 91 K2
Evenwood Gate Dur 91 K2
Evercreech Somset 22 E5
Everingham E R Yk 86 E7

Everleigh Wilts....24 C3
Everley N York....93 K9
Eversholt C Beds....44 E5
Evershot Dorset....10 E4
Eversley Hants....31 Q10
Eversley Cross Hants....31 R10
Everthorpe E R Yk....86 K9
Everton C Beds....56 D10
Everton Hants....12 D6
Everton Lpool....75 K5
Everton Notts....78 H5
Everton D & G....98 D3
Evesbatch Herefs....52 C11
Evesham Worcs....42 B3
Evington C Leic....66 G11
Ewden Village Sheff....77 P4
Ewell Surrey....33 J9
Ewell Minnis Kent....17 N2
Ewelme Oxon....31 N4
Ewen Gloucs....30 B3
Ewenny V Glam....27 L7
Ewerby Lincs....68 C3
Ewerby Thorpe Lincs....68 C3
Ewhurst Surrey....31 D6
Ewhurst Green E Susx....16 D6
Ewhurst Green Surrey....14 F3
Ewloe Flints....75 J10
Ewloe Green Flints....75 J10
Ewood Bl w D....83 P10
Ewood Bridge Lancs....84 B11
Eworthy Devon....7 N6
Ewshot Hants....25 P3
Ewyas Harold Herefs....40 E6
Exbourne Devon....8 B4
Exbury Hants....12 G5
Exceat E Susx....15 P11
Exebridge Somset....20 E8
Exelby N York....91 M9
Exeter Devon....8 H6
Exeter Airport Devon....9 J6
Exeter Services Devon....8 H6
Exford Somset....20 D6
Exfordsgreen Shrops....63 M11
Exhall Warwks....53 L9
Exhall Warwks....54 B3
Exlade Street Oxon....31 N6
Exley Head C Brad....84 F7
Exminster Devon....8 H7
Exmoor National Park....20 D5
Exmouth Devon....8 H9
Exning Suffk....57 M7
Exted Kent....17 J2
Exton Devon....9 J7
Exton Hants....25 K9
Exton Rutlnd....67 M10
Exton Somset....20 E6
Exwick Devon....8 G6
Eyam Derbys....77 N8
Eydon Nhants....54 E10
Eye C Pete....68 E11
Eye Herefs....51 N8
Eye Suffk....58 H6
Eye Green C Pete....68 E11
Eyemouth Border....117 L8
Eyeworth C Beds....45 J3
Eyhorne Street Kent....34 E11
Eyke Suffk....59 L10
Eynesbury Cambs....56 D9
Eynsford Kent....33 P9
Eynsham Oxon....43 J10
Eype Dorset....10 C6
Eyre Highld....134 G5
Eythorne Kent....17 N1
Eyton Herefs....51 N8
Eyton Shrops....51 L9
Eyton Shrops....63 L9
Eyton Shrops....63 M7
Eyton Wrexhm....63 K3
Eyton on Severn Shrops....63 P11
Eyton upon the Weald Moors Wrekin....64 C9

F

Faccombe Hants....30 H10
Faceby N York....91 R6
Fachwen Powys....62 G9
Facit Lancs....84 D11
Fackley Notts....78 D11
Faddiley Ches E....63 P2
Fadmoor N York....92 D9
Faerdre Swans....26 G2
Faifley W Duns....113 P6
Failand N Som....28 G8
Failford S Ayrs....104 H4
Failsworth Oldham....76 G3
Fairbourne Gwynd....61 K8
Fairburn N York....85 P9
Fairfield Derbys....77 K9
Fairfield Herefs....16 G5
Fairfield Worcs....52 H5
Fairfield Park Herts....44 H5
Fairford Gloucs....30 D2
Fairford Park Gloucs....30 D2
Fairgirth D & G....96 H7
Fair Green Norfk....69 M8
Fairhaven Lancs....82 H9
Fair Isle Shet....147 h10
Fair Isle Airport Shet....147 h10
Fairlands Surrey....32 D11
Fairlie N Ayrs....113 J10
Fairlight E Susx....16 F8
Fairlight Cove E Susx....16 F8
Fairmile Devon....9 L5
Fairmile Surrey....32 G10
Fairmilehead C Edin....115 N8
Fair Oak Hants....24 H9
Fairoak Staffs....64 E5
Fair Oak Green Hants....31 N10
Fairseat Kent....34 A10
Fairstead Essex....46 D8
Fairstead Norfk....69 M8
Fairstead Norfk....71 K7
Fairwarp E Susx....15 N5
Fairwater Cardif....27 N7
Fairy Cross Devon....18 H8
Fakenham Norfk....70 D6
Fakenham Magna Suffk....58 D6
Fala Mdloth....116 B9
Fala Dam Mdloth....116 B9
Falcut Nhants....43 M3
Faldingworth Lincs....79 N8
Faldouët Jersey....13 d2
Falfield S Glos....29 K4
Falkenham Suffk....47 N4
Falkirk Falk....114 F5
Falkirk Wheel Falk....114 F5
Falkland Fife....124 E11
Fallburn S Lans....106 C2
Fallgate Derbys....78 B11
Fallin Stirlg....114 G4
Fallodon Nthumb....109 K5
Fallowfield Manch....76 F5
Fallowfield Nthumb....99 P4
Falmer E Susx....15 L9
Falmouth Cnwll....3 K8
Falnash Border....107 K8
Falsgrave N York....93 L9
Falstone Nthumb....108 B2
Fanagmore Highld....148 E6
Fancott C Beds....44 F7
Fanellan Highld....137 N7
Fangdale Beck N York....92 B8
Fangfoss E R Yk....86 E4

Fanmore Ag & B....119 L4
Fannich Lodge Highld....136 H3
Fans Border....107 P2
Far Bletchley M Keyn....44 B5
Farcet Cambs....56 D2
Far Cotton Nhants....55 J9
Farden Shrops....51 P5
Fareham Hants....13 J3
Farewell Staffs....65 K10
Far Forest Worcs....52 D6
Farforth Lincs....80 F8
Far Green Gloucs....29 M2
Faringdon Oxon....30 G3
Farington Lancs....83 M10
Farlam Cumb....98 H6
Farleigh N Som....28 G8
Farleigh Surrey....33 L10
Farleigh Hungerford Somset....29 N11
Farleigh Wallop Hants....25 K4
Farlesthorpe Lincs....81 J9
Farleton Cumb....89 N9
Farleton Lancs....83 N2
Farley Derbys....77 P11
Farley Staffs....65 K3
Farley Wilts....24 C7
Farley Green Suffk....57 P10
Farley Green Surrey....14 F2
Farley Hill Wokam....31 Q9
Farleys End Gloucs....41 M8
Farlington C Port....13 M4
Farlington N York....86 B2
Farlow Shrops....52 B4
Farmborough BaNES....29 K10
Farmbridge End Essex....46 A9
Farmcote Gloucs....42 C6
Farmcote Shrops....52 E2
Farmington Gloucs....42 D8
Farmoor Oxon....43 K10
Far Moor Wigan....75 N3
Farms Common Cnwll....2 H7
Farm Town Leics....66 C9
Farmtown Moray....140 D5
Farnah Green Derbys....65 Q3
Farnborough Gt Lon....33 N9
Farnborough Hants....32 C11
Farnborough W Berk....31 J6
Farnborough Warwks....54 C10
Farnborough Park Hants....32 C11
Farncombe Surrey....14 D2
Farndish Bed....55 M8
Farndon Ches W....63 L1
Farndon Notts....67 J2
Farne Islands Nthumb....109 L2
Farnell Angus....125 M2
Farnham Dorset....23 L10
Farnham Essex....45 N7
Farnham N York....85 M3
Farnham Suffk....59 M8
Farnham Surrey....25 P4
Farnham Common Bucks....32 D5
Farnham Green Essex....45 N6
Farnham Royal Bucks....32 D6
Farningham Kent....33 Q9
Farnley Leeds....85 K8
Farnley N York....85 J5
Farnley Tyas Kirk....77 M1
Farnsfield Notts....78 G12
Farnworth Bolton....76 D2
Farnworth Halton....75 N6
Far Oakridge Gloucs....42 H4
Farr Highld....130 F1
Farr Highld....138 C9
Farr Highld....150 C4
Farraline Highld....137 P11
Farrington Devon....9 J4
Farrington Gurney BaNES....22 E2
Far Sawrey Cumb....89 L6
Farsley Leeds....85 J8
Farther Howegreen Essex....34 E2
Farthing Green Essex....16 E2
Farthinghoe Nhants....43 L4
Farthingloe Kent....17 N3
Farthingstone Nhants....54 G9
Farthing Street Gt Lon....33 M9
Fartown Kirk....84 H11
Farway Devon....9 M6
Fasnacloich Ag & B....121 J3
Fasnakyle Highld....137 K10
Fassfern Highld....128 E8
Fatfield Sundld....100 H7
Faugh Cumb....98 G7
Fauld Staffs....65 M6
Fauldhouse W Loth....114 G9
Faulkbourne Essex....46 D8
Faulkland Somset....22 G2
Fauls Shrops....63 Q6
Faversham Kent....34 H10
Fawdington N York....91 Q12
Fawdon N u Ty....100 G4
Fawdon Nthumb....108 G6
Fawfieldhead Staffs....77 K11
Fawkham Green Kent....33 Q9
Fawler Oxon....42 H9
Fawley Bucks....31 Q5
Fawley Hants....12 G4
Fawley W Berk....30 H6
Fawley Chapel Herefs....41 J6
Fawnog Flints....74 H10
Fawsley Nhants....54 F9
Faxfleet E R Yk....86 F10
Faygate W Susx....15 J4
Fazakerley Lpool....75 L4
Fazeley Staffs....65 M11
Fearby N York....91 K10
Fearn Highld....146 E9
Fearnan P & K....123 J4
Fearnbeg Highld....135 N4
Fearnhead Warrtn....76 B5
Fearnmore Highld....135 N4
Fearnoch Ag & B....112 D5
Featherstone Staffs....64 H11
Featherstone Wakefd....85 N11
Feckenham Worcs....53 J8
Feering Essex....46 F7
Feetham N York....90 G7
Feizor N York....84 B2
Felbridge Surrey....15 L3
Felbrigg Norfk....71 J4
Felcourt Surrey....15 M3
Felden Herts....44 F9
Felindre Carmth....38 A4
Felindre Carmth....38 E4
Felindre Carmth....38 H6
Felindre Cerdgn....49 J9
Felindre Powys....50 G4
Felindre Powys....50 G4
Felindre Swans....38 F11
Felindre Farchog Pembks....37 J3
Felinfach Cerdgn....49 J9
Felinfach Powys....39 P5
Felinfoel Carmth....38 D11
Felingwm Isaf Carmth....38 D7
Felingwm Uchaf Carmth....38 D7
Felin-newydd Powys....39 Q4
Felixkirk N York....91 Q10
Felixstowe Suffk....47 N5
Felixstowe Ferry Suffk....47 N5
Felkington Nthumb....117 L12
Felkirk Wakefd....78 C1
Felling Gatesd....100 H6
Fell Lane C Brad....84 F7
Fell Side Cumb....98 C10
Felmersham Bed....55 N9
Felmingham Norfk....71 K6

Felpham W Susx....14 D11
Felsham Suffk....58 D9
Felsted Essex....46 B7
Feltham Gt Lon....32 G6
Felthamhill Surrey....32 G6
Felthorpe Norfk....70 H8
Felton Herefs....51 P11
Felton N Som....28 H9
Felton Nthumb....109 K9
Felton Butler Shrops....63 L8
Feltwell Norfk....57 N2
Fenay Bridge Kirk....85 J12
Fence Lancs....84 B8
Fence Rothm....78 D6
Fence Houses Sundld....101 J8
Fencott Oxon....43 M8
Fendike Corner Lincs....81 J11
Fen Ditton Cambs....57 J8
Fen Drayton Cambs....56 G7
Fen End Lincs....68 E8
Fen End W Mids....53 N6
Fenham Nthumb....108 H2
Feniscliffe Bl w D....83 P10
Fen15cowles Bl w D....83 P10
Feniton Devon....9 L5
Fenn Green Shrops....52 E4
Fenn Street Medway....34 D7
Fenny Bentley Derbys....65 M2
Fenny Bridges Devon....9 L5
Fenny Compton Warwks....54 C11
Fenny Drayton Leics....54 B1
Fenny Stratford M Keyn....44 C5
Fenrother Nthumb....109 K11
Fenstanton Cambs....56 F7
Fenstead End Suffk....57 Q10
Fen Street Norfk....58 E2
Fen Street Suffk....58 H8
Fenton C Stke....64 G3
Fenton Cambs....56 F5
Fenton Cumb....98 G7
Fenton Lincs....67 L2
Fenton Lincs....79 L8
Fenton Notts....79 K7
Fenton Nthumb....108 F3
Fenton Barns E Loth....116 C12
Fenwick Donc....86 B12
Fenwick E Ayrs....104 H1
Fenwick Nthumb....100 D4
Fenwick Nthumb....108 H2
Feock Cnwll....3 K7
Feolin Ferry Ag & B....111 K7
Fergushill N Ayrs....104 H1
Feriniquarrie Highld....134 C6
Fermain Bay Guern....12 c3
Fern Angus....132 D12
Ferndale Rhondd....27 N3
Ferndown Dorset....11 M4
Ferness Highld....138 H7
Fernham Oxon....30 G4
Fernhill Heath Worcs....52 F9
Fernhurst W Susx....14 C5
Fernie Fife....124 F9
Ferniegair S Lans....114 D10
Fernilea Highld....134 H4
Fernilee Derbys....77 J8
Fernwood Notts....67 K2
Ferrensby N York....85 M3
Ferriby Sluice N Linc....86 H11
Ferrindonald Highld....127 M3
Ferring W Susx....14 F10
Ferrybridge Wakefd....85 P10
Ferrybridge Services Wakefd....85 P10
Ferryden Angus....125 P2
Ferryhill Dur....100 H11
Ferryhill Station Dur....100 H12
Ferry Point Highld....146 D8
Ferryside Carmth....38 A9
Ferrytown Highld....146 D7
Fersfield Norfk....58 F4
Fersit Highld....129 L8
Feshiebridge Highld....130 F3
Fetcham Surrey....32 G11
Fetlar Shet....147 k3
Fetterangus Abers....141 N6
Fettercairn Abers....132 G9
Fewcott Oxon....43 L6
Fewston N York....85 J4
Ffairfach Carmth....38 F7
Ffair Rhos Cerdgn....49 M7
Ffald-y-Brenin Carmth....38 F3
Ffarmers Carmth....38 G3
Ffawyddog Powys....40 B8
Ffestiniog Gwynd....61 M4
Ffestiniog Railway Gwynd....61 L4
Ffordd-las Denbgs....74 F10
Fforest Carmth....26 H2
Fforest Gôch Neath....26 H2
Ffostrasol Cerdgn....48 F11
Ffrith Flints....63 J1
Ffynnonddewi Cerdgn....48 F10
Ffynnongroyw Flints....74 F7
Ffynnon-oer Cerdgn....49 J10
Fickleshole Surrey....33 M10
Fiddington Gloucs....41 Q5
Fiddington Somset....21 K5
Fiddleford Dorset....22 H10
Fiddlers Green Cnwll....3 K3
Fiddlers Hamlet Essex....33 N2
Field Staffs....65 J4
Field Broughton Cumb....89 L10
Field Dalling Norfk....70 E4
Fieldhead Cumb....98 F10
Field Head Leics....66 E10
Fifehead Magdalen Dorset....22 H9
Fifehead Neville Dorset....11 J3
Fifehead St Quintin Dorset....11 J3
Fife Keith Moray....140 C6
Fifield Oxon....42 F8
Fifield W & M....32 C7
Fifield Wilts....23 P4
Figheldean Wilts....23 P4
Filands Wilts....29 Q5
Filby Norfk....71 P9
Filey N York....93 M10
Filgrave M Keyn....55 L11
Filkins Oxon....42 F10
Filleigh Devon....19 N8
Fillingham Lincs....79 N6
Fillongley Warwks....53 P5
Filmore Hill Hants....25 L6
Filton S Glos....29 J6
Fimber E R Yk....86 G3
Finavon Angus....125 D11
Fincham Norfk....69 L11
Finchampstead Wokam....31 Q9
Fincharn Ag & B....120 G12
Finchdean Hants....25 M10
Finchingfield Essex....46 B5
Finchley Gt Lon....33 K4
Findern Derbys....65 Q6
Findhorn Moray....139 J4
Findhorn Bridge Highld....138 G10
Findochty Moray....140 D4
Findo Gask P & K....123 P9
Findon Abers....133 N5
Findon W Susx....14 G9
Findon Mains Highld....137 P4
Findrack House Abers....132 F3
Finedon Nhants....55 M6
Fingal Street Suffk....59 J6
Fingask P & K....124 D9
Fingest Bucks....31 Q4

Finghall N York....91 K9
Fingland Cumb....97 Q7
Fingland D & G....105 Q6
Finglesham Kent....35 P11
Fingringhoe Essex....47 J7
Finkle Street Barns....77 P4
Finlarig Stirlg....122 F6
Finmere Oxon....43 N5
Finnart P & K....122 E1
Finningham Suffk....58 F7
Finningley Donc....78 H4
Finsbay W Isls....152 e6
Finstall Worcs....52 H6
Finsthwaite Cumb....89 L7
Finstock Oxon....42 H8
Finstown Ork....147 c4
Fintry Abers....141 J5
Fintry Stirlg....114 D4
Finzean Abers....132 F5
Fionnphort Ag & B....119 J8
Fionnsbhagh W Isls....152 e6
Firbank Cumb....89 Q8
Firbeck Rothm....78 F6
Firby N York....86 D2
Firby N York....91 M9
Firgrove Rochdl....76 G3
Firle E Susx....15 N9
Firsby Lincs....81 J11
Firsdown Wilts....24 C7
Fir Tree Dur....100 F11
Fishbourne IoW....13 J6
Fishbourne W Susx....13 M4
Fishbourne Roman Palace W Susx....13 P4
Fishburn Dur....101 K11
Fishcross Clacks....114 G2
Fisher W Susx....14 B10
Fisherford Abers....140 G8
Fisher's Pond Hants....24 H9
Fisher's Row Lancs....83 K5
Fisherstreet W Susx....14 D4
Fisherton Highld....138 D5
Fisherton S Ayrs....104 E6
Fisherton de la Mere Wilts....23 M6
Fisherwick Staffs....65 M10
Fishery Estate W & M....32 C6
Fishguard Pembks....37 J3
Fishlake Donc....78 G1
Fishleigh Devon....7 Q4
Fishmere End Lincs....68 E5
Fishnish Pier Ag & B....120 C4
Fishpond Bottom Dorset....10 B5
Fishponds Brisl....29 J7
Fishtoft Lincs....68 G4
Fishtoft Drove Lincs....68 F2
Fishwick Lancs....83 M9
Fiskavaig Highld....134 F9
Fiskerton Lincs....79 P9
Fiskerton Notts....67 J2
Fitling E R Yk....87 N8
Fittleton Wilts....23 P3
Fittleworth W Susx....14 E7
Fitton End Cambs....68 H9
Fitz Shrops....63 M8
Fitzhead Somset....20 H7
Fitzroy Somset....21 K8
Fitzwilliam Wakefd....85 N12
Five Ash Down E Susx....15 N6
Five Ashes E Susx....15 Q6
Five Bells Somset....20 H5
Five Bridges Herefs....41 K2
Fivecrosses Ches W....75 N8
Fivehead Somset....21 M9
Fivelanes Cnwll....7 J4
Five Lanes Cnwll....28 H4
Five Oak Green Kent....16 B2
Five Oaks Jersey....13 c2
Five Oaks W Susx....14 G5
Five Roads Carmth....38 D10
Five Wents Kent....34 E12
Flack's Green Essex....46 D8
Flackwell Heath Bucks....32 C4
Fladbury Worcs....42 A2
Fladdabister Shet....147 i8
Flagg Derbys....77 L10
Flamborough E R Yk....87 N1
Flamborough Head E R Yk....87 N1
Flamingo Land Theme Park N York....92 F10
Flamstead Herts....44 F8
Flamstead End Herts....45 L11
Flansham W Susx....14 D10
Flanshaw Wakefd....85 L10
Flappit Spring C Brad....84 F8
Flasby N York....84 E4
Flash Staffs....77 J10
Flashader Highld....134 F5
Flaunden Herts....32 E2
Flawborough Notts....67 K2
Flawith N York....85 P2
Flax Bourton N Som....28 H8
Flaxby N York....85 M4
Flaxley Gloucs....41 K8
Flaxmere Ches W....75 N9
Flaxpool Somset....21 J6
Flaxton N York....86 C3
Fleckney Leics....54 G2
Flecknoe Warwks....54 D7
Fleet Dorset....10 H7
Fleet Hants....13 J4
Fleet Hants....25 P3
Fleet Lincs....68 H7
Fleetend Hants....13 J4
Fleet Hargate Lincs....68 H7
Fleetwood Lancs....82 H5
Fleggburgh Norfk....71 N9
Flemingston V Glam....27 N8
Flemington S Lans....114 B9
Flempton Suffk....57 Q7
Fletchersbridge Cnwll....6 G11
Fletcher's Green Kent....33 P12
Fletchertown Cumb....97 P9
Fletching E Susx....15 M6
Fleur-de-lis Caerph....27 P3
Flexbury Cnwll....7 J3
Flexford Surrey....32 D12
Flimby Cumb....97 L11
Flimwell E Susx....16 D4
Flint Flints....74 H9
Flintham Notts....67 J3
Flint Mountain Flints....74 H9
Flint's Green Solhll....53 P5
Flishinghurst Kent....16 D3
Flitcham Norfk....69 N7
Flitton C Beds....44 F5
Flitwick C Beds....44 F5
Flixborough N Linc....86 F12
Flixborough Stather N Linc....86 F12
Flixton Gt Man....76 E4
Flixton N York....93 L11
Flixton Suffk....59 L4
Flockton Kirk....85 K12
Flockton Green Kirk....85 K12
Flodden Nthumb....108 E3
Flodigarry Highld....142 G10
Flookburgh Cumb....89 K11
Flordon Norfk....59 J1
Flore Nhants....54 G8

Flotterton Nthumb....108 G9
Flowers Green E Susx....16 B8
Flowton Suffk....47 K2
Flushdyke Wakefd....85 L11
Flushing Cnwll....3 K8
Fluxton Devon....9 K6
Flyford Flavell Worcs....52 H9
Fobbing Thurr....34 C5
Fochabers Moray....139 Q4
Fochriw Caerph....39 Q10
Fockerby N Linc....86 F11
Foddington Somset....22 D7
Foel Powys....62 D9
Foelgastell Carmth....38 E8
Foel y Dyffryn Brdgnd....27 K3
Fogathorpe E R Yk....86 D7
Fogo Border....116 H11
Fogwatt Moray....139 N4
Foindle Highld....148 E7
Folda Angus....131 M11
Fole Staffs....65 K5
Foleshill Covtry....54 B4
Folke Dorset....22 F10
Folkestone Kent....17 M4
Folkingham Lincs....67 Q5
Folksworth Cambs....56 C3
Folkton N York....93 L10
Folla Rule Abers....140 H9
Follifoot N York....85 M5
Folly Powys....50 H6
Folly Gate Devon....7 Q5
Folly Hill Surrey....25 P4
Fonmon V Glam....27 N9
Fonthill Bishop Wilts....23 L7
Fonthill Gifford Wilts....23 K7
Fontmell Magna Dorset....23 J10
Fontmell Parva Dorset....23 J10
Fontwell W Susx....14 C9
Font-y-gary V Glam....27 N9
Foolow Derbys....77 M8
Foots Cray Gt Lon....33 N8
Forbestown Abers....131 Q2
Forcett N York....91 K4
Ford Ag & B....120 G12
Ford Bucks....43 Q9
Ford Derbys....78 C7
Ford Devon....5 K6
Ford Devon....5 N8
Ford Devon....18 H8
Ford Gloucs....42 C6
Ford Nthumb....108 F2
Ford Shrops....63 L9
Ford Somset....20 H7
Ford Somset....22 D3
Ford Staffs....65 K1
Ford W Susx....14 E10
Ford Wilts....29 N7
Forda Devon....7 P6
Fordcombe Kent....15 P3
Fordell Fife....115 L4
Forden Powys....62 H12
Ford End Essex....46 B8
Forder Green Devon....5 N3
Ford Green Lancs....83 L6
Fordham Cambs....57 M6
Fordham Essex....46 H6
Fordham Norfk....69 M12
Fordham Heath Essex....46 H6
Ford Heath Shrops....63 L10
Fordingbridge Hants....23 P10
Fordon E R Yk....93 L11
Fordoun Abers....133 J9
Ford's Green Suffk....58 F7
Fordstreet Essex....46 G6
Ford Street Somset....21 J10
Fordton Devon....8 H5
Fordwells Oxon....42 G9
Fordwich Kent....35 L10
Fordyce Abers....140 E3
Forebridge Staffs....64 H7
Foremark Derbys....65 Q7
Forest Guern....12 c3
Forest N York....91 M6
Forest Becks Lancs....84 B5
Forestburn Gate Nthumb....108 H10
Forest Chapel Ches E....76 H9
Forest Coal Pit Mons....40 C7
Forest Gate Gt Lon....33 M5
Forest Green Surrey....14 G3
Forest Hall N Tyne....100 H4
Forest Hill Gt Lon....33 M7
Forest Hill Oxon....43 M10
Forest-in-Teesdale Dur....99 N12
Forest Lane Head N York....85 M3
Forest Mill Clacks....114 H2
Forest of Bowland Lancs....83 P4
Forest of Dean Gloucs....41 K9
Forest Row E Susx....15 M4
Forest Side IoW....12 H7
Forestside W Susx....25 N11
Forest Town Notts....78 F11
Forfar Angus....125 J3
Forgandenny P & K....124 B9
Forge Powys....61 N12
Forge Hammer Torfn....28 C3
Forge Side Torfn....40 C10
Forgie Moray....140 B5
Forgieside Moray....140 B5
Forgue Abers....140 F7
Forhill Worcs....53 J5
Formby Sefton....75 J2
Forncett End Norfk....58 G2
Forncett St Mary Norfk....58 H2
Forncett St Peter Norfk....58 H2
Fornham All Saints Suffk....57 Q7
Fornham St Martin Suffk....58 B7
Fornighty Highld....138 H5
Forres Moray....139 J4
Forsbrook Staffs....64 H4
Forse Highld....151 N8
Forshaw Heath Warwks....53 K6
Forsinard Highld....150 F8
Forss Highld....151 J3
Forteviot P & K....123 Q10
Fort Augustus Highld....129 L4
Forthampton Gloucs....41 P5
Fort George Highld....138 D5
Forth S Lans....114 G10
Fort Hommet Guern....12 b2
Forth Rail Bridge C Edin....115 L5
Forth Road Bridge C Edin....115 L5
Fortingall P & K....123 J4
Forton Hants....24 H3
Forton Lancs....83 L5
Forton Shrops....63 M9
Forton Somset....9 Q4
Forton Staffs....64 E7
Fortrie Abers....140 F6
Fort Richmond Guern....12 b2
Fortrose Highld....138 D5
Fortuneswell Dorset....10 G9
Fort William Highld....128 F9
Forty Green Bucks....32 D4
Forty Hill Gt Lon....33 L3
Forward Green Suffk....58 G9
Fosbury Wilts....24 E2
Foscot Oxon....42 E7
Foscote Nhants....43 N3
Fosdyke Lincs....68 F5
Fosdyke Bridge Lincs....68 F6
Foss P & K....123 K3
Fossebridge Gloucs....42 C9
Foss-y-ffin Cerdgn....48 G8
Fosterhouses Donc....86 C12

Foster Street Essex....45 P10
Foston Derbys....65 M6
Foston Leics....54 G2
Foston Lincs....67 L4
Foston N York....86 C2
Foston on the Wolds E R Yk....87 L4
Fotherby Lincs....80 F5
Fothergill Cumb....97 L11
Fotheringhay Nhants....55 Q2
Foula Shet....147 a7
Foula Airport Shet....147 h8
Foulbridge Cumb....98 E8
Foulby Wakefd....85 N11
Foulden Border....117 L10
Foulden Norfk....69 Q12
Foul End Warwks....53 N2
Foul Mile E Susx....16 A8
Foulness Island Essex....34 H4
Foulridge Lancs....84 D7
Foulsham Norfk....70 F7
Fountainhall Border....116 B11
Four Ashes Solhll....53 M6
Four Ashes Staffs....52 E3
Four Ashes Staffs....64 G10
Four Ashes Suffk....58 F6
Four Cabots Guern....12 c2
Four Crosses Powys....62 H8
Four Crosses Staffs....64 H10
Four Elms Kent....15 N1
Four Foot Somset....22 D6
Four Forks Somset....21 K6
Four Gates Bolton....76 B2
Four Gotes Cambs....69 J9
Four Lane End Barns....77 P3
Four Lane Ends Ches W....75 P1
Four Lanes Cnwll....2 H7
Fourlanes End Ches E....76 E1
Four Marks Hants....25 L6
Four Mile Bridge IoA....72 D8
Four Oaks E Susx....16 D6
Four Oaks Gloucs....41 L6
Four Oaks Solhll....53 L3
Four Oaks Solhll....53 N4
Fourpenny Highld....146 E9
Four Points W Berk....31 L6
Four Roads Carmth....38 C10
Four Shire Stone Warwks....42 F5
Four Throws Kent....16 D5
Four Wents Kent....34 A12
Fovant Wilts....23 M7
Foveran Abers....141 N11
Fowey Cnwll....3 R4
Fowley Common Warrtn....76 C4
Fowlhall Kent....16 C2
Fowlis Angus....124 G6
Fowlis Wester P & K....123 N8
Fowlmere Cambs....45 M2
Fownhope Herefs....41 J5
Fox Corner Surrey....32 D11
Foxcote Gloucs....42 B8
Foxcote Somset....22 G2
Foxdale IoM....102 c5
Foxearth Essex....46 E3
Foxendown Kent....34 B9
Foxfield Cumb....88 G9
Foxham Wilts....29 P7
Fox Hatch Essex....33 Q3
Foxhills Hants....12 E2
Foxhole Cnwll....3 M4
Foxholes N York....93 K9
Foxhunt Green E Susx....15 P7
Foxley Nhants....54 G10
Foxley Norfk....70 F8
Foxley Wilts....29 P5
Foxlydiate Worcs....53 J7
Fox Street Essex....47 J6
Foxt Staffs....65 J3
Foxton Cambs....56 H11
Foxton Dur....91 N1
Foxton Leics....54 H2
Foxton N York....91 P7
Foxup N York....90 E11
Foxwist Green Ches W....76 B10
Foxwood Shrops....52 B5
Foy Herefs....41 J7
Foyers Highld....137 N11
Foynesfield Highld....138 G5
Fraddam Cnwll....2 F7
Fraddon Cnwll....3 M3
Fradley Staffs....65 M10
Fradswell Staffs....65 J6
Fraisthorpe E R Yk....87 M3
Framfield E Susx....15 N6
Framingham Earl Norfk....71 K11
Framingham Pigot Norfk....71 K11
Framlingham Suffk....59 K8
Frampton Dorset....10 H5
Frampton Lincs....68 F4
Frampton Cotterell S Glos....29 K6
Frampton Mansell Gloucs....41 Q11
Frampton-on-Severn Gloucs....41 M10
Frampton West End Lincs....68 E4
Framsden Suffk....59 J8
Framwellgate Moor Dur....100 H9
Franche Worcs....52 F5
Frandley Ches W....76 B8
Frankaborough Devon....7 N6
Frankby Wirral....74 H6
Frankfort Norfk....71 L7
Franklands Gate Herefs....41 Q11
Frankley Worcs....52 H4
Frankley Services Worcs....53 J4
Frankton Warwks....54 C6
Frank's Bridge Powys....50 G9
Frankton Warwks....54 C6
Frant E Susx....15 Q4
Fraserburgh Abers....141 N2
Frating Essex....47 J6
Frating Green Essex....47 K7
Fratton C Port....13 L4
Freathy Cnwll....4 F6
Freckenham Suffk....57 M5
Freckleton Lancs....83 K9
Freebirch Derbys....77 Q9
Freeby Leics....67 K8
Freefolk Hants....24 H4
Freehay Staffs....65 J4
Freeland Oxon....43 J9
Freethorpe Norfk....71 N11
Freethorpe Common Norfk....71 N11
Freiston Lincs....68 G3
Fremington Devon....19 K6
Fremington N York....90 H7
Frenchay S Glos....29 J6
Frenchbeer Devon....8 D7
French Street Kent....33 N11
Frenich P & K....123 J3
Frensham Surrey....25 P5
Freshfield Sefton....75 J2
Freshford Wilts....29 M10
Freshwater IoW....12 G7
Freshwater Bay IoW....12 G7
Freshwater East Pembks....37 K11
Fressingfield Suffk....59 K5
Freston Suffk....47 K5
Freswick Highld....151 Q3
Fretherne Gloucs....41 M9
Frettenham Norfk....71 K8
Freuchie Fife....124 F11
Freystrop Pembks....37 J8

Friar Park Sandw....53 J2
Friar's Gate E Susx....15 P4
Friars' Hill N York....92 F9
Friar Waddon Dorset....10 G7
Friday Bridge Cambs....69 J11
Friday Street Suffk....59 K8
Friday Street Suffk....59 L10
Friday Street Suffk....59 M8
Friday Street Surrey....14 G2
Fridaythorpe E R Yk....86 G3
Friden Derbys....77 M11
Friendly Calder....84 F10
Friern Barnet Gt Lon....33 K4
Friesthorpe Lincs....79 Q7
Frieston Lincs....67 M3
Frieth Bucks....31 R4
Friezeland Notts....66 D3
Frilford Oxon....31 J3
Frilsham W Berk....31 L8
Frimley Surrey....32 C11
Frimley Green Surrey....32 C11
Frindsbury Medway....34 C8
Fring Norfk....69 P5
Fringford Oxon....43 M6
Frinsted Kent....34 F11
Frinton-on-Sea Essex....47 M7
Friockheim Angus....125 L3
Friog Gwynd....61 K9
Frisby on the Wreake Leics....66 H8
Friskney Lincs....69 J1
Friskney Eaudike Lincs....69 J1
Friston E Susx....15 Q11
Friston Suffk....59 N8
Fritchley Derbys....66 B2
Frith Bank Lincs....68 F3
Frith Common Worcs....52 C7
Frithelstock Devon....19 J9
Frithelstock Stone Devon....19 J9
Frithend Hants....25 P5
Frithsden Herts....44 E9
Frithville Lincs....68 F2
Frittenden Kent....16 E3
Frittiscombe Devon....5 N8
Fritton Norfk....59 J2
Fritton Norfk....71 P12
Fritwell Oxon....43 L6
Frizinghall C Brad....84 H8
Frizington Cumb....88 D3
Frocester Gloucs....41 M11
Frodesley Shrops....63 N12
Frodsham Ches W....75 N8
Frogden Border....108 D3
Frog End Cambs....56 M2
Frog End Cambs....57 K9
Froggatt Derbys....77 N8
Frogham Hants....23 Q10
Frogham Kent....35 N12
Frogmore Devon....5 N8
Frognall Lincs....68 C10
Frogpool Cnwll....3 J6
Frog Pool Worcs....52 E7
Frogwell Cnwll....4 E3
Frolesworth Leics....54 E3
Frome Somset....22 G4
Frome St Quintin Dorset....10 F4
Fromes Hill Herefs....41 M2
Fron Gwynd....60 H1
Fron Gwynd....60 H6
Fron Powys....50 D2
Fron Powys....62 G11
Froncysyllte Wrexhm....63 J4
Fron-goch Gwynd....61 Q4
Fron Isaf Wrexhm....63 J4
Frostenden Suffk....59 P4
Frosterley Dur....100 C11
Froxfield C Beds....44 D5
Froxfield Wilts....30 G9
Froxfield Green Hants....25 M8
Fryern Hill Hants....24 G9
Fryerning Essex....34 B2
Fryton N York....92 E11
Fuinary Highld....120 B3
Fulbeck Lincs....67 N2
Fulbourn Cambs....57 K9
Fulbrook Oxon....42 F9
Fulflood Hants....24 H7
Fulford C York....86 B5
Fulford Somset....21 K8
Fulford Staffs....64 H5
Fulham Gt Lon....33 J7
Fulking W Susx....15 J8
Fullaford Devon....19 N6
Fuller's Moor Ches W....63 N1
Fuller Street Essex....46 C8
Fuller Street Kent....33 Q11
Fullerton Hants....24 F5
Fulletby Lincs....80 F9
Fullready Warwks....42 G2
Full Sutton E R Yk....86 D4
Fullwood E Ayrs....113 N11
Fulmer Bucks....32 E5
Fulmodeston Norfk....70 E6
Fulnetby Lincs....79 P8
Fulney Lincs....68 E7
Fulstone Kirk....77 M2
Fulstow Lincs....80 F4
Fulwell Oxon....42 H7
Fulwood Lancs....83 M8
Fulwood Notts....78 D12
Fulwood Sheff....77 P6
Fulwood Somset....21 J8
Fundenhall Norfk....58 H1
Funtington W Susx....13 M3
Funtley Hants....13 J3
Funtullich P & K....123 J8
Furleigh Cross Dorset....10 C5
Furley Devon....9 P4
Furnace Ag & B....112 F1
Furnace Carmth....26 D2
Furnace Cerdgn....49 L12
Furnace End Warwks....53 N3
Furner's Green E Susx....15 M5
Furness Vale Derbys....77 J7
Furneux Pelham Herts....45 M6
Further Quarter Kent....16 E3
Furtho Nhants....43 Q3
Furzehill Devon....19 N3
Furzehill Dorset....11 N4
Furzeley Corner Hants....13 L2
Furze Platt W & M....32 B6
Furzley Hants....24 D10
Fyfett Somset....21 K10
Fyfield Essex....45 Q10
Fyfield Hants....24 D4
Fyfield Oxon....31 J3
Fyfield Wilts....30 C8
Fyfield Wilts....30 D9
Fyfield Bavant Wilts....23 M8
Fylingthorpe N York....93 J6
Fyning W Susx....25 N10
Fyvie Abers....141 J8

G

Gabroc Hill E Ayrs....113 N11
Gaddesby Leics....66 H9
Gaddesden Row Herts....44 F9
Gadfa IoA....72 H6

Gadgirth S Ayrs 104 G5
Gadlas Shrops 63 L5
Gaer Powys 40 A7
Gaerllwyd Mons 28 F3
Gaerwen IoA 72 H9
Gagingwell Oxon 43 J6
Gailes N Ayrs 104 F3
Gainford Dur 91 K3
Gainsborough Lincs 79 K6
Gainsford End Essex 46 C4
Gairloch Highld 143 L9
Gairlochy Highld 128 G2
Gairneybridge P & K 115 L2
Gaisgill Cumb 89 Q6
Gaitsgill Cumb 98 E9
Galashiels Border 107 M3
Galgate Lancs 83 L4
Galhampton Somset 22 E7
Gallanachbeg Ag & B 120 F7
Gallanachmore Ag & B 120 F7
Gallantry Bank Ches E 63 N1
Gallatown Fife 115 P2
Galley Common Warwks 53 P7
Galleywood Essex 46 C11
Gallovie Highld 129 P6
Galloway Forest Park 95 N1
Gallowfauld Angus 125 J4
Gallowhill P & K 124 D5
Gallows Green Essex 46 G6
Gallows Green Worcs 52 H8
Gallowstree Common Oxon 31 P6
Galltair Highld 135 P11
Gallt-y-foel Gwynd 73 K11
Gally Hill Hants 25 P3
Gallypot Street E Susx 15 N4
Galmisdale Highld 127 J7
Galmpton Devon 5 L8
Galmpton Torbay 5 Q5
Galphay N York 91 L12
Galston E Ayrs 105 J2
Gamballs Green Staffs 77 J10
Gamblesby Cumb 99 J13
Gambles Green Essex 46 D8
Gamesley Derbys 77 J5
Gamlingay Cambs 56 E10
Gamlingay Cinques Cambs 56 E10
Gamlingay Great Heath Cambs 56 D10
Gammersgill N York 90 H10
Gamrie Abers 141 J3
Gamston Notts 66 F5
Gamston Notts 78 H8
Ganarew Herefs 40 H8
Ganavan Bay Ag & B 120 F6
Gang Cnwll 4 D3
Ganllwyd Gwynd 61 M7
Gannachy Angus 132 F10
Ganstead E R Yk 87 L8
Ganthorpe N York 86 C1
Ganton N York 93 K11
Ganwick Corner Herts 33 J2
Gappah Devon 8 G9
Garbity Moray 139 P5
Garboldisham Norfk 58 E4
Garbole Highld 138 D11
Garchory Abers 131 P2
Garden City Flints 75 K10
Gardeners Green Wokham 32 B9
Gardenstown Abers 141 J3
Garden Village Sheff 77 N4
Garderhouse Shet 147 i7
Gardham E R Yk 86 H7
Gare Hill Somset 22 H5
Garelochhead Ag & B 113 J3
Garford Oxon 31 J3
Garforth Leeds 85 M8
Gargrave N York 84 D4
Gargunnock Stirlg 114 C2
Garlic Street Norfk 59 J4
Garlieston D & G 95 N9
Garlinge Kent 35 P8
Garlinge Green Kent 35 K11
Garlogie Abers 133 J3
Garmond Abers 141 K5
Garmouth Moray 139 P4
Garmston Shrops 63 Q11
Garndolbenmaen Gwynd 60 H3
Garnett Bridge Cumb 89 P7
Garnfadryn Gwynd 60 D5
Garnswllt Swans 38 F9
Garn-yr-erw Torfn 40 B9
Garrabost W Isls 152 h3
Garralburn Moray 140 D5
Garrallan E Ayrs 105 L10
Garras Cnwll 2 H9
Garreg Gwynd 61 K4
Garrigill Cumb 99 L10
Garriston N York 91 K8
Garroch D & G 96 C2
Garrochtrie D & G 94 G10
Garrochty Ag & B 112 G10
Garros Highld 135 J3
Garsdale Cumb 90 B9
Garsdale Head Cumb 90 B9
Garsdon Wilts 29 Q5
Garshall Green Staffs 64 H5
Garsington Oxon 43 M10
Garstang Lancs 83 L6
Garston Herts 32 G2
Garston Lpool 75 L7
Garswood St Hel 75 P4
Gartachossan Ag & B 110 H9
Gartcosh N Lans 114 C7
Garth Brdgnd 27 K4
Garth Mons 28 D4
Garth Powys 50 C10
Garth Powys 51 J6
Garth Wrexhm 63 J4
Garthamlock C Glas 114 B8
Garthbrengy Powys 39 P6
Gartheli Cerdgn 49 K9
Garthmyl Powys 62 G12
Garthorpe Leics 67 L8
Garthorpe N Linc 79 N7
Garth Row Cumb 89 N9
Garths Cumb 89 N9
Gartly Abers 140 D9
Gartmore Stirlg 113 Q2
Gartness N Lans 114 E8
Gartness Stirlg 113 P4
Gartocharn W Duns 113 M4
Garton E R Yk 87 P8
Garton-on-the-Wolds E R Yk 86 H3
Gartymore Highld 147 J2
Garva Bridge Highld 129 P5
Garvald Border 115 K11
Garvald E Loth 116 D7
Garvan Highld 127 P2
Garvard Ag & B 111 J3
Garve Highld 137 L3
Garvellachs Ag & B 120 C10
Garvestone Norfk 70 F10
Garvock Inver 113 K7
Garway Herefs 40 F7
Garway Common Herefs 40 G7
Garway Hill Herefs 40 F6
Garyvard W Isls 152 g4
Gasper Wilts 22 G7
Gastard Wilts 29 J8
Gasthorpe Norfk 58 E4

Gaston Green Essex 45 P8
Gatcombe IoW 12 H8
Gatebeck Cumb 89 N9
Gate Burton Lincs 79 L7
Gateforth N York 85 R9
Gateford Notts 78 F7
Gatehead E Ayrs 104 G2
Gate Helmsley N York 86 C4
Gatehouse Nthumb 108 C12
Gatehouse of Fleet D & G 96 C7
Gateley Norfk 70 E7
Gatenby N York 91 N9
Gatesgarth Cumb 88 G4
Gateshaw Border 108 C5
Gateshead Gatesd 100 G6
Gates Heath Ches W 75 M11
Gateside Angus 125 J4
Gateside E Rens 113 P9
Gateside Fife 124 D11
Gateside N Ayrs 113 M10
Gathurst Wigan 75 P2
Gatley Stockp 76 F6
Gatton Surrey 33 K11
Gattonside Border 107 N3
Gatwick Airport W Susx 15 K3
Gaufron Powys 50 D7
Gaulby Leics 66 H12
Gauldry Fife 124 H8
Gaulkthorn Lancs 83 R10
Gaultree Norfk 69 J10
Gaunt's Common Dorset 11 N4
Gaunt's End Essex 45 Q6
Gaunton's Bank Ches E 63 P3
Gautby Lincs 80 D9
Gavinton Border 116 H11
Gawber Barns 77 Q2
Gawcott Bucks 43 P5
Gawsworth Ches E 76 G9
Gawthorpe Wakefd 85 K11
Gawthrop Cumb 90 A9
Gawthwaite Cumb 88 H9
Gay Bowers Essex 46 C11
Gaydon Warwks 54 B10
Gayhurst M Keyn 44 B2
Gayle N York 90 D9
Gayles N York 91 J5
Gay Street W Susx 14 F7
Gayton Nhants 54 H9
Gayton Norfk 69 N8
Gayton Staffs 64 H6
Gayton Wirral 75 J7
Gayton le Marsh Lincs 80 H7
Gayton Thorpe Norfk 69 P8
Gaywood Norfk 69 M7
Gazeley Suffk 57 N8
Gear Cnwll 2 H9
Gearraidh Bhaird W Isls 152 g4
Gearraidh na h-Aibhne W Isls 152 f3
Geary Highld 134 E3
Gedding Suffk 58 D9
Geddington Nhants 55 M4
Gedling Notts 66 G4
Gedney Lincs 68 H7
Gedney Broadgate Lincs 68 H7
Gedney Drove End Lincs 69 J6
Gedney Dyke Lincs 68 H7
Gedney Hill Lincs 68 G10
Gee Cross Tamesd 76 H5
Geeston Rutlnd 67 N11
Geldeston Norfk 59 M2
Gelli Rhondd 27 M3
Gelli Torfn 28 C4
Gellifor Denbgs 74 F11
Gelligaer Caerph 27 Q3
Gelligroes Caerph 28 A3
Gelligron Neath 38 H10
Gellilydan Gwynd 61 L4
Gellinudd Neath 38 H11
Gelly Pembks 37 L6
Gellyburn P & K 124 C5
Gellywen Carmth 37 P6
Gelston D & G 96 F6
Gelston Lincs 67 M3
Gembling E R Yk 87 L4
Gentleshaw Staffs 65 K10
Georgefield D & G 107 J11
George Green Bucks 32 E6
Georgeham Devon 19 J5
Georgemas Junction Station Highld 151 L5
George Nympton Devon 19 N8
Georgetown Blae G 39 Q10
Georgia Cnwll 2 D7
Georth Ork 147 c3
Gerlan Gwynd 73 L10
Germansweek Devon 7 N6
Germoe Cnwll 2 F8
Gerrans Cnwll 3 L7
Gerrards Cross Bucks 32 E5
Gerrick R & Cl 92 E4
Gestingthorpe Essex 46 E4
Geuffordd Powys 62 H9
Gib Hill Ches W 76 B8
Gibraltar Lincs 81 K12
Gibsmere Notts 67 J2
Giddeahall Wilts 29 P7
Giddy Green Dorset 11 K7
Gidea Park Gt Lon 33 P4
Gidleigh Devon 8 D7
Giffnock E Rens 113 Q9
Gifford E Loth 116 C7
Giffordtown Fife 124 F10
Giggleswick N York 84 B2
Gigha Ag & B 111 N11
Gilberdyke E R Yk 86 F9
Gilbert's End Worcs 41 N3
Gilbert Street Hants 25 L7
Gilchriston E Loth 116 C8
Gilcrux Cumb 97 M10
Gildersome Leeds 85 K9
Gildingwells Rothm 78 F6
Gileston V Glam 27 N9
Gilfach Caerph 27 R3
Gilfach Goch Brdgnd 27 M4
Gilfachrheda Cerdgn 48 G9
Gilgarran Cumb 88 D2
Gill Cumb 98 F12
Gillamoor N York 92 D8
Gillan Cnwll 3 J9
Gillen Highld 134 E4
Gillesbie D & G 106 F11
Gilling East N York 92 C11
Gillingham Dorset 22 H8
Gillingham Medway 34 D8
Gillingham Norfk 59 N2
Gilling West N York 91 K6
Gillock Highld 151 M5
Gillow Heath Staffs 76 G12
Gills Highld 151 P2
Gill's Green Kent 16 D4
Gilmanscleuch Border 107 J3
Gilmerton C Edin 115 P7
Gilmerton P & K 123 N6
Gilmonby Dur 90 G4
Gilmorton Leics 54 F3
Gilsland Nthumb 99 M3
Gilson Warwks 53 M3
Gilstead C Brad 85 J8
Gilston Border 116 B10
Gilston Herts 45 M9
Gilston Park Herts 45 M9
Giltbrook Notts 66 D3

Gilwern Mons 40 C9
Gimingham Norfk 71 K5
Gingers Green E Susx 16 A8
Gipping Suffk 58 G8
Gipsey Bridge Lincs 68 F2
Girdle Toll N Ayrs 104 F2
Girlington C Brad 84 H8
Girlsta Shet 147 i7
Girsby N York 91 N5
Girthon D & G 96 C7
Girton Cambs 56 H8
Girton Notts 79 K10
Girvan S Ayrs 104 C10
Gisburn Lancs 84 B5
Gisleham Suffk 59 P3
Gislingham Suffk 58 G6
Gissing Norfk 58 H3
Gittisham Devon 9 L5
Gladestry Powys 51 L6
Gladsmuir E Loth 116 B6
Glais Swans 26 G2
Glaisdale N York 92 F5
Glamis Angus 124 H3
Glanaber Gwynd 61 L2
Glanaman Carmth 38 G9
Glan-Duar Carmth 38 D3
Glandwr Pembks 37 N5
Glan-Dwyfach Gwynd 60 H3
Glandyfi Cerdgn 61 L11
Glangrwyney Powys 40 C8
Glanllynfi Brdgnd 27 K4
Glanmule Powys 50 G3
Glan-rhyd Pembks 37 M2
Glan-rhyd Powys 39 J10
Glanton Nthumb 108 H7
Glanton Pike Nthumb 108 H7
Glanvilles Wootton Dorset 10 G3
Glan-y-don Flints 74 G8
Glan-y-llyn Rhondd 27 Q5
Glan-y-nant Powys 50 C4
Glan-yr-afon Gwynd 62 B4
Glan-yr-afon Gwynd 62 D3
Glan-yr-afon IoA 73 K7
Glan-yr-afon Swans 38 F10
Glan-y-wern Gwynd 61 K5
Glapthorn Nhants 55 P3
Glapwell Derbys 78 D10
Glasbury Powys 40 A4
Glascoed Denbgs 74 D9
Glascoed Mons 40 D11
Glascote Staffs 65 M11
Glascwm Powys 50 G10
Glasfryn Conwy 62 C2
Glasgow C Glas 113 R8
Glasgow Airport Rens 113 P8
Glasgow Prestwick Airport S Ayrs 104 G4
Glasgow Science Centre C Glas 113 Q8
Glasinfryn Gwynd 73 K10
Glasnacardoch Bay Highld 127 M5
Glasnakille Highld 127 K2
Glasphein Highld 134 C6
Glaspwll Powys 49 M1
Glassburn Highld 137 N8
Glassenbury Kent 16 D3
Glassford S Lans 114 C10
Glasshouse Gloucs 41 L7
Glasshouse Hill Gloucs 41 L7
Glasshouses N York 85 J2
Glasslaw Abers 141 K4
Glasson Cumb 97 Q6
Glasson Lancs 83 L5
Glassonby Cumb 98 H10
Glasterlaw Angus 125 L3
Glaston Rutlnd 67 M12
Glastonbury Somset 22 C5
Glatton Cambs 56 C3
Glazebrook Warrtn 76 C4
Glazebury Warrtn 76 C4
Glazeley Shrops 52 D3
Gleadless Sheff 78 B7
Gleadsmoss Ches E 76 H10
Gleaston Cumb 82 G1
Gledhow Leeds 85 L8
Gledpark D & G 96 C8
Gledrid Shrops 63 J5
Glemsford Suffk 58 B11
Glenallachie Moray 139 N8
Glenancross Highld 127 M9
Glenaros House Ag & B 119 P4
Glen Auldyn IoM 102 d3
Glenbarr Ag & B 103 J2
Glenbarry Abers 140 E5
Glenbeg Highld 127 K11
Glenbervie Abers 133 J8
Glenboig N Lans 114 C7
Glenborrodale Highld 127 L12
Glenbranter Ag & B 112 F2
Glenbreck Border 106 D5
Glenbrittle Highld 134 G11
Glenbuck E Ayrs 105 N4
Glencally Angus 131 L12
Glencaple D & G 97 K4
Glencarse P & K 124 D8
Glencoe Highld 121 L2
Glencothe Border 106 E4
Glencraig Fife 115 M2
Glencrosh D & G 105 P12
Glendale Highld 134 C6
Glendaruel Ag & B 112 A4
Glendevon P & K 123 P12
Glendoe Lodge Highld 129 L2
Glendoick P & K 124 E8
Glenduckie Fife 124 F9
Glenegedale Ag & B 110 H11
Glenelg Highld 135 P12
Glenerney Moray 139 J6
Glenfarg P & K 124 C10
Glenfield Leics 66 E11
Glenfinnan Highld 128 C6
Glenfintaig Lodge Highld 128 H7
Glenfoot P & K 124 D9
Glenfyne Lodge Ag & B 120 H12
Glengarnock N Ayrs 113 L10
Glengolly Highld 151 L3
Glengorm Castle Ag & B 119 M1
Glengrasco Highld 134 H7
Glenholm Border 106 E3
Glenhoul D & G 105 M11
Glenisla Angus 131 N12
Glenkin Ag & B 112 G5
Glenkindie Abers 132 C2
Glenlivet Moray 139 M10
Glenlochar D & G 96 E6
Glenlomond P & K 124 D11
Glenluce D & G 94 H6
Glenmassen Ag & B 112 F4
Glenmavis N Lans 114 D8
Glen Maye IoM 102 b6
Glenmore Ag & B 120 F5
Glenmore Highld 134 H6
Glenmore Lodge Highld 130 H2
Glen Nevis House Highld 128 G10
Glenochil Clacks 114 F2
Glen Parva Leics 66 F12
Glenquiech Angus 132 C12
Glenralloch Ag & B 112 A2
Glenridding Cumb 89 K3
Glenrothes Fife 115 N1

Glenshero Lodge Highld 129 P6
Glenstriven Ag & B 112 G5
Glentham Lincs 79 Q5
Glentrool D & G 95 L3
Glen Trool Lodge D & G 95 M2
Glentruim House Highld 130 C5
Glentworth Lincs 79 N6
Glenuig Highld 127 M9
Glen Vine IoM 102 d5
Glenwhilly D & G 94 H4
Glespin S Lans 105 Q4
Glewstone Herefs 40 H7
Glinton C Pete 68 C11
Glooston Leics 55 J2
Glossop Derbys 77 J5
Gloster Hill Nthumb 109 L9
Gloucester Gloucs 41 N8
Gloucester Services Gloucs 41 N9
Gloucestershire Airport Gloucs 41 P7
Glusburn N York 84 F6
Glutt Lodge Highld 150 H9
Gluvian Cnwll 3 M2
Glympton Oxon 43 J7
Glynarthen Cerdgn 48 E11
Glyn Ceiriog Wrexhm 62 H4
Glyncoch Rhondd 27 P4
Glyncorrwg Neath 27 K2
Glynde E Susx 15 N9
Glyndebourne E Susx 15 N8
Glyndyfrdwy Denbgs 62 G4
Glynneath Neath 39 L11
Glyntaff Rhondd 27 P4
Glyntawe Powys 39 K8
Glynteg Carmth 38 A4
Gnosall Staffs 64 F8
Gnosall Heath Staffs 64 F8
Goadby Leics 67 J12
Goadby Marwood Leics 67 K7
Goatacre Wilts 30 B7
Goathill Dorset 22 F9
Goathland N York 92 G6
Goathurst Somset 21 L6
Goathurst Common Kent 33 P12
Goat Lees Kent 34 H5
Gobowen Shrops 63 J6
Godalming Surrey 14 D2
Goddard's Corner Suffk 59 K7
Goddard's Green Kent 16 E4
Goddards Green W Susx 15 K5
Godden Green Kent 33 Q11
Godford Cross Devon 9 K5
Godington Oxon 43 N6
Godley Tamesd 76 H5
Godmanchester Cambs 56 E6
Godmanstone Dorset 10 H5
Godmersham Kent 35 J12
Godney Somset 22 B5
Godolphin Cross Cnwll 2 F8
Godre'r-graig Neath 38 H10
Godshill Hants 24 B10
Godshill IoW 13 J8
Godstone Staffs 65 J5
Godstone Surrey 33 L11
Godsworthy Devon 7 P9
Godwinscroft Hants 12 C5
Goetre Mons 40 D10
Goff's Oak Herts 45 L11
Gogar C Edin 115 L7
Goginan Cerdgn 49 M4
Golan Gwynd 61 J4
Golant Cnwll 3 R4
Golberdon Cnwll 4 F7
Golborne Wigan 75 Q4
Golcar Kirk 84 G12
Goldcliff Newpt 28 E6
Golden Cross E Susx 15 P8
Golden Green Kent 16 B1
Golden Grove Carmth 38 D8
Goldenhill C Stke 64 F2
Golden Pot Hants 25 M5
Golden Valley Derbys 66 C2
Golders Green Gt Lon 33 J5
Goldfinch Bottom W Berk 31 L9
Goldhanger Essex 46 F10
Gold Hill Cambs 57 K2
Gold Hill Dorset 23 J10
Golding Shrops 63 P11
Goldington Bed 55 Q10
Goldsborough N York 85 M4
Goldsborough N York 92 G4
Golds Green Sandw 53 J2
Goldsithney Cnwll 2 E8
Goldstone Shrops 64 D6
Goldthorpe Barns 78 D3
Goldworthy Devon 18 H9
Golford Kent 16 D3
Golford Green Kent 16 D3
Gollanfield Highld 138 E5
Gollinglith Foot N York 91 K10
Golly Wrexhm 75 K12
Golsoncott Somset 20 E6
Golspie Highld 146 E5
Gomeldon Wilts 23 N5
Gomersal Kirk 85 J10
Gomshall Surrey 14 F2
Gonalston Notts 66 H3
Gonerby Hill Foot Lincs 67 M4
Gonfirth Shet 147 i6
Goodameavy Devon 4 H4
Good Easter Essex 46 A9
Gooderstone Norfk 69 P11
Goodleigh Devon 19 L6
Goodmanham E R Yk 86 G6
Goodmayes Gt Lon 33 N5
Goodnestone Kent 35 J11
Goodnestone Kent 35 N12
Goodrich Herefs 40 H8
Goodrington Torbay 5 Q5
Goodshaw Lancs 84 B10
Goodshaw Fold Lancs 84 B10
Goodstone Devon 8 E10
Goodwick Pembks 36 H3
Goodworth Clatford Hants 24 F5
Goodwood W Susx 14 C9
Goodyers End Warwks 53 Q4
Goole E R Yk 86 D10
Goole Fields E R Yk 86 D11
Goom's Hill Worcs 53 J9
Goonbell Cnwll 2 H4
Goonhavern Cnwll 3 K4
Goonvrea Cnwll 2 H4
Goosecruives Abers 133 J7
Gooseford Devon 8 E6
Goose Green Essex 47 L6
Goose Green Kent 34 B12
Goose Green Kent 16 B2
Goose Green S Glos 29 K9
Goose Green W Susx 14 H6
Goose Green Wigan 75 P3
Gooseham Cnwll 18 E8
Goosehill Green Worcs 52 H8
Goosey Oxon 30 H4
Goosnargh Lancs 83 M8
Goostrey Ches E 76 E9
Gorddinog Conwy 73 L9
Gordon Border 107 Q1

Gordon Arms Hotel Border 107 J5
Gordonstown Abers 140 E5
Gordonstown Abers 140 H8
Gore Powys 51 M2
Gorebridge Mdloth 115 Q9
Gorefield Cambs 68 H9
Gore Pit Essex 46 F8
Gores Wilts 30 C10
Gore Street Kent 35 N9
Goring Oxon 31 M6
Goring-by-Sea W Susx 14 G10
Goring Heath Oxon 31 N6
Gorleston on Sea Norfk 71 Q11
Gorrachie Abers 140 H4
Gorran Churchtown Cnwll 3 N6
Gorran Haven Cnwll 3 N6
Gorran High Lanes Cnwll 3 M6
Gorrig Cerdgn 38 B2
Gors Cerdgn 49 K5
Gorsedd Flints 74 G8
Gorse Hill Swindn 30 D5
Gorseinon Swans 26 E3
Gorsebank Derbys 65 P2
Gorsgoch Cerdgn 48 H10
Gorslas Carmth 38 E9
Gorsley Gloucs 41 K6
Gorsley Common Herefs 41 K6
Gorstage Ches W 75 Q9
Gorstan Highld 137 L3
Gorstella Ches W 75 K11
Gorsty Hill Staffs 65 L6
Gorten Ag & B 120 B6
Gosbeck Suffk 58 H9
Gosberton Lincs 68 D5
Gosberton Clough Lincs 68 D6
Gosfield Essex 46 D6
Gosford Devon 9 L5
Gosforth Cumb 88 E6
Gosforth N u Ty 100 G4
Gosling Street Somset 22 C6
Gosmore Herts 44 H6
Gospel End Staffs 52 F2
Gospel Green W Susx 14 D4
Gosport Hants 13 J5
Gossard's Green C Beds 44 D3
Gossington Gloucs 41 L11
Goswick Nthumb 117 N12
Gotham Notts 66 E6
Gotherington Gloucs 41 Q6
Gotton Somset 21 K7
Goudhurst Kent 16 C3
Goulceby Lincs 80 E8
Gourdas Abers 141 J7
Gourdie C Dund 124 G6
Gourdon Abers 133 K10
Gourock Inver 113 K6
Govan C Glas 113 Q8
Goveton Devon 5 L6
Govilon Mons 40 C9
Gowdall E R Yk 86 B10
Gower Highld 137 N4
Gower Swans 26 D4
Gowerton Swans 26 E3
Gowkhall Fife 115 J3
Gowthorpe E R Yk 86 E4
Goxhill E R Yk 87 M7
Goxhill N Linc 87 M10
Goytre Neath 27 J4
Grabhair W Isls 152 g4
Graby Lincs 68 B6
Grade Cnwll 3 J10
Gradeley Green Ches E 63 Q2
Graffham W Susx 14 C7
Grafham Cambs 56 C7
Grafham Surrey 14 G2
Grafton Herefs 40 G4
Grafton N York 85 N3
Grafton Oxon 30 G1
Grafton Shrops 63 M8
Grafton Worcs 42 A4
Grafton Worcs 51 P8
Grafton Flyford Worcs 52 H9
Grafton Regis Nhants 43 P3
Grafton Underwood Nhants 55 M5
Grafty Green Kent 16 F1
Graianrhyd Denbgs 74 H12
Graig Conwy 73 P9
Graig Denbgs 74 D9
Graigfechan Denbgs 62 F2
Grain Medway 34 F7
Grains Bar Oldham 76 H2
Grainsby Lincs 80 E4
Grainthorpe Lincs 80 H4
Grampound Cnwll 3 M5
Grampound Road Cnwll 3 M4
Gramsdal W Isls 152 c9
Gramsdale W Isls 152 c9
Granborough Bucks 43 Q7
Granby Notts 67 J5
Grandborough Warwks 54 E7
Grand Chemins Jersey 13 c2
Grandes Rocques Guern 12 c1
Grandtully P & K 123 N3
Grange Cumb 88 H3
Grange Medway 34 D8
Grange P & K 124 F8
Grange Wirral 74 H6
Grange Crossroads Moray 140 D5
Grange Hall Moray 139 K4
Grangehall S Lans 106 C2
Grange Hill Essex 33 N3
Grangemill Derbys 77 N12
Grange Moor Kirk 85 J12
Grangemouth Falk 114 F4
Grange of Lindores Fife 124 E9
Grange-over-Sands Cumb 89 L11
Grangepans Falk 115 J4
Grange Park Nhants 55 J8
Grangetown R & Cl 92 B3
Grange Villa Dur 100 G8
Gransmoor E R Yk 87 L4
Gransmore Green Essex 46 C7
Granston Pembks 36 G3
Grantchester Cambs 56 H9
Grantham Lincs 67 M4
Granton C Edin 115 N6
Grantown-on-Spey Highld 139 J10
Grantsfield Herefs 51 N8
Grantshouse Border 116 H6
Grappenhall Warrtn 76 C6
Grasby Lincs 80 B3
Grasmere Cumb 89 K5
Grasscroft Oldham 76 H2
Grassendale Lpool 75 L7
Grassgarth Cumb 98 E11
Grass Green Essex 46 C4
Grassington N York 84 F2
Grassmoor Derbys 78 C10
Grassthorpe Notts 79 K10
Grateley Hants 24 E5
Gratwich Staffs 65 J5
Graveley Cambs 56 E8
Graveley Herts 45 J6

Gravelsbank Shrops 63 K12
Graveney Kent 35 J9
Gravesend Kent 34 B7
Gravir W Isls 152 g4
Grayingham Lincs 79 P4
Grayrigg Cumb 89 P7
Grays Thurr 34 A7
Grayshott Hants 14 C4
Grayson Green Cumb 88 C2
Grayswood Surrey 14 D4
Graythorpe Hartpl 92 B3
Grazeley Wokham 31 P9
Greasbrough Rothm 78 C4
Greasby Wirral 75 J6
Greasley Notts 66 D3
Great Abington Cambs 57 K11
Great Addington Nhants 55 N6
Great Alne Warwks 53 L8
Great Altcar Lancs 75 L2
Great Amwell Herts 45 L9
Great Asby Cumb 89 R4
Great Ashfield Suffk 58 E7
Great Ayton N York 92 A4
Great Baddow Essex 46 C10
Great Badminton S Glos 29 M6
Great Bardfield Essex 46 B5
Great Barford Bed 56 C10
Great Barr Sandw 53 K2
Great Barrington Gloucs 42 F8
Great Barrow Ches W 75 M10
Great Barton Suffk 58 C7
Great Barugh N York 92 F11
Great Bavington Nthumb 100 C2
Great Bealings Suffk 59 J11
Great Bedwyn Wilts 30 F9
Great Bentley Essex 47 K7
Great Billing Nhants 55 K8
Great Bircham Norfk 69 R5
Great Blakenham Suffk 58 G10
Great Blencow Cumb 98 F11
Great Bolas Wrekin 64 B8
Great Bookham Surrey 32 H11
Great Bourton Oxon 43 K3
Great Bowden Leics 55 J3
Great Bradley Suffk 57 N10
Great Braxted Essex 46 F9
Great Bricett Suffk 58 F10
Great Brickhill Bucks 44 C5
Great Bridgeford Staffs 64 G7
Great Brington Nhants 54 H7
Great Bromley Essex 47 K6
Great Broughton Cumb 97 L12
Great Broughton N York 92 A5
Great Budworth Ches W 76 C8
Great Burdon Darltn 91 N3
Great Burstead Essex 34 B4
Great Busby N York 92 A5
Great Canfield Essex 45 R7
Great Carlton Lincs 80 H6
Great Casterton Rutlnd 67 P10
Great Chalfield Wilts 29 P9
Great Chart Kent 16 H2
Great Chatwell Staffs 64 E9
Great Chell C Stke 64 F2
Great Chesterford Essex 45 P3
Great Cheverell Wilts 29 R10
Great Chishill Cambs 45 M4
Great Clacton Essex 47 L8
Great Cliffe Wakefd 85 L12
Great Clifton Cumb 97 L12
Great Coates NE Lin 80 E2
Great Comberton Worcs 41 Q3
Great Comp Kent 34 A11
Great Corby Cumb 98 F7
Great Cornard Suffk 46 F4
Great Cowden E R Yk 87 N7
Great Coxwell Oxon 30 G4
Great Cransley Nhants 55 L5
Great Cressingham Norfk 69 R11
Great Crosthwaite Cumb 88 H2
Great Cubley Derbys 65 L5
Great Cumbrae Island N Ayrs 112 H10
Great Dalby Leics 67 J9
Great Denham Bed 55 P11
Great Doddington Nhants 55 M8
Great Doward Herefs 40 H8
Great Dunham Norfk 70 C9
Great Dunmow Essex 46 A7
Great Durnford Wilts 23 N5
Great Easton Essex 45 R6
Great Easton Leics 55 L2
Great Eccleston Lancs 83 J7
Great Edstone N York 92 E10
Great Ellingham Norfk 58 F1
Great Elm Somset 22 G3
Great Everdon Nhants 54 F9
Great Eversden Cambs 56 G10
Great Fencote N York 91 M8
Great Finborough Suffk 58 F9
Greatford Lincs 68 B9
Great Fransham Norfk 70 D9
Great Gaddesden Herts 44 E9
Greatgate Staffs 65 K4
Great Gidding Cambs 56 C4
Great Givendale E R Yk 86 E4
Great Glemham Suffk 59 L8
Great Glen Leics 54 G1
Great Gonerby Lincs 67 M4
Great Gransden Cambs 56 E9
Great Green Cambs 56 E11
Great Green Norfk 59 K3
Great Green Suffk 58 D9
Great Green Suffk 58 E6
Great Habton N York 92 F11
Great Hale Lincs 68 B3
Great Hallingbury Essex 45 P8
Greatham Hants 25 M7
Greatham Hartpl 91 R2
Greatham W Susx 14 F8
Great Hampden Bucks 32 B2
Great Harrowden Nhants 55 M6
Great Harwood Lancs 83 Q8
Great Haseley Oxon 43 N10
Great Hatfield E R Yk 87 M6
Great Haywood Staffs 64 H7
Great Heck N York 86 B11
Great Henny Essex 46 E4
Great Hinton Wilts 29 P10
Great Hockham Norfk 70 E12
Great Holland Essex 47 M8
Great Horkesley Essex 46 H5
Great Hormead Herts 45 M5
Great Horton C Brad 84 H8
Great Horwood Bucks 43 Q5
Great Houghton Barns 78 D2
Great Houghton Nhants 55 K9
Great Hucklow Derbys 77 L8
Great Kelk E R Yk 87 L4
Great Kimble Bucks 44 B10
Great Kingshill Bucks 32 C3
Great Langdale Cumb 89 J5
Great Langton N York 91 M7
Great Leighs Essex 46 C8
Great Limber Lincs 80 D3
Great Linford M Keyn 44 B3
Great Livermere Suffk 58 C6
Great Longstone Derbys 77 M9
Great Lumley Dur 100 H8
Great Lyth Shrops 63 M11
Great Malvern Worcs 41 M3
Great Maplestead Essex 46 E5
Great Marton Bpool 82 H8

Great Massingham Norfk 69 Q7
Great Melton Norfk 70 H10
Great Meols Wirral 74 H5
Great Milton Oxon 43 N11
Great Missenden Bucks 32 C2
Great Mitton Lancs 83 Q7
Great Mongeham Kent 35 P12
Great Moulton Norfk 58 H3
Great Munden Herts 45 L7
Great Musgrave Cumb 90 C4
Great Ness Shrops 63 L8
Great Notley Essex 46 D7
Great Oak Mons 40 E9
Great Oakley Essex 47 M6
Great Oakley Nhants 55 L3
Great Offley Herts 44 G6
Great Ormside Cumb 90 B3
Great Orton Cumb 98 D7
Great Ouseburn N York 85 N3
Great Oxendon Nhants 55 J4
Great Oxney Green Essex 46 B10
Great Palgrave Norfk 70 C9
Great Park N u Ty 100 G4
Great Pardon Essex 45 N10
Great Parndon Essex 45 N10
Great Paxton Cambs 56 D8
Great Plumpton Lancs 83 J8
Great Plumstead Norfk 71 L9
Great Ponton Lincs 67 M6
Great Potheridge Devon 19 K10
Great Preston Leeds 85 N9
Great Purston Nhants 43 L4
Great Raveley Cambs 56 E4
Great Rissington Gloucs 42 E7
Great Rollright Oxon 42 G5
Great Ryburgh Norfk 70 E7
Great Ryle Nthumb 108 G7
Great Ryton Shrops 63 M12
Great Saling Essex 46 C6
Great Salkeld Cumb 98 G11
Great Sampford Essex 46 B4
Great Saredon Staffs 64 H11
Great Saughall Ches W 75 K9
Great Shefford W Berk 30 H7
Great Shelford Cambs 57 J10
Great Smeaton N York 91 N6
Great Snoring Norfk 70 E6
Great Somerford Wilts 29 R5
Great Soudley Shrops 64 D6
Great Stainton Darltn 91 N2
Great Stambridge Essex 34 F4
Great Staughton Cambs 56 C8
Great Steeping Lincs 80 H10
Great Stoke S Glos 29 J6
Great Stonar Kent 35 P10
Greatstone-on-Sea Kent 17 K6
Great Strickland Cumb 89 P2
Great Stukeley Cambs 56 E6
Great Sturton Lincs 80 D8
Great Sutton Ches W 75 L8
Great Sutton Shrops 51 N4
Great Swinburne Nthumb 99 P3
Great Tew Oxon 43 J6
Great Tey Essex 46 F6
Great Thurlow Suffk 57 N10
Great Torrington Devon 19 J9
Great Tosson Nthumb 108 G9
Great Totham Essex 46 F9
Great Totham Essex 46 F9
Great Tows Lincs 80 E5
Great Urswick Cumb 88 H11
Great Wakering Essex 34 G4
Great Waldingfield Suffk 46 G3
Great Walsingham Norfk 70 D5
Great Waltham Essex 46 B8
Great Warford Ches E 76 E8
Great Warley Essex 33 R4
Great Washbourne Gloucs 42 A5
Great Weeke Devon 8 E7
Great Welnetham Suffk 58 C9
Great Wenham Suffk 47 J4
Great Whittington Nthumb 100 C4
Great Wigborough Essex 46 G8
Great Wilbraham Cambs 57 K9
Great Wilne Derbys 66 C6
Great Wishford Wilts 23 N6
Great Witchingham Norfk 70 G8
Great Witcombe Gloucs 41 Q8
Great Witley Worcs 52 D7
Great Wolford Warwks 42 F4
Greatworth Nhants 43 L3
Great Wratting Suffk 57 N11
Great Wymondley Herts 45 J6
Great Wyrley Staffs 64 H11
Great Wytheford Shrops 63 P8
Great Yarmouth Norfk 71 Q10
Great Yeldham Essex 46 D4
Grebby Lincs 80 H10
Greeba IoM 102 d5
Green Bank Cumb 89 K10
Greenbottom Cnwll 3 J5
Greenburn W Loth 114 H9
Greencroft Hall Dur 100 F8
Green Cross Surrey 14 B3
Green Down Somset 22 B3
Green End Bed 55 P11
Green End Bed 56 B8
Green End Bed 56 C10
Green End Cambs 56 C4
Green End Cambs 56 G8
Green End Herts 45 K5
Green End Herts 45 L7
Green End Warwks 53 N3
Greenend Oxon 42 H7
Green End Warwks 53 N3
Greenfield Ag & B 113 K3
Greenfield C Beds 44 F4
Greenfield Flints 74 H8
Greenfield Highld 128 H4
Greenfield Oldham 77 J3
Greenfield Oxon 31 P4
Greengairs N Lans 114 E7
Greengates C Brad 85 J8
Greenhalgh Lancs 83 J8
Greenham Somset 20 H9
Green Hammerton N York 85 P4
Greenhaugh Nthumb 108 C12
Green Head Cumb 98 E9
Greenhead Nthumb 99 M5
Green Heath Staffs 65 J5
Greenheys Salfd 76 C3
Greenhill Derbys 78 B8
Greenhill Falk 114 E6
Greenhill Herefs 52 D11
Greenhill Kent 35 M9
Greenhill S Lans 106 C3
Green Hill Wilts 30 B5
Greenhillocks Derbys 66 C2
Greenhills S Lans 114 A10
Greenhithe Kent 34 B8
Greenholm E Ayrs 105 K2
Greenhouse Border 107 P5
Greenhow Hill N York 84 H2
Greenland Highld 151 N3

166 Greenland – Hazelwood

Greenland Sheff 78 C6
Greenlands Bucks 31 Q5
Green Lane Devon 8 E9
Green Lane Worcs 53 K7
Greenlaw Border 116 G12
Greenlea D & G 97 L3
Greenloaning P & K 123 L11
Green Moor Barns 77 P4
Greenmount Bury 84 B12
Green Oak E R Yk 86 E9
Greenock Inver 113 K6
Greenodd Cumb 89 J10
Green Ore Somset 22 D3
Green Quarter Cumb 89 M6
Greensgate Norfk 70 G9
Greenshields S Lans 106 D1
Greenside Gatesd 100 E6
Greenside Kirk 85 J12
Greens Norton Nhants 54 H10
Greenstead Green Essex 46 E6
Greensted Essex 45 P11
Green Street E Susx 16 D8
Green Street Gloucs 41 P8
Green Street Herts 32 H3
Green Street Herts 45 N7
Green Street Worcs 52 G11
Green Street Green Gt Lon 33 N9
Green Street Green Kent 33 Q8
Greenstreet Green Suffk 58 F10
Green Tye Herts 45 N8
Greenway Gloucs 41 L5
Greenway Somset 21 M8
Greenway V Glam 27 P7
Greenway Worcs 52 D6
Greenwich Gt Lon 33 M7
Greenwich Maritime Gt Lon 33 M7
Greet Gloucs 42 B6
Greete Shrops 51 P6
Greetham Lincs 80 F9
Greetham Rutlnd 67 M9
Greetland Calder 84 G11
Gregson Lane Lancs 83 N10
Greinton Somset 21 N6
Grenaby IoM 102 c6
Grendon Nhants 55 L8
Grendon Warwks 65 P12
Grendon Green Herefs 51 Q9
Grendon Underwood Bucks 43 P7
Grenofen Devon 7 P10
Grenoside Sheff 77 Q5
Greosabhagh W Isls 152 e6
Gresford Wrexhm 63 K1
Gresham Norfk 70 H4
Greshornish Highld 134 F5
Gressenhall Norfk 70 E9
Gressenhall Green Norfk 70 E9
Gressingham Lancs 83 M1
Gresty Green Ches E 64 D1
Greta Bridge Dur 90 H4
Gretna D & G 98 C5
Gretna Green D & G 98 C5
Gretna Services D & G 98 C4
Gretton Gloucs 42 B5
Gretton Nhants 55 M2
Gretton Shrops 51 N2
Grewelthorpe N York 91 L11
Grey Friars Suffk 59 P6
Greygarth N York 91 K12
Grey Green N Linc 79 K2
Greylake Somset 21 N6
Greylees Lincs 67 P3
Greyrigg D & G 106 E12
Greys Green Oxon 31 P6
Greysouthen Cumb 97 L12
Greystoke Cumb 98 F12
Greystone Angus 125 K4
Greywell Hants 25 M3
Gribb Dorset 10 B4
Gribthorpe E R Yk 86 E8
Griff Warwks 54 B3
Griffithstown Torfn 28 C3
Griffydam Leics 66 C8
Griggs Green Hants 25 P7
Grimeford Village Lancs 76 B1
Grimesthorpe Sheff 78 B6
Grimethorpe Barns 78 C2
Grimley Worcs 52 F8
Grimmet S Ayrs 104 F7
Grimoldby Lincs 80 G6
Grimpo Shrops 63 K7
Grimsargh Lancs 83 N8
Grimsby NE Lin 80 E2
Grimscote Nhants 54 G10
Grimscott Cnwll 7 K3
Grimshader W Isls 152 g4
Grimshaw Bl w D 83 Q10
Grimshaw Green Lancs 75 N1
Grimsthorpe Lincs 67 P7
Grimston E R Yk 87 P8
Grimston Leics 66 H8
Grimston Norfk 69 N7
Grimstone Dorset 10 G6
Grimstone End Suffk 58 D7
Grinacombe Moor Devon 7 N6
Grindale E R Yk 87 L1
Grindle Shrops 64 D11
Grindleford Derbys 77 N8
Grindleton Lancs 84 A6
Grindley Brook Shrops 63 N4
Grindlow Derbys 77 M8
Grindon Nthumb 117 K12
Grindon S on T 91 P2
Grindon Staffs 65 K1
Grindon Hill Nthumb 99 M5
Grindonrigg Nthumb 108 E1
Gringley on the Hill Notts 79 J5
Grinsdale Cumb 98 D6
Grinshill Shrops 63 N7
Grinton N York 90 H7
Griomaisiader W Isls 152 g4
Grishipoll Ag & B 118 G1
Grisling Common E Susx 15 N6
Gristhorpe N York 93 M10
Griston Norfk 70 D12
Gritley Ork 147 d5
Grittenham Wilts 30 B6
Grittleton Wilts 29 P6
Grizebeck Cumb 88 H9
Grizedale Cumb 89 K8
Groby Leics 66 E10
Groes Conwy 74 D10
Groes-faen Rhondd 27 P6
Groesffordd Gwynd 60 D4
Groesffordd Powys 39 P6
Groesffordd Marli Denbgs 74 D9
Groeslon Gwynd 60 H1
Groeslon Gwynd 73 J11
Groes-lwyd Powys 62 H10
Groes-Wen Caerph 27 Q5
Grogarry W Isls 152 c10
Grogport Ag & B 112 B12
Groigearraidh W Isls 152 c10
Gromford Suffk 59 M9
Gronant Flints 74 F7
Groombridge E Susx 15 P3
Grosebay W Isls 152 e6
Grosmont Mons 40 E7
Grosmont N York 92 G6
Groton Suffk 46 G3
Grotton Oldham 76 H3
Grouville Jersey 13 d3
Grove Bucks 44 C7
Grove Dorset 10 H10
Grove Kent 35 M10
Grove Notts 79 J8
Grove Oxon 31 J4
Grove Pembks 37 J10
Grove Green Kent 34 D11
Grovenhurst Kent 16 C3
Grove Park Gt Lon 33 M8
Grovesend S Glos 29 K4
Grovesend Swans 26 E2
Grubb Street Kent 33 Q8
Gruinard Highld 143 P7
Gruinart Ag & B 110 G8
Grula Highld 134 G10
Gruline Ag & B 119 P5
Grumbla Cnwll 2 C8
Grundisburgh Suffk 59 J10
Gruting Shet 147 h7
Grutness Shet 147 i10
Gualachulain Highld 121 L4
Guanockgate Lincs 68 G10
Guardbridge Fife 125 J9
Guarlford Worcs 41 N3
Guay P & K 123 P3
Guernsey Guern 12 c2
Guernsey Airport Guern 12 b3
Guestling Green E Susx 16 E8
Guestling Thorn E Susx 16 E7
Guestwick Norfk 70 F7
Guide Bridge Tamesd 76 G4
Guide Post Nthumb 100 H1
Guilden Morden Cambs 45 K3
Guilden Sutton Ches W 75 M10
Guildford Surrey 14 E1
Guildstead Kent 34 E10
Guildtown P & K 124 C6
Guilsborough Nhants 54 H6
Guilsfield Powys 62 H10
Guilton Kent 35 N10
Guiltreehill S Ayrs 104 G7
Guineaford Devon 19 K6
Guisborough R & Cl 92 C4
Guiseley Leeds 85 J7
Guist Norfk 70 E7
Guiting Power Gloucs 42 C7
Gullane E Loth 116 C5
Gulling Green Suffk 58 B9
Gulval Cnwll 2 D8
Gulworthy Devon 7 N10
Gumfreston Pembks 37 L10
Gumley Leics 54 H3
Gummow's Shop Cnwll 3 L3
Gunby E R Yk 86 D8
Gunby Lincs 67 M8
Gunby Lincs 81 J10
Gundleton Hants 25 K7
Gun Green Kent 16 D4
Gun Hill E Susx 15 Q8
Gun Hill Warwks 53 P3
Gunn Devon 19 M7
Gunnerside N York 90 F7
Gunnerton Nthumb 99 P3
Gunness N Linc 79 L1
Gunnislake Cnwll 7 N10
Gunnista Shet 147 j7
Gunthorpe C Pete 68 D11
Gunthorpe N Linc 79 K4
Gunthorpe Norfk 70 F5
Gunthorpe Notts 66 H3
Gunton Suffk 59 Q2
Gunwalloe Cnwll 2 G10
Gupworthy Somset 20 F6
Gurnard IoW 12 H6
Gurnett Ches E 76 G9
Gurney Slade Somset 22 E3
Gurnos Powys 39 J10
Gushmere Kent 35 J11
Gussage All Saints Dorset 11 N3
Gussage St Andrew Dorset 23 L10
Gussage St Michael Dorset 11 N2
Guston Kent 17 P2
Gutcher Shet 147 j3
Guthrie Angus 125 L3
Guyhirn Cambs 68 H11
Guyhirn Gull Cambs 68 G11
Guy's Marsh Dorset 23 J9
Guyzance Nthumb 109 K9
Gwaenysgor Flints 74 F7
Gwalchmai IoA 72 F8
Gwastadnant Gwynd 73 K12
Gwaun-Cae-Gurwen Carmth 38 G9
Gwbert on Sea Cerdgn 48 B10
Gwealavellan Cnwll 2 F6
Gweek Cnwll 2 H9
Gwehelog Mons 40 E10
Gwenddwr Powys 39 P3
Gwennap Cnwll 3 J6
Gwennap Mining District Cnwll 3 J6
Gwenter Cnwll 3 J11
Gwernaffield Flints 74 H10
Gwernesney Mons 40 F11
Gwernogle Carmth 38 D5
Gwernymynydd Flints 74 H11
Gwersyllt Wrexhm 63 K2
Gwespyr Flints 74 F7
Gwindra Cnwll 3 M4
Gwinear Cnwll 2 F7
Gwithian Cnwll 2 F6
Gwredog IoA 72 G6
Gwrhay Caerph 28 B3
Gwyddelwern Denbgs 62 E3
Gwyddgrug Carmth 38 C4
Gwynfryn Wrexhm 63 J2
Gwystre Powys 50 E7
Gwytherin Conwy 73 Q11
Gyfelia Wrexhm 63 K3
Gyrn Goch Gwynd 60 F2

H

Habberley Shrops 63 L11
Habberley Worcs 52 E5
Habergham Lancs 84 C8
Habertoft Lincs 81 J10
Habin W Susx 25 P8
Habrough NE Lin 80 C1
Hacconby Lincs 68 B7
Haceby Lincs 67 P5
Hacheston Suffk 59 L9
Hackbridge Gt Lon 33 K9
Hackenthorpe Sheff 78 C7
Hackford Norfk 70 F11
Hackforth N York 91 L8
Hack Green Ches E 64 C3
Hackland Ork 147 c4
Hackleton Nhants 55 K9
Hacklinge Kent 35 P12
Hackman's Gate Worcs 52 G5
Hackness N York 93 K8
Hackness Somset 21 M4
Hackney Gt Lon 33 L5
Hackthorn Lincs 79 N7
Hackthorpe Cumb 89 N2
Hacton Gt Lon 33 Q5
Hadden Border 108 C3
Haddenham Bucks 43 Q10
Haddenham Cambs 57 J5
Haddington E Loth 116 C6
Haddington Lincs 79 M11
Haddiscoe Norfk 59 N1
Haddo Abers 141 K8
Haddon Cambs 56 C2
Hade Edge Kirk 77 L3
Hadfield Derbys 77 J4
Hadham Cross Herts 45 M8
Hadham Ford Herts 45 N7
Hadleigh Essex 34 E5
Hadleigh Suffk 47 J3
Hadleigh Heath Suffk 46 H3
Hadley Worcs 52 F8
Hadley Wrekin 64 C10
Hadley End Staffs 65 L8
Hadley Wood Gt Lon 33 J3
Hadlow Kent 34 B12
Hadlow Down E Susx 15 P6
Hadnall Shrops 63 N8
Hadrian's Wall 100 B4
Hadstock Essex 45 Q3
Hadston Nthumb 109 L9
Hadzor Worcs 52 H8
Haffenden Quarter Kent 16 F3
Hafodunos Conwy 73 Q10
Hafod-y-bwch Wrexhm 63 K3
Hafod-y-coed Blae G 28 B2
Hafodyrynys Caerph 28 B3
Haggate Lancs 84 C8
Haggbeck Cumb 98 F3
Haggersta Shet 147 i7
Haggerston Nthumb 108 G1
Haggington Hill Devon 19 L4
Haggs Falk 114 E5
Hagley Herefs 40 H3
Hagley Worcs 52 G4
Hagmore Green Suffk 46 G4
Hagnaby Lincs 80 G11
Hagnaby Lincs 81 J7
Hagworthingham Lincs 80 G10
Haigh Wigan 75 Q2
Haighton Green Lancs 83 M8
Haile Cumb 88 D5
Hailes Gloucs 42 B6
Hailey Herts 45 L9
Hailey Oxon 31 N5
Hailey Oxon 42 H9
Hailsham E Susx 15 Q9
Hail Weston Cambs 56 C8
Hainault Gt Lon 33 N4
Haine Kent 35 P9
Hainford Norfk 71 J8
Hainton Lincs 80 D7
Hainworth C Brad 84 G7
Haisthorpe E R Yk 87 L2
Hakin Pembks 36 H9
Halam Notts 66 H1
Halbeath Fife 115 L3
Halberton Devon 20 F10
Halcro Highld 151 M4
Hale Cumb 89 N11
Hale Halton 75 M7
Hale Hants 24 C9
Hale Somset 22 G8
Hale Surrey 25 P4
Hale Traffd 76 E6
Hale Bank Halton 75 N7
Hale Barns Traffd 76 E6
Hale Green E Susx 15 Q8
Hale Nook Lancs 83 J6
Hales Norfk 59 M1
Hales Staffs 64 D5
Halesgate Lincs 68 F7
Hales Green Derbys 65 M4
Halesowen Dudley 52 H4
Hales Place Kent 35 L10
Hale Street Kent 16 B1
Halesville Essex 34 F4
Halesworth Suffk 59 M5
Halewood Knows 75 M6
Halford Devon 8 F10
Halford Shrops 51 M4
Halford Warwks 42 F3
Halfpenny Cumb 89 N9
Halfpenny Green Staffs 52 F2
Halfpenny Houses N York 91 L10
Halfway Carmth 38 F5
Halfway Carmth 39 K5
Halfway Sheff 78 C7
Halfway W Berk 31 J8
Halfway Bridge W Susx 14 D6
Halfway House Shrops 63 K10
Halfway Houses Kent 34 G8
Halifax Calder 84 G10
Halket E Ayrs 113 N10
Halkirk Highld 151 L5
Halkyn Flints 74 H9
Hall E Rens 113 N10
Hallam Fields Derbys 66 D4
Halland E Susx 15 P7
Hallaton Leics 55 K1
Hallatrow BaNES 29 K11
Hallbankgate Cumb 98 H6
Hallbeck Cumb 89 Q9
Hall Cliffe Wakefd 85 L11
Hall Cross Lancs 83 K9
Hall Dunnerdale Cumb 88 G7
Hallen S Glos 28 H6
Hall End Bed 44 E3
Hall End C Beds 44 F4
Hallfield Gate Derbys 78 C12
Hallgarth Dur 101 J9
Hallglen Falk 114 G5
Hall Green Birm 53 L4
Hallin Highld 134 D4
Halling Medway 34 C9
Hallington Lincs 80 F6
Hallington Nthumb 100 C3
Halliwell Bolton 76 C2
Halloughton Notts 66 H2
Hallow Worcs 52 F9
Hallow Heath Worcs 52 F8
Hallsands Devon 5 N9
Hall's Green Essex 45 M10
Hall's Green Herts 45 K6
Hallthwaites Cumb 88 G9
Hallworthy Cnwll 6 H7
Hallyne Border 106 G2
Halmer End Staffs 64 E2
Halmond's Frome Herefs 52 C11
Halmore Gloucs 41 L11
Halnaker W Susx 14 C9
Halsall Lancs 75 L2
Halse Nhants 43 M4
Halse Somset 21 J8
Halsetown Cnwll 2 D7
Halsham E R Yk 87 P9
Halsinger Devon 19 K6
Halstead Essex 46 E5
Halstead Kent 33 N10
Halstead Leics 67 J11
Halstock Dorset 10 E3
Halsway Somset 20 H6
Haltcliff Bridge Cumb 98 D11
Haltham Lincs 80 E11
Haltoft End Lincs 68 G3
Halton Bucks 44 C9
Halton Halton 75 P7
Halton Lancs 83 L2
Halton Leeds 85 M8
Halton Nthumb 100 C5
Halton Wrexhm 63 J4
Halton East N York 84 F4
Halton Fenside Lincs 80 H11
Halton Gill N York 90 E11
Halton Green Lancs 83 L2
Halton Holegate Lincs 80 H10
Halton Lea Gate Nthumb 99 J6
Halton Quay Cnwll 4 F4
Halton Shields Nthumb 100 C4
Halton West N York 84 C4
Haltwhistle Nthumb 99 K5
Halvana Cnwll 7 J9
Halvergate Norfk 71 N10
Halwell Devon 5 N6
Halwill Devon 7 N5
Halwill Junction Devon 7 N5
Ham Devon 9 N4
Ham Gloucs 29 K3
Ham Gloucs 41 R7
Ham Gt Lon 32 H8
Ham Kent 35 P11
Ham Somset 21 L8
Ham Somset 22 F4
Ham Wilts 30 G9
Hambleden Bucks 31 R5
Hambledon Hants 25 L10
Hambledon Surrey 14 D3
Hamble-le-Rice Hants 12 H3
Hambleton Lancs 83 J7
Hambleton N York 85 Q9
Hambleton Moss Side Lancs 83 J7
Hambridge Somset 21 N9
Hambrook S Glos 29 K6
Hambrook W Susx 13 N3
Ham Common Dorset 22 H8
Hameringham Lincs 80 F10
Hamerton Cambs 56 C5
Ham Green Herefs 41 M3
Ham Green Kent 16 F5
Ham Green Kent 34 E8
Ham Green N Som 28 H7
Ham Green Worcs 53 J8
Ham Hill Kent 34 C10
Hamilton S Lans 114 D10
Hamilton Services S Lans 114 D10
Hamlet Dorset 10 F3
Hamlins E Susx 15 Q9
Hammerpot W Susx 14 F9
Hammersmith Gt Lon 33 J6
Hammerwich Staffs 65 K10
Hammerwood E Susx 15 N3
Hammond Street Herts 45 L10
Hammoon Dorset 22 H10
Hamnavoe Shet 147 i8
Hampden Park E Susx 15 R10
Hamperden End Essex 45 Q5
Hampnett Gloucs 42 C8
Hampole Donc 78 E2
Hampreston Dorset 11 P5
Hampsfield Cumb 89 L10
Hampson Green Lancs 83 L4
Hampstead Gt Lon 33 J5
Hampstead Norreys W Berk 31 L7
Hampsthwaite N York 85 K3
Hampton C Pete 56 D2
Hampton Devon 9 P5
Hampton Gt Lon 32 G8
Hampton Kent 35 L8
Hampton Shrops 52 D3
Hampton Swindn 30 E4
Hampton Worcs 42 B3
Hampton Bishop Herefs 40 H4
Hampton Court Palace Gt Lon 32 H8
Hampton Fields Gloucs 29 P2
Hampton Green Ches W 63 N2
Hampton Heath Ches W 63 N2
Hampton-in-Arden Solhll 53 M4
Hampton Loade Shrops 52 D3
Hampton Lovett Worcs 52 G7
Hampton Lucy Warwks 53 N9
Hampton Magna Warwks 53 N7
Hampton on the Hill Warwks 53 N8
Hampton Poyle Oxon 43 L8
Hampton Wick Gt Lon 32 H8
Hamptworth Wilts 24 D9
Hamrow Norfk 70 D7
Hamsey E Susx 15 M8
Hamsey Green Surrey 33 L10
Hamstall Ridware Staffs 65 L8
Hamstead Birm 53 K2
Hamstead IoW 12 F6
Hamstead Marshall W Berk 31 J9
Hamsterley Dur 100 E12
Hamsterley Dur 100 E7
Hamstreet Kent 16 H4
Ham Street Somset 22 D6
Hamwood N Som 28 E11
Hamworthy BCP 11 N6
Hanbury Staffs 65 M6
Hanbury Worcs 52 H7
Hanby Lincs 67 P6
Hanchet End Suffk 46 B2
Hanchurch Staffs 64 F4
Handa Island Highld 148 D7
Handale R & Cl 92 E4
Hand and Pen Devon 9 K5
Handbridge Ches W 75 L10
Handcross W Susx 15 J5
Handforth Ches E 76 F7
Hand Green Ches W 75 P11
Handley Ches W 75 M12
Handley Derbys 78 B11
Handley Green Essex 46 B11
Handsacre Staffs 65 K9
Handsworth Birm 53 K3
Handsworth Sheff 78 C6
Handy Cross Bucks 32 B4
Hanford C Stke 64 F4
Hanford Dorset 11 K3
Hanging Heaton Kirk 85 K10
Hanging Houghton Nhants 55 J6
Hanging Langford Wilts 23 M6
Hangleton Br & H 15 K9
Hangleton W Susx 14 F10
Hanham S Glos 29 K8
Hankelow Ches E 64 C3
Hankerton Wilts 29 R4
Hankham E Susx 16 A9
Hanley C Stke 64 G3
Hanley Castle Worcs 41 N3
Hanley Child Worcs 52 C7
Hanley Swan Worcs 41 N3
Hanley William Worcs 52 C7
Hanlith N York 84 D3
Hanmer Wrexhm 63 M4
Hannaford Devon 19 L7
Hannah Lincs 81 J8
Hannington Hants 25 J2
Hannington Nhants 55 K6
Hannington Swindn 30 E4
Hannington Wick Swindn 30 E3
Hanscombe End C Beds 44 G5
Hanslope M Keyn 44 A2
Hanthorpe Lincs 68 B7
Hanwell Gt Lon 32 H6
Hanwell Oxon 43 J3
Hanwood Shrops 63 M10
Hanworth Gt Lon 32 G8
Hanworth Norfk 71 J5
Happendon S Lans 105 Q3
Happendon Services S Lans 105 Q3
Happisburgh Norfk 71 M6
Happisburgh Common Norfk 71 M6
Hapsford Ches W 75 M9
Hapton Lancs 84 B9
Hapton Norfk 58 H1
Harberton Devon 5 N5
Harbertonford Devon 5 N5
Harbledown Kent 35 K10
Harborne Birm 53 J4
Harborough Magna Warwks 54 D5
Harbottle Nthumb 108 E9
Harbourneford Devon 5 M4
Harbours Hill Worcs 52 H7
Harbridge Hants 12 B3
Harbridge Green Hants 12 B3
Harbury Warwks 54 B8
Harby Leics 67 J6
Harby Notts 79 L9
Harcombe Devon 8 G8
Harcombe Devon 9 M7
Harcombe Bottom Devon 9 Q5
Harden C Brad 84 G7
Harden Wsall 65 J12
Hardendale Cumb 89 P4
Hardenhuish Wilts 29 P7
Hardgate Abers 133 J4
Hardgate D & G 96 G5
Hardgate N York 85 K3
Hardgate W Duns 113 P7
Hardham W Susx 14 E7
Hardhorn Lancs 83 J8
Hardingham Norfk 70 F11
Hardingstone Nhants 55 J9
Hardington Somset 22 G3
Hardington Mandeville Somset 10 D2
Hardington Marsh Somset 10 D3
Hardington Moor Somset 22 C11
Hardisworthy Devon 18 E9
Hardley Hants 12 G4
Hardley Street Norfk 71 M12
Hardmead M Keyn 55 M11
Hardraw N York 90 D8
Hardsough Lancs 84 B11
Hardstoft Derbys 78 D11
Hardway Hants 13 K4
Hardway Somset 22 G6
Hardwick Bucks 44 A8
Hardwick Cambs 56 G9
Hardwick Nhants 55 L7
Hardwick Norfk 59 J3
Hardwick Oxon 42 H10
Hardwick Oxon 43 M6
Hardwick Rothm 78 D6
Hardwick Wsall 65 K12
Hardwicke Gloucs 41 M9
Hardwicke Gloucs 41 P6
Hardwick Hall Derbys 78 D11
Hardwick Village Notts 78 G8
Hardy's Green Essex 46 G7
Harebeating E Susx 15 Q8
Hareby Lincs 80 G10
Hare Croft C Brad 84 G8
Harefield Gt Lon 32 F4
Hare Green Essex 47 K6
Hare Hatch Wokham 32 A7
Harehill Derbys 65 M5
Harehills Leeds 85 L8
Harehope Nthumb 108 H6
Harelaw Border 107 N5
Harelaw D & G 98 E3
Harelaw Dur 100 F7
Hareplain Kent 16 E3
Harescough Cumb 99 J9
Harescombe Gloucs 41 N9
Haresfield Gloucs 41 N9
Harestock Hants 24 H7
Hare Street Essex 33 P2
Hare Street Essex 45 M9
Hare Street Herts 45 M6
Harewood Leeds 85 L6
Harewood End Herefs 40 H6
Harford Devon 5 K5
Hargate Norfk 58 G2
Hargatewall Derbys 77 L8
Hargrave Ches W 75 N11
Hargrave Nhants 55 P6
Hargrave Suffk 57 P8
Harker Cumb 98 E6
Harkstead Suffk 47 L5
Harlaston Staffs 65 N10
Harlaxton Lincs 67 L6
Harlech Gwynd 61 K6
Harlech Castle Gwynd 61 K6
Harlescott Shrops 63 N9
Harlesden Gt Lon 33 J6
Harlesthorpe Derbys 78 E8
Harleston Devon 5 N7
Harleston Norfk 59 K4
Harleston Suffk 58 F8
Harlestone Nhants 54 H8
Harle Syke Lancs 84 C8
Harley Rothm 78 B4
Harley Shrops 63 Q11
Harlington C Beds 44 E5
Harlington Donc 78 D3
Harlington Gt Lon 32 F7
Harlosh Highld 134 E7
Harlow Essex 45 N9
Harlow Carr RHS N York 85 L4
Harlow Hill Nthumb 100 D4
Harlthorpe E R Yk 86 D8
Harlton Cambs 56 G10
Harlyn Cnwll 6 C9
Harman's Cross Dorset 11 N8
Harmby N York 91 J9
Harmer Green Herts 45 J8
Harmer Hill Shrops 63 N8
Harmondsworth Gt Lon 32 F7
Harmston Lincs 79 N11
Harnage Shrops 63 P11
Harnham Nthumb 100 D2
Harnhill Gloucs 30 C2
Harold Hill Gt Lon 33 Q4
Haroldston West Pembks 36 G7
Haroldswick Shet 147 k2
Harold Wood Gt Lon 33 Q4
Harome N York 92 D10
Harpenden Herts 44 G9
Harpford Devon 9 L7
Harpham E R Yk 87 K3
Harpley Norfk 69 Q7
Harpley Worcs 52 C8
Harpole Nhants 54 H8
Harpsdale Highld 151 L5
Harpsden Oxon 31 Q6
Harpswell Lincs 79 M6
Harpurhey Manch 76 F3
Harpur Hill Derbys 77 K9
Harraby Cumb 98 E7
Harracott Devon 19 L8
Harrapool Highld 135 M11
Harrietfield P & K 123 P7
Harrietsham Kent 34 F11
Harringay Gt Lon 33 K5
Harrington Cumb 88 C2
Harrington Lincs 80 G9
Harrington Nhants 55 J5
Harringworth Nhants 55 M1
Harris W Isls 152 e6
Harriseahead Staffs 64 F1
Harriston Cumb 97 N10
Harrogate N York 85 L4
Harrold Bed 55 N9
Harrop Dale Oldham 77 J2
Harrow Gt Lon 32 H5
Harrowbarrow Cnwll 7 M10
Harrowden Bed 44 F2
Harrowgate Village Darltn 91 M3
Harrow Green Suffk 58 C9
Harrow Hill Gloucs 41 K8
Harrow on the Hill Gt Lon 32 H5
Harrow Weald Gt Lon 32 H4
Harston Cambs 56 H10
Harston Leics 67 L6
Harswell E R Yk 86 F7
Hart Hartpl 101 L11
Hartburn Nthumb 100 E1
Hartburn S on T 91 P3
Hartest Suffk 58 B10
Hartfield E Susx 15 N4
Hartford Cambs 56 E6
Hartford Ches W 76 B9
Hartford Somset 20 E7
Hartfordbridge Hants 31 Q10
Hartford End Essex 46 B8
Hartforth N York 91 K5
Hartgrove Dorset 23 J9
Harthill Ches W 63 N1
Harthill N Lans 114 G8
Harthill Rothm 78 E7
Harthope D & G 106 D7
Hartington Derbys 77 L11
Hartington Nthumb 108 G12
Hartland Devon 18 E8
Hartland Quay Devon 18 E8
Hartlebury Worcs 52 F6
Hartlepool Hartpl 101 M11
Hartley Cumb 90 C5
Hartley Kent 16 D4
Hartley Kent 33 R9
Hartley Nthumb 101 J3
Hartley Green Kent 33 R9
Hartley Green Staffs 64 H6
Hartley Wespall Hants 31 P10
Hartley Wintney Hants 31 Q11
Hartlip Kent 34 E9
Hartoft End N York 92 F8
Harton N York 86 D3
Harton S Tyne 101 K5
Harton Shrops 51 N3
Hartpury Gloucs 41 M7
Hartshead Kirk 85 J10
Hartshead Moor Services Calder 85 J10
Hartshill C Stke 64 F3
Hartshill Warwks 53 Q2
Hartshorne Derbys 65 Q8
Hartside Nthumb 108 F6
Hartsop Cumb 89 L4
Hart Station Hartpl 101 M11
Hartswell Somset 20 H8
Hartwell Nhants 55 K10
Hartwith N York 85 J3
Hartwood N Lans 114 F9
Hartwoodmyres Border 107 L5
Harvel Kent 34 B9
Harvington Worcs 52 G6
Harvington Worcs 53 K10
Harwell Notts 78 H5
Harwell Oxon 31 K4
Harwich Essex 47 N5
Harwood Bolton 76 D2
Harwood Dur 99 M11
Harwood Nthumb 108 G11
Harwood Dale N York 93 K7
Harwood Lee Bolton 76 D1
Harworth Notts 78 G5
Hasbury Dudley 52 H4
Hascombe Surrey 14 E3
Haselbech Nhants 54 H5
Haselbury Plucknett Somset 10 D3
Haseley Warwks 53 N7
Haseley Green Warwks 53 N7
Haseley Knob Warwks 53 N6
Haselor Warwks 53 L9
Hasfield Gloucs 41 N6
Hasguard Pembks 36 G8
Hasholme E R Yk 86 F8
Haskayne Lancs 75 K2
Hasketon Suffk 59 K10
Hasland Derbys 78 C9
Haslemere Surrey 14 C4
Haslingden Lancs 84 B10
Haslingfield Cambs 56 H10
Haslington Ches E 64 D1
Hassall Ches E 76 E12
Hassall Green Ches E 76 E12
Hassell Street Kent 17 K2
Hassingham Norfk 71 M11
Hassness Cumb 88 G3
Hassocks W Susx 15 K7
Hassop Derbys 77 N9
Haste Hill Surrey 14 C4
Haster Highld 151 P6
Hasthorpe Lincs 81 J9
Hastingleigh Kent 17 K2
Hastings E Susx 16 E9
Hastings Somset 21 M10
Hastingwood Essex 45 N10
Hastoe Herts 44 C9
Haswell Dur 101 K9
Haswell Plough Dur 101 K10
Hatch C Beds 56 C11
Hatch Beauchamp Somset 21 M9
Hatch End Bed 55 Q8
Hatch End Gt Lon 32 G4
Hatchet Gate Hants 12 F4
Hatching Green Herts 44 G9
Hatchmere Ches W 75 P9
Hatcliffe NE Lin 80 D4
Hatfield Donc 78 H2
Hatfield Herefs 51 Q8
Hatfield Herts 45 J10
Hatfield Worcs 52 G10
Hatfield Broad Oak Essex 45 Q8
Hatfield Heath Essex 45 P8
Hatfield Peverel Essex 46 D9
Hatfield Woodhouse Donc 78 H2
Hatford Oxon 30 H3
Hatherden Hants 24 E3
Hatherleigh Devon 7 Q4
Hathern Leics 66 E8
Hatherop Gloucs 42 D10
Hathersage Derbys 77 N7
Hathersage Booths Derbys 77 N7
Hatherton Ches E 64 C3
Hatherton Staffs 64 H10
Hatley St George Cambs 56 E10
Hatt Cnwll 4 F4
Hattersley Tamesd 77 J5
Hattingley Hants 25 L6
Hatton Abers 141 P8
Hatton Angus 125 J4
Hatton Derbys 65 N6
Hatton Gt Lon 32 G7
Hatton Lincs 80 D8
Hatton Shrops 51 M3
Hatton Warrtn 75 Q7
Hatton Warwks 53 N7
Hatton Heath Ches W 75 M11
Hatton of Fintray Abers 133 K1
Haugh E Ayrs 105 J5
Haugh Lincs 80 H8
Haugh Rochdl 76 H1
Haugham Lincs 80 G7
Haughhead E Duns 114 A5
Haugh Head Nthumb 108 G4
Haughley Suffk 58 F8
Haughley Green Suffk 58 F8
Haugh of Glass Moray 140 C8
Haugh of Urr D & G 96 G5
Haughs of Kinnaird Angus 125 M1
Haughton Ches E 75 P12
Haughton Notts 78 H9
Haughton Powys 63 J8
Haughton Shrops 52 C1
Haughton Shrops 63 L7
Haughton Shrops 63 P9
Haughton Shrops 64 D10
Haughton Staffs 64 F8
Haughton Green Tamesd 76 H5
Haughton le Skerne Darltn 91 M3
Haultwick Herts 45 L7
Haunton Staffs 65 N10
Hautes Croix Jersey 13 c1
Hauxton Cambs 56 H10
Havannah Ches E 76 F10
Havant Hants 13 M3
Haven Herefs 51 L10
Haven Bank Lincs 68 E2
Haven Side E R Yk 87 M9
Havenstreet IoW 13 J6
Havercroft Wakefd 78 C1
Haverfordwest Pembks 37 J7
Haverhill Suffk 46 B3
Haverigg Cumb 88 F11
Havering-atte-Bower Gt Lon 33 P4
Haversham M Keyn 44 B3
Haverthwaite Cumb 89 K10
Haverton Hill S on T 91 R2
Havyatt N Som 28 G10
Havyatt Somset 22 C6
Hawarden Flints 75 K10
Hawbridge Worcs 52 G10
Hawbush Green Essex 46 D7
Hawcoat Cumb 88 G12
Hawen Cerdgn 48 E11
Hawes N York 90 E9
Hawe's Green Norfk 71 K12
Hawford Worcs 52 F8
Hawick Border 107 M7
Hawkchurch Devon 9 Q5
Hawkedon Suffk 57 Q10
Hawkenbury Kent 16 E2
Hawkeridge Wilts 23 J3
Hawkerland Devon 9 K7
Hawker's Cove Cnwll 6 C9
Hawkesbury S Glos 29 M5
Hawkesbury Warwks 54 B4
Hawkesbury Upton S Glos 29 M5
Hawkes End Covtry 53 P4
Hawk Green Stockp 76 H6
Hawkhill Nthumb 109 L7
Hawkhurst Kent 16 D5
Hawkhurst Common E Susx 15 P7
Hawkinge Kent 17 M3
Hawkley Hants 25 N7
Hawkley Wigan 75 P3
Hawkridge Somset 20 D7
Hawksdale Cumb 98 D8
Hawkshaw Bury 84 A12
Hawkshead Cumb 89 K7
Hawkshead Hill Cumb 89 K7
Hawksland S Lans 105 Q2
Hawkspur Green Essex 46 B5
Hawkstone Shrops 63 P6
Hawkswick N York 84 E1
Hawksworth Leeds 85 J7
Hawksworth Notts 67 J3
Hawkwell Essex 34 E4
Hawkwell Nthumb 100 D4
Hawley Hants 32 B10
Hawley Kent 33 Q8
Hawling Gloucs 42 C7
Hawnby N York 92 B9
Haworth C Brad 84 F8
Hawridge Bucks 44 D10
Hawstead Suffk 58 C9
Hawstead Green Suffk 58 C9
Hawthorn Dur 101 K9
Hawthorn Hants 25 L6
Hawthorn Rhondd 27 Q5
Hawthorn Hill Br For 32 B7
Hawthorn Hill Lincs 68 D1
Hawthorpe Lincs 67 P7
Hawton Notts 67 K2
Haxby C York 86 B4
Haxby Gates C York 86 B4
Haxey N Linc 79 K4
Haxey Carr N Linc 79 J3
Haxted Surrey 15 M2
Haxton Wilts 23 P3
Hay Cnwll 3 N4
Hay Cnwll 6 E10
Haydock St Hel 75 P4
Haydon BaNES 22 F3
Haydon Dorset 22 F10
Haydon Somset 21 L8
Haydon Bridge Nthumb 99 N5
Haydon Wick Swindn 30 D5
Haye Cnwll 4 E3
Hayes Gt Lon 32 G6
Hayes Gt Lon 33 M9
Hayes End Gt Lon 32 F6
Hayfield Ag & B 121 K8
Hayfield Derbys 77 J6
Hayfield Green Donc 78 G4
Haygate Wrekin 64 B10
Hay Green Norfk 69 K8
Hayhillock Angus 125 K4
Hayle Cnwll 2 E7
Hayle Port Cnwll 2 E7
Hayley Green Dudley 52 H4
Hayling Island Hants 13 M4
Haymoor Green Ches E 64 C2
Hayne Devon 8 E7
Hayne Devon 20 E10
Haynes C Beds 44 G3
Haynes Church End C Beds 44 F3
Haynes West End C Beds 44 F4
Hay-on-Wye Powys 40 B3
Hayscastle Pembks 36 H5
Hayscastle Cross Pembks 36 H5
Haysden Kent 15 Q2
Hay Street Herts 45 M6
Hayton Cumb 97 M10
Hayton Cumb 98 G7
Hayton E R Yk 86 F6
Hayton Notts 79 J7
Hayton's Bent Shrops 51 N4
Haytor Vale Devon 8 E9
Haytown Devon 18 G10
Haywards Heath W Susx 15 L6
Haywood Donc 78 F1
Haywood Herefs 40 G5
Haywood Oaks Notts 66 G1
Hazards Green E Susx 16 C8
Hazelbank S Lans 114 F12
Hazelbury Bryan Dorset 10 H3
Hazeleigh Essex 46 E11
Hazelford Notts 67 J2
Hazel Grove Stockp 76 G6
Hazelhurst Tamesd 76 H4
Hazelslade Staffs 65 J9
Hazel Street Kent 16 C3
Hazel Stub Suffk 46 B3
Hazelton Walls Fife 124 G8
Hazelwood Derbys 65 Q3

Hazlemere Bucks...32 C3
Hazlerigg N u Ty...100 G4
Hazles Staffs...65 J3
Hazleton Gloucs...42 C8
Heacham Norfk...69 N5
Headbourne Worthy Hants...24 H7
Headbrook Herefs...51 J9
Headcorn Kent...16 E2
Headingley Leeds...85 L8
Headington Oxon...43 L10
Headlam Dur...91 K3
Headlesscross N Lans...114 A9
Headless Cross Worcs...53 J7
Headley Hants...25 P6
Headley Hants...31 L10
Headley Surrey...32 H11
Headley Down Hants...25 P6
Headley Heath Worcs...53 K5
Headon Devon...7 L4
Headon Notts...79 J8
Heads Nook Cumb...98 G7
Heage Derbys...66 B2
Healaugh N York...85 P6
Healaugh N York...90 E8
Heald Green Stockp...76 F6
Heale Devon...19 M4
Heale Somset...21 K9
Heale Somset...21 M8
Healey N York...91 K10
Healey Nthumb...100 C6
Healey Rochdl...84 D12
Healey Wakefd...85 K11
Healeyfield Dur...100 D8
Healing NE Lin...80 D2
Heamoor Cnwll...2 C8
Heanor Derbys...66 C3
Heanton Punchardon Devon...19 K6
Heapham Lincs...79 L6
Hearn Hants...25 P6
Heart of Scotland Services N Lans...114 A9
Hearts Delight Kent...34 F10
Heasley Mill Devon...19 P7
Heaste Highld...135 L12
Heath Derbys...78 D10
Heath Wakefd...85 M11
Heath and Reach C Beds...44 C6
Heath Common W Susx...14 G8
Heathcote Derbys...77 L11
Heathcote Shrops...64 C6
Heath End Bucks...32 C3
Heath End Hants...31 J10
Heath End Leics...66 B8
Heath End Warwks...53 N6
Heather Leics...66 C10
Heathfield Cambs...45 K9
Heathfield E Susx...15 Q6
Heathfield N York...84 H2
Heathfield Somset...21 J8
Heathfield Village Oxon...43 J8
Heath Green Worcs...53 K6
Heath Hall D & G...97 K2
Heath Hayes & Wimblebury Staffs...65 J10
Heath Hill Shrops...64 E9
Heath House Somset...21 P4
Heathrow Airport Gt Lon...32 F6
Heathstock Devon...9 N4
Heathton Shrops...52 F2
Heath Town Wolves...64 H12
Heathwaite N York...91 R6
Heatley Staffs...65 K7
Heatley Warrtn...76 C2
Heaton Bolton...84 H8
Heaton C Brad...84 H8
Heaton Lancs...83 B4
Heaton N u Ty...100 H5
Heaton Staffs...76 H11
Heaton Chapel Stockp...76 F5
Heaton Mersey Stockp...76 F5
Heaton Norris Stockp...76 F5
Heaton's Bridge Lancs...75 L1
Heaverham Kent...33 Q10
Heaviley Stockp...76 H6
Heavitree Devon...8 H6
Hebburn S Tyne...101 J5
Hebden N York...84 F3
Hebden Bridge Calder...84 E9
Hebden Green Ches W...76 B10
Hebing End Herts...45 K9
Hebron Carmth...37 N5
Hebron IoA...72 G7
Hebron Nthumb...109 K11
Heckfield Hants...31 P10
Heckfield Green Suffk...59 J5
Heckfordbridge Essex...46 G7
Heckington Lincs...68 C3
Heckmondwike Kirk...85 J10
Heddington Wilts...30 A9
Heddon-on-the-Wall Nthumb...100 E5
Hedenham Norfk...59 L2
Hedge End Hants...24 H10
Hedgerley Bucks...32 D5
Hedgerley Green Bucks...32 D5
Hedging Somset...21 L7
Hedley on the Hill Nthumb...100 D6
Hednesford Staffs...65 J10
Hedon E R Yk...87 M9
Hedsor Bucks...32 C5
Heeley Sheff...78 B7
Hegdon Hill Herefs...51 Q10
Heglibister Shet...147 i6
Heighington Darltn...91 L2
Heighington Lincs...79 P10
Heightington Worcs...52 E6
Heiton Border...108 B4
Hele Devon...5 M3
Hele Devon...8 H4
Hele Devon...19 K4
Hele Somset...21 J8
Hele Lane Devon...8 E3
Helebridge Cnwll...7 J4
Helensburgh Ag & B...113 K5
Helenton S Ayrs...104 G3
Helford Cnwll...3 J9
Helford Passage Cnwll...3 J9
Helhoughton Norfk...70 C7
Helions Bumpstead Essex...46 B3
Hellaby Rothm...78 E6
Helland Cnwll...6 F10
Hellandbridge Cnwll...6 F10
Hell Corner W Berk...31 K7
Hellescott Cnwll...7 K7
Hellesdon Norfk...71 J9
Hellesveor Cnwll...2 D6
Hellidon Nhants...54 N4
Hellifield N York...84 C4
Hellingly E Susx...15 Q9
Hellington Norfk...71 L11
Helm Nthumb...109 K10
Helmdon Nhants...43 M3
Helme Kirk...77 L4
Helmingham Suffk...59 J9
Helmington Row Dur...100 F11
Helmsdale Highld...147 L12
Helmshore Lancs...84 B11
Helmsley N York...92 C10
Helperby N York...85 R1
Helperthorpe N York...86 H1
Helpringham Lincs...68 C4

Helpston C Pete...68 C11
Helsby Ches W...75 N8
Helsey Lincs...81 K9
Helston Cnwll...2 G9
Helstone Cnwll...6 F8
Helton Cumb...89 N2
Helwith N York...90 H4
Helwith Bridge N York...84 B1
Hemblington Norfk...71 L10
Hemerdon Devon...5 J9
Hemingbrough N York...86 C9
Hemingby Lincs...80 E9
Hemingfield Barns...78 C3
Hemingford Abbots Cambs...56 F6
Hemingford Grey Cambs...56 F6
Hemingstone Suffk...58 H10
Hemington Leics...66 D6
Hemington Nhants...56 D3
Hemington Somset...22 G3
Hemley Suffk...47 N3
Hemlington Middsb...92 A4
Hempholme E R Yk...87 K5
Hempnall Norfk...59 K2
Hempnall Green Norfk...59 K2
Hempriggs Moray...139 K3
Hempstead Essex...46 B4
Hempstead Medway...34 D9
Hempstead Norfk...70 G5
Hempstead Norfk...71 N6
Hempsted Gloucs...41 N8
Hempton Norfk...70 D7
Hempton Oxon...43 J5
Hemsby Norfk...71 P8
Hemswell Lincs...79 M5
Hemswell Cliff Lincs...79 N6
Hemsworth Wakefd...78 C1
Hemyock Devon...21 J10
Henbury Bristl...29 J7
Henbury Ches E...76 G9
Hendersyde Border...5 M6
Hendomen Powys...50 H1
Hendon Gt Lon...33 J4
Hendon Sundld...101 K7
Hendra Cnwll...2 H7
Hendra Cnwll...6 C9
Hendre Brdgnd...27 M6
Hendre Flints...74 G10
Hendy Carmth...38 E11
Heneglwys IoA...72 G8
Henfield W Susx...14 G8
Henford Devon...7 M6
Henfynyw Cerdgn...48 G9
Henghurst Kent...16 G3
Hengoed Caerph...27 R3
Hengoed Powys...50 H10
Hengoed Shrops...63 J6
Hengrave Suffk...58 B7
Henham Essex...45 Q6
Heniarth Powys...62 F10
Henlade Somset...21 L8
Henley Dorset...10 H4
Henley Gloucs...41 P8
Henley Shrops...51 M3
Henley Shrops...51 P5
Henley Somset...21 P7
Henley Suffk...59 H10
Henley W Susx...25 N5
Henley Green Covtry...54 B4
Henley-in-Arden Warwks...53 M7
Henley Park Surrey...32 D11
Henley's Down E Susx...16 C8
Henley Street Kent...34 B9
Henllan Cerdgn...38 A4
Henllan Denbgs...77 N6
Henllan Amgoed Carmth...37 N6
Henllys Torfn...28 C4
Henlow C Beds...44 H4
Hennock Devon...8 F8
Henny Street Essex...46 F4
Henryd Conwy...73 N9
Henry's Moat (Castell Hendre) Pembks...37 K5
Hensall N York...86 B10
Henshaw Nthumb...99 L5
Hensingham Cumb...88 C3
Henstead Suffk...59 P3
Hensting Hants...24 H9
Henstridge Somset...22 G9
Henstridge Ash Somset...22 G9
Henstridge Marsh Somset...22 B12
Henton Oxon...43 Q11
Henton Somset...22 C4
Henwick Worcs...52 F9
Henwood Cnwll...7 K10
Henwood Oxon...43 K11
Heogerrig Myr Td...39 N10
Heol-las Swans...26 G3
Heol Senni Powys...39 L7
Heol-y-Cyw Brdgnd...27 M5
Hepburn Nthumb...108 H5
Hepple Nthumb...108 H8
Hepscott Nthumb...100 G1
Heptonstall Calder...84 E9
Hepworth Kirk...77 M2
Hepworth Suffk...58 E6
Herbrandston Pembks...36 G9
Hereford Herefs...40 G4
Hereson Kent...35 Q9
Heribusta Highld...142 D11
Heriot Border...115 R10
Hermiston C Edin...115 M7
Hermitage Border...107 M10
Hermitage Dorset...10 G3
Hermitage W Berk...31 M8
Hermitage W Susx...13 N4
Hermit Hill Barns...77 Q3
Hermon Carmth...38 A5
Hermon IoA...72 F10
Hermon Pembks...37 N4
Herne Kent...35 L9
Herne Bay Kent...35 L9
Herne Common Kent...35 L9
Herne Hill Gt Lon...33 K7
Herne Pound Kent...34 B11
Herner Devon...19 L7
Hernhill Kent...35 J10
Herodsfoot Cnwll...6 H10
Heronden Kent...35 N11
Herongate Essex...34 A4
Heronsford S Ayrs...94 G2
Heronsgate Herts...32 E3
Herriard Hants...25 L4
Herringfleet Suffk...59 P1
Herring's Green Bed...44 F4
Herringswell Suffk...57 N5
Herringthorpe Rothm...78 D5
Herrington Sundld...101 J7
Hersden Kent...35 M10
Hersham Surrey...32 G9
Herstmonceux E Susx...15 Q8
Herston Dorset...11 N9
Herston Ork...147 C6
Hertford Herts...45 L9
Hertford Heath Herts...45 L9
Hertingfordbury Herts...45 K9
Hesketh Bank Lancs...83 L9
Hesketh Lane Lancs...83 N7
Hesket Newmarket Cumb...98 C7
Heskin Green Lancs...83 M12
Hesleden Dur...101 L10

Hesleden N York...90 E11
Hesley Donc...78 G5
Hesleyside Nthumb...99 M2
Heslington C York...86 B5
Hessay C York...85 Q4
Hessenford Cnwll...4 D5
Hessett Suffk...58 D8
Hessle E R Yk...87 H6
Hessle Wakefd...85 N11
Hest Bank Lancs...83 L2
Hestley Green Suffk...58 H7
Heston Gt Lon...32 G7
Heston Services Gt Lon...32 G7
Hestwall Ork...147 b4
Heswall Wirral...75 J7
Hethe Oxon...43 M6
Hethersett Norfk...70 H11
Hethersgill Cumb...98 L9
Hetherside Cumb...98 E5
Hetherson Green Ches W...63 N3
Hethpool Nthumb...108 E4
Hett Dur...100 H11
Hetton N York...84 E3
Hetton-le-Hole Sundld...101 J8
Hetton Steads Nthumb...108 G3
Heugh Nthumb...100 E4
Heughhead Abers...132 B2
Heugh Head Border...117 K9
Heveningham Suffk...59 L6
Hever Kent...15 N2
Heversham Cumb...89 M10
Hevingham Norfk...71 J8
Hewas Water Cnwll...3 N4
Hewelsfield Gloucs...40 H11
Hewenden C Brad...84 G8
Hewish N Som...28 E9
Hewish Somset...10 C3
Hewood Dorset...9 Q4
Hexham Nthumb...99 P5
Hextable Kent...33 P8
Hexthorpe Donc...78 F3
Hexton Herts...44 G5
Hexworthy Cnwll...7 M6
Hexworthy Devon...8 C10
Hey Lancs...84 C6
Heybridge Essex...34 B3
Heybridge Essex...46 E10
Heybridge Basin Essex...46 F10
Heybrook Bay Devon...4 F7
Heydon Cambs...45 N4
Heydon Norfk...70 G7
Heydour Lincs...67 P4
Hey Houses Lancs...82 H9
Heylipoll Ag & B...118 B3
Heylor Shet...147 H4
Heyrod Tamesd...76 H4
Heysham Lancs...83 K3
Heyshaw N York...85 J3
Heyshott W Susx...14 C7
Heyside Oldham...76 H2
Heytesbury Wilts...23 K5
Heythrop Oxon...42 H6
Heywood Rochdl...76 F2
Heywood Wilts...23 J3
Hibaldstow N Linc...79 N3
Hickleton Donc...78 D3
Hickling Norfk...71 N7
Hickling Notts...66 H6
Hickling Green Norfk...71 N7
Hickling Heath Norfk...71 N7
Hickling Pastures Notts...66 H6
Hickmans Green Kent...35 J11
Hicks Forstal Kent...35 L9
Hickstead W Susx...15 K7
Hidcote Bartrim Gloucs...42 F3
Hidcote Boyce Gloucs...42 E3
High Ackworth Wakefd...85 N11
Higham Barns...77 P2
Higham Derbys...78 C12
Higham Kent...34 E7
Higham Lancs...84 B8
Higham Suffk...47 J4
Higham Suffk...57 Q6
Higham Dykes Nthumb...100 E3
Higham Ferrers Nhants...55 N7
Higham Gobion C Beds...44 G5
Higham Hill Gt Lon...33 L4
Higham on the Hill Leics...54 C2
Highampton Devon...7 M4
Highams Park Gt Lon...33 M4
High Ardwell D & G...94 F9
High Auldgirth D & G...106 B12
High Bankhill Cumb...98 H10
High Beach Essex...33 M3
High Bentham N York...83 P1
High Bewaldeth Cumb...97 P11
High Bickington Devon...19 L9
High Biggins Cumb...89 P11
High Birkwith N York...90 C11
High Blantyre S Lans...114 C10
High Bonnybridge Falk...114 E5
High Borrans Cumb...89 L6
High Bradley N York...84 G6
High Bray Devon...19 N6
Highbridge Hants...24 H9
Highbridge Somset...21 M4
Highbrook W Susx...15 L5
High Brooms Kent...15 Q2
High Bullen Devon...19 K9
Highburton Kirk...77 M1
Highbury Gt Lon...33 K5
Highbury Somset...22 G4
High Buston Nthumb...109 L8
High Callerton Nthumb...100 F4
High Catton E R Yk...86 D4
Highclere Hants...31 J10
Highcliffe BCP...12 C6
High Close Dur...91 K4
High Cogges Oxon...42 H10
High Common Norfk...70 E11
High Coniscliffe Darltn...91 L4
High Crosby Cumb...98 F6
High Cross Cnwll...3 L5
High Cross E Ayrs...113 M12
High Cross Hants...25 M8
High Cross Herts...45 L8
Highcross Lancs...82 H7
High Cross W Susx...15 J7
High Cross Warwks...53 M5
High Drummore D & G...94 G11
High Dubmire Sundld...101 J8
High Easter Essex...46 A8
High Eggborough N York...85 Q10
High Ellington N York...91 K10
Higher Alham Somset...22 F4
Higher Ansty Dorset...11 J4
Higher Ballam Lancs...83 L8
Higher Bartle Lancs...83 L8
Higher Berry End C Beds...44 D5
Higher Bockhampton Dorset...11 H6
Higher Brixham Torbay...5 Q6
Higher Burrowton Devon...9 J5
Higher Burwardsley Ches W...75 N12
Higher Chillington Somset...10 B3
Higher Clovelly Devon...18 F8
Higher Coombe Dorset...10 E6
Higher Disley Ches E...76 H7
Higher Folds Wigan...76 C3

Higherford Lancs...84 C7
Higher Gabwell Devon...5 Q3
Higher Halstock Leigh Dorset...10 D3
Higher Harpers Lancs...84 B7
Higher Heysham Lancs...83 K3
Higher Hurdsfield Ches E...76 H8
Higher Irlam Salfd...76 D5
Higher Kingcombe Dorset...10 E5
Higher Kinnerton Flints...75 K11
Higher Marston Ches W...76 C8
Higher Muddiford Devon...19 L6
Higher Nyland Dorset...22 G9
Higher Ogden Rochdl...76 H1
Higher Pentire Cnwll...2 G9
Higher Penwortham Lancs...83 L9
Higher Prestacott Devon...7 M5
Higher Studfold N York...84 B1
Higher Town Cnwll...3 K5
Higher Town Cnwll...6 H8
Higher Town IoS...2 b1
Higher Tregantle Cnwll...4 E6
Higher Walton Lancs...83 N9
Higher Walton Warrtn...75 Q7
Higher Wambrook Somset...9 P3
Higher Waterston Dorset...10 H5
Higher Whatcombe Dorset...11 K4
Higher Wheelton Lancs...83 N10
Higher Whitley Ches W...76 B7
Higher Wincham Ches W...76 C8
Higher Wraxall Dorset...10 E4
Higher Wych Ches W...63 N3
High Etherley Dur...91 K1
High Ferry Lincs...68 G2
Highfield E R Yk...86 D8
Highfield Gatesd...100 F6
Highfield N Ayrs...113 L11
Highfields Donc...78 E2
High Flats Kirk...77 N2
High Garrett Essex...46 D6
Highgate E Susx...15 M4
Highgate Gt Lon...33 K5
Highgate Kent...16 D3
High Grange Dur...100 F12
High Grantley N York...85 L1
High Green Cumb...89 L6
High Green E R Yk...85 Q4
High Green Norfk...58 H3
High Green Norfk...70 H11
High Green Sheff...77 Q4
High Green Suffk...58 C8
High Green Suffk...58 C8
High Halden Kent...16 F3
High Halstow Medway...34 D7
High Ham Somset...21 P7
High Harrington Cumb...88 D2
High Harrogate N York...85 L4
High Haswell Dur...101 J9
High Hatton Shrops...63 Q7
High Hauxley Nthumb...109 M9
High Hawsker N York...93 J5
High Hesket Cumb...98 F9
High Hoyland Barns...77 P2
High Hunsley E R Yk...86 H8
High Hurstwood E Susx...15 P5
High Hutton N York...86 E2
High Ireby Cumb...97 P10
High Kelling Norfk...70 G4
High Kilburn N York...92 B10
High Killerby N York...93 L10
High Knipe Cumb...89 N3
High Lands Dur...91 J2
Highlane Ches E...76 G10
Highlane Derbys...78 C7
High Lane Rochdl...76 H6
High Lanes Cnwll...2 F7
High Laver Essex...45 P10
Highlaws Cumb...97 N8
Highleadon Gloucs...41 M7
High Legh Ches E...76 C7
Highleigh W Susx...13 N6
High Leven S on T...91 Q4
Highley Shrops...52 E4
High Littleton BaNES...29 K10
High Lorton Cumb...88 G2
High Marishes N York...92 G11
High Marnham Notts...79 K9
High Melton Donc...78 E3
High Mickley Nthumb...100 D6
Highmoor Cumb...31 P5
Highmoor Cross Oxon...31 P5
Highmoor Hill Mons...28 F4
High Moorsley Sundld...101 J8
Highnam Gloucs...41 M8
Highnam Green Gloucs...41 M8
High Newport Sundld...101 K7
High Newton Cumb...89 L9
High Nibthwaite Cumb...89 J9
High Offley Staffs...64 F7
High Ongar Essex...45 Q11
High Onn Staffs...64 F9
High Park Corner Essex...47 J7
High Pennyvenie E Ayrs...105 J10
High Post Wilts...23 P6
Highridge N Som...28 H9
High Roding Essex...45 R8
High Row Cumb...89 K2
High Row Cumb...98 D11
High Salter Lancs...83 N1
High Salvington W Susx...14 G9
High Scales Cumb...97 N9
High Seaton Cumb...97 L12
High Shaw N York...90 E8
High Side Cumb...97 P12
High Spen Gatesd...100 E6
Highstead Kent...35 M9
Highsted Kent...34 F10
High Stoop Dur...100 E9
High Street Cnwll...3 N4
High Street Kent...16 D4
High Street Suffk...59 M8
High Street Suffk...59 N9
Highstreet Green Surrey...14 D5
Hightae D & G...97 K2
Highter's Heath Birm...53 K5
High Throston Hartpl...101 M11
High Town Hants...13 J2
Hightown Ches W...76 G11
Hightown Hants...12 B4
Hightown Sefton...75 J3
High Town Staffs...65 J9
Hightown Green Suffk...58 E9
High Toynton Lincs...80 F9
High Trewhitt Nthumb...108 G8
High Urpeth Dur...100 G7
High Valleyfield Fife...114 H4
High Warden Nthumb...99 M5
Highway Herefs...51 M10
Highway Wilts...30 B7
Highweek Devon...8 B8
High Westwood Dur...100 E7
Highwood Essex...46 B11
Highwood Hill Gt Lon...33 J4
High Woolaston Gloucs...29 J2
High Worsall N York...91 P5
Highworth Swindn...30 E4

High Wray Cumb...89 K7
High Wych Herts...45 N9
High Wycombe Bucks...32 B4
Hilborough Norfk...70 B12
Hilcote Derbys...78 D12
Hilcott Wilts...30 C10
Hildenborough Kent...15 Q1
Hildersham Cambs...57 K11
Hilderstone Staffs...64 H5
Hilderthorpe E R Yk...87 M2
Hilfield Dorset...10 G4
Hilgay Norfk...57 M1
Hill S Glos...29 K3
Hill Warwks...54 D7
Hillam N York...85 Q9
Hillbeck Cumb...90 C4
Hillborough Kent...35 M8
Hill Brow Hants...25 N8
Hillbutts Dorset...11 N4
Hill Chorlton Staffs...64 E4
Hillclifflane Derbys...65 P3
Hill Common Norfk...71 N7
Hill Common Somset...21 J8
Hill Deverill Wilts...23 J5
Hilldyke Lincs...68 G3
Hill End Dur...100 C11
Hill End Fife...115 J2
Hill End Gloucs...41 P4
Hillend Fife...115 L4
Hillend Mdloth...115 N8
Hillend N Lans...114 E8
Hillend Swans...26 B4
Hillersland Gloucs...41 J8
Hillerton Devon...8 D5
Hillesden Bucks...43 P6
Hillesley Gloucs...29 M4
Hillfarrance Somset...21 J8
Hill Green Kent...34 E10
Hillgrove W Susx...14 D5
Hillhampton Herefs...41 J2
Hillhead Abers...140 F8
Hillhead Devon...5 Q6
Hill Head Hants...13 J4
Hill Head S Lans...106 C2
Hillhead of Cocklaw Abers...141 Q7
Hilliard's Cross Staffs...65 M10
Hilliclay Highld...151 L4
Hillingdon Gt Lon...32 F6
Hillington C Glas...113 P8
Hillington Norfk...69 N7
Hillis Corner IoW...12 H6
Hillmorton Warwks...54 E6
Hillock Vale Lancs...84 A9
Hill of Beath Fife...115 L3
Hill of Fearn Highld...146 E9
Hillowton D & G...96 F5
Hillpool Worcs...52 G5
Hillpound Hants...25 K10
Hill Ridware Staffs...65 K8
Hillside Abers...133 M5
Hillside Angus...132 H12
Hillside Devon...5 L4
Hill Side Kirk...85 J1
Hill Side Worcs...52 D8
Hills Town Derbys...78 D9
Hillstreet Hants...24 E10
Hillswick Shet...147 h4
Hill Top Dur...90 G2
Hill Top Hants...12 F4
Hill Top Kirk...77 K1
Hill Top Sandw...53 J2
Hill Top Wakefd...85 M12
Hillwell Shet...147 i9
Hilmarton Wilts...30 B7
Hilperton Wilts...29 N10
Hilperton Marsh Wilts...29 N10
Hilsea C Port...13 J4
Hilston E R Yk...87 P8
Hiltingbury Hants...24 H9
Hilton Border...117 K11
Hilton Cambs...56 F7
Hilton Cumb...90 B3
Hilton Derbys...65 N5
Hilton Dorset...11 J4
Hilton Dur...91 K2
Hilton Highld...146 F10
Hilton S on T...91 Q4
Hilton Shrops...52 E2
Hilton Park Services Staffs...64 H11
Himbleton Worcs...52 H9
Himley Staffs...52 G2
Hincaster Cumb...89 N10
Hinchley Wood Surrey...32 H9
Hinckley Leics...54 C2
Hinderclay Suffk...58 F5
Hinderwell N York...92 H3
Hindford Shrops...63 K5
Hindhead Surrey...14 C4
Hindhead Tunnel Surrey...14 C4
Hindle Fold Lancs...83 Q8
Hindley Nthumb...100 D6
Hindley Wigan...76 C3
Hindley Green Wigan...76 C3
Hindlip Worcs...52 G9
Hindolveston Norfk...70 F6
Hindon Wilts...23 K7
Hindringham Norfk...70 E5
Hingham Norfk...70 F11
Hinksford Staffs...52 F3
Hinstock Shrops...64 C7
Hintlesham Suffk...47 J3
Hinton Gloucs...41 K11
Hinton Hants...12 C5
Hinton Herefs...40 D4
Hinton S Glos...29 M7
Hinton Shrops...52 C4
Hinton Admiral Hants...12 C5
Hinton Ampner Hants...25 K8
Hinton Blewett BaNES...29 J11
Hinton Charterhouse BaNES...29 M10
Hinton Cross Worcs...42 B4
Hinton-in-the-Hedges Nhants...43 M4
Hinton Marsh Hants...25 K8
Hinton Martell Dorset...11 N3
Hinton on the Green Worcs...42 B4
Hinton Parva Swindn...30 F6
Hinton St George Somset...21 P11
Hinton St Mary Dorset...22 G10
Hinton Waldrist Oxon...30 H2
Hints Shrops...51 N5
Hints Staffs...65 M11
Hinwick Bed...55 M8
Hinxhill Kent...17 J3
Hinxton Cambs...45 J4
Hinxworth Herts...45 J4
Hipperholme Calder...84 H10
Hipsburn Nthumb...109 L7
Hipswell N York...91 K7
Hirn Abers...132 H5
Hirnant Powys...62 E8
Hirst Nthumb...109 M12
Hirst Courtney N York...86 B10
Hirwaen Denbgs...74 F11
Hirwaun Rhondd...39 N9
Hiscott Devon...19 K8
Histon Cambs...56 H8
Hitcham Suffk...58 E10
Hitcham Causeway Suffk...58 E10

Hitcham Street Suffk...58 E10
Hitchin Herts...44 H6
Hither Green Gt Lon...33 L7
Hittisleigh Devon...8 D5
Hive E R Yk...86 F9
Hixon Staffs...65 J7
Hoaden Kent...35 N10
Hoar Cross Staffs...65 L7
Hoarwithy Herefs...40 H6
Hoath Kent...35 M9
Hobarris Shrops...51 K5
Hobbles Green Suffk...57 N10
Hobbs Cross Essex...33 N2
Hobbs Cross Essex...45 P9
Hobkirk Border...107 P7
Hobland Hall Norfk...71 Q11
Hobsick Notts...66 D2
Hobson Dur...100 F7
Hoby Leics...66 H8
Hockering Norfk...70 G9
Hockerton Notts...79 J12
Hockley Ches E...76 H7
Hockley Covtry...53 P5
Hockley Essex...34 E4
Hockley Staffs...65 N12
Hockley Heath Solhll...53 M6
Hockliffe C Beds...44 D6
Hockwold cum Wilton Norfk...57 P3
Hockworthy Devon...20 G9
Hoddesdon Herts...45 L10
Hoddlesden Bl w D...83 Q10
Hoddom Cross D & G...97 N3
Hoddom Mains D & G...97 N3
Hodgehill Ches E...76 F9
Hodgeston Pembks...37 K10
Hodnet Shrops...63 Q6
Hodsock Notts...78 G6
Hodsoll Street Kent...34 A9
Hodson Swindn...30 E6
Hodthorpe Derbys...78 E8
Hoe Norfk...70 E9
Hoe Benham W Berk...31 J8
Hoe Gate Hants...25 K10
Hoff Cumb...89 R3
Hogben's Hill Kent...35 J11
Hoggards Green Suffk...58 C9
Hoggeston Bucks...44 A7
Hoggrill's End Warwks...53 N2
Hog Hill E Susx...16 F7
Hoghton Lancs...83 N9
Hoghton Bottoms Lancs...83 N10
Hognaston Derbys...65 P2
Hogsthorpe Lincs...81 K9
Holbeach Lincs...68 G7
Holbeach Bank Lincs...68 G6
Holbeach Clough Lincs...68 G6
Holbeach Drove Lincs...68 G8
Holbeach Hurn Lincs...68 G6
Holbeach St Johns Lincs...68 G8
Holbeach St Mark's Lincs...68 G6
Holbeach St Matthew Lincs...68 H6
Holbeck Notts...78 F9
Holbeck Woodhouse Notts...78 F9
Holberrow Green Worcs...53 J9
Holbeton Devon...5 K6
Holborn Gt Lon...33 K6
Holborough Kent...34 C9
Holbrook Derbys...66 B3
Holbrook S York...78 D7
Holbrook Suffk...47 L4
Holbrook Moor Derbys...66 B3
Holbrooks Covtry...53 Q4
Holburn Nthumb...108 G3
Holbury Hants...12 F4
Holcombe Devon...8 H9
Holcombe Somset...22 F3
Holcombe Rogus Devon...20 G9
Holcot Nhants...55 K7
Holden Lancs...84 B6
Holdenby Nhants...54 H7
Holden Gate Calder...84 D10
Holder's Green Essex...46 B6
Holdgate Shrops...51 Q3
Holdingham Lincs...67 Q3
Holditch Dorset...9 R4
Holdsworth Calder...84 G9
Holehouse Derbys...77 K5
Hole-in-the-Wall Herefs...41 J6
Holemoor Devon...7 M4
Hole Street W Susx...14 G8
Holford Somset...21 J5
Holgate C York...86 B4
Holker Cumb...89 K11
Holkham Norfk...70 C3
Hollacombe Devon...7 M5
Holland Fen Lincs...68 E2
Holland Lees Lancs...75 N2
Holland-on-Sea Essex...47 M8
Hollandstoun Ork...147 f1
Hollee D & G...97 R4
Hollesley Suffk...47 P3
Hollicombe Torbay...5 Q5
Hollingbourne Kent...34 E11
Hollingrove E Susx...16 C6
Hollington Derbys...65 N4
Hollington Staffs...65 K4
Hollingworth Tamesd...77 J4
Hollins Bury...76 F2
Hollins Derbys...77 P8
Hollins Staffs...64 H4
Hollinsclough Staffs...77 K10
Hollins End Sheff...78 C7
Hollins Green Warrtn...76 C4
Hollins Lane Lancs...83 L3
Hollinswood Wrekin...64 D10
Hollocombe Devon...19 N10
Holloway Derbys...65 Q1
Holloway Gt Lon...33 K5
Holloway Wilts...23 J7
Hollowell Nhants...54 G6
Hollowmoor Heath Ches W...75 M10
Hollows D & G...98 E3
Hollybush Caerph...39 P10
Hollybush E Ayrs...104 G4
Hollybush Herefs...41 M4
Holly End Norfk...69 J11
Holly Green Worcs...41 P3
Hollyhurst Ches E...63 P3
Hollywood Worcs...53 K5
Holmbridge Kirk...77 L3
Holmbury St Mary Surrey...14 H2
Holmbush Cnwll...3 Q3
Holmcroft Staffs...64 G7
Holme Cambs...56 E3
Holme Cumb...89 N11
Holme Kirk...77 L3
Holme N Linc...79 M2
Holme N York...91 P9
Holme Notts...79 K12
Holme Chapel Lancs...84 C9
Holme Green N York...85 Q5
Holme Hale Norfk...70 C10
Holme Lacy Herefs...40 H5
Holme Marsh Herefs...51 L9

Holme next the Sea Norfk...69 N3
Holme on the Wolds E R Yk...86 H6
Holme Pierrepont Notts...66 G4
Holmer Herefs...40 G3
Holmer Green Bucks...32 C3
Holme St Cuthbert Cumb...97 M9
Holmes Chapel Ches E...76 E10
Holmesfield Derbys...77 Q8
Holmes Hill E Susx...15 P8
Holmeswood Lancs...83 K12
Holmethorpe Surrey...33 K12
Holme upon Spalding Moor E R Yk...86 E7
Holmewood Derbys...78 C10
Holmfield Calder...84 G9
Holmfirth Kirk...77 L2
Holmhead E Ayrs...105 K6
Holmpton E R Yk...87 Q10
Holmrook Cumb...88 E8
Holmshurst E Susx...16 C6
Holmside Dur...100 G8
Holmwrangle Cumb...98 H8
Holne Devon...5 L3
Holnest Dorset...10 G3
Holnicote Somset...20 E4
Holsworthy Devon...7 L4
Holsworthy Beacon Devon...7 L3
Holt Dorset...11 P4
Holt Norfk...70 G4
Holt Wilts...29 P10
Holt Worcs...52 F8
Holt Wrexhm...63 L1
Holtby C York...86 C4
Holt End Worcs...53 K7
Holt Fleet Worcs...52 F8
Holt Green Lancs...75 L3
Holt Heath Dorset...11 P4
Holt Heath Worcs...52 F8
Holton Oxon...43 M10
Holton Somset...22 F8
Holton cum Beckering Lincs...80 C7
Holton Heath Dorset...11 M6
Holton le Clay Lincs...80 B6
Holton le Moor Lincs...79 P4
Holton St Mary Suffk...47 J4
Holt Street Kent...35 N12
Holtye E Susx...15 N3
Holway Flints...74 G8
Holwell Dorset...10 H2
Holwell Herts...44 H5
Holwell Leics...67 J7
Holwell Oxon...42 F10
Holwick Dur...90 E1
Holworth Dorset...11 J8
Holy Cross Worcs...52 G5
Holyfield Essex...45 L11
Holyhead IoA...72 D7
Holy Island IoA...72 D7
Holy Island Nthumb...109 J1
Holymoorside Derbys...77 Q10
Holyport W & M...32 C7
Holystone Nthumb...108 G8
Holytown N Lans...114 D9
Holywell Cambs...56 G6
Holywell Cnwll...3 J3
Holywell Dorset...10 E5
Holywell Flints...74 G8
Holywell Nthumb...101 J3
Holywell Warwks...53 M7
Holywell Green Calder...84 G11
Holywell Lake Somset...20 H8
Holywell Row Suffk...57 N5
Holywood D & G...97 J2
Holywood Village D & G...97 J2
Homer Shrops...64 B12
Homer Green Sefton...75 K3
Homersfield Suffk...59 K3
Homescales Cumb...89 N9
Hom Green Herefs...41 J7
Homington Wilts...23 P8
Honeyborough Pembks...37 J9
Honeybourne Worcs...42 D3
Honeychurch Devon...8 D4
Honey Hill Kent...35 K10
Honeystreet Wilts...30 C10
Honey Tye Suffk...46 G4
Honiley Warwks...53 N6
Honing Norfk...71 L7
Honingham Norfk...70 G10
Honington Lincs...67 N3
Honington Suffk...58 D6
Honington Warwks...42 G3
Honiton Devon...9 M5
Honley Kirk...77 L1
Honnington Wrekin...64 D9
Hoo Kent...35 N10
Hoobrook Worcs...52 F6
Hood Green Barns...77 P3
Hood Hill Rothm...78 B4
Hooe C Plym...4 H6
Hooe E Susx...16 C8
Hoo End Herts...44 H7
Hoo Green Ches E...76 D7
Hoohill Bpool...82 H7
Hook Cambs...56 H2
Hook Devon...9 N5
Hook E R Yk...86 E10
Hook Gt Lon...32 H9
Hook Hants...12 H4
Hook Hants...25 M3
Hook Pembks...37 J8
Hook Wilts...30 C5
Hook-a-Gate Shrops...63 M10
Hook Bank Worcs...41 P3
Hooke Dorset...10 E4
Hook End Essex...33 Q2
Hookgate Staffs...64 E5
Hook Green Kent...16 C4
Hook Green Kent...34 B8
Hook Norton Oxon...42 H5
Hook Street Gloucs...29 K2
Hook Street Wilts...30 C5
Hookway Devon...8 G5
Hookwood Surrey...15 J2
Hooley Surrey...33 K11
Hooley Bridge Rochdl...76 F1
Hoo Meavy Devon...4 H3
Hoo St Werburgh Medway...34 D8
Hooton Ches W...75 L8
Hooton Levitt Rothm...78 E5
Hooton Pagnell Donc...78 D2
Hooton Roberts Rothm...78 D4
Hopcrofts Holt Oxon...43 K7
Hope Derbys...77 M7
Hope Devon...5 L8
Hope Flints...75 K12
Hope Powys...63 J10
Hope Shrops...63 K10
Hope Staffs...65 L1
Hope Bagot Shrops...51 Q5
Hope Bowdler Shrops...51 N2
Hope End Green Essex...45 Q7
Hopehouse Border...107 J6
Hopeman Moray...139 J4
Hope Mansell Herefs...41 K8
Hopesay Shrops...51 L4

Hopetown Wakefd....85 N10
Hope under Dinmore Herefs....51 N10
Hopgrove C York....86 B4
Hopperton N York....85 N4
Hop Pole Lincs....68 D9
Hopsford Warwks....54 C4
Hopstone Shrops....52 E2
Hopton Derbys....65 N2
Hopton Shrops....63 L8
Hopton Staffs....64 H7
Hopton Suffk....58 E5
Hopton Cangeford Shrops....51 P4
Hopton Castle Shrops....51 L5
Hoptonheath Shrops....51 L5
Hopton on Sea Norfk....71 Q12
Hopton Wafers Shrops....52 B3
Hopwas Staffs....65 M11
Hopwood Rochdl....76 F2
Hopwood Park Services Worcs....53 J6
Horam E Susx....15 Q7
Horbling Lincs....68 C5
Horbury Wakefd....85 L11
Horcott Gloucs....30 D2
Horden Dur....101 L10
Horderley Shrops....51 L3
Hordle Hants....12 D6
Hordley Shrops....63 L8
Horeb Carmth....38 D10
Horeb Cerdgn....38 B3
Horfield Bristl....29 J7
Horham Suffk....59 J6
Horkesley Heath Essex....46 H6
Horkstow N Linc....87 J11
Horley Oxon....43 J3
Horley Surrey....15 K2
Hornblotton Green Somset....22 D6
Hornby Lancs....83 N2
Hornby N York....91 L8
Hornby N York....91 N5
Horncastle Lincs....80 E10
Hornchurch Gt Lon....33 P5
Horncliffe Nthumb....117 K11
Horndean Border....117 K11
Horndean Hants....25 M10
Horndon Devon....7 P8
Horndon on the Hill Thurr....34 B6
Horne Surrey....15 L2
Horner Somset....20 D4
Horne Row Essex....46 D10
Horners Green Suffk....46 H3
Horney Common E Susx....15 N6
Horn Hill Bucks....32 E4
Horning Norfk....71 L8
Horninghold Leics....55 K1
Horninglow Staffs....65 N7
Horningsea Cambs....57 J8
Horningsham Wilts....22 H5
Horningtoft Norfk....70 D7
Horningtops Cnwll....4 D3
Hornsbury Somset....9 Q3
Hornsby Cumb....98 G8
Hornsbygate Cumb....98 G8
Horns Cross Devon....18 H8
Horns Cross E Susx....16 E6
Hornsea E R Yk....87 M6
Hornsey Gt Lon....33 N4
Horn's Green Gt Lon....33 N10
Horn Street Kent....17 L4
Hornton Oxon....42 H3
Horpit Swindn....30 E5
Horra Shet....147 J3
Horrabridge Devon....4 H3
Horringer Suffk....58 B8
Horringford IoW....13 J7
Horrocks Fold Bolton....76 C1
Horrocksford Lancs....83 P6
Horsacott Devon....19 K7
Horsebridge Devon....7 M9
Horsebridge E Susx....15 Q8
Horsebridge Hants....24 E7
Horsebridge Shrops....63 L11
Horsebridge Staffs....64 H1
Horsebrook Staffs....64 G10
Horsecastle N Som....28 F9
Horsedown Cnwll....2 F7
Horsehay Wrekin....64 C10
Horseheath Cambs....45 R2
Horsehouse N York....90 H10
Horsell Surrey....32 E10
Horseman's Green Wrexhm....63 M4
Horsenden Bucks....43 R11
Horsey Norfk....71 P7
Horsey Somset....21 M5
Horsey Corner Norfk....71 N7
Horsford Norfk....71 J9
Horsforth Leeds....85 K7
Horsham W Susx....14 H5
Horsham Worcs....52 D9
Horsham St Faith Norfk....71 J9
Horsington Lincs....80 D10
Horsington Somset....22 F8
Horsley Derbys....66 C3
Horsley Gloucs....29 N3
Horsley Nthumb....100 E5
Horsley Nthumb....108 D10
Horsley Cross Essex....47 K6
Horsleycross Street Essex....47 K6
Horsley-Gate Derbys....77 P8
Horsleyhill Border....107 N6
Horsley's Green Bucks....31 R3
Horsley Woodhouse Derbys....66 C3
Horsmonden Kent....16 C3
Horspath Oxon....43 M10
Horstead Norfk....71 K8
Horsted Keynes W Susx....15 M5
Horton Bucks....44 C8
Horton Dorset....11 P3
Horton Lancs....84 C5
Horton Nthants....55 J9
Horton S Glos....29 M5
Horton Shrops....63 M6
Horton Somset....21 M10
Horton Staffs....76 H12
Horton Surrey....32 H10
Horton Swans....26 C6
Horton W & M....32 E7
Horton Wilts....30 B9
Horton Wrekin....64 C9
Horton Cross Somset....21 M10
Horton-cum-Studley Oxon....43 M9
Horton Green Ches W....63 M2
Horton Heath Hants....24 H4
Horton-in-Ribblesdale N York....90 C12
Horwich Bolton....76 C1
Horwich End Derbys....77 J7
Horwood Devon....19 K8
Hoscar Lancs....75 M1
Hoscote Border....107 J7
Hose Leics....67 J6
Hosey Hill Kent....33 N11
Hosh P & K....123 L8
Hoswick Shet....147 i9
Hotham E R Yk....86 G8
Hothfield Kent....16 G2

Hoton Leics....66 F7
Hott Nthumb....99 L1
Hough Ches E....64 D2
Hough Ches E....76 F8
Hougham Lincs....67 M3
Hough End Leeds....85 K8
Hough Green Halton....75 M5
Hough-on-the-Hill Lincs....67 M3
Houghton Cambs....56 F6
Houghton Cumb....98 E6
Houghton Hants....24 E7
Houghton Nthumb....100 E5
Houghton Pembks....37 J9
Houghton W Susx....14 E8
Houghton Conquest C Beds....44 F3
Houghton Gate Dur....100 H8
Houghton Green E Susx....16 G6
Houghton Green Warrtn....76 C4
Houghton le Side Darltn....91 L2
Houghton-le-Spring Sundld....101 J8
Houghton on the Hill Leics....66 H11
Houghton Regis C Beds....44 E7
Houghton St Giles Norfk....70 D5
Hound Green Hants....31 Q10
Houndslow Border....116 E11
Houndsmoor Somset....20 H8
Houndwood Border....117 J8
Hounslow Gt Lon....32 G7
Househill Highld....138 G5
Houses Hill Kirk....85 J11
Housieside Abers....141 L10
Houston Rens....113 M8
Houstry Highld....151 L9
Houton Ork....147 b5
Hove Br & H....15 K10
Hove Edge Calder....84 H10
Hoveringham Notts....66 H3
Hoveton Norfk....71 L8
Hovingham N York....92 D11
Howbrook Barns....77 Q4
How Caple Herefs....41 J6
Howden E R Yk....86 D9
Howden-le-Wear Dur....100 F11
Howe Highld....151 P4
Howe IoM....102 b7
Howe N York....91 N10
Howe Norfk....71 K12
Howe Bridge Wigan....76 C3
Howe Green Essex....46 D11
Howegreen Essex....34 E2
Howell Lincs....68 C3
Howe of Teuchar Abers....141 J6
Howes D & G....97 N5
Howe Street Essex....46 C5
Howe Street Essex....46 C8
Howey Powys....50 E9
Howgate Cumb....88 C2
Howgate Mdloth....115 N9
Howgill Lancs....84 B6
Howick Nthumb....109 L6
Howle Wrekin....64 C7
Howle Hill Herefs....41 J7
Howlett End Essex....45 Q5
Howley Somset....9 P3
How Mill Cumb....98 G2
Howmore W Isls....152 b10
Hownam Border....108 C6
Howrigg Cumb....98 D8
Howsham N Linc....87 K11
Howsham N York....86 D3
Howt Green Kent....34 F9
Howton Herefs....40 F6
Howtown Cumb....89 L3
How Wood Herts....44 G11
Howwood Rens....113 M9
Hoxa Ork....147 c6
Hoxne Suffk....58 H5
Hoy Ork....147 b5
Hoylake Wirral....74 H6
Hoyland Barns....78 B4
Hoyland Common Barns....78 B4
Hoylandswaine Barns....77 N3
Hoyle W Susx....14 C7
Hoyle Mill Barns....78 B2
Hubberholme N York....90 F11
Hubberston Pembks....36 H9
Hubbert's Bridge Lincs....68 E3
Huby N York....85 K6
Huby N York....85 R2
Huccaby Devon....8 C10
Hucclecote Gloucs....41 P8
Hucking Kent....34 E10
Hucknall Notts....66 C2
Huddersfield Kirk....84 H12
Huddington Worcs....52 H9
Huddlesford Staffs....65 M11
Hudnall Herts....44 D9
Hudswell N York....91 K7
Huggate E R Yk....86 G4
Hugglescote Leics....66 C9
Hughenden Valley Bucks....32 B3
Hughley Shrops....51 P1
Hugh Town IoS....2 b2
Huish Devon....7 P2
Huish Devon....9 D9
Huish Champflower Somset....20 G7
Huish Episcopi Somset....21 P8
Hùisinis W Isls....152 d5
Huisinish W Isls....152 d5
Hulcote C Beds....44 D4
Hulcote Nhants....54 H10
Hulcott Bucks....44 B8
Hulham Devon....9 J8
Hulland Derbys....65 N3
Hulland Ward Derbys....65 N3
Hullavington Wilts....29 P6
Hull Bridge E R Yk....87 K7
Hullbridge Essex....34 E3
Hull, Kingston upon C Hull....87 K9
Hulme Manch....76 F4
Hulme Staffs....64 H3
Hulme Warrtn....75 Q5
Hulme End Staffs....77 L11
Hulme Walfield Ches E....76 D7
Hulse Heath Ches E....76 D6
Hulton Lane Ends Bolton....76 C3
Hulverstone IoW....12 F8
Hulver Street Suffk....59 P3
Humber Devon....8 H5
Humber Herefs....51 P9
Humber Bridge N Linc....87 J10
Humberside Airport N Linc....80 B2
Humberston NE Lin....80 F3
Humberstone C Leic....66 G11
Humberton N York....85 N1
Humbie E Loth....116 B9
Humbleton E R Yk....87 N8
Humbleton Nthumb....108 H4
Humby Lincs....67 P5
Hume Border....108 A1
Humshaugh Nthumb....99 P4
Huna Highld....151 Q2
Huncoat Lancs....84 B9
Huncote Leics....66 E12
Hundalee Border....107 Q6
Hundall Derbys....77 Q8
Hunderthwaite Dur....90 G2
Hundle Houses Lincs....68 E1
Hundleby Lincs....80 G10

Hundle Houses Lincs....68 E1
Hundleton Pembks....37 J10
Hundon Suffk....57 P11
Hundred End Lancs....83 K10
Hundred House Powys....50 F10
Hungarton Leics....66 H10
Hungerford Hants....23 Q11
Hungerford Somset....20 G5
Hungerford W Berk....30 H8
Hungerford Newtown W Berk....30 H8
Hunger Hill Bolton....76 C2
Hunger Hill Lancs....75 P1
Hungerstone Herefs....40 F5
Hungerton Lincs....67 L6
Hungryhatton Shrops....64 C7
Hunmanby N York....93 M11
Hunningham Warwks....54 B7
Hunnington Worcs....52 H4
Hunsbury Hill Nhants....55 M9
Hunsdon Herts....45 M9
Hunsingore N York....85 N4
Hunslet Leeds....85 L9
Hunsonby Cumb....98 H11
Hunstanton Norfk....69 N4
Hunstanworth Dur....100 D9
Hunsterson Ches E....64 C3
Hunston Suffk....58 E7
Hunston W Susx....13 Q4
Hunston Green Suffk....58 E7
Hunstrete BaNES....29 K10
Hunt End Worcs....53 J8
Hunter's Inn Devon....19 M4
Hunter's Quay Ag & B....112 H5
Huntham Somset....21 M8
Hunthill Lodge Angus....132 D10
Huntingdon Cambs....56 E6
Huntingfield Suffk....59 L6
Huntingford Dorset....22 H7
Huntington C York....86 B4
Huntington Ches W....75 M10
Huntington E Loth....116 C6
Huntington Herefs....40 G3
Huntington Staffs....64 H9
Huntingtowerfield P & K....124 C9
Huntley Gloucs....41 L8
Huntly Abers....140 E8
Hunton Hants....24 H5
Hunton Kent....16 C1
Hunton N York....91 K8
Hunton Bridge Herts....32 F2
Hunt's Corner Norfk....58 F3
Huntscott Somset....20 E4
Hunt's Cross Lpool....75 M7
Hunts Green Bucks....44 C11
Hunts Green Warwks....53 M1
Huntsham Devon....20 D9
Huntshaw Devon....19 K9
Huntshaw Cross Devon....19 K9
Huntspill Somset....21 M4
Huntstile Somset....21 L6
Huntworth Somset....21 M6
Hunwick Dur....100 F11
Hunworth Norfk....70 F5
Hurcott Somset....21 N10
Hurdcott Wilts....23 Q6
Hurdsfield Ches E....76 H9
Hurley W & M....32 B5
Hurley Warwks....53 N1
Hurley Bottom W & M....32 B6
Hurley Common Warwks....53 N1
Hurlford E Ayrs....104 H2
Hurlston Green Lancs....75 L1
Hurn BCP....11 Q5
Hurn's End Lincs....68 H2
Hursley Hants....24 G8
Hurst Dorset....11 J7
Hurst N York....90 H6
Hurst Somset....21 P9
Hurst Wokham....31 R8
Hurstbourne Priors Hants....24 G4
Hurstbourne Tarrant Hants....24 F2
Hurst Green E Susx....16 C5
Hurst Green Essex....47 K8
Hurst Green Lancs....83 Q7
Hurst Green Surrey....33 M12
Hurst Hill Dudley....52 H2
Hurstley Herefs....51 K11
Hurstpierpoint W Susx....15 K7
Hurst Wickham W Susx....15 K7
Hurstwood Lancs....84 C9
Hurtiso Ork....147 d5
Hurtmore Surrey....14 D2
Hurworth Burn Dur....101 K11
Hurworth-on-Tees Darltn....91 M5
Hurworth Place Darltn....91 M5
Hury Dur....90 F3
Husbands Bosworth Leics....54 G4
Husborne Crawley C Beds....44 D4
Husthwaite N York....92 B11
Hutcherleigh Devon....6 H9
Hut Green N York....85 R10
Huthwaite Notts....78 D11
Hutoft Lincs....81 K8
Hutton Border....117 K10
Hutton Cumb....89 L1
Hutton E R Yk....87 J4
Hutton Essex....34 B3
Hutton Lancs....83 L10
Hutton N Som....28 D10
Hutton Bonville N York....91 N7
Hutton Buscel N York....93 K10
Hutton Conyers N York....91 N11
Hutton Cranswick E R Yk....87 J5
Hutton End Cumb....98 F12
Hutton Hang N York....91 K9
Hutton Henry Dur....101 L11
Hutton-le-Hole N York....92 E8
Hutton Lowcross R & Cl....92 C4
Hutton Magna Dur....91 J4
Hutton Mulgrave N York....92 G5
Hutton Roof Cumb....89 P11
Hutton Roof Cumb....98 D11
Hutton Rudby N York....91 Q11
Hutton Sessay N York....91 Q11
Hutton Wandesley N York....85 R5
Huxham Devon....8 H5
Huxham Green Somset....21 Q6
Huxley Ches W....75 N11
Huyton Knows....75 M4
Hycemoor Cumb....88 E9
Hyde Gloucs....41 P11
Hyde Hants....23 Q10
Hyde Tamesd....76 H5
Hyde Heath Bucks....32 D2
Hyde Lea Staffs....64 G8
Hydestile Surrey....14 D3
Hykeham Moor Lincs....79 M10
Hylands House & Park Essex....46 B11
Hyndford Bridge S Lans....106 B1
Hynish Ag & B....118 D5
Hyssington Powys....51 K2
Hystfield Gloucs....41 L5
Hythe Essex....46 H7
Hythe Hants....12 G5
Hythe Kent....17 L4
Hythe Somset....21 P3
Hythe End W & M....32 E7
Hyton Cumb....88 E9

I
Ibberton Dorset....11 J3
Ible Derbys....77 N12
Ibsley Hants....12 B3
Ibstock Leics....66 C10
Ibstone Bucks....31 Q4
Ibthorpe Hants....24 F3
Iburndale N York....92 H5
Ibworth Hants....25 J2
Icelton N Som....28 E9
Ichrachan Ag & B....121 J6
Ickburgh Norfk....57 Q2
Ickenham Gt Lon....32 F5
Ickford Bucks....43 N10
Ickham Kent....35 M10
Ickleford Herts....44 H5
Icklesham E Susx....16 F7
Ickleton Cambs....45 P6
Icklingham Suffk....57 P5
Ickornshaw N York....84 G6
Ickwell Green C Beds....44 G3
Icomb Gloucs....42 G7
Idbury Oxon....42 F8
Iddesleigh Devon....7 N3
Ide Devon....8 G6
Ideford Devon....8 H5
Ide Hill Kent....33 N12
Iden E Susx....16 G6
Iden Green Kent....16 D3
Iden Green Kent....16 E4
Idle C Brad....85 J7
Idless Cnwll....3 K5
Idlicote Warwks....42 H4
Idmiston Wilts....24 C6
Idole Carmth....38 B8
Idridgehay Derbys....65 P2
Idrigill Highld....134 E5
Idstone Oxon....30 F5
Iffley Oxon....43 L11
Ifield W Susx....15 J3
Ifold W Susx....14 E4
Iford BCP....12 B6
Iford E Susx....15 M9
Ifton Heath Shrops....63 K5
Ightfield Shrops....63 Q4
Ightham Kent....33 Q11
Iken Suffk....59 N9
Ilam Staffs....65 L2
Ilchester Somset....22 C9
Ilderton Nthumb....108 G5
Ilford Gt Lon....33 N5
Ilford Somset....21 M10
Ilfracombe Devon....19 K4
Ilkeston Derbys....66 D4
Ilketshall St Andrew Suffk....59 M3
Ilketshall St John Suffk....59 M3
Ilketshall St Lawrence Suffk....59 M4
Ilketshall St Margaret Suffk....59 L4
Ilkley C Brad....84 H6
Illand Cnwll....7 K9
Illey Dudley....52 H4
Illidge Green Ches E....76 E11
Illingworth Calder....84 G9
Illogan Cnwll....2 G6
Illston on the Hill Leics....66 H12
Ilmer Bucks....43 Q10
Ilmington Warwks....42 G4
Ilminster Somset....21 M10
Ilsington Devon....8 E9
Ilsington Dorset....11 J6
Ilston Swans....26 E4
Ilton N York....91 K11
Ilton Somset....21 M10
Imachar N Ayrs....103 M2
Immingham NE Lin....87 M12
Immingham Dock NE Lin....87 M12
Impington Cambs....56 H8
Ince Ches W....75 M8
Ince Blundell Sefton....75 K3
Ince-in-Makerfield Wigan....75 Q3
Inchbae Lodge Hotel Highld....145 K11
Inchbare Angus....132 H11
Inchberry Moray....139 P5
Incheril Highld....136 E3
Inchinnan Rens....113 P7
Inchlaggan Highld....128 G4
Inchmichael P & K....124 E8
Inchmore Highld....137 P7
Inchnacardoch Highld....129 K10
Inchnadamph Highld....148 F12
Inchture P & K....124 F7
Inchvuilt Highld....137 J8
Inchyra P & K....124 D8
Indian Queens Cnwll....3 M3
Ingatestone Essex....34 B2
Ingbirchworth Barns....77 N3
Ingerthorpe N York....85 L2
Ingestre Staffs....64 H7
Ingham Lincs....79 N7
Ingham Norfk....71 M7
Ingham Suffk....58 C6
Ingham Corner Norfk....71 M7
Ingleborough Norfk....69 J9
Ingleby Derbys....66 B6
Ingleby Arncliffe N York....91 Q6
Ingleby Barwick S on T....91 Q4
Ingleby Cross N York....91 Q6
Ingleby Greenhow N York....92 C5
Ingleigh Green Devon....8 B3
Inglesbatch BaNES....29 L11
Inglesham Swindn....30 E3
Ingleston D & G....97 K3
Ingleton Dur....91 M3
Ingleton N York....90 A12
Inglewhite Lancs....83 M7
Ingmanthorpe N York....85 N5
Ingoe Nthumb....100 D3
Ingol Lancs....83 L9
Ingoldisthorpe Norfk....69 N5
Ingoldmells Lincs....81 K10
Ingoldsby Lincs....67 P6
Ingram Nthumb....108 H6
Ingrave Essex....34 B4
Ingrow C Brad....84 F7
Ings Cumb....89 M7
Ingst S Glos....29 J5
Ingthorpe Rutlnd....67 N9
Ingworth Norfk....71 J6
Inkberrow Worcs....53 J9
Inkerman Dur....100 E10
Inkhorn Abers....141 M8
Inkpen W Berk....30 H9
Inkstack Highld....151 N3
Inmarsh Wilts....29 Q10
Innellan Ag & B....112 H7
Innerleithen Border....107 J2
Innerleven Fife....115 Q1
Innermessan D & G....94 F6
Innerwick E Loth....116 H6
Innesmill Moray....139 P3
Insch Abers....140 F10
Insh Highld....130 E4
Inskip Lancs....83 L7
Inskip Moss Side Lancs....83 L7
Instow Devon....19 J7
Insworke Cnwll....5 J5
Intake Sheff....78 C4
Inver Abers....131 N4
Inver Highld....146 F8
Inver P & K....123 P4
Inverailort Highld....127 P8
Inverallochy Abers....141 P3
Inveran Highld....145 N5
Inveraray Ag & B....121 L6
Inverarish Highld....135 K8
Inverarity Angus....125 J4
Inverarnan Stirlg....121 Q9
Inverasdale Highld....143 L8
Inverbeg Ag & B....113 L2
Inverbervie Abers....133 N10
Inverboyndie Abers....140 G3
Invercreran House Hotel Ag & B....121 J3
Inverdruie Highld....130 G2
Inveresk E Loth....115 Q6
Inveresragan Ag & B....121 J6
Inverey Abers....131 K6
Inverfarigaig Highld....137 P11
Inverfolla Ag & B....120 H4
Invergarry Highld....129 K4
Invergeldie P & K....123 J7
Invergloy Highld....128 H6
Invergordon Highld....138 C2
Invergowrie P & K....124 G7
Inverguseran Highld....127 N3
Inverhadden P & K....122 H1
Inverie Highld....127 P4
Inverinan Ag & B....121 J9
Inverinate Highld....136 C11
Inverkeilor Angus....125 N3
Inverkeithing Fife....115 L5
Inverkeithny Abers....140 F6
Inverkip Inver....113 J7
Inverkirkaig Highld....144 D1
Inverlael Highld....144 H8
Inverlair Highld....129 K8
Inverliever Lodge Ag & B....120 G11
Inverlochy Ag & B....121 M7
Invermark Angus....132 C8
Invermoriston Highld....129 M1
Invernaver Highld....150 C4
Inverneill Ag & B....112 B5
Inverness Highld....138 C7
Inverness Airport Highld....138 E5
Invernettie Abers....141 Q7
Invernoaden Ag & B....112 G2
Inveroran Hotel Ag & B....121 P4
Inverquharity Angus....124 H1
Inverquhomery Abers....141 N6
Inverroy Highld....129 J8
Inversanda Highld....128 C12
Invershiel Highld....136 C12
Invershin Highld....145 N6
Invershore Highld....151 N9
Inversnaid Hotel Stirlg....122 B11
Inveruglas Ag & B....121 Q11
Inveruglass Highld....130 E4
Inverurie Abers....141 J11
Inwardleigh Devon....7 P3
Inworth Essex....46 F8
Iochdar W Isls....152 b10
Iona Ag & B....119 J8
Iping W Susx....14 C6
iPort Logistics Park Donc....78 F4
Ipplepen Devon....5 P3
Ipsden Oxon....31 N5
Ipstones Staffs....65 J2
Ipswich Suffk....47 L3
Irby Wirral....75 J7
Irby in the Marsh Lincs....81 J11
Irby upon Humber NE Lin....80 D3
Irchester Nhants....55 M7
Ireby Cumb....97 P10
Ireby Lancs....89 Q11
Ireland C Beds....44 G3
Ireleth Cumb....88 H11
Ireshopeburn Dur....99 N10
Ireton Wood Derbys....65 P3
Irlam Salfd....76 D5
Irnham Lincs....67 P7
Iron Acton S Glos....29 K5
Iron Bridge Cambs....57 J1
Ironbridge Wrekin....64 C11
Iron Cross Warwks....53 K10
Ironmacannie D & G....96 D3
Irons Bottom Surrey....15 J2
Ironville Derbys....66 C2
Irstead Norfk....71 M8
Irthington Cumb....98 G6
Irthlingborough Nhants....55 N6
Irton N York....93 K10
Irvine N Ayrs....104 F2
Isauld Highld....150 H4
Isbister Shet....147 i3
Isbister Shet....147 k5
Isfield E Susx....15 N7
Isham Nhants....55 M6
Isington Hants....25 N5
Islandpool Worcs....52 F4
Islay Ag & B....110 H6
Islay Airport Ag & B....110 H11
Isle Abbotts Somset....21 N9
Isle Brewers Somset....21 N9
Isleham Cambs....57 M5
Isle of Dogs Gt Lon....33 M6
Isle of Grain Medway....34 F7
Isle of Lewis W Isls....152 f3
Isle of Man IoM....102 e4
Isle of Man Ronaldsway Airport IoM....102 c7
Isle of Mull Ag & B....119 Q6
Isle of Purbeck Dorset....11 N8
Isle of Sheppey Kent....34 H8
Isle of Skye Highld....134 G8
Isle of Thanet Kent....35 P9
Isle of Walney Cumb....82 D2
Isle of Whithorn D & G....95 N11
Isle of Wight IoW....13 J7
Isleornsay Highld....127 M2
Isles of Scilly St Mary's Airport IoS....2 b2
Islesteps D & G....97 K4
Islet Village Guern....12 c1
Isleworth Gt Lon....32 H7
Isley Walton Leics....66 C7
Islibhig W Isls....152 d3
Islington Gt Lon....33 M5
Islip Nhants....55 N5
Islip Oxon....43 L9
Islivig W Isls....152 d3
Isombridge Wrekin....63 P9
Istead Rise Kent....34 B8
Itchen Abbas Hants....25 J6
Itchen Stoke Hants....25 J6
Itchingfield W Susx....14 G5
Itchington S Glos....29 K5
Itteringham Norfk....70 H6
Itton Devon....7 Q4
Itton Mons....28 G3
Itton Common Mons....28 G3
Ivegill Cumb....98 E10
Ivelet N York....90 H7
Iver Bucks....32 F6
Iver Heath Bucks....32 E6
Iveston Dur....100 F8
Ivinghoe Bucks....44 C8
Ivinghoe Aston Bucks....44 D8
Ivington Herefs....51 N10
Ivington Green Herefs....51 M10
Ivybridge Devon....5 N5

Ivychurch Kent....17 J5
Ivy Cross Dorset....23 J8
Ivy Hatch Kent....33 Q11
Ivy Todd Norfk....70 C10
Iwade Kent....34 F9
Iwerne Courtney Dorset....23 J10
Iwerne Minster Dorset....23 J10
Ixworth Suffk....58 D6
Ixworth Thorpe Suffk....58 D6

J
Jack Green Lancs....83 N10
Jack Hill N York....85 J5
Jack-in-the-Green Devon....9 J6
Jacksdale Notts....66 D2
Jackson Bridge Kirk....77 M2
Jackson's Bush Hants....24 D6
Jackton S Lans....113 R10
Jacobstow Cnwll....6 H5
Jacobstowe Devon....8 A4
Jacobs Well Surrey....32 E11
Jameston Pembks....37 L10
Jamestown Highld....137 N4
Jamestown W Duns....113 M5
Janetstown Highld....151 M10
Janetstown Highld....151 Q6
Jardine Hall D & G....106 E12
Jarrow S Tyne....101 J5
Jarvis Brook E Susx....15 P5
Jasper's Green Essex....46 C6
Jawcraig Falk....114 F6
Jaywick Essex....47 L9
Jealott's Hill Br For....32 B7
Jeater Houses N York....91 Q8
Jedburgh Border....107 Q6
Jeffreyston Pembks....37 L9
Jemimaville Highld....138 D3
Jerbourg Guern....12 c3
Jersey Jersey....13 c2
Jersey Airport Jersey....13 b2
Jersey Marine Neath....26 H3
Jerusalem Lincs....79 J9
Jesmond N u Ty....100 H5
Jevington E Susx....15 Q10
Jingle Street Mons....40 G9
Jockey End Herts....44 F9
Jodrell Bank Ches E....76 E9
Johnby Cumb....98 E11
John Lennon Airport Lpool....75 M7
John o' Groats Highld....151 Q2
Johns Cross E Susx....16 D6
Johnshaven Abers....133 J11
Johnston Pembks....36 H9
Johnstone D & G....106 H9
Johnstone Rens....113 N8
Johnstonebridge D & G....106 E11
Johnstown Carmth....38 B8
Johnstown Wrexhm....63 J3
Joppa C Edin....115 P6
Joppa Cerdgn....49 J2
Joppa S Ayrs....104 G6
Jordans Bucks....32 D4
Jordanston Pembks....36 H4
Jordanthorpe Sheff....78 B7
Joyden's Wood Kent....33 P8
Jubilee Corner Kent....16 E1
Jump Barns....78 B4
Jumper's Town E Susx....15 N4
Juniper Nthumb....100 D6
Juniper Green C Edin....115 M7
Jura Ag & B....111 L4
Jurassic Coast Devon....9 Q7
Jurby IoM....102 e3
Jurston Devon....8 D8

K
Kaber Cumb....90 C4
Kaimend S Lans....114 H12
Kames Ag & B....112 E7
Kames E Ayrs....105 M4
Kea Cnwll....3 K6
Keadby N Linc....79 L1
Keal Cotes Lincs....80 G11
Kearby Town End N York....85 M6
Kearsley Bolton....76 D3
Kearsney Kent....17 N2
Kearstwick Cumb....89 P10
Kearton N York....90 H7
Keasden N York....83 R3
Keaton Devon....5 N6
Keckwick Halton....75 P7
Keddington Lincs....80 G6
Keddington Corner Lincs....80 G6
Kedington Suffk....46 C2
Kedleston Derbys....65 P4
Keelby Lincs....80 D2
Keele Staffs....64 E3
Keele Services Staffs....64 E3
Keeley Green Bed....44 E3
Keelham C Brad....84 F8
Keeres Green Essex....45 Q8
Keeston Pembks....36 H6
Keevil Wilts....29 Q10
Kegworth Leics....66 D7
Kehelland Cnwll....2 G5
Keig Abers....140 F12
Keighley C Brad....84 F7
Keilarsbrae Clacks....114 G2
Keillour P & K....123 N7
Keiloch Abers....131 M6
Keils Ag & B....111 L7
Keinton Mandeville Somset....22 D7
Keir Mill D & G....105 Q10
Keirsleywell Row Nthumb....99 L8
Keisby Lincs....67 P6
Keisley Cumb....90 B2
Keiss Highld....151 P4
Keith Moray....140 C5
Keithick P & K....124 D5
Keithock Angus....132 H11
Keithtown Highld....137 P5
Kelbrook Lancs....84 D6
Kelby Lincs....67 P4
Keld Cumb....89 M1
Keld N York....90 F7
Keld Head N York....92 F10
Keldholme N York....92 F9
Kelfield N Linc....79 L3
Kelfield N York....86 B7
Kelham Notts....79 K12
Kelhead D & G....97 P4
Kellacott Devon....7 M6
Kellamergh Lancs....83 J10
Kellas Angus....125 J5
Kellas Moray....139 M5
Kellaton Devon....5 R8
Kelleth Cumb....89 P6
Kelling Norfk....70 F4
Kellington N York....85 Q10
Kelloe Dur....101 J11
Kelloholm D & G....105 N11
Kells Cumb....88 C3
Kelly Devon....7 L6
Kelly Bray Cnwll....7 L10

Kelmarsh Nhants....55 J5
Kelmscott Oxon....30 F2
Kelsale Suffk....59 M7
Kelsall Ches W....75 N10
Kelshall Herts....45 L4
Kelsick Cumb....97 P8
Kelso Border....108 B3
Kelstedge Derbys....77 Q11
Kelstern Lincs....80 E6
Kelsterton Flints....75 J9
Kelston BaNES....29 L8
Keltneyburn P & K....123 K3
Kelton D & G....97 K4
Kelty Fife....115 L2
Kelvedon Essex....46 F7
Kelvedon Hatch Essex....33 Q3
Kelynack Cnwll....2 B8
Kemacott Devon....19 M4
Kemback Fife....124 H10
Kemberton Shrops....64 D11
Kemble Gloucs....30 A3
Kemble Wick Gloucs....29 R3
Kemerton Worcs....41 Q4
Kemeys Commander Mons....40 D10
Kemnay Abers....132 H1
Kempe's Corner Kent....17 J2
Kempley Gloucs....41 K6
Kempley Green Gloucs....41 K6
Kempsey Worcs....52 F10
Kempsford Gloucs....30 D3
Kemps Green Warwks....53 L6
Kempshott Hants....25 J3
Kempston Bed....55 P11
Kempston Hardwick Bed....44 E3
Kempton Shrops....51 K4
Kemp Town Br & H....15 L10
Kemsing Kent....33 Q10
Kemsley Kent....34 F9
Kemsley Street Kent....34 E10
Kenardington Kent....16 H4
Kenchester Herefs....40 F3
Kencot Oxon....42 F10
Kendal Cumb....89 N8
Kenderchurch Herefs....40 E6
Kenfig Brdgnd....27 M5
Kenfig Hill Brdgnd....27 M5
Kenilworth Warwks....53 P6
Kenley Gt Lon....33 L10
Kenley Shrops....63 P12
Kenmore Highld....135 N4
Kenmore P & K....123 K4
Kenn Devon....8 H7
Kenn N Som....28 F9
Kennacraig Ag & B....112 C7
Kennall Vale Cnwll....3 J7
Kennards House Cnwll....7 K8
Kenneggy Cnwll....2 F9
Kennerleigh Devon....8 F3
Kennet Clacks....114 G2
Kennethmont Abers....140 E10
Kennett Cambs....57 N7
Kenniford Devon....8 H7
Kenninghall Norfk....58 F3
Kennington Kent....17 J2
Kennington Oxon....43 L11
Kennoway Fife....124 G12
Kenny Somset....21 M9
Kenny Hill Suffk....57 M5
Kennythorpe N York....86 E2
Kenovay Ag & B....118 C5
Kensaleyre Highld....134 G5
Kensington Gt Lon....33 K7
Kensington Palace Gt Lon....33 K7
Kensworth C Beds....44 E8
Kensworth Common C Beds....44 E8
Kentallen Highld....121 J1
Kentchurch Herefs....40 F6
Kentford Suffk....57 N7
Kent Green Ches E....76 F12
Kentisbeare Devon....9 K3
Kentisbury Devon....19 M4
Kentisbury Ford Devon....19 M4
Kentish Town Gt Lon....33 L6
Kentmere Cumb....89 M6
Kenton Devon....8 H6
Kenton Gt Lon....32 H5
Kenton N u Ty....100 H5
Kenton Suffk....59 J7
Kenton Bankfoot N u Ty....100 G4
Kentra Highld....127 M10
Kents Bank Cumb....89 J11
Kent's Green Gloucs....41 L7
Kent's Oak Hants....24 E8
Kent Street E Susx....16 D7
Kent Street Kent....34 B11
Kenwick Shrops....63 M6
Kenwyn Cnwll....3 K5
Kenyon Warrtn....76 B5
Keoldale Highld....149 J3
Keppoch Highld....136 C11
Kepwick N York....91 Q8
Keresley Covtry....53 Q4
Kermincham Ches E....76 E10
Kernborough Devon....5 P8
Kerne Bridge Herefs....41 J8
Kerrera Ag & B....120 F7
Kerridge Ches E....76 H8
Kerridge-end Ches E....76 H8
Kerris Cnwll....2 C9
Kerry Powys....50 H3
Kerrycroy Ag & B....112 G9
Kersall Notts....78 H11
Kersbrook Devon....9 K8
Kerscott Devon....19 M8
Kersey Suffk....46 H3
Kersey Tye Suffk....46 H3
Kersey Upland Suffk....46 H3
Kershader W Isls....152 g4
Kershopefoot Cumb....98 F2
Kersoe Worcs....42 A4
Kerswell Devon....9 K3
Kerswell Green Worcs....41 N2
Kesgrave Suffk....47 M3
Kessingland Suffk....59 R3
Kessingland Beach Suffk....59 R3
Kestle Cnwll....3 N5
Kestle Mill Cnwll....3 L4
Keston Gt Lon....33 N9
Keswick Cumb....89 J1
Keswick Norfk....71 L8
Ketsby Lincs....80 G8
Kettering Nhants....55 L5
Ketteringham Norfk....70 H11
Kettins P & K....124 D5
Kettlebaston Suffk....58 E10
Kettlebridge Fife....124 H11
Kettlebrook Staffs....65 N11
Kettleburgh Suffk....59 K8
Kettle Green Herts....45 M7
Kettleholm D & G....97 N3
Kettleness N York....92 H4
Kettleshulme Ches E....77 J8
Kettlesing N York....85 K4
Kettlesing Bottom N York....85 K4
Kettlestone Norfk....70 D6
Kettlethorpe Lincs....79 L9
Kettletoft Ork....147 e2
Kettlewell N York....90 H12
Kew Gt Lon....33 K7
Kew Royal Botanic Gardens Gt Lon....32 H7
Kewstoke N Som....28 D9

Kexbrough – Laversdale 169

Kexbrough Barns 77 P2
Kexby C York 86 C5
Kexby Lincs 79 L6
Key Green Ches E 76 G11
Key Green N York 92 G6
Keyham Leics 66 H11
Keyhaven Hants 12 E6
Keyingham E R Yk 87 N10
Keymer W Susx 15 K8
Keynsham BaNES 29 K8
Keysoe Bed 55 Q8
Keysoe Row Bed 56 B8
Keyston Cambs 55 P5
Key Street Kent 34 F9
Keyworth Notts 66 G6
Kibbear Somset 21 K9
Kibblesworth Gatesd 100 G7
Kibworth Beauchamp Leics 54 H2
Kibworth Harcourt Leics 54 H2
Kidbrooke Gt Lon 33 M7
Kidburngill Cumb 88 E2
Kiddemore Green Staffs 64 F10
Kidderminster Worcs 52 F5
Kiddington Oxon 43 J7
Kidd's Moor Norfk 70 G11
Kidlington Oxon 43 K9
Kidmore End Oxon 31 P6
Kidsdale D & G 95 N11
Kidsgrove Staffs 64 F1
Kidstones N York 90 F10
Kidwelly Carmth 38 B10
Kiel Crofts Ag & B 120 G5
Kielder Nthumb 107 Q11
Kielder Forest 107 P12
Kiells Ag & B 111 J7
Kilbarchan Rens 113 M8
Kilbeg Highld 127 M3
Kilberry Ag & B 111 Q8
Kilbirnie N Ayrs 113 L10
Kilbride Ag & B 111 Q5
Kilbride Ag & B 112 F7
Kilbuiack Moray 139 K4
Kilburn Derbys 66 C3
Kilburn Gt Lon 33 J6
Kilburn N York 92 A11
Kilby Leics 54 G2
Kilchamaig Ag & B 112 B9
Kilchattan Ag & B 111 J2
Kilchattan Ag & B 112 G10
Kilcheran Ag & B 120 F5
Kilchoan Highld 127 J11
Kilchoman Ag & B 110 F8
Kilchrenan Ag & B 121 K8
Kilconquhar Fife 125 K12
Kilcot Gloucs 41 L6
Kilcoy Highld 137 Q5
Kilcreggan Ag & B 113 K5
Kildale N York 92 C5
Kildalloig Ag & B 103 K6
Kildary Highld 146 D10
Kildavaig Ag & B 112 E8
Kildavanan Ag & B 112 F8
Kildonan Highld 146 G1
Kildonan N Ayrs 103 Q5
Kildonan Lodge Highld 150 G12
Kildonnan Highld 127 J7
Kildrochet House D & G 94 F7
Kildrummy Abers 140 D12
Kildwick N York 84 F6
Kilfinan Ag & B 112 D5
Kilfinnan Highld 129 J5
Kilford Denbgs 74 E10
Kilgetty Pembks 37 M9
Kilgrammie S Ayrs 104 E9
Kilgwrrwg Common Mons 28 G3
Kilham E R Yk 87 K2
Kilham Nthumb 108 E3
Kilkenneth Ag & B 118 C4
Kilkenzie Ag & B 103 J5
Kilkerran Ag & B 103 K6
Kilkhampton Cnwll 7 J2
Killamarsh Derbys 78 D7
Killay Swans 26 F4
Killearn Stirlg 113 Q4
Killen Highld 138 C4
Killerby Darltn 91 K3
Killerton Devon 9 J5
Killichonan P & K 122 F1
Killiechonate Highld 129 J8
Killiechronan Ag & B 119 P4
Killiecrankie P & K 130 G11
Killilan Highld 136 C10
Killimster Highld 151 P5
Killin Stirlg 122 F6
Killinghall N York 85 L3
Killington Cumb 89 Q9
Killington Devon 19 N4
Killington Lake Services Cumb 89 P8
Killingworth N Tyne 100 H4
Killiow Cnwll 3 K6
Killochyett Border 116 B12
Kilmacolm Inver 113 M7
Kilmahog Stirlg 122 G11
Kilmahumaig Ag & B 112 A3
Kilmaluag Highld 142 E10
Kilmany Fife 124 H8
Kilmarnock E Ayrs 104 H2
Kilmartin Ag & B 112 B2
Kilmaurs E Ayrs 104 G2
Kilmelford Ag & B 120 F10
Kilmersdon Somset 22 F3
Kilmeston Hants 25 K8
Kilmichael Ag & B 103 J5
Kilmichael Glassary Ag & B 112 C3
Kilmichael of Inverlussa Ag & B 112 A4
Kilmington Devon 9 P5
Kilmington Wilts 22 H6
Kilmington Common Wilts 22 H6
Kilmington Street Wilts 22 H6
Kilmorack Highld 137 N7
Kilmore Ag & B 120 G8
Kilmore Highld 127 M3
Kilmory Ag & B 111 P6
Kilmory Highld 127 J10
Kilmory N Ayrs 103 P5
Kilmuir Highld 134 D6
Kilmuir Highld 138 C6
Kilmuir Highld 142 D11
Kilmuir Highld 146 D10
Kilmun Ag & B 112 H5
Kilnave Ag & B 110 G7
Kilncadzow S Lans 114 F11
Kilndown Kent 16 C4
Kiln Green Wokham 32 A6
Kilnhill Cumb 97 P11
Kilnhouses Ches W 76 B10
Kilnhurst Rothm 78 D4
Kilninver Ag & B 120 F8
Kiln Pit Hill Nthumb 100 D7
Kilnsea E R Yk 87 R12
Kilnsey N York 84 E2
Kilnwick E R Yk 87 J5
Kilnwick Percy E R Yk 86 F5
Kiloran Ag & B 111 J2
Kilpatrick N Ayrs 103 N4
Kilpeck Herefs 40 F5
Kilpin E R Yk 86 E10
Kilpin Pike E R Yk 86 E10
Kilrenny Fife 125 L11
Kilsby Nhants 54 F6
Kilspindie P & K 124 E7
Kilstay D & G 94 G10
Kilsyth N Lans 114 C6
Kiltarlity Highld 137 N7
Kilton R & Cl 92 E3
Kilton Somset 21 J4
Kilton Thorpe R & Cl 92 E3
Kilvaxter Highld 142 D11
Kilve Somset 21 J5
Kilvington Notts 67 K4
Kilwinning N Ayrs 104 E1
Kimberley Norfk 70 G11
Kimberley Notts 66 E3
Kimberworth Rothm 78 C5
Kimblesworth Dur 100 H9
Kimble Wick Bucks 44 A10
Kimbolton Cambs 56 B7
Kimbolton Herefs 51 N8
Kimcote Leics 54 F3
Kimmeridge Dorset 11 M9
Kimmerston Nthumb 108 F3
Kimpton Hants 24 D4
Kimpton Herts 44 H8
Kimworthy Devon 18 F10
Kinbrace Highld 150 F10
Kinbuck Stirlg 123 K11
Kincaple Fife 125 J9
Kincardine Fife 114 G4
Kincardine Highld 145 N7
Kincardine Bridge Fife 114 G4
Kincardine O'Neil Abers 132 F4
Kinclaven P & K 124 C5
Kincorth C Aber 133 M4
Kincorth House Moray 139 J3
Kincraig Highld 130 F3
Kincraigie P & K 123 P3
Kindallachan P & K 123 P3
Kinerarach Ag & B 111 P10
Kineton Gloucs 42 C6
Kineton Warwks 53 Q10
Kinfauns P & K 124 D8
Kingarth Ag & B 112 G10
Kingcausie Abers 133 L4
Kingcoed Mons 40 F10
Kingerby Lincs 79 Q5
Kingford Devon 7 K3
Kingham Oxon 42 F7
Kingholm Quay D & G 97 K3
Kinghorn Fife 115 N4
Kinglassie Fife 115 N2
Kingoodie P & K 124 G7
King's Acre Herefs 40 G3
Kingsand Cnwll 4 G6
Kingsash Bucks 44 C10
Kingsbarns Fife 125 L10
Kingsbridge Devon 5 M8
Kingsbridge Somset 20 F6
Kings Bridge Swans 26 E3
King's Bromley Staffs 65 L9
Kingsburgh Highld 134 G5
Kingsbury Gt Lon 32 H5
Kingsbury Warwks 53 N1
Kingsbury Episcopi Somset 21 P9
King's Caple Herefs 40 H6
Kingsclere Hants 31 L10
King's Cliffe Nhants 55 P1
Kings Clipstone Notts 78 G10
Kingscote Gloucs 29 N3
Kingscott Devon 19 K9
King's Coughton Warwks 53 K9
Kingscross N Ayrs 103 R4
Kingsdon Somset 22 C8
Kingsdown Kent 17 Q1
Kingsdown Swindn 30 D5
Kingsdown Wilts 29 N9
Kingseat Abers 141 L12
Kingseat Fife 115 L3
Kingsey Bucks 43 Q10
Kingsfold W Susx 14 H4
Kingsford C Aber 133 K3
Kingsford E Ayrs 113 N11
Kingsford Worcs 52 F4
Kingsgate Kent 35 Q8
Kings Green Gloucs 41 M5
Kingshall Street Suffk 58 D8
Kingsheanton Devon 19 L6
King's Heath Birm 53 K4
Kings Hill Kent 34 B11
King's Hill Wsall 52 H1
Kings House Hotel Highld 121 P2
Kingshurst Solhll 53 M3
Kingside Hill Cumb 97 N8
Kingskerswell Devon 5 P3
Kingskettle Fife 124 F11
Kingsland Dorset 10 C5
Kingsland Herefs 51 M8
Kingsland IoA 72 D7
Kings Langley Herts 44 F11
Kingsley Ches W 75 P9
Kingsley Hants 25 N6
Kingsley Staffs 65 J3
Kingsley Green W Susx 14 C5
Kingsley Holt Staffs 65 J3
Kingsley Park Nhants 55 J8
Kingslow Shrops 52 E1
King's Lynn Norfk 69 M8
Kings Meaburn Cumb 89 Q2
Kingsmead Hants 25 K10
King's Mills Guern 12 b2
King's Moss St Hel 75 N3
Kingsmuir Angus 125 J3
Kings Muir Border 106 H2
Kingsmuir Fife 125 K11
Kings Newnham Warwks 54 D5
King's Newton Derbys 66 C7
Kingsnorth Kent 16 H3
King's Norton Birm 53 K5
King's Norton Leics 66 H12
Kings Nympton Devon 19 N9
King's Pyon Herefs 51 M10
Kings Ripton Cambs 56 E5
King's Somborne Hants 24 F7
King's Stag Dorset 10 H3
King's Stanley Gloucs 41 N11
King's Sutton Nhants 43 K4
Kingstanding Birm 53 K2
Kingsteignton Devon 8 F10
King Sterndale Derbys 77 K9
Kingsthorne Herefs 40 G5
Kingsthorpe Nhants 55 J8
Kingston Cambs 56 G9
Kingston Cnwll 7 L9
Kingston Devon 5 K7
Kingston Devon 9 K7
Kingston Dorset 11 J3
Kingston Dorset 11 M9
Kingston E Loth 116 D5
Kingston Hants 12 B4
Kingston IoW 13 J8
Kingston Kent 35 M12
Kingston W Susx 14 F10
Kingston Bagpuize Oxon 31 J3
Kingston Blount Oxon 31 Q2
Kingston Deverill Wilts 23 J6
Kingstone Herefs 40 F5
Kingstone Somset 21 N10
Kingstone Staffs 65 K6
Kingstone Winslow Oxon 30 F5
Kingston Lacy House & Gardens Dorset 11 N4
Kingston Lisle Oxon 30 G5
Kingston near Lewes E Susx 15 M9
Kingston on Soar Notts 66 E6
Kingston on Spey Moray 139 Q3
Kingston Russell Dorset 10 F6
Kingston St Mary Somset 21 K7
Kingston Seymour N Som 28 E9
Kingston Stert Oxon 31 Q2
Kingston upon Hull C KuH 87 K9
Kingston upon Thames Gt Lon 32 H8
Kingstown Cumb 98 E6
King's Walden Herts 44 H7
Kingswear Devon 5 Q6
Kingswells C Aber 133 L3
Kings Weston Bristl 28 H7
Kingswinford Dudley 52 G3
Kingswood Bucks 43 P8
Kingswood Gloucs 29 M4
Kingswood Kent 34 E12
Kingswood Powys 62 H11
Kingswood S Glos 29 K7
Kingswood Somset 20 H6
Kingswood Surrey 33 J11
Kingswood Warwks 53 M6
Kingswood Brook Warwks 53 M6
Kingswood Common Herefs 51 J10
Kingswood Common Staffs 64 F11
Kings Worthy Hants 24 H7
Kingthorpe Lincs 80 C8
Kington Herefs 51 J9
Kington S Glos 29 J4
Kington Worcs 53 J9
Kington Langley Wilts 29 Q7
Kington Magna Dorset 22 G9
Kington St Michael Wilts 29 P7
Kingussie Highld 130 D4
Kingweston Somset 22 C7
Kinharrachie Abers 141 M9
Kinharvie D & G 97 J5
Kinkell Bridge P & K 123 N9
Kinknockie Abers 141 N7
Kinleith C Edin 115 M8
Kinlet Shrops 52 D4
Kinloch Highld 126 G4
Kinloch Highld 148 H9
Kinloch Highld 149 M6
Kinloch P & K 124 C4
Kinlochard Stirlg 122 D12
Kinlochbervie Highld 148 F5
Kinlocheil Highld 128 D8
Kinlochewe Highld 136 E3
Kinloch Hourn Highld 128 C3
Kinlochlaggan Highld 129 P6
Kinlochleven Highld 128 H12
Kinlochmoidart Highld 127 M9
Kinlochnanuagh Highld 127 N7
Kinloch Rannoch P & K 122 H1
Kinloss Moray 139 K3
Kinmel Bay Conwy 74 D7
Kinmuck Abers 141 K12
Kinmundy Abers 133 L1
Kinnabus Ag & B 102 B1
Kinnadie Abers 141 N7
Kinnaird P & K 123 N1
Kinneff Abers 133 K9
Kinnelhead D & G 106 D9
Kinnell Angus 125 M3
Kinnerley Shrops 63 K8
Kinnersley Herefs 51 K10
Kinnersley Worcs 41 P3
Kinnerton Powys 50 H8
Kinnerton Shrops 51 L1
Kinnerton Green Flints 75 K11
Kinnesswood P & K 124 D12
Kinninvie Dur 90 H2
Kinnordy Angus 124 G2
Kinoulton Notts 66 H6
Kinross P & K 124 C12
Kinrossie P & K 124 D6
Kinross Services P & K 124 C12
Kinsbourne Green Herts 44 G8
Kinsey Heath Ches E 64 C4
Kinsham Herefs 51 K7
Kinsham Worcs 41 Q4
Kinsley Wakefd 85 N12
Kinson BCP 11 P5
Kintail Highld 136 D12
Kintbury W Berk 30 H9
Kintessack Moray 139 J4
Kintillo P & K 124 C9
Kinton Herefs 51 L6
Kinton Shrops 63 L8
Kintore Abers 133 J1
Kintour Ag & B 111 K11
Kintra Ag & B 110 H11
Kintra Ag & B 119 K8
Kintraw Ag & B 120 F11
Kintyre Ag & B 103 K2
Kinveachy Highld 138 G12
Kinver Staffs 52 F4
Kiplin N York 91 M7
Kippax Leeds 85 N9
Kippen Stirlg 114 B2
Kippford D & G 96 G7
Kipping's Cross Kent 16 B3
Kirbister Ork 147 c5
Kirby Bedon Norfk 71 K11
Kirby Bellars Leics 67 J8
Kirby Cane Norfk 59 M2
Kirby Corner Covtry 53 P5
Kirby Cross Essex 47 M7
Kirby Fields Leics 66 E11
Kirby Green Norfk 59 M2
Kirby Grindalythe N York 86 G2
Kirby Hill N York 85 N2
Kirby Hill N York 91 J5
Kirby Knowle N York 91 Q9
Kirby-le-Soken Essex 47 M7
Kirby Misperton N York 92 F10
Kirby Muxloe Leics 66 E11
Kirby Sigston N York 91 P8
Kirby Underdale E R Yk 86 E3
Kirby Wiske N York 91 P9
Kirdford W Susx 14 E5
Kirk Highld 151 N5
Kirkabister Shet 147 j8
Kirkandrews D & G 96 C8
Kirkandrews upon Eden Cumb 98 D6
Kirkbampton Cumb 98 C7
Kirkbean D & G 97 K6
Kirk Bramwith Donc 78 G1
Kirkbride Cumb 97 P7
Kirkbridge N York 91 L8
Kirkbuddo Angus 125 K4
Kirkburn Border 107 J2
Kirkburn E R Yk 86 H4
Kirkburton Kirk 77 M1
Kirkby Knows 75 L4
Kirkby Lincs 79 Q5
Kirkby N York 92 B5
Kirkby Fleetham N York 91 M8
Kirkby Green Lincs 80 B12
Kirkby-in-Ashfield Notts 78 E12
Kirkby-in-Furness Cumb 88 H10
Kirkby la Thorpe Lincs 68 B3
Kirkby Lonsdale Cumb 89 P11
Kirkby Malham N York 84 D3
Kirkby Mallory Leics 66 D12
Kirkby Malzeard N York 91 L11
Kirkby Mills N York 92 E9
Kirkbymoorside N York 92 E9
Kirkby on Bain Lincs 80 E11
Kirkby Overblow N York 85 L5
Kirkby Stephen Cumb 90 C5
Kirkby Thore Cumb 89 Q2
Kirkby Underwood Lincs 67 Q7
Kirkby Wharf N York 85 Q7
Kirkby Woodhouse Notts 66 E1
Kirkcaldy Fife 115 P3
Kirkcambeck Cumb 98 G4
Kirkchrist D & G 96 D8
Kirkcolm D & G 94 E4
Kirkconnel D & G 105 N7
Kirkconnell D & G 97 K5
Kirkcowan D & G 95 L6
Kirkcudbright D & G 96 D8
Kirkdale Lpool 75 K5
Kirk Deighton N York 85 N5
Kirk Ella E R Yk 87 J9
Kirkfieldbank S Lans 105 R1
Kirkgunzeon D & G 96 H5
Kirk Hallam Derbys 66 D4
Kirkham Lancs 83 K9
Kirkham N York 86 D2
Kirkhamgate Wakefd 85 L10
Kirk Hammerton N York 85 P4
Kirkharle Nthumb 100 C2
Kirkhaugh Nthumb 99 K8
Kirkheaton Kirk 85 J11
Kirkheaton Nthumb 100 C3
Kirkhill Highld 137 P7
Kirkhope S Lans 106 C8
Kirkhouse Cumb 98 H6
Kirkhouse Green Donc 78 G1
Kirkibost Highld 135 K12
Kirkinch P & K 124 F4
Kirkinner D & G 95 M8
Kirkintilloch E Duns 114 B6
Kirk Ireton Derbys 65 P2
Kirkland Cumb 88 E3
Kirkland Cumb 99 J11
Kirkland D & G 105 N7
Kirkland D & G 105 Q11
Kirkland D & G 106 D11
Kirkland Guards Cumb 97 N10
Kirk Langley Derbys 65 P4
Kirkleatham R & Cl 92 C2
Kirklevington S on T 91 Q5
Kirkley Suffk 59 Q2
Kirklington N York 91 N10
Kirklington Notts 78 H12
Kirklinton Cumb 98 E5
Kirkliston C Edin 115 L6
Kirkmabreck D & G 95 N7
Kirkmaiden D & G 94 G11
Kirk Merrington Dur 100 H12
Kirk Michael IoM 102 d4
Kirkmichael P & K 131 K12
Kirkmichael S Ayrs 104 F8
Kirkmuirhill S Lans 105 P1
Kirknewton Nthumb 108 E4
Kirknewton W Loth 115 L8
Kirkney Abers 140 D9
Kirk of Shotts N Lans 114 F8
Kirkoswald Cumb 98 H10
Kirkoswald S Ayrs 104 D8
Kirkpatrick D & G 106 B11
Kirkpatrick Durham D & G 96 F4
Kirkpatrick-Fleming D & G 98 C4
Kirk Sandall Donc 78 G2
Kirksanton Cumb 88 F10
Kirk Smeaton N York 85 Q12
Kirkstall Leeds 85 K8
Kirkstead Lincs 80 D11
Kirkstile Abers 140 E9
Kirkstile D & G 107 K11
Kirkstone Pass Inn Cumb 89 L5
Kirkstyle Highld 151 P2
Kirkthorpe Wakefd 85 M11
Kirkton Abers 140 G10
Kirkton D & G 97 K2
Kirkton Fife 124 G8
Kirkton Highld 135 Q10
Kirkton Highld 136 C7
Kirkton P & K 123 N9
Kirkton Manor Border 106 G2
Kirkton of Airlie Angus 124 F3
Kirkton of Auchterhouse Angus 124 G5
Kirkton of Barevan Highld 138 F6
Kirkton of Collace P & K 124 D6
Kirkton of Glenbuchat Abers 132 B1
Kirkton of Kingoldrum Angus 124 G2
Kirkton of Lethendy P & K 124 C4
Kirkton of Logie Buchan Abers 141 N10
Kirkton of Maryculter Abers 133 K4
Kirkton of Menmuir Angus 132 E11
Kirkton of Monikie Angus 125 K5
Kirkton of Rayne Abers 140 H10
Kirkton of Skene Abers 133 K3
Kirkton of Tealing Angus 124 H5
Kirkton of Tough Abers 132 F2
Kirktown Abers 141 N3
Kirktown Abers 141 Q5
Kirktown of Alvah Abers 140 G4
Kirktown of Bourtie Abers 141 K10
Kirktown of Fetteresso Abers 133 K7
Kirktown of Mortlach Moray 139 P8
Kirktown of Slains Abers 141 P10
Kirkurd Border 106 F1
Kirkwall Ork 147 c4
Kirkwall Airport Ork 147 d5
Kirkwhelpington Nthumb 100 C1
Kirk Yetholm Border 108 D4
Kirmington N Linc 80 B1
Kirmond le Mire Lincs 80 D5
Kirn Ag & B 112 H6
Kirriemuir Angus 124 H2
Kirstead Green Norfk 59 L1
Kirtlebridge D & G 97 P4
Kirtling Cambs 57 M9
Kirtling Green Cambs 57 N9
Kirtlington Oxon 43 K8
Kirtomy Highld 150 D4
Kirton Lincs 68 F4
Kirton Notts 78 H10
Kirton Suffk 47 N4
Kirton End Lincs 68 F4
Kirtonhill W Duns 113 M6
Kirton Holme Lincs 68 E4
Kirton in Lindsey N Linc 79 M4
Kirwaugh D & G 95 M7
Kishorn Highld 135 Q8
Kislingbury Nhants 54 H9
Kitebrook Warwks 42 F5
Kite Green Warwks 53 M7
Kites Hardwick Warwks 54 D7
Kitleigh Cnwll 7 J5
Kitt Green Wigan 75 P3
Kittisford Somset 20 H9
Kittle Swans 26 E4
Kitt's Green Birm 53 M3
Kittybrewster C Aber 133 M3
Kitwood Hants 25 L7
Kivernoll Herefs 40 G5
Kiveton Park Rothm 78 E7
Knaith Lincs 79 L7
Knaith Park Lincs 79 L6
Knap Corner Dorset 22 H8
Knaphill Surrey 32 D10
Knapp Somset 21 L8
Knapp Hill Hants 24 G8
Knapthorpe Notts 79 J12
Knapton C York 85 R5
Knapton N York 92 H11
Knapton Norfk 71 L5
Knapton Green Herefs 51 M10
Knapwell Cambs 56 F8
Knaresborough N York 85 M4
Knarsdale Nthumb 99 K7
Knaven Abers 141 L7
Knayton N York 91 Q9
Knebworth Herts 45 J7
Knedlington E R Yk 86 D9
Kneesall Notts 78 H11
Kneeton Notts 66 H3
Knelston Swans 26 C4
Knenhall Staffs 64 G5
Knettishall Suffk 58 E4
Knightacott Devon 19 M5
Knightcote Warwks 54 C9
Knightley Staffs 64 E7
Knightley Dale Staffs 64 F7
Knighton BCP 11 P5
Knighton C Leic 66 G12
Knighton Devon 4 H7
Knighton Dorset 10 F2
Knighton Powys 51 J6
Knighton Somset 21 K4
Knighton Staffs 64 D2
Knighton Staffs 64 D7
Knighton Wilts 30 G8
Knighton on Teme Worcs 52 B6
Knightsbridge Gloucs 41 P6
Knightsmill Cnwll 6 F8
Knightwick Worcs 52 D9
Knill Herefs 51 J8
Knipoch Ag & B 120 F8
Knipton Leics 67 K6
Knitsley Dur 100 E8
Kniveton Derbys 65 N2
Knock Cumb 89 R1
Knock Highld 127 M2
Knock Moray 140 E5
Knock W Isls 152 g3
Knockally Highld 151 L10
Knockan Highld 144 F3
Knockando Moray 139 M7
Knockbain Highld 137 P7
Knockbain Highld 138 B5
Knock Castle N Ayrs 113 J8
Knockdee Highld 151 L4
Knockdow Ag & B 112 G6
Knockdown Wilts 29 N5
Knockeen S Ayrs 104 F10
Knockenkelly N Ayrs 103 Q4
Knockentiber E Ayrs 104 G2
Knockhall Kent 33 Q7
Knockholt Kent 33 N10
Knockholt Pound Kent 33 N10
Knockin Shrops 63 K7
Knockinlaw E Ayrs 104 H2
Knockmill Kent 33 Q10
Knocknain D & G 94 D5
Knockrome Ag & B 111 M7
Knocksharry IoM 102 c4
Knocksheen D & G 96 C2
Knockvennie Smithy D & G 96 F4
Knodishall Suffk 59 N8
Knodishall Common Suffk 59 N8
Knole Somset 22 B8
Knole Park S Glos 29 J6
Knolls Green Ches E 76 E8
Knolton Wrexhm 63 L4
Knook Wilts 23 L5
Knossington Leics 67 K10
Knott End-on-Sea Lancs 83 J6
Knotting Bed 55 P8
Knotting Green Bed 55 P8
Knottingley Wakefd 85 Q10
Knotty Ash Lpool 75 L5
Knotty Green Bucks 32 D4
Knowbury Shrops 51 P6
Knowe D & G 95 K4
Knowehead D & G 105 L11
Knoweside S Ayrs 104 E7
Knowle Bristl 29 J8
Knowle Devon 8 E4
Knowle Devon 9 J3
Knowle Devon 9 K8
Knowle Devon 19 J6
Knowle Shrops 51 P6
Knowle Solhll 53 M5
Knowle Somset 20 F5
Knowle Cross Devon 9 K5
Knowlefield Cumb 98 E7
Knowle Green Lancs 83 P7
Knowle Hill Surrey 32 E9
Knowle St Giles Somset 9 Q2
Knowle Village Hants 13 J3
Knowle Wood Calder 84 D10
Knowl Green Essex 46 D3
Knowl Hill W & M 32 B6
Knowlton Dorset 11 N3
Knowlton Kent 35 N11
Knowsley Knows 75 M4
Knowsley Safari Park Knows 75 M5
Knowstone Devon 20 C8
Knox N York 85 L4
Knox Bridge Kent 16 D3
Knoydart Highld 127 P4
Knucklas Powys 51 J6
Knuston Nhants 55 M7
Knutsford Ches E 76 D8
Knutsford Services Ches E 76 D8
Knutton Staffs 64 F3
Krumlin Calder 84 G11
Kuggar Cnwll 2 H11
Kyleakin Highld 135 N10
Kyle of Lochalsh Highld 135 N10
Kylerhea Highld 135 P11
Kylesku Highld 148 F10
Kylesmorar Highld 127 P6
Kyles Scalpay W Isls 152 f6
Kylestrome Highld 148 F9
Kynaston Herefs 41 K4
Kynaston Shrops 63 K8
Kynnersley Wrekin 64 C9
Kyre Green Worcs 51 Q8
Kyre Park Worcs 52 B8
Kyrewood Worcs 51 Q7
Kyrle Somset 20 G9

L

La Bellieuse Guern 12 c3
Lacasaigh W Isls 152 f4
Lacasdal W Isls 152 g3
Laceby NE Lin 80 D2
Lacey Green Bucks 32 B2
Lach Dennis Ches W 76 D9
Lackenby R & Cl 92 B3
Lackford Suffk 57 Q6
Lackford Green Suffk 57 Q6
Lacock Wilts 29 Q8
Ladbroke Warwks 54 C9
Ladderedge Staffs 64 H1
Laddingford Kent 16 C1
Lade Bank Lincs 68 H1
Ladock Cnwll 3 L4
Lady Ork 147 e2
Ladybank Fife 124 F11
Ladycross Cnwll 7 L7
Ladygill S Lans 106 B4
Lady Hall Cumb 88 G9
Ladykirk Border 117 K11
Ladyridge Herefs 41 J5
Lady's Green Suffk 57 P9
Ladywood Birm 53 K3
Ladywood Worcs 52 F8
La Fontenelle Guern 12 d1
La Fosse Guern 12 c3
Lag D & G 96 H1
Laga Highld 127 L12
Lagavulin Ag & B 111 J12
Lagg N Ayrs 103 P5
Laggan Highld 129 K5
Laggan Highld 130 B5
Lagganlia Highld 130 F4
La Greve Guern 12 c1
La Grève de Lecq Jersey 13 a1
La Hougue Bie Jersey 13 d2
La Houguette Guern 12 b2
Laid Highld 149 J5
Laide Highld 143 N7
Laig Highld 126 H7
Laigh Clunch E Ayrs 113 N11
Laigh Fenwick E Ayrs 104 H1
Laigh Glenmuir E Ayrs 105 L6
Laighstonehall S Lans 114 C10
Laindon Essex 34 B4
Lairg Highld 145 N4
Laisterdyke C Brad 85 J8
Laithes Cumb 98 F11
Lake Devon 7 P7
Lake Devon 19 L7
Lake IoW 13 K8
Lake Wilts 23 P5
Lake District Cumb 88 H4
Lake District National Park Cumb 88 H4
Lakenheath Suffk 57 N4
Laker's Green Surrey 14 E4
Lakes End Norfk 57 K1
Lakeside Cumb 89 K9
Laleham Surrey 32 F8
Laleston Brdgnd 27 L6
Lamanva Cnwll 3 J8
Lamarsh Essex 46 F4
Lamas Norfk 71 K7
Lambden Border 108 B1
Lamberhurst Kent 16 B4
Lamberhurst Down Kent 16 B4
Lamberton Border 117 L9
Lambeth Gt Lon 33 K6
Lambfair Green Suffk 57 N10
Lambley Notts 66 G3
Lambley Nthumb 99 K6
Lambourn W Berk 30 G6
Lambourne End Essex 33 N3
Lambourn Woodlands W Berk 30 G7
Lamb Roe Lancs 83 Q7
Lambs Green W Susx 15 J3
Lambston Pembks 36 H7
Lamellion Cnwll 4 C4
Lamerton Devon 7 N9
Lamesley Gatesd 100 G7
Lamington S Lans 106 C4
Lamlash N Ayrs 103 Q4
Lamonby Cumb 98 E11
Lamorick Cnwll 3 P2
Lamorna Cnwll 2 C9
Lamorran Cnwll 3 L6
Lampen Cnwll 4 B3
Lampeter Cerdgn 49 K11
Lampeter Velfrey Pembks 37 M7
Lamphey Pembks 37 K10
Lamplugh Cumb 88 E3
Lamport Nhants 55 J6
Lamyatt Somset 22 F6
Lana Devon 7 K3
Lana Devon 7 L5
Lanark S Lans 106 A1
Lancaster Lancs 83 L3
Lancaster Services Lancs 83 L5
Lancaut Gloucs 28 H3
Lanchester Dur 100 F9
Lancing W Susx 14 H10
L'Ancresse Guern 12 c1
Landbeach Cambs 57 J7
Landcross Devon 19 J8
Landerberry Abers 133 J3
Landford Wilts 24 D9
Land-hallow Highld 151 M10
Landimore Swans 26 C4
Landkey Devon 19 L7
Landore Swans 26 G3
Landrake Cnwll 4 E4
Landscove Devon 5 N3
Land's End Cnwll 2 B9
Land's End Airport Cnwll 2 B8
Landshipping Pembks 37 K8
Landue Cnwll 7 L9
Landulph Cnwll 4 F4
Landwade Suffk 57 M7
Lane Cnwll 3 K2
Laneast Cnwll 7 J8
Lane Bottom Lancs 84 C8
Lane End Bucks 32 A4
Lane End Cnwll 6 F11
Lane End Hants 25 J8
Lane End Kent 33 Q8
Lane End Lancs 84 C6
Lane End Warrtn 76 C5
Lane End Wilts 22 H4
Lane Ends Derbys 65 N6
Lane Ends Lancs 84 B9
Lane Ends N York 84 E6
Lane Green Staffs 64 G11
Laneham Notts 79 K8
Lane Head Dur 91 J4
Lanehead Dur 99 N10
Lanehead Nthumb 99 M1
Lane Head Wigan 76 B4
Lane Head Wsall 64 H12
Lane Heads Lancs 83 K7
Lanercost Cumb 98 H5
Laneshaw Bridge Lancs 84 D7
Lane Side Lancs 84 B10
Langaford Devon 7 M5
Langal Highld 127 N10
Langaller Somset 21 L8
Langar Notts 67 J5
Langbank Rens 113 M6
Langbar N York 84 G5
Langbaurgh N York 92 B4
Langcliffe N York 84 B2
Langdale End N York 93 J8
Langdon Cnwll 7 K6
Langdon Beck Dur 99 N12
Langdown Hants 12 G3
Langdyke Fife 124 G11
Langenhoe Essex 46 H8
Langford C Beds 44 H3
Langford Devon 9 K4
Langford Essex 46 E10
Langford Notts 79 K12
Langford Oxon 42 F11
Langford Budville Somset 20 H9
Langham Dorset 22 H8
Langham Essex 46 H5
Langham Norfk 70 E4
Langham Rutlnd 67 L10
Langham Suffk 58 E6
Langho Lancs 83 Q8
Langholm D & G 98 D1
Langland Swans 26 F5
Langlee Border 107 M3
Langley Ches E 76 H9
Langley Derbys 66 D3
Langley Gloucs 42 B6
Langley Hants 12 G4
Langley Herts 45 J7
Langley Kent 34 E12
Langley Nthumb 99 M6
Langley Oxon 42 G8
Langley Rochdl 76 F2
Langley Slough 32 E6
Langley Somset 20 H7
Langley W Susx 25 P7
Langley Warwks 53 M8
Langley Burrell Wilts 29 Q7
Langley Castle Nthumb 99 N6
Langley Common Derbys 65 P5
Langley Green Derbys 65 P4
Langley Green Essex 46 F7
Langley Green Warwks 53 M8
Langley Heath Kent 34 E12
Langley Lower Green Essex 45 N5
Langley Marsh Somset 20 G7
Langley Mill Derbys 66 D3
Langley Moor Dur 100 G10
Langley Park Dur 100 G9
Langley Street Norfk 71 M11
Langley Upper Green Essex 45 N5
Langley Vale Surrey 33 J10
Langney E Susx 16 A10
Langold Notts 78 F6
Langore Cnwll 7 K7
Langport Somset 21 P8
Langrick Lincs 68 E2
Langridge BaNES 29 L8
Langridgeford Devon 19 L9
Langrigg Cumb 97 N9
Langrish Hants 25 M8
Langsett Barns 77 N4
Langside P & K 123 K10
Langstone Hants 13 M4
Langstone Newpt 28 E4
Langthorne N York 91 L8
Langthorpe N York 85 M2
Langthwaite N York 90 G6
Langtoft E R Yk 87 J2
Langtoft Lincs 68 C9
Langton Dur 91 K3
Langton Lincs 80 E10
Langton Lincs 80 G9
Langton N York 86 E2
Langton by Wragby Lincs 80 C8
Langton Green Kent 15 Q3
Langton Green Suffk 58 H6
Langton Herring Dorset 10 F8
Langton Long Blandford Dorset 11 L4
Langton Matravers Dorset 11 N9
Langtree Devon 19 J10
Langtree Week Devon 19 J10
Langwathby Cumb 98 H11
Langwell House Highld 151 K12
Langwith Derbys 78 E9
Langwith Junction Derbys 78 E10
Langworth Lincs 79 Q8
Lanhydrock House & Gardens Cnwll 3 Q2
Lanivet Cnwll 3 P2
Lanjeth Cnwll 3 N4
Lank Cnwll 6 F9
Lanlivery Cnwll 3 Q3
Lanner Cnwll 2 H6
Lanoy Cnwll 7 K9
Lanreath Cnwll 4 B5
Lansallos Cnwll 4 B6
Lanteglos Cnwll 6 F8
Lanteglos Highway Cnwll 4 A6
Lanton Border 107 P5
Lanton Nthumb 108 E3
La Passee Guern 12 c1
Lapford Devon 8 D3
Laphroaig Ag & B 111 J12
Lapley Staffs 64 G9
La Pulente Jersey 13 a2
Lapworth Warwks 53 M6
Larachbeg Highld 120 D3
Larbert Falk 114 F5
Larbreck Lancs 83 K7
Largie Abers 140 F9
Largiemore Ag & B 112 D4
Largoward Fife 125 J11
Largs N Ayrs 113 J9
Largybeg N Ayrs 103 Q5
Largymore N Ayrs 103 R5
Larkbeare Devon 9 K5
Larkfield Inver 113 K6
Larkfield Kent 34 C10
Larkhall S Lans 114 D11
Larkhill Wilts 23 P4
Larling Norfk 58 E3
La Rocque Jersey 13 d3
La Rousaillerie Guern 12 c2
Lartington Dur 90 G3
Lasborough Gloucs 29 N3
Lasham Hants 25 L5
Lashbrook Devon 7 M3
Lashbrook Devon 7 N4
Lashenden Kent 16 E3
Lask Edge Staffs 76 G12
Lasswade Mdloth 115 P8
Lastingham N York 92 E8
Latcham Somset 21 P4
Latchford Herts 45 M7
Latchford Oxon 31 N2
Latchford Warrtn 76 B6
Latchingdon Essex 34 F2
Latchley Cnwll 7 M10
Lately Common Warrtn 76 C4
Lathbury M Keyn 44 C3
Latheron Highld 151 M10
Latheronwheel Highld 151 M10
Lathom Lancs 75 M2
Lathones Fife 125 J11
Latimer Bucks 32 E3
Latteridge S Glos 29 K5
Lattiford Somset 22 F8
Latton Wilts 30 C3
Lauder Border 116 C11
Laugharne Carmth 37 Q8
Laughterton Lincs 79 L8
Laughton E Susx 15 P8
Laughton Leics 54 H3
Laughton Lincs 67 Q6
Laughton Lincs 79 L4
Laughton-en-le-Morthen Rothm 78 E6
Launcells Cnwll 7 J4
Launcells Cross Cnwll 7 K4
Launceston Cnwll 7 L8
Launton Oxon 43 M7
Laurencekirk Abers 132 H10
Laurieston D & G 96 D5
Laurieston Falk 114 G5
Lavendon M Keyn 55 M10
Lavenham Suffk 58 D10
Lavernock V Glam 28 A8
Laversdale Cumb 98 F6

Laverstock Wilts...23 P7
Laverstoke Hants...24 H4
Laverton Gloucs...42 C4
Laverton N York...91 L12
Laverton Somset...22 H3
La Villette Guern...12 c3
Lavister Wrexhm...75 L12
Law S Lans...114 E10
Lawers P & K...122 H5
Lawford Essex...47 K5
Lawford Somset...21 J6
Law Hill S Lans...114 E11
Lawhitton Cnwll...7 L8
Lawkland N York...84 A2
Lawkland Green N York...84 B2
Lawley Wrekin...64 C10
Lawnhead Staffs...64 F7
Lawrence Weston Bristl...28 H6
Lawrenny Pembks...37 K9
Lawshall Suffk...58 C10
Lawshall Green Suffk...58 C10
Lawton Herefs...51 M9
Laxay W Isls...152 f4
Laxdale W Isls...152 g3
Laxey IoM...102 f5
Laxfield Suffk...59 L6
Laxford Bridge Highld...148 F7
Laxo Shet...147 j5
Laxton E R Yk...86 E10
Laxton Nhants...55 N1
Laxton Notts...79 J10
Laycock C Brad...84 F7
Layer Breton Essex...46 G8
Layer-de-la-Haye Essex...46 G8
Layer Marney Essex...46 G8
Layham Suffk...47 J4
Layland's Green W Berk...30 H9
Laymore Dorset...10 J4
Layter's Green Bucks...32 E4
Laytham E R Yk...86 D7
Laythes Cumb...97 P7
Lazenby R & Cl...92 C3
Lazonby Cumb...98 G10
Lea Derbys...77 Q12
Lea Herefs...41 K7
Lea Lincs...79 L6
Lea Shrops...51 K3
Lea Wilts...29 Q5
Leachkin Highld...138 B7
Leadburn Border...115 N10
Leadenham Lincs...67 N2
Leaden Roding Essex...45 Q9
Leadgate Cumb...100 K9
Leadgate Dur...100 E8
Leadgate Nthumb...100 E6
Leadhills S Lans...106 A7
Leadingcross Green Kent...34 F12
Leadmill Derbys...77 N7
Leafield Oxon...42 G8
Leagrave Luton...44 F7
Leahead Ches W...76 C10
Lea Heath Staffs...65 J7
Leake N York...91 Q8
Leake Common Side Lincs...68 H2
Lealholm N York...92 F5
Lealholm Side N York...92 F5
Lealt Highld...135 J4
Leam Derbys...77 N8
Lea Marston Warwks...53 M2
Leamington Hastings Warwks...54 D7
Leamington Spa Warwks...53 Q7
Leamside Dur...101 J9
Leap Cross E Susx...15 Q9
Leasgill Cumb...89 M10
Leasingham Lincs...67 Q2
Leasingthorne Dur...100 H12
Leatherhead Surrey...32 G11
Leathley N York...85 K6
Leaton Shrops...63 M8
Leaton Wrekin...63 Q10
Lea Town Lancs...83 L9
Leaveland Kent...34 H11
Leavenheath Suffk...46 G4
Leavening N York...86 E3
Leaves Green Gt Lon...33 M10
Lea Yeat Cumb...90 C9
Lebberston N York...93 M10
Le Bigard Guern...12 b3
Le Bourg Guern...12 c3
Le Bourg Jersey...13 d3
Lechlade on Thames Gloucs...30 E2
Lecht Gruinart Ag & B...110 G7
Leck Lancs...89 Q11
Leckbuie P & K...123 J5
Leckford Hants...24 F6
Leckhampstead Bucks...43 P4
Leckhampstead W Berk...31 J7
Leckhampstead Thicket W Berk...31 J7
Leckhampton Gloucs...41 Q8
Leckmelm Highld...144 F7
Leckwith V Glam...27 R7
Leconfield E R Yk...87 J6
Ledaig Ag & B...120 G5
Ledburn Bucks...44 D8
Ledbury Herefs...41 L4
Leddington Gloucs...41 L5
Ledgemoor Herefs...51 L10
Ledicot Herefs...51 L8
Ledmore Highld...144 G3
Ledsham Ches W...75 K9
Ledsham Leeds...85 P9
Ledston Leeds...85 N9
Ledstone Devon...5 M7
Ledston Luck Leeds...85 N9
Ledwell Oxon...43 J6
Lee Devon...19 J4
Lee Gt Lon...33 M7
Lee Hants...24 F9
Lee Shrops...63 L6
Leebotwood Shrops...51 N1
Lee Brockhurst Shrops...63 P7
Leece Cumb...82 G1
Lee Chapel Essex...34 C5
Lee Clump Bucks...44 C10
Lee Common Bucks...44 C11
Leeds Kent...34 E11
Leeds Leeds...85 L8
Leeds Bradford Airport Leeds...85 K7
Leeds Castle Kent...34 E11
Leedstown Cnwll...2 F7
Lee Green Ches E...76 C11
Leek Staffs...77 J12
Leek Wootton Warwks...53 P7
Lee Mill Devon...5 J3
Leeming C Brad...84 F8
Leeming N York...91 M9
Leeming Bar N York...91 M8
Lee Moor Devon...5 J3
Lee-on-the-Solent Hants...13 J5
Lees C Brad...84 F7
Lees Derbys...65 N5
Lees Oldham...76 H3
Lees Green Derbys...65 N5
Leesthorpe Leics...67 K9
Leeswood Flints...75 J11
Leetown P & K...124 E8
Leftwich Ches W...76 C9
Legar Powys...40 B8
Legbourne Lincs...80 G7
Legburthwaite Cumb...89 J3

Legerwood Border...107 P1
Legoland W & M...32 D7
Le Gron Guern...12 b3
Legsby Lincs...80 C6
Le Haguais Jersey...13 c3
Le Hocq Jersey...13 d3
Leicester C Leic...66 F11
Leicester Forest East Leics...66 E11
Leicester Forest East Services Leics...66 E11
Leigh Devon...19 P11
Leigh Dorset...10 F3
Leigh Gloucs...41 P6
Leigh Kent...15 Q2
Leigh Shrops...63 K11
Leigh Surrey...15 J1
Leigh Wigan...76 C4
Leigh Wilts...30 C4
Leigh Worcs...52 E10
Leigh Beck Essex...34 G6
Leigh Delamere Wilts...29 P6
Leigh Delamere Services Wilts...29 P6
Leigh Green Kent...16 F4
Leigh Knoweglass S Lans...114 B11
Leighland Chapel Somset...20 G6
Leigh-on-Sea Sthend...34 E5
Leigh Park Hants...13 M3
Leigh Sinton Worcs...52 E10
Leighswood Wsall...65 K12
Leighterton Gloucs...29 N4
Leighton N York...91 K11
Leighton Powys...62 H11
Leighton Shrops...63 Q11
Leighton Somset...22 F4
Leighton Bromswold Cambs...56 C5
Leighton Buzzard C Beds...44 C6
Leigh upon Mendip Somset...22 F4
Leigh Woods N Som...28 H8
Leinthall Earls Herefs...51 M7
Leinthall Starkes Herefs...51 M7
Leintwardine Herefs...51 L6
Leire Leics...54 E3
Leiston Suffk...59 N8
Leith C Edin...115 N6
Leitholm Border...108 C1
Lelant Cnwll...2 E7
Lelley E R Yk...87 N8
Lem Hill Worcs...52 D5
Lempitlaw Border...108 C3
Lemreway W Isls...152 g5
Lemsford Herts...45 J9
Lenchwick Worcs...42 B2
Lendalfoot S Ayrs...104 C11
Lendrick Stirlg...122 F11
Lendrum Terrace Abers...141 Q7
Lenham Kent...34 F12
Lenham Heath Kent...34 G12
Lenie Highld...137 N10
Lennel Border...108 D2
Lennox Plunton D & G...96 C8
Lennoxtown E Duns...114 B6
Lent Bucks...32 D6
Lenton C Nott...66 F4
Lenton Lincs...67 P6
Lenwade Norfk...70 G8
Lenzie E Duns...114 B7
Leochel-Cushnie Abers...132 E2
Leomansley Staffs...65 L10
Leominster Herefs...51 N9
Leonard Stanley Gloucs...41 N11
Leoville Jersey...13 a1
Lepe Hants...12 G5
Lephin Highld...134 C6
Leppington N York...86 E3
Lepton Kirk...85 J12
Lerags Ag & B...120 F7
L'Erée Guern...12 b2
Lerryn Cnwll...4 A5
Lerwick Shet...147 j7
Les Arquêts Guern...12 b3
Lesbury Nthumb...109 L7
Les Hubits Guern...12 c3
Leslie Abers...140 F11
Leslie Fife...115 N1
Les Lohiers Guern...12 b2
Lesmahagow S Lans...105 Q2
Les Murchez Guern...12 b3
Lesnewth Cnwll...6 G6
Les Nicolles Guern...12 c3
Les Quartiers Guern...12 c2
Les Quennevais Jersey...13 a2
Les Sages Guern...12 b3
Lessingham Norfk...71 M6
Lessonhall Cumb...97 P8
Lestowder Cnwll...3
Les Villets Guern...12 b3
Leswalt D & G...94 E5
L'Etacq Jersey...13 a1
Letchmore Heath Herts...32 G3
Letchworth Garden City Herts...45 J5
Letcombe Bassett Oxon...30 H5
Letcombe Regis Oxon...30 H5
Letham Angus...125 K3
Letham Border...107 Q8
Letham Falk...114 G4
Letham Fife...124 F10
Letham Grange Angus...125 M4
Lethenty Abers...140 F11
Lethenty Abers...141 K8
Letheringham Suffk...59 K9
Letheringsett Norfk...70 F4
Lettaford Devon...8 D8
Letterewe Highld...143 P11
Letterfearn Highld...136 B11
Letterfinlay Lodge Hotel Highld...129 J6
Lettermorar Highld...127 N6
Letters Highld...144 F7
Lettershaw S Lans...106 B6
Letterston Pembks...36 H4
Lettoch Highld...139 J12
Lettoch Highld...139 K9
Letton Herefs...40 D2
Letton Herefs...51 L7
Lett's Green Kent...33 N10
Letwell Rothm...78 F6
Leuchars Fife...125 J8
Leumrabhagh W Isls...152 g5
Leurbost W Isls...152 g4
Levalsa Meor Cnwll...3 N5
Levedale Staffs...64 G9
Level's Green Essex...45 N7
Leven E R Yk...87 L6
Leven Fife...115 Q1
Levens Cumb...89 M9
Levens Green Herts...45 L7
Levenshulme Manch...76 H3
Levenwick Shet...147 i9
Leverburgh W Isls...152 d6
Leverington Cambs...68 H10
Leverstock Green Herts...44 F10
Leverton Lincs...68 H3
Le Villocq Guern...12 c2
Levington Suffk...47 M4
Levisham N York...92 G8
Levishie Highld...137 M5
Lew Oxon...42 G10
Lewannick Cnwll...7 K8
Lewdown Devon...7 N7
Lewes E Susx...15 N9

Leweston Pembks...36 H6
Lewisham Gt Lon...33 M7
Lewiston Highld...137 N10
Lewistown Brdgnd...27 M5
Lewis Wych Herefs...51 M9
Lewknor Oxon...31 P3
Leworthy Devon...7 L4
Leworthy Devon...19 N6
Lewson Street Kent...34 G10
Lewth Lancs...83 L8
Lewtrenchard Devon...7 N7
Lexden Essex...46 G6
Lexworthy Somset...21 L6
Ley Cnwll...4 B3
Leybourne Kent...34 B10
Leyburn N York...91 J8
Leycett Staffs...64 E3
Leygreen Herts...44 H7
Ley Hill Bucks...44 E11
Leyland Lancs...83 M10
Leylodge Abers...133 J2
Leys Abers...141 N5
Leys P & K...124 E5
Leysdown-on-Sea Kent...35 J8
Leysmill Angus...125 M3
Leys of Cossans Angus...124 H3
Leysters Herefs...51 P8
Leyton Gt Lon...33 M5
Leytonstone Gt Lon...33 M5
Lezant Cnwll...7 L9
Lezerea Cnwll...2 H8
Lhanbryde Moray...139 P4
Libanus Powys...39 N6
Libberton S Lans...106 C1
Libbery Worcs...52 H9
Liberton C Edin...115 N7
Lichfield Staffs...65 L10
Lickey Worcs...53 J5
Lickey End Worcs...52 H6
Lickey Rock Worcs...52 H6
Lickfold W Susx...14 C5
Liddaton Green Devon...7 N8
Liddesdale Highld...127 P12
Liddington Swindn...30 E6
Lidgate Derbys...77 P8
Lidgate Suffk...57 N9
Lidget Donc...78 G4
Lidgett Notts...78 G10
Lidham Hill E Susx...16 E7
Lidlington C Beds...44 E4
Lidsey W Susx...14 D10
Lidsing Kent...34 D10
Liff Angus...124 G6
Lifford Birm...53 K5
Lifton Devon...7 M8
Liftondown Devon...7 L7
Lighthorne Warwks...53 Q9
Lighthorne Heath Warwks...54 B9
Lightwater Surrey...32 D10
Lightwater Valley Theme Park N York...91 M11
Lightwood C Stke...64 G4
Lightwood Green Ches E...64 B4
Lightwood Green Wrexhm...63 L4
Lilbourne Nhants...54 F5
Lilburn Tower Nthumb...108 G5
Lilleshall Wrekin...64 D9
Lilley Herts...44 G6
Lilley W Berk...31 J6
Lilliesleaf Border...107 N5
Lillingstone Dayrell Bucks...43 P4
Lillingstone Lovell Bucks...43 P4
Lillington Dorset...22 E11
Lilliput BCP...11 P7
Lilstock Somset...21 J4
Lilyhurst Shrops...64 D9
Limbrick Lancs...83 N10
Limbury Luton...44 F7
Limebrook Herefs...51 L7
Limefield Bury...76 E1
Limekilnburn S Lans...114 C11
Limekilns Fife...115 K5
Limerigg Falk...114 F7
Limerstone IoW...12 G8
Lime Street Worcs...41 N5
Limington Somset...22 C9
Limmerhaugh E Ayrs...105 L4
Limpenhoe Norfk...71 M11
Limpley Stoke Wilts...29 M10
Limpsfield Surrey...33 M11
Limpsfield Chart Surrey...33 M12
Linby Notts...66 E2
Linchmere W Susx...14 B5
Lincluden D & G...97 K3
Lincoln Lincs...79 N9
Lincomb Worcs...52 F7
Lincombe Devon...5 M8
Lincombe Devon...19 K4
Lindale Cumb...89 L10
Lindal in Furness Cumb...88 H11
Lindfield W Susx...15 L5
Lindford Hants...25 P6
Lindley Kirk...84 H11
Lindley N York...85 K5
Lindores Fife...124 F9
Lindow End Ches E...76 H6
Lindridge Worcs...52 C7
Lindsell Essex...46 B6
Lindsey Suffk...46 H3
Lindsey Tye Suffk...46 H3
Liney Somset...21 N6
Linford Hants...11 M3
Linford Thurr...34 B6
Lingbob C Brad...84 G8
Lingdale R & Cl...92 D3
Lingen Herefs...51 L7
Lingfield Surrey...15 M2
Lingwood Norfk...71 M10
Liniclate W Isls...152 c9
Linicro Highld...134 G2
Linkend Worcs...41 N5
Linkenholt Hants...30 H10
Linkhill Kent...16 E5
Linkinhorne Cnwll...7 L10
Linktown Fife...115 N3
Linkwood Moray...139 K2
Linley Shrops...51 K2
Linley Green Herefs...52 C11
Linleygreen Shrops...52 C1
Linlithgow W Loth...114 H6
Linshiels Nthumb...108 E8
Linsidemore Highld...145 M5
Linslade C Beds...44 C7
Linstead Parva Suffk...59 L5
Linstock Cumb...98 E6
Linthurst Worcs...53 J6
Linthwaite Kirk...84 G12
Lintlaw Border...117 J9
Lintmill Moray...140 D3
Linton Border...108 C4
Linton Cambs...45 Q3
Linton Derbys...65 N9
Linton Herefs...41 K6
Linton Kent...34 D12
Linton Leeds...85 N6
Linton N York...84 G2
Linton Nthumb...109 L11
Linton Heath Derbys...65 N9
Linton Hill Herefs...41 K7
Linton-on-Ouse N York...85 P3
Linwood Hants...11 M3
Linwood Lincs...80 B6

Linwood Rens...113 N8
Lionacleit W Isls...152 c9
Lional W Isls...152 h1
Lions Green E Susx...15 Q7
Liphook Hants...25 P7
Lipley Shrops...64 D5
Liscard Wirral...75 J5
Liscombe Somset...20 D7
Liskeard Cnwll...4 C4
Lismore Ag & B...120 F4
Liss Hants...25 N8
Lissett E R Yk...87 L4
Liss Forest Hants...25 N7
Lissington Lincs...80 D7
Liston Essex...46 E3
Lisvane Cardif...28 B6
Liswerry Newpt...28 D5
Litcham Norfk...70 C8
Litchard Brdgnd...27 M6
Litchborough Nhants...54 G10
Litchfield Hants...24 G3
Litherland Sefton...75 K4
Litlington Cambs...45 K3
Litlington E Susx...15 P10
Little Abington Cambs...57 K10
Little Addington Nhants...55 N6
Little Airies D & G...95 M8
Little Almshoe Herts...44 H6
Little Alne Warwks...53 L8
Little Altcar Sefton...75 J2
Little Amwell Herts...45 L9
Little Asby Cumb...90 A5
Little Aston Staffs...65 K12
Little Atherfield IoW...12 H9
Little Ayton N York...92 B5
Little Baddow Essex...46 D10
Little Badminton S Glos...29 N5
Little Bampton Cumb...98 B7
Little Bardfield Essex...46 B5
Little Barford Bed...56 D9
Little Barningham Norfk...70 H5
Little Barrington Gloucs...42 E9
Little Barrow Ches W...75 M9
Little Barugh N York...92 F10
Little Bavington Nthumb...100 C3
Little Bealings Suffk...59 J11
Littlebeck N York...92 H6
Little Bedwyn Wilts...30 G9
Little Bentley Essex...47 K6
Little Berkhamsted Herts...45 K10
Little Billing Nhants...55 M8
Little Billington C Beds...44 D7
Little Birch Herefs...40 G5
Little Bispham Bpool...82 H7
Little Blakenham Suffk...58 G11
Little Blencow Cumb...98 F11
Little Bloxwich Wsall...65 J11
Little Bognor W Susx...14 E7
Little Bolehill Derbys...65 P1
Little Bollington Ches E...76 D6
Little Bookham Surrey...32 G11
Littleborough Devon...8 F3
Littleborough Notts...79 K7
Littleborough Rochdl...84 D12
Littlebourne Kent...35 M10
Little Bourton Oxon...43 K3
Little Bradley Suffk...57 N10
Little Brampton Herefs...51 J8
Little Brampton Shrops...51 L4
Little Braxted Essex...46 E8
Little Brechin Angus...132 F11
Littlebredy Dorset...10 F7
Little Brickhill M Keyn...44 C5
Little Bridgeford Staffs...64 G7
Little Brington Nhants...54 H8
Little Bromley Essex...47 K6
Little Broughton Cumb...97 M11
Little Budworth Ches W...75 Q10
Littleburn Highld...138 B5
Little Burstead Essex...34 B4
Little Bytham Lincs...67 P8
Little Canfield Essex...45 Q7
Little Carlton Lincs...80 H6
Little Carlton Notts...79 K12
Little Casterton Rutlnd...67 P10
Little Catwick E R Yk...87 L6
Little Catworth Cambs...56 B6
Little Cawthorpe Lincs...80 G7
Little Chalfont Bucks...32 E3
Little Chart Kent...16 G2
Little Chesterford Essex...45 P3
Little Cheveney Kent...16 C2
Little Cheverell Wilts...23 L3
Little Chishill Cambs...45 M4
Little Clacton Essex...47 L8
Little Clanfield Oxon...30 F2
Little Clifton Cumb...88 E1
Little Coates NE Lin...80 E2
Little Comberton Worcs...41 Q3
Little Common E Susx...16 C9
Little Comp Kent...34 B11
Little Compton Warwks...42 F6
Little Corby Cumb...98 F6
Little Cornard Suffk...46 F4
Littlecott Wilts...23 P3
Little Cowarne Herefs...51 Q10
Little Coxwell Oxon...30 G4
Little Crakehall N York...91 L8
Little Cransley Nhants...55 L6
Little Cressingham Norfk...70 C12
Little Crosby Sefton...75 K3
Little Crosthwaite Cumb...88 H1
Little Cubley Derbys...65 M5
Little Dalby Leics...67 K9
Littledean Gloucs...41 L9
Little Dewchurch Herefs...40 H5
Little Ditton Cambs...57 M9
Little Doward Herefs...40 H8
Littledown Hants...30 H10
Little Downham Cambs...57 K4
Little Driffield E R Yk...87 J4
Little Dunham Norfk...70 C9
Little Dunkeld P & K...123 P4
Little Dunmow Essex...46 C7
Little Durnford Wilts...23 N7
Little Easton Essex...45 R7
Little Eaton Derbys...66 B4
Little Ellingham Norfk...70 E12
Little Everdon Nhants...54 F9
Little Eversden Cambs...56 G10
Little Faringdon Oxon...42 E10
Little Fencote N York...91 M8
Little Fenton N York...85 P8
Little Fransham Norfk...70 D9
Little Gaddesden Herts...44 D9
Little Garway Herefs...40 F7
Little Gidding Cambs...56 C4
Little Glemham Suffk...59 L9
Little Gorsley Herefs...41 K7
Little Gransden Cambs...56 E9
Little Green Notts...67 J3
Little Green Somset...22 F4
Little Grimsby Lincs...80 F5
Little Gringley Notts...79 J7
Little Habton N York...92 F10
Little Hadham Herts...45 N7
Little Hale Lincs...68 B3
Little Hallam Derbys...66 D4
Little Hallingbury Essex...45 P8
Littleham Devon...8 B8
Littleham Devon...18 H6
Little Hampden Bucks...44 B11

Littlehampton W Susx...14 E10
Little Hanford Dorset...11 K2
Little Harrowden Nhants...55 L6
Little Haseley Oxon...31 N2
Little Hatfield E R Yk...87 M6
Little Hautbois Norfk...71 K8
Little Haven Pembks...36 G8
Little Haven W Susx...14 H4
Little Hay Staffs...65 L11
Little Hayfield Derbys...77 J6
Little Haywood Staffs...65 J8
Little Heath Staffs...64 G8
Little Heath W Berk...31 N4
Littlehempston Devon...5 N4
Little Hereford Herefs...51 P7
Little Horkesley Essex...46 G5
Little Hormead Herts...45 M6
Little Horsted E Susx...15 N7
Little Horton Wilts...30 B10
Little Horwood Bucks...43 P6
Little Houghton Barns...78 C2
Little Houghton Nhants...55 L8
Littlehoughton Nthumb...109 L6
Little Hucklow Derbys...77 M8
Little Hulton Salfd...76 D3
Little Hungerford W Berk...31 L7
Little Hutton N York...91 Q11
Little Irchester Nhants...55 M7
Little Kelk E R Yk...87 K3
Little Keyford Somset...22 H4
Little Kimble Bucks...44 B10
Little Kineton Warwks...53 Q10
Little Kingshill Bucks...32 C3
Little Knox D & G...96 G6
Little Langdale Cumb...89 J6
Little Langford Wilts...23 N6
Little Laver Essex...45 Q9
Little Leigh Ches W...76 B8
Little Leighs Essex...46 C8
Little Lever Bolton...76 D2
Little Linford M Keyn...44 B3
Little Load Somset...21 P8
Little London Bucks...43 N9
Little London Cambs...56 H1
Little London E Susx...15 Q8
Little London Essex...45 M6
Little London Gloucs...41 L8
Little London Hants...24 F3
Little London Hants...31 N10
Little London Leeds...85 J7
Little London Lincs...68 E7
Little London Lincs...68 H7
Little London Norfk...69 N11
Little London Norfk...71 J7
Little London Powys...50 E3
Little Longstone Derbys...77 M9
Little Malvern Worcs...41 M4
Little Mancot Flints...75 K10
Little Maplestead Essex...46 E5
Little Marcle Herefs...41 K4
Little Marland Devon...19 K11
Little Marlow Bucks...32 C5
Little Massingham Norfk...69 Q7
Little Melton Norfk...70 H10
Little Mill Mons...40 D11
Little Milton Oxon...31 N2
Little Missenden Bucks...32 C3
Littlemoor Derbys...78 B11
Littlemoor Dorset...10 H8
Little Moor Somset...21 M7
Littlemore Oxon...43 L11
Littlemoss Tamesd...76 H3
Little Musgrave Cumb...90 C4
Little Ness Shrops...63 L8
Little Neston Ches W...75 J8
Little Newcastle Pembks...37 J5
Little Newsham Dur...91 J3
Little Norton Somset...21 P11
Little Oakley Essex...47 M6
Little Oakley Nhants...55 M3
Little Odell Bed...55 N9
Little Offley Herts...44 G6
Little Ormside Cumb...90 B3
Little Orton Cumb...98 D6
Little Ouse Cambs...57 M3
Little Ouseburn N York...85 P3
Littleover C Derb...66 B5
Little Oxendon Nhants...55 J4
Little Packington Warwks...53 N4
Little Pattenden Kent...16 C2
Little Paxton Cambs...56 D8
Little Petherick Cnwll...6 D10
Little Plumpton Lancs...83 J8
Little Plumstead Norfk...71 L9
Little Ponton Lincs...67 M5
Littleport Cambs...57 L3
Littleport Bridge Cambs...57 L3
Little Posbrook Hants...13 J4
Little Potheridge Devon...19 K10
Little Preston Leeds...85 L9
Little Preston Nhants...54 E9
Little Raveley Cambs...56 E5
Little Reedness E R Yk...86 E10
Little Ribston N York...85 M4
Little Rissington Gloucs...42 D8
Little Rollright Oxon...42 G6
Little Rowsley Derbys...77 N10
Little Ryburgh Norfk...70 E6
Little Ryle Nthumb...108 G6
Little Ryton Shrops...63 N11
Little Salkeld Cumb...98 H11
Little Sampford Essex...46 B5
Little Sandhurst Br For...32 B10
Little Saredon Staffs...64 H10
Little Saughall Ches W...75 L10
Little Saxham Suffk...57 Q8
Little Scatwell Highld...137 L4
Little Shelford Cambs...57 J10
Little Shrewley Warwks...53 N7
Little Silver Devon...8 B4
Little Singleton Lancs...83 J8
Little Skipwith N York...86 C7
Little Smeaton N York...85 Q11
Little Snoring Norfk...70 E6
Little Sodbury S Glos...29 M6
Little Sodbury End S Glos...29 M5
Little Somborne Hants...24 F7
Little Somerford Wilts...29 Q5
Little Soudley Shrops...64 D7
Little Stainforth N York...84 B2
Little Stainton Darltn...91 N3
Little Stanion Nhants...55 M3
Little Staughton Bed...56 B8
Little Steeping Lincs...80 H11
Little Stoke Staffs...64 G5
Littlestone-on-Sea Kent...17 K6
Little Stonham Suffk...58 G8
Little Stretton Leics...67 J11
Little Stretton Shrops...51 M2
Little Strickland Cumb...89 P3
Little Stukeley Cambs...56 C5
Little Sugnall Staffs...64 F5
Little Sutton Ches W...75 K8
Little Sutton Shrops...51 P4
Little Swinburne Nthumb...99 Q3
Little Sypland D & G...96 D7
Little Tew Oxon...42 H7
Little Tey Essex...46 F7
Little Thetford Cambs...57 K5
Little Thirkleby N York...91 Q11
Little Thornage Norfk...70 F4
Little Thornton Lancs...83 J7
Little Thorpe Dur...101 L4
Littlethorpe Leics...54 E1
Littlethorpe N York...85 L1
Little Thurlow Suffk...57 N10
Little Thurlow Green Suffk...57 N10
Little Thurrock Thurr...34 A7
Littleton Angus...124 G3
Littleton BaNES...28 H9
Littleton D & G...96 D7
Littleton Dorset...11 L4
Littleton Hants...24 G7
Littleton Somset...22 C7
Littleton Surrey...14 D1
Littleton Surrey...32 F8
Littleton Drew Wilts...29 N6
Littleton-on-Severn S Glos...29 J4
Littleton Pannell Wilts...23 M3
Little Torrington Devon...19 J10
Little Totham Essex...46 F9
Little Town Cumb...88 H3
Little Town Lancs...83 P8
Little Town Warrtn...76 B5
Little Twycross Leics...65 Q11
Little Urswick Cumb...88 H12
Little Wakering Essex...34 G5
Little Walden Essex...45 Q3
Little Waldingfield Suffk...46 G3
Little Walsingham Norfk...70 D5
Little Waltham Essex...46 C9
Little Warley Essex...33 R4
Little Washbourne Gloucs...42 A5
Little Weighton E R Yk...87 J8
Little Welnetham Suffk...58 C9
Little Welton Lincs...80 F6
Little Wenham Suffk...47 K4
Little Wenlock Wrekin...64 C10
Little Weston Somset...22 C8
Little Whitefield IoW...13 K7
Little Whittingham Green Suffk...59 K5
Littlewick Green W & M...32 B6
Little Wilbraham Cambs...57 K9
Little Windsor Dorset...10 C4
Little Witcombe Gloucs...41 P8
Little Witley Worcs...52 F8
Little Wittenham Oxon...31 M4
Little Wolford Warwks...42 F5
Littleworth Bed...55 Q10
Littleworth Oxon...30 G3
Littleworth Staffs...64 H7
Littleworth Staffs...65 J9
Littleworth W Susx...14 H7
Littleworth Worcs...52 G10
Littleworth Common Bucks...32 D5
Little Wratting Suffk...46 C2
Little Wymington Bed...55 N7
Little Wymondley Herts...45 J6
Little Wyrley Staffs...65 J11
Little Wytheford Shrops...63 P8
Little Yeldham Essex...46 D4
Littley Green Essex...46 C8
Litton Derbys...77 M8
Litton N York...90 E12
Litton Somset...22 D2
Litton Cheney Dorset...10 E6
Liurbost W Isls...152 g4
Liverpool Lpool...75 K5
Liverpool Maritime Mercantile City Lpool...75 K6
Liversedge Kirk...85 J10
Liverton Devon...8 C9
Liverton R & Cl...92 E3
Liverton Mines R & Cl...92 E3
Liverton Street Kent...34 F12
Livingston W Loth...115 K7
Livingston Village W Loth...115 J8
Lixwm Flints...74 G9
Lizard Cnwll...2 H12
Llaingoch IoA...72 C7
Llaithddu Powys...50 E5
Llan Powys...61 Q12
Llanaber Gwynd...61 K8
Llanaelhaearn Gwynd...60 F3
Llanafan Cerdgn...49 M6
Llanafan-Fawr Powys...50 C9
Llanafan-fechan Powys...50 D10
Llanallgo IoA...72 H6
Llananno Powys...50 E6
Llanarmon Gwynd...60 G4
Llanarmon Dyffryn Ceiriog Wrexhm...62 G6
Llanarmon-yn-Ial Denbgs...74 G12
Llanarth Cerdgn...48 G9
Llanarth Mons...40 E9
Llanarthne Carmth...38 D7
Llanasa Flints...74 F7
Llanbabo IoA...72 F6
Llanbadarn Fawr Cerdgn...49 K4
Llanbadarn Fynydd Powys...50 F5
Llanbadarn-y-garreg Powys...50 F11
Llanbadoc Mons...28 E2
Llanbadrig IoA...72 F5
Llanbeder Newpt...28 E4
Llanbedr Gwynd...61 K7
Llanbedr Powys...39 Q2
Llanbedr Powys...40 B9
Llanbedr-Dyffryn-Clwyd Denbgs...74 G11
Llanbedrgoch IoA...72 H7
Llanbedrog Gwynd...60 E6
Llanbedr-y-Cennin Conwy...73 N10
Llanberis Gwynd...73 K11
Llanbethêry V Glam...27 P8
Llanbister Powys...50 F6
Llanblethian V Glam...27 N7
Llanboidy Carmth...37 P5
Llanbradach Caerph...27 Q4
Llancadle V Glam...27 P8
Llancarfan V Glam...27 P8
Llancayo Mons...40 E11
Llancloudy Herefs...40 G7
Llancynfelyn Cerdgn...49 L2
Llandaff Cardif...27 Q7
Llandanwg Gwynd...61 K7
Llandarcy Neath...26 H3
Llandawke Carmth...37 N6
Llanddaniel Fab IoA...72 H9
Llanddarog Carmth...38 C8
Llanddeiniol Cerdgn...49 K6
Llanddeiniolen Gwynd...73 J10
Llandderfel Gwynd...62 D6
Llanddeusant Carmth...38 H4
Llanddeusant IoA...72 E6
Llanddew Powys...39 N5
Llanddewi Swans...26 C6
Llanddewi Brefi Cerdgn...49 M9
Llanddewi'r Cwm Powys...50 E11
Llanddewi Rhydderch Mons...40 D9
Llanddewi Velfrey Pembks...37 M7

Llanddewi Ystradenni Powys...50 F7
Llanddoged Conwy...73 P11
Llanddona IoA...73 J8
Llanddowror Carmth...37 P7
Llanddulas Conwy...74 B8
Llanddwywe Gwynd...61 K8
Llanddyfnan IoA...72 H8
Llandecwyn Gwynd...61 K5
Llandefaelog Powys...39 N5
Llandefaelog-Tre'r-Graig Powys...39 Q6
Llandefalle Powys...39 Q4
Llandegfan IoA...73 J9
Llandegla Denbgs...74 H2
Llandegley Powys...50 F8
Llandegveth Mons...28 D3
Llandegwning Gwynd...60 D6
Llandeilo Carmth...38 F7
Llandeilo Graban Powys...39 Q3
Llandeilo'r Fan Powys...39 L5
Llandeloy Pembks...36 G5
Llandenny Mons...28 E2
Llandevaud Newpt...28 E4
Llandevenny Mons...28 F5
Llandinabo Herefs...40 G6
Llandinam Powys...50 D4
Llandissilio Pembks...37 M5
Llandogo Mons...40 H10
Llandough V Glam...27 M7
Llandough V Glam...27 R8
Llandovery Carmth...39 J5
Llandow V Glam...27 M7
Llandre Carmth...38 G3
Llandre Cerdgn...49 K3
Llandre Isaf Pembks...37 M5
Llandrillo Denbgs...62 E5
Llandrillo-yn-Rhos Conwy...73 P7
Llandrindod Wells Powys...50 E8
Llandrinio Powys...63 J8
Llandudno Conwy...73 N7
Llandudno Junction Conwy...73 N8
Llandulas Powys...39 L3
Llandwrog Gwynd...60 G1
Llandybie Carmth...38 E6
Llandyfaelog Carmth...38 B9
Llandyfriog Cerdgn...37 Q2
Llandyfrydog IoA...72 H6
Llandygai Gwynd...73 K9
Llandygwydd Cerdgn...37 P2
Llandynan Denbgs...62 G2
Llandyrnog Denbgs...74 F10
Llandyssil Powys...50 F2
Llandysul Cerdgn...38 B3
Llanedeyrn Cardif...28 B3
Llanedi Carmth...38 E8
Llaneglwys Powys...39 P4
Llanegryn Gwynd...61 K11
Llanegwad Carmth...38 D7
Llaneilian IoA...72 H5
Llanelian-yn-Rhôs Conwy...73 Q8
Llanelidan Denbgs...62 F2
Llanelieu Powys...40 A5
Llanellen Mons...40 D9
Llanelli Carmth...26 D3
Llanelltyd Gwynd...61 M8
Llanelly Mons...40 B8
Llanelly Hill Mons...40 B9
Llanelwedd Powys...50 E10
Llanenddwyn Gwynd...61 K7
Llanengan Gwynd...60 D7
Llanerch Gwynd...62 B9
Llanerchymedd IoA...72 G6
Llanerfyl Powys...62 C11
Llanfachraeth IoA...72 E7
Llanfachreth Gwynd...61 N7
Llanfaelog IoA...72 E7
Llanfaelrhys Gwynd...60 C7
Llanfaenor Mons...40 F9
Llanfaes IoA...73 K8
Llanfaes Powys...39 N6
Llanfaethlu IoA...72 E6
Llanfair Caereinion Powys...62 F11
Llanfair Clydogau Cerdgn...49 M9
Llanfair Dyffryn Clwyd Denbgs...62 F1
Llanfairfechan Conwy...73 L9
Llanfair Kilgeddin Mons...40 D10
Llanfair-Nant-Gwyn Pembks...37 M3
Llanfairpwllgwyngyll IoA...73 J9
Llanfair Talhaiarn Conwy...74 C9
Llanfair Waterdine Shrops...50 H5
Llanfairynghornwy IoA...72 E5
Llanfair-yn-Neubwll IoA...72 E7
Llanfallteg Carmth...37 M6
Llanfallteg West Carmth...37 M6
Llanfarian Cerdgn...49 K5
Llanfechain Powys...62 G9
Llanfechell IoA...72 F5
Llanferres Denbgs...74 G11
Llanfigael IoA...72 E7
Llanfihangel-ar-arth Carmth...38 C4
Llanfihangel Glyn Myfyr Conwy...62 D2
Llanfihangel Nant Bran Powys...39 M5
Llanfihangel-nant-Melan Powys...50 G9
Llanfihangel Rhydithon Powys...50 G7
Llanfihangel Rogiet Mons...28 F5
Llanfihangel Tal-y-llyn Powys...39 Q6
Llanfihangel-uwch-Gwili Carmth...38 D7
Llanfihangel-y-Creuddyn Cerdgn...49 L5
Llanfihangel-yng-Ngwynfa Powys...62 E9
Llanfihangel yn Nhowyn IoA...72 E8
Llanfihangel-y-pennant Gwynd...61 J3
Llanfihangel-y-pennant Gwynd...61 L10
Llanfihangel-y-traethau Gwynd...61 K5
Llanfilo Powys...39 Q5
Llanfoist Mons...40 C9
Llanfor Gwynd...61 Q5
Llanfrechfa Torfn...28 D4
Llanfrothen Gwynd...61 L4
Llanfrynach Powys...39 N6
Llanfwrog Denbgs...62 F1
Llanfwrog IoA...72 E6
Llanfyllin Powys...62 F9
Llanfynydd Carmth...38 E6
Llanfynydd Flints...75 J12
Llanfyrnach Pembks...37 N4
Llangadfan Powys...62 D10
Llangadog Carmth...38 G5
Llangadwaladr IoA...72 F10
Llangadwaladr Powys...62 F7

Llangaffo IoA 72 G10
Llangain Carmth 38 B8
Llangammarch Wells
Powys 39 M2
Llangan V Glam 27 M7
Llangarron Herefs 40 H7
Llangasty-Talyllyn Powys ..39 Q6
Llangathen Carmth 38 E7
Llangattock Powys 40 B8
Llangattock Lingoed
Mons 40 E7
Llangattock-Vibon-Avel
Mons 40 F10
Llangedwyn Powys 62 G7
Llangefni IoA 72 G8
Llangeinor Brdgnd 27 L5
Llangeitho Cerdgn 49 K8
Llangeler Carmth 38 B4
Llangelynin Gwynd 61 K10
Llangendeirne Carmth 38 C9
Llangennech Carmth 26 C4
Llangennith Swans 26 C4
Llangenny Powys 40 C8
Llangernyw Conwy 73 Q10
Llangian Gwynd 60 E6
Llangiwg Neath 38 H10
Llangloffan Pembks 36 H4
Llanglydwen Carmth 37 N5
Llangoed IoA 73 K8
Llangoedmor Cerdgn 48 C11
Llangollen Denbgs 62 H4
Llangolman Pembks 37 M5
Llangors Powys 39 Q6
Llangorwen Cerdgn 49 K6
Llangovan Mons 40 F10
Llangower Gwynd 62 D3
Llangrannog Cerdgn 48 E10
Llangristiolus IoA 72 G9
Llangrove Herefs 40 H8
Llangua Mons 40 E8
Llangunllo Powys 50 H6
Llangunnor Carmth 38 C7
Llangurig Powys 50 B5
Llangwm Conwy 62 C3
Llangwm Mons 28 F2
Llangwm Pembks 37 J8
Llangwnnadl Gwynd 60 C5
Llangwyfan Denbgs 74 F10
Llangwyllog IoA 72 G8
Llangwyryfon Cerdgn 49 K10
Llangybi Cerdgn 49 K10
Llangybi Gwynd 60 G4
Llangybi Mons 28 E3
Llangyfelach Swans 26 B3
Llangynhafal Denbgs 74 F11
Llangynidr Powys 39 R8
Llangynin Carmth 37 R2
Llangynllo Cerdgn 37 R2
Llangynog Carmth 37 R9
Llangynog Powys 62 E7
Llangynwyd Brdgnd 27 K5
Llanhamlach Powys 39 P6
Llanharan Rhondd 27 L6
Llanharry Rhondd 27 N6
Llanhennock Mons 28 E2
Llanhilleth Blae G 28 B2
Llanidan IoA 72 H10
Llanidloes Powys 50 C4
Llaniestyn Gwynd 60 D5
Llanigon Powys 40 A6
Llanilar Cerdgn 49 K6
Llanilid Rhondd 27 M6
Llanina Cerdgn 48 F8
Llanio Cerdgn 49 L9
Llanishen Cardif 28 A6
Llanishen Mons 40 G11
Llanllechid Gwynd 73 K10
Llanlleonfel Powys 50 C10
Llanllowell Mons 28 E3
Llanllugan Powys 62 E11
Llanllwch Carmth 38 B8
Llanllwchaiarn Powys 50 F2
Llanllwni Carmth 38 D4
Llanllyfni Gwynd 60 H2
Llanmadoc Swans 26 C4
Llanmaes V Glam 27 M8
Llanmartin Newpt 28 E4
Llanmerewig Powys 50 G2
Llanmihangel V Glam 27 M8
Llanmiloe Carmth 37 P9
Llanmorlais Swans 26 C4
Llannefydd Conwy 73 K8
Llannon Carmth 38 E10
Llannor Gwynd 60 F5
Llanon Cerdgn 48 H7
Llanover Mons 40 D9
Llanpumsaint Carmth 38 B6
Llanrhaeadr-ym-
Mochnant Powys 62 F7
Llanrhian Pembks 36 H4
Llanrhidian Swans 26 D4
Llanrhos Conwy 73 N7
Llanrhychwyn Conwy 73 N11
Llanrhyddlad IoA 72 E6
Llanrhystud Cerdgn 48 H7
Llanrothal Herefs 40 G8
Llanrug Gwynd 73 J11
Llanrumney Cardif 28 B6
Llanrwst Conwy 73 P11
Llansadurnen Carmth 37 Q8
Llansadwrn Carmth 38 G5
Llansadwrn IoA 73 J8
Llansaint Carmth 38 B10
Llansamlet Swans 26 B3
Llansanffraid Glan
Conwy Conwy 73 P8
Llansannan Conwy 74 C10
Llansannor V Glam 27 M7
Llansantffraed Powys 39 Q7
Llansantffraed-
Cwmdeuddwr Powys 50 C7
Llansantffraed-in-Elvel
Powys 39 F9
Llansantffraid Cerdgn 49 J7
Llansantffraid-ym-
Mechain Powys 62 H8
Llansawel Carmth 38 F4
Llansilin Powys 62 H6
Llansoy Mons 40 F11
Llanspyddid Powys 39 N6
Llanstadwell Pembks 37 R8
Llansteffan Carmth 37 R8
Llanstephan Powys 39 Q3
Llantarnam Torfn 28 D4
Llanteg Pembks 37 N8
Llanthewy Skirrid Mons ..40 D8
Llanthony Mons 40 D7
Llantilio-Crossenny
Mons 40 E8
Llantilio Pertholey Mons ..40 D8
Llantood Pembks 37 M2
Llantrisant IoA 72 F7
Llantrisant Mons 28 E3
Llantrisant Rhondd 27 P6
Llantrithyd V Glam 27 N7
Llantwit Fardre Rhondd ...27 P5
Llantwit Major V Glam ...27 M8
Llantysilio Denbgs 62 H3
Llanuwchllyn Gwynd 61 Q6
Llanvaches Newpt 28 F4
Llanvair Discoed Mons ...28 F4
Llanvapley Mons 40 E9
Llanvetherine Mons 40 E8
Llanveynoe Herefs 40 D5
Llanvihangel Crucorney
Mons 40 D7

Llanvihangel Gobion
Mons 40 D9
Llanvihangel-Ystern-
Llewern Mons 40 F9
Llanwarne Herefs 40 G6
Llanwddyn Powys 62 D8
Llanwenarth Mons 40 C8
Llanwenog Cerdgn 38 D3
Llanwern Newpt 28 E5
Llanwinio Carmth 37 P5
Llanwnda Gwynd 72 H12
Llanwnda Pembks 36 H3
Llanwnnen Cerdgn 38 D2
Llanwnog Powys 50 D2
Llanwonno Rhondd 27 N3
Llanwrda Carmth 38 H5
Llanwrin Powys 61 N11
Llanwrthwl Powys 50 D8
Llanwrtyd Powys 49 Q11
Llanwrtyd Wells Powys ...39 L2
Llanyblodwel Shrops 62 H7
Llanybri Carmth 37 R8
Llanybydder Carmth 38 D3
Llanycefn Pembks 37 L6
Llanychaer Pembks 37 J3
Llanycil Gwynd 62 B5
Llanycrwys Carmth 38 F3
Llanymawddwy Gwynd ...62 B8
Llanymynech Powys 62 H7
Llanynghenedl IoA 72 E7
Llanynys Denbgs 74 F11
Llan-y-pwll Wrexhm 63 L2
Llanyre Powys 50 E8
Llanystumdwy Gwynd 60 H4
Llanywern Powys 39 Q6
Llawhaden Pembks 37 L7
Llawnt Shrops 62 H6
Llawryglyn Powys 50 C2
Llay Wrexhm 63 K1
Llechcynfarwy IoA 72 F7
Llechfaen Powys 39 P6
Llechrhyd Caerph 39 Q10
Llechryd Cerdgn 37 N2
Llechylched IoA 72 F7
Lledrod Cerdgn 49 L6
Lleyn Peninsula Gwynd ...60 E5
Llidiardau Gwynd 61 Q4
Llidiartnenog Carmth 38 E4
Llidiart-y-parc Denbgs 62 F3
Llithfaen Gwynd 60 F4
Lloc Flints 74 G8
Llowes Powys 40 B3
Llwydcoed Rhondd 39 N10
Llwydiarth Powys 62 E9
Llwyncelyn Cerdgn 48 G8
Llwyndafydd Cerdgn 48 E9
Llwynderw Powys 62 H11
Llwyn-drain Pembks 37 P4
Llwyn-du Mons 40 C8
Llwyndyrys Gwynd 60 F4
Llwyngwril Gwynd 61 K10
Llwynhendy Carmth 26 E2
Llwynmawr Wrexhm 62 H5
Llwyn-on Myr Td 39 N9
Llwyn-y-brain Carmth 37 N7
Llwyn-y-groes Cerdgn 49 K9
Llwynypia Rhondd 27 N4
Llynclys Shrops 63 J7
Llynfaes IoA 72 G8
Llyn-y-pandy Flints 74 H10
Llysfaen Conwy 74 B8
Llyswen Cerdgn 48 G8
Llyswen Powys 39 Q4
Llysworney V Glam 27 M7
Llys-y-frân Pembks 37 K6
Llywel Powys 39 K6
Load Brook Sheff 77 P1
Loan Falk 114 H6
Loanend Nthumb 117 L11
Loanhead Mdloth 115 P8
Loaningfoot D & G 97 J7
Loans S Ayrs 104 F3
Lobb Devon 19 J6
Lobhillcross Devon 7 N4
Lochailort Highld 127 P8
Lochaline Highld 120 C4
Lochans D & G 94 F7
Locharbriggs D & G 97 K2
Lochavich Ag & B 120 H9
Lochawe Ag & B 120 H7
Loch Baghasdail W Isls ..152 c11
Lochboisdale W Isls 152 c11
Lochbuie Ag & B 119 Q8
Lochcarron Highld 136 B8
Lochdon Ag & B 120 D6
Lochdonhead Ag & B 120 D6
Lochead Ag & B 111 R6
Lochearnhead Stirlg 122 G8
Lochee C Dund 124 H6
Locheilside Station
Highld 128 D8
Lochend Highld 137 Q8
Lochfoot D & G 97 J3
Lochgair Ag & B 112 D3
Lochgelly Fife 115 M3
Lochgilphead Ag & B 112 C3
Lochgoilhead Ag & B 113 J1
Lochieheads Fife 124 E10
Lochill Moray 139 M2
Lochindorb Lodge Highld 138 H9
Lochinver Highld 148 C12
Loch Lomond and The
Trossachs National
Park 122 D10
Loch Loyal Lodge Highld 149 N7
Lochluichart Highld 137 K3
Lochmaben D & G 97 M2
Lochmaddy W Isls 152 d8
Loch nam Madadh W Isls 152 d8
Lochore Fife 115 M2
Lochranza N Ayrs 112 D11
Lochside Abers 132 H11
Lochside D & G 97 J3
Lochside Highld 138 C5
Lochskipport W Isls 152 c10
Lochslin Highld 146 F9
Lochton S Ayrs 95 J2
Lochty Angus 132 E11
Lochty Fife 125 K11
Lochuisge Highld 120 E2
Lochwinnoch Rens 113 L9
Lockwood D & G 106 D10
Lockengate Cnwll 3 P2
Lockerbie D & G 97 N1
Lockeridge Wilts 30 D9
Lockerley Hants 24 E8
Locking N Som 28 E10
Locking Stumps Warrtn ...76 B5
Lockington E R Yk 87 J4
Lockington Leics 66 D7
Lockleywood Shrops 64 C6
Locksbottom Gt Lon 33 M9
Locks Green IoW 12 G6
Locks Heath Hants 9 Q5
Lockton N York 92 H3
Loddington Leics 66 H2
Loddington Nhants 55 H8
Loddiswell Devon 7 J9
Loddon Norfk 71 M12
Lode Cambs 57 K8

Lode Heath Solhll 53 M4
Loders Dorset 10 D6
Lodsworth W Susx 14 C6
Lofthouse Leeds 85 L10
Lofthouse N York 91 J12
Lofthouse Gate Wakefd ..85 L10
Loftus R & Cl 92 E3
Logan E Ayrs 105 L6
Loganbeck Cumb 88 G8
Loganlea W Loth 114 H9
Loggerheads Staffs 64 D5
Logie Angus 132 H11
Logie Fife 124 H8
Logie Coldstone Abers ..132 C3
Logie Newton Abers 140 G8
Logie Pert Angus 132 G11
Logierait P & K 123 N2
Logierieve Abers 141 M10
Login Carmth 37 N6
Lolworth Cambs 56 G8
Lonbain Highld 135 M5
Londesborough E R Yk ...86 F6
London Gt Lon 33 L6
London Apprentice Cnwll ..3 N4
London Beach Kent 16 F3
London Colney Herts 44 H11
Londonderry N York 91 M9
London End Bucks 55 M7
London Gateway
Services Gt Lon 32 H3
London Gatwick Airport
W Susx 15 K3
London Heathrow
Airport Gt Lon 32 F7
London Luton Airport
Luton 44 G7
London Oxford Airport
Oxon 43 K8
London Southend
Airport Essex 34 F4
London Stansted
Airport Essex 45 Q7
Londonthorpe Lincs 67 M4
London Zoo ZSL Gt Lon ..33 K6
Londubh Highld 143 M9
Lonemore Highld 143 L9
Long Ashton N Som 28 H8
Long Bank Worcs 52 E6
Long Bennington Lincs ...67 L3
Longbenton N Tyne 100 H4
Longborough Gloucs 42 E6
Long Bredy Dorset 10 D6
Longbridge Birm 53 J5
Longbridge Warwks 54 G2
Longbridge Deverill Wilts .23 J5
Long Buckby Nhants 54 G7
Longburgh Cumb 98 C6
Longburton Dorset 22 E8
Long Cause Devon 5 N4
Long Clawson Leics 67 J7
Longcliffe Derbys 65 N1
Longcombe Devon 5 P5
Long Common Hants 24 H10
Long Compton Staffs 64 F7
Long Compton Warwks ..42 G5
Longcot Oxon 30 F4
Long Crendon Bucks 43 P10
Long Crichel Dorset 11 N3
Longcroft Cumb 97 P6
Longcross Surrey 32 E9
Longden Shrops 63 M11
Longden Common
Shrops 63 M11
Long Ditton Surrey 32 H9
Longdon Staffs 65 K9
Longdon Worcs 41 N4
Longdon Green Staffs 65 K9
Longdon Heath Worcs ...41 N4
Longdon upon Tern
Wrekin 63 Q9
Longdown Devon 8 H6
Longdowns Cnwll 3 J7
Long Drax N York 86 D9
Long Duckmanton
Derbys 78 D9
Long Eaton Derbys 66 D5
Longfield Kent 33 R8
Longford Covtry 54 B4
Longford Derbys 65 N5
Longford Gloucs 41 N7
Longford Gt Lon 32 F7
Longford Kent 33 P11
Longford Shrops 64 B5
Longford Wrekin 64 D8
Longforgan P & K 124 F7
Longformacus Border ...116 F10
Longframlington Nthumb 109 J9
Long Green Ches W 75 N9
Long Green Worcs 41 N5
Longham Dorset 11 P5
Longham Norfk 70 D9
Long Hanborough Oxon ..43 J9
Longhaven Abers 141 Q8
Long Hedges Lincs 68 H2
Longhirst Nthumb 109 L12
Longhope Gloucs 41 K8
Longhope Ork 147 b6
Longhorsley Nthumb 109 J11
Longhoughton Nthumb ..109 L7
Long Itchington Warwks ..54 F7
Longlands Cumb 98 B11
Longlane Derbys 65 N5
Long Lawford Warwks ...54 D5
Longleat Safari &
Adventure Park Wilts ..22 H4
Longlevens Gloucs 41 N8
Longley Calder 84 G10
Longley Kirk 77 L2
Longley Green Worcs 52 D10
Longleys P & K 124 F4
Long Load Somset 21 P8
Longmanhill Abers 140 H3
Long Marston Herts 44 C8
Long Marston N York 85 Q5
Long Marston Warwks ...53 M11
Long Marton Cumb 89 Q2
Long Meadowend Shrops .51 L4
Long Melford Suffk 58 D2
Longmoor Camp Hants ..25 N7
Longmorn Moray 139 N4
Longmoss Ches E 76 G9
Long Newnton Gloucs 29 N4
Long Newton E Loth 116 C8
Longnewton on T 91 P3
Longney Gloucs 41 M9
Longniddry E Loth 116 B6
Longnor Shrops 63 N12
Longnor Staffs 77 K10
Longparish Hants 24 G5
Longpark Cumb 98 E6
Long Preston N York 84 C4
Longridge Lancs 83 N9
Longridge Staffs 64 G8
Longridge W Loth 114 H9
Longriggend N Lans 114 E7
Long Riston E R Yk 87 L7
Longrock Cnwll 2 D8
Longsdon Derbys 64 H1
Longshaw Wigan 75 P3
Long Sight Oldham 76 G2
Longside Abers 141 P6
Longslow Shrops 64 C5
Longstanton Cambs 56 H7
Longstock Hants 24 F6

Longstone Pembks 37 M8
Longstowe Cambs 56 F9
Long Stratton Norfk 59 J2
Long Street M Keyn 55 K11
Long Sutton Hants 25 M4
Long Sutton Lincs 68 H7
Long Sutton Somset 21 P8
Longthorpe C Pete 56 C1
Long Thurlow Suffk 58 F7
Longthwaite Cumb 89 L2
Longton C Stke 64 G3
Longton Lancs 83 L10
Longtown Cumb 98 D4
Longtown Herefs 40 D6
Longueville Jersey 13 c3
Longville in the Dale
Shrops 51 P2
Long Waste Wrekin 64 B9
Long Whatton Leics 66 D7
Longwick Bucks 43 Q10
Long Wittenham Oxon ...31 L4
Longwitton Nthumb 108 H12
Longwood D & G 96 G3
Longworth Oxon 30 H2
Longyester E Loth 116 C8
Lôn-las Swans 38 H10
Lonmay Abers 141 N4
Lonmore Highld 134 C6
Looe Cnwll 4 C6
Loose Kent 34 D12
Loosebeare Devon 8 D4
Loosegate Lincs 68 H7
Loosley Row Bucks 32 B3
Lootcherbrae Abers 140 F5
Lopcombe Corner Wilts ..24 D6
Lopen Somset 21 P10
Loppington Shrops 63 M6
Lorbottle Nthumb 108 G8
Lordington W Susx 13 N3
Lordsbridge Norfk 69 L9
Lordshill C Sotn 24 F10
Lords Wood Medway 34 D10
Lornty P & K 124 D4
Loscoe Derbys 66 C3
Loscombe Dorset 10 D5
Losgaintir W Isls 152 e6
Lossiemouth Moray 147 N11
Lostford Shrops 64 B5
Lostock Gralam Ches W ..76 C8
Lostock Green Ches W ...76 C9
Lostock Hall Lancs 83 M10
Lostock Hall Fold Bolton .76 C2
Lostock Junction Bolton ..76 C3
Lostwithiel Cnwll 3 R3
Lothbeg Highld 146 G3
Lothersdale N York 84 E6
Lothmore Highld 146 H3
Loudwater Bucks 32 C4
Loughborough Leics 66 E8
Loughor Swans 26 E3
Loughton Essex 33 M3
Loughton M Keyn 44 B4
Loughton Shrops 52 A4
Lound Lincs 67 Q8
Lound Notts 78 H6
Lound Suffk 71 P12
Louth Lincs 80 F6
Loveclough Lancs 84 B9
Lovedean Hants 25 L10
Lover Wilts 24 C9
Loversall Donc 78 F4
Loves Green Essex 46 B10
Lovesome Hill N York 91 N1
Loveston Pembks 37 L9
Lovington Somset 22 D7
Low Ackworth Wakefd ...85 P11
Low Angerton Nthumb .100 E1
Lowbands Gloucs 41 M5
Low Barbeth D & G 94 E5
Low Barlings Lincs 80 B9
Low Bell End N York 92 E7
Low Bentham N York 83 P7
Low Biggins Cumb 89 P11
Low Borrowbridge Cumb .89 N6
Low Bradfield Sheff 77 N5
Low Bradley N York 84 F5
Low Braithwaite Cumb ...98 E10
Low Burnham N Linc 79 K3
Low Buston Nthumb 109 L8
Lowca Cumb 88 C2
Low Catton E R Yk 86 D4
Low Coniscliffe Darltn ...91 L4
Low Crosby Cumb 98 F6
Lowdham Notts 67 J3
Low Dinsdale Darltn 91 N4
Lowe Shrops 63 N6
Lowe Hill Staffs 65 J1
Low Ellington N York 91 L10
Lower Aisholt Somset 21 K6
Lower Ansty Dorset 11 J4
Lower Apperley Gloucs ...41 N6
Lower Arboll Highld 146 F9
Lower Arncott Oxon 43 M8
Lower Assendon Oxon 31 Q5
Lower Badcall Highld 148 E8
Lower Ballam Lancs 83 J9
Lower Bartle Lancs 83 L8
Lower Basildon W Berk ...31 M6
Lower Bearwood Herefs ..51 L9
Lower Beeding W Susx ...15 J5
Lower Benefield Nhants ..55 N3
Lower Bentley Worcs 53 J7
Lower Beobridge Shrops .52 E2
Lower Birchwood Derbys .66 C2
Lower Boddington
Nhants 54 D10
Lower Boscaswell Cnwll ...2 B7
Lower Bourne Surrey 25 P4
Lower Brailes Warwks 42 G4
Lower Breakish Highld ..135 M11
Lower Bredbury Stockp ...76 G3
Lower Broadheath Worcs .52 F9
Lower Broxwood Herefs ..51 L9
Lower Buckenhill Herefs ..40 H3
Lower Bullingham Herefs .40 G4
Lower Burgate Hants 23 R9
Lower Burrowton Devon ..9 J5
Lower Burton Herefs 51 M9
Lower Caldecote C Beds ..44 H2
Lower Canada N Som 28 E10
Lower Catesby Nhants 54 E9
Lower Chapel Powys 39 N4
Lower Chicksgrove Wilts ..23 L7
Lower Chute Wilts 24 D4
Lower Clapton Gt Lon 33 L5
Lower Clent Worcs 52 H5
Lower Common Hants 31 Q10
Lower Creedy Devon 8 H4
Lower Crossings Derbys ..77 K7
Lower Cumberworth Kirk .77 N3
Lower Darwen Bl w D 83 Q10
Lower Dean Bed 55 N7
Lower Denby Kirk 77 N3
Lower Diabaig Highld ...135 P4
Lower Dicker E Susx 15 Q8
Lower Dinchope Shrops ...51 K4
Lower Down Shrops 51 J4
Lower Dunsforth N York ..85 Q3
Lower Egleton Herefs 41 J3
Lower Elkstone Staffs 77 K12

Lower Ellastone Staffs 65 L4
Lower End Bucks 43 P10
Lower End M Keyn 44 D4
Lower End Nhants 55 K9
Lower End Nhants 55 L8
Lower Everleigh Wilts 24 C2
Lower Exbury Hants 12 G5
Lower Eythorne Kent 35 N12
Lower Failand N Som 28 G7
Lower Farringdon Hants ..25 M6
Lower Feltham Gt Lon 32 G7
Lower Fittleworth W Susx .14 E7
Lower Foxdale IoM 102 c5
Lower Frankton Shrops ...63 L6
Lower Freystrop Pembks .37 J8
Lower Froyle Hants 25 N4
Lower Gabwell Devon 5 Q3
Lower Gledfield Highld ..145 N7
Lower Godney Somset 21 Q5
Lower Gornal Dudley 52 G2
Lower Gravenhurst
C Beds 44 G5
Lower Green Herts 44 H5
Lower Green Herts 45 M5
Lower Green Kent 15 Q3
Lower Green Kent 16 A2
Lower Green Norfk 70 E5
Lower Green Staffs 64 G12
Lower Green Suffk 57 P7
Lower Hacheston Suffk ...59 L9
Lower Halstock Leigh
Dorset 10 E3
Lower Halstow Kent 34 F9
Lower Hamworthy BCP ...11 N6
Lower Hardres Kent 35 L11
Lower Harpton Herefs 51 J8
Lower Hartlip Kent 34 E9
Lower Hartshay Derbys ...66 C2
Lower Hartwell Bucks 43 R9
Lower Hatton Staffs 64 F5
Lower Hawthwaite Cumb .88 G9
Lower Hergest Herefs 51 J9
Lower Heyford Oxon 43 K7
Lower Heysham Lancs 83 K3
Lower Higham Kent 34 C8
Lower Holbrook Suffk 47 L5
Lower Hordley Shrops 63 L6
Lower Horncroft W Susx .14 E7
Lowerhouse Lancs 84 B8
Lower Houses Kirk 84 H12
Lower Howsell Worcs 52 E11
Lower Irlam Salfd 76 D5
Lower Kilburn Derbys 66 B4
Lower Kilcott Gloucs 29 M4
Lower Killeyan Ag & B ..102 B1
Lower Kingcombe Dorset .10 E5
Lower Kingswood Surrey .33 J10
Lower Kinnerton Ches W .75 K11
Lower Langford N Som ...28 F10
Lower Largo Fife 124 H12
Lower Leigh Staffs 65 J5
Lower Lemington Gloucs .42 F5
Lower Llanfadog Powys ..50 C7
Lower Lovacott Devon 19 K8
Lower Loxhore Devon 19 M6
Lower Lydbrook Gloucs ..41 J8
Lower Lye Herefs 51 L7
Lower Machen Newpt 28 B5
Lower Maes-coed Herefs .40 D5
Lower Mannington
Dorset 11 P4
Lower Marston Somset ...22 G4
Lower Meend Gloucs 40 H10
Lower Merridge Somset ..21 K6
Lower Middleton
Cheney Nhants 43 L3
Lower Milton Somset 22 C4
Lower Moor Worcs 42 C4
Lower Morton S Glos 29 K4
Lower Nazeing Essex 45 M10
Lower Norton Warwks 53 N8
Lower Nyland Dorset 22 G9
Lower Penarth V Glam ...28 A8
Lower Penn Staffs 52 G1
Lower Pennington Hants .12 E6
Lower Penwortham
Lancs 83 M10
Lower Peover Ches E 76 D9
Lower Place Rochdl 76 G1
Lower Pollicott Bucks 43 P9
Lower Quinton Warwks ..42 E2
Lower Rainham Medway .34 E9
Lower Raydon Suffk 47 J4
Lower Roadwater Somset .20 G5
Lower Salter Lancs 83 N4
Lower Seagry Wilts 29 N6
Lower Sheering Essex 45 P9
Lower Shelton C Beds 44 E3
Lower Shiplake Oxon 31 Q6
Lower Shuckburgh
Warwks 54 D8
Lower Slaughter Gloucs ..42 D7
Lower Soothill Kirk 85 K10
Lower Soudley Gloucs 41 K9
Lower Standen Kent 17 M3
Lower Stanton St
Quintin Wilts 29 Q6
Lower Stoke Medway 34 E7
Lower Stondon C Beds ...44 H5
Lower Stone Gloucs 29 K3
Lower Stonnall Staffs 65 M5
Lower Stow Bedon Norfk .58 E2
Lower Street E Susx 16 C8
Lower Street Norfk 71 K5
Lower Street Suffk 57 Q10
Lower Street Suffk 58 G10
Lower Stretton Warrtn ...76 B7
Lower Stroud Dorset 10 C5
Lower Sundon C Beds 44 F6
Lower Swanwick Hants ...12 H3
Lower Swell Gloucs 42 D6
Lower Tadmarton Oxon ..43 J4
Lower Tale Devon 9 K4
Lower Tasburgh Norfk ...59 J1
Lower Tean Staffs 65 J4
Lower Thurlton Norfk 71 N2
Lower Town Cnwll 2 G8
Lower Town Devon 5 N4
Lower Town Herefs 41 M3
Lower Town Pembks 37 J3
Lower Treluswell Cnwll 3 J7
Lower Trebullett Cnwll 7 L9
Lower Tysoe Warwks 42 H3
Lower Ufford Suffk 59 L10
Lower Upcott Devon 8 H9
Lower Upham Hants 25 J9
Lower Upnor Medway 34 D8
Lower Vexford Somset ...20 H6
Lower Walton Warrtn 76 A6
Lower Waterston Dorset ..11 J5
Lower Weare Somset 21 Q3
Lower Weedon Nhants ...54 F9
Lower Welson Herefs 51 J10
Lower Westmancote
Worcs 42 B4
Lower Whatcombe
Dorset 11 K4
Lower Whatley Somset ...22 G4
Lower Whitley Ches W ...75 Q8
Lower Wick Gloucs 29 L3
Lower Wield Hants 25 J5
Lower Willingdon E Susx .15 Q10
Lower Withington Ches E .76 E10
Lower Woodend Bucks ...32 B5

Lower Woodford Wilts 23 P6
Lower Wraxall Dorset 10 E4
Lower Wyche Worcs 41 N3
Lower Wyke C Brad 84 H10
Lowesby Leics 67 J10
Lowestoft Suffk 59 Q2
Loweswater Cumb 88 F3
Low Fell Gatesd 100 H6
Lowfield Heath W Susx ...15 K3
Low Gartachorrans Stirlg 113 P4
Low Gettbridge Cumb 98 G6
Low Grantley N York 85 K1
Low Green N York 85 J3
Low Green N York 91 J3
Low Habberley Worcs 52 E5
Low Ham Somset 21 P7
Low Harrogate N York 85 L4
Low Hawsker N York 93 J5
Low Hesket Cumb 98 F9
Low Hutton N York 86 E3
Lowick Cumb 89 J9
Lowick Nhants 55 N4
Lowick Nthumb 108 G2
Lowick Bridge Cumb 89 J9
Lowick Green Cumb 89 J9
Low Knipe Cumb 89 N3
Low Laithe N York 85 J2
Lowlands Dur 91 J2
Lowlands Torfn 28 C3
Low Langton Lincs 80 C8
Low Leighton Derbys 77 J6
Low Lorton Cumb 88 F2
Low Marishes N York 92 G11
Low Marnham Notts 79 K10
Low Middleton Nthumb ..109 J3
Low Mill N York 92 D7
Low Moor C Brad 84 H9
Low Moorsley Sundld ...101 J9
Low Moresby Cumb 88 C3
Low Newton Cumb 89 L10
Low Row Cumb 97 P9
Low Row Cumb 98 D11
Low Row N York 90 H6
Low Row Cumb 99 Q7
Low Salchrie D & G 94 E5
Low Santon N Linc 79 N1
Low Street Norfk 71 L7
Low Street Thurr 34 B7
Low Tharston Norfk 59 J2
Lowther Cumb 89 N3
Lowthorpe E R Yk 87 K3
Lowton Somset 20 G8
Lowton Wigan 76 B4
Lowton Common Wigan ..76 B4
Lowton St Mary's Wigan .76 B4
Low Torry Fife 115 J5
Low Toynton Lincs 80 E9
Low Valley Barns 78 C3
Low Wood Cumb 89 K10
Low Worsall N York 91 P5
Low Wray Cumb 89 K6
Loxbeare Devon 20 E10
Loxhill Surrey 14 E3
Loxhore Devon 19 M5
Loxhore Cott Devon 19 M6
Loxley Warwks 53 N10
Loxley Green Staffs 65 K6
Loxter Herefs 41 L3
Loxton N Som 21 N2
Loxwood W Susx 14 E4
Lubenham Leics 54 H3
Lucasgate Lincs 68 H3
Lucas Green Surrey 32 D10
Luccombe Somset 20 E4
Luccombe Village IoW 13 K9
Lucker Nthumb 109 J4
Luckett Cnwll 7 M10
Lucking Street Essex 46 E5
Luckington Wilts 29 N5
Lucklawhill Fife 124 H8
Lucknam Wilts 29 N6
Luckwell Bridge Somset ..20 D5
Lucton Herefs 51 M8
Lucy Cross N York 91 L4
Ludag W Isls 152 c12
Ludborough Lincs 80 F4
Ludbrook Devon 5 L9
Ludchurch Pembks 37 M8
Luddenden Calder 84 F10
Luddenden Foot Calder ..84 F10
Luddenham Court Kent ..34 H9
Luddesdown Kent 34 B9
Luddington N Linc 86 F12
Luddington Warwks 53 N10
Luddington in the Brook
Nhants 56 B4
Ludford Lincs 80 D6
Ludford Shrops 51 N6
Ludgershall Bucks 43 N8
Ludgershall Wilts 24 D3
Ludgvan Cnwll 2 D8
Ludham Norfk 71 M8
Ludlow Shrops 51 N5
Ludney Somset 21 N11
Ludwell Wilts 23 K9
Ludworth Dur 101 J10
Luffenhall Herts 45 K6
Luffincott Devon 7 L6
Luffness E Ayrs 116 C5
Lugar E Ayrs 105 L5
Luggate Burn E Loth 116 E6
Lugg Green Herefs 51 M8
Luggiebank N Lans 114 D7
Lugton E Ayrs 113 N10
Lugwardine Herefs 40 H3
Luib Highld 135 K10
Lulham Herefs 40 F3
Lullington Derbys 65 N9
Lullington E Susx 15 Q10
Lullington Somset 22 G3
Lulsgate Bottom N Som ..28 H9
Lulsley Worcs 52 D9
Lulworth Camp Dorset ...11 J8
Lumb Calder 84 F10
Lumb Lancs 84 B10
Lumbutts Calder 84 D10
Lumby N York 85 P9
Lumphanan Abers 132 F3
Lumphinnans Fife 115 M3
Lumsden Abers 140 D11
Lunan Angus 125 N2
Lunanhead Angus 125 J2
Luncarty P & K 124 C7
Lund E R Yk 86 H5
Lund N York 86 D7
Lundie Angus 124 F6
Lundin Links Fife 124 H12
Lundin Mill Fife 124 H12
Lundy Devon 18 C4
Lundy Green Norfk 59 K2
Lunga Ag & B 120 D3
Lunna Shet 147 j5
Lunsford Kent 34 C10
Lunsford's Cross E Susx ..16 C8
Lunt Sefton 75 K3
Luntley Herefs 51 L9
Luppitt Devon 9 P4
Lupridge Devon 5 M8
Lupset Wakefd 85 K11
Lupton Cumb 89 N9
Lurgashall W Susx 14 D5

Lurley Devon 20 E10
Lusby Lincs 80 G10
Luscombe Devon 5 N5
Luson Devon 5 J7
Luss Ag & B 113 M3
Lussagiven Ag & B 111 N4
Lusta Highld 134 E4
Lustleigh Devon 8 E8
Luston Herefs 51 N8
Luthermuir Abers 132 G10
Luthrie Fife 124 G9
Lutley Dudley 52 G4
Luton Devon 8 H6
Luton Devon 9 K4
Luton Luton 44 F7
Luton Airport Luton 44 G7
Luton Medway 34 D9
Lutterworth Leics 54 E4
Lutton Devon 5 J5
Lutton Devon 5 L4
Lutton Lincs 68 H7
Lutton Nhants 56 C3
Luxborough Somset 20 F6
Luxley Gloucs 41 L6
Luxulyan Cnwll 3 P3
Luzley Tamesd 76 H3
Lybster Highld 151 N9
Lydbury North Shrops ...51 K3
Lydcott Devon 19 N6
Lydd Kent 17 J5
Lydd Airport Kent 17 J6
Lydden Kent 17 N2
Lydden Kent 35 P9
Lyddington Rutlnd 55 L1
Lydd-on-Sea Kent 17 K5
Lydeard St Lawrence
Somset 20 H7
Lyde Green Hants 31 P11
Lydford Devon 7 P8
Lydford on Fosse Somset .22 D7
Lydgate Calder 84 D10
Lydgate Rochdl 84 E12
Lydham Shrops 51 K2
Lydiard Green Wilts 30 C5
Lydiard Millicent Wilts ...30 C5
Lydiard Tregoze Swindn .30 C5
Lydiate Sefton 75 L3
Lydiate Ash Worcs 52 H5
Lydlinch Dorset 22 G10
Lydney Gloucs 41 K11
Lydstep Pembks 37 L11
Lye Dudley 52 G4
Lye Cross N Som 28 G10
Lye Green Bucks 44 D11
Lye Green E Susx 15 P4
Lye Green Warwks 53 M7
Lye Head Worcs 52 D6
Lye's Green Wilts 22 H4
Lyford Oxon 30 H3
Lymbridge Green Kent ...17 K2
Lyme Regis Dorset 9 Q6
Lyminge Kent 17 L3
Lymington Hants 12 E5
Lyminster W Susx 14 E10
Lymm Warrtn 76 C6
Lymm Services Warrtn ...76 C7
Lympne Kent 17 K4
Lympsham Somset 21 M2
Lympstone Devon 9 J8
Lynbridge Devon 19 M4
Lynch Hall Wilts 130 E4
Lynch Green Norfk 70 H11
Lyndhurst Hants 12 F4
Lyndon Rutlnd 67 M11
Lyne Border 106 G12
Lyne Surrey 32 E9
Lyneal Shrops 63 M5
Lyne Down Herefs 41 K5
Lyneham Devon 8 F9
Lyneham Oxon 42 F7
Lyneham Wilts 30 B6
Lyneholmeford Cumb 98 H4
Lynemouth Nthumb 109 M11
Lyne of Skene Abers 133 J2
Lynesack Dur 90 H2
Lyness Ork 147 b6
Lyng Norfk 70 F8
Lyng Somset 21 M7
Lynmouth Devon 19 P3
Lynn Staffs 65 K11
Lynn Wrekin 64 E9
Lynsted Kent 34 G10
Lynstone Cnwll 7 J4
Lynton Devon 19 N3
Lynton Cross Devon 19 K5
Lyon's Gate Dorset 10 G4
Lyonshall Herefs 51 K9
Lytchett Matravers
Dorset 11 M6
Lytchett Minster Dorset ..11 M6
Lyth Highld 151 N4
Lytham Lancs 82 H9
Lytham St Annes Lancs ...82 H9
Lythbank Shrops 63 M10
Lythe N York 92 H4
Lythmore Highld 151 J3

M

Mabe Burnthouse Cnwll 3 J7
Mablethorpe Lincs 81 K7
Macclesfield Ches E 76 G9
Macduff Abers 140 H3
Macharioch Ag & B 103 K8
Machen Caerph 28 B4
Machrie N Ayrs 103 N3
Machrihanish Ag & B ...102 H5
Machrins Ag & B 111 J3
Machynlleth Powys 61 N12
Machynys Carmth 26 D3
Mackworth Derbys 65 P5
Macmerry E Loth 116 B7
Maddaford Devon 7 Q6
Madderty P & K 123 N8
Maddington Wilts 23 N5
Madehurst W Susx 14 E8
Madeley Staffs 64 E3
Madeley Wrekin 64 C11
Madeley Heath Staffs 64 E3
Madford Devon 9 M3
Madingley Cambs 56 H8
Madley Herefs 40 F4
Madresfield Worcs 52 E11
Madron Cnwll 2 D8
Maenaddwyn IoA 72 H7
Maenan Conwy 73 N10
Maenclochog Pembks 37 L4
Maendy V Glam 27 N7
Maenporth Cnwll 3 K8
Maentwrog Gwynd 61 L4
Maer Cnwll 7 J4
Maer Staffs 64 E5
Maerdy Carmth 38 G6
Maerdy Conwy 62 C3
Maerdy Rhondd 27 M3
Maesbrook Shrops 63 J7
Maesbury Shrops 63 K6
Maesbury Marsh Shrops ..63 K6
Maes-glas Newpt 28 C5
Maesgwynne Carmth 37 N6
Maeshafn Denbgs 74 H11

Maesllyn Cerdgn 38 A3
Maesmynis Powys 39 N2
Maesmynis Powys 50 E10
Maesteg Brdgnd 27 K4
Maesybont Carmth 38 E8
Maesycwmmer Caerph 27 R3
Magdalen Laver Essex 45 P10
Maggieknockater Moray 139 P7
Maggots End Essex 45 N6
Magham Down E Susx 15 R8
Maghull Sefton 75 L3
Magor Mons 28 F5
Magor Services Mons 28 F5
Maidenbower W Susx 15 K4
Maiden Bradley Wilts 22 H5
Maidencombe Torbay 5 Q3
Maidenhayne Devon 9 P6
Maiden Head N Som 28 N9
Maidenhead W & M 32 C6
Maiden Law Dur 100 F8
Maiden Newton Dorset 10 F5
Maidens S Ayrs 104 D8
Maiden's Green Br For 32 C8
Maidenwell Lincs 80 F8
Maidford Nhants 54 G10
Maids Moreton Bucks 34 D11
Maidstone Kent 34 D11
Maidstone Services Kent 34 L1
Maidwell Nhants 55 J5
Mail Shet 147 j7
Maindee Newpt 28 D5
Mainland Ork 147 c4
Mainland Shet 147 i6
Mainsforth Dur 101 J12
Mains of Balhall Angus 132 D11
Mains of Balnakettle
    Abers 132 F9
Mains of Dalvey Highld 139 L9
Mains of Haulkerton
    Abers 132 H9
Mains of Lesmoir Abers 140 D10
Mains of Melgunds
    Angus 125 L2
Mainsriddle D & G 97 J3
Mainstone Shrops 51 J3
Maisemore Gloucs 41 N7
Major's Green Worcs 53 L5
Makeney Derbys 66 B3
Malborough Devon 5 L8
Malcoff Derbys 77 K7
Malden Rushett Gt Lon 32 E6
Maldon Essex 46 E10
Malham N York 84 D3
Maligar Highld 134 H3
Mallaig Highld 127 M5
Mallaigvaig Highld 127 M5
Malleny Mills C Edin 115 L8
Mallows Green Essex 45 N6
Malltraeth IoA 72 G10
Mallwyd Gwynd 61 Q9
Malmesbury Wilts 29 Q5
Malmsmead Devon 20 B4
Malpas Ches W 63 N3
Malpas Cnwll 3 K6
Malpas Newpt 28 D4
Malshanger Hants 25 J3
Malswick Gloucs 41 L7
Maltby Lincs 80 F7
Maltby Rothm 78 E5
Maltby S on T 91 Q4
Maltby le Marsh Lincs 81 J7
Malting Green Essex 46 F2
Maltman's Hill Kent 16 F2
Malton N York 92 F12
Malvern Worcs 41 M2
Malvern Hills 41 M3
Malvern Link Worcs 52 E11
Malvern Wells Worcs 41 M3
Mamble Worcs 52 C6
Mamhilad Mons 40 D11
Manaccan Cnwll 3 J9
Manafon Powys 62 F11
Manais W Isls 152 e6
Manaton Devon 8 L8
Manby Lincs 80 H6
Mancetter Warwks 53 Q1
Manchester Manch 76 F4
Manchester Airport Manch 76 F7
Mancot Flints 75 K10
Mandally Highld 129 K4
Manea Cambs 57 J3
Maney Birm 53 L2
Manfield N York 91 L4
Mangersta W Isls 152 d3
Mangerton Dorset 10 D5
Mangotsfield S Gloucs 29 K7
Mangrove Green Herts 44 G7
Mangurstadh W Isls 152 d3
Manhay Cnwll 2 H8
Manish W Isls 152 e6
Mankinholes Calder 84 E10
Manley Ches W 75 N9
Manmoel Caerph 40 A11
Mannal Ag & B 118 D5
Manningford Bohune
    Wilts 30 D10
Manningford Bruce Wilts 30 D10
Manningham C Brad 84 H8
Mannings Heath W Susx 14 H5
Mannington Dorset 11 P4
Manningtree Essex 47 K5
Mannofield C Aber 133 M3
Manorbier Pembks 37 L11
Manorbier Newton
    Pembks 37 K10
Manordeilo Carmth 38 G6
Manorhill Border 107 Q3
Manorowen Pembks 36 H3
Manor Park Gt Lon 33 M5
Mansell Gamage Herefs 40 E3
Mansell Lacy Herefs 40 F3
Mansergh Cumb 89 P10
Mansfield E Ayrs 105 L7
Mansfield Notts 78 E11
Mansfield Woodhouse
    Notts 78 E11
Mansriggs Cumb 89 J10
Manston Dorset 22 H10
Manston Kent 35 Q9
Manston Leeds 85 M8
Manswood Dorset 11 P4
Manthorpe Lincs 67 N5
Manthorpe Lincs 68 C9
Manton N Linc 79 M3
Manton Notts 78 E10
Manton Rutlnd 67 L11
Manton Wilts 30 E8
Manuden Essex 45 P6
Manwood Green Essex 45 N9
Maperton Somset 22 F8
Maplebeck Notts 78 H11
Maple Cross Herts 32 E4
Mapledurham Oxon 31 N6
Mapledurwell Hants 25 M3
Maplehurst W Susx 14 H5
Maplescombe Kent 33 Q9
Mapleton Derbys 65 M3
Mapleton Kent 15 N1
Mapperley Derbys 66 C4
Mapperley Park C Nott 66 F3
Mapperton Dorset 10 D5
Mappleborough Green
    Warwks 53 K7

Mappleton E R Yk 87 N6
Maplewell Barns 77 Q2
Mappowder Dorset 10 H3
Marazanvose Cnwll 3 K4
Marazion Cnwll 2 E8
Marbhig W Isls 152 g4
Marbury Ches E 63 P3
March Cambs 56 H1
March S Lans 106 C2
Marcham Oxon 31 K3
Marchamley Shrops 63 Q6
Marchamley Wood
    Shrops 63 Q6
Marchington Staffs 65 L6
Marchington Woodlands
    Staffs 65 L6
Marchros Gwynd 60 E7
Marchwiel Wrexhm 63 K3
Marchwood Hants 12 H3
Marcross V Glam 27 L8
Marden Herefs 40 H2
Marden Kent 16 D2
Marden Wilts 30 C10
Marden Ash Essex 45 Q11
Marden Beech Kent 16 C2
Marden Thorn Kent 16 E8
Marden's Hill E Susx 15 P4
Mardlebury Herts 45 K8
Mardy Mons 40 D8
Marefield Leics 67 K10
Mareham le Fen Lincs 80 E11
Mareham on the Hill
    Lincs 80 F10
Marehay Derbys 66 C3
Marehill W Susx 14 F7
Maresfield E Susx 15 N6
Marfleet C KuH 87 L9
Marford Wrexhm 75 K12
Margam Neath 27 J5
Margaret Marsh Dorset 22 H9
Margaret Roding Essex 45 Q9
Margaretting Essex 34 B2
Margaretting Tye Essex 34 B2
Margate Kent 35 P8
Margnaheglish N Ayrs 103 Q3
Margrie D & G 96 C8
Margrove Park R & Cl 92 D4
Marham Norfk 69 N10
Marhamchurch Cnwll 7 J4
Marholm C Pete 68 C11
Marian-glas IoA 72 H7
Mariansleigh Devon 19 P9
Marine Town Kent 34 G7
Marionburgh Abers 132 H3
Marishader Highld 135 J3
Maristow Devon 4 G4
Marjoriebanks D & G 97 M2
Mark Somset 21 N4
Markbeech Kent 15 N2
Markby Lincs 81 J8
Mark Causeway Somset 21 N4
Mark Cross E Susx 15 Q4
Markeaton C Derb 65 Q5
Market Bosworth Leics 66 C11
Market Deeping Lincs 68 C10
Market Drayton Shrops 64 C5
Market Harborough
    Leics 55 J3
Market Lavington Wilts 23 M3
Market Overton Rutlnd 67 M9
Market Rasen Lincs 80 B6
Market Stainton Lincs 80 E7
Market Warsop Notts 78 F10
Market Weighton E R Yk 86 G7
Market Weston Suffk 58 E5
Markfield Leics 66 D10
Markham Caerph 28 A2
Markham Moor Notts 78 J9
Markinch Fife 115 P1
Markington N York 85 J2
Markle E Loth 116 D6
Marksbury BaNES 29 K10
Mark's Corner IoW 12 H6
Marks Tey Essex 46 F7
Markwell Cnwll 4 E5
Markyate Herts 44 F8
Marlborough Wilts 30 E8
Marlbrook Herefs 51 N9
Marlbrook Worcs 52 H5
Marlcliff Warwks 53 L10
Marldon Devon 5 P4
Marle Green E Susx 15 Q7
Marlesford Suffk 59 L9
Marley Kent 35 L12
Marley Kent 35 P11
Marley Green Ches E 63 P3
Marley Hill Gatesd 100 G6
Marlingford Norfk 70 H10
Marloes Pembks 36 F9
Marlow Bucks 32 B5
Marlow Herefs 51 L5
Marlow Bottom Bucks 32 B5
Marlpit Hill Kent 15 N2
Marlpits E Susx 15 N5
Marlpits E Susx 16 C8
Marlpool Derbys 66 D3
Marnhull Dorset 22 H9
Marple Stockp 76 H6
Marple Bridge Stockp 76 H6
Marr Donc 78 E3
Marrick N York 90 H7
Marros Carmth 37 N9
Marsden Kirk 77 K1
Marsden S Tyne 101 K5
Marsden Height Lancs 84 C8
Marsett N York 90 H9
Marsh Bucks 44 A10
Marsh C Brad 84 F8
Marsh Devon 9 P3
Marshall's Heath Herts 44 H8
Marshalswick Herts 44 H9
Marsham Norfk 71 J7
Marsh Baldon Oxon 31 M3
Marsh Benham W Berk 31 J9
Marshborough Kent 35 P11
Marshbrook Shrops 51 N3
Marshchapel Lincs 80 G4
Marsh Farm Luton 44 F7
Marshfield Newpt 28 C6
Marshfield S Glos 29 M7
Marshgate Cnwll 6 H6
Marsh Gibbon Bucks 43 P7
Marsh Green Devon 9 K6
Marsh Green Kent 15 N2
Marsh Green Wrekin 63 Q9
Marshland St James
    Norfk 69 K10
Marsh Lane Derbys 78 C8
Marsh Lane Gloucs 41 J10
Marshside Sefton 83 J11
Marsh Street Somset 20 F4
Marston Dorset 10 J6
Marske N York 91 J6
Marske-by-the-Sea
    R & Cl 92 D2
Marsland Green Wigan 76 C4
Marston Ches W 76 C10
Marston Herefs 51 L9
Marston Lincs 67 M3
Marston Oxon 43 L10
Marston Staffs 64 G8
Marston Staffs 64 H7
Marston Warwks 53 N2
Marston Wilts 29 Q10
Marston Green Solhll 53 M4
Marston Jabbet Warwks 54 C2

Marston Magna Somset 22 D9
Marston Meysey Wilts 30 D3
Marston Montgomery
    Derbys 65 L5
Marston Moretaine
    C Beds 44 E3
Marston on Dove Derbys 65 N6
Marston St Lawrence
    Nhants 43 L3
Marston Stannett Herefs 51 P9
Marston Trussell Nhants 54 H3
Marstow Herefs 40 H8
Marsworth Bucks 44 C8
Marten Wilts 30 G10
Marthall Ches E 76 E8
Martham Norfk 71 N8
Martin Hants 23 N9
Martin Kent 17 P1
Martin Lincs 80 C11
Martin Lincs 80 E10
Martindale Cumb 89 L3
Martin Dales Lincs 80 D11
Martin Drove End Hants 23 N9
Martinhoe Devon 19 N4
Martin Hussingtree
    Worcs 52 G8
Martinscroft Warrtn 76 C6
Martinstown Dorset 10 G7
Martlesham Suffk 47 N2
Martlesham Heath Suffk 47 M3
Martletwy Pembks 37 K8
Martley Worcs 52 D8
Martock Somset 21 P9
Marton Ches E 76 F10
Marton Ches E 76 B10
Marton Cumb 88 H11
Marton E R Yk 87 M1
Marton E R Yk 87 M7
Marton Lincs 79 L7
Marton Middsb 92 B3
Marton N York 85 N3
Marton N York 92 G10
Marton Shrops 63 J11
Marton Warwks 54 C7
Marton-le-Moor N York 85 M1
Martyr's Green Surrey 32 F11
Martyr Worthy Hants 24 H7
Marwell Wildlife Hants 24 H9
Marwick Ork 147 b3
Marwood Devon 19 L6
Marybank Highld 137 N5
Maryburgh Highld 137 P4
Marygold Border 116 H9
Maryhill C Glas 113 Q7
Marykirk Abers 132 G11
Maryland Mons 40 G10
Marylebone Gt Lon 33 J6
Marylebone Wigan 75 P2
Marypark Moray 139 M8
Maryport Cumb 97 L11
Maryport D & G 94 E11
Marystow Devon 7 N8
Mary Tavy Devon 7 N9
Maryton Angus 125 N2
Marywell Abers 132 F5
Marywell Abers 133 M4
Marywell Angus 125 M4
Masham N York 91 L10
Mashbury Essex 46 B9
Mason N u Ty 100 Q3
Masongill N York 89 Q11
Mastin Moor Derbys 78 D8
Matching Essex 45 P9
Matching Green Essex 45 P9
Matching Tye Essex 45 P9
Matfen Nthumb 100 D4
Matfield Kent 16 C2
Mathern Mons 28 H4
Mathon Herefs 41 L2
Mathry Pembks 36 G4
Matlask Norfk 70 H5
Matlock Derbys 77 P11
Matlock Bank Derbys 77 P11
Matlock Bath Derbys 77 P11
Matlock Dale Derbys 77 P12
Matson Gloucs 41 N8
Matterdale End Cumb 89 L2
Mattersey Notts 78 H6
Mattersey Thorpe Notts 78 H6
Mattingley Hants 31 Q10
Mattishall Norfk 70 H10
Mattishall Burgh Norfk 70 G10
Mauchline E Ayrs 105 J4
Maud Abers 141 M6
Maufant Jersey 13 d2
Maugersbury Gloucs 42 E7
Maughold IoM 102 g4
Mauld Highld 137 L8
Maulden C Beds 44 F4
Maulds Meaburn Cumb 89 Q3
Maunby N York 91 N9
Maund Bryan Herefs 51 P10
Maundown Somset 20 F8
Mautby Norfk 71 P9
Mavesyn Ridware Staffs 65 K9
Mavis Enderby Lincs 80 G10
Mawbray Cumb 97 M9
Mawdesley Lancs 83 L12
Mawdlam Brdgnd 27 J6
Mawgan Cnwll 2 H9
Mawgan Porth Cnwll 6 B11
Maw Green Ches E 76 D12
Mawla Cnwll 2 H5
Mawnan Cnwll 3 J8
Mawnan Smith Cnwll 3 J8
Mawsley Nhants 55 K5
Mawthorpe Lincs 81 J9
Maxey C Pete 68 C10
Maxstoke Warwks 53 N3
Maxted Street Kent 17 K2
Maxton Border 107 P4
Maxton Kent 17 N1
Maxwelltown D & G 97 J3
Maxworthy Cnwll 7 J6
Mayals Swans 26 F4
May Bank Staffs 64 F3
Maybole S Ayrs 104 F8
Maybury Surrey 32 E10
Mayes Green Surrey 14 G3
Mayfield E Susx 15 Q5
Mayfield Mdloth 115 Q8
Mayfield Staffs 65 M3
Mayford Surrey 32 E11
May Hill Gloucs 41 L7
Mayland Essex 46 G11
Maylandsea Essex 46 F11
Maynard's Green E Susx 15 Q7
Maypole Birm 53 L5
Maypole Kent 35 M9
Maypole Mons 40 G8
Maypole Green Norfk 59 N2
Maypole Green Suffk 58 D9
Maypole Green Suffk 59 K9
May's Green Oxon 31 Q6
May's Green Surrey 32 F11
Mead Devon 18 D9
Meadgate BaNES 29 K10
Meadle Bucks 44 A10
Meadowtown Shrops 63 K12
Meadwell Devon 7 M8
Meaford Staffs 64 F5
Mealabost W Isls 152 g3
Meal Bank Cumb 89 N7
Mealrigg Cumb 97 M12

Mealsgate Cumb 97 P10
Meanwood Leeds 85 L8
Mearbeck N York 84 B3
Meare Somset 21 P5
Meare Green Somset 21 L9
Meare Green Somset 21 M8
Mearns E Rens 113 Q10
Mears Ashby Nhants 55 L7
Measham Leics 65 Q9
Meath Green Surrey 15 K2
Meathop Cumb 89 L10
Meaux E R Yk 87 L7
Meavaig W Isls 152 e6
Meavy Devon 4 H3
Medbourne Leics 55 K2
Medburn Nthumb 100 E4
Meddon Devon 18 D10
Meden Vale Notts 78 F9
Medlam Lincs 68 F11
Medlar Lancs 83 K8
Medmenham Bucks 32 A5
Medomsley Dur 100 E7
Medstead Hants 25 L6
Medway Services
    Medway 34 E9
Meerbrook Staffs 77 J11
Meer Common Herefs 51 K10
Meesden Herts 45 M5
Meeson Wrekin 64 C8
Meeth Devon 7 Q3
Meeting Green Suffk 57 P9
Meeting House Hill Norfk 71 L6
Meidrim Carmth 37 Q6
Meifod Powys 62 G9
Meigle P & K 124 F4
Meikle Carco D & G 105 P7
Meikle Earnock S Lans 114 C10
Meikle Kilmory Ag & B 112 F9
Meikle Obney P & K 123 Q5
Meikleour P & K 124 D5
Meikle Wartle Abers 140 H9
Meinciau Carmth 38 C9
Meir C Stke 64 H4
Meir Heath Staffs 64 H4
Melbost W Isls 152 g3
Melbourn Cambs 45 M3
Melbourne Derbys 66 C7
Melbourne E R Yk 86 D6
Melbur Cnwll 3 L5
Melbury Devon 18 G9
Melbury Abbas Dorset 23 K9
Melbury Bubb Dorset 10 E4
Melbury Osmond Dorset 10 E3
Melbury Sampford
    Dorset 10 E4
Melchbourne Bed 55 P7
Melcombe Bingham
    Dorset 11 J4
Meldon Devon 7 Q6
Meldon Nthumb 100 E1
Meldon Park Nthumb 100 E1
Meldreth Cambs 45 M2
Meldrum Stirlg 114 C1
Melfort Ag & B 120 F10
Meliden Denbgs 74 E7
Melinau Pembks 37 N8
Melin-byrhedyn Powys 61 P12
Melincourt Neath 39 K11
Melin-y-coed Conwy 73 P11
Melin-y-ddol Powys 62 F10
Melin-y-wig Denbgs 62 E2
Melkinthorpe Cumb 89 P2
Melkridge Nthumb 99 L5
Melksham Wilts 29 P9
Mellangoose Cnwll 2 H8
Mell Green W Berk 31 K7
Mellguards Cumb 98 F9
Melling Lancs 83 N1
Melling Sefton 75 L4
Melling Mount Sefton 75 L3
Mellis Suffk 58 G6
Mellon Charles Highld 143 M7
Mellon Udrigle Highld 143 N6
Mellor Lancs 83 P9
Mellor Stockp 77 J5
Mellor Brook Lancs 83 P9
Mells Somset 22 H4
Mells Suffk 59 M5
Melmerby Cumb 99 J10
Melmerby N York 90 H9
Melmerby N York 91 N11
Melness Highld 149 M4
Melon Green Suffk 58 C9
Melplash Dorset 10 D5
Melrose Border 107 N3
Melsetter Ork 147 b6
Melsonby N York 91 K5
Meltham Kirk 77 L2
Meltham Mills Kirk 77 L2
Melton E R Yk 86 H10
Meltonby E R Yk 86 E5
Melton Constable Norfk 70 F5
Melton Mowbray Leics 67 J8
Melton Ross N Linc 79 Q2
Melvaig Highld 143 K8
Melverley Shrops 63 K9
Melverley Green Shrops 63 K9
Melvich Highld 150 F4
Membury Devon 9 P4
Memsie Abers 141 N4
Memus Angus 124 H1
Menabilly Cnwll 3 N4
Menagissey Cnwll 2 H5
Menai Bridge IoA 73 J9
Mendham Suffk 59 K4
Mendip Hills 22 C3
Mendlesham Suffk 58 G7
Mendlesham Green Suffk 58 F8
Menheniot Cnwll 4 D4
Menithwood Worcs 52 D7
Menna Cnwll 3 M4
Mennock D & G 105 N8
Menston C Brad 85 J6
Menstrie Clacks 114 F2
Mentmore Bucks 44 C8
Meoble Highld 127 P9
Meole Brace Shrops 63 N10
Meols Wirral 74 H6
Meonstoke Hants 25 K9
Meopham Kent 34 C9
Meopham Green Kent 34 C9
Meopham Station Kent 34 C9
Mepal Cambs 56 H4
Meppershall C Beds 44 G4
Merbach Herefs 40 D3
Mere Ches E 76 D7
Mere Wilts 22 H6
Mere Brow Lancs 83 K11
Mereclough Lancs 84 C9
Mere Green Birm 53 L2
Mere Green Worcs 52 H8
Mere Heath Ches W 76 C9
Meresborough Medway 34 E9
Mereworth Kent 34 B11
Mergie Abers 132 H4
Meriden Solhll 53 N4
Merkadale Highld 134 G7
Merley BCP 11 P5
Merlin's Bridge Pembks 37 J8
Merrington Shrops 63 N8
Merrion Pembks 36 H11
Merriott Somset 21 N11
Merrivale Devon 7 N9
Merrow Surrey 32 F11

Merry Field Hill Dorset 11 N4
Merry Hill Herts 32 G3
Merryhill Wolves 52 G1
Merry Lees Leics 66 D11
Merrymeet Cnwll 4 D3
Mersea Island Essex 47 K3
Mersey Crossing Halton 75 N7
Mersham Kent 17 J3
Merstham Surrey 33 K11
Merston W Susx 14 C10
Merstone IoW 13 J8
Merther Cnwll 3 L5
Merthyr Carmth 38 A7
Merthyr Cynog Powys 39 N4
Merthyr Dyfan V Glam 27 Q8
Merthyr Mawr Brdgnd 27 J8
Merthyr Tydfil Myr Td 27 P7
Merthyr Vale Myr Td 27 P8
Merton Devon 19 K11
Merton Gt Lon 33 J8
Merton Norfk 70 D12
Merton Oxon 43 M8
Meshaw Devon 19 P9
Messing Essex 46 F8
Messingham N Linc 79 M3
Metfield Suffk 59 L4
Metherell Cnwll 4 F3
Metheringham Lincs 79 Q11
Methil Fife 115 Q1
Methilhill Fife 115 Q1
Methley Leeds 85 N10
Methley Junction Leeds 85 N10
Methlick Abers 141 K8
Methven P & K 123 P7
Methwold Norfk 57 P2
Methwold Hythe Norfk 57 N2
Mettingham Suffk 59 M3
Metton Norfk 71 J5
Mevagissey Cnwll 3 P5
Mexborough Donc 78 D4
Mey Highld 151 N2
Meysey Hampton Gloucs 30 D2
Miabhaig W Isls 152 e3
Michaelchurch Herefs 40 H7
Michaelchurch Escley
    Herefs 40 D5
Michaelchurch-on-
    Arrow Powys 50 H10
Michaelstone-y-Fedw
    Newpt 28 C5
Michaelstow Cnwll 6 F9
Michaelwood Services
    Gloucs 29 L3
Michelcombe Devon 5 L3
Micheldever Hants 24 H5
Micheldever Station
    Hants 24 H5
Michelmersh Hants 24 F8
Mickfield Suffk 58 H8
Micklebring Donc 78 E5
Mickleby N York 92 G4
Micklefield Leeds 85 N9
Micklefield Green Herts 32 E3
Mickleham Surrey 32 H11
Mickleover C Derb 65 P5
Micklethwaite C Brad 84 G7
Micklethwaite Cumb 98 C8
Mickleton Dur 90 F2
Mickleton Gloucs 42 F3
Mickletown Leeds 85 N9
Mickle Trafford Ches W 75 M9
Mickley Derbys 77 Q8
Mickley N York 91 L11
Mickley Green Suffk 58 B9
Mickley Square Nthumb 100 D6
Mid Ardlaw Abers 141 M3
Midbea Ork 147 c2
Mid Beltie Abers 132 F4
Mid Bockhampton BCP 12 B5
Mid Calder W Loth 115 K8
Mid Clyth Highld 151 P9
Mid Culbeuchly Abers 140 G3
Middle Assendon Oxon 31 N6
Middle Aston Oxon 43 K6
Middle Barton Oxon 43 J6
Middlebie D & G 97 Q3
Middlebridge P & K 130 E2
Middle Chinnock Somset 21 Q10
Middle Claydon Bucks 43 P6
Middlecliffe Barns 78 C2
Middlecott Devon 8 D7
Middle Duntisbourne
    Gloucs 41 R10
Middleham N York 91 J9
Middle Handley Derbys 78 C8
Middle Harling Norfk 58 E3
Middlehill Cnwll 4 D3
Middlehill Wilts 29 M8
Middlehope Shrops 51 N3
Middle Kames Ag & B 112 H3
Middle Littleton Worcs 42 C2
Middle Madeley Staffs 64 D3
Middle Maes-coed
    Herefs 40 D4
Middlemarsh Dorset 10 G4
Middle Mayfield Staffs 65 L3
Middle Mill Pembks 36 F5
Middlemoor Devon 7 M8
Middle Quarter Kent 16 E3
Middle Rasen Lincs 80 B6
Middle Rocombe Devon 5 Q3
Middle Salter Lancs 83 N3
Middlesbrough Middsb 92 A3
Middlesceugh Cumb 98 E10
Middleshaw Cumb 89 N9
Middlesmoor N York 91 J12
Middle Stoford Somset 21 J9
Middle Stoke Medway 34 E7
Middlestone Dur 100 H10
Middlestone Moor Dur 100 H10
Middle Stoughton
    Somset 21 P3
Middlestown Wakefd 85 K11
Middle Street Gloucs 41 M10
Middle Taphouse Cnwll 4 B4
Middlethird Border 107 R1
Middleton Ag & B 118 A8
Middleton Cumb 89 Q8
Middleton Derbys 65 P1
Middleton Derbys 77 M11
Middleton Essex 46 F4
Middleton Hants 24 H5
Middleton Herefs 51 P7
Middleton Lancs 83 K3
Middleton Leeds 85 L9
Middleton N York 84 H4
Middleton N York 92 C6
Middleton Nhants 55 L2
Middleton Norfk 69 L8
Middleton Nthumb 100 E1
Middleton Nthumb 117 P4
Middleton P & K 124 C7
Middleton Rochdl 76 F2
Middleton Shrops 51 N6
Middleton Shrops 63 J8
Middleton Suffk 59 P7
Middleton Swans 26 B6
Middleton Warwks 53 M2
Middleton Cheney Nhants 43 L3
Middleton Green Staffs 64 H5
Middleton Hall Nthumb 108 H3
Middleton-in-Teesdale
    Dur 90 F2
Middleton Moor Suffk 59 P7

Middleton One Row
    Darltn 91 N4
Middleton-on-Leven
    N York 91 Q5
Middleton-on-Sea
    W Susx 14 D10
Middleton on the Hill
    Herefs 51 P7
Middleton on the Wolds
    E R Yk 86 H5
Middleton Park C Aber 133 M2
Middleton Priors Shrops 52 B3
Middleton Quernhow
    N York 91 N11
Middleton St George
    Darltn 91 N4
Middleton Scriven
    Shrops 52 C3
Middleton Stoney Oxon 43 L7
Middleton Tyas N York 91 L5
Middle Town IoS 2 b3
Middletown Cumb 88 C5
Middletown Powys 63 K9
Middle Tysoe Warwks 42 H3
Middle Wallop Hants 24 D7
Middlewich Ches E 76 C10
Middle Winterslow Wilts 24 D7
Middlewood Cnwll 7 K9
Middle Woodford Wilts 23 N5
Middlewood Green Suffk 58 G8
Middle Yard Gloucs 41 N11
Middlezoy Somset 21 N7
Middridge Dur 91 M2
Midford BaNES 29 M10
Midge Hall Lancs 83 L9
Midgeholme Cumb 99 Q6
Midgham W Berk 31 M9
Midgley Calder 84 F10
Midgley Wakefd 85 K12
Midhopestones Sheff 77 N4
Midhurst W Susx 14 C6
Mid Lavant W Susx 13 Q3
Midlem Border 107 N4
Mid Mains Highld 137 M8
Midmar Abers 132 G3
Midney Somset 21 P8
Midpark Ag & B 112 F9
Midsomer Norton BaNES 22 F3
Midtown Highld 149 M4
Midville Lincs 80 G12
Mid Yell Shet 147 j3
Migdale Highld 146 C7
Migvie Abers 132 C3
Milarrochy Stirlg 113 M1
Milborne Port Somset 22 F9
Milborne St Andrew
    Dorset 11 K5
Milborne Wick Somset 22 F9
Milbourne Nthumb 100 E3
Milbourne Wilts 29 Q5
Milburn Cumb 89 Q2
Milbury Heath S Glos 29 K4
Milby N York 85 N2
Milcombe Oxon 43 J5
Milden Suffk 46 G2
Mildenhall Suffk 57 N6
Mildenhall Wilts 30 E8
Milebrook Powys 51 K6
Milebush Kent 16 D2
Mile Elm Wilts 30 A8
Mile End Essex 46 H6
Mile End Gloucs 41 J9
Mile End Suffk 59 L3
Mileham Norfk 70 D8
Mile Oak Br & H 15 J9
Mile Oak Staffs 65 M11
Miles Hope Herefs 51 P7
Milesmark Fife 115 K4
Miles Platting Manch 76 F4
Mile Town Kent 34 G7
Milfield Nthumb 108 H3
Milford Derbys 66 B3
Milford Devon 18 E9
Milford Powys 62 E1
Milford Staffs 64 H8
Milford Surrey 14 D2
Milford Haven Pembks 36 H9
Milford on Sea Hants 12 D6
Milkwall Gloucs 41 J10
Millais Jersey 13 a1
Milland W Susx 25 N8
Mill Bank Calder 84 F11
Millbeck Cumb 88 H2
Millbreck Abers 141 N7
Millbridge Surrey 25 P5
Millbrook C Beds 44 E4
Millbrook C Soton 24 F10
Millbrook Cnwll 4 F6
Millbrook Jersey 13 b2
Millbrook Tamesd 76 H4
Mill Brow Stockp 76 H6
Millburn Abers 133 L4
Millcombe Devon 5 N7
Mill Common Norfk 71 L11
Mill Common Norfk 59 N4
Millcorner E Susx 16 E6
Millcraig Highld 145 P11
Mill Cross Devon 5 M4
Milldale Staffs 65 L1
Mill End Bucks 31 R5
Mill End Cambs 57 L8
Mill End Herts 45 L5
Millend Gloucs 41 M10
Miller's Dale Derbys 77 L9
Millers Green Derbys 65 Q2
Miller's Green Essex 45 Q10
Millerston C Glas 114 B8
Millgate Lancs 84 C11
Mill Green Cambs 46 B3
Mill Green Essex 34 B2
Mill Green Herts 45 J9
Mill Green Lincs 68 E7
Mill Green Norfk 58 H4
Mill Green Suffk 58 C6
Mill Green Suffk 58 D10
Mill Green Suffk 59 K8
Millhalf Herefs 40 C3
Millhayes Devon 9 N4
Millhead Lancs 83 L1
Millheugh S Lans 114 D11
Mill Hill E Susx 16 A9
Mill Hill Gt Lon 33 J3
Millhouse Ag & B 112 G7
Millhouse Cumb 98 G10
Millhousebridge D & G 97 M3
Millhouse Green Barns 77 M3
Millhouses Sheff 77 Q5
Millhouses Barns 78 C3
Millikenpark Rens 113 M7
Mill Lane Hants 25 M3
Millmeece Staffs 64 E5
Millness Cumb 89 N10
Mill of Drummond P & K 123 N9
Mill of Haldane W Duns 113 M4
Millom Cumb 88 G10

Millook Cnwll 6 H5
Millpool Cnwll 2 F8
Millpool Cnwll 6 G10
Millport N Ayrs 112 H10
Mill Side Cumb 89 N10
Mill Street Kent 34 C11
Mill Street Suffk 58 F6
Millthorpe Derbys 77 P8
Millthrop Cumb 89 Q8
Milltimber C Aber 133 L4
Milltown Abers 131 M2
Milltown Abers 132 D1
Milltown Cnwll 3 Q3
Milltown D & G 98 D3
Milltown Derbys 78 B11
Milltown Devon 19 L6
Milltown Highld 135 N7
Milltown of Auchindoun
    Moray 139 Q8
Milltown of Campfield
    Abers 132 G4
Milltown of Edinvillie
    Moray 139 N8
Milltown of Learney
    Abers 132 G4
Milltown of Rothiemay
    Moray 140 E6
Milnathort P & K 124 C11
Milngavie E Duns 113 Q6
Milnrow Rochdl 76 G1
Milnthorpe Cumb 89 N10
Milnthorpe Wakefd 85 M11
Milovaig Highld 134 C6
Milson Shrops 52 B6
Milstead Kent 34 F10
Milston Wilts 23 Q4
Milthorpe Nhants 43 M3
Milton C Stke 64 G3
Milton Cambs 57 J8
Milton Cumb 98 H6
Milton D & G 95 J7
Milton D & G 96 G4
Milton Derbys 66 B8
Milton Highld 137 N9
Milton Highld 137 Q6
Milton Highld 146 D10
Milton Inver 113 C12
Milton Kent 34 C8
Milton Moray 139 M12
Milton Moray 140 D2
Milton N Som 28 D10
Milton Newpt 28 E5
Milton Notts 78 H9
Milton Oxon 43 K5
Milton Oxon 43 K5
Milton P & K 131 K12
Milton Pembks 37 K10
Milton Somset 21 P8
Milton Stirlg 113 P1
Milton Abbas Dorset 11 K4
Milton Abbot Devon 7 M9
Milton Bridge Mdloth 115 N8
Milton Bryan C Beds 44 D6
Milton Clevedon Somset 22 F6
Milton Combe Devon 4 G3
Milton Common Oxon 43 N11
Milton Damerel Devon 18 H10
Milton End Gloucs 30 D2
Milton End Gloucs 41 L9
Milton Ernest Bed 55 P9
Milton Green Ches W 75 M12
Milton Hill Oxon 31 K4
Milton Keynes M Keyn 44 B4
Milton Lilbourne Wilts 30 E10
Milton Malsor Nhants 55 J9
Milton Morenish P & K 122 G5
Milton of Auchinhove
    Abers 132 E4
Milton of Balgonie Fife 115 Q1
Milton of Buchanan
    Stirlg 113 N3
Milton of Campsie
    E Duns 114 B6
Milton of Finavon Angus 125 K1
Milton of Leys Highld 138 C7
Milton of Murtle C Aber 133 L4
Milton on Stour Dorset 22 G8
Milton Regis Kent 34 F9
Milton Street E Susx 15 P10
Milton-under-
    Wychwood Oxon 42 F8
Milverton Somset 20 H8
Milverton Warwks 53 P7
Milwich Staffs 64 H6
Milwr Flints 74 G8
Minard Ag & B 112 G2
Minchington Dorset 23 L10
Minchinhampton Gloucs 29 P2
Mindrum Nthumb 108 D3
Minehead Somset 20 F3
Minera Wrexhm 63 J2
Minety Wilts 30 B4
Minffordd Gwynd 61 L4
Mingarrypark Highld 127 M10
Mingary Lincs 80 F11
Miningsby Lincs 80 F11
Minions Cnwll 7 K10
Minishant S Ayrs 104 F7
Minllyn Gwynd 61 Q9
Minnigaff D & G 95 M5
Minnonie Abers 141 K4
Minshull Vernon Ches E 76 C11
Minskip N York 85 M2
Minstead Hants 12 D3
Minsted W Susx 25 N8
Minster Kent 34 G7
Minster Kent 35 Q9
Minsterley Shrops 63 L11
Minster Lovell Oxon 42 G9
Minsterworth Gloucs 41 M8
Minster-on-Sea Kent 34 G8
Minterne Magna Dorset 10 G4
Minterne Parva Dorset 10 G4
Minting Lincs 80 D9
Mintlaw Abers 141 N6
Minto Border 107 N6
Minton Shrops 51 M2
Minwear Pembks 37 K8
Minworth Birm 53 M2
Mirehouse Cumb 88 C4
Mireland Highld 151 P4
Mirfield Kirk 85 J11
Miserden Gloucs 41 Q10
Miskin Rhondd 27 P3
Misson Notts 78 H5
Misterton Leics 54 F4
Misterton Notts 79 J5
Misterton Somset 10 C2
Mistley Essex 47 K5
Mistley Heath Essex 47 K5
Mitcham Gt Lon 33 J8
Mitcheldean Gloucs 41 K8
Mitchell Cnwll 3 L3
Mitchellslacks D & G 106 C10
Mitchel Troy Mons 40 G9
Mitford Nthumb 100 F1
Mithian Cnwll 3 J4
Mitton Staffs 64 F9
Mixbury Oxon 43 M5
Moats Tye Suffk 58 E9
Mobberley Ches E 76 E8
Mobberley Staffs 65 K4

Moccas – Newton 173

Moccas Herefs 40 E3
Mochdre Conwy 73 P8
Mochdre Powys 50 E3
Mochrum D & G 95 L9
Mockbeggar Hants 12 B3
Mockbeggar Kent 16 C1
Mockerkin Cumb 88 E2
Modbury Devon 5 L6
Moddershall Staffs 64 G5
Moelfre IoA 72 H6
Moelfre Powys 62 G6
Moel Tryfan Gwynd 60 H1
Moffat D & G 106 E8
Mogador Surrey 33 J11
Moggerhanger C Beds 56 C10
Moira Leics 65 P9
Molash Kent 35 J12
Mol-chlach Highld 126 H2
Mold Flints 74 H11
Moldgreen Kirk 84 H12
Molehill Green Essex 45 Q7
Molehill Green Essex 46 C7
Molescroft E R Yk 87 J7
Molesden Nthumb 100 F1
Molesworth Cambs 55 Q5
Moll Highld 135 K9
Molland Devon 20 C7
Mollington Ches W 75 L9
Mollington Oxon 54 D11
Mollinsburn N Lans 114 C7
Monachty Cerdgn 48 H8
Mondynes Abers 133 J8
Monewden Suffk 59 K9
Moneydie P & K 123 Q7
Moneyrow Green W & M 32 C7
Moniaive D & G 105 P11
Monifieth Angus 125 K6
Monikie Angus 125 K5
Monimail Fife 124 F10
Monington Pembks 37 M2
Monk Bretton Barns 78 B2
Monken Hadley Gt Lon 33 J3
Monk Fryston N York 85 Q9
Monkhide Herefs 41 J3
Monkhill Cumb 98 D6
Monkhopton Shrops 52 B2
Monkland Herefs 51 M9
Monkleigh Devon 19 J9
Monknash V Glam 27 L8
Monkokehampton Devon 7 Q4
Monkseaton N Tyne 101 J4
Monks Eleigh Suffk 58 E11
Monk's Gate W Susx 14 H5
Monks Heath Ches E 76 F9
Monk Sherborne Hants 31 M11
Monks Horton Kent 17 K3
Monksilver Somset 20 G6
Monks Kirby Warwks 54 D4
Monk Soham Suffk 59 J7
Monkspath Solhll 53 L5
Monks Risborough Bucks 44 A10
Monksthorpe Lincs 80 H10
Monk Street Essex 45 R6
Monkswood Mons 40 D11
Monkton Devon 9 M4
Monkton Kent 35 N9
Monkton S Ayrs 104 F4
Monkton S Tyne 101 J5
Monkton V Glam 27 M8
Monkton Combe BaNES 29 M10
Monkton Deverill Wilts 23 J6
Monkton Farleigh Wilts 29 N9
Monkton Heathfield Somset 21 L8
Monkton Up Wimborne Dorset 23 M10
Monkton Wyld Dorset 9 Q5
Monkwearmouth Sundld 101 K6
Monkwood Hants 25 L7
Monmore Green Wolves 52 H1
Monmouth Mons 40 G9
Monnington on Wye Herefs 40 E3
Monreith D & G 95 L10
Montacute Somset 22 C10
Montcliffe Bolton 76 C1
Montford Shrops 63 L9
Montford Bridge Shrops 63 M9
Montgarrie Abers 140 E12
Montgomery Powys 50 H1
Monton Salfd 76 E4
Montrose Angus 125 P1
Mont Saint Guern 12 b2
Monxton Hants 24 E4
Monyash Derbys 77 L10
Monymusk Abers 132 G1
Monzie P & K 123 M8
Moodiesburn N Lans 114 C7
Moonzie Fife 124 G9
Moor Allerton Leeds 85 L7
Moorbath Dorset 10 C6
Moorby Lincs 80 F11
Moorcot Herefs 51 K9
Moor Crichel Dorset 11 N3
Moordown BCP 11 Q6
Moore Halton 75 P7
Moor End C Beds 44 D7
Moor End Calder 84 F9
Moor End Devon 8 C3
Moorend Gloucs 41 L11
Moor End Lancs 83 J6
Moor End N York 86 B7
Moorends Donc 86 C12
Moorgreen Hants 24 H10
Moor Green Herts 45 L6
Moorgreen Notts 66 D3
Moorhall Derbys 77 P8
Moorhampton Herefs 40 E2
Moorhead C Brad 84 H8
Moor Head Leeds 85 K9
Moorhouse Cumb 98 B8
Moorhouse Cumb 98 D7
Moorhouse Donc 78 D2
Moorhouse Notts 79 J10
Moorhouse Bank Surrey 33 M11
Moorland Somset 21 M7
Moorlinch Somset 21 N6
Moor Monkton N York 85 Q4
Moor Row Cumb 88 D4
Moor Row Cumb 97 P8
Moorsholm R & Cl 92 E4
Moorside Dorset 22 H9
Moorside Dur 100 E8
Moor Side Lancs 83 K8
Moor Side Lancs 83 L8
Moorside Leeds 85 K8
Moor Side Lincs 80 E12
Moorside Oldham 76 H2
Moorstock Kent 17 K3
Moor Street Birm 53 J4
Moor Street Medway 34 E9
Moorswater Cnwll 4 C4
Moorthorpe Wakefd 78 D2
Moortown Devon 7 P10
Moortown Hants 12 B4
Moortown IoW 12 G8
Moortown Leeds 85 L7
Moortown Lincs 79 Q4
Moortown Wrekin 63 Q8
Morangie Highld 146 D8
Morar Highld 127 M6
Morborne Cambs 56 C2
Morchard Bishop Devon 8 E3
Morchard Road Devon 8 E4
Morcombelake Dorset 10 B6
Morcott Rutlnd 67 M12
Morda Shrops 63 J6
Morden Dorset 11 M5
Morden Gt Lon 33 J8
Mordiford Herefs 40 H4
Mordon Dur 91 N1
More Shrops 51 K2
Morebath Devon 20 E8
Morebattle Border 108 C5
Morecambe Lancs 83 K2
Moredon Swindn 30 D5
Morefield Highld 144 E6
Morehall Kent 17 M3
Moreleigh Devon 5 M6
Morenish P & K 122 G6
Moresby Parks Cumb 88 D3
Morestead Hants 24 H8
Moreton Dorset 11 K7
Moreton Essex 45 P10
Moreton Herefs 51 N8
Moreton Oxon 43 P10
Moreton Staffs 64 E8
Moreton Staffs 65 L6
Moreton Wirral 75 J6
Moreton Corbet Shrops 63 P7
Moretonhampstead Devon 8 E7
Moreton-in-Marsh Gloucs 42 E5
Moreton Jeffries Herefs 51 Q11
Moretonmill Shrops 63 P7
Moreton Morrell Warwks 53 P9
Moreton on Lugg Herefs 40 G3
Moreton Paddox Warwks 53 P9
Moreton Pinkney Nhants 54 F11
Moreton Say Shrops 64 B5
Moreton Valence Gloucs 41 M9
Morfa Cerdgn 48 E10
Morfa Bychan Gwynd 61 J5
Morfa Dinlle Gwynd 72 G12
Morfa Glas Neath 39 K10
Morfa Nefyn Gwynd 60 D4
Morganstown Cardif 27 Q6
Morgan's Vale Wilts 24 C9
Morham E Loth 116 D7
Moriah Cerdgn 49 K5
Morland Cumb 89 P2
Morley Ches E 76 F7
Morley Derbys 66 C4
Morley Dur 91 J1
Morley Leeds 85 K9
Morley Green Ches E 76 F7
Morley St Botolph Norfk 70 G12
Mornick Cnwll 7 L10
Morningside C Edin 115 N7
Morningside N Lans 114 E10
Morningthorpe Norfk 59 J2
Morpeth Nthumb 100 G1
Morphie Abers 132 H11
Morrey Staffs 65 L8
Morridge Side Staffs 65 J1
Morriston Swans 26 G3
Morston Norfk 70 E3
Mortehoe Devon 19 J4
Morthen Rothm 78 D6
Mortimer W Berk 31 N9
Mortimer Common W Berk 31 N9
Mortimer's Cross Herefs 51 M8
Mortimer West End Hants 31 N9
Mortlake Gt Lon 32 H7
Morton Cumb 98 E7
Morton Cumb 98 F10
Morton Derbys 78 C11
Morton IoW 13 K7
Morton Lincs 68 B7
Morton Lincs 79 K5
Morton Lincs 79 M11
Morton Notts 67 J2
Morton Shrops 63 J7
Morton-on-Swale N York 91 N8
Morton on the Hill Norfk 70 G9
Morton Tinmouth Dur 91 K2
Morvah Cnwll 2 C7
Morval Cnwll 4 C5
Morvich Highld 136 D11
Morville Shrops 52 C2
Morville Heath Shrops 52 C2
Morwenstow Cnwll 18 D10
Mosborough Sheff 78 C7
Moscow E Ayrs 105 J2
Mose Shrops 52 D3
Mosedale Cumb 98 D11
Moseley Birm 53 K4
Moseley Wolves 52 H1
Moseley Worcs 52 E8
Moses Gate Bolton 76 D2
Moss Ag & B 118 C4
Moss Donc 86 B12
Moss Wrexhm 63 J2
Mossat Abers 140 D12
Mossbank Shet 147 j5
Moss Bank St Hel 75 N4
Mossbay Cumb 88 C1
Mossblown S Ayrs 104 G5
Mossbrow Traffd 76 D6
Mossburnford Border 107 Q6
Mossdale D & G 96 D4
Mossdale E Ayrs 105 J9
Moss Edge Lancs 83 K6
Moss End Ches E 76 C8
Mossend N Lans 114 D9
Mosser Mains Cumb 88 F2
Mossley Ches E 76 G11
Mossley Tamesd 76 H3
Mosspaul Hotel Border 107 L10
Moss Side Cumb 97 P8
Moss-side Highld 138 F5
Moss Side Lancs 83 J9
Moss Side Sefton 75 L3
Mosstodloch Moray 139 Q4
Mossyard D & G 95 Q8
Mossy Lea Lancs 75 P1
Mosterton Dorset 10 C4
Moston Manch 76 G3
Moston Shrops 63 P7
Moston Green Ches E 76 D11
Mostyn Flints 74 G7
Motcombe Dorset 23 J8
Mothecombe Devon 5 K7
Motherby Cumb 98 E12
Motherwell N Lans 114 D10
Motspur Park Gt Lon 33 J9
Mottingham Gt Lon 33 M8
Mottisfont Hants 24 E8
Mottisfont Hants 24 E8
Mottistone IoW 12 G8
Mottram in Longdendale Tamesd 77 J5
Mottram St Andrew Ches E 76 G8
Mouilpied Guern 12 c3
Mouldsworth Ches W 75 N9
Moulin P & K 123 N1
Moulsecoomb Br & H 15 L9
Moulsford Oxon 31 M5
Moulsoe M Keyn 44 C3
Moultavie Highld 145 P11
Moulton Ches W 76 C9
Moulton Lincs 68 F7
Moulton N York 91 L6
Moulton Nhants 55 K7
Moulton Suffk 57 N8
Moulton V Glam 27 P8
Moulton Chapel Lincs 68 E8
Moulton St Mary Norfk 71 M10
Moulton Seas End Lincs 68 F6
Mount Cnwll 3 J3
Mount Cnwll 4 A3
Mount Kirk 84 G11
Mountain C Brad 84 G9
Mountain Ash Rhondd 27 P3
Mountain Cross Border 115 L12
Mountain Street Kent 35 J11
Mount Ambrose Cnwll 2 H6
Mount Bures Essex 46 F5
Mountfield E Susx 16 C7
Mountgerald Highld 137 P3
Mount Hawke Cnwll 2 H5
Mount Hermon Cnwll 2 H11
Mountjoy Cnwll 3 L2
Mount Lothian Mdloth 115 N10
Mountnessing Essex 34 A3
Mounton Mons 28 G4
Mount Pleasant Ches E 76 F12
Mount Pleasant Derbys 65 P8
Mount Pleasant Derbys 65 Q2
Mount Pleasant Dur 100 H11
Mount Pleasant E R Yk 87 N7
Mount Pleasant E Susx 15 M7
Mount Pleasant Norfk 58 E2
Mount Pleasant Suffk 57 P11
Mount Pleasant Worcs 53 J7
Mountsorrel Leics 66 F9
Mount Sorrel Wilts 23 M8
Mount Tabor Calder 84 G9
Mousehole Cnwll 2 D9
Mouswald D & G 97 L4
Mow Cop Ches E 76 F12
Mowhaugh Border 108 C5
Mowmacre Hill C Leic 66 F10
Mowsley Leics 54 G3
Moy Highld 129 M8
Moy Highld 138 E9
Moyle Highld 136 B12
Moylegrove Pembks 48 A11
Muasdale Ag & B 103 J2
Muchalls Abers 133 L6
Much Birch Herefs 40 G5
Much Cowarne Herefs 41 J2
Much Dewchurch Herefs 40 G5
Muchelney Somset 21 P8
Muchelney Ham Somset 21 P8
Much Hadham Herts 45 M8
Much Hoole Lancs 83 L10
Much Hoole Town Lancs 83 L10
Muchlarnick Cnwll 4 C5
Much Marcle Herefs 41 K5
Much Wenlock Shrops 64 B12
Muck Highld 126 G8
Mucking Thurr 34 B6
Muckleburgh Collection Norfk 70 G3
Muckleford Dorset 10 G6
Mucklestone Staffs 64 D5
Muckley Shrops 52 B1
Muckton Lincs 80 G7
Muddiford Devon 19 L6
Muddles Green E Susx 15 Q8
Mudeford BCP 12 C6
Mudford Somset 22 D9
Mudford Sock Somset 22 D9
Mudgley Somset 21 P4
Mud Row Kent 34 H8
Mugdock Stirlg 113 Q6
Mugeary Highld 134 H8
Mugginton Derbys 65 P4
Muggintonlane End Derbys 65 P3
Muggleswick Dur 100 D8
Muirden Abers 140 H5
Muirdrum Angus 125 L5
Muiresk Abers 140 G6
Muirhead Angus 124 G6
Muirhead Fife 124 F11
Muirhead N Lans 114 C7
Muirhouses Falk 115 J5
Muirkirk E Ayrs 105 N4
Muirmill Stirlg 114 D4
Muir of Fowlis Abers 132 E2
Muir of Miltonduff Moray 139 M4
Muir of Ord Highld 137 P6
Muirshearlich Highld 128 G8
Muirtack Abers 141 N8
Muirton P & K 123 N10
Muirton Mains Highld 137 M5
Muirton of Ardblair P & K 124 D4
Muker N York 90 F7
Mulbarton Norfk 71 J12
Mulben Moray 139 Q6
Mulfra Cnwll 2 D7
Mull Ag & B 119 Q6
Mullacott Cross Devon 19 K4
Mullion Cnwll 2 H10
Mullion Cove Cnwll 2 G11
Mumby Lincs 81 K9
Munderfield Row Herefs 52 C10
Munderfield Stocks Herefs 52 C10
Mundesley Norfk 71 L5
Mundford Norfk 57 Q2
Mundham Norfk 59 L1
Mundon Hill Essex 46 F11
Mundy Bois Kent 16 G1
Mungrisdale Cumb 98 D12
Munlochy Highld 138 B5
Munnoch N Ayrs 113 K11
Munsley Herefs 41 K3
Munslow Shrops 51 N3
Murchington Devon 8 C7
Murcot Worcs 42 C4
Murcott Oxon 43 M8
Murcott Wilts 29 Q4
Murkle Highld 151 L3
Murlaggan Highld 128 D6
Murrell Green Hants 25 N2
Murroes Angus 125 J5
Murrow Cambs 68 G10
Mursley Bucks 44 B6
Murston Kent 34 G9
Murthill Angus 125 J1
Murthly P & K 124 C5
Murton C York 86 C5
Murton Cumb 90 C2
Murton Dur 101 K9
Murton N Tyne 101 J4
Murton Nthumb 117 L11
Murton Swans 26 E4
Musbury Devon 9 P6
Muscoates N York 92 E10
Musselburgh E Loth 115 Q7
Muston Leics 67 K5
Muston N York 93 M10
Mustow Green Worcs 52 F6
Muswell Hill Gt Lon 33 K4
Mutehill D & G 96 E8
Mutford Suffk 59 P3
Muthill P & K 123 M9
Mutterton Devon 9 J4
Muxton Wrekin 64 D9
Mybster Highld 151 L6
Myddfai Carmth 39 J6
Myddle Shrops 63 M7
Mydroilyn Cerdgn 48 G9
Myerscough Lancs 83 L7
Mylor Cnwll 3 K7
Mylor Bridge Cnwll 3 K7
Mynachlog ddu Pembks 37 N4
Myndd-llan Flints 74 G9
Myndtown Shrops 51 L3
Mynydd Bach Cerdgn 49 M5
Mynydd-bach Mons 28 G3
Mynydd-Bach Swans 26 G3
Mynyddgarreg Carmth 38 C10
Mynydd Isa Flints 75 J11
Mynydd Llandygai Gwynd 73 K10
Mynytho Gwynd 60 E6
Myrebird Abers 132 H4
Myredykes Border 107 P10
Mytchett Surrey 32 C11
Mytholm Calder 84 E9
Mytholmroyd Calder 84 F10
Mythop Lancs 83 J8
Myton-on-Swale N York 85 N2

N

Naast Highld 143 M8
Nab's Head Lancs 83 N9
Na Buirgh W Isls 152 d6
Naburn C York 86 B6
Naccolt Kent 17 J2
Nackington Kent 35 L11
Nacton Suffk 47 M4
Nafferton E R Yk 87 K3
Nag's Head Gloucs 29 P3
Nailbridge Gloucs 41 K8
Nailsbourne Somset 21 K7
Nailsea N Som 28 G8
Nailstone Leics 66 C10
Nailsworth Gloucs 29 N2
Nairn Highld 138 G5
Nalderswood Surrey 15 J2
Nancegollan Cnwll 2 G8
Nancledra Cnwll 2 D7
Nanhoron Gwynd 60 D6
Nannerch Flints 74 G9
Nanpantan Leics 66 E8
Nanpean Cnwll 3 N3
Nanquidno Cnwll 2 B8
Nanstallon Cnwll 6 F11
Nant-ddu Powys 39 N8
Nanternis Cerdgn 48 F9
Nantgaredig Carmth 38 D7
Nantgarw Rhondd 27 Q5
Nant-glas Powys 50 D7
Nantglyn Denbgs 74 D11
Nantgwyn Powys 50 D5
Nant Gwynant Gwynd 61 L2
Nantlle Gwynd 60 H2
Nantmawr Shrops 63 J7
Nantmel Powys 50 E7
Nantmor Gwynd 61 K3
Nant Peris Gwynd 73 K12
Nantwich Ches E 64 C2
Nant-y-Bwch Blae G 39 Q9
Nantycaws Carmth 38 C8
Nant-y-derry Mons 40 D10
Nantyffyllon Brdgnd 27 K4
Nantyglo Blae G 40 B9
Nant-y-gollen Shrops 62 H6
Nant-y-moel Brdgnd 27 M4
Nant-y-pandy Conwy 73 M9
Naphill Bucks 32 B3
Napleton Worcs 52 F11
Nappa N York 84 C4
Napton on the Hill Warwks 54 D8
Narberth Pembks 37 L7
Narborough Leics 54 E1
Narborough Norfk 69 P9
Narkurs Cnwll 4 E5
Nasareth Gwynd 60 H2
Naseby Nhants 54 H5
Nash Bucks 43 Q5
Nash Gt Lon 33 M9
Nash Herefs 51 K8
Nash Newpt 28 D6
Nash Shrops 51 Q6
Nash End Worcs 52 E4
Nashes Green Hants 25 L4
Nash Lee Bucks 44 B10
Nash Street Kent 34 B8
Nassington Nhants 55 Q1
Nastend Gloucs 41 M10
Nasty Herts 45 L7
Nateby Cumb 90 C5
Nateby Lancs 83 L6
National Memorial Arboretum Staffs 65 M9
National Motor Museum (Beaulieu) Hants 12 F4
National Space Centre C Leic 66 F10
Natland Cumb 89 N9
Naughton Suffk 58 F10
Naunton Gloucs 42 D7
Naunton Worcs 41 P4
Naunton Beauchamp Worcs 52 H10
Navenby Lincs 79 N12
Navestock Essex 33 P3
Navestock Side Essex 33 Q3
Navidale Highld 147 J2
Navity Highld 138 E3
Nawton N York 92 D9
Nayland Suffk 46 H5
Nazeing Essex 45 M10
Nazeing Gate Essex 45 M10
Neacroft Hants 12 C5
Neal's Green Warwks 53 Q4
Neap Shet 147 j6
Near Cotton Staffs 65 K3
Near Sawrey Cumb 89 K7
Neasden Gt Lon 33 J5
Neasham Darltn 91 N5
Neath Neath 26 H3
Neatham Hants 25 M5
Neatishead Norfk 71 L8
Nebo Cerdgn 49 J7
Nebo Conwy 61 P1
Nebo Gwynd 60 H2
Nebo IoA 72 H5
Necton Norfk 70 C10
Nedd Highld 148 D10
Nedderton Nthumb 100 G2
Nedging Suffk 58 E11
Nedging Tye Suffk 58 F11
Needham Norfk 59 J4
Needham Market Suffk 58 G9
Needham Street Suffk 57 N7
Needingworth Cambs 56 G6
Neen Savage Shrops 52 C5
Neen Sollars Shrops 52 C6
Neenton Shrops 52 B3
Nefyn Gwynd 60 E4
Neilston E Rens 113 P10
Nelson Caerph 27 Q3
Nelson Lancs 84 C7
Nemphlar S Lans 105 Q1
Nempnett Thrubwell BaNES 28 H10
Nenthall Cumb 99 L9
Nenthead Cumb 99 M9
Nenthorn Border 107 R2
Neopardy Devon 8 E5
Nep Town W Susx 15 J8
Nerabus Ag & B 110 F10
Nercwys Flints 74 H11
Nerston S Lans 114 B10
Nesbit Nthumb 108 F3
Nesfield N York 84 G5
Ness Ches W 75 J8
Nesscliffe Shrops 63 L8
Neston Ches W 75 J8
Neston Wilts 29 P8
Netchwood Shrops 52 B2
Nether Abington S Lans 106 B5
Nether Alderley Ches E 76 F8
Netheravon Wilts 23 P4
Nether Blainslie Border 107 N1
Netherbrae Abers 141 J4
Nether Broughton Leics 66 H7
Netherburn S Lans 114 E11
Netherbury Dorset 10 D5
Netherby Cumb 98 E4
Netherby N York 85 M6
Nether Cerne Dorset 10 G5
Nethercleuch D & G 97 M1
Nether Compton Dorset 22 D10
Nethercote Warwks 54 E8
Nethercott Devon 7 L5
Nethercott Devon 19 J5
Nether Crimond Abers 141 K11
Nether Dallachy Moray 139 Q3
Netherend Gloucs 29 J2
Nether Exe Devon 8 H5
Netherfield E Susx 16 C7
Netherfield Leics 66 F9
Netherfield Notts 66 G4
Nether Fingland S Lans 106 B7
Nethergate N Linc 79 J4
Nethergate Norfk 70 F6
Netherhampton Wilts 23 P7
Nether Handley Derbys 78 C8
Nether Handwick Angus 124 G4
Nether Haugh Rothm 78 C4
Netherhay Dorset 10 C4
Nether Headon Notts 79 J8
Nether Heage Derbys 66 B2
Nether Heyford Nhants 54 H9
Nether Kellet Lancs 83 L2
Nether Kinmundy Abers 141 P7
Netherland Green Staffs 65 L6
Nether Langwith Notts 78 E9
Netherlaw D & G 96 F9
Netherley Abers 133 K6
Nethermill D & G 106 D12
Nethermuir Abers 141 L7
Netherne-on-the-Hill Surrey 33 K11
Netheroyd Hill Kirk 84 H11
Nether Padley Derbys 77 N8
Nether Poppleton C York 85 R4
Nether Row Cumb 98 C10
Netherseal Derbys 65 P9
Nether Silton N York 91 Q8
Nether Skyborry Shrops 51 J6
Nether Stowey Somset 21 K5
Nether Street Essex 45 Q9
Netherstreet Wilts 29 R9
Netherthong Kirk 77 L2
Netherthorpe Derbys 78 D9
Netherton Angus 125 L1
Netherton Devon 8 G10
Netherton Dudley 52 H3
Netherton Hants 30 H10
Netherton Herefs 40 H6
Netherton Kirk 77 L1
Netherton N Lans 114 E10
Netherton Nthumb 108 F8
Netherton Oxon 31 J2
Netherton P & K 124 C2
Netherton Sefton 75 K4
Netherton Shrops 52 D4
Netherton Stirlg 113 Q5
Netherton Wakefd 85 L11
Netherton Worcs 42 A3
Nethertown Cumb 88 C5
Nethertown Highld 151 Q1
Nethertown Lancs 83 Q8
Nethertown Staffs 65 L8
Netherurd Border 115 K12
Nether Wallop Hants 24 E6
Nether Wasdale Cumb 88 F6
Nether Welton Cumb 98 D9
Nether Westcote Gloucs 42 E7
Nether Whitacre Warwks 53 N2
Nether Whitecleuch S Lans 105 Q6
Nether Winchendon Bucks 43 Q9
Netherwitton Nthumb 108 H11
Nethy Bridge Highld 139 J11
Netley Hants 12 G3
Netley Marsh Hants 24 E10
Nettlebed Oxon 31 P5
Nettlebridge Somset 22 E4
Nettlecombe Dorset 10 E6
Nettlecombe IoW 13 J9
Nettleden Herts 44 E9
Nettleham Lincs 79 P8
Nettlestead Kent 34 B12
Nettlestead Green Kent 34 B12
Nettlestone IoW 13 K6
Nettlesworth Dur 100 H8
Nettleton Lincs 80 B4
Nettleton Wilts 29 N6
Nettleton Shrub Wilts 29 N7
Netton Devon 5 J7
Netton Wilts 23 P6
Neuadd Carmth 38 G7
Neuadd-ddu Powys 50 C5
Nevendon Essex 34 D4
Nevern Pembks 37 L3
Nevill Holt Leics 55 K2
New Abbey D & G 97 K5
New Aberdour Abers 141 L3
New Addington Gt Lon 33 M9
Newall Leeds 85 J6
New Alresford Hants 25 K7
New Alyth P & K 124 E3
Newark C Pete 68 D12
Newark Ork 147 e2
Newark-on-Trent Notts 67 K1
New Arram E R Yk 87 J6
Newarthill N Lans 114 E9
New Ash Green Kent 33 R9
New Balderton Notts 67 K2
Newbarn Kent 17 L3
New Barn Kent 34 A8
New Barnet Gt Lon 33 K3
New Barton Nhants 55 L8
Newbattle Mdloth 115 P8
New Bewick Nthumb 108 H6
Newbie D & G 97 N5
Newbiggin Cumb 88 H3
Newbiggin Cumb 89 Q1
Newbiggin Cumb 98 F12
Newbiggin Cumb 98 H8
Newbiggin Dur 90 E1
Newbiggin Dur 100 F8
Newbiggin N York 90 F8
Newbiggin N York 90 G9
Newbiggin-by-the-Sea Nthumb 109 M12
Newbigging Angus 124 F4
Newbigging Angus 124 H5
Newbigging Angus 125 K5
Newbigging S Lans 115 J12
Newbiggin-on-Lune Cumb 90 B6
New Bilton Warwks 54 D5
Newbold Derbys 78 B9
Newbold Leics 66 C8
Newbold on Avon Warwks 54 D5
Newbold on Stour Warwks 42 F2
Newbold Pacey Warwks 53 P9
Newbold Revel Warwks 54 D4
Newbold Verdon Leics 66 D11
New Bolingbroke Lincs 80 F12
Newborough C Pete 68 D11
Newborough IoA 72 G10
Newborough Staffs 65 L7
Newbottle Nhants 43 L4
Newbottle Sundld 101 J8
New Boultham Lincs 79 N9
Newbourne Suffk 47 N3
New Bradwell M Keyn 44 B3
New Brampton Derbys 78 B9
New Brancepeth Dur 100 G10
Newbridge C Edin 115 L7
Newbridge Caerph 28 B3
Newbridge Cerdgn 48 H9
Newbridge Cnwll 2 C8
Newbridge Cnwll 3 K6
Newbridge D & G 97 J2
Newbridge Hants 24 E10
Newbridge IoW 12 G7
New Bridge N York 92 G9
Newbridge Oxon 31 J2
Newbridge Wrexhm 63 J4
Newbridge Green Worcs 41 N4
Newbridge-on-Usk Mons 28 E3
Newbridge-on-Wye Powys 50 D9
New Brighton Flints 75 J10
New Brighton Wirral 75 K5
New Brinsley Notts 66 D2
New Brotton R & Cl 92 E3
Newbrough Nthumb 99 N5
New Broughton Wrexhm 63 K2
New Buckenham Norfk 58 G3
Newbuildings Devon 8 E4
Newburgh Abers 141 M4
Newburgh Abers 141 N10
Newburgh Fife 124 E9
Newburgh Lancs 75 N2
Newburn N u Ty 100 F5
New Bury Bolton 76 D3
Newbury Somset 22 F3
Newbury W Berk 31 K9
Newbury Wilts 22 H5
Newbury Park Gt Lon 33 N5
Newby Cumb 89 P2
Newby Lancs 84 B6
Newby N York 83 Q1
Newby N York 92 A4
Newby N York 93 K8
Newby Bridge Cumb 89 K9
Newby Cross Cumb 98 D7
Newby East Cumb 98 F6
Newby Head Cumb 89 P2
New Byth Abers 141 K5
Newby West Cumb 98 D7
Newby Wiske N York 91 N9
Newcastle Mons 40 F8
Newcastle Shrops 50 H4
Newcastle Airport Nthumb 100 F4
Newcastle Emlyn Carmth 37 Q2
Newcastleton Border 107 M12
Newcastle-under-Lyme Staffs 64 F3
Newcastle upon Tyne N u Ty 100 G5
Newchapel Pembks 37 P3
Newchapel Staffs 64 F1
Newchapel Surrey 15 L2
New Charlton Gt Lon 33 M7
New Cheriton Hants 25 K8
Newchurch Blae G 40 A9
Newchurch Herefs 51 K10
Newchurch IoW 13 J7
Newchurch Kent 17 J4
Newchurch Mons 28 G3
Newchurch Powys 50 H10
Newchurch Staffs 65 L7
Newchurch in Pendle Lancs 84 B7
New Costessey Norfk 71 J10
New Cowper Cumb 97 M9
Newcraighall C Edin 115 P7
New Crofton Wakefd 85 M11
New Cross Cerdgn 49 L5
New Cross Gt Lon 33 L7
New Cross Somset 21 P9
New Cumnock E Ayrs 105 L7
New Cut E Susx 16 E7
New Deer Abers 141 L6
New Delaval Nthumb 100 H2
New Delph Oldham 77 J2
New Denham Bucks 32 F5
Newdigate Surrey 14 H2
New Duston Nhants 54 H8
New Earswick C York 86 B4
New Eastwood Notts 66 D3
New Edlington Donc 78 E4
New Elgin Moray 139 N3
New Ellerby E R Yk 87 M7
Newell Green Br For 32 C8
New Eltham Gt Lon 33 N8
New End Worcs 53 K8
Newenden Kent 16 E5
New England C Pete 68 D12
New England Essex 46 C3
Newent Gloucs 41 L6
New Farnley Leeds 85 K9
New Ferry Wirral 75 K6
Newfield Dur 100 G11
Newfield Dur 100 G8
Newfield Highld 146 D9
New Fletton C Pete 56 D1
New Forest National Park 12 D3
Newfound Hants 25 K3
New Fryston Wakefd 85 P10
Newgale Pembks 36 G6
New Galloway D & G 96 D3
Newgate Norfk 70 F4
Newgate Street Herts 45 K10
New Gilston Fife 125 J11
New Grimsby IoS 2 b1
Newhall Ches E 63 Q3
Newhall Derbys 65 P8
Newham Nthumb 109 K4
New Hartley Nthumb 100 H3
Newhaven C Edin 115 N6
Newhaven Derbys 77 M11
Newhaven E Susx 15 N10
New Haw Surrey 32 F9
New Hedges Pembks 37 M10
New Herrington Sundld 101 J7
Newhey Rochdl 76 H1
New Holkham Norfk 70 C4
New Holland N Linc 87 K10
Newholm N York 92 H5
New Houghton Derbys 78 E10
New Houghton Norfk 69 Q6
Newhouse N Lans 114 E9
New Houses N York 90 C12
New Houses Wigan 75 P3
New Hutton Cumb 89 P8
New Hythe Kent 34 C10
Newick E Susx 15 M6
Newingreen Kent 17 K4
Newington Kent 17 L3
Newington Kent 34 F9
Newington Oxon 31 M3
Newington Shrops 51 M4
Newington Bagpath Gloucs 29 N3
New Inn Carmth 38 C4
New Inn Torfn 28 D2
New Invention Shrops 51 J5
New Lakenham Norfk 71 J10
New Lanark S Lans 106 A1
New Lanark Village S Lans 106 A1
Newland C KuH 87 K9
Newland Cumb 89 J10
Newland E R Yk 86 E9
Newland Gloucs 40 H9
Newland N York 86 C10
Newland Oxon 42 H9
Newland Somset 20 C6
Newland Worcs 52 E11
Newlandrig Mdloth 115 Q9
Newlands Border 107 M11
Newlands Cumb 98 D10
Newlands Nthumb 100 E7
Newlands of Dundurcas Moray 139 P6
New Lane Lancs 75 M1
New Lane End Warrtn 76 B5
New Langholm D & G 98 D1
New Leake Lincs 80 H12
New Leeds Abers 141 N5
New Lodge Barns 78 B2
New Longton Lancs 83 L10
New Luce D & G 94 H5
Newlyn Cnwll 2 D9
Newmachar Abers 141 L12
Newmains N Lans 114 E10
New Malden Gt Lon 33 J8
Newman's End Essex 45 P9
Newman's Green Suffk 46 F3
Newmarket Suffk 57 M8
Newmarket W Isls 152 g3
New Marske R & Cl 92 C2
New Marston Oxon 43 L10
New Marton Shrops 63 K5
New Mill Abers 133 J7
Newmill Border 107 L7
New Mill Cnwll 2 D7
New Mill Herts 44 C9
New Mill Kirk 77 M2
Newmill Moray 140 C5
Newmillerdam Wakefd 85 L12
Newmill of Inshewan Angus 132 C12
Newmills C Edin 115 L8
New Mills Cnwll 3 L4
New Mills Derbys 77 J6
Newmills Fife 115 J4
Newmills Mons 40 G10
New Mills Powys 62 E12
Newmiln P & K 124 C7
Newmilns E Ayrs 105 K2
New Milton Hants 12 D6
New Mistley Essex 47 K5
New Moat Pembks 37 L5
Newnes Shrops 63 L5
Newney Green Essex 46 B10
Newnham Hants 25 M3
Newnham Herts 45 J4
Newnham Kent 34 G11
Newnham Nhants 54 F9
Newnham Bridge Worcs 52 B7
Newnham on Severn Gloucs 41 L9
New Ollerton Notts 78 H10
New Oscott Birm 53 L2
New Pitsligo Abers 141 L5
New Polzeath Cnwll 6 D9
Newport Cnwll 7 L7
Newport Dorset 11 L6
Newport E R Yk 86 F9
Newport Essex 45 P5
Newport Gloucs 29 L3
Newport Highld 151 L11
Newport IoW 12 H7
Newport Newpt 28 D5
Newport Norfk 71 P8
Newport Pembks 37 L3
Newport Wrekin 64 D8
Newport-on-Tay Fife 124 H7
Newport Pagnell M Keyn 44 B3
Newport Pagnell Services M Keyn 44 B3
Newpound Common W Susx 14 F5
New Prestwick S Ayrs 104 F5
New Quay Cerdgn 48 F8
Newquay Cnwll 3 K2
New Quay Essex 46 H7
Newquay Zoo Cnwll 3 K2
New Rackheath Norfk 71 K9
New Radnor Powys 50 H8
New Rent Cumb 98 F11
New Ridley Nthumb 100 D6
New Road Side N York 84 E6
New Romney Kent 17 J6
New Rossington Donc 78 G4
New Row Cerdgn 49 M6
New Row Lancs 83 P7
New Sauchie Clacks 114 G2
Newsbank Ches E 76 F10
Newseat Abers 140 H9
Newsham Lancs 83 L8
Newsham N York 91 J5
Newsham N York 91 P10
Newsham Nthumb 100 H2
New Sharlston Wakefd 85 M11
Newsholme E R Yk 86 D9
Newsholme Lancs 84 C5
New Shoreston Nthumb 109 K3
New Silksworth Sundld 101 K7
New Skelton R & Cl 92 D3
Newsome Kirk 84 H12
New Somerby Lincs 67 M5
New Springs Wigan 75 Q2
Newstead Border 107 N3
Newstead Notts 66 E2
Newstead Nthumb 109 J4
New Stevenston N Lans 114 D9
New Street Herefs 51 K9
New Swanington Leics 66 C9
Newthorpe N York 85 P8
Newthorpe Notts 66 D3
New Thundersley Essex 34 D4
Newtimber W Susx 15 K8
Newtoft Lincs 79 P6
Newton Ag & B 112 F2
Newton Border 107 P5
Newton Brdgnd 27 K7
Newton C Beds 45 J3
Newton Cambs 56 H10
Newton Cambs 68 H9
Newton Cardif 28 B6
Newton Ches W 75 L10
Newton Ches W 75 N11
Newton Ches W 75 N8
Newton Cumb 88 H12
Newton Derbys 78 D12
Newton Herefs 40 D5
Newton Herefs 51 L7
Newton Herefs 51 N10
Newton Highld 137 Q6
Newton Highld 138 D6
Newton Highld 138 E3
Newton Highld 151 Q6
Newton Lancs 82 H8
Newton Lancs 89 P11
Newton Lincs 67 P5
Newton Mdloth 115 P7
Newton Moray 139 M3
Newton Moray 139 Q3
Newton N York 92 H11
Newton Nhants 55 L4
Newton Norfk 70 B9
Newton Notts 66 H4
Newton Nthumb 100 D5

Newton Nthumb 108 F8
Newton S Lans 106 B3
Newton S Lans 114 C9
Newton Sandw 53 J2
Newton Shrops 63 M6
Newton Somset 20 H6
Newton Staffs 65 J7
Newton Suffk 46 G3
Newton W Loth 115 K6
Newton Warwks 54 E5
Newton Wilts 24 C9
Newton Abbot Devon 8 F10
Newton Arlosh Cumb 97 P7
Newton Aycliffe Dur 91 M2
Newton Bewley Hartpl 91 Q1
Newton Blossomville M Keyn 55 M10
Newton Bromswold Nhants P7
Newton Burgoland Leics 66 B10
Newton-by-the-Sea • Nthumb 109 L5
Newton by Toft Lincs 79 P6
Newton Ferrers Devon 5 J7
Newton Ferry W Isls 152 c7
Newton Flotman Norfk 63 J1
Newtongrange Mdloth 115 P8
Newton Green Mons 28 G8
Newton Harcourt Leics 54 G1
Newton Heath Manch 76 G4
Newtonhill Abers 133 L5
Newton Hill Wakefd 85 L10
Newton-in-Bowland Lancs 83 Q5
Newton Kyme N York 85 P6
Newton-le-Willows N York 91 L9
Newton-le-Willows St Hel 75 Q4
Newtonloan Mdloth 115 P8
Newton Longville Bucks 44 B5
Newton Mearns E Rens 113 Q10
Newtonmill Angus 132 F11
Newtonmore Highld 130 C4
Newton Morrell N York 91 L5
Newton Mountain Pembks 37 J9
Newton Mulgrave N York 92 F4
Newton of Balcanquhal P & K 124 D10
Newton of Balcormo Fife 125 K12
Newton-on-Ouse N York 85 Q3
Newton-on-Rawcliffe N York 92 G8
Newton on the Hill Shrops 63 N7
Newton-on-the-Moor Nthumb 109 K8
Newton on Trent Lincs 79 L9
Newton Poppleford Devon 9 L7
Newton Purcell Oxon 43 N5
Newton Regis Warwks 65 P10
Newton Reigny Cumb 98 F12
Newton St Cyres Devon 8 G5
Newton St Faith Norfk 71 J8
Newton St Loe BaNES 29 K8
Newton St Petrock Devon 18 H11
Newton Solney Derbys 65 P7
Newton Stacey Hants 24 G5
Newton Stewart D & G 95 M5
Newton Tony Wilts 24 C5
Newton Tracey Devon 19 K8
Newton under Roseberry R & Cl 92 B4
Newton Underwood Nthumb 100 F1
Newton upon Derwent E R Yk 86 D5
Newton Valence Hants 25 M7
Newton Wamphray D & G 106 E10
Newton with Scales Lancs 83 K9
Newtown BCP 11 P6
Newtown Blae G 40 A9
Newtown Ches W 75 N8
Newtown Cnwll 2 h2
Newtown Cnwll 7 K9
Newtown Cumb 89 N2
Newtown Cumb 97 M8
Newtown Cumb 98 E6
Newtown Cumb 98 G6
Newtown D & G 105 P8
Newtown Derbys 77 J7
Newtown Devon 9 K5
Newtown Devon 19 P8
Newtown Dorset 10 D4
New Town Dorset 11 N3
New Town Dorset 23 L10
New Town Dorset 23 L9
New Town E Susx 15 N7
Newtown Gloucs 41 K11
Newtown Hants 25 K10
Newtown Hants 31 K9
Newtown Hants 40 H5
Newtown Herefs 41 J3
Newtown Herefs 51 K8
Newtown Highld 129 L3
Newtown IoW 12 G6
New Town Nhants 55 N5
Newtown Nthumb 108 G5
Newtown Nthumb 108 G8
Newtown Nthumb 108 G9
Newtown Powys P3
Newtown Rhondd 27 P3
Newtown Shrops 63 M7
Newtown Shrops 63 N6
Newtown Somset 21 L10
Newtown Staffs 65 J11
Newtown Staffs 76 G11
Newtown Wigan 75 P3
Newtown Wilts 23 K7
New Town Wilts 30 G8
Newtown Wilts 30 G9
Newtown Worcs 52 G9
Newtown-in-St Martin Cnwll 3 J10
Newtown Linford Leics 66 E10
Newtown of Beltrees Rens 113 M9
Newtown St Boswells Border 107 P3
Newtown Unthank Leics 66 E11
New Tredegar Caerph 39 Q11
New Trows S Lans 105 Q2
New Tupton Derbys 78 C10
Newtyle Angus 124 F5
New Walsoken Cambs 69 J10
New Waltham NE Lin 80 F3
New Whittington Derbys 78 C8
New Winton E Loth 116 B7
New Yatt Oxon 42 H9
Newyears Green Gt Lon 32 F5
Newyork Ag & B 120 H10
New York Lincs 68 E1
New York N Tyne 101 J4
New York N York 85 J3
Nextend Herefs 51 K9
Neyland Pembks 37 J8
Niarbyl IoM 102 b6
Nibley Gloucs 41 K10
Nibley S Glos 29 L6
Nibley Green Gloucs 29 L3
Nicholashayne Devon 20 H10

Nicholaston Swans 26 D5
Nickies Hill Cumb 98 G5
Nidd N York 85 L3
Nigg C Aber 133 M4
Nigg Highld 146 E10
Nigg Ferry Highld 146 E11
Nimlet BaNES 29 M8
Ninebanks Nthumb 99 M7
Nine Elms Swindn 30 C5
Nine Wells Pembks 36 F5
Ninfield E Susx 16 C8
Ningwood IoW 12 F7
Nisbet Border 107 Q5
Nisbet Hill Border 116 H11
Niton IoW 12 H9
Nitshill C Glas 113 P9
Noah's Ark Kent 33 Q10
Noak Bridge Essex 34 C4
Noak Hill Gt Lon 33 P3
Noblethorpe Barns 77 P3
Nobold Shrops 63 M10
Nobottle Nhants 54 H8
Nocton Lincs 79 Q11
Nogdam End Norfk 71 M12
Noke Oxon 43 L9
Nolton Pembks 36 G7
Nolton Haven Pembks 36 G7
No Man's Heath Ches W 63 N3
No Man's Heath Warwks 65 P10
No Man's Land Cnwll 4 D5
Nomansland Devon 20 C10
Nomansland Wilts 24 D10
Noneley Shrops 63 N6
Nonington Kent 35 N11
Nook Cumb 89 N10
Nook Cumb 98 F2
Norbiton Gt Lon 32 H8
Norbreck Bpool 82 H7
Norbridge Herefs 41 L3
Norbury Ches E 63 P3
Norbury Derbys 65 L4
Norbury Gt Lon 33 K8
Norbury Shrops 51 L2
Norbury Staffs 64 F1
Norbury Common Ches E 63 P2
Norbury Junction Staffs 64 E7
Norchard Worcs 52 F7
Norcott Brook Ches W 75 Q7
Norcross Lancs 82 H7
Nordelph Norfk 69 K12
Norden Rochdl 84 C12
Nordley Shrops 52 C1
Norfolk Broads Norfk 71 Q10
Norham Nthumb 117 K11
Norland Town Calder 84 G10
Norley Ches W 75 P9
Norleywood Hants 12 F5
Norlington E Susx 15 N8
Normanby Lincs 79 P6
Normanby N Linc 86 G12
Normanby N York 92 G10
Normanby R & Cl 92 B3
Normanby le Wold Lincs 80 C5
Normandy Surrey 32 D12
Normans Bay E Susx 16 B9
Norman's Green Devon 9 K4
Normanton C Derb 65 Q5
Normanton Leics 67 K4
Normanton Notts 66 H1
Normanton RutInd 67 M11
Normanton Wakefd 85 M10
Normanton Wilts 23 P5
Normanton le Heath Leics 66 B9
Normanton on Cliffe Lincs 67 N3
Normanton on Soar Notts 66 E7
Normanton on the Wolds Notts 66 G5
Normanton on Trent Notts 79 K10
Normoss Lancs 82 H7
Norney Surrey 14 D2
Norrington Common Wilts 29 P9
Norris Green Cnwll 4 P9
Norris Green Lpool 75 L5
Norris Hill Leics 65 Q9
Norristhorpe Kirk 85 J10
Northacre Norfk 58 E1
Northall Bucks 44 D7
Northallerton N York 91 N8
Northall Green Norfk 70 E9
Northam C Sotn 24 G11
Northam Devon 19 J7
Northampton Nhants 55 J8
Northampton Worcs 52 F7
Northampton Services Nhants 55 J8
North Anston Rothm 78 E7
North Ascot Br For 32 C8
North Aston Oxon 43 K6
Northaw Herts 45 K11
Northay Somset 9 P3
North Baddesley Hants 24 F9
North Ballachulish Highld 128 E12
North Barrow Somset 22 E7
North Barsham Norfk 70 D5
Northbay W Isls 152 b13
North Benfleet Essex 34 D4
North Berwick E Loth 116 D4
North Bitchburn Dur 100 F11
North Blyth Nthumb 101 J2
North Boarhunt Hants 13 K3
North Bockhampton BCP 12 B5
Northborough C Pete 68 C10
Northbourne Kent 35 P11
North Bovey Devon 8 D8
North Bradley Wilts 23 J2
North Brentor Devon 7 P8
North Brewham Somset 22 G6
North Bridge Surrey 14 D3
Northbridge Street E Susx 16 C6
Northbrook Hants 24 H5
Northbrook Oxon 43 K7
North Brook End Cambs 45 K3
North Buckland Devon 19 J5
North Burlingham Norfk 71 M10
North Cadbury Somset 22 E7
North Carlton Lincs 79 N8
North Carlton Notts 78 E7
North Cave E R Yk 86 G8
North Cerney Gloucs 42 B10
North Chailey E Susx 15 M6
Northchapel W Susx 14 D6
North Charford Hants 24 C9
North Charlton Nthumb 109 K5
North Cheam Gt Lon 33 J9
North Cheriton Somset 22 F7
North Chideock Dorset 10 C6
Northchurch Herts 44 E10
North Cliffe E R Yk 86 G8
North Clifton Notts 79 K9
North Close Dur 100 H11
North Cockerington Lincs 80 G6
North Connel Ag & B 120 G6
North Cornelly Brdgnd 27 K6
North Corner Cnwll 3 J10
North Cotes Lincs 80 H4
Northcott Devon 7 L6
Northcott Devon 20 H10
North Country Cnwll 2 H5

Northcourt Oxon 31 K3
North Cove Suffk 59 P3
North Cowton N York 91 M6
North Crawley M Keyn 44 C3
North Cray Gt Lon 33 N8
North Creake Norfk 70 C4
North Curry Somset 21 M8
North Dalton E R Yk 86 H5
North Deighton N York 85 N5
Northdown Kent 35 Q8
North Downs 34 G1
North Duffield N York 86 C8
Northedge Derbys 78 B10
North Elham Kent 17 L2
North Elkington Lincs 80 F5
North Elmham Norfk 70 E8
North Elmsall Wakefd 78 D1
Northend Bucks 31 Q4
North End C Port 13 L4
North End Cumb 97 P8
North End E R Yk 87 M7
North End E R Yk 87 P9
North End Essex 46 B8
North End Hants 23 N10
North End Hants 25 K7
North End Leics 66 F9
North End Lincs 68 E4
North End Lincs 79 P4
North End Lincs 80 F3
North End Lincs 80 H6
North End N Linc 87 L10
North End N Som 28 F9
North End Nhants 55 N7
North End Norfk 58 E2
North End Nthumb 109 J9
North End Sefton 75 J3
North End W Susx 14 G10
North End W Susx 14 G9
Northend Warwks 54 C10
Northenden Manch 76 F6
Northend Woods Bucks 32 C4
North Erradale Highld 143 K9
North Evington C Leic 66 G11
North Fambridge Essex 34 E3
North Featherstone Wakefd 85 M11
North Ferriby E R Yk 87 J10
Northfield Birm 53 J5
Northfield C Aber 133 L3
Northfield E R Yk 87 J10
Northfields Lincs 67 P10
Northfleet Kent 34 B7
North Frodingham E R Yk 87 L5
North Gorley Hants 12 B2
North Green Norfk 59 J3
North Green Suffk 59 L8
North Green Suffk 59 M7
North Greetwell Lincs 79 P9
North Grimston N York 86 F2
North Halling Medway 34 C9
North Hayling Hants 13 M4
North Hazelrigg Nthumb 108 H3
North Heasley Devon 19 P7
North Heath W Susx 14 F6
North Hele Devon 20 G8
North Hill Cnwll 7 K9
North Hillingdon Gt Lon 32 F5
North Hinksey Village Oxon 43 K10
North Holmwood Surrey 14 H1
North Huish Devon 5 L5
North Hykeham Lincs 79 N10
Northiam E Susx 16 E5
Northill C Beds 44 G2
Northington Gloucs 41 L10
Northington Hants 25 J6
North Kelsey Lincs 79 P3
North Kessock Highld 138 B6
North Killingholme N Linc 87 L11
North Kilvington N York 91 P9
North Kilworth Leics 54 G4
North Kingston Hants 12 B4
North Kyme Lincs 68 C2
North Lancing W Susx 14 H9
North Landing E R Yk 93 P12
Northlands Lincs 68 G2
Northleach Gloucs 42 D9
North Lee Bucks 44 B10
North Lees N York 91 M12
Northleigh Devon 9 M5
North Leigh Kent 17 K1
North Leigh Oxon 42 H9
North Leverton with Habblesthorpe Notts 79 K7
Northlew Devon 7 P5
North Littleton Worcs 53 K11
North Lopham Norfk 58 F4
North Luffenham RutInd 67 M11
North Marden W Susx 25 P10
North Marston Bucks 43 Q7
North Middleton Mdloth 115 Q9
North Middleton Nthumb 108 G5
North Millbrex Abers 141 K7
North Milmain D & G 94 F7
North Molton Devon 19 P7
Northmoor Oxon 43 J11
North Moreton Oxon 31 M4
Northmuir Angus 124 H2
North Mundham W Susx 14 C10
North Muskham Notts 79 K12
North Newbald E R Yk 86 G8
North Newington Oxon 43 J4
North Newnton Wilts 30 D11
North Newton Somset 21 L7
Northney Hants 13 M4
North Nibley Gloucs 29 L3
North Oakley Hants 25 J2
North Ockendon Gt Lon 33 Q5
Northolt Gt Lon 32 G5
Northolt Airport Gt Lon 32 F5
Northop Flints 74 H10
Northop Hall Flints 75 J10
Northorpe Lincs 68 B5
Northorpe Lincs 68 D5
Northorpe Lincs 79 M4
North Otterington N York 91 N9
Northover Somset 21 N7
Northover Somset 22 C8
North Owersby Lincs 79 Q5
Northowram Calder 84 H10
North Perrott Somset 10 D2
North Petherton Somset 21 L7
North Petherwin Cnwll 7 L7
North Pickenham Norfk 70 C10
North Piddle Worcs 52 H9
North Poorton Dorset 10 D5
Northport Dorset 11 M7
North Poulner Hants 12 B4
North Queensferry Fife 115 L5
North Radworthy Devon 19 P6
North Rauceby Lincs 67 P3
Northrepps Norfk 71 K4
North Reston Lincs 80 G7
North Rigton N York 85 L5
North Ripley Hants 12 B5
North Rode Ches E 76 G10
North Ronaldsay Ork 147 f1

North Ronaldsay Airport Ork 147 f1
North Row Cumb 97 P11
North Runcton Norfk 69 M9
North Scale Cumb 82 F1
North Scarle Lincs 79 L10
North Seaton Nthumb 100 H1
North Seaton Colliery Nthumb 100 H1
North Shian Ag & B 120 G4
North Shields N Tyne 101 J4
North Shoebury Sthend 34 G5
North Shore Bpool 82 H8
North Side C Pete 68 E12
North Side Cumb 97 K12
North Skelton R & Cl 92 D3
North Somercotes Lincs 80 H4
North Stainley N York 91 M11
North Stainmore Cumb 90 D4
North Stifford Thurr 33 Q6
North Stoke BaNES 29 L8
North Stoke Oxon 31 M6
North Stoke W Susx 14 F8
North Street Cambs 57 J7
North Street Hants 23 P9
North Street Hants 25 L7
North Street Kent 34 H11
North Street Medway 34 E7
North Street W Berk 31 N8
North Sunderland Nthumb 109 K3
North Tamerton Cnwll 7 K5
North Tawton Devon 8 C4
North Third Stirlg 114 D3
North Thoresby Lincs 80 F4
North Togston Nthumb 109 L9
North Tolsta W Isls 152 h2
North Town Devon 7 P9
North Town Somset 22 D5
North Town W & M 32 C6
North Tuddenham Norfk 70 F9
North Uist W Isls 152 b8
Northumberland
National Park Nthumb 99 M2
North Walbottle N u Ty 100 F5
North Walsham Norfk 71 K6
North Waltham Hants 25 J4
North Warnborough Hants 25 M3
Northway Somset 21 J7
North Weald Bassett Essex 45 P11
North Wheatley Notts 79 J6
North Whilborough Devon 5 P3
North Wick BaNES 28 H9
Northwich Ches W 76 C9
North Widcombe BaNES 28 H10
North Willingham Lincs 80 C6
North Wingfield Derbys 78 C10
North Witham Lincs 67 M8
Northwold Norfk 57 P1
Northwood C Stke 64 G2
Northwood Derbys 77 P10
Northwood Gt Lon 32 F4
Northwood IoW 12 H6
Northwood Shrops 63 M5
Northwood Green Gloucs 41 L8
North Wootton Dorset 22 E10
North Wootton Norfk 69 M7
North Wootton Somset 22 C5
North Wraxall Wilts 29 N7
North Wroughton Swindn 30 D6
Norton Donc 85 Q12
Norton E Susx 15 N10
Norton Gloucs 41 P7
Norton Halton 75 P7
Norton Hants 24 H5
Norton Herts 45 J5
Norton IoW 12 E7
Norton Mons 40 F7
Norton N Som 28 D9
Norton Nhants 54 F8
Norton Notts 78 F9
Norton Powys 51 J7
Norton S on T 91 Q2
Norton Sheff 78 B7
Norton Shrops 51 M4
Norton Shrops 52 B4
Norton Shrops 63 P10
Norton Shrops 64 D12
Norton Suffk 58 E8
Norton Swans 26 F5
Norton W Susx 14 C10
Norton W Susx 14 C9
Norton Wilts 29 P5
Norton Worcs 52 G11
Norton Worcs 53 K11
Norton Bavant Wilts 23 J5
Norton Bridge Staffs 64 F6
Norton Canes Staffs 65 J11
Norton Canes Services Staffs 65 K10
Norton Canon Herefs 40 E2
Norton Corner Norfk 70 G6
Norton Disney Lincs 79 M11
Norton Ferris Wilts 22 H6
Norton Fitzwarren Somset 21 K8
Norton Green IoW 12 E7
Norton Hawkfield BaNES 28 H9
Norton Heath Essex 45 N10
Norton in Hales Shrops 64 D4
Norton-Juxta-Twycross Leics 65 Q10
Norton-le-Clay N York 85 N1
Norton-le-Moors C Stke 64 G2
Norton Lindsey Warwks 53 N8
Norton Little Green Suffk 58 E8
Norton Malreward BaNES 29 J9
Norton Mandeville Essex 45 Q10
Norton-on-Derwent N York 86 E1
Norton St Philip Somset 22 H2
Norton Subcourse Norfk 59 N1
Norton sub Hamdon Somset 21 P10
Norton Wood Herefs 51 L11
Norwell Notts 79 K11
Norwell Woodhouse Notts 79 J11
Norwich Norfk 71 J10
Norwich Airport Norfk 71 J9
Norwick Shet 147 k2
Norwood Clacks 114 F3
Norwood Derbys 78 D7
Norwood Kent 17 J4
Norwood End Essex 45 Q10
Norwood Green Calder 84 H10
Norwood Hill Surrey 15 J2
Norwoodside Cambs 57 J1
Noseley Leics 55 J1
Noss Mayo Devon 5 J7
Nosterfield N York 91 M10
Nosterfield End Cambs 46 B3
Nostie Highld 135 Q10
Notgrove Gloucs 42 D7
Nottage Brdgnd 27 K7
Notter Cnwll 4 D4

Nottingham C Nott 66 F4
Nottington Dorset 10 G8
Notton Wakefd 77 Q1
Notton Wilts 29 P8
Nounsley Essex 46 D9
Noutard's Green Worcs 52 E8
Nowton Suffk 58 C8
Nox Shrops 63 L10
Nuffield Oxon 31 N5
Nunburnholme E R Yk 86 G6
Nuncargate Notts 66 E1
Nunclose Cumb 98 F9
Nuneaton Warwks 54 B2
Nuneham Courtenay Oxon 31 L2
Nunhead Gt Lon 33 L7
Nunkeeling E R Yk 87 L5
Nun Monkton N York 85 Q4
Nunney Somset 22 G5
Nunney Catch Somset 22 G5
Nunnington Herefs 40 H3
Nunnington N York 92 D11
Nunsthorpe NE Lin 80 E2
Nunthorpe C York 86 B5
Nunthorpe Middsb 92 B4
Nunthorpe Village Middsb 92 B4
Nunton Wilts 23 P8
Nunwick N York 91 N11
Nunwick Nthumb 99 N3
Nupdown S Glos 29 J3
Nup End Bucks 44 B8
Nupend Gloucs 41 M10
Nuptown Br For 32 C7
Nursling Hants 24 F10
Nursted Hants 25 N9
Nursteed Wilts 30 B10
Nurton Staffs 64 F12
Nutbourne W Susx 13 M5
Nutbourne W Susx 14 F7
Nutfield Surrey 33 K12
Nuthall Notts 66 E4
Nuthampstead Herts 45 M5
Nuthurst W Susx 14 H5
Nutley E Susx 15 N5
Nutley Hants 25 K5
Nuttall Bury 84 B12
Nutwell Donc 78 G3
Nybster Highld 151 Q4
Nyetimber W Susx 14 C11
Nyewood W Susx 25 N9
Nymans W Susx 15 K5
Nymet Rowland Devon 8 D3
Nymet Tracey Devon 8 D5
Nympsfield Gloucs 29 N2
Nynehead Somset 21 J8
Nythe Somset 21 P6
Nyton W Susx 14 D9

Oadby Leics 66 G12
Oad Street Kent 34 F10
Oakall Green Worcs 52 E8
Oakamoor Staffs 65 K3
Oakbank W Loth 115 K8
Oak Cross Devon 7 Q5
Oakdale Caerph 28 B3
Oake Somset 21 J8
Oaken Staffs 64 F11
Oakenclough Lancs 83 M6
Oakengates Wrekin 64 C10
Oakenholt Flints 75 J9
Oakenshaw Dur 100 F10
Oakenshaw Kirk 85 J9
Oakerthorpe Derbys 66 C1
Oakford Cerdgn 48 G9
Oakford Devon 20 E9
Oakfordbridge Devon 20 E9
Oakgrove Ches E 76 G10
Oakham RutInd 67 L10
Oakhanger Ches E 64 D1
Oakhanger Hants 25 N6
Oakhill Somset 22 E4
Oakhurst Kent 33 Q12
Oakington Cambs 56 H8
Oaklands Powys 50 G10
Oakle Street Gloucs 41 M8
Oakley Bed 55 P9
Oakley Bucks 43 P9
Oakley Fife 115 J3
Oakley Hants 25 J3
Oakley Suffk 58 H5
Oakley Green W & M 32 D7
Oakley Park Powys 50 D3
Oakridge Lynch Gloucs 41 Q11
Oaks Lancs 83 P8
Oaks Shrops 63 L11
Oaksey Wilts 30 A4
Oaks Green Derbys 65 M5
Oakshaw Ford Cumb 98 H3
Oakshott Hants 25 M8
Oakthorpe Leics 65 Q9
Oak Tree Darltn 91 N4
Oakwood C Derb 66 B4
Oakwood Nthumb 99 P5
Oakworth C Brad 84 F7
Oare Kent 34 H9
Oare Somset 19 P4
Oare W Berk 31 K7
Oare Wilts 30 D9
Oasby Lincs 67 P4
Oath Somset 21 M8
Oathlaw Angus 125 J2
Oatlands Park Surrey 32 F9
Oban Ag & B 120 F6
Oban Airport Ag & B 120 G6
Obley Shrops 51 K5
Obney P & K 123 P5
Oborne Dorset 22 E9
Obthorpe Lincs 68 B8
Occold Suffk 58 H6
Occumster Highld 151 N9
Ochiltree S Ayrs 105 J3
Ockbrook Derbys 66 C5
Ocker Hill Sandw 52 H2
Ockeridge Worcs 52 E8
Ockham Surrey 32 F11
Ockle Highld 127 K10
Ockley Surrey 14 G3
Ocle Pychard Herefs 41 J2
Octon E R Yk 87 J2
Odcombe Somset 21 P10
Odd Down BaNES 29 M10
Oddendale Cumb 89 Q6
Oddingley Worcs 52 G9
Oddington Gloucs 42 E6
Oddington Oxon 43 L8
Odell Bed 55 N8
Odham Devon 7 N4
Odiham Hants 25 M4
Odsal C Brad 84 H9
Odsey Cambs 45 J4
Odstock Wilts 23 P8
Odstone Leics 66 C10
Offchurch Warwks 54 C8
Offenham Worcs 53 K11
Offerton Stockp 76 G6
Offerton Sundld 101 J7
Offham E Susx 15 N8
Offham Kent 34 B11
Offham W Susx 14 E9
Offleymarsh Staffs 64 E6
Offord Cluny Cambs 56 D8

Offord D'Arcy Cambs 56 D7
Offton Suffk 58 F10
Offwell Devon 9 M5
Ogbourne Maizey Wilts 30 E8
Ogbourne St Andrew Wilts 30 E8
Ogbourne St George Wilts 30 E7
Ogden Calder 84 G9
Ogle Nthumb 100 G2
Oglet Lpool 75 M7
Ogmore V Glam 27 L7
Ogmore-by-Sea V Glam 27 K7
Ogmore Vale Brdgnd 27 M3
Okeford Fitzpaine Dorset 11 K3
Okehampton Devon 8 B6
Okewood Hill Surrey 14 G3
Olchard Devon 8 G9
Old Nhants 55 K6
Old Aberdeen C Aber 133 M3
Old Alresford Hants 25 K6
Oldany Highld 148 D10
Old Auchenbrack D & G 105 P10
Old Basford C Nott 66 F3
Old Basing Hants 25 L3
Old Beetley Norfk 70 E8
Oldberrow Warwks 53 L7
Old Bewick Nthumb 108 H5
Old Bolingbroke Lincs 80 G10
Old Bramhope Leeds 85 K6
Old Brampton Derbys 77 Q9
Old Bridge of Urr D & G 96 F5
Old Buckenham Norfk 58 F2
Old Burghclere Hants 31 K10
Oldbury Kent 33 Q11
Oldbury Sandw 53 J3
Oldbury Shrops 52 D2
Oldbury Warwks 53 P2
Oldbury Naite S Glos 29 J4
Oldbury-on-Severn S Glos 29 J4
Oldbury on the Hill Gloucs 29 N5
Old Byland N York 91 Q10
Old Cantley Donc 78 G3
Old Cassop Dur 101 J2
Oldcastle Mons 40 D7
Oldcastle Heath Ches W 63 N3
Old Catton Norfk 71 J9
Old Clee NE Lin 80 F2
Old Cleeve Somset 20 G5
Old Colwyn Conwy 73 Q8
Oldcotes Notts 78 F6
Old Coulsdon Gt Lon 33 K10
Old Dailly S Ayrs 104 D10
Old Dalby Leics 66 H7
Old Dam Derbys 77 L8
Old Deer Abers 141 M6
Old Ditch Somset 22 C3
Old Edlington Donc 78 E4
Old Eldon Dur 91 L1
Old Ellerby E R Yk 87 M7
Old Felixstowe Suffk 47 P4
Oldfield C Brad 84 F7
Oldfield Worcs 52 F7
Old Fletton C Pete 56 D1
Oldford Somset 22 H3
Old Forge Herefs 41 H8
Old Furnace Herefs 40 H8
Old Glossop Derbys 77 K5
Old Goole E R Yk 86 D10
Old Grimsby IoS 2 b1
Old Hall Green Herts 45 L7
Oldhall Green Suffk 58 C9
Old Hall Street Norfk 71 L5
Oldham Oldham 76 G3
Oldhamstocks E Loth 116 G7
Old Harlow Essex 45 N9
Old Heath Essex 46 H7
Old Hunstanton Norfk 69 M3
Old Hutton Cumb 89 N9
Old Inns Services N Lans 114 C6
Old Kea Cnwll 3 L6
Old Kilpatrick W Duns 113 N6
Old Knebworth Herts 45 K7
Old Lakenham Norfk 71 J11
Oldland S Glos 29 K8
Old Langho Lancs 83 Q8
Old Laxey IoM 102 f5
Old Leake Lincs 68 H2
Old Malton N York 92 G12
Oldmeldrum Abers 141 K10
Old Milverton Warwks 53 P7
Oldmixon N Som 28 D10
Old Newton Suffk 58 F8
Old Oxted Surrey 33 M12
Old Portlethen Abers 133 M5
Old Quarrington Dur 101 J3
Old Radford C Nott 66 F4
Old Radnor Powys 51 J9
Old Rayne Abers 140 G11
Old Romney Kent 17 J5
Old Shoreham W Susx 15 J9
Oldshoremore Highld 148 G5
Old Soar N York 92 A11
Old Sodbury S Glos 29 M6
Old Somerby Lincs 67 N5
Oldstead N York 92 B10
Old Stratford Nhants 43 Q3
Old Struan P & K 130 E11
Old Swarland Nthumb 109 K9
Old Swinford Dudley 52 G4
Old Tebay Cumb 89 Q6
Old Thirsk N York 91 Q10
Old Town Calder 84 F9
Old Town Cumb 89 P10
Old Town Cumb 98 G11
Old Town E Susx 15 P10
Old Town IoS 2 b2
Old Trafford Traffd 76 F4
Old Tupton Derbys 78 C10
Old Warden C Beds 44 G3
Oldways End Somset 20 D7
Old Weston Cambs 56 B5
Old Wick Highld 151 Q6
Old Windsor W & M 32 D8
Old Wives Lees Kent 34 H11
Old Woking Surrey 32 E11
Old Wolverton M Keyn 44 A3
Old Woodhall Lincs 80 D11
Old Woods Shrops 63 M8
Oldwhat Abers 141 K6
Olgrinmore Highld 151 K6
Olive Green Staffs 65 L8
Oliver's Battery Hants 24 H7
Ollaberry Shet 147 h4
Ollach Highld 135 J8
Ollerton Ches E 76 E8
Ollerton Notts 78 F10
Ollerton Shrops 64 B7
Olmarch Cerdgn 49 L9
Olmstead Green Cambs 46 B3
Olney M Keyn 55 M9
Olrig Highld 151 M3
Olton Solhll 53 M4
Olveston S Glos 29 J5
Ombersley Worcs 52 F8
Ompton Notts 78 G10
Once Brewed Nthumb 99 L5
Onchan IoM 102 e5

Onecote Staffs 65 K1
Onehouse Suffk 58 F9
Onen Mons 40 F9
Ongar Street Herefs 51 L7
Onibury Shrops 51 M5
Onich Highld 128 E12
Onllwyn Neath 39 K9
Onneley Staffs 64 D4
Onslow Green Essex 46 B8
Onslow Village Surrey 14 D1
Onston Ches W 75 P9
Openwoodgate Derbys 66 B3
Opinan Abers 143 K10
Orbliston Moray 139 P4
Orbost Highld 134 D7
Orby Lincs 81 J10
Orchard Portman Somset 21 K8
Orcheston Wilts 23 N4
Orcop Herefs 40 G6
Orcop Hill Herefs 40 G6
Ord Abers 140 F4
Ordhead Abers 132 G2
Ordie Abers 132 D3
Ordiequish Moray 139 Q4
Ordley Nthumb 99 Q6
Ordsall Notts 78 H8
Ore E Susx 16 E8
Oreleton Common Herefs 51 N7
Oreton Shrops 52 C4
Orford Suffk 59 N10
Orford Warrtn 75 Q5
Organford Dorset 11 M6
Orgreave Staffs 65 L9
Orkney Islands Ork 147 c4
Orkney Neolithic Ork 147 b5
Orlestone Kent 16 H4
Orleton Herefs 51 N7
Orleton Worcs 52 C7
Orlingbury Nhants 55 L6
Ormathwaite Cumb 88 H2
Ormesby R & Cl 92 B3
Ormesby St Margaret Norfk 71 P9
Ormesby St Michael Norfk 71 P9
Ormiscaig Highld 143 M7
Ormiston E Loth 116 A7
Ormsaigmore Highld 126 H11
Ormsary Ag & B 111 Q7
Ormskirk Lancs 75 L2
Ornsby Hill Dur 100 F8
Oronsay Ag & B 110 H3
Orphir Ork 147 b5
Orpington Gt Lon 33 N9
Orrell Sefton 75 K4
Orrell Wigan 75 P3
Orrell Post Wigan 75 P3
Orrisdale IoM 102 d3
Orroland D & G 96 F9
Orsett Thurr 34 B5
Orslow Staffs 64 E9
Orston Notts 67 J4
Orthwaite Cumb 97 Q11
Ortner Lancs 83 M4
Orton Cumb 89 Q5
Orton Nhants 55 L5
Orton Staffs 52 F2
Orton Longueville C Pete 56 D1
Orton-on-the-Hill Leics 65 P11
Orton Rigg Cumb 98 D8
Orton Waterville C Pete 56 C1
Orwell Cambs 56 G10
Osbaldeston Lancs 83 P9
Osbaldeston Green Lancs 83 P9
Osbaldwick C York 86 B6
Osbaston Leics 66 C11
Osbaston Shrops 63 K7
Osborne IoW 12 H6
Osborne House IoW 13 J6
Osbournby Lincs 67 Q5
Oscroft Ches W 75 N10
Ose Highld 134 F7
Osgathorpe Leics 66 C8
Osgodby Lincs 79 Q5
Osgodby N York 86 B8
Osgodby N York 93 L11
Oskaig Highld 135 K8
Oskamull Ag & B 119 K6
Osmaston Derbys 65 M3
Osmington Dorset 10 H8
Osmington Mills Dorset 10 H8
Osmondthorpe N York 91 Q7
Osney C Oxon 43 K10
Ospringe Kent 34 H10
Ossett Wakefd 85 K11
Ossington Notts 79 J10
Ostend Essex 34 G3
Osterley Gt Lon 32 H7
Oswaldkirk N York 92 C11
Oswaldtwistle Lancs 83 P10
Oswestry Shrops 63 J6
Otford Kent 33 P11
Otham Kent 34 D11
Otham Hole Kent 34 E11
Otherton Staffs 64 H9
Othery Somset 21 N7
Otley Leeds 85 J5
Otley Suffk 59 J9
Otley Green Suffk 59 J9
Otterbourne Hants 24 H8
Otterburn N York 84 C4
Otterburn Nthumb 108 E11
Otter Ferry Ag & B 112 E4
Otterham Cnwll 6 H5
Otterhampton Somset 21 J5
Otterham Quay Kent 34 E9
Otterham Station Cnwll 6 H5
Otternish W Isls 152 c7
Ottershaw Surrey 32 E10
Otterswick Shet 147 j4
Otterton Devon 9 K7
Otterwood Hants 12 H4
Ottery St Mary Devon 9 L5
Ottinge Kent 17 L2
Ottringham E R Yk 87 P10
Oughterby Cumb 98 C7
Oughtershaw N York 90 D10
Oughterside Cumb 97 M10
Oughtibridge Sheff 77 P5
Oughtrington Warrtn 76 C6
Oulston N York 92 B12
Oulton Cumb 98 C7
Oulton Leeds 85 M9
Oulton Norfk 70 H6
Oulton Staffs 64 G5
Oulton Staffs 64 G7
Oulton Suffk 59 Q2
Oulton Broad Suffk 59 Q2
Oulton Street Norfk 70 H7
Oundle Nhants 55 P3
Our Dynamic Earth C Edin 115 N6
Ousby Cumb 99 J11
Ousden Suffk 57 P8
Ousefleet E R Yk 86 F10
Ouston Dur 100 H7
Outchester Nthumb 109 J3
Out Elmstead Kent 35 M12
Outgate Cumb 89 L7
Outhgill Cumb 90 C7
Outhill Warwks 53 L7
Outlands Staffs 64 E6
Outlane Kirk 84 G11
Out Newton E R Yk 87 R10

Out Rawcliffe Lancs...83 J7
Out Skerries Shet...147 k5
Outwell Norfk...69 K11
Outwick Hants...P10
Outwood Surrey...15 K2
Outwood Wakefd...85 L10
Outwood Gate Bury...76 E2
Outwoods Leics...66 C8
Outwoods Staffs...64 E8
Ouzlewell Green Leeds...85 M10
Over Calder...84 G10
Over Cambs...56 G6
Over Ches W...76 B10
Over S Glos...41 N8
Over S Glos...29 J6
Over Burrows Derbys...65 N4
Overbury Worcs...41 Q4
Overcombe Dorset...10 H8
Over Compton Dorset...22 D10
Over End Cambs...56 B2
Overgreen Derbys...77 Q9
Over Green Warwks...53 M2
Over Haddon Derbys...77 M10
Over Kellet Lancs...83 M1
Over Kiddington Oxon...43 J7
Overleigh Somset...22 B6
Overley Staffs...65 M9
Over Monnow Mons...40 G9
Over Norton Oxon...42 G6
Over Peover Ches E...76 E9
Overpool Ches W...75 L8
Overscaig Highld...149 G10
Over Silton N York...91 Q8
Oversland Kent...35 J11
Oversley Green Warwks...53 L9
Overstone Nhants...55 K7
Over Stowey Somset...21 J6
Overstrand Norfk...71 K4
Over Stratton Somset...21 P10
Overstreet Wilts...23 N6
Over Tabley Ches E...76 D7
Overthorpe Nhants...43 K4
Overton C Aber...133 L2
Overton Ches W...75 N8
Overton Hants...24 H3
Overton Lancs...83 K4
Overton N York...85 Q4
Overton Shrops...51 N6
Overton Swans...26 C5
Overton Wakefd...85 K12
Overton Wrexhm...63 K4
Overton Bridge Wrexhm...63 K4
Overtown Lancs...84 C9
Overtown N Lans...114 E10
Overtown Swindn...30 D6
Overtown Wakefd...85 M12
Over Wallop Hants...24 D6
Over Whitacre Warwks...53 N2
Over Woodhouse Derbys...78 D9
Over Worton Oxon...43 J6
Overy Oxon...31 M3
Oving Bucks...43 Q7
Oving W Susx...14 C10
Ovingdean Br & H...15 L10
Ovingham Nthumb...100 E6
Ovington Dur...91 J4
Ovington Essex...46 D3
Ovington Hants...25 J7
Ovington Norfk...70 D11
Ovington Nthumb...100 D5
Ower Hants...12 H4
Ower Hants...24 E7
Owermoigne Dorset...11 J7
Owlbury Shrops...51 K2
Owlerton Sheff...77 Q6
Owl's Green Suffk...59 K7
Owlsmoor Br For...32 B10
Owlswick Bucks...43 R10
Owmby Lincs...79 P6
Owmby Lincs...79 Q3
Owslebury Hants...24 H8
Owston Donc...78 F1
Owston Leics...67 K10
Owston Ferry N Linc...79 K4
Owstwick E R Yk...87 Q9
Owthorne E R Yk...87 R9
Owthorpe Notts...66 H5
Owton Manor Hartpl...101 M12
Oxborough Norfk...69 P11
Oxbridge Dorset...10 D5
Oxcombe Lincs...80 F8
Oxcroft Derbys...78 D9
Oxen End Essex...46 B6
Oxenholme Cumb...89 N9
Oxenhope C Brad...84 F8
Oxen Park Cumb...89 J9
Oxenpill Somset...21 P5
Oxenton Gloucs...41 Q5
Oxenwood Wilts...30 G10
Oxford Oxon...43 L10
Oxford Airport Oxon...43 K8
Oxford Services Oxon...43 N10
Oxhey Herts...32 G3
Oxhill Dur...100 F8
Oxhill Warwks...42 G2
Oxley Wolves...64 G11
Oxley Green Essex...46 F9
Oxley's Green E Susx...16 C6
Oxlode Cambs...57 J3
Oxnam Border...108 A6
Oxnead Norfk...71 J7
Oxshott Surrey...32 G10
Oxshott Heath Surrey...32 G10
Oxspring Barns...77 P3
Oxted Surrey...33 M11
Oxton Border...116 C10
Oxton N York...85 Q6
Oxton Notts...66 G2
Oxton Wirral...75 J6
Oxwich Swans...26 D5
Oxwich Green Swans...26 D5
Oxwick Norfk...70 D7
Oykel Bridge Highld...145 J5
Oyne Abers...140 G10
Oystermouth Swans...26 F5
Ozleworth Gloucs...29 M4

P

Pabail W Isls...152 h3
Packers Hill Dorset...10 H3
Packington Leics...66 B9
Packmoor C Stke...76 F1
Packmores Warwks...53 P7
Padanaram Angus...124 H2
Padbury Bucks...43 P5
Paddington Gt Lon...33 K6
Paddington Warrtn...76 B6
Paddlesworth Kent...17 M3
Paddlesworth Kent...34 B10
Paddock Wood Kent...16 B2
Paddolgreen Shrops...63 N6
Padfield Derbys...77 J4
Padgate Warrtn...76 B6
Padham Green Essex...34 B3
Padiham Lancs...84 B8
Padside N York...84 H3
Padstow Cnwll...6 C9
Padworth W Berk...31 M9
Page Bank Dur...100 G11

Pagham W Susx...14 C11
Paglesham Essex...34 G4
Paignton Torbay...5 Q4
Pailton Warwks...54 D4
Paine's Cross E Susx...16 A6
Painleyhill Staffs...65 J5
Painscastle Powys...40 A2
Painshawfield Nthumb...100 D6
Painsthorpe E R Yk...86 F4
Painswick Gloucs...41 P9
Painter's Forstal Kent...34 H10
Paisley Rens...113 P8
Pakefield Suffk...59 Q3
Pakenham Suffk...58 D7
Pale Gwynd...62 D5
Pale Green Essex...46 B3
Palestine Hants...24 D5
Paley Street W & M...32 B7
Palfrey Wsall...53 J1
Palgrave Suffk...58 G5
Pallington Dorset...11 J6
Palmersbridge Cnwll...6 H9
Palmers Green Gt Lon...33 K4
Palmerston E Ayrs...105 J6
Palmerstown V Glam...27 Q8
Palnackie D & G...96 G7
Palnure D & G...95 N5
Palterton Derbys...78 D10
Pamber End Hants...31 M10
Pamber Green Hants...31 M10
Pamber Heath Hants...31 M10
Pamington Gloucs...41 Q5
Pamphill Dorset...11 M5
Pampisford Cambs...57 J11
Panborough Somset...21 Q4
Panbride Angus...125 L6
Pancrasweek Devon...7 K4
Pancross V Glam...27 P8
Pandy Caerph...27 Q5
Pandy Gwynd...61 Q6
Pandy Mons...40 D7
Pandy Powys...62 B11
Pandy Wrexhm...62 H5
Pandy'r Capel Denbgs...62 F2
Pandy Tudur Conwy...73 Q11
Panfield Essex...46 C6
Pangbourne W Berk...31 N6
Pangdean W Susx...15 K8
Panks Bridge Herefs...52 B11
Pannal N York...85 L5
Pannal Ash N York...85 L4
Panshash Flints...74 G8
Pant Shrops...63 J8
Pantasaph Flints...74 G8
Pant Glas Gwynd...60 H3
Pantglas Powys...49 N1
Pant-Gwyn Carmth...38 C4
Pant-lasau Swans...26 G2
Pant Mawr Powys...49 P4
Panton Lincs...80 D8
Pant-pastynog Denbgs...74 E11
Pantperthog Gwynd...61 N11
Pant-y-dwr Powys...50 D6
Pant-y-ffridd Powys...62 G11
Pantyffynnon Carmth...38 F9
Pantygaseg Torfn...28 C2
Pantygelli Mons...40 D8
Pant-y-gog Brdgnd...27 J4
Pantymenyn Carmth...37 N4
Pant-y-mwyn Flints...74 H10
Panxworth Norfk...71 M9
Papa Stour Shet...147 h4
Papa Stour Airport Shet...147 g6
Papa Westray Ork...147 d1
Papa Westray Airport Ork...147 d1
Papcastle Cumb...97 M12
Papigoe Highld...151 Q6
Papple E Loth...116 D7
Papplewick Notts...66 F2
Papworth Everard Cambs...56 F8
Papworth St Agnes Cambs...56 E8
Par Cnwll...3 Q4
Paramour Street Kent...35 N10
Parbold Lancs...75 N2
Parbrook Somset...22 D6
Parbrook W Susx...14 F6
Parc Gwynd...61 Q5
Parciliyn Cerdgn...48 D10
Parc Seymour Newpt...28 F4
Pardshaw Cumb...88 E2
Parham Suffk...59 L8
Park D & G...106 B11
Park Nthumb...99 K6
Park Bottom Cnwll...2 H6
Park Bridge Tamesd...76 H3
Park Corner E Susx...15 P4
Park Corner Oxon...31 P5
Park Corner W & M...32 B6
Park End Bed...55 N10
Parkend Gloucs...41 J10
Park End Nthumb...99 N3
Parker's Green Kent...15 R1
Parkeston Essex...47 M5
Parkeston Quay Essex...47 M5
Park Farm Kent...16 H3
Parkgate Ches W...75 J8
Parkgate Cumb...98 D12
Parkgate D & G...106 D12
Parkgate Essex...16 C8
Parkgate Essex...46 B6
Park Gate Hants...13 J3
Parkgate Kent...16 F4
Park Gate Kent...16 F4
Park Gate Leeds...85 J7
Parkgate Surrey...15 J2
Park Gate Worcs...52 H6
Parkhall W Duns...113 P7
Parkham Devon...19 H9
Parkham Ash Devon...18 G9
Park Head Derbys...66 B3
Park Hill Gloucs...28 H2
Parkhouse Mons...40 G11
Parkmill Swans...26 E4
Park Royal Gt Lon...32 H6
Parkside N Lans...114 E9
Parkside Wrexhm...63 L1
Parkstone BCP...11 Q6
Park Street Herts...32 H1
Park Street W Susx...14 G5
Parley Green BCP...11 Q5
Parmoor Bucks...31 R4
Parracombe Devon...19 N4
Parrog Pembks...37 K3
Parsonby Cumb...97 N10
Parson Cross Sheff...77 Q5
Parson Drove Cambs...68 G10
Parson's Heath Essex...46 H6
Parson's Hill Derbys...65 P7
Partick C Glas...113 Q8
Partington Traffd...76 D5
Partney Lincs...80 H10
Parton Cumb...88 C2
Partridge Green W Susx...14 H7
Partrishow Powys...40 C7
Parwich Derbys...65 M1
Paslow Wood Common Essex...45 Q11

Passenham Nhants...43 Q4
Passfield Hants...25 P6
Passingford Bridge Essex...33 P3
Paston C Pete...68 D11
Paston Norfk...71 L5
Pasturefields Staffs...65 J7
Patchacott Devon...7 N5
Patcham Br & H...15 K9
Patchetts Green Herts...32 G3
Patching W Susx...14 F9
Patchole Devon...19 M5
Patchway S Glos...29 J6
Pateley Bridge N York...84 H2
Paternoster Heath Essex...46 G8
Pathe Somset...21 N7
Pathhead Fife...115 P3
Pathhead Mdloth...115 R8
Pathlow Warwks...53 N9
Patmore Heath Herts...45 N6
Patna E Ayrs...104 H7
Patney Wilts...30 C10
Patrick IoM...102 c5
Patrick Brompton N York...91 K8
Patricroft Salfd...76 D4
Patrington E R Yk...87 P11
Patrington Haven E R Yk...87 P11
Patrixbourne Kent...35 L11
Patterdale Cumb...89 L4
Pattingham Staffs...64 F12
Pattishall Nhants...54 H10
Pattiswick Green Essex...46 E6
Patton Shrops...51 P2
Patton Bridge Cumb...89 P7
Paul Cnwll...2 D9
Paulerspury Nhants...43 P3
Paull E R Yk...87 M10
Paulton BaNES...29 K11
Paultons Park Hants...24 E7
Paunton Herefs...52 C10
Pauperhaugh Nthumb...108 H10
Pave Lane Wrekin...64 H9
Pavenham Bed...55 N9
Pawlett Somset...21 L5
Pawston Nthumb...108 D3
Paxford Gloucs...42 E4
Paxton Border...117 L10
Payden Street Kent...34 G11
Payhembury Devon...9 L4
Paynter's Lane End Cnwll...2 G6
Paythorne Lancs...84 B5
Paytoe Herefs...51 L6
Peacehaven E Susx...15 M10
Peak Dale Derbys...77 K8
Peak District National Park...77 M5
Peak Forest Derbys...77 L8
Peak Hill Lincs...68 E9
Peakirk C Pete...68 D11
Pearson's Green Kent...16 C2
Peartree Green Herefs...41 N5
Peasedown St John BaNES...29 L11
Peasehill Derbys...66 C2
Peaseland Green Norfk...70 F9
Peasemore W Berk...31 K6
Peasenhall Suffk...59 M7
Pease Pottage W Susx...15 J4
Pease Pottage Services W Susx...15 J4
Peaslake Surrey...14 F2
Peasley Cross St Hel...75 N5
Peasmarsh E Susx...16 F6
Peasmarsh Somset...21 M11
Peasmarsh Surrey...14 E2
Peathill Abers...141 M3
Peatling Magna Leics...54 F2
Peatling Parva Leics...54 F3
Peaton Shrops...51 N4
Pebmarsh Essex...46 E5
Pebsham E Susx...16 D9
Pebworth Worcs...42 D2
Pecket Well Calder...84 E9
Peckforton Ches E...75 P12
Peckham Gt Lon...33 L7
Peckleton Leics...66 D12
Pedairffordd Powys...62 F7
Pedlinge Kent...17 L4
Pedmore Dudley...52 G4
Pedwell Somset...21 P6
Peebles Border...106 H2
Peel IoM...102 c5
Peel Lancs...83 J9
Peel Common Hants...13 J3
Peene Kent...17 L3
Peening Quarter Kent...16 F5
Peggs Green Leics...66 C8
Pegsdon C Beds...44 G5
Pegswood Nthumb...109 L12
Pegwell Kent...35 Q9
Peinchorran Highld...135 J9
Peinlich Highld...134 G4
Pelcomb Pembks...36 H7
Pelcomb Bridge Pembks...36 H7
Pelcomb Cross Pembks...36 H7
Peldon Essex...46 H8
Pell Green E Susx...16 B4
Pelsall Wsall...65 J11
Pelsall Wood Wsall...65 J11
Pelton Dur...100 G7
Pelton Fell Dur...100 H8
Pelutho Cumb...97 M8
Pelynt Cnwll...4 H4
Pemberton Carmth...26 D2
Pemberton Wigan...75 P3
Pembles Cross Kent...16 F1
Pembrey Carmth...25 Q2
Pembridge Herefs...51 L9
Pembroke Pembks...37 J10
Pembroke Dock Pembks...37 J10
Pembrokeshire Coast National Park Pembks...36 G6
Pembury Kent...16 A3
Pen-allt Herefs...40 H6
Penallt Mons...40 H10
Penally Pembks...37 M10
Penare Cnwll...3 N6
Penarth V Glam...28 B8
Penblewin Pembks...37 M7
Pen-bont Rhydybeddau Cerdgn...49 L4
Penbryn Cerdgn...48 D10
Pencader Carmth...38 C4
Pencaenewydd Gwynd...60 G4
Pencarnisiog IoA...72 F9
Pencarreg Carmth...38 E3
Pencarrow Cnwll...6 G8
Pencelli Powys...39 P7
Pen-clawdd Swans...26 D3
Pencoed Brdgnd...27 M6
Pencombe Herefs...51 Q10
Pencoyd Herefs...40 H6
Pencraig Herefs...40 H7
Pencraig Powys...62 E7
Pendeen Cnwll...2 B8
Penderyn Rhondd...39 M10
Pendine Carmth...37 P7
Pendlebury Salfd...76 E3
Pendleton Lancs...84 B7
Pendock Worcs...41 M5
Pendomer Somset...10 D2
Pendoylan V Glam...27 P7
Pendre Brdgnd...27 L6
Penegoes Powys...61 N12

Penelewey Cnwll...3 K6
Pen-ffordd Pembks...37 L6
Pengam Caerph...27 R3
Pengam Cardif...28 B7
Penge Gt Lon...33 L8
Pengelly Cnwll...6 F8
Pengenffordd Powys...40 A6
Pengorffwysfa IoA...72 H5
Pengover Green Cnwll...4 G4
Pengwern Denbgs...74 D8
Penhale Cnwll...2 H10
Penhale Cnwll...3 K3
Penhale Cnwll...4 F6
Penhallow Cnwll...2 H4
Penhalurick Cnwll...2 H7
Penhalvean Cnwll...2 H7
Penhill Swindn...30 D5
Penhow Newpt...28 F4
Penhurst E Susx...16 C7
Peniarth Gwynd...61 K11
Penicuik Mdloth...115 N9
Peniel Carmth...38 C7
Peniel Denbgs...74 E11
Penifiler Highld...135 J2
Peninver Ag & B...103 K5
Penisarwaun Gwynd...73 J11
Penistone Barns...77 N3
Penjerrick Cnwll...3 J7
Penketh Warrtn...75 P6
Penkill S Ayrs...104 D10
Penkridge Staffs...64 H9
Penlean Cnwll...7 J3
Penleigh Wilts...23 J3
Penley Wrexhm...63 L4
Penllergaer Swans...26 F3
Pen-llyn IoA...72 F7
Penllyn V Glam...27 M7
Pen-lon IoA...72 G10
Penmachno Conwy...61 N2
Penmaen Caerph...27 P3
Penmaen Swans...26 D4
Penmaenan Conwy...73 M8
Penmaenmawr Conwy...73 M8
Penmaenpool Gwynd...61 M8
Penmark V Glam...27 Q8
Penmon IoA...73 K7
Penmorfa Gwynd...61 J4
Penmynydd IoA...72 H9
Penn Bucks...32 C4
Penn Wolves...52 G2
Pennal Gwynd...61 M12
Pennan Abers...141 K3
Pennant Cerdgn...48 H8
Pennant Denbgs...62 E5
Pennant Powys...61 N2
Pennant-Melangell Powys...62 D7
Pennar Pembks...37 J10
Pennard Swans...26 E5
Pennerley Shrops...63 K12
Pennicott Devon...8 H4
Pennines...84 B8
Pennington Cumb...88 H11
Pennington Hants...12 E6
Pennington Green Wigan...76 B2
Pennorth Powys...39 Q7
Penn Street Bucks...32 C3
Pennsylvania S Glos...29 M7
Penny Bridge Cumb...89 J10
Pennycross Ag & B...119 L7
Pennygate Norfk...71 L7
Pennyghael Ag & B...119 N7
Pennyglen S Ayrs...104 E7
Penny Green Derbys...78 E8
Penny Hill Lincs...68 G7
Pennymoor Devon...8 H2
Pennywell Sundld...101 J7
Penparc Cerdgn...48 C11
Penparcau Cerdgn...49 K4
Penpedairheol Caerph...27 P3
Penpedairheol Mons...40 D11
Penpergwm Mons...40 D10
Penperlleni Mons...40 D10
Penpethy Cnwll...6 E6
Penpillick Cnwll...3 Q3
Penpol Cnwll...3 K6
Penpoll Cnwll...4 A6
Penponds Cnwll...2 G7
Penpont Cnwll...6 D9
Penpont D & G...105 Q11
Penpont Powys...39 M6
Penquit Devon...5 K6
Penrest Cnwll...7 L9
Penrherber Carmth...37 Q3
Pen-rhiw Pembks...37 Q3
Penrhiwceiber Rhondd...27 P3
Pen Rhiwfawr Neath...38 H10
Penrhiwllan Cerdgn...38 B3
Penrhiw-pal Cerdgn...48 E10
Penrhos Gwynd...60 E5
Penrhos IoA...72 D7
Penrhos Mons...40 F9
Penrhos garnedd Gwynd...73 J9
Penrhyn Bay Conwy...73 P7
Penrhyn-coch Cerdgn...49 L4
Penrhyndeudraeth Gwynd...61 K4
Penrhyn-side Conwy...73 P7
Penrhys Rhondd...27 N3
Penrice Swans...26 D5
Penrioch N Ayrs...112 C10
Penrith Cumb...98 G12
Penrose Cnwll...6 C10
Penruddock Cumb...89 L1
Penryn Cnwll...3 J7
Pensarn Conwy...74 C8
Pensax Worcs...52 D7
Pensby Wirral...75 J6
Penselwood Somset...22 F7
Pensford BaNES...29 J9
Pensham Worcs...41 Q3
Penshaw Sundld...101 J7
Penshurst Kent...15 R2
Penshurst Station Kent...15 P2
Pensilva Cnwll...4 G3
Pensnett Dudley...52 G3
Penstone Devon...8 G4
Penstrowed Powys...50 E2
Pentewan Cnwll...3 N5
Pentir Gwynd...73 J10
Pentire Cnwll...3 J1
Pentlepoir Pembks...37 M9
Pentlow Essex...46 D3
Pentlow Street Essex...46 E3
Pentney Norfk...69 R9
Penton Grafton Hants...24 D3
Penton Mewsey Hants...24 D3
Pentraeth IoA...72 H8
Pentre Denbgs...74 F11
Pentre Flints...75 K10
Pentre Mons...40 E10
Pentre Powys...50 G3
Pentre Powys...50 G5
Pentre Powys...62 F11
Pentre Rhondd...27 M3
Pentre Shrops...63 J8
Pentre Wrexhm...63 J4
Pentre-bâch Cerdgn...38 H3
Pentre Bach Flints...74 H8
Pentrebach Myr Td...27 M2
Pentre-bach Powys...39 P11

Pentrebeirdd Powys...62 G9
Pentre Berw IoA...72 H9
Pentre-bont Conwy...61 N2
Pentre-cagel Carmth...37 R2
Pentre-celyn Denbgs...62 G2
Pentre-celyn Powys...62 B11
Pentre-chwyth Swans...26 G3
Pentre-clawdd Shrops...63 J6
Pentre-cwrt Carmth...38 B4
Pentredwr Denbgs...62 H3
Pentrefelin Gwynd...61 J4
Pentrefelin IoA...72 G5
Pentre Ffwrndan Flints...75 J9
Pentrefoelas Conwy...61 Q2
Pentregalar Pembks...37 M4
Pentregat Cerdgn...48 F10
Pentre-Gwenlais Carmth...38 F8
Pentre Gwynfryn Gwynd...61 K7
Pentre Halkyn Flints...74 H9
Pentre Hodrey Shrops...51 K5
Pentre Isaf Conwy...74 D9
Pentre Llanrhaeadr Denbgs...74 E11
Pentre Llifior Powys...50 G1
Pentre-llwyn-llwyd Powys...50 C9
Pentre-llyn Cerdgn...49 K6
Pentre-llyn-cymmer Conwy...62 D2
Pentre-Maw Powys...62 B11
Pentre Meyrick V Glam...27 M7
Pentre-piod Torfn...40 C11
Pentre-poeth Newpt...28 C5
Pentre'r-bryn Cerdgn...48 F9
Pentre'r-felin Cerdgn...49 K11
Pentre'r Felin Conwy...73 P10
Pentre'r-felin Powys...39 L5
Pentre Saron Denbgs...74 D11
Pentre-tafarn-y-fedw Conwy...73 P11
Pentre ty gwyn Carmth...39 K4
Pentrich Derbys...66 C2
Pentridge Dorset...23 M10
Pen-twyn Caerph...28 B2
Pen-twyn Mons...40 H10
Pen-twyn Torfn...40 C11
Pentwynmaur Caerph...28 B3
Pentyrch Cardif...27 Q6
Penwithick Cnwll...3 N4
Penwood Hants...31 J10
Penwyllt Powys...39 K8
Penybanc Carmth...38 F7
Penybont Powys...50 F8
Penybontfawr Powys...62 F7
Pen-y-bont Powys...62 H7
Pen-y-bryn Pembks...37 N2
Pen-y-bryn Wrexhm...63 J3
Pen-y-cae Powys...39 K9
Penycae Wrexhm...63 J3
Pen-y-cae-mawr Mons...28 F3
Penycaerau Gwynd...60 C6
Pen-y-cefn Flints...74 F8
Pen-y-clawdd Mons...40 F10
Pen-y-coedcae Rhondd...27 P5
Penycwm Pembks...36 G6
Pen-y-fai Brdgnd...27 L6
Pen-y-felin Flints...74 G9
Pen-y-ffordd Flints...74 G9
Penyffordd Flints...75 J11
Pen-y-ffridd Gwynd...72 H12
Pen-y-garn Cerdgn...49 K3
Pen-y-Garnedd Powys...62 F7
Pen-y-graig Gwynd...60 C5
Penygraig Rhondd...27 N4
Penygroes Carmth...38 E7
Penygroes Gwynd...60 H2
Pen-y-Gwryd Gwynd...61 L1
Pen-y-lan V Glam...27 N7
Pen-y-Mynydd Carmth...38 C11
Penymynydd Flints...75 J11
Pen-y-pass Gwynd...61 L1
Pen-yr-Heol Mons...40 E9
Penysarn IoA...72 G5
Pen-y-stryt Denbgs...62 H2
Penywaun Rhondd...39 M10
Penzance Cnwll...2 D8
Peopleton Worcs...52 H10
Peover Heath Ches E...76 E9
Peper Harow Surrey...14 D2
Peplow Shrops...64 B7
Pepper's Green Essex...46 A9
Pepperstock C Beds...44 F8
Perceton N Ayrs...104 F2
Percyhorner Abers...141 M3
Perelle Guern...12 b2
Perham Down Wilts...24 D3
Periton Somset...20 H4
Perivale Gt Lon...32 H6
Perkins Village Devon...9 J6
Perkinsville Dur...100 H7
Perlethorpe Notts...78 E8
Perranarworthal Cnwll...3 J7
Perranporth Cnwll...2 H4
Perranuthnoe Cnwll...2 E8
Perranwell Cnwll...3 J6
Perranwell Cnwll...3 J6
Perran Wharf Cnwll...3 J7
Perranzabuloe Cnwll...3 J4
Perrott's Brook Gloucs...42 B10
Perry Birm...53 K2
Perry-side Conwy...73 P7
Perrys Rhondd...26 D5
Perry Barr Birm...53 K2
Perry Green Essex...45 N8
Perry Green Herts...45 N8
Perry Green Wilts...29 N4
Perryston Hill Herefs...41 K6
Pershall Staffs...64 E6
Pershore Worcs...41 Q2
Pertenhall Bed...56 B7
Perth P & K...124 C2
Perthy Shrops...63 L5
Perton Herefs...41 K6
Perton Staffs...64 F12
Pertwood Wilts...23 K6
Peterborough C Pete...68 D12
Peterborough Services Cambs...56 C2
Peterchurch Herefs...40 H4
Peterculter C Aber...133 K4
Peterhead Abers...141 Q6
Peterlee Dur...101 L10
Petersfield Hants...25 M8
Peter's Green Herts...44 G8
Petersham Gt Lon...32 H7
Peters Marland Devon...19 J10
Peterstone Wentlooge Newpt...28 C6
Peterston-super-Ely V Glam...27 P7
Peterstow Herefs...40 H7
Peters Village Kent...34 C9
Petham Kent...35 K11
Petherwin Gate Cnwll...7 K7
Petrockstow Devon...19 J10
Petsoe End M Keyn...55 M10
Pett E Susx...16 F8
Pettaugh Suffk...58 H9
Petterden Angus...124 H5
Pettinain S Lans...106 C2
Pettistree Suffk...59 L10
Petton Devon...20 F8
Petton Shrops...63 M7
Petts Wood Gt Lon...33 N8
Petty Abers...140 H9

Pettycur Fife...115 N4
Petty France S Glos...29 M5
Pettymuk Abers...141 L11
Petworth W Susx...14 D6
Pevensey E Susx...16 B10
Pevensey Bay E Susx...16 B10
Pewsey Wilts...30 D10
Pewsham Wilts...29 Q8
Pheasant's Hill Bucks...31 R5
Phepson Worcs...52 H8
Philadelphia Sundld...101 J8
Philham Devon...18 E9
Philiphaugh Border...107 L4
Phillack Cnwll...2 F7
Philleigh Cnwll...3 L6
Philpot End Essex...45 R8
Phocle Green Herefs...41 M6
Phoenix Green Hants...25 N2
Pibsbury Somset...21 P8
Pica Cumb...88 D2
Piccadilly Warwks...53 N1
Piccotts End Herts...44 F9
Pickburn Donc...78 E2
Pickering N York...92 F10
Picket Piece Hants...24 F4
Picket Post Hants...12 C3
Picket Twenty Hants...24 F4
Pickford Covtry...53 P4
Pickford Green Covtry...53 P4
Pickhill N York...91 N10
Picklescott Shrops...63 M12
Pickmere Ches E...76 C8
Pickney Somset...21 K7
Pickstock Wrekin...64 D7
Pickwell Devon...19 J5
Pickwell Leics...67 K10
Pickwick Wilts...29 P8
Pickworth Lincs...67 Q5
Pickworth Rutlnd...67 P8
Picton Ches W...75 M9
Picton Flints...74 F7
Picton N York...91 P5
Piddinghoe E Susx...15 N10
Piddington Bucks...32 A3
Piddington Nhants...55 K9
Piddington Oxon...43 N8
Piddlehinton Dorset...11 J5
Piddletrenthide Dorset...11 J5
Pidley Cambs...56 H5
Piercebridge Darltn...91 L4
Pierowall Ork...147 c1
Piff's Elm Gloucs...41 P6
Pigdon Nthumb...109 J12
Pigeon Green Warwks...53 N8
Pig Oak Dorset...11 N4
Pig Street Herefs...51 L11
Pikehall Derbys...77 M12
Pilford Dorset...11 N4
Pilgrims Hatch Essex...33 Q3
Pilham Lincs...79 L5
Pill N Som...28 H7
Pillaton Cnwll...4 E4
Pillatonmill Cnwll...4 E4
Pilleth Powys...51 J8
Pilley Barns...77 Q4
Pilley Hants...12 E5
Pilley Bailey Hants...12 E5
Pillgwenlly Newpt...28 D5
Pillhead Devon...19 J8
Pilling Lancs...83 J5
Pilling Lane Lancs...83 J5
Pilning S Glos...28 H5
Pilot Inn Kent...17 K7
Pilsbury Derbys...77 L11
Pilsdon Dorset...10 C5
Pilsgate C Pete...67 Q11
Pilsley Derbys...78 C12
Pilsley Derbys...78 C11
Pilson Green Norfk...71 M9
Piltdown E Susx...15 N6
Pilton Devon...19 L6
Pilton Nhants...55 P3
Pilton Rutlnd...67 M11
Pilton Somset...22 D5
Pilton Green Swans...26 C5
Pimbo Lancs...75 N3
Pimlico Herts...44 F9
Pimlico Lancs...83 R6
Pimlico Nhants...43 N4
Pimperne Dorset...11 L3
Pinchbeck Lincs...68 E6
Pinchbeck Bars Lincs...68 C6
Pinchbeck West Lincs...86 C11
Pinchinthorpe R & Cl...92 C11
Pincock Lancs...83 M11
Pinfold Lancs...75 L1
Pinford End Suffk...58 C9
Pinged Carmth...38 D11
Pingewood W Berk...31 P8
Pin Green Herts...45 K4
Pinhoe Devon...9 K6
Pinkett's Booth Covtry...53 P4
Pinkney Wilts...29 P5
Pinley Birm...54 D11
Pinley Green Warwks...53 P8
Pin Mill Suffk...47 M4
Pinminnoch S Ayrs...104 C11
Pinmore S Ayrs...104 D11
Pinn Devon...9 L7
Pinner Gt Lon...32 G4
Pinner Green Gt Lon...32 G4
Pinsley Green Ches E...63 P3
Pinvin Worcs...52 H11
Pinwherry S Ayrs...104 D12
Pinxton Derbys...66 E1
Pipe and Lyde Herefs...40 G3
Pipe Aston Herefs...51 M6
Pipe Gate Shrops...64 D4
Pipehill Staffs...65 J11
Piperdam Angus...124 F6
Piperhill Highld...138 E6
Pipers Pool Cnwll...7 J8
Pipewell Nhants...55 L3
Pippacott Devon...19 K6
Pippin Street Lancs...83 N10
Pipton Powys...39 R4
Pirbright Surrey...32 D11
Pirbright Camp Surrey...32 D11
Pirnie Border...107 Q4
Pirnmill N Ayrs...112 C12
Pirton Herts...44 G5
Pirton Worcs...52 G11
Pisgah Cerdgn...49 L5
Pishill Oxon...31 P4
Pistyll Gwynd...60 E4
Pitagowan P & K...123 Q2
Pitblae Abers...141 N3
Pitcairngreen P & K...123 Q6
Pitcalnie Highld...146 E10
Pitcaple Abers...140 H10
Pitcarity Angus...131 Q11
Pitchcombe Gloucs...41 N10
Pitchcott Bucks...43 Q7
Pitch Green Bucks...31 R3
Pitch Place Surrey...32 D11
Pitch Place Surrey...14 D2
Pitcombe Somset...22 E6
Pitcox E Loth...116 E6
Pitcur P & K...124 E5

Pitfichie Abers...132 G1
Pitglassie Abers...140 H7
Pitgrudy Highld...146 E7
Pitlessie Fife...124 G11
Pitlochry P & K...123 N1
Pitmachie Abers...140 G10
Pitmain Highld...130 D4
Pitmedden Abers...141 L10
Pitmedden Garden Abers...141 L10
Pitminster Somset...21 K9
Pitmuies Angus...125 L3
Pitmunie Abers...132 G1
Pitney Somset...21 P7
Pitroddie P & K...124 E7
Pitscottie Fife...124 H10
Pitsea Essex...34 C5
Pitses Oldham...76 H3
Pitsford Nhants...55 J7
Pitstone Bucks...44 D8
Pitt Devon...20 G10
Pitt Hants...24 G8
Pittarrow Abers...132 H9
Pitt Court Gloucs...29 M3
Pittentrail Highld...146 D7
Pittenweem Fife...125 L12
Pitteuchar Fife...115 P1
Pittington Dur...101 J9
Pittodrie House Hotel Abers...140 H11
Pitton Wilts...24 C7
Pitt's Wood Kent...33 R12
Pittulie Abers...141 M2
Pityme Cnwll...6 D9
Pity Me Dur...100 H9
Pivington Kent...16 G2
Pixey Green Suffk...59 K5
Pixham Surrey...32 H12
Plains N Lans...114 E8
Plain Street Cnwll...6 E8
Plaish Shrops...51 N1
Plaistow Gt Lon...33 M6
Plaistow W Susx...14 E5
Plaitford Hants...24 C9
Plank Lane Wigan...76 B4
Plas Cymyran IoA...72 E8
Plastow Green Hants...31 L10
Platt Bridge Wigan...75 Q3
Platt Lane Shrops...63 N5
Platts Heath Kent...34 F12
Plawsworth Dur...100 H8
Plaxtol Kent...33 R11
Playden E Susx...16 G6
Playford Suffk...59 J11
Play Hatch Oxon...31 Q7
Playing Place Cnwll...3 K6
Playley Green Gloucs...41 M5
Plealey Shrops...63 M10
Plean Stirlg...114 F4
Pleasance Fife...124 E10
Pleasington Bl w D...83 P10
Pleasley Derbys...78 E10
Pleasleyhill Notts...78 E11
Pleasurewood Hills Suffk...59 Q1
Pleck Dorset...10 H3
Pledgdon Green Essex...45 Q6
Pledwick Wakefd...85 M12
Plemstall Ches W...75 M9
Plenmeller Nthumb...99 M6
Pleshey Essex...46 A8
Plockton Highld...135 P9
Plowden Shrops...51 L3
Plox Green Shrops...63 L11
Pluckley Kent...16 G2
Pluckley Station Kent...16 G2
Pluckley Thorne Kent...16 G2
Plucks Gutter Kent...35 N9
Plumbland Cumb...97 N10
Plumgarths Cumb...89 M8
Plumley Ches E...76 D8
Plump Hill Gloucs...41 K8
Plumpton Cumb...89 J11
Plumpton E Susx...15 L8
Plumpton Nhants...54 F11
Plumpton Green E Susx...15 L7
Plumpton Head Cumb...89 Q10
Plumstead Gt Lon...33 N6
Plumstead Norfk...70 H5
Plumstead Green Norfk...70 H5
Plumtree Notts...66 G5
Plumtree Green Kent...16 E2
Plungar Leics...67 J5
Plurenden Kent...16 G3
Plush Dorset...10 H4
Plusha Cnwll...7 J8
Plushabridge Cnwll...7 K10
Plwmp Cerdgn...48 F10
Plymouth C Plym...4 F6
Plympton C Plym...5 J5
Plymstock C Plym...4 H5
Plymtree Devon...9 K4
Pockley N York...92 D9
Pocklington E R Yk...86 F6
Pode Hole Lincs...68 D8
Podimore Somset...22 B8
Podington Bed...55 N8
Podmore Staffs...64 E5
Point Clear Essex...47 J9
Pointon Lincs...68 C6
Pokesdown BCP...11 Q6
Polbain Highld...144 C3
Polbathic Cnwll...4 D6
Polbeth W Loth...115 J8
Polbrock Cnwll...6 E11
Poldark Mine Cnwll...2 H8
Polebrook Nhants...55 Q3
Pole Elm Worcs...52 F11
Polegate E Susx...15 Q10
Pole Moor Kirk...84 G12
Polesden Lacey Surrey...32 G12
Polesworth Warwks...65 N11
Polgiga Cnwll...2 B9
Polglass Highld...144 C4
Polgooth Cnwll...3 N4
Polgown D & G...105 N9
Poling W Susx...14 F10
Poling Corner W Susx...14 F9
Polkerris Cnwll...3 Q4
Pollard Street Norfk...71 L5
Pollington E R Yk...86 B10
Polloch Highld...127 P10
Pollokshaws C Glas...113 Q9
Pollokshields C Glas...113 Q8
Polmassick Cnwll...3 N5
Polmear Cnwll...3 Q4
Polmont Falk...114 G6
Polnish Highld...127 N8
Polperro Cnwll...4 F6
Polruan Cnwll...4 B6
Polsham Somset...22 C4
Polstead Suffk...46 G4
Polstead Heath Suffk...46 H4
Poltalloch Ag & B...112 B2
Poltescoe Cnwll...2 H11
Poltimore Devon...9 J5
Polton Mdloth...115 N8
Polwarth Border...116 G11
Polyphant Cnwll...7 K8
Polzeath Cnwll...6 D9
Pomathorn Mdloth...115 N9
Pomeroy Derbys...77 L11
Ponde Powys...39 Q4
Pondersbridge Cambs...56 F2
Ponders End Gt Lon...33 L3

Place	County	Page	Grid
Ponsanooth	Cnwll	3	J7
Ponsonby	Cumb	88	E5
Ponsongath	Cnwll	3	J11
Ponsworthy	Devon	8	D10
Pont Abraham Services	Carmth	38	E10
Pontac	Jersey	13	d3
Pontamman	Carmth	38	F9
Pontantwn	Carmth	38	C9
Pontardawe	Neath	38	H11
Pontarddulais	Swans	38	G9
Pont-ar-Hydfer	Powys	39	K6
Pont-ar-llechau	Carmth	38	H7
Pontarsais	Carmth	38	C6
Pontblyddyn	Flints	75	J11
Pons Cyfyng	Conwy	73	M12
Pontcysyllte Aqueduct	Wrexhm	63	J4
Pont Dolgarrog	Conwy	73	N10
Pontdolgoch	Powys	50	C2
Pont-Ebbw	Newpt	28	G5
Pontefract	Wakefd	85	P11
Ponteland	Nthumb	100	H4
Ponterwyd	Cerdgn	49	N4
Pontesbury	Shrops	63	L11
Pontesbury Hill	Shrops	63	L11
Pontesford	Shrops	63	L11
Pontfadog	Wrexhm	62	H4
Pontfaen	Pembks	37	K4
Pont-faen	Powys	39	N5
Pontgarreg	Cerdgn	48	E10
Pontgarreg	Pembks	37	M2
Ponthenri	Carmth	38	C10
Ponthir	Torfn	28	D4
Ponthirwaun	Cerdgn	48	D11
Pontllanfraith	Caerph	28	A3
Pontlliw	Swans	26	F2
Pontllyfni	Gwynd	60	G2
Pontlottyn	Caerph	39	Q10
Pont Morlais	Carmth	38	E10
Pontnêddfêchan	Neath	39	L6
Pontnewydd	Torfn	28	C3
Pontnewynydd	Torfn	28	C2
Pont Pen-y-benglog	Gwynd	73	L11
Pontrhydfendigaid	Cerdgn	49	M7
Pont Rhyd-sarn	Gwynd	61	Q6
Pont Rhyd-y-cyff	Brdgnd	27	K4
Pont-rhyd-y-fen	Neath	27	J2
Pontrhydygroes	Cerdgn	49	M6
Pontrhydyrun	Torfn	28	C3
Pontrilas	Herefs	40	E6
Pont Robert	Powys	62	F9
Ponts Green	E Susx	16	C8
Pontshaen	Cerdgn	38	C2
Pontshill	Herefs	41	K7
Pontsticill	Myr Td	39	P9
Pont Walby	Neath	39	L10
Pontwelly	Carmth	38	B4
Pontyates	Carmth	38	C10
Pontyberem	Carmth	38	D9
Pont-y-blew	Wrexhm	63	K4
Pontybodkin	Flints	75	J11
Pontyclun	Rhondd	27	N6
Pontycymer	Brdgnd	27	L4
Pontyglasier	Pembks	37	M3
Pontygwaith	Rhondd	27	M3
Pontygynon	Pembks	37	M3
Pontymister	Caerph	28	C4
Pont-y-pant	Conwy	61	N1
Pontypool	Torfn	28	C2
Pontypridd	Rhondd	27	P4
Pont-yr-hafod	Pembks	36	H5
Pont-yr-Rhyl	Brdgnd	27	L4
Pontywaun	Caerph	28	B4
Pool	Cnwll	2	G6
Pool	IoS	2	b2
Poole	BCP	11	N7
Poole Keynes	Gloucs	30	A3
Poolewe	Highld	143	M9
Pooley Bridge	Cumb	89	M2
Pooley Street	Norfk	58	F4
Poolfold	Staffs	76	G11
Pool Head	Herefs	51	P10
Poolhill	Gloucs	41	L6
Pool in Wharfedale	Leeds	85	K6
Pool of Muckhart	Clacks	114	H1
Pool Quay	Powys	63	J10
Pool Street	Essex	46	C4
Pooting's	Kent	15	N1
Popham	Hants	25	J4
Poplar	Gt Lon	33	L6
Poplar Street	Suffk	59	N7
Porchfield	IoW	12	G6
Poringland	Norfk	71	L10
Porkellis	Cnwll	2	H8
Porlock	Somset	20	D4
Porlock Weir	Somset	20	D4
Portachoillan	Ag & B	111	Q8
Port-an-Eorna	Highld	135	P9
Port Appin	Ag & B	120	G4
Port Askaig	Ag & B	111	K7
Portavadie	Ag & B	112	D7
Portbury	N Som	28	H7
Port Carlisle	Cumb	97	P6
Port Charlotte	Ag & B	110	F9
Portchester	Hants	13	K4
Port Clarence	S on T	91	R2
Port Driseach	Ag & B	112	E6
Port Ellen	Ag & B	110	H12
Port Elphinstone	Abers	141	J11
Portencalzie	D & G	94	E4
Portencross	N Ayrs	112	H11
Port Erin	IoM	102	b7
Portesham	Dorset	10	F7
Portessie	Moray	140	C3
Port e Vullen	IoM	102	f3
Portfield Gate	Pembks	36	H7
Portgate	Devon	7	M7
Port Gaverne	Cnwll	6	E8
Port Glasgow	Inver	113	L6
Portgordon	Moray	140	B3
Portgower	Highld	146	H2
Porth	Cnwll	3	K2
Porth	Rhondd	27	N4
Porthallow	Cnwll	3	J9
Porthallow	Cnwll	4	C6
Porthcawl	Brdgnd	27	J6
Porthcothan	Cnwll	6	B10
Porthcurno	Cnwll	2	B9
Porthdinllaen	Gwynd	60	D4
Port Henderson	Highld	143	K10
Porthgain	Pembks	36	F4
Porthgwarra	Cnwll	2	B9
Porthill	Staffs	64	F2
Porthkea	Cnwll	3	K6
Porthkerry	V Glam	27	P9
Porthleven	Cnwll	2	G9
Porthmadog	Gwynd	61	J4
Porthmeor	Cnwll	2	C7
Porth Navas	Cnwll	3	J9
Portholland	Cnwll	3	N6
Porthoustock	Cnwll	3	K9
Porthpean	Cnwll	3	P4
Porthtowan	Cnwll	2	F6
Porthwgan	Wrexhm	63	L3
Porthyrhyd	Carmth	38	D8
Porth-y-Waen	Shrops	63	J7
Portincaple	Ag & B	113	J3
Portinfer	Jersey	13	a1
Portington	E R Yk	86	E9
Portinnisherrich	Ag & B	121	J10
Portinscale	Cumb	88	H2
Port Isaac	Cnwll	6	E8
Portishead	N Som	28	G7
Portknockie	Moray	140	D2
Portland	Dorset	10	G10
Portlethen	Abers	133	M5
Portling	D & G	96	H7
Portloe	Cnwll	3	M6
Port Logan	D & G	94	G10
Portmahomack	Highld	146	G8
Portmeirion	Gwynd	61	K5
Portmellon	Cnwll	3	P5
Port Mòr	Highld	126	G8
Portmore	Hants	12	E5
Port Mulgrave	N York	92	G3
Portnacroish	Ag & B	120	H3
Portnaguran	W Isls	152	h3
Portnahaven	Ag & B	110	E10
Portnalong	Highld	134	F9
Port nan Giuran	W Isls	152	h3
Port nan Long	W Isls	152	c7
Port Nis	W Isls	152	h1
Portobello	C Edin	115	P6
Portobello	Gatesd	100	H7
Portobello	Wolves	52	H1
Port of Menteith	Stirlg	113	R1
Port o' Ness	W Isls	152	h1
Porton	Wilts	24	C6
Portontown	Devon	7	M9
Portpatrick	D & G	94	E7
Port Quin	Cnwll	6	C6
Port Ramsay	Ag & B	120	G4
Portreath	Cnwll	2	G5
Portreath Harbour	Cnwll	2	G5
Portree	Highld	134	H7
Port Righ	Ag & B	103	L2
Port St Mary	IoM	102	b7
Portscatho	Cnwll	3	L7
Portsea	C Port	13	L5
Portskerra	Highld	150	F3
Portskewett	Mons	28	G5
Portslade	Br & H	15	J10
Portslade-by-Sea	Br & H	15	J10
Portslogan	D & G	94	E6
Portsmouth	C Port	13	L5
Portsmouth	Calder	84	C9
Portsmouth Arms	Devon	19	M9
Portsmouth Dockyard	C Port	13	K4
Port Soderick	IoM	102	d6
Port Solent	C Port	13	L5
Portsonachan Hotel	Ag & B	121	K8
Portsoy	Abers	140	F3
Port Sunlight	Wirral	75	K7
Portswood	C Sotn	24	G10
Port Talbot	Neath	27	J4
Portuairk	Highld	126	H10
Portway	Herefs	40	G3
Portway	Herefs	40	G5
Portway	Sandw	52	H3
Portway	Worcs	53	K6
Port Wemyss	Ag & B	110	E11
Port William	D & G	95	L9
Portwrinkle	Cnwll	4	E6
Porwerrock	D & G	95	P7
Posbury	Devon	8	F5
Posenhall	Shrops	64	C11
Poslingford	Suffk	57	P11
Posso	Border	106	G3
Postbridge	Devon	8	C9
Postcombe	Oxon	31	P2
Post Green	Dorset	11	M6
Postling	Kent	17	L3
Postwick	Norfk	71	L10
Potarch	Abers	132	F5
Potsgrove	C Beds	44	D6
Potten End	Herts	44	D8
Potten Street	Kent	35	N9
Potter Brompton	N York	93	J5
Pottergate Street	Norfk	58	H2
Potterhanworth	Lincs	79	Q10
Potterhanworth Booths	Lincs	79	Q10
Potter Heigham	Norfk	71	N8
Potterne	Wilts	30	A10
Potterne Wick	Wilts	30	A10
Potter Row	Bucks	44	C11
Potters Bar	Herts	33	J2
Potters Brook	Lancs	83	L5
Potter's Cross	Staffs	52	F4
Potters Crouch	Herts	44	G10
Potter's Green	E Susx	16	A6
Potter's Green	Covtry	54	B4
Potter's Green	Herts	45	L7
Pottersheath	Herts	45	J7
Potters Marston	Leics	54	E1
Potter Somersal	Derbys	65	L6
Potterspury	Nhants	43	Q3
Potter Street	Essex	45	N10
Potterton	Abers	133	M1
Potterton	Leeds	85	N7
Potthorpe	Norfk	70	D7
Pottle Street	Wilts	22	H5
Potto	N York	91	Q6
Potton	C Beds	56	D10
Pott Row	Norfk	69	N8
Pott's Green	Essex	46	F7
Pott Shrigley	Ches E	76	H8
Poughill	Cnwll	7	D11
Poughill	Devon	8	G3
Poulner	Hants	12	B3
Poulshot	Wilts	29	K10
Poulton	Gloucs	30	C2
Poulton	Wirral	75	J5
Poulton-le-Fylde	Lancs	82	H7
Poulton Priory	Gloucs	30	C2
Pound Bank	Worcs	52	D6
Poundbury	Dorset	10	G6
Poundffald	Swans	26	E3
Poundgate	E Susx	15	P5
Pound Green	E Susx	15	P6
Pound Green	Suffk	57	N10
Pound Green	Worcs	52	D5
Pound Hill	W Susx	15	K4
Poundon	Bucks	43	N6
Poundsbridge	Kent	15	R2
Poundsgate	Devon	8	D10
Poundstock	Cnwll	7	J4
Pound Street	Hants	31	K10
Pounsley	E Susx	15	P6
Pouton	D & G	95	N9
Pouy Street	Suffk	59	M6
Povey Cross	Surrey	15	K2
Powburn	Nthumb	108	H6
Powderham	Devon	8	H6
Powerstock	Dorset	10	D5
Powfoot	D & G	97	N5
Pow Green	Herefs	41	L3
Powhill	Cumb	97	P7
Powick	Worcs	52	F10
Powmill	P & K	115	J2
Poxwell	Dorset	10	H8
Poyle	Slough	32	F6
Poynings	W Susx	15	J8
Poyntington	Dorset	22	E9
Poynton	Ches E	76	G7
Poynton	Wrekin	63	P9
Poynton Green	Wrekin	63	P9
Poyston Cross	Pembks	37	J6
Poystreet Green	Suffk	58	E9
Praa Sands	Cnwll	2	F9
Pratt's Bottom	Gt Lon	33	N10
Praze-an-Beeble	Cnwll	2	G7
Predannack Wollas	Cnwll	2	G11
Prees	Shrops	63	P5
Preesall	Lancs	83	J6
Prees Green	Shrops	63	P6
Preesgweene	Shrops	63	J5
Prees Heath	Shrops	63	P4
Prees Higher Heath	Shrops	63	P5
Prees Lower Heath	Shrops	63	P5
Prendwick	Nthumb	108	G7
Pren-gwyn	Cerdgn	38	C3
Prenteg	Gwynd	61	K4
Prenton	Wirral	75	J6
Prescot	Knows	75	M5
Prescott	Devon	20	H10
Prescott	Shrops	63	M8
Prescott	Shrops	52	H4
Presnerb	Angus	131	M11
Pressen	Nthumb	108	D3
Prestatyn	Denbgs	74	F7
Prestbury	Ches E	76	G8
Prestbury	Gloucs	41	R7
Presteigne	Powys	51	K8
Prestleigh	Somset	22	E5
Prestolee	Bolton	76	D3
Preston	Border	116	H10
Preston	Br & H	15	K9
Preston	Devon	8	F10
Preston	Dorset	10	H8
Preston	E R Yk	87	M9
Preston	Gloucs	30	B2
Preston	Herts	44	H7
Preston	Kent	34	H10
Preston	Kent	35	N10
Preston	Lancs	83	M9
Preston	Nthumb	109	K5
Preston	Rutlnd	67	L11
Preston	Shrops	63	N9
Preston	Somset	20	H6
Preston	Torbay	5	Q4
Preston	Wilts	30	B7
Preston	Wilts	30	F7
Preston Bagot	Warwks	53	M7
Preston Bissett	Bucks	43	N6
Preston Bowyer	Somset	21	J8
Preston Brockhurst	Shrops	63	P7
Preston Brook	Halton	75	P7
Preston Candover	Hants	25	K5
Preston Capes	Nhants	54	F9
Preston Crowmarsh	Oxon	31	N4
Preston Deanery	Nhants	55	K9
Preston Green	Warwks	53	M7
Preston Gubbals	Shrops	63	N8
Preston Montford	Shrops	63	M9
Preston on Stour	Warwks	53	M10
Preston on Tees	S on T	91	Q4
Preston on the Hill	Halton	75	P7
Preston on Wye	Herefs	40	E3
Prestonpans	E Loth	115	P6
Preston Patrick	Cumb	89	N10
Preston Plucknett	Somset	22	C10
Preston St Mary	Suffk	58	D10
Preston Street	Kent	35	N10
Preston-under-Scar	N York	90	H8
Preston upon the Weald Moors	Wrekin	64	C9
Preston Wynne	Herefs	40	H2
Prestwich	Bury	76	F3
Prestwick	Nthumb	100	F4
Prestwick	S Ayrs	104	F5
Prestwick Airport	S Ayrs	104	G4
Prestwood	Bucks	32	C2
Prestwood	Staffs	52	F3
Price Town	Brdgnd	27	M4
Prickwillow	Cambs	57	L4
Priddy	Somset	22	C3
Priestacott	Devon	7	N3
Priestcliffe	Derbys	77	L9
Priestcliffe Ditch	Derbys	77	L9
Priest Hutton	Lancs	89	N12
Priestland	E Ayrs	105	K2
Priestley Green	Calder	84	H10
Priest Weston	Shrops	51	J1
Priestwood Green	Kent	34	B9
Primethorpe	Leics	54	E2
Primrose Green	Norfk	70	G9
Primrosehill	Border	116	H9
Primrose Hill	Cambs	56	G3
Primrose Hill	Derbys	78	C12
Primrose Hill	Dudley	52	H3
Primrose Hill	Lancs	75	L2
Primsidemill	Border	108	C4
Prince of Wales Bridge	Mons	28	G5
Princes Gate	Pembks	37	M8
Princes Risborough	Bucks	44	A11
Princethorpe	Warwks	54	C6
Princetown	Devon	8	B10
Prinsted	W Susx	13	N4
Prion	Denbgs	74	E11
Prior Rigg	Cumb	98	F4
Priors Halton	Shrops	51	N5
Priors Hardwick	Warwks	54	D9
Priorslee	Wrekin	64	D10
Priors Marston	Warwks	54	E9
Priors Norton	Gloucs	41	N7
Priory Wood	Herefs	40	C3
Prisk	V Glam	27	N7
Priston	BaNES	29	L10
Pristow Green	Norfk	58	H3
Prittlewell	Sthend	34	F5
Privett	Hants	25	L8
Prixford	Devon	19	K6
Probus	Cnwll	3	M5
Prora	E Loth	116	C5
Prospect	Cumb	97	M10
Prospidnick	Cnwll	2	G8
Protstonhill	Abers	141	M3
Prudhoe	Nthumb	100	E6
Prussia Cove	Cnwll	2	F9
Pubil	P & K	122	D4
Publow	BaNES	29	J9
Puckeridge	Herts	45	M7
Puckington	Somset	21	N9
Pucklechurch	S Glos	29	L7
Puckrup	Gloucs	41	P4
Puddinglake	Ches W	76	D9
Puddington	Ches W	75	J9
Puddledock	Norfk	58	F2
Puddletown	Dorset	11	L7
Pudleston	Herefs	51	P8
Pudsey	Leeds	85	K8
Pulborough	W Susx	14	F7
Puleston	Wrekin	64	D7
Pulford	Ches W	75	L12
Pulham	Dorset	10	H3
Pulham Market	Norfk	59	J4
Pulham St Mary	Norfk	59	J4
Pullens Green	S Glos	29	J5
Pulloxhill	C Beds	44	F5
Pumpherston	W Loth	115	M7
Pumsaint	Carmth	38	G4
Puncheston	Pembks	37	K4
Puncknowle	Dorset	10	D6
Punnett's Town	E Susx	16	A7
Purbrook	Hants	13	L3
Purfleet	Thurr	33	Q6
Puriton	Somset	21	M5
Purleigh	Essex	46	E11
Purley	Gt Lon	33	K9
Purley on Thames	W Berk	31	N7
Purlogue	Shrops	51	J5
Purlpit	Wilts	29	P9
Purls Bridge	Cambs	57	J3
Purse Caundle	Dorset	22	F10
Purshull Green	Worcs	52	G6
Purslow	Shrops	51	K4
Purston Jaglin	Wakefd	85	N11
Purtington	Somset	10	B3
Purton	Gloucs	41	K10
Purton	Gloucs	41	L11
Purton	Wilts	30	C5
Purton Stoke	Wilts	30	C4
Pury End	Nhants	43	P3
Pusey	Oxon	30	H3
Putley	Herefs	41	K4
Putley Green	Herefs	41	K4
Putloe	Gloucs	41	M9
Putney	Gt Lon	33	J7
Putsborough	Devon	19	J5
Puttenham	Herts	44	C8
Puttenham	Surrey	14	D1
Puttock End	Essex	46	E4
Putton	Dorset	10	G8
Putts Corner	Devon	9	M5
Puxley	Nhants	43	Q3
Puxton	N Som	28	G9
Pwll	Carmth	26	D2
Pwllcrochan	Pembks	36	H10
Pwll-du	Mons	40	C9
Pwll-glâs	Denbgs	62	F1
Pwllgloyw	Powys	39	N5
Pwllheli	Gwynd	60	F5
Pwllmeyric	Mons	28	H4
Pwll-trap	Carmth	37	P7
Pwll-y-glaw	Neath	27	J4
Pydew	Conwy	73	N8
Pye Bridge	Derbys	66	D2
Pyecombe	W Susx	15	K8
Pye Corner	Newpt	28	D5
Pye Green	Staffs	65	J9
Pyle	Brdgnd	27	J6
Pyleigh	Somset	20	H7
Pylle	Somset	22	E6
Pymoor	Cambs	57	J3
Pymore	Dorset	10	D6
Pyrford	Surrey	32	E10
Pyrton	Oxon	31	P3
Pytchley	Nhants	55	L6
Pyworthy	Devon	7	K4
Q			
Quabbs	Shrops	50	H4
Quadring	Lincs	68	E5
Quadring Eaudike	Lincs	68	E5
Quainton	Bucks	43	Q7
Quaker's Yard	Myr Td	27	P3
Quaking Houses	Dur	100	F8
Quantock Hills	Somset	21	J6
Quarff	Shet	147	i8
Quarley	Hants	24	D5
Quarndon	Derbys	66	B4
Quarr Hill	IoW	13	J6
Quarrier's Village	Inver	113	M8
Quarrington	Lincs	67	Q3
Quarrington Hill	Dur	101	J10
Quarrybank	Ches W	75	P10
Quarry Bank	Dudley	52	H3
Quarrywood	Moray	139	M3
Quarter	N Ayrs	113	J9
Quarter	S Lans	114	D11
Quatford	Shrops	52	D2
Quatt	Shrops	52	D3
Quebec	Dur	100	F9
Quedgeley	Gloucs	41	N9
Queen Adelaide	Cambs	57	L4
Queenborough	Kent	34	F8
Queen Camel	Somset	22	D9
Queen Charlton	BaNES	29	K9
Queen Dart	Devon	20	D10
Queen Elizabeth Forest Park	Stirlg	122	H6
Queenhill	Worcs	41	P4
Queen Oak	Dorset	22	H7
Queen's Bower	IoW	13	J8
Queensbury	C Brad	84	G9
Queensferry	Flints	75	K10
Queensferry Crossing	Fife	115	L5
Queen's Head	Shrops	63	L7
Queen's Hills	Norfk	70	H9
Queenslie	C Glas	114	B8
Queen's Park	Bed	55	P10
Queen's Park	Nhants	55	J8
Queen Street	Kent	16	C2
Queen Street	Wilts	30	C5
Queenzieburn	N Lans	114	C6
Quendon	Essex	45	P4
Queniborough	Leics	66	G9
Quenington	Gloucs	42	D11
Quernmore	Lancs	83	M3
Queslett	Birm	53	K2
Quethiock	Cnwll	4	D4
Quick's Green	W Berk	31	M7
Quidenham	Norfk	58	F3
Quidhampton	Hants	25	J3
Quidhampton	Wilts	23	N7
Quina Brook	Shrops	63	N5
Quinton	Dudley	52	H3
Quinton	Nhants	55	K10
Quinton Green	Nhants	55	K10
Quintrell Downs	Cnwll	3	L2
Quixhall	Staffs	65	L4
Quixwood	Border	116	H10
Quoditch	Devon	7	M5
Quoig	P & K	123	J2
Quoisley	Ches E	63	P3
Quorn	Leics	66	F9
Quothquan	S Lans	106	C2
Quoyburray	Ork	147	d5
Quoyloo	Ork	147	b4
R			
Raasay	Highld	135	K7
Rabbit's Cross	Kent	16	D1
Rableyheath	Herts	45	J8
Raby	Cumb	97	P8
Raby	Wirral	75	K8
Rachan Mill	Border	106	A3
Rachub	Gwynd	73	K10
Rackenford	Devon	20	D10
Rackham	W Susx	14	F7
Rackheath	Norfk	71	K9
Racks	D & G	97	J3
Rackwick	Ork	147	a5
Radbourne	Derbys	65	P5
Radcliffe	Bury	76	D3
Radcliffe	Nthumb	109	L9
Radcliffe on Trent	Notts	66	G4
Radclive	Bucks	43	N5
Radcot	Oxon	30	G2
Raddery	Highld	138	C4
Raddington	Somset	20	G8
Radernie	Fife	125	J11
Radford	Covtry	53	C4
Radford Semele	Warwks	53	Q8
Radlet	Somset	21	K6
Radlett	Herts	32	H2
Radley	Devon	19	P8
Radley	Oxon	31	L3
Radley	W Berk	30	H7
Radmore Green	Ches E	63	Q1
Radnage	Bucks	31	R4
Radstock	BaNES	22	F2
Radstone	Nhants	43	M4
Radway	Warwks	54	B11
Radwell	Bed	55	P9
Radwell	Herts	45	J4
Radwinter	Essex	45	R4
Radwinter End	Essex	45	R4
Radyr	Cardif	27	Q6
RAF College (Cranwell)	Lincs	67	P2
Rafford	Moray	139	K4
RAF Museum Cosford	Shrops	64	E11
RAF Museum Hendon	Gt Lon	33	J4
Ragdale	Leics	66	H8
Ragdon	Shrops	51	M2
Raginnis	Cnwll	2	D9
Raglan	Mons	40	F10
Ragnall	Notts	79	K9
Raigbeg	Highld	138	G10
Rainbow Hill	Worcs	52	F9
Rainford	St Hel	75	N3
Rainham	Gt Lon	33	Q6
Rainham	Medway	34	E9
Rainhill	St Hel	75	N6
Rainhill Stoops	St Hel	75	N6
Rainow	Ches E	76	H9
Rainsough	Bury	76	E3
Rainton	N York	91	N11
Rainworth	Notts	78	F12
Raisbeck	Cumb	89	Q5
Raise	Cumb	99	K9
Raithby	Lincs	80	F7
Raithby	Lincs	80	G10
Raithwaite	N York	92	G4
Rake	Hants	25	P8
Rakewood	Rochdl	84	D12
Ralia	Highld	130	C5
Ram	Carmth	38	E2
Ramasaig	Highld	134	C7
Rame	Cnwll	2	H9
Rame	Cnwll	4	F7
Ram Hill	S Glos	29	K6
Ram Lane	Kent	16	H2
Rampisham	Dorset	10	D4
Rampside	Cumb	82	G2
Rampton	Cambs	56	H7
Rampton	Notts	79	K8
Ramsbottom	Bury	84	B11
Ramsbury	Wilts	30	F8
Ramscraigs	Highld	151	L11
Ramsdean	Hants	25	M9
Ramsdell	Hants	31	M10
Ramsden	Oxon	42	H8
Ramsden	Worcs	41	Q2
Ramsden Bellhouse	Essex	34	C3
Ramsden Heath	Essex	34	C3
Ramsey	Cambs	56	F3
Ramsey	Essex	47	M5
Ramsey	IoM	102	f3
Ramsey Forty Foot	Cambs	56	F3
Ramsey Heights	Cambs	56	E4
Ramsey Island	Essex	46	G10
Ramsey Island	Pembks	36	D6
Ramsey Mereside	Cambs	56	E3
Ramsey St Mary's	Cambs	56	E3
Ramsgate	Kent	35	Q9
Ramsgill	N York	91	K11
Ramshaw	Dur	91	K2
Ramshaw	Dur	99	Q9
Ramsholt	Suffk	47	P3
Ramshope	Nthumb	108	B9
Ramshorn	Staffs	65	K3
Ramsley	Devon	8	D6
Ramsnest Common	Surrey	14	D3
Ranby	Lincs	80	D8
Ranby	Notts	78	G7
Rand	Lincs	80	B8
Randwick	Gloucs	41	N10
Ranfurly	Rens	113	M8
Rangemore	Staffs	65	M7
Rangeworthy	S Glos	29	L5
Rankinston	E Ayrs	104	H7
Ranksborough	Rutlnd	67	L10
Rank's Green	Essex	46	C8
Rannoch Station	P & K	122	C3
Ranscombe	Somset	20	D5
Ranskill	Notts	78	G6
Ranton	Staffs	64	G8
Ranton Green	Staffs	64	G7
Ranworth	Norfk	71	M9
Raploch	Stirlg	114	G2
Rapness	Ork	147	d2
Rapps	Somset	21	M9
Rascarrel	D & G	96	G8
Rashfield	Ag & B	112	H5
Rashwood	Worcs	52	G7
Raskelf	N York	91	N12
Rassau	Blae G	39	R9
Rastrick	Calder	84	H10
Ratagan	Highld	136	C11
Ratby	Leics	66	E11
Ratcliffe Culey	Leics	54	B1
Ratcliffe on Soar	Notts	66	E6
Ratcliffe on the Wreake	Leics	66	G9
Rathen	Abers	141	N4
Rathillet	Fife	124	H9
Rathmell	N York	84	B3
Ratho	C Edin	115	L7
Ratho Station	C Edin	115	L7
Rathven	Moray	140	C3
Ratlake	Hants	24	G8
Ratley	Warwks	42	H2
Ratling	Kent	35	M11
Ratlinghope	Shrops	51	L1
Rattar	Highld	151	M2
Ratten Row	Cumb	98	C10
Ratten Row	Cumb	98	E8
Ratten Row	Lancs	83	K6
Rattery	Devon	5	M4
Rattlesden	Suffk	58	E9
Ratton Village	E Susx	15	Q10
Rattray	P & K	124	D4
Raughton	Cumb	98	H8
Raughton Head	Cumb	98	H9
Raunds	Nhants	55	R6
Ravenfield	Rothm	78	D5
Ravenglass	Cumb	88	D9
Ravenhills Green	Worcs	52	E9
Raveningham	Norfk	59	N1
Ravenscar	N York	93	J6
Ravenscraig	N Lans	114	E10
Ravensden	Bed	55	P9
Ravenseat	N York	90	D6
Ravenshead	Notts	78	F11
Ravensmoor	Ches E	63	Q2
Ravensthorpe	Kirk	85	K11
Ravensthorpe	Nhants	54	H6
Ravenstone	Leics	66	C9
Ravenstone	M Keyn	55	L10
Ravenstonedale	Cumb	90	B6
Ravenstruther	S Lans	114	G12
Ravensworth	N York	91	J5
Raw	N York	93	J5
Rawcliffe	C York	86	A4
Rawcliffe	E R Yk	86	C10
Rawcliffe Bridge	E R Yk	86	C11
Rawdon	Leeds	85	J7
Rawling Street	Kent	34	F11
Rawmarsh	Rothm	78	D4
Rawnsley	Staffs	65	J9
Rawreth	Essex	34	D4
Rawridge	Devon	9	N3
Rawtenstall	Lancs	84	B10
Raydon	Suffk	47	J4
Raylees	Nthumb	108	E11
Rayleigh	Essex	34	E4
Raymond's Hill	Devon	9	R5
Rayne	Essex	46	C6
Raynes Park	Gt Lon	33	J8
Reach	Cambs	57	L7
Read	Lancs	84	A8
Reading	Readg	31	P7
Reading Services	W Berk	31	P8
Reading Street	Kent	16	G4
Reading Street	Kent	35	Q8
Reagill	Cumb	89	P3
Realwa	Cnwll	2	F7
Rearquhar	Highld	146	D6
Rearsby	Leics	66	G9
Rease Heath	Ches E	63	Q2
Reay	Highld	150	H4
Reculver	Kent	35	M8
Red Ball	Devon	20	H10
Redberth	Pembks	37	L9
Redbourn	Herts	44	G8
Redbourne	N Linc	79	N4
Redbrook	Gloucs	40	H9
Redbrook	Wrexhm	63	N4
Redbrook Street	Kent	16	G3
Redburn	Highld	138	E6
Redburn	Nthumb	99	L5
Redcar	R & Cl	92	C2
Redcastle	D & G	96	G6
Redcastle	Highld	137	Q6
Red Dial	Cumb	97	Q9
Redding	Falk	114	G6
Reddingmuirhead	Falk	114	G6
Reddish	Stockp	76	G5
Redditch	Worcs	53	K7
Rede	Suffk	57	R10
Redenhall	Norfk	59	J4
Redenham	Hants	24	E3
Redesmouth	Nthumb	99	N2
Redford	Abers	133	J10
Redford	W Susx	25	P9
Redfordgreen	Border	107	K6
Redgate	Rhondd	27	N5
Redgorton	P & K	124	B7
Redgrave	Suffk	58	F5
Redhill	Abers	133	J3
Redhill	Herts	45	K5
Redhill	N Som	28	H9
Redhill	Surrey	33	K12
Red Hill	Warwks	53	L9
Redisham	Suffk	59	N4
Redland	Bristl	29	J7
Redland	Ork	147	c4
Redlingfield	Suffk	59	J6
Redlingfield Green	Suffk	59	J6
Red Lodge	Suffk	57	N6
Red Lumb	Rochdl	84	C12
Redlynch	Somset	22	F6
Redlynch	Wilts	24	C9
Redmain	Cumb	97	N11
Redmarley	Worcs	52	E7
Redmarley D'Abitot	Gloucs	41	M5
Redmarshall	S on T	91	P3
Redmile	Leics	67	K5
Redmire	N York	90	H8
Redmyre	Abers	133	J8
Rednal	Birm	53	J5
Rednal	Shrops	63	L7
Redpath	Border	107	P3
Redpoint	Highld	135	N2
Red Post	Cnwll	7	K4
Red Rock	Wigan	75	P2
Red Roses	Carmth	37	N7
Red Row	Nthumb	109	L10
Redruth	Cnwll	2	H6
Redstocks	Wilts	29	Q9
Redstone	P & K	124	C7
Redstone Cross	Pembks	37	L7
Red Street	Staffs	64	F2
Redvales	Bury	76	E2
Red Wharf Bay	IoA	72	H6
Redwick	Newpt	28	F5
Redwick	S Glos	28	H5
Redworth	Darltn	91	L2
Reed	Herts	45	L5
Reedham	Norfk	71	N11
Reedness	E R Yk	86	E10
Reeds Beck	Lincs	80	D10
Reeds Holme	Lancs	84	B10
Reepham	Lincs	79	P9
Reepham	Norfk	70	G8
Reeth	N York	90	H7
Reeves Green	Solhll	53	N5
Regaby	IoM	102	f3
Regil	N Som	28	H9
Reiff	Highld	143	P2
Reigate	Surrey	33	J12
Reighton	N York	93	N11
Reinigeadal	W Isls	152	f5
Reisque	Abers	141	L11
Reiss	Highld	151	P5
Rejerrah	Cnwll	3	K3
Releath	Cnwll	2	G8
Relubbus	Cnwll	2	F8
Relugas	Moray	139	J6
Remenham	Wokham	31	Q5
Remenham Hill	Wokham	31	Q6
Rempstone	Notts	66	F7
Rendcomb	Gloucs	42	B9
Rendham	Suffk	59	M8
Rendlesham	Suffk	59	L10
Renfrew	Rens	113	Q8
Renhold	Bed	55	P9
Renishaw	Derbys	78	C8
Rennington	Nthumb	109	K6
Renton	W Duns	113	M6
Renwick	Cumb	98	H9
Repps	Norfk	71	N8
Repton	Derbys	66	B6
Rescassa	Cnwll	3	N6
Rescorla	Cnwll	3	N4
Resipole Burn	Highld	127	N11
Reskadinnick	Cnwll	2	F6
Resolis	Highld	138	C3
Resolven	Neath	39	K11
Rest and be thankful	Ag & B	121	M10
Reston	Border	117	J9
Restronguet	Cnwll	3	K7
Reswallie	Angus	125	K3
Retew	Cnwll	3	M4
Retford	Notts	78	H7
Retire	Cnwll	3	N3
Rettendon	Essex	34	D3
Retyn	Cnwll	3	L3
Revesby	Lincs	80	F11
Rew	Devon	5	M8
Rew	Devon	8	E10
Rewe	Devon	8	H5
Rew Street	IoW	12	H6
Rexon	Devon	7	M7
Reydon	Suffk	59	P5
Reymerston	Norfk	70	F11
Reynalton	Pembks	37	L9
Reynoldston	Swans	26	C4
Rezare	Cnwll	7	L9
Rhadyr	Mons	40	E11
Rhandirmwyn	Carmth	39	J3
Rhayader	Powys	50	D7
Rheindown	Highld	137	P6
Rhenigidale	W Isls	152	f5
Rhes-y-cae	Flints	74	G9
Rhewl	Denbgs	62	E1
Rhewl	Denbgs	74	F11
Rhewl Mostyn	Flints	74	G7
Rhiconich	Highld	148	G5
Rhicullen	Highld	146	C10
Rhigos	Rhondd	39	L10
Rhiwbina	Cardif	27	R6
Rhiwbryfdir	Gwynd	61	M3
Rhiwderyn	Newpt	28	C5
Rhiwen	Gwynd	73	J11
Rhiwinder	Rhondd	27	N5
Rhiwlas	Gwynd	62	C5
Rhiwlas	Gwynd	73	K10
Rhiwlas	Powys	62	H6
Rhiwsaeson	Rhondd	27	P6
Rhode	Somset	21	L6
Rhoden Green	Kent	16	B2
Rhodes Minnis	Kent	17	L2
Rhodiad-y-brenin	Pembks	36	E5
Rhonehouse	D & G	96	F6
Rhoose	V Glam	27	P9
Rhos	Carmth	38	B5
Rhos	Denbgs	74	F11
Rhos	Neath	38	H11
Rhosaman	Carmth	38	H9
Rhosbeirio	IoA	72	F5
Rhoscefnhir	IoA	73	J8
Rhoscolyn	IoA	72	D8
Rhoscrowther	Pembks	36	H10
Rhosddu	Wrexhm	63	J2
Rhos-ddu	Gwynd	60	D5
Rhosdylluan	Gwynd	61	Q5
Rhosesmor	Flints	74	H10
Rhos-fawr	Gwynd	60	F5
Rhosgadfan	Gwynd	72	H12
Rhosgoch	IoA	72	G5
Rhosgoch	Powys	50	G11
Rhos Haminiog	Cerdgn	49	J8
Rhoshill	Pembks	37	N2
Rhoshirwaun	Gwynd	60	C6
Rhoslan	Gwynd	60	H4
Rhoslefain	Gwynd	61	K10
Rhosllanerchrugog	Wrexhm	63	J3
Rhôs Lligwy	IoA	72	H6
Rhosmaen	Carmth	38	G7
Rhosmeirch	IoA	72	H8
Rhosneigr	IoA	72	E8
Rhosnesni	Wrexhm	63	K2
Rhôs-on-Sea	Conwy	73	P7
Rhosrobin	Wrexhm	63	J2
Rhossili	Swans	26	B5
Rhostrehwfa	IoA	72	G8
Rhostryfan	Gwynd	72	H12
Rhostyllen	Wrexhm	63	J3
Rhosybol	IoA	72	G6
Rhos-y-brithdir	Powys	62	G8
Rhosygadfa	Shrops	63	J5
Rhos-y-garth	Cerdgn	49	L6
Rhos-y-gwaliau	Gwynd	62	C5
Rhos-y-llan	Gwynd	60	D5
Rhosymedre	Wrexhm	63	J4
Rhos-y-meirch	Powys	51	J7
Rhu	Ag & B	113	K4
Rhuallt	Denbgs	74	E8
Rhubodach	Ag & B	112	F6
Rhuddall Heath	Ches W	75	P11
Rhuddlan	Cerdgn	38	D3
Rhuddlan	Denbgs	74	D8
Rhulen	Powys	50	G11
Rhunahaorine	Ag & B	111	Q11
Rhyd	Gwynd	61	L4
Rhydargaeau	Carmth	38	C6
Rhydcymerau	Carmth	38	F4
Rhydd	Worcs	41	N3
Rhyd-Ddu	Gwynd	61	J2
Rhydding	Neath	26	G2
Rhydgaled	Conwy	74	C11
Rhydlanfair	Conwy	61	P2
Rhydlewis	Cerdgn	48	E11
Rhydlios	Gwynd	60	C6
Rhydlydan	Conwy	62	C3
Rhydowen	Cerdgn	38	C2
Rhydroser	Cerdgn	49	J7
Rhydspence	Herefs	40	C3
Rhydtalog	Flints	62	H1
Rhyd-uchaf	Gwynd	62	C4
Rhyd-y-clafdy	Gwynd	60	F5
Rhydycroesau	Shrops	62	H5
Rhydyfelin	Cerdgn	49	K5
Rhydyfelin	Rhondd	27	P5
Rhyd-y-foel	Conwy	74	C8
Rhydyfro	Neath	38	H10
Rhyd-y-groes	Gwynd	73	K10
Rhydymain	Gwynd	61	P6
Rhyd-y-meirch	Mons	40	D10
Rhydymwyn	Flints	74	H10
Rhyd-yr-onnen	Gwynd	61	K11
Rhyd-y-sarn	Gwynd	61	M4
Rhyl	Denbgs	74	D7
Rhymney	Caerph	39	Q9
Rhynd	P & K	124	C8
Rhynie	Abers	140	D10
Rhynie	Highld	146	E9
Ribbesford	Worcs	52	E6
Ribbleton	Lancs	83	M9
Ribby	Lancs	83	J9
Ribchester	Lancs	83	P8
Riber	Derbys	77	P11
Riby	Lincs	80	D2
Riccall	N York	86	B8
Riccarton	Border	107	N10
Riccarton	E Ayrs	104	H3
Richards Castle	Herefs	51	N6
Richings Park	Bucks	32	F6
Richmond	Gt Lon	32	H7
Richmond	N York	91	K6
Richmond	Sheff	78	C7
Rich's Holford	Somset	20	H6
Rickerscote	Staffs	64	H8
Rickford	N Som	28	G10
Rickham	Devon	5	M8
Rickinghall	Suffk	58	F5
Rickling	Essex	45	P5
Rickling Green	Essex	45	P6
Rickmansworth	Herts	32	F3
Riddell	Border	107	N5
Riddings	Derbys	66	C2
Riddlecombe	Devon	19	M10
Riddlesden	C Brad	84	G6
Ridge	BaNES	28	H11
Ridge	Dorset	11	M7
Ridge	Herts	33	J2
Ridge	Wilts	23	K7
Ridge Green	Surrey	15	K2
Ridge Lane	Warwks	53	P2

Ridge Row Kent....17 M2
Ridgeway Derbys....78 C7
Ridgeway Worcs....53 K8
Ridgeway Cross Herefs....41 L2
Ridgewell Essex....46 C3
Ridgewood E Susx....15 H4
Ridgmont C Beds....44 D4
Riding Mill Nthumb....100 C6
Ridley Kent....34 A9
Ridley Nthumb....99 M5
Ridley Green Ches E....69 P1
Ridlington Norfk....71 L6
Ridlington Rutlnd....57 L2
Ridlington Street Norfk....71 L6
Ridsdale Nthumb....99 P1
Rievaulx N York....92 C9
Rigg D & G....98 C5
Rigend N Lans....114 D7
Righoul Highld....138 G5
Rigmadon Park Cumb....89 P9
Rigsby Lincs....80 H8
Rigside S Lans....105 R3
Riley Green Lancs....83 N10
Rileyhill Staffs....65 L9
Rilla Mill Cnwll....7 K10
Rillaton Cnwll....7 K10
Rillington N York....92 H11
Rimington Lancs....84 B6
Rimpton Somset....22 B9
Rimswell E R Yk....87 P9
Rinaston Pembks....37 J5
Rindleford Shrops....52 D2
Ringford D & G....96 E7
Ringinglow Sheff....77 P7
Ringland Norfk....70 H9
Ringles Cross E Susx....15 L5
Ringlestone Kent....34 F11
Ringley Bolton....76 E3
Ringmer E Susx....15 N8
Ringmore Devon....5 K7
Ringmore Devon....8 H10
Ringorm Moray....139 N7
Ring's End Cambs....68 H11
Ringsfield Suffk....59 M3
Ringsfield Corner Suffk....59 N3
Ringshall Herts....44 E9
Ringshall Suffk....58 F10
Ringshall Stocks Suffk....58 F10
Ringstead Nhants....55 N5
Ringstead Norfk....69 M4
Ringwood Hants....13 L4
Ringwould Kent....17 P1
Rinmore Abers....132 C1
Rinsey Cnwll....2 F9
Rinsey Croft Cnwll....2 F9
Ripe E Susx....15 P9
Ripley Derbys....66 C2
Ripley Hants....12 B5
Ripley N York....85 L3
Ripley Surrey....32 F11
Riplingham E R Yk....86 H9
Riplington Hants....25 L8
Ripon N York....85 L1
Rippingale Lincs....68 B6
Ripple Kent....35 P12
Ripple Worcs....41 P4
Ripponden Calder....84 F11
Risabus Ag & B....102 B1
Risbury Herefs....51 N9
Risby N Linc....86 G12
Risby Suffk....57 Q7
Risca Caerph....28 B4
Rise E R Yk....87 M7
Riseden Kent....16 A5
Riseden Kent....16 C4
Risegate Lincs....68 D6
Riseholme Lincs....79 N8
Risehow Cumb....97 L11
Riseley Bed....55 P8
Riseley Wokham....31 P9
Rishangles Suffk....58 H7
Rishton Lancs....83 Q9
Rishworth Calder....84 F11
Rising Bridge Lancs....84 B10
Risley Derbys....66 C5
Risley Warrtn....76 C5
Risplith N York....85 K1
Rivar Wilts....30 G10
Rivenhall End Essex....46 E8
River Kent....17 N2
River W Susx....14 D6
River Bank Cambs....57 K7
Riverford Highld....137 P5
Riverhead Kent....33 P11
Rivers Corner Dorset....22 H10
Rivington Lancs....83 N12
Rivington Services Lancs....76 B1
Roachill Devon....20 C9
Roade Nhants....55 J10
Road Green Norfk....59 K2
Roadhead Cumb....98 G3
Roadside Highld....105 K6
Roadside Highld....151 L4
Roadwater Somset....20 G6
Roag Highld....134 E7
Roa Island Cumb....82 F7
Roan of Craigoch S Ayrs....104 E9
Roast Green Essex....45 N5
Roath Cardif....28 B7
Roberton Border....107 L7
Roberton S Lans....106 B4
Robertsbridge E Susx....16 C6
Roberttown Kirk....85 J10
Robeston Wathen Pembks....37 L7
Robgill Tower D & G....97 Q4
Robin Hood Lancs....75 Q2
Robin Hood Leeds....85 L9
Robinhood End Essex....46 C4
Robin Hood's Bay N York....93 J6
Roborough Devon....4 H4
Roborough Devon....19 L10
Robroyston C Glas....114 B7
Roby Knows....75 M5
Roby Mill Lancs....75 N2
Rocester Staffs....65 L4
Roch Pembks....36 G6
Rochdale Rochdl....76 G1
Roche Cnwll....3 M3
Rochester Medway....34 D8
Rochester Nthumb....108 D10
Rochford Essex....34 F4
Rochford Worcs....52 B7
Rock Gate Pembks....36 G6
Rock Cnwll....6 D9
Rock Neath....27 J4
Rock Nthumb....109 K6
Rock W Susx....14 G8
Rock Worcs....52 D6
Rockbeare Devon....9 J6
Rockcliffe Cumb....98 D6
Rockcliffe D & G....96 E7
Rockcliffe Cross Cumb....98 D6
Rock End Staffs....76 G12
Rock Ferry Wirral....75 K6
Rockfield Highld....146 G8
Rockfield Mons....40 G8
Rockford Devon....19 P4
Rockford Hants....13 M3
Rockgreen Shrops....51 N5
Rockhampton S Glos....29 K4
Rockhead Cnwll....6 F7

Rockhill Shrops....51 J5
Rock Hill Worcs....52 H7
Rockingham Nhants....55 L2
Rockland All Saints Norfk....58 E1
Rockland St Mary Norfk....71 L11
Rockland St Peter Norfk....58 E1
Rockley Notts....78 H8
Rockley Wilts....30 D8
Rockliffe Lancs....84 C10
Roden Wrekin....63 P9
Rodhuish Somset....20 F6
Rodington Wrekin....63 P9
Rodington Heath Wrekin....63 P9
Rodley Gloucs....41 M9
Rodley Leeds....85 K8
Rodmarton Gloucs....29 Q3
Rodmell E Susx....15 M9
Rodmersham Kent....34 G10
Rodmersham Green Kent....34 G10
Rodney Stoke Somset....22 B3
Rodsley Derbys....65 M4
Rodway Somset....21 L5
Roecliffe N York....85 M2
Roe Cross Tamesd....77 J4
Roe Green Herts....45 J10
Roe Green Herts....45 K5
Roe Green Salfd....76 D3
Roehampton Gt Lon....33 J7
Roffey W Susx....14 F5
Rogart Highld....146 C5
Rogate W Susx....25 P8
Roger Ground Cumb....89 K7
Rogerstone Newpt....28 C5
Roghadal W Isls....152 d7
Rogiet Mons....28 F5
Roke Oxon....31 N4
Roker Sundld....101 K6
Rollesby Norfk....71 N9
Rolleston Leics....67 J12
Rolleston Notts....67 J2
Rolleston on Dove Staffs....65 N6
Rolston E R Yk....87 N6
Rolstone N Som....28 E10
Rolvenden Kent....16 E4
Rolvenden Layne Kent....16 E5
Romaldkirk Dur....90 G2
Romanby N York....91 N8
Romanno Bridge Border....115 L11
Romansleigh Devon....19 P9
Romden Castle Kent....16 F2
Romesdal Highld....134 G5
Romford Dorset....11 P3
Romford Gt Lon....33 P5
Romiley Stockp....76 H5
Romney Street Kent....33 Q10
Romsey Hants....24 F8
Romsley Shrops....52 E4
Romsley Worcs....52 H5
Rona Highld....135 L4
Ronachan Ag & B....111 Q10
Rood Ashton Wilts....29 P11
Rookhope Dur....99 P9
Rookley IoW....12 H8
Rooks Bridge Somset....21 N3
Rooks Nest Somset....20 H6
Rookwith N York....91 L9
Roos E R Yk....87 P9
Roose Cumb....82 F7
Roosebeck Cumb....82 G7
Roothams Green Bed....56 B9
Ropley Hants....25 L7
Ropley Dean Hants....25 L7
Ropley Soke Hants....25 L7
Ropsley Lincs....67 N5
Rora Abers....141 P6
Rorrington Shrops....63 J12
Rosarie Moray....140 B6
Rose Cnwll....3 J4
Roseacre Lancs....83 K8
Rose Ash Devon....20 B9
Rosebank S Lans....114 E11
Rosebush Pembks....37 L5
Rosecare Cnwll....6 H5
Rosecliston Cnwll....3 K3
Rosedale Abbey N York....92 F8
Rose Green Suffk....46 G4
Rose Green Suffk....46 G4
Rose Green W Susx....14 C11
Rosehall Highld....145 L5
Rosehearty Abers....141 M2
Rose Hill Lancs....84 B9
Rose Hill E Susx....15 M7
Rosehill Shrops....63 M9
Roseisle Moray....139 L2
Roselands E Susx....16 A10
Rosemarket Pembks....37 J9
Rosemarkie Highld....138 D4
Rosemary Lane Devon....21 J10
Rosemount P & K....124 D4
Rosenannon Cnwll....6 D11
Rosenithon Cnwll....3 K10
Roser's Cross E Susx....15 Q7
Rosevean Cnwll....3 P3
Rosevine Cnwll....3 L7
Rosewarne Cnwll....2 F7
Rosewell Mdloth....115 P9
Roseworth S on T....91 P2
Roseworthy Cnwll....2 F7
Rosgill Cumb....89 N3
Roskestal Cnwll....2 B10
Roskhill Highld....134 E7
Roskorwell Cnwll....3 K9
Rosley Cumb....98 C9
Roslin Mdloth....115 N9
Rosliston Derbys....65 N9
Rosneath Ag & B....113 K5
Ross D & G....96 C9
Ross Nthumb....109 J2
Rossett Wrexhm....75 L12
Rossett Green N York....85 L4
Rossington Donc....78 G4
Ross-on-Wye Herefs....41 J7
Roster Highld....151 N8
Rostherne Ches E....76 D6
Rosthwaite Cumb....88 H4
Roston Derbys....65 M4
Rosudgeon Cnwll....2 E8
Rosyth Fife....115 L4
Rothbury Nthumb....108 H9
Rotherby Leics....66 H8
Rotherfield E Susx....15 Q5
Rotherfield Greys Oxon....31 P6
Rotherfield Peppard Oxon....31 P6
Rotherham Rothm....78 C5
Rothersthorpe Nhants....55 J9
Rotherwick Hants....25 P2
Rothes Moray....139 P6

Rothesay Ag & B....112 G8
Rothiebrisbane Abers....141 J8
Rothiemurchus Lodge Highld....130 H3
Rothienorman Abers....140 H8
Rothley Leics....66 F9
Rothley Nthumb....108 G12
Rothmaise Abers....140 G9
Rothwell Leeds....85 M9
Rothwell Lincs....80 C4
Rothwell Nhants....55 K4
Rotsea E R Yk....87 K5
Rottal Lodge Angus....132 B10
Rottingdean Br & H....15 L10
Rottington Cumb....88 C4
Roucan D & G....97 L3
Roud IoW....12 H8
Rougham Norfk....70 B8
Rougham Suffk....58 D8
Rough Close Staffs....64 G4
Rough Common Kent....35 K10
Roughlee Lancs....84 C7
Roughpark Abers....131 Q2
Roughton Lincs....80 E10
Roughton Norfk....71 J5
Roughton Shrops....52 D2
Roughway Kent....34 A11
Roundbush Essex....34 F2
Round Bush Herts....32 G3
Roundbush Green Essex....45 Q8
Round Green Luton....44 G7
Roundham Somset....10 C3
Roundhay Leeds....85 M8
Rounds Green Sandw....52 H3
Round Street Kent....34 B8
Roundstreet Common W Susx....14 F5
Roundswell Devon....19 K7
Roundway Wilts....30 B9
Roundyhill Angus....124 H3
Rousay Ork....147 c3
Rousdon Devon....9 P6
Rousham Oxon....43 K8
Rous Lench Worcs....53 J10
Routenburn N Ayrs....113 J9
Routh E R Yk....87 K7
Rout's Green Bucks....31 R3
Row Cnwll....6 G9
Row Cumb....89 M9
Row Cumb....99 J11
Rowanburn D & G....98 E3
Rowardennan Stirlg....113 M2
Rowarth Derbys....77 J6
Row Ash Hants....25 J10
Rowberrow Somset....28 F11
Rowborough IoW....12 H8
Rowde Wilts....29 N10
Rowden Devon....8 C5
Rowen Conwy....73 N9
Rowfield Derbys....65 M2
Rowfoot Nthumb....99 K6
Rowford Somset....21 K8
Row Green Essex....46 D7
Rowhedge Essex....47 J7
Rowhook W Susx....14 G4
Rowington Warwks....53 M7
Rowland Derbys....77 M9
Rowland's Castle Hants....13 M3
Rowlands Gill Gatesd....100 F6
Rowledge Surrey....25 P5
Rowley Dur....100 E8
Rowley E R Yk....86 H8
Rowley Shrops....63 J11
Rowley Regis Sandw....52 H3
Rowlstone Herefs....40 E6
Rowly Surrey....14 F3
Rowner Hants....13 K4
Rowney Green Worcs....53 K6
Rownhams Hants....24 F10
Rownhams Services Hants....24 F10
Rowrah Cumb....88 E3
Rowsham Bucks....44 B8
Rowsley Derbys....77 N10
Rowstock Oxon....31 K4
Rowston Lincs....80 B12
Rowthorne Derbys....78 D10
Rowton Ches W....75 M11
Rowton Shrops....51 L4
Rowton Shrops....63 N10
Rowton Wrekin....63 Q8
Row Town Surrey....32 E9
Roxburgh Border....108 A4
Roxby N Linc....86 G11
Roxby N York....92 F3
Roxton Bed....56 C9
Roxwell Essex....46 B10
Royal Leamington Spa Warwks....53 Q7
Royal Oak Darltn....91 L2
Royal Oak Lancs....75 L3
Royal's Green Ches E....64 B4
Royal Sutton Coldfield Birm....53 L1
Royal Tunbridge Wells Kent....15 Q3
Royal Wootton Bassett Wilts....30 C6
Royal Yacht Britannia C Edin....115 N6
Roy Bridge Highld....129 J8
Roydhouse Kirk....77 N1
Roydon Essex....45 M9
Roydon Norfk....58 G2
Roydon Norfk....69 N7
Roydon Hamlet Essex....45 M10
Royston Barns....78 B1
Royston Herts....45 L4
Royton Oldham....76 G2
Rozel Jersey....13 d1
Ruabon Wrexhm....63 J3
Ruaig Ag & B....118 E3
Ruan High Lanes Cnwll....3 M7
Ruan Lanihorne Cnwll....3 L6
Ruan Major Cnwll....2 H11
Ruan Minor Cnwll....2 H11
Ruardean Gloucs....41 J8
Ruardean Hill Gloucs....41 K8
Ruardean Woodside Gloucs....41 J8
Rubery Birm....53 J5
Rubha Ban W Isls....152 c12
Ruckcroft Cumb....98 G9
Ruckhall Herefs....40 F7
Ruckinge Kent....17 J4
Ruckland Lincs....80 F8
Ruckley Shrops....63 P12
Rudbaxton Pembks....37 J5
Rudby N York....91 Q5
Rudchester Nthumb....100 E5
Ruddington Notts....66 F5
Ruddle Gloucs....41 K9
Ruddlemoor Cnwll....3 M4
Rudford Gloucs....41 M7
Rudge Somset....23 J3
Rudgeway S Glos....29 J5
Rudgwick W Susx....14 F4
Rudhall Herefs....41 J6
Rudheath Ches W....76 C9
Rudheath Woods Ches E....76 F8
Rudley Green Essex....46 E11
Rudloe Wilts....29 N8
Rudry Caerph....28 B5
Rudston E R Yk....87 K3
Rudyard Staffs....76 H12

Ruecastle Border....107 P6
Rufford Lancs....83 K12
Rufford Abbey Notts....78 G10
Rufforth C York....85 Q5
Rug Denbgs....62 E3
Rugby Warwks....54 E5
Rugeley Staffs....65 K8
Ruigh'riabhach Highld....144 C6
Ruisgarry W Isls....152 f1
Ruishton Somset....21 L8
Ruisigearraidh W Isls....152 d7
Ruislip Gt Lon....32 F5
St Allen Cnwll....3 K4
St Andrew Guern....12 c2
St Andrews Fife....125 K9
St Andrews Botanic Garden Fife....125 K9
St Andrews Major V Glam....27 Q8
St Andrews Well Dorset....10 D6
St Anne's Lancs....82 H9
St Ann's D & G....106 H11
St Ann's Chapel Cnwll....7 M10
St Ann's Chapel Cnwll....5 L7
St Anthony-in-Meneage Cnwll....3 J9
St Anthony's Hill E Susx....16 A10
St Arvans Mons....28 H3
St Asaph Denbgs....74 E9
St Athan V Glam....27 N9
St Aubin Jersey....13 b2
St Austell Cnwll....3 M4
St Bees Cumb....88 C4
St Blazey Cnwll....3 M4
St Blazey Gate Cnwll....3 M4
St Boswells Border....107 P4
St Brelade Jersey....13 a2
St Brelade's Bay Jersey....13 a3
St Breock Cnwll....6 E10
St Breward Cnwll....6 G9
St Briavels Gloucs....40 H10
St Brides Pembks....36 F8
St Bride's Major V Glam....27 L7
St Brides Netherwent Mons....28 F4
St Brides-super-Ely V Glam....27 P7
St Brides Wentlooge Newpt....28 C6
St Budeaux C Plym....4 G5
Saintbury Gloucs....42 C4
St Buryan Cnwll....2 C9
St Catherine BaNES....29 M8
St Catherines Ag & B....121 L11
St Chloe Gloucs....41 N11
St Clears Carmth....37 Q7
St Cleer Cnwll....4 C4
St Clement Cnwll....3 L5
St Clement Jersey....13 d3
St Clether Cnwll....7 J8
St Colmac Ag & B....112 F8
St Columb Major Cnwll....3 M3
St Columb Minor Cnwll....3 K2
St Columb Road Cnwll....3 M3
St Combs Abers....141 P3
St Cross South Elmham Suffk....59 L4
St Cyrus Abers....133 J11
St David's P & K....123 N9
St David's Pembks....36 E5
St Davids Cathedral Pembks....36 D5
St Day Cnwll....2 H6
St Decumans Somset....20 G5
St Dennis Cnwll....3 M3
St Devereux Herefs....40 F5
St Dogmaels Pembks....48 B11
St Dogwells Pembks....37 J5
St Dominick Cnwll....4 F3
St Donat's V Glam....27 M8
St Edith's Marsh Wilts....29 N9
St Endellion Cnwll....6 E9
St Enoder Cnwll....3 L3
St Erme Cnwll....3 L4
St Erney Cnwll....4 E6
St Erth Cnwll....2 E7
St Erth Praze Cnwll....2 E7
St Ervan Cnwll....6 C10
St Eval Cnwll....6 C11
St Ewe Cnwll....3 N5
St Fagans Cardif....27 Q7
St Fagans: National History Museum Cardif....27 Q7
St Fergus Abers....141 Q5
St Fillans P & K....122 H5
St Florence Pembks....37 L10
St Gennys Cnwll....6 H5
St George Conwy....74 D8
St Georges N Som....28 E9
St George's V Glam....27 Q7
St George's Hill Surrey....32 F10
St Germans Cnwll....4 E6
St Giles in the Wood Devon....19 K9
St Giles-on-the-Heath Devon....7 L7
St Gluvia's Cnwll....3 K7
St Harmon Powys....50 D6
St Helen Auckland Dur....91 K1
St Helens Cumb....97 L11
St Helens E Susx....16 E8
St Helens IoW....13 K7
St Helens St Hel....75 N5
St Helier Gt Lon....33 J9
St Helier Jersey....13 c2
St Hilary Cnwll....2 E7
St Hilary V Glam....27 N8
Saint Hill Devon....9 Q3
Saint Hill W Susx....15 L4
St Illtyd Blae G....40 B11
St Ippolyts Herts....44 H6
St Ishmael's Pembks....36 G9
St Issey Cnwll....6 D10
St Ive Cnwll....4 D3
St Ive Cross Cnwll....4 D3
St Ives Cambs....56 E6
St Ives Cnwll....2 E6
St Ives Dorset....11 Q4
St James Norfk....71 K8
St James's End Nhants....55 J8
St James South Elmham Suffk....59 L4
St Jidgey Cnwll....6 D10
St John Cnwll....4 F6
St John Jersey....13 b1
St Johns Dur....100 D11
St John's E Susx....15 P4
St John's IoM....102 c5
St John's Kent....33 P11
St Johns Surrey....32 E10
St Johns Worcs....52 F10
St John's Chapel Devon....19 K7
St John's Chapel Dur....99 N10
St John's Fen End Norfk....69 K9
St John's Highway Norfk....69 K9
St John's Kirk S Lans....106 C3
St John's Town of Dalry D & G....96 C2
St John's Wood Gt Lon....33 K6
St Judes IoM....102 e3
St Just Cnwll....2 B8
St Just-in-Roseland Cnwll....3 L6
St Just Mining District Cnwll....2 B8
St Katherines Abers....141 J9
St Keverne Cnwll....3 K10
St Kew Cnwll....6 F9
St Kew Highway Cnwll....6 F9
St Keyne Cnwll....4 C4
St Lawrence Cnwll....3 M3
St Lawrence Essex....46 G11
St Lawrence IoW....12 H9
St Lawrence Jersey....13 b1
St Lawrence Kent....35 Q9
St Leonards Bucks....44 C10
St Leonards Dorset....11 Q4
St Leonards E Susx....16 E9

St Leonard's Street Kent....34 B11
St Levan Cnwll....2 B10
St Lythans V Glam....27 Q8
St Mabyn Cnwll....6 F10
St Madoes P & K....124 D8
St Margarets Herefs....40 E5
St Margarets Herts....45 M9
St Margaret's at Cliffe Kent....17 P2
St Margaret's Hope Ork....147 c6
St Margaret South Elmham Suffk....59 L4
St Marks IoM....102 d6
St Martin Cnwll....3 J9
St Martin Cnwll....4 C6
St Martin Guern....12 c2
St Martin Jersey....13 d2
St Martin's IoS....2 c1
St Martin's P & K....124 D7
St Martin's Shrops....63 K5
St Martin's Moor Shrops....63 K5
St Mary Bourne Hants....24 G3
St Marychurch Torbay....5 Q3
St Mary Church V Glam....27 N8
St Mary Cray Gt Lon....33 N8
St Mary Hill V Glam....27 M7
St Mary in the Marsh Kent....17 J5
St Mary's IoS....2 b2
St Mary's Ork....147 c5
St Mary's Hoo Medway....34 E7
St Mary's Platt Kent....34 A11
St Maughans Mons....40 F8
St Maughans Green Mons....40 G8
St Mawes Cnwll....3 L8
St Mawgan Cnwll....6 C11
St Mellion Cnwll....4 F4
St Mellons Cardif....28 B6
St Merryn Cnwll....6 C10
St Mewan Cnwll....3 N4
St Michael Caerhays Cnwll....3 N6
St Michael Church Somset....21 M7
St Michael Penkevil Cnwll....3 L5
St Michaels Kent....16 E4
St Michaels Worcs....51 N7
St Michael's Mount Cnwll....2 E8
St Michael's on Wyre Lancs....83 K7
St Michael South Elmham Suffk....59 L4
St Minver Cnwll....6 D9
St Monans Fife....116 C1
St Neot Cnwll....4 B3
St Neots Cambs....56 D8
St Newlyn East Cnwll....3 K3
St Nicholas Pembks....36 H3
St Nicholas V Glam....27 P7
St Nicholas-at-Wade Kent....35 N9
St Ninians Stirlg....114 E3
St Olaves Norfk....71 N12
St Osyth Essex....47 K8
St Ouen Jersey....13 a1
St Owen's Cross Herefs....40 H7
St Paul's Cray Gt Lon....33 N8
St Paul's Walden Herts....44 H7
St Peter Jersey....13 b2
St Peter Port Guern....12 c2
St Peter's Guern....12 b2
St Peter's Kent....35 Q8
St Peter's Hill Cambs....56 E6
St Petrox Pembks....37 J11
St Pinnock Cnwll....4 B4
St Quivox S Ayrs....104 G5
St Ruan Cnwll....2 H11
St Sampson Guern....12 d1
St Saviour Guern....12 b2
St Saviour Jersey....13 c2
St Stephen Cnwll....3 M4
St Stephens Cnwll....4 F5
St Stephens Cnwll....7 L7
St Teath Cnwll....6 F8
St Thomas Devon....9 M6
St Tudy Cnwll....6 F9
St Twynnells Pembks....37 J11
St Veep Cnwll....4 A6
St Vigeans Angus....125 M4
St Wenn Cnwll....6 D11
St Weonards Herefs....40 G7
St Winnow Cnwll....3 Q3
St y-Nyll V Glam....27 P7
Salcombe Devon....5 M7
Salcombe Regis Devon....9 M7
Salcott-cum-Virley Essex....46 G9
Sale Traffd....76 E5
Saleby Lincs....81 J8
Sale Green Worcs....52 H9
Salehurst E Susx....16 C6
Salem Carmth....38 F6
Salem Cerdgn....49 L4
Salen Ag & B....119 P4
Salen Highld....127 M11
Salesbury Lancs....83 P8
Salford C Beds....44 D4
Salford Oxon....42 G6
Salford Salfd....76 E4
Salford Priors Warwks....53 K10
Salfords Surrey....15 K2
Salhouse Norfk....71 L9
Saline Fife....115 J3
Salisbury Wilts....23 N7
Salisbury Plain Wilts....23 N4
Salkeld Dykes Cumb....98 G10
Salle Norfk....70 H7
Salmonby Lincs....80 G9
Salperton Gloucs....42 C7
Salph End Bed....55 Q9
Salsburgh N Lans....114 E8
Salt Staffs....64 H6
Salta Cumb....97 M9
Saltaire C Brad....84 H7
Saltash Cnwll....4 F5
Saltburn Highld....146 C11
Saltburn-by-the-Sea R & Cl....92 D3
Saltby Leics....67 L6
Salt Coates Cumb....97 P7
Saltcotes Lancs....83 J9
Saltdean Br & H....15 M10
Salterbeck Cumb....97 L11
Salterforth Lancs....84 D6
Salterton Wilts....23 N5
Saltfleet Lincs....81 J4
Saltfleetby All Saints Lincs....81 J5
Saltfleetby St Clement Lincs....81 K4
Saltfleetby St Peter Lincs....81 J5
Saltford BaNES....29 K8
Salthouse Norfk....70 G3
Saltley Birm....53 L3
Saltmarshe E R Yk....86 D10
Saltney Flints....75 K11
Salton N York....92 E10

Saltrens Devon....19 J9
Saltwick Nthumb....100 F2
Saltwood Kent....17 L4
Salvation W Susx....14 G9
Salwarpe Worcs....52 G8
Salway Ash Dorset....10 C5
Sambourne Warwks....53 K8
Sambrook Wrekin....64 D7
Samlesbury Lancs....83 N9
Samlesbury Bottoms Lancs....83 N9
Sampford Arundel Somset....20 H9
Sampford Brett Somset....20 H5
Sampford Courtenay Devon....8 B4
Sampford Peverell Devon....20 H9
Sampford Spiney Devon....7 P10
Samsonlane Ork....147 e3
Samson's Corner Essex....47 K8
Samuelston E Loth....116 B7
Sanaigmore Ag & B....110 D7
Sancreed Cnwll....2 C8
Sancton E R Yk....86 G7
Sand Somset....21 P4
Sandaig Highld....127 N4
Sandal Magna Wakefd....85 M11
Sanday Ork....147 e2
Sanday Airport Ork....147 e2
Sandbach Ches E....76 D11
Sandbach Services Ches E....76 E11
Sandbank Ag & B....112 H5
Sandbanks BCP....11 P7
Sandend Abers....140 E3
Sanderstead Gt Lon....33 L10
Sandford Cumb....90 B3
Sandford Devon....8 F4
Sandford Dorset....11 M7
Sandford Hants....12 B4
Sandford IoW....12 H8
Sandford N Som....28 F10
Sandford S Lans....105 N1
Sandford Shrops....63 K7
Sandford Shrops....63 P5
Sandford-on-Thames Oxon....43 L10
Sandford Orcas Dorset....22 E9
Sandford St Martin Oxon....43 J7
Sandgate Kent....17 M4
Sandhaven Abers....141 M2
Sandhead D & G....94 G8
Sandhills Rothm....78 D4
Sandford Dorset....10 G3
Sandhills Leeds....85 M7
Sandhills Oxon....43 L10
Sandhills Surrey....14 D3
Sandhoe Nthumb....100 B5
Sandhole Ag & B....112 E2
Sand Hole E R Yk....86 F8
Sandholme E R Yk....86 F9
Sandholme Lincs....68 G5
Sandhurst Br For....32 B10
Sandhurst Gloucs....41 P7
Sandhurst Kent....16 E5
Sandhurst Cross Kent....16 D5
Sand Hutton N York....86 C5
Sandhutton N York....91 P10
Sandiacre Derbys....66 D5
Sandilands Lincs....81 K7
Sandiway Ches W....75 Q9
Sandleheath Hants....23 P9
Sandleigh Oxon....31 K2
Sandling Kent....34 B11
Sandlow Green Ches E....76 E10
Sandness Shet....147 h6
Sandon Essex....46 C10
Sandon Herts....45 L5
Sandon Staffs....64 H6
Sandown IoW....12 H8
Sandplace Cnwll....4 C5
Sandridge Herts....44 H9
Sandringham Norfk....69 N6
Sandsend N York....92 H4
Sandside Cumb....89 L10
Sandtoft N Linc....79 J2
Sandway Kent....34 F12
Sandwich Kent....35 P10
Sandwich Bay Kent....35 Q11
Sandwick Cumb....89 L3
Sandwick Shet....147 i9
Sandwick W Isls....152 g3
Sandwith Cumb....88 C4
Sandwith Newtown Cumb....88 C4
Sandy C Beds....56 D10
Sandy Bank Lincs....80 E1
Sandycroft Flints....75 K10
Sandy Cross Herefs....52 C9
Sandy Cross Herefs....52 C9
Sandyford D & G....106 G11
Sandygate IoM....102 e3
Sandygate IoW....102 e3
Sandy Haven Pembks....36 G9
Sandyhills D & G....96 H6
Sandylands Lancs....83 K3
Sandy Lane C Brad....84 H8
Sandylane Swans....26 E4
Sandy Lane Wilts....29 Q8
Sandy Lane Wrexhm....63 L4
Sandy Park Devon....8 D7
Sandysike Cumb....98 D5
Sandyway Herefs....40 G6
Sangobeg Highld....149 J3
Sangomore Highld....149 J3
Sankey Bridges Warrtn....75 P6
Sankyn's Green Worcs....52 E7
Sanna Highld....126 H10
Sannabhaig W Isls....152 g3
Sannox N Ayrs....112 C12
Sanquhar D & G....105 P8
Santon Cumb....88 E6
Santon IoM....102 d6
Santon Bridge Cumb....88 E6
Santon Downham Suffk....58 B4
Sapcote Leics....54 D2
Sapey Common Herefs....52 C8
Sapiston Suffk....58 D5
Sapley Cambs....56 E6
Sapperton Derbys....65 M5
Sapperton Gloucs....41 Q11
Sapperton Lincs....67 P5
Saracen's Head Lincs....68 G7
Sarclet Highld....151 Q8
Sarisbury Hants....12 H4
Sarn Brdgnd....27 L6
Sarn Powys....50 H2
Sarnau Carmth....37 L6
Sarnau Cerdgn....48 E10
Sarnau Gwynd....62 B5
Sarnau Powys....39 M9
Sarnau Powys....62 G7
Sarn Bach Gwynd....60 E7
Sarnesfield Herefs....51 L10
Sarn Mellteyrn Gwynd....60 D6
Sarn Park Services Brdgnd....27 L6
Sarn-wen Powys....63 J8

Saron Carmth....38 B4
Saron Carmth....38 F9
Saron Gwynd....72 H12
Saron Gwynd....73 J10
Sarratt Herts....32 F2
Sarre Kent....35 Q8
Sarsden Oxon....42 G7
Sarson Hants....24 E4
Satley Dur....100 E9
Satron N York....90 F7
Satterleigh Devon....19 N4
Satterthwaite Cumb....89 K8
Satwell Oxon....31 P6
Sauchen Abers....132 H2
Saucher P & K....124 C6
Sauchieburn Abers....132 G10
Saul Gloucs....41 M10
Saundby Notts....79 K6
Saundersfoot Pembks....37 M9
Saunderton Bucks....44 A11
Saunderton Station
  Bucks....32 A3
Saunton Devon....19 J6
Sausthorpe Lincs....80 G10
Saverley Green Staffs....64 H4
Savile Town Kirk....85 K11
Sawbridge Warwks....54 E7
Sawbridgeworth Herts....45 M8
Sawdon N York....93 J9
Sawley Derbys....66 D6
Sawley Lancs....84 B6
Sawley N York....85 K9
Sawston Cambs....57 J11
Sawtry Cambs....56 C4
Saxby Leics....67 K9
Saxby Lincs....79 P6
Saxby All Saints N Linc....87 J12
Saxelbye Leics....66 H8
Saxham Street Suffk....58 G8
Saxilby Lincs....79 M8
Saxlingham Norfk....76 E4
Saxlingham Green Norfk....59 K1
Saxlingham Nethergate
  Norfk....59 J1
Saxlingham Thorpe
  Norfk....59 J1
Saxmundham Suffk....59 M8
Saxondale Notts....66 H4
Saxon Street Cambs....57 N9
Saxtead Suffk....59 K7
Saxtead Green Suffk....59 K8
Saxtead Little Green
  Suffk....59 K7
Saxthorpe Norfk....70 G6
Saxton N York....85 P8
Sayers Common W Susx....15 K7
Scackleton N York....92 D12
Scadabay W Isls....152 e6
Scadabhagh W Isls....152 e6
Scafell Pike Cumb....88 G8
Scaftworth Notts....78 H5
Scagglethorpe N York....92 G12
Scalasaig Ag & B....111 J4
Scalby E R Yk....86 F9
Scalby N York....93 K8
Scald End Bed....55 J6
Scaldwell Nhants....55 J6
Scaleby Cumb....98 F5
Scalebyhill Cumb....98 F5
Scale Houses Cumb....98 H9
Scales Cumb....88 H12
Scales Cumb....89 K1
Scalesceugh Cumb....98 F8
Scalford Leics....67 J7
Scaling N York....92 F4
Scaling Dam R & Cl....92 F4
Scalloway Shet....147 i7
Scalpay Highld....135 K4
Scalpay W Isls....152 h6
Scamblesby Lincs....80 E8
Scammonden Kirk....84 F12
Scamodale Highld....127 Q9
Scampston N York....92 H11
Scampton Lincs....79 N8
Scaniport Highld....138 B8
Scapegoat Hill Kirk....84 G12
Scarba Ag & B....120 D12
Scarborough N York....93 L9
Scarcewater Cnwll....3 M4
Scarcliffe Derbys....78 E10
Scarcroft Leeds....85 M7
Scarfskerry Highld....151 N2
Scargill Dur....90 H4
Scarinish Ag & B....118 E4
Scarisbrick Lancs....75 L1
Scarness Cumb....97 P12
Scarning Norfk....70 D9
Scarrington Notts....66 H4
Scarth Hill Lancs....75 M2
Scarthingwell N York....85 P8
Scartho NE Lin....80 E2
Scatsta Airport Shet....147 i5
Scaur D & G....96 G7
Scawby N Linc....79 N3
Scawsby Donc....78 E3
Scawthorpe Donc....78 F2
Scawton N York....92 B10
Scayne's Hill W Susx....15 L6
Scethrog Powys....39 Q6
Scholar Green Ches E....76 F12
Scholes Kirk....77 M2
Scholes Kirk....85 J10
Scholes Leeds....85 M8
Scholes Rothm....78 C5
Scholes Wigan....75 N3
School Aycliffe Dur....91 L2
School Green C Brad....84 H8
School Green Ches W....76 B11
Schoolgreen Wokham....31 Q9
School House Dorset....10 B4
Scissett Kirk....77 N2
Scleddau Pembks....36 H4
Scofton Notts....78 G8
Scole Norfk....58 H5
Scone P & K....124 C7
Sconser Highld....135 J4
Scoonie Fife....115 Q3
Scopwick Lincs....79 Q12
Scoraig Highld....144 C6
Scorborough E R Yk....87 K4
Scorrier Cnwll....2 H6
Scorriton Devon....5 L3
Scorton Lancs....83 L7
Scorton N York....91 K6
Sco Ruston Norfk....71 K8
Scotby Cumb....98 F7
Scotch Corner N York....91 L6
Scotch Corner Rest
  Area N York....91 L6
Scotforth Lancs....83 L3
Scot Hay Staffs....64 F3
Scothern Lincs....79 P8
Scotland Lincs....67 P6
Scotland Gate Nthumb....100 H1
Scotlandwell P & K....115 M1
Scot Lane End Bolton....76 B2
Scotscalder Station
  Highld....151 K5
Scotsdike Cumb....98 F4
Scot's Gap Nthumb....100 D1
Scotsmill Abers....140 E12
Scotstoun C Glas....113 Q8
Scotswood N u Ty....100 G5
Scotter Lincs....79 L4
Scotterthorpe Lincs....79 L3

Scottish Seabird Centre
  E Loth....116 D4
Scottish Wool Centre
  Stirlg....113 Q1
Scottlethorpe Lincs....67 Q8
Scotton Lincs....79 M4
Scotton N York....85 L3
Scotton N York....91 K7
Scottow Norfk....71 K7
Scoulton Norfk....70 C11
Scounslow Green Staffs....65 K6
Scourie Highld....148 E7
Scourie More Highld....148 D8
Scousburgh Shet....147 i9
Scouthead Oldham....76 H3
Scrabster Highld....151 K3
Scraesburgh Border....107 Q6
Scrafield Lincs....80 F10
Scrainwood Nthumb....108 F8
Scrane End Lincs....68 G4
Scraptoft Leics....66 G11
Scratby Norfk....71 P9
Scrayingham N York....86 D3
Scrays E Susx....16 D7
Scredington Lincs....68 B4
Scremby Lincs....80 H10
Scremerston Nthumb....117 M11
Screveton Notts....67 J3
Scrivelsby Lincs....80 E10
Scriven N York....85 M3
Scrooby Notts....78 G5
Scropton Derbys....65 M6
Scrub Hill Lincs....68 E1
Scruton N York....91 M8
Scuggate Cumb....98 F3
Scullomie Highld....149 N4
Sculthorpe Norfk....70 C6
Scunthorpe N Linc....79 M2
Scurlage Swans....26 C5
Sea Somset....21 M10
Seaborough Dorset....10 C3
Seabridge Staffs....64 F3
Seabrook Kent....17 L4
Seaburn Sundld....101 K6
Seacombe Wirral....75 K5
Seacroft Leeds....85 M8
Seacroft Lincs....81 L11
Seadyke Lincs....68 F5
Seafield W Loth....115 J8
Seaford E Susx....15 N11
Seaforth Sefton....75 K4
Seagrave Leics....66 G8
Seagry Heath Wilts....29 Q6
Seaham Dur....101 K8
Seahouses Nthumb....109 L3
Seal Kent....33 Q11
Sealand Flints....75 K10
Seale Surrey....14 C1
Seamer N York....91 R5
Seamer N York....93 K10
Seamill N Ayrs....113 J12
Sea Palling Norfk....71 N7
Searby Lincs....79 Q3
Seasalter Kent....35 K9
Seascale Cumb....88 D6
Seathwaite Cumb....88 H8
Seathwaite Cumb....88 H7
Seatle Cumb....89 K10
Seatoller Cumb....88 H4
Seaton Cnwll....4 D6
Seaton Cumb....97 K12
Seaton Devon....6 H5
Seaton Dur....101 K8
Seaton E R Yk....87 M6
Seaton Kent....35 M10
Seaton Nthumb....101 J3
Seaton Rutlnd....55 M1
Seaton Burn N Tyne....100 G3
Seaton Carew Hartpl....101 M12
Seaton Delaval Nthumb....100 H3
Seaton Ross E R Yk....86 E7
Seaton Sluice Nthumb....101 J3
Seatown Dorset....10 C6
Seave Green N York....92 B7
Seaview IoW....13 K6
Seaville Cumb....97 N7
Seavington St Mary
  Somset....21 N10
Seavington St Michael
  Somset....21 N10
Sebastopol Torfn....28 C3
Sebergham Cumb....98 D10
Seckington Warwks....65 N11
Second Severn Crossing
  Mons....28 G5
Sedbergh Cumb....89 Q8
Sedbury Gloucs....28 H4
Sedbusk N York....90 E8
Sedgeberrow Worcs....42 B4
Sedgebrook Lincs....67 L4
Sedge Fen Suffk....57 N4
Sedgefield Dur....91 N1
Sedgeford Norfk....69 N5
Sedgehill Wilts....23 J8
Sedgemoor Services
  Somset....21 N3
Sedgley Dudley....52 G2
Sedgley Park Bury....76 F3
Sedgwick Cumb....89 N9
Sedlescombe E Susx....16 D7
Sedrup Bucks....44 A9
Seed Kent....34 G11
Seend Wilts....29 Q10
Seend Cleeve Wilts....29 Q10
Seer Green Bucks....32 D4
Seething Norfk....59 L1
Sefton Sefton....75 K3
Seghill Nthumb....100 H3
Seighford Staffs....64 G8
Seion Gwynd....73 J10
Seisdon Staffs....52 F2
Selattyn Shrops....63 J5
Selborne Hants....25 N6
Selby N York....86 B9
Selham W Susx....14 E6
Selhurst Gt Lon....33 L9
Selkirk Border....107 M4
Sellack Herefs....40 H6
Sellafield Station Cumb....88 D7
Sellafirth Shet....147 J3
Sellan Cnwll....2 C8
Sellick's Green Somset....21 K9
Sellindge Kent....17 J3
Selling Kent....35 J11
Sells Green Wilts....29 Q10
Selly Oak Birm....53 K4
Selmeston E Susx....15 P9
Selsdon Gt Lon....33 L10
Selsey W Susx....13 Q6
Selsfield Common
  W Susx....15 L4
Selside Cumb....89 N7
Selside N York....90 C11
Selsley Gloucs....41 N9
Selsted Kent....17 M2
Selston Notts....66 D2
Selworthy Somset....20 E4
Semer Suffk....46 H2
Semington Wilts....29 P10
Semley Wilts....23 J8
Sempringham Lincs....68 C5
Send Surrey....32 E11
Send Marsh Surrey....32 E11
Senghenydd Caerph....27 Q9
Sennen Cnwll....2 B9

Sennen Cove Cnwll....2 B9
Sennybridge Powys....39 L6
Serlby Notts....78 G6
Sessay N York....91 Q11
Setchey Norfk....69 M9
Setley Hants....12 E5
Seton Mains E Loth....116 B6
Settle N York....84 B2
Settrington N York....86 F1
Seven Ash Somset....21 J7
Sevenhampton Gloucs....42 B7
Sevenhampton Swindn....30 E4
Seven Kings Gt Lon....33 N5
Sevenoaks Kent....33 P11
Sevenoaks Weald Kent....33 P12
Seven Sisters Neath....39 K10
Seven Springs Gloucs....41 Q8
Seven Star Green Essex....46 G6
Severn Beach S Glos....28 H5
Severn Bridge S Glos....28 H4
Severn Stoke Worcs....41 P3
Severn View Services
  S Glos....28 H4
Sevick End Bed....56 B10
Sevington Kent....17 J3
Sewards End Essex....45 Q4
Sewardstonebury Essex....33 M3
Sewell C Beds....44 D8
Sewerby E R Yk....87 M2
Seworgan Cnwll....2 H8
Sewstern Leics....67 M8
Sexhow N York....91 Q5
Sgalpaigh W Isls....152 f6
Sgiogarstaigh W Isls....152 h1
Shabbington Bucks....43 N10
Shackerley Shrops....64 F11
Shackerstone Leics....66 B10
Shacklecross Derbys....66 C5
Shackleford Surrey....14 D2
Shade Calder....84 D10
Shader W Isls....152 g1
Shadforth Dur....101 J10
Shadingfield Suffk....59 N4
Shadoxhurst Kent....16 H3
Shadwell Leeds....85 M7
Shadwell Norfk....58 D4
Shaftenhoe End Herts....45 M4
Shaftesbury Dorset....23 J9
Shafton Donc....78 F2
Shafton Two Gates Barns....78 C2
Shakerley Wigan....76 C3
Shalbourne Wilts....30 G9
Shalcombe IoW....12 F7
Shalden Hants....25 M5
Shalden Green Hants....25 M5
Shaldon Devon....6 C8
Shalfleet IoW....12 G7
Shalford Essex....46 C6
Shalford Surrey....14 E1
Shalford Green Essex....46 C6
Shallowford Staffs....64 G6
Shalmsford Street Kent....35 K11
Shalstone Bucks....43 N4
Shamley Green Surrey....14 E2
Shandford Angus....132 D11
Shandon Ag & B....113 K4
Shandwick Highld....146 F10
Shangton Leics....55 J1
Shankhouse Nthumb....100 H3
Shanklin IoW....13 K8
Shantron Ag & B....113 L4
Shap Cumb....89 P4
Shapinsay Ork....147 d4
Shapwick Dorset....11 M4
Shapwick Somset....21 P6
Shard End Birm....53 M3
Shardlow Derbys....66 C6
Shareshill Staffs....64 H11
Sharlston Wakefd....85 N11
Sharlston Common
  Wakefd....85 N11
Sharman's Cross Solhll....53 L5
Sharnal Street Medway....34 D7
Sharnbrook Bed....55 N8
Sharneyford Lancs....84 C10
Sharnford Leics....54 F2
Sharnhill Green Dorset....10 H4
Sharoe Green Lancs....83 M8
Sharow N York....91 N12
Sharpenhoe C Beds....44 F5
Sharperton Nthumb....108 C2
Sharp Green Norfk....71 N8
Sharpness Gloucs....41 L9
Sharpthorne W Susx....15 L3
Sharpton Cnwll....7 K10
Sharpway Gate Worcs....52 H7
Sharrington Norfk....70 E5
Shatterford Worcs....52 E4
Shatterling Kent....35 N10
Shatton Derbys....77 M7
Shaugh Prior Devon....4 H4
Shave Cross Dorset....10 C5
Shavington Ches E....64 C2
Shaw C Brad....84 F8
Shaw Oldham....76 H2
Shaw Swindn....30 D5
Shaw W Berk....31 K8
Shaw Wilts....29 P9
Shawbirch Wrekin....64 B9
Shawbost W Isls....152 f2
Shawbury Shrops....63 P8
Shawclough Rochdl....84 D12
Shaw Common Gloucs....41 L6
Shawdon Hill Nthumb....108 H7
Shawell Leics....54 F5
Shawford Hants....24 H8
Shawforth Lancs....84 D11
Shaw Green Herts....45 K5
Shaw Green Lancs....83 M11
Shaw Green N York....85 K5
Shawhead D & G....96 H3
Shaw Mills N York....85 K3
Shawsburn S Lans....114 L11
Shear Cross Wilts....23 J5
Shearington D & G....97 L5
Shearsby Leics....54 G2
Shearston Somset....21 L7
Shebbear Devon....7 N3
Shebdon Staffs....64 E7
Shebster Highld....151 J4
Shedfield Hants....25 J7
Sheen Staffs....77 L11
Sheepbridge Derbys....78 B9
Sheep Hill Dur....100 F7
Sheepridge Kirk....84 H11
Sheepscar Leeds....85 L8
Sheepscombe Gloucs....41 P9
Sheepstor Devon....5 J3
Sheepwash Devon....7 J3
Sheepwash Nthumb....100 H1
Sheepway N Som....28 G7
Sheepy Magna Leics....65 Q12
Sheepy Parva Leics....65 Q11
Sheering Essex....45 P9
Sheerness Kent....34 G7
Sheerwater Surrey....32 E10
Sheet Hants....25 N8
Sheffield Sheff....78 B6
Sheffield Bottom W Berk....31 M9
Sheffield Green E Susx....15 M6
Sheffield Park E Susx....15 M5
Shefford C Beds....44 G4
Shefford Woodlands
  W Berk....30 H8

Sheigra Highld....148 E4
Sheinton Shrops....63 Q11
Shelderton Shrops....51 L5
Sheldon Birm....53 L4
Sheldon Derbys....77 M10
Sheldon Devon....9 L3
Sheldwich Kent....34 H11
Sheldwich Lees Kent....34 H11
Shelf Calder....84 H9
Shelfanger Norfk....58 G4
Shelfield Warwks....53 L8
Shelfield Wsall....65 J11
Shelford Notts....66 H4
Shelford Warwks....54 C3
Shellacres Nthumb....108 E1
Shelley Essex....45 Q10
Shelley Kirk....77 M2
Shelley Suffk....47 J4
Shelley Far Bank Kirk....77 M2
Shellingford Oxon....30 G4
Shellow Bowells Essex....45 R10
Shelsley Beauchamp
  Worcs....52 D8
Shelsley Walsh Worcs....52 D8
Shelton Bed....55 N7
Shelton Norfk....59 J2
Shelton Notts....67 K3
Shelton Shrops....63 M9
Shelton Green Norfk....59 J3
Shelton Lock C Derb....66 B6
Shelton Under Harley
  Staffs....64 F4
Shelve Shrops....63 K12
Shelwick Herefs....40 H3
Shenfield Essex....33 R3
Shenington Oxon....42 H3
Shenley Herts....32 H2
Shenley Brook End
  M Keyn....44 B5
Shenleybury Herts....44 H11
Shenley Church End
  M Keyn....44 B4
Shenmore Herefs....40 E4
Shennanton D & G....95 L5
Shenstone Staffs....65 L11
Shenstone Worcs....52 F6
Shenstone Woodend
  Staffs....65 L12
Shenton Leics....66 C12
Shenval Moray....139 M10
Shepeau Stow Lincs....68 F9
Shephall Herts....45 J8
Shepherd's Bush Gt Lon....33 J6
Shepherd's Green Oxon....31 P6
Shepherds Patch Gloucs....41 M9
Shepherdswell Kent....17 N1
Shepley Kirk....77 J12
Shepperdine S Glos....29 J3
Shepperton Surrey....32 F9
Shepreth Cambs....56 H11
Shepshed Leics....66 D8
Shepton Beauchamp
  Somset....21 N9
Shepton Mallet Somset....22 E5
Shepton Montague
  Somset....22 F7
Shepway Kent....34 D11
Sheraton Dur....101 L11
Sherborne Dorset....22 E10
Sherborne Gloucs....42 E8
Sherborne St John Hants....25 J3
Sherbourne Warwks....53 N8
Sherburn Dur....101 J10
Sherburn N York....93 J11
Sherburn Hill Dur....101 J10
Sherburn in Elmet
  N York....85 P9
Shere Surrey....14 F1
Shereford Norfk....70 C7
Sherfield English Hants....24 D9
Sherfield on Loddon
  Hants....31 P10
Sherfin Lancs....84 B10
Sherford Devon....5 N8
Sherford Somset....21 K8
Sheriffhales Shrops....64 D9
Sheriff Hutton N York....86 C2
Sheringham Norfk....70 H3
Sherington M Keyn....44 C2
Shermanbury W Susx....14 H6
Shernborne Norfk....69 N6
Sherrington Wilts....23 L5
Sherston Wilts....29 N5
Sherwood C Nott....66 D4
Sherwood Forest Notts....78 G11
Shetland Islands Shet....147 i6
Shettleston C Glas....114 B8
Shevington Wigan....75 P2
Shevington Moor Wigan....75 P2
Shevington Vale Wigan....75 N2
Sheviock Cnwll....4 E6
Shibden Head C Brad....84 G9
Shide IoW....12 H7
Shidlaw Nthumb....108 C2
Shiel Bridge Highld....136 C12
Shieldaig Highld....135 P5
Shieldhill D & G....97 L3
Shieldhill Falk....114 G6
Shieldhill House Hotel
  S Lans....106 C2
Shields N Lans....114 D10
Shielfoot Highld....127 M10
Shielhill Angus....124 H1
Shielhill Inver....113 K7
Shifford Oxon....42 H11
Shifnal Shrops....64 D10
Shilbottle Nthumb....109 K8
Shildon Dur....91 L1
Shillford E Rens....113 N10
Shillingford Devon....20 D8
Shillingford Oxon....31 M4
Shillingford Abbot Devon....8 G7
Shillingford St George
  Devon....8 G7
Shillingstone Dorset....11 K2
Shillington C Beds....44 G5
Shillmoor Nthumb....108 D6
Shilton Oxon....42 F10
Shilton Warwks....54 C4
Shimpling Norfk....58 G4
Shimpling Suffk....58 C10
Shimpling Street Suffk....58 C10
Shincliffe Dur....100 C10
Shiney Row Sundld....101 J8
Shinfield Wokham....31 Q8
Shingay Cambs....45 K2
Shingle Street Suffk....47 Q3
Shinnersbridge Devon....5 N4
Shinness Highld....145 M2
Shipbourne Kent....33 Q12
Shipdham Norfk....70 E10
Shipham Somset....28 C11
Shiphay Torbay....5 P4
Shiplake Oxon....31 Q7
Shiplake Row Oxon....31 Q7
Shiplate N Som....28 C10
Shipley C Brad....84 H7
Shipley Derbys....66 D3
Shipley Shrops....52 F2
Shipley W Susx....14 G6
Shipley Bridge Surrey....15 K2
Shipley Hatch Kent....16 H2
Shipmeadow Suffk....59 M3

Shippea Hill Station
  Cambs....57 M4
Shippon Oxon....31 K3
Shipston-on-Stour
  Warwks....42 F4
Shipton Bucks....43 Q6
Shipton Gloucs....42 B8
Shipton N York....85 Q3
Shipton Shrops....51 P2
Shipton Bellinger Hants....24 C4
Shipton Gorge Dorset....10 D6
Shipton Green W Susx....13 P5
Shipton Moyne Gloucs....29 N4
Shipton-on-Cherwell
  Oxon....43 K8
Shiptonthorpe E R Yk....86 F6
Shipton-under-
  Wychwood Oxon....42 G8
Shirburn Oxon....31 P3
Shirdley Hill Lancs....75 K1
Shire Cumb....99 J11
Shirebrook Derbys....78 E10
Shiregreen Sheff....78 B5
Shirehampton Bristl....28 H7
Shiremoor N Tyne....101 J4
Shirenewton Mons....28 G4
Shire Oak Wsall....65 K11
Shireoaks Notts....78 F7
Shirkoak Kent....16 G4
Shirland Derbys....78 C12
Shirlett Shrops....52 C1
Shirley C Sotn....24 F10
Shirley Derbys....65 N4
Shirley Gt Lon....33 L9
Shirley Solhll....53 L5
Shirl Heath Herefs....51 M8
Shirrell Heath Hants....25 J10
Shirwell Devon....19 L6
Shiskine N Ayrs....103 N4
Shittlehope Dur....100 C10
Shobdon Herefs....51 L8
Shobley Hants....12 G3
Shobrooke Devon....8 G4
Shoby Leics....66 H8
Shocklach Ches W....63 M2
Shocklach Green Ches W....63 M2
Shoeburyness Sthend....34 G5
Sholden Kent....35 P12
Sholing C Sotn....12 G2
Shoot Hill Shrops....63 L9
Shop Cnwll....6 C12
Shop Cnwll....18 E10
Shopwyke W Susx....14 C9
Shore Rochdl....84 D11
Shoreditch Gt Lon....33 L6
Shoreditch Somset....21 K9
Shoreham Kent....33 P10
Shoreham-by-Sea
  W Susx....15 J10
Shoresdean Nthumb....117 L12
Shoreswood Nthumb....117 L12
Shorley Hants....25 K8
Shorncote Gloucs....30 B3
Shorne Kent....34 C8
Shortacross Cnwll....4 D5
Shortbridge E Susx....15 N6
Shortfield Common
  Surrey....25 P5
Shortgate E Susx....15 P8
Short Heath Birm....53 L2
Shortheath Hants....25 N6
Short Heath Wsall....64 H12
Shortlanesend Cnwll....3 K5
Shortstown Bed....44 F1
Shorwell IoW....12 G8
Shoscombe BaNES....29 L11
Shotesham Norfk....71 K12
Shotgate Essex....34 D4
Shotley Suffk....47 M4
Shotley Bridge Dur....100 D7
Shotleyfield Nthumb....100 D7
Shotley Gate Suffk....47 M5
Shotley Street Suffk....47 M5
Shottenden Kent....35 J11
Shottermill Surrey....14 C4
Shottery Warwks....53 M9
Shotteswell Warwks....43 J3
Shottisham Suffk....47 N3
Shottle Derbys....65 Q3
Shottlegate Derbys....65 Q3
Shotton Dur....91 N2
Shotton Dur....101 K10
Shotton Flints....75 K10
Shotton Nthumb....100 H4
Shotton Nthumb....108 D4
Shotton Colliery Dur....101 K10
Shotts N Lans....114 F9
Shotwick Ches W....75 K9
Shougle Moray....139 M5
Shouldham Norfk....69 M10
Shouldham Thorpe Norfk....69 M10
Shoulton Worcs....52 F9
Shover's Green E Susx....16 B5
Shraleybrook Staffs....64 E3
Shrawardine Shrops....63 L8
Shrawley Worcs....52 F7
Shreding Green Bucks....32 E6
Shrewley Warwks....53 N7
Shrewsbury Shrops....63 M9
Shrewton Wilts....23 N5
Shripney W Susx....14 D10
Shrivenham Oxon....30 F4
Shropham Norfk....58 E2
Shroton Dorset....23 J10
Shrub End Essex....46 H6
Shucknall Herefs....41 J3
Shudy Camps Cambs....46 A3
Shuna Highld....120 E11
Shurdington Gloucs....41 Q8
Shurlock Row W & M....32 B7
Shurnock Worcs....53 J8
Shurrery Highld....151 J5
Shurrery Lodge Highld....151 J5
Shurton Somset....21 J4
Shustoke Warwks....53 N3
Shute Devon....6 H4
Shute Devon....9 N5
Shutford Oxon....42 H4
Shut Heath Staffs....64 G7
Shuthonger Gloucs....41 P5
Shutlanger Nhants....43 P3
Shutterton Devon....8 H9
Shutt Green Staffs....64 F10
Shuttington Warwks....65 N11
Shuttlewood Derbys....78 D9
Shuttleworth Bury....84 B11
Siabost W Isls....152 f2
Siadar W Isls....152 g1
Sibbertoft Nhants....54 H4
Sibdon Carwood Shrops....51 L3
Sibford Ferris Oxon....42 H4
Sibford Gower Oxon....42 H4
Sible Hedingham Essex....46 D4
Sibley's Green Essex....46 A6
Sibsey Lincs....68 G2
Sibsey Fenside Lincs....68 G2
Sibson Cambs....56 B1
Sibson Leics....66 B12
Sibster Highld....151 Q5
Sibthorpe Notts....67 J3
Sibton Suffk....59 N7
Sicklesmere Suffk....58 C8
Sicklinghall N York....85 L5
Sidbrook Somset....21 L8
Sidbury Devon....9 L6
Sidbury Shrops....52 C3
Sid Cop Barns....78 C2
Sidcup Gt Lon....33 N8
Siddick Cumb....97 K12
Siddington Ches E....76 F9
Siddington Gloucs....30 B2
Sidemoor Worcs....52 H6
Sidestrand Norfk....71 K4
Sidford Devon....9 L7
Sidlesham W Susx....13 Q5
Sidley E Susx....16 C9
Sidmouth Devon....9 L7
Siefton Shrops....51 N4
Sigford Devon....8 E10
Sigglesthorne E R Yk....87 M6
Sigingstone V Glam....27 M8
Signet Oxon....42 F9
Silchester Hants....31 N10
Sileby Leics....66 G9
Silecroft Cumb....88 F10
Silfield Norfk....70 G12
Silian Cerdgn....49 J10
Silkstead Hants....24 G8
Silkstone Barns....77 P3
Silkstone Common Barns....77 P3
Silk Willoughby Lincs....67 Q4
Silloth Cumb....97 M7
Silpho N York....93 K8
Silsden C Brad....84 F6
Silsoe C Beds....44 F4
Silton Dorset....22 H7
Silverburn Mdloth....115 M9
Silverdale Lancs....89 M11
Silverdale Staffs....64 E3
Silver End Essex....46 E8
Silverford Abers....141 J3
Silvergate Norfk....71 H6
Silverlace Green Suffk....59 L8
Silverley's Green Suffk....59 K5
Silverstone Nhants....43 M3
Silver Street Kent....34 F10
Silver Street Somset....22 C7
Silverton Devon....8 H4
Silvington Shrops....52 B5
Simister Bury....76 F3
Simmondley Derbys....77 J5
Simonburn Nthumb....99 N3
Simonsbath Somset....19 P5
Simonstone Lancs....84 B8
Simonstone N York....90 E8
Simprim Border....117 J12
Simpson M Keyn....44 C4
Simpson Cross Pembks....36 H6
Sinclair's Hill Border....116 H11
Sinclairston E Ayrs....105 J6
Sinderby N York....91 N10
Sinderhope Nthumb....99 N8
Sinderland Green Traffd....76 D6
Sindlesham Wokham....31 Q8
Sinfin C Derb....66 B6
Singleborough Bucks....43 Q5
Single Street Gt Lon....33 N10
Singleton Lancs....83 K7
Singleton W Susx....14 C8
Singlewell Kent....34 B8
Sinkhurst Green Kent....16 E2
Sinnarhard Abers....132 D2
Sinnington N York....92 F9
Sinton Worcs....52 F9
Sinton Green Worcs....52 F8
Sipson Gt Lon....32 F7
Sirhowy Blae G....39 Q9
Sissinghurst Kent....16 D3
Siston S Glos....29 K7
Sitcott Devon....7 L6
Sithney Cnwll....2 G8
Sithney Common Cnwll....2 G8
Sithney Green Cnwll....2 G8
Sittingbourne Kent....34 F9
Six Ashes Shrops....52 E3
Six Bells Blae G....40 B11
Six Hills Leics....66 H8
Sixhills Lincs....80 C6
Six Mile Bottom Cambs....57 L9
Sixmile Cottages Kent....17 K2
Sixpenny Handley Dorset....23 M10
Six Rues Jersey....13 b1
Sizewell Suffk....59 P8
Skaill Ork....147 d5
Skara Brae Ork....147 b4
Skares E Ayrs....105 K5
Skateraw Abers....133 L6
Skateraw E Loth....116 G6
Skeabost Highld....134 G6
Skeeby N York....91 K6
Skeffington Leics....67 J11
Skeffling E R Yk....87 Q11
Skegby Notts....78 D11
Skegness Lincs....81 L11
Skelbo Highld....146 E9
Skelbo Street Highld....146 E9
Skelbrooke Donc....78 E1
Skeldyke Lincs....68 G5
Skellingthorpe Lincs....79 M9
Skellorn Green Ches E....76 G7
Skellow Donc....78 E1
Skelmanthorpe Kirk....77 N2
Skelmersdale Lancs....75 M2
Skelmorlie N Ayrs....113 J8
Skelpick Highld....150 C5
Skelston D & G....96 G1
Skelton C York....86 B4
Skelton Cumb....98 F11
Skelton E R Yk....86 D9
Skelton N York....91 K6
Skelton R & Cl....92 D3
Skelton on Ure N York....85 M2
Skelwith Bridge Cumb....89 K6
Skendleby Lincs....81 K9
Skene House Abers....133 J2
Skenfrith Mons....40 F7
Skerne E R Yk....87 K4
Skerray Highld....149 P3
Skerricha Highld....148 F6
Skerton Lancs....83 L3
Sketchley Leics....54 C2
Sketty Swans....26 F3
Skewen Neath....26 G3
Skewsby N York....86 B1
Skeyton Norfk....71 K7
Skeyton Corner Norfk....71 K7
Skiall Highld....151 J3
Skidbrooke Lincs....80 H5
Skidbrooke North End
  Lincs....80 H5
Skidby E R Yk....87 J8
Skigersta W Isls....152 h1
Skilgate Somset....20 E8
Skillington Lincs....67 M7
Skinburness Cumb....97 M7
Skinflats Falk....114 G6
Skinidin Highld....134 C6
Skinners Green W Berk....31 J9
Skinningrove R & Cl....92 E2
Skipness Ag & B....112 C9
Skipper's Bridge D & G....98 D2

Skiprigg Cumb....98 E10
Skipsea E R Yk....87 M4
Skipsea Brough E R Yk....87 M4
Skipton N York....84 E5
Skipton-on-Swale N York....91 N10
Skipwith N York....86 C7
Skirlaugh E R Yk....87 L7
Skirling Border....106 E2
Skirmett Bucks....31 Q5
Skirpenbeck E R Yk....86 D4
Skirwith Cumb....99 J11
Skirwith N York....90 D11
Skirza Highld....151 Q3
Skitby Cumb....98 E5
Skittle Green Bucks....43 Q10
Skokholm Island Pembks....36 D9
Skomer Island Pembks....36 B8
Skulamus Highld....135 M11
Skyborry Green Shrops....51 J6
Skye Green Essex....46 F7
Skye of Curr Highld....138 H11
Skyreholme N York....84 G3
Slack Calder....84 E9
Slackcote Oldham....76 H2
Slack Head Cumb....89 M11
Slackholme End Lincs....81 K9
Slacks of Cairnbanno
  Abers....141 K7
Slad Gloucs....41 P10
Slade Devon....9 L3
Slade Devon....19 K4
Slade Swans....26 C8
Slade End Oxon....31 M4
Slade Green Gt Lon....33 P7
Slade Heath Staffs....64 G11
Slade Hooton Rothm....78 E6
Sladesbridge Cnwll....6 E10
Slades Green Worcs....41 N5
Slaggyford Nthumb....99 K8
Slaidburn Lancs....83 Q5
Slaithwaite Kirk....84 G12
Slaley Derbys....77 P12
Slaley Nthumb....100 B7
Slamannan Falk....114 F7
Slapton Bucks....44 D7
Slapton Devon....5 N7
Slapton Nhants....43 N2
Slattocks Rochdl....76 G2
Slaugham W Susx....15 J5
Slaughterford Wilts....29 N7
Slawston Leics....55 K2
Sleaford Hants....25 P6
Sleaford Lincs....67 Q3
Sleagill Cumb....89 P3
Sleap Shrops....63 N7
Sleapford Wrekin....64 B8
Sleasdairidh Highld....145 P6
Slebech Pembks....37 K7
Sledge Green Worcs....41 N5
Sledmere E R Yk....86 H2
Sleetbeck Cumb....98 G3
Sleight Dorset....11 N5
Sleightholme Dur....90 F5
Sleights N York....92 H5
Slepe Dorset....11 M6
Slickly Highld....151 P3
Sliddery N Ayrs....103 N5
Sligachan Highld....135 J10
Sligrachan Ag & B....112 H3
Slimbridge Gloucs....41 L11
Slindon Staffs....64 F6
Slindon W Susx....14 D9
Slinfold W Susx....14 G4
Sling Gwynd....41 J10
Slingsby N York....92 E11
Slip End C Beds....44 F8
Slip End Herts....45 K4
Slipton Nhants....55 N5
Slitting Mill Staffs....65 J9
Slockavullin Ag & B....112 B2
Sloley Norfk....71 K7
Sloncombe Devon....8 D7
Sloothby Lincs....81 K9
Slough Slough....32 D6
Slough Green Somset....21 K9
Slough Green W Susx....15 K5
Slumbay Highld....136 A9
Slyfield Green Surrey....32 E12
Slyne Lancs....83 L3
Smailholm Border....107 P4
Smallbridge Rochdl....84 D12
Smallbrook Gloucs....28 G5
Smallbrook Gloucs....29 J10
Smallburgh Norfk....71 L7
Smallburn E Ayrs....105 M4
Smalldale Derbys....77 L8
Smalldale Derbys....77 M7
Small Dole W Susx....14 H7
Smalley Derbys....66 C4
Smalley Common Derbys....66 C4
Smalley Green Derbys....66 C4
Smallfield Surrey....15 L2
Small Heath Birm....53 L3
Small Hythe Kent....16 E4
Smallridge Devon....9 P4
Smallthorne C Stke....64 G2
Smallwood Ches E....76 E11
Small Wood Hey Lancs....83 J5
Smallworth Norfk....58 F4
Smannell Hants....24 E3
Smardale Cumb....90 C6
Smarden Kent....16 F2
Smarden Bell Kent....16 F2
Smart's Hill Kent....15 Q2
Smeafield Nthumb....108 H2
Smeatharpe Devon....9 M3
Smeeth Kent....17 J3
Smeeton Westerby Leics....54 H2
Smelthouses N York....85 J2
Smerral Highld....151 L10
Smestow Staffs....52 F2
Smethwick Sandw....53 J3
Smethwick Green Ches E....76 F11
Smirisary Highld....127 L9
Smisby Derbys....66 B8
Smith End Green Worcs....52 E10
Smithfield Cumb....98 F5
Smith Green Lancs....83 L4
Smithies Barns....77 Q2
Smithincott Devon....9 K2
Smith's End Herts....45 M4
Smith's Green Essex....45 Q7
Smith's Green Essex....45 Q4
Smithstown Highld....143 J9
Smithton Highld....138 D7
Smithy Bridge Rochdl....84 D12
Smithy Green Ches E....76 E8
Smithy Green Stockp....76 G6
Smithy Houses Derbys....66 C3
Smockington Leics....54 D4
Smoo Highld....149 J3
Smythe's Green Essex....46 G8
Snade D & G....96 G1
Snailbeach Shrops....63 L11
Snailwell Cambs....57 M7
Snainton N York....93 J10
Snaith E R Yk....86 E10
Snake Pass Inn Derbys....77 L5
Snape N York....91 M9
Snape Suffk....59 M9
Snape Green Lancs....83 J11
Snape Street Suffk....59 M9
Snaresbrook Gt Lon....33 M5

Snarestone – Stoney Stratton 179

Snarestone Leics 65 Q10
Snarford Lincs 79 P7
Snargate Kent 16 H5
Snave Kent 16 H5
Sneachill Worcs 52 G10
Snead Powys 51 K2
Sneath Common Norfk 58 H3
Sneaton N York 92 H5
Sneatonthorpe N York 92 H5
Snelland Lincs 79 Q7
Snelson Ches E 76 E8
Snelston Derbys 65 L3
Snetterton Norfk 58 E2
Snettisham Norfk 69 N5
Snibston Leics 66 C9
Snig's End Gloucs 41 M6
Snitter Nthumb 108 G9
Snitterby Lincs 79 N5
Snitterfield Warwks 53 N8
Snitterton Derbys 77 P11
Snitton Shrops 51 P5
Snoadhill Kent 16 G2
Snodhill Herefs 40 D4
Snodland Kent 34 C10
Snoll Hatch Kent 16 B1
Snowden Hill Barns 77 N4
Snowdon Gwynd 61 K1
Snowdon Kent 35 N12
Snowdonia National Park 61 P6
Snow End Herts 45 M5
Snowshill Gloucs 42 C5
Snow Street Norfk 58 G4
Soake Hants 13 L2
Soar Cardif 27 P6
Soar Devon 5 L9
Soar Powys 39 M5
Soay Highld 126 H2
Soberton Hants 25 K10
Soberton Heath Hants 25 K10
Sockbridge Cumb 89 M1
Sockburn Darltn 91 N5
Sodom Denbgs 74 F9
Sodylt Bank Shrops 63 K4
Soham Cambs 57 L6
Soham Cotes Cambs 57 L6
Solas W Isls 152 c7
Solbury Pembks 36 H8
Soldon Devon 7 L3
Soldon Cross Devon 7 L3
Soldridge Hants 25 L6
Sole Street Kent 17 K1
Sole Street Kent 34 B9
Solihull Solhll 53 M5
Sollers Dilwyn Herefs 51 M9
Sollers Hope Herefs 41 J5
Sollom Lancs 83 K11
Solva Pembks 36 F6
Solwaybank D & G 98 C3
Somerby Leics 67 K10
Somerby Lincs 79 Q2
Somercotes Derbys 66 C1
Somerford BCP 12 B6
Somerford Keynes Gloucs 30 B3
Somerley W Susx 13 P5
Somerleyton Suffk 59 P1
Somersal Herbert Derbys 65 L5
Somersby Lincs 80 G9
Somersham Cambs 56 G5
Somersham Suffk 58 G11
Somerton Oxon 43 K6
Somerton Somset 22 C7
Somerton Suffk 57 Q10
Somerwood Shrops 63 P9
Sompting W Susx 14 H10
Sompting Abbotts W Susx 14 H9
Sonning Wokham 31 Q7
Sonning Common Oxon 31 P6
Sonning Eye Oxon 31 Q7
Sontley Wrexhm 63 K3
Sopley Hants 12 B5
Sopwell Herts 44 H10
Sopworth Wilts 29 N5
Sorbie D & G 95 N9
Sordale Highld 151 L4
Sorisdale Ag & B 126 E11
Sorn E Ayrs 105 K4
Sornhill E Ayrs 105 J3
Sortat Highld 151 N4
Sotby Lincs 80 D8
Sots Hole Lincs 80 C11
Sotterley Suffk 59 N4
Soughton Flints 74 H10
Soulbury Bucks 44 C6
Soulby Cumb 89 M2
Soulby Cumb 90 B4
Souldern Oxon 43 L5
Souldrop Bed 55 N8
Sound Ches E 64 B3
Sound Muir Moray 140 B5
Soundwell S Glos 29 K7
Sourton Devon 7 P6
Soutergate Cumb 88 H10
South Acre Norfk 69 Q9
South Alkham Kent 17 N2
Southall Gt Lon 32 G6
South Allington Devon 5 N9
South Alloa Falk 114 F3
Southam Gloucs 41 R6
Southam Warwks 54 C8
South Ambersham W Susx 14 C7
Southampton C Sotn 24 G11
Southampton Airport Hants 24 G10
South Anston Rothm 78 E7
South Ascot W & M 32 C8
South Ashford Kent 16 H2
South Baddesley Hants 12 F5
South Ballachulish Highld 121 K1
South Bank C York 86 B5
South Bank R & Cl 92 B3
South Barrow Somset 22 E8
South Beddington Gt Lon 33 K9
South Beer Cnwll 7 K6
South Benfleet Essex 34 D5
South Bockhampton BCP 12 B5
Southborough Gt Lon 33 M9
Southborough Kent 15 Q2
Southbourne BCP 12 B6
Southbourne W Susx 13 N4
South Bowood Dorset 10 C5
South Bramwith Donc 78 G1
South Brent Devon 5 L5
South Brewham Somset 22 G6
South Broomhill Nthumb 109 L10
Southburgh Norfk 70 E11
South Burlingham Norfk 71 M10
Southburn E R Yk 87 J4
South Cadbury Somset 22 E8
South Carlton Lincs 79 N8
South Carlton Notts 78 F7
South Cave E R Yk 86 G9
South Cerney Gloucs 30 B3
South Chailey E Susx 15 M7
South Chard Somset 9 Q4
South Charlton Nthumb 109 K6
South Cheriton Somset 22 F8
South Church Dur 91 L1
Southchurch Sthend 34 F5
South Cleatlam Dur 91 J3
South Cliffe E R Yk 86 G8
South Clifton Notts 79 K9
South Cockerington Lincs 80 G6
South Cornelly Brdgnd 27 K6
Southcott Cnwll 6 H6
Southcott Devon 7 Q6
Southcott Devon 8 E8
Southcott Devon 19 J10
Southcott Wilts 30 E10
Southcourt Bucks 44 A9
South Cove Suffk 59 P4
South Creake Norfk 70 C5
South Crosland Kirk 77 L1
South Croxton Leics 66 H10
South Dalton E R Yk 86 H6
South Darenth Kent 33 Q8
South Dell W Isls 152 g1
South Downs National Park 15 L9
South Duffield N York 86 C8
South Earlswood Surrey 15 K1
Southease E Susx 15 M10
South Elkington Lincs 80 F6
South Elmsall Wakefd 78 D1
Southend Ag & B 103 J8
South End E R Yk 87 R11
South End Hants 23 N10
South End Herefs 41 L3
South End N Linc 87 L11
South End Norfk 58 E3
Southend Wilts 30 E7
Southend Airport Essex 34 F4
Southend-on-Sea Sthend 34 F4
Southernby Cumb 98 D10
Southernden Kent 16 F2
Southerndown V Glam 27 L7
Southerness D & G 97 K7
South Erradale Highld 143 K11
Southerton Devon 9 K6
Southery Norfk 57 M2
South Fambridge Essex 34 F3
South Fawley W Berk 30 H6
South Ferriby N Linc 87 J11
South Field E R Yk 87 J10
Southfield Falk 114 F7
Southfleet Kent 33 R8
Southford IoW 13 J9
Southgate Gt Lon 33 K3
Southgate Norfk 69 N5
Southgate Norfk 70 C5
Southgate Norfk 70 H7
Southgate Swans 26 E5
South Godstone Surrey 15 L1
South Gorley Hants 12 B3
South Gosforth N u Ty 100 G5
South Green Essex 34 B4
South Green Essex 47 J8
South Green Kent 34 E10
South Green Norfk 70 F10
South Green Suffk 58 H5
South Gyle C Edin 115 M7
South Hanningfield Essex 34 C3
South Harting W Susx 25 N9
South Hayling Hants 13 M5
South Hazelrigg Nthumb 108 H3
South Heath Bucks 44 C11
South Heighton E Susx 15 N10
South Hetton Dur 101 K9
South Hiendley Wakefd 78 C1
South Hill Cnwll 7 L10
South Hill Somset 21 Q8
South Hinksey Oxon 43 L11
South Hole Devon 18 E9
South Holmwood Surrey 14 H2
South Hornchurch Gt Lon 33 P5
South Horrington Somset 22 D4
South Huish Devon 5 L8
South Hykeham Lincs 79 M10
South Hylton Sundld 101 J7
Southill C Beds 44 H3
Southington Hants 25 J3
South Kelsey Lincs 79 P4
South Kessock Highld 138 C6
South Killingholme N Linc 87 L12
South Kilvington N York 91 P10
South Kilworth Leics 54 G4
South Kirkby Wakefd 78 D2
South Knighton Devon 8 F10
South Kyme Lincs 68 D2
Southleigh Devon 9 N6
South Leigh Oxon 43 J10
South Leverton Notts 79 K7
South Littleton Worcs 42 C2
South Lopham Norfk 58 F4
South Luffenham Rutlnd 67 M11
South Lynn Norfk 69 M8
South Malling E Susx 15 N8
South Marston Swindn 30 E5
South Merstham Surrey 33 K12
South Middleton Nthumb 108 G5
South Milford N York 85 P9
South Milton Devon 5 L8
South Mimms Herts 33 J2
South Mimms Services Herts 33 J2
Southminster Essex 34 G2
South Molton Devon 19 N8
South Moor Dur 100 F8
Southmoor Oxon 31 J3
South Moreton Oxon 31 M5
Southmuir Angus 124 H2
South Mundham W Susx 14 C10
South Muskham Notts 79 K12
South Newbald E R Yk 86 G8
South Newington Oxon 43 J5
South Newton Wilts 23 N6
South Normanton Derbys 78 D12
South Norwood Gt Lon 33 L8
South Nutfield Surrey 15 K1
South Ockendon Thurr 33 Q6
Southoe Cambs 56 D8
Southolt Suffk 59 J7
South Ormsby Lincs 80 G8
Southorpe C Pete 67 Q11
South Ossett Wakefd 85 L11
South Otterington N York 91 N9
Southover Dorset 10 F6
Southover E Susx 16 B6
South Owersby Lincs 79 Q5
Southowram Calder 84 H10
South Park Surrey 15 J1
South Perrott Dorset 10 D3
South Petherton Somset 21 P10
South Petherwin Cnwll 7 K8
South Pickenham Norfk 70 C11
South Pill Cnwll 4 F5
South Pool Devon 5 N8
South Poorton Dorset 10 E5
Southport Sefton 82 H11
South Queensferry C Edin 115 L6
South Radworthy Devon 19 P7
South Rauceby Lincs 67 P3
South Raynham Norfk 70 C7
South Reddish Stockp 76 G5
Southrepps Norfk 71 K5
South Reston Lincs 80 H7
Southrey Lincs 80 C10
South Ronaldsay Ork 147 c6
Southrop Gloucs 42 E11
Southrope Hants 25 L4
South Runcton Norfk 69 M10
South Scarle Notts 79 L11
Southsea C Port 13 L5
Southsea Wrexhm 63 J2
South Shian Ag & B 120 G4
South Shields S Tyne 101 K5
South Shore Bpool 82 H8
Southside Dur 91 J1
South Somercotes Lincs 80 H5
South Stainley N York 85 L3
South Stifford Thurr 33 Q7
South Stoke BaNES 29 M10
South Stoke Oxon 31 M5
South Stoke W Susx 14 E9
South Stour Kent 17 J3
South Street Kent 34 B9
South Street Kent 35 J10
South Street Kent 35 K9
South Tarbrax S Lans 115 J10
South Tawton Devon 8 C6
South Tehidy Cnwll 2 G6
South Thoresby Lincs 80 H8
South Thorpe Dur 91 J4
South Town Hants 25 L6
Southtown Norfk 71 Q11
Southtown Somset 21 M10
South Uist W Isls 152 c10
Southwaite Cumb 98 F9
Southwaite Services Cumb 98 F9
South Walsham Norfk 71 M9
Southwark Gt Lon 33 L6
South Warnborough Hants 25 M4
Southwater W Susx 14 H5
Southwater Street W Susx 14 H5
Southway C Plym 4 G4
Southway Somset 22 C5
South Weald Essex 33 Q3
Southwell Dorset 10 G10
Southwell Notts 66 H1
South Weston Oxon 31 P3
South Wheatley Cnwll 7 J6
South Wheatley Notts 79 J6
Southwick Hants 13 K3
Southwick Nhants 55 P2
Southwick Somset 21 N4
Southwick Sundld 101 K6
Southwick W Susx 15 J10
Southwick Wilts 23 J2
South Widcombe BaNES 29 J11
South Wigston Leics 54 F1
South Willesborough Kent 17 J3
South Willingham Lincs 80 D7
South Wingate Dur 101 K11
South Wingfield Derbys 66 B1
South Witham Lincs 67 M8
Southwold Suffk 59 P5
South Wonston Hants 24 H6
Southwood Norfk 71 M11
Southwood Somset 22 D6
South Woodham Ferrers Essex 34 E3
South Wootton Norfk 69 M7
South Wraxall Wilts 29 N9
South Zeal Devon 8 C6
Sovereign Harbour E Susx 16 B10
Sowerby Calder 84 F10
Sowerby N York 91 Q10
Sowerby Bridge Calder 84 G10
Sowerby Row Cumb 98 E10
Sower Carr Lancs 83 J6
Sowerhill Somset 20 D8
Sowhill Torfn 28 C2
Sowley Green Suffk 57 N10
Sowood Calder 84 G11
Sowton Devon 4 H4
Sowton Devon 9 J6
Soyland Town Calder 84 F11
Spa Common Norfk 71 K5
Spain's End Essex 46 B4
Spalding Lincs 68 E7
Spaldington E R Yk 86 E8
Spaldwick Cambs 56 C6
Spalford Notts 79 L10
Spanby Lincs 68 B4
Spanish Green Hants 31 P10
Sparham Norfk 70 G8
Sparhamill Norfk 70 G8
Spark Bridge Cumb 89 J9
Sparket Cumb 89 L2
Sparkford Somset 22 E8
Sparkhill Birm 53 L4
Sparkwell Devon 5 J5
Sparrow Green Norfk 70 D9
Sparrowpit Derbys 77 K7
Sparrows Green E Susx 16 B4
Sparsholt Hants 24 G7
Sparsholt Oxon 30 H5
Spartylea Nthumb 99 N8
Spath Staffs 65 K5
Spaunton N York 92 E9
Spaxton Somset 21 K6
Spean Bridge Highld 128 H8
Spear Hill W Susx 14 G7
Spearywell Hants 24 E8
Speen Bucks 32 B2
Speen W Berk 31 K8
Speeton N York 93 N11
Speke Lpool 75 M7
Speldhurst Kent 15 Q2
Spellbrook Herts 45 N8
Spelmonden Kent 16 C3
Spelsbury Oxon 42 H7
Spen Kirk 85 J10
Spencers Wood Wokham 31 P9
Spen Green Ches E 76 F11
Spennithorne N York 91 J9
Spennymoor Dur 100 H11
Spernall Warwks 53 K8
Spetchley Worcs 52 G10
Spetisbury Dorset 11 M4
Spexhall Suffk 59 M4
Spey Bay Moray 139 Q3
Speybridge Highld 139 J10
Speyview Moray 139 N7
Spilsby Lincs 80 H10
Spindlestone Nthumb 109 J3
Spinkhill Derbys 78 D8
Spinningdale Highld 146 B7
Spion Kop Notts 78 F10
Spirthill Wilts 30 A7
Spital Wirral 75 K7
Spital Hill Donc 78 G5
Spital in the Street Lincs 79 N6
Spithurst E Susx 15 M7
Spittal E Loth 116 B6
Spittal E R Yk 86 E5
Spittal Highld 151 L6
Spittal Nthumb 117 M11
Spittal Pembks 37 J6
Spittalfield P & K 124 C5
Spittal of Glenmuick Abers 131 P7
Spittal of Glenshee P & K 131 J10
Spittal-on-Rule Border 107 P6
Spixworth Norfk 71 K9
Splatt Cnwll 6 D9
Splatt Cnwll 7 J7
Splatt Devon 8 B4
Splayne's Green E Susx 15 M6
Splott Cardif 28 B7
Spofforth N York 85 M5
Spondon C Derb 66 C5
Spon Green Flints 75 J11
Spooner Row Norfk 58 G1
Sporle Norfk 70 C10
Spott E Loth 116 F6
Spottiswoode Border 116 E11
Spratton Nhants 55 J6
Spreakley Surrey 25 P5
Spreyton Devon 8 D5
Spriddlestone Devon 4 H6
Spridlington Lincs 79 P7
Springburn C Glas 114 A7
Springfield D & G 98 C4
Springfield Essex 46 C10
Springfield Fife 124 G10
Springhill Staffs 64 H11
Springhill Staffs 65 K11
Springholm D & G 96 G4
Springside N Ayrs 104 G2
Springthorpe Lincs 79 L6
Spring Vale Barns 77 N3
Springwell Sundld 100 H6
Sproatley E R Yk 87 M8
Sproston Green Ches W 76 D10
Sprotbrough Donc 78 E3
Sproughton Suffk 47 K3
Sprouston Border 108 B3
Sprowston Norfk 71 K9
Sproxton Leics 67 L7
Sproxton N York 92 C10
Spunhill Shrops 63 L5
Spurstow Ches E 75 P12
Spyway Dorset 10 E6
Square and Compass Pembks 36 G4
Stableford Shrops 52 D1
Stableford Staffs 64 E4
Stacey Bank Sheff 77 P5
Stackhouse N York 84 B2
Stackpole Pembks 37 J11
Stackpole Elidor Pembks 37 J11
Stacksford Norfk 58 F3
Stacksteads Lancs 84 C11
Staddiscombe C Plym 4 H6
Staddlethorpe E R Yk 86 F9
Staden Derbys 77 K9
Stadhampton Oxon 31 M3
Stadhlaigearraidh W Isls 152 b10
Staffield Cumb 98 G9
Staffin Highld 135 J2
Stafford Staffs 64 G7
Stafford Services (northbound) Staffs 64 G6
Stafford Services (southbound) Staffs 64 G6
Stagsden Bed 55 N11
Stainborough Barns 77 Q3
Stainburn Cumb 88 D1
Stainburn N York 85 K5
Stainby Lincs 67 M7
Staincross Barns 77 Q2
Staindrop Dur 91 J3
Staines-upon-Thames Surrey 32 E8
Stainfield Lincs 68 B6
Stainfield Lincs 80 C9
Stainforth Donc 78 G1
Stainforth N York 84 B2
Staining Lancs 82 H8
Stainland Calder 84 G11
Stainsacre N York 93 J5
Stainsby Derbys 78 D10
Stainton Cumb 89 M1
Stainton Cumb 89 N9
Stainton Cumb 98 D7
Stainton Donc 78 F5
Stainton Dur 90 H3
Stainton Middsb 91 Q4
Stainton N York 91 J7
Stainton by Langworth Lincs 79 Q8
Staintondale N York 93 K7
Stainton le Vale Lincs 80 D5
Stainton with Adgarley Cumb 88 H12
Stair Cumb 88 H2
Stair E Ayrs 104 H5
Stairfoot Barns 78 B3
Stairhaven D & G 95 J7
Staithes N York 92 F3
Stakeford Nthumb 100 H1
Stake Pool Lancs 83 K5
Stakes Hants 13 M3
Stalbridge Dorset 22 G10
Stalbridge Weston Dorset 22 G10
Stalham Norfk 71 M7
Stalham Green Norfk 71 M7
Stalisfield Green Kent 34 G11
Stalland Common Norfk 58 F1
Stallen Dorset 22 E10
Stallingborough NE Lin 80 D1
Stalling Busk N York 90 E9
Stallington Staffs 64 H4
Stalmine Lancs 83 J6
Stalmine Moss Side Lancs 83 J6
Stalybridge Tamesd 76 H4
Stambourne Essex 46 C4
Stambourne Green Essex 46 C4
Stamford Lincs 67 P10
Stamford Nthumb 109 L6
Stamford Bridge Ches W 75 M10
Stamford Bridge E R Yk 86 D4
Stamfordham Nthumb 100 D4
Stamford Hill Gt Lon 33 L5
Stanah Lancs 83 J6
Stanborough Herts 45 J9
Stanbridge C Beds 44 D7
Stanbridge Dorset 11 N4
Stanbury C Brad 84 F8
Stand Bury 76 E3
Stand N Lans 114 D7
Standburn Falk 114 G6
Standeford Staffs 64 G10
Standen Kent 16 F3
Standen Street Kent 16 E5
Standerwick Somset 22 H3
Standford Hants 25 P6
Standingstone Cumb 97 L11
Standish Gloucs 41 M10
Standish Wigan 75 P2
Standish Lower Ground Wigan 75 P2
Standlake Oxon 43 J11
Standon Hants 24 G8
Standon Herts 45 M7
Standon Staffs 64 E5
Standon Green End Herts 45 L7
Standwell Green Suffk 58 H6
Stane N Lans 114 F9
Stanfield Norfk 70 D8
Stanford C Beds 44 H3
Stanford Kent 17 K3
Stanford Shrops 63 K9
Stanford Bishop Herefs 52 C10
Stanford Bridge Worcs 52 D7
Stanford Bridge Wrekin 64 D7
Stanford Dingley W Berk 31 M8
Stanford in the Vale Oxon 30 H4
Stanford le Hope Thurr 34 B6
Stanford on Avon Nhants 54 F5
Stanford on Soar Notts 66 E8
Stanford on Teme Worcs 52 D7
Stanford Rivers Essex 33 P2
Stanfree Derbys 78 D9
Stanghow R & Cl 92 D4
Stanground C Pete 56 D1
Stanhill Lancs 83 Q9
Stanhoe Norfk 69 Q5
Stanhope Border 106 F4
Stanhope Dur 100 C10
Stanhope Kent 16 H3
Stanhope Bretby Derbys 65 P8
Stanion Nhants 55 M3
Stanklin Worcs 52 F6
Stanley Derbys 66 C4
Stanley Dur 100 F7
Stanley Notts 78 D11
Stanley P & K 124 C6
Stanley Shrops 52 D4
Stanley Staffs 64 H2
Stanley Wakefd 85 M10
Stanley Common Derbys 66 C4
Stanley Crook Dur 100 F10
Stanley Ferry Wakefd 85 M10
Stanley Gate Lancs 75 M3
Stanley Moor Staffs 64 G2
Stanley Pontlarge Gloucs 42 B5
Stanmer Br & H 15 L9
Stanmore Gt Lon 32 H4
Stanmore Hants 24 H7
Stanmore W Berk 31 K6
Stannersburn Nthumb 99 L1
Stanningfield Suffk 58 C9
Stanningley Leeds 85 K8
Stannington Nthumb 100 G2
Stannington Sheff 77 P6
Stannington Station Nthumb 100 G2
Stansbatch Herefs 51 K8
Stansfield Suffk 57 P10
Stanshope Staffs 65 L1
Stanstead Suffk 58 B11
Stanstead Abbotts Herts 45 M9
Stansted Kent 33 R10
Stansted Airport Essex 45 Q7
Stansted Mountfitchet Essex 45 P6
Stanton Derbys 65 P8
Stanton Gloucs 42 C5
Stanton Mons 40 D7
Stanton Nthumb 109 J11
Stanton Staffs 65 L3
Stanton Suffk 58 E6
Stanton by Bridge Derbys 66 B7
Stanton by Dale Derbys 66 D4
Stanton Drew BaNES 29 J9
Stanton Fitzwarren Swindn 30 E4
Stanton Harcourt Oxon 43 J10
Stanton Hill Notts 78 D11
Stanton in Peak Derbys 77 N11
Stanton Lacy Shrops 51 N5
Stanton Lees Derbys 77 N11
Stanton Long Shrops 51 P2
Stanton-on-the-Wolds Notts 66 G6
Stanton Prior BaNES 29 K10
Stanton St Bernard Wilts 30 C10
Stanton St John Oxon 43 M10
Stanton St Quintin Wilts 29 P6
Stanton Street Suffk 58 D7
Stanton under Bardon Leics 66 D10
Stanton upon Hine Heath Shrops 63 P7
Stanton Wick BaNES 29 J10
Stantway Gloucs 41 L9
Stanwardine in the Field Shrops 63 L7
Stanwardine in the Wood Shrops 63 M6
Stanway Essex 46 G7
Stanway Gloucs 42 C5
Stanway Green Essex 46 G7
Stanway Green Suffk 59 K6
Stanwell Surrey 32 F7
Stanwell Moor Surrey 32 F7
Stanwick Nhants 55 N6
Stanwick St John N York 91 K4
Stanwix Cumb 98 E7
Staoinebrig W Isls 152 b10
Stape N York 92 G8
Stapehill Dorset 11 P5
Stapeley Ches E 64 C2
Stapenhill Staffs 65 N8
Staple Kent 35 N11
Staple Cross Devon 20 G9
Staplecross E Susx 16 D6
Staplefield W Susx 15 K5
Staple Fitzpaine Somset 21 L9
Stapleford Cambs 57 J10
Stapleford Herts 45 K8
Stapleford Leics 67 K8
Stapleford Lincs 79 L12
Stapleford Notts 66 D5
Stapleford Wilts 23 N6
Stapleford Abbotts Essex 33 P3
Stapleford Tawney Essex 33 P3
Staplegrove Somset 21 K8
Staplehay Somset 21 K9
Staple Hill Worcs 52 H6
Staplehurst Kent 16 D2
Staplers IoW 12 H7
Staplestreet Kent 35 J10
Stapleton Cumb 98 G4
Stapleton Herefs 51 K7
Stapleton Leics 54 C1
Stapleton N York 91 M4
Stapleton Shrops 63 M11
Stapleton Somset 21 P9
Stapley Somset 21 K10
Staploe Bed 56 C8
Staplow Herefs 41 L3
Star Fife 124 F12
Star IoA 72 H9
Star Pembks 37 P3
Star Somset 28 F10
Starbeck N York 85 L4
Starbotton N York 90 F11
Starcross Devon 9 J8
Stareton Warwks 53 Q6
Starkholmes Derbys 77 P12
Starlings Green Essex 45 N5
Starr's Green E Susx 16 D8
Starston Norfk 59 J4
Start Devon 5 N8
Startforth Dur 90 H3
Startley Wilts 29 Q6
Statenborough Kent 35 P11
Statham Warrtn 76 C6
Stathe Somset 21 N7
Stathern Leics 67 K6
Station Town Dur 101 K11
Staughton Green Cambs 56 C7
Staughton Highway Cambs 56 C8
Staunton Gloucs 40 H9
Staunton Gloucs 41 M6
Staunton in the Vale Notts 67 K3
Staunton on Arrow Herefs 51 L8
Staunton on Wye Herefs 40 E3
Staveley Cumb 89 M7
Staveley Derbys 78 C8
Staveley N York 85 M3
Staveley-in-Cartmel Cumb 89 K9
Staverton Devon 5 N4
Staverton Gloucs 41 P7
Staverton Nhants 54 E8
Staverton Wilts 29 N10
Staverton Bridge Gloucs 41 P7
Stawell Somset 21 N6
Stawley Somset 20 G9
Staxigoe Highld 151 Q6
Staxton N York 93 K11
Staylittle Cerdgn 49 L3
Staylittle Powys 50 B2
Staynall Lancs 83 J6
Staythorpe Notts 67 J1
Stead C Brad 84 H6
Stean N York 90 H12
Stearsby N York 86 B1
Steart Somset 21 L4
Stebbing Essex 46 B7
Stebbing Green Essex 46 C7
Stechford Birm 53 L3
Stede Quarter Kent 16 F3
Stedham W Susx 14 B6
Steel Nthumb 99 P6
Steel Cross E Susx 15 P4
Steelend Fife 115 J3
Steele Road Border 107 N11
Steel Green Cumb 88 G11
Steel Heath Shrops 63 P5
Steen's Bridge Herefs 51 P9
Steep Hants 25 N8
Steephill IoW 13 J9
Steep Lane Calder 84 F10
Steeple Dorset 11 L8
Steeple Essex 46 G11
Steeple Ashton Wilts 29 P11
Steeple Aston Oxon 43 K6
Steeple Barton Oxon 43 K7
Steeple Bumpstead Essex 46 B3
Steeple Claydon Bucks 43 P6
Steeple Gidding Cambs 56 C4
Steeple Langford Wilts 23 M6
Steeple Morden Cambs 45 K3
Steep Marsh Hants 25 N8
Steeton C Brad 84 F6
Stein Highld 134 E4
Stella Gatesd 100 F5
Stelling Minnis Kent 17 L1
Stembridge Somset 21 P9
Stenalees Cnwll 3 P3
Stenhouse D & G 105 P11
Stenhousemuir Falk 114 F5
Stenigot Lincs 80 E7
Stenscholl Highld 134 H2
Stenson Fields Derbys 65 Q6
Stenton E Loth 116 E6
Steornabhagh W Isls 152 g3
Stepaside Pembks 37 M9
Stepford D & G 96 H2
Stepney Gt Lon 33 L6
Stepping Hill Stockp 76 G6
Steppingley C Beds 44 E4
Stepps N Lans 114 B7
Sternfield Suffk 59 M8
Stert Wilts 30 B10
Stetchworth Cambs 57 M9
Stevenage Herts 45 J6
Steven's Crouch E Susx 16 C8
Stevenston N Ayrs 104 E1
Steventon Hants 25 J4
Steventon Oxon 31 K4
Steventon End Essex 45 Q3
Stevington Bed 55 N10
Stewartby Bed 44 E3
Stewartfield S Lans 114 B10
Stewarton Ag & B 103 J6
Stewarton E Ayrs 113 N12
Stewkley Bucks 44 B6
Stewley Somset 21 M9
Stewton Lincs 80 G6
Steyne Cross IoW 13 L7
Steyning W Susx 14 H8
Steynton Pembks 36 H9
Stibb Cnwll 7 J3
Stibbard Norfk 70 E6
Stibb Cross Devon 18 H10
Stibb Green Wilts 30 F10
Stibbington Cambs 56 B1
Stichill Border 108 B2
Sticker Cnwll 3 N4
Stickford Lincs 80 G11
Sticklepath Devon 8 C6
Sticklepath Somset 20 G6
Stickling Green Essex 45 N5
Stickney Lincs 80 G12
Stiffkey Norfk 70 E4
Stifford Clays Thurr 34 A6
Stifford's Bridge Herefs 52 D11
Stiff Street Kent 34 F10
Stile Bridge Kent 16 D1
Stileway Somset 21 P5
Stilligarry W Isls 152 b10
Stillingfleet N York 86 B7
Stillington N York 86 A2
Stillington S on T 91 P2
Stilton Cambs 56 C3
Stinchcombe Gloucs 29 L3
Stinsford Dorset 10 H6
Stiperstones Shrops 63 L12
Stirchley Birm 53 K4
Stirchley Wrekin 64 C10
Stirling Abers 141 Q7
Stirling Stirlg 114 E2
Stirling Castle Stirlg 114 E2
Stirling Services Stirlg 114 E3
Stirtloe Cambs 56 D7
Stirton N York 84 E5
Stisted Essex 46 D7
Stitchcombe Wilts 30 F8
Stithians Cnwll 3 J7
Stivichall Covtry 53 Q5
Stixwould Lincs 80 D10
St Michaels Fife 125 J8
Stoak Ches W 75 M9
Stobo Border 106 G2
Stoborough Dorset 11 M7
Stoborough Green Dorset 11 M7
Stobs Castle Border 107 M8
Stobswood Nthumb 109 L10
Stock Essex 34 C3
Stock N Som 28 F10
Stockbridge Hants 24 F6
Stockbriggs S Lans 105 P2
Stockbury Kent 34 E10
Stockcross W Berk 31 J8
Stockdalewath Cumb 98 E9
Stocker's Hill Kent 34 G12
Stockerston Leics 55 L1
Stock Green Worcs 53 J9
Stocking Herefs 41 J5
Stockingford Warwks 53 Q2
Stocking Pelham Herts 45 N6
Stockland Devon 9 N4
Stockland Bristol Somset 21 K4
Stockland Green Kent 15 Q2
Stockleigh English Devon 8 F3
Stockleigh Pomeroy Devon 8 G4
Stockley Wilts 30 A9
Stockley Hill Herefs 40 E4
Stocklinch Somset 21 N10
Stockmoor Herefs 51 L9
Stockport Stockp 76 G5
Stocksbridge Sheff 77 N4
Stocksfield Nthumb 100 D6
Stockton Herefs 51 N8
Stockton Norfk 59 M2
Stockton Shrops 52 D1
Stockton Shrops 63 J12
Stockton Shrops 64 D12
Stockton Warwks 54 D8
Stockton Wilts 23 L6
Stockton Wrekin 64 E9
Stockton Brook Staffs 64 G2
Stockton Heath Warrtn 75 Q6
Stockton-on-Tees S on T 91 Q3
Stockton on Teme Worcs 52 D7
Stockton on the Forest C York 86 C4
Stockwell Gloucs 41 Q9
Stockwell End Wolves 64 G12
Stockwell Heath Staffs 65 K8
Stockwood Bristl 29 J8
Stockwood Dorset 10 F3
Stock Wood Worcs 53 J9
Stodday Lancs 83 L3
Stodmarsh Kent 35 M10
Stody Norfk 70 F5
Stoer Highld 148 B11
Stoford Somset 22 D10
Stoford Wilts 23 N6
Stogumber Somset 20 H6
Stogursey Somset 21 K5
Stoke Covtry 54 B5
Stoke Devon 18 E8
Stoke Hants 13 M4
Stoke Hants 24 F3
Stoke Medway 34 E7
Stoke Abbott Dorset 10 C5
Stoke Albany Nhants 55 K3
Stoke Ash Suffk 58 G6
Stoke Bardolph Notts 66 G4
Stoke Bliss Worcs 52 C8
Stoke Bruerne Nhants 55 J10
Stoke-by-Clare Suffk 46 C3
Stoke-by-Nayland Suffk 46 H4
Stoke Canon Devon 8 H5
Stoke Charity Hants 24 H5
Stoke Climsland Cnwll 7 L10
Stoke Cross Herefs 52 B10
Stoke D'Abernon Surrey 32 G10
Stoke Doyle Nhants 55 P3
Stoke Dry Rutlnd 55 L1
Stoke Edith Herefs 41 J3
Stoke End Warwks 53 M1
Stoke Farthing Wilts 23 N8
Stoke Ferry Norfk 69 N12
Stoke Fleming Devon 5 P7
Stokeford Dorset 11 L7
Stoke Gabriel Devon 5 P5
Stoke Gifford S Glos 29 J6
Stoke Golding Leics 54 C1
Stoke Goldington M Keyn 55 L11
Stoke Green Bucks 32 D6
Stokeham Notts 79 K8
Stoke Hammond Bucks 44 C6
Stoke Heath Shrops 64 C6
Stoke Heath Worcs 52 H7
Stoke Holy Cross Norfk 71 J11
Stokeinteignhead Devon 8 G10
Stoke Lacy Herefs 52 B10
Stoke Lyne Oxon 43 M6
Stoke Mandeville Bucks 44 B9
Stokenchurch Bucks 31 Q3
Stoke Newington Gt Lon 33 L5
Stokenham Devon 5 N8
Stoke-on-Trent C Stke 64 G3
Stoke Orchard Gloucs 41 Q6
Stoke Poges Bucks 32 D6
Stoke Pound Worcs 52 H7
Stoke Prior Herefs 51 N9
Stoke Prior Worcs 52 H7
Stoke Rivers Devon 19 M6
Stoke Rochford Lincs 67 M7
Stoke Row Oxon 31 P5
Stoke St Gregory Somset 21 M8
Stoke St Mary Somset 21 L9
Stoke St Michael Somset 22 F4
Stoke St Milborough Shrops 51 P4
Stokesay Shrops 51 M4
Stokesby Norfk 71 N10
Stokesley N York 92 B5
Stoke sub Hamdon Somset 21 Q10
Stoke Talmage Oxon 31 P2
Stoke Trister Somset 22 G7
Stoke upon Tern Shrops 64 B6
Stoke-upon-Trent C Stke 64 G3
Stoke Wake Dorset 11 J3
Stoke Wharf Worcs 52 H7
Stolford Somset 21 K4
Stondon Massey Essex 33 Q2
Stone Bucks 43 R9
Stone Gloucs 29 K3
Stone Kent 33 Q7
Stone Rothm 78 F6
Stone Somset 22 D6
Stone Staffs 64 G5
Stone Worcs 52 F5
Stonea Cambs 57 J2
Stone Allerton Somset 21 N3
Ston Easton Somset 22 E3
Stonebridge N Som 28 E10
Stonebridge Norfk 58 D2
Stonebridge Warwks 53 N4
Stone Bridge Corner C Pete 68 E12
Stonebroom Derbys 78 C11
Stone Chair Calder 84 H9
Stone Cross E Susx 15 P5
Stone Cross E Susx 15 R10
Stone Cross E Susx 16 B4
Stone Cross Kent 15 P3
Stone Cross Kent 17 J3
Stone Cross Kent 35 P11
Stonecross Green Suffk 58 B9
Stonecrouch Kent 16 C4
Stone-edge-Batch N Som 28 G8
Stoneferry C KuH 87 L9
Stonefield Castle Hotel Ag & B 112 C7
Stonegate E Susx 16 B5
Stonegate N York 92 F5
Stonegrave N York 92 D11
Stonehall Worcs 52 G11
Stonehaugh Nthumb 99 M3
Stonehaven Abers 133 L7
Stonehenge Wilts 23 P5
Stone Hill Donc 78 H2
Stonehouse C Plym 4 G6
Stone House Cumb 90 C9
Stonehouse Gloucs 41 N10
Stonehouse Nthumb 99 K6
Stonehouse S Lans 114 D12
Stone in Oxney Kent 16 G5
Stoneleigh Warwks 53 Q6
Stoneley Green Ches E 63 Q2
Stonely Cambs 56 B7
Stoner Hill Hants 25 M8
Stonesby Leics 67 K7
Stonesfield Oxon 43 J8
Stones Green Essex 47 L6
Stone Street Kent 33 Q11
Stone Street Suffk 46 G4
Stone Street Suffk 46 H3
Stone Street Suffk 59 M4
Stonestreet Green Kent 17 J3
Stonethwaite Cumb 88 H4
Stonewells Moray 139 P3
Stonewood Kent 33 Q8
Stoneybridge W Isls 152 b10
Stoneybridge Worcs 52 H5
Stoneyburn W Loth 114 H8
Stoney Cross Hants 12 D2
Stoneygate C Leic 66 G11
Stoneyhills Essex 34 G3
Stoneykirk D & G 94 F7
Stoney Middleton Derbys 77 N8
Stoney Stanton Leics 54 D2
Stoney Stoke Somset 22 F7
Stoney Stratton Somset 22 F5

Stoney Stretton Shrops 63 L10
Stoneywood C Aber 133 L2
Stoneywood Falk 114 K5
Stonham Aspal Suffk 58 H8
Stonnall Staffs 65 K11
Stonor Oxon 31 Q5
Stonton Wyville Leics 55 J2
Stony Cross Herefs 51 P7
Stony Cross Herefs 52 D11
Stonyford Hants 24 E10
Stony Houghton Derbys ...78 E10
Stony Stratford M Keyn ...43 R4
Stonywell Staffs 65 K9
Stoodleigh Devon 19 M7
Stoodleigh Devon 20 E9
Stop 24 Services Kent 17 K3
Stopham W Susx 14 E7
Stopsley Luton 44 G7
Stoptide Cnwll 6 D9
Storeton Wirral 75 J7
Storeyard Green Herefs ...41 L3
Stornoway W Isls 152 g3
Stornoway Airport W Isls .152 g3
Storridge Herefs 52 D11
Storrington W Susx 14 H8
Storth Cumb 89 M10
Storwood E R Yk 86 D6
Stotfield Moray 147 M11
Stotfold C Beds 45 J4
Stottesdon Shrops 52 C4
Stoughton Leics 66 G11
Stoughton Surrey 32 D12
Stoughton W Susx 13 P2
Stoulton Worcs 52 G10
Stourbridge Dudley 52 G4
Stourhead Wilts 22 H6
Stourpaine Dorset 11 L3
Stourport-on-Severn
  Worcs 52 E6
Stour Provost Dorset 22 H9
Stour Row Dorset 22 H9
Stourton Leeds 85 K9
Stourton Staffs 52 F4
Stourton Warwks 42 G4
Stourton Wilts 22 H6
Stourton Caundle Dorset ..22 G10
Stout Somset 21 P7
Stove Shet 147 i9
Stoven Suffk 59 N4
Stow Border 116 B12
Stow Lincs 79 L7
Stow Bardolph Norfk 69 M11
Stow Bedon Norfk 58 E1
Stowbridge Norfk 69 L10
Stow-cum-Quy Cambs 57 K8
Stowe Gloucs 40 H10
Stowe Shrops 51 K6
Stowe by Chartley Staffs ..65 J7
Stowehill Nhants 54 C9
Stowell Somset 22 F9
Stowey BaNES 29 J10
Stowford Devon 7 N5
Stowford Devon 9 L7
Stowford Devon 19 M5
Stowlangtoft Suffk 58 E7
Stow Longa Cambs 56 B6
Stow Maries Essex 34 E2
Stowmarket Suffk 58 F9
Stow-on-the-Wold
  Gloucs 42 E6
Stowting Kent 17 K2
Stowting Common Kent 17 K2
Stowupland Suffk 58 G8
Straanruie Highld 131 J1
Strachan Abers 132 G6
Strachur Ag & B 112 G1
Stradbroke Suffk 59 J6
Stradbrook Wilts 23 K3
Stradishall Suffk 57 P10
Stradsett Norfk 69 M11
Stragglethorpe Lincs 67 M2
Stragglethorpe Notts 66 G5
Straight Soley Wilts 30 G8
Straiton Mdloth 115 N8
Straiton S Ayrs 104 G9
Straloch Abers 141 L11
Straloch P & K 131 J11
Stramshall Staffs 65 K11
Strang IoM 102 e5
Strangeways Salfd 76 F4
Strangford Herefs 41 J6
Stranraer D & G 94 F6
Strata Florida Cerdgn 49 N7
Stratfield Mortimer
  W Berk 31 N9
Stratfield Saye Hants 31 P10
Stratfield Turgis Hants 31 P10
Stratford C Beds 56 D11
Stratford Gt Lon 33 M5
Stratford St Andrew
  Suffk 59 M8
Stratford St Mary Suffk 47 J5
Stratford sub Castle
  Wilts 23 P7
Stratford Tony Wilts 23 N8
Stratford-upon-Avon
  Warwks 53 M9
Strath Highld 143 L9
Strathan Highld 144 D1
Strathan Highld 149 M4
Strathaven S Lans 114 C12
Strathblane Stirlg 113 Q5
Strathcanaird Highld 144 E5
Strathcarron Highld 136 C7
Strathcoil Ag & B 120 C7
Strathdon Abers 131 Q2
Strathkinness Fife 125 J9
Strathloanhead W Loth ...114 G7
Strathmashie House
  Highld 129 Q6
Strathmiglo Fife 124 E11
Strathpeffer Highld 137 N4
Strathtay P & K 123 M2
Strathwhillan N Ayrs 103 Q3
Strathy Highld 150 H3
Strathy Inn Highld 150 E3
Strathyre Stirlg 122 F9
Stratton Cnwll 7 J3
Stratton Dorset 10 M8
Stratton Gloucs 42 B11
Stratton Audley Oxon 43 M6
Stratton-on-the-Fosse
  Somset 22 F3
Stratton St Margaret
  Swindn 30 E5
Stratton St Michael Norfk ..59 J2
Stratton Strawless Norfk ...71 J8
Stream Somset 20 G5
Streat E Susx 15 L8
Streatham Gt Lon 33 K8
Streatley C Beds 44 F6
Streatley W Berk 31 M6
Street Devon 9 M7
Street Lancs 83 M5
Street N York 92 E6
Street Somset 21 N6
Street Ashton Warwks 54 D4
Street Dinas Shrops 63 K6
Street End E Susx 16 C9
Street End Kent 35 L11
Street End W Susx 13 P5
Street Gate Gatesd 100 G6
Streethay Staffs 65 L10
Street Houses N York 85 Q6

Streetlam N York 91 M7
Street Lane Derbys 66 C3
Streetly Wsall 53 K1
Streetly End Cambs 57 L11
Street on the Fosse
  Somset 22 E5
Stretford Shrops 51 M3
Strelitz P & K 124 D5
Strelley Notts 66 E4
Strensall C York 86 B3
Strensham Worcs 41 Q4
Strensham Services
  (northbound) Worcs 41 P3
Strensham Services
  (southbound) Worcs 41 P4
Stretcholt Somset 21 L4
Strete Devon 5 P7
Stretford Herefs 51 M9
Stretford Herefs 51 N9
Stretford Traffd 76 E5
Strethall Essex 45 N4
Stretham Cambs 57 K6
Strettington W Susx 14 C9
Stretton Ches W 63 M2
Stretton Derbys 78 C11
Stretton Rutlnd 67 N9
Stretton Staffs 64 G10
Stretton Staffs 65 N7
Stretton Warrtn 76 B7
Stretton en le Field Leics ..65 P10
Stretton Grandison
  Herefs 41 K3
Stretton-on-Dunsmore
  Warwks 54 C6
Stretton on Fosse
  Warwks 42 E4
Stretton Sugwas Herefs ...40 G3
Stretton under Fosse
  Warwks 54 D4
Stretton Westwood
  Shrops 51 Q1
Strichen Abers 141 M5
Strines Stockp 76 H6
Stringston Somset 21 J3
Strixton Nhants 55 M8
Stroat Gloucs 28 H3
Strollamus Highld 135 K10
Stroma Highld 151 Q1
Stromeferry Highld 136 B9
Stromness Ork 147 b4
Stronaba Highld 128 H7
Stronachlachar Stirlg 122 C10
Stronafian Ag & B 112 F5
Strone Ag & B 113 J5
Strone Highld 128 G8
Strone Highld 137 P10
Stronmilchan Ag & B 121 M7
Stronsay Ork 147 e3
Stronsay Airport Ork 147 e3
Strontian Highld 127 P12
Strood Kent 16 E4
Strood Medway 34 C8
Strood Green Surrey 14 H1
Strood Green W Susx 14 E4
Stroud Gloucs 41 N10
Stroud Hants 25 M8
Stroude Surrey 32 E8
Stroud Green Essex 34 F4
Stroud Green Gloucs 41 N10
Stroxton Lincs 67 M6
Struan Highld 134 F8
Struan P & K 130 E11
Strubby Lincs 81 J7
Strumpshaw Norfk 71 M10
Strutherhill S Lans 114 D11
Struthers Fife 124 H11
Struy Highld 137 L8
Stryd-y-Facsen IoA 72 E7
Stryt-issa Wrexhm 63 J3
Stuartfield Abers 141 N7
Stubbers Green Wsall 53 K11
Stubbington Hants 13 J4
Stubbins Lancs 84 B11
Stubbs Green Norfk 59 K1
Stubhampton Dorset 23 K10
Stubley Derbys 77 Q8
Stubshaw Cross Wigan 75 P4
Stubton Lincs 67 L2
Stuckton Hants 23 Q10
Studfold N York 84 B1
Stud Green W & M 32 C7
Studham C Beds 44 E8
Studholme Cumb 98 B7
Studland Dorset 11 P8
Studley Warwks 53 K8
Studley Wilts 29 Q8
Studley Common Warwks ..53 K8
Studley Roger N York 85 L1
Studley Royal N York 85 L1
Studley Royal Park &
  Fountains Abbey
  N York 85 K2
Stuntney Cambs 57 K5
Stunts Green E Susx 16 A8
Sturbridge Staffs 64 F6
Sturgate Lincs 79 L6
Sturmer Essex 46 C3
Sturminster Common
  Dorset 22 H11
Sturminster Marshall
  Dorset 11 M5
Sturminster Newton
  Dorset 22 H10
Sturry Kent 35 L9
Sturton N Linc 79 N3
Sturton by Stow Lincs 79 M7
Sturton le Steeple Notts ...79 K7
Stuston Suffk 58 H5
Stutton N York 85 P7
Stutton Suffk 47 L5
Styal Ches E 76 F6
Stydd Lancs 83 P8
Stynie Moray 139 Q4
Styrrup Notts 78 G5
Succoth Ag & B 121 P11
Suckley Worcs 52 D10
Suckley Green Worcs 52 D10
Sudborough Nhants 55 N4
Sudbourne Suffk 59 N10
Sudbrook Lincs 67 N3
Sudbrook Mons 28 G9
Sudbrooke Lincs 79 P8
Sudbury Derbys 65 M5
Sudbury Gt Lon 32 H5
Sudbury Suffk 46 F3
Sudden Rochdl 76 G1
Sudgrove Gloucs 41 Q10
Suffield N York 93 K8
Suffield Norfk 71 J5
Sugdon Wrekin 63 Q9
Sugnall Staffs 64 E6
Sugwas Pool Herefs 40 F3
Suisnish Highld 135 K11
Sulby IoM 102 d3
Sulgrave Nhants 43 L3
Sulham W Berk 31 N6
Sulhamstead W Berk 31 N8
Sulhamstead Abbots
  W Berk 31 N8
Sulhamstead Bannister
  W Berk 31 N8
Sullington W Susx 14 F7
Sullom Shet 147 i5
Sullom Voe Shet 147 i5
Sully V Glam 27 Q8

Sumburgh Airport Shet ..147 i10
Summerbridge N York 85 J3
Summercourt Cnwll 3 L3
Summerfield Norfk 69 P4
Summerfield Worcs 52 F6
Summer Heath Bucks 31 Q4
Summerhill Pembks 37 M9
Summerhill Staffs 65 K11
Summer Hill Wrexhm 63 K1
Summerhouse Darltn 91 M3
Summerlands Cumb 89 N3
Summerley Derbys 78 B8
Summersdale W Susx 14 B9
Summerseat Bury 84 B12
Summertown Oxon 43 L10
Summit Oldham 76 G2
Summit Rochdl 84 D11
Sunbiggin Cumb 89 Q5
Sunbury-on-Thames
  Surrey 32 G8
Sundaywell D & G 96 G3
Sunderland Ag & B 110 F8
Sunderland Cumb 97 M11
Sunderland Lancs 83 K4
Sunderland Bridge Dur ...100 H10
Sundhope Border 107 J5
Sundon Park Luton 44 F6
Sundridge Kent 33 N11
Sunk Island E R Yk 87 P11
Sunningdale W & M 32 D9
Sunninghill W & M 32 D9
Sunningwell Oxon 31 K2
Sunniside Dur 100 F10
Sunniside Gatesd 100 G6
Sunny Brow Dur 100 F11
Sunnyhill C Derb 65 Q6
Sunnyhurst Bl w D 83 P10
Sunnylaw Stirlg 114 E2
Sunnymead Oxon 43 L9
Sunton Wilts 24 D2
Surbiton Gt Lon 32 H9
Surfleet Lincs 68 E6
Surfleet Seas End Lincs 68 E6
Surlingham Norfk 71 L11
Surrex Essex 46 F7
Sustead Norfk 71 J5
Susworth Lincs 79 L3
Sutcombe Devon 7 L3
Sutcombemill Devon 7 L3
Sutterby Lincs 81 K8
Sutterton Lincs 68 E4
Sutton C Beds 45 J2
Sutton C Pete 68 B12
Sutton Cambs 56 H5
Sutton Devon 5 D4
Sutton Donc 78 F1
Sutton E Susx 15 P11
Sutton Gt Lon 33 J9
Sutton Kent 35 P12
Sutton N York 85 P10
Sutton Norfk 71 M7
Sutton Notts 67 J5
Sutton Oxon 43 J10
Sutton Pembks 36 H7
Sutton Shrops 52 D3
Sutton Shrops 63 N10
Sutton Shrops 64 C6
Sutton St Hel 75 P5
Sutton Suffk 47 P2
Sutton W Susx 14 D8
Sutton Abinger Surrey 14 G2
Sutton-at-Hone Kent 33 Q8
Sutton Bassett Nhants 55 J2
Sutton Benger Wilts 29 Q6
Sutton Bingham Somset 10 E2
Sutton Bonington Notts 66 E7
Sutton Bridge Lincs 69 J8
Sutton Cheney Leics 66 C12
Sutton Coldfield Birm 53 L1
Sutton Courtenay Oxon 31 L3
Sutton Crosses Lincs 68 H7
Sutton cum Lound Notts 78 H7
Sutton Fields Notts 66 E7
Sutton Green Surrey 32 E11
Sutton Green Wrexhm 63 M3
Sutton Howgrave N York ...91 M11
Sutton-in-Ashfield Notts ...78 F10
Sutton-in-Craven N York ...84 F6
Sutton in the Elms Leics ...54 E2
Sutton Lane Ends Ches E ...76 H9
Sutton Maddock Shrops 64 D12
Sutton Mallet Somset 21 N6
Sutton Mandeville Wilts 23 L7
Sutton Manor St Hel 75 P5
Sutton Marsh Herefs 40 H3
Sutton Montis Somset 22 E9
Sutton-on-Hull C KuH 87 L8
Sutton on Sea Lincs 81 K7
Sutton-on-the-Forest
  N York 86 A2
Sutton on the Hill Derbys ..65 N5
Sutton on Trent Notts 79 K10
Sutton Poyntz Dorset 10 H8
Sutton St Edmund Lincs 68 H9
Sutton St James Lincs 68 H8
Sutton St Nicholas
  Herefs 40 H3
Sutton Scotney Hants 24 H6
Sutton Street Kent 34 E11
Sutton-under-Brailes
  Warwks 42 G4
Sutton-under-
  Whitestonecliffe
  N York 91 Q10
Sutton upon Derwent
  E R Yk 86 D6
Sutton Valence Kent 16 E1
Sutton Veny Wilts 23 K5
Sutton Waldron Dorset 23 B4
Sutton Weaver Ches W 75 P8
Sutton Wick BaNES 28 D7
Sutton Wick Oxon 31 K3
Swaby Lincs 80 G8
Swadlincote Derbys 65 P8
Swaffham Norfk 70 B10
Swaffham Bulbeck
  Cambs 57 L8
Swaffham Prior Cambs 57 L8
Swafield Norfk 71 K6
Swainby N York 91 Q6
Swainshill Herefs 40 F3
Swainsthorpe Norfk 71 J12
Swainswick BaNES 29 M8
Swalcliffe Oxon 42 H4
Swalecliffe Kent 35 K9
Swallow Lincs 80 D3
Swallow Beck Lincs 79 N10
Swallowcliffe Wilts 23 M7
Swallowfield Wokham 31 P9
Swallownest Rothm 78 B6
Swallows Cross Essex 33 R3
Swampton Hants 24 G3
Swanage Dorset 11 P9
Swanbourne Bucks 44 A6
Swanbridge V Glam 27 R9
Swancote Shrops 52 D2
Swan Green Ches W 76 D9
Swanland E R Yk 87 J9
Swanley Kent 33 P8
Swanley Village Kent 33 P8
Swanmore Hants 25 K10

Swannington Leics 66 C9
Swannington Norfk 70 H8
Swanpool Lincs 79 N10
Swanscombe Kent 33 R7
Swansea Swans 26 F8
Swansea Airport Swans 26 E4
Swansea West Services
  Swans 26 F2
Swan Street Essex 46 F6
Swanton Abbot Norfk 71 K7
Swanton Morley Norfk 70 F8
Swanton Novers Norfk 70 F6
Swanton Street Kent 34 F10
Swan Valley Sandw 53 J2
Swan Village Sandw 53 J2
Swanwick Derbys 66 C2
Swanwick Hants 13 J5
Swarby Lincs 67 P4
Swardeston Norfk 71 J11
Swarkestone Derbys 66 B6
Swarland Nthumb 109 K9
Swarraton Hants 25 J6
Swartha C Brad 84 F6
Swarthmoor Cumb 88 H11
Swaton Lincs 68 C3
Swavesey Cambs 56 G7
Sway Hants 12 D5
Swayfield Lincs 67 N7
Swaythling C Sotn 24 G10
Sweet Green Worcs 52 C8
Sweetham Devon 8 G5
Sweethaws E Susx 15 N4
Sweetlands Corner Kent ...16 D2
Sweets Cnwll 6 H5
Sweetshouse Cnwll 3 Q2
Swefling Suffk 59 L8
Swepstone Leics 66 B10
Swerford Oxon 42 H5
Swettenham Ches E 76 E10
Swffryd Blae G 28 B3
Swift's Green Kent 16 F2
Swilland Suffk 59 J10
Swillbrook Lancs 83 L8
Swillington Leeds 85 M9
Swimbridge Devon 19 M7
Swimbridge Newland
  Devon 19 L7
Swinbrook Oxon 42 G9
Swincliffe Kirk 85 J9
Swincliffe N York 85 K4
Swincombe Devon 19 N5
Swindale Cumb 89 N4
Swinden N York 84 C4
Swinderby Lincs 79 L11
Swindon Gloucs 41 Q7
Swindon Nthumb 108 F10
Swindon Staffs 52 F3
Swindon Swindn 30 D5
Swine E R Yk 87 L8
Swinefleet E R Yk 86 E10
Swineford S Glos 29 L8
Swineshead Bed 55 Q7
Swineshead Lincs 68 E3
Swineshead Bridge
  Lincs 68 D4
Swiney Highld 151 M9
Swinford Leics 54 F5
Swinford Oxon 43 J10
Swingfield Minnis Kent 17 M2
Swingfield Street Kent 17 M2
Swingleton Green Suffk 46 G2
Swinhoe Nthumb 109 K4
Swinhope Lincs 80 D4
Swinithwaite N York 90 H9
Swinmore Common
  Herefs 41 K3
Swinscoe Staffs 65 L3
Swinside Cumb 88 H2
Swinstead Lincs 67 P7
Swinthorpe Lincs 79 P8
Swinton Border 117 J11
Swinton N York 91 L11
Swinton N York 92 F12
Swinton Rothm 78 D4
Swinton Salfd 76 E3
Swithland Leics 66 F9
Swordale Highld 137 Q3
Swordland Highld 127 P6
Swordly Highld 150 D4
Sworton Heath Ches E 76 C7
Swydd-ffynnon Cerdgn 49 M7
Swyncombe Oxon 31 P4
Swynnerton Staffs 64 F5
Swyre Dorset 10 E7
Sycharth Powys 62 H7
Sychnant Powys 50 D9
Sychtyn Powys 62 C10
Sydallt Wrexhm 63 K1
Syde Gloucs 41 Q9
Sydenham Gt Lon 33 L8
Sydenham Oxon 43 Q11
Sydenham Damerel
  Devon 7 M9
Sydenhurst Surrey 14 D4
Syderstone Norfk 70 B6
Sydling St Nicholas
  Dorset 10 F5
Sydmonton Hants 31 K10
Sydnal Lane Shrops 64 E11
Syerston Notts 67 J3
Syke Rochdl 84 D12
Sykehouse Donc 86 B11
Syleham Suffk 59 J5
Sylen Carmth 38 D10
Symbister Shet 147 j6
Symington S Ayrs 104 G3
Symington S Lans 106 C3
Symondsbury Dorset 10 C6
Symonds Yat (East)
  Herefs 40 H8
Symonds Yat (West)
  Herefs 40 H8
Sympson Green C Brad 85 J7
Synderford Dorset 10 B4
Synod Inn Cerdgn 48 F9
Syre Highld 149 P8
Syreford Gloucs 42 B7
Syresham Nhants 43 N3
Syston Leics 66 G10
Syston Lincs 67 M4
Sytchampton Worcs 52 F7
Sywell Nhants 55 K7

T

Tabley Hill Ches E 76 D8
Tackley Oxon 43 K7
Tacolneston Norfk 58 H2
Tadcaster N York 85 P6
Taddington Derbys 77 L9
Taddington Gloucs 42 C5
Taddiport Devon 19 J9
Tadley Hants 31 M10
Tadlow Cambs 56 F11
Tadmarton Oxon 43 J4
Tadwick BaNES 29 L8
Tadworth Surrey 33 J11
Tafarnaubach Blae G 39 Q9
Tafarn-y-bwlch Pembks 37 L3
Tafarn-y-Gelyn Denbgs 74 G11
Taff's Well Rhondd 27 N7
Tafolwern Powys 62 B11
Taibach Neath 26 H6
Taibach Neath 26 H6
Tain Highld 146 F3
Tain Highld 151 M3
Tai'n Lôn Gwynd 60 G2
Tairbeart W Isls 152 e5
Tai'r Bull Powys 39 N6
Tairgwaith Neath 38 H9
Takeley Essex 45 Q7
Takeley Street Essex 45 Q7
Talachddu Powys 39 P5
Talacre Flints 74 F7
Talaton Devon 9 K5
Talbenny Pembks 36 G8
Talbot Green Rhondd 27 N6
Talbot Village BCP 11 P6
Taleford Devon 9 L5
Talerddig Powys 62 C12
Talgarreg Cerdgn 48 G10
Talgarth Powys 39 R5
Talisker Highld 134 F10
Talke Staffs 64 F2
Talke Pits Staffs 64 F2
Talkin Cumb 98 G2
Talladale Highld 143 N11
Talla Linnfoots Border 106 F6
Tallaminnock S Ayrs 104 G10
Tallarn Green Wrexhm 63 M3
Teesside Park S on T 91 Q3
Tallentire Cumb 97 L11
Talley Carmth 38 F5
Tallington Lincs 68 B10
Tallwrn Wrexhm 63 J3
Talmine Highld 149 M4
Talog Carmth 37 Q5
Talsarn Cerdgn 49 J9
Talsarn Powys 49 J9
Talsarnau Gwynd 61 K5
Talskiddy Cnwll 6 C11
Talwrn IoA 72 H8
Talwrn Wrexhm 63 L3
Tal-y-bont Cerdgn 49 L3
Tal-y-bont Conwy 73 N10
Tal-y-bont Gwynd 61 K8
Tal-y-bont Gwynd 73 K9
Talybont-on-Usk Powys 39 Q7
Tal-y-Cafn Conwy 73 N10
Tal-y-coed Mons 40 F8
Talygarn Rhondd 27 N6
Tal-y-llyn Gwynd 61 M10
Talysarn Gwynd 60 H2
Tal-y-Waun Torfn 40 C10
Talywern Powys 61 M11
Tamar Valley Mining
  District Devon 4 F3
Tamer Lane End Wigan 76 B3
Tamerton Foliot C Plym 4 G4
Tamworth Staffs 65 M1
Tamworth Green Lincs 68 G4
Tamworth Services
  Warwks 65 N12
Tancred N York 85 P3
Tancredston Pembks 36 G5
Tandridge Surrey 33 L12
Tanfield Dur 100 F7
Tanfield Lea Dur 100 F7
Tangasdale W Isls 152 b13
Tangiers Pembks 37 J7
Tangley Hants 24 E3
Tangmere W Susx 14 C9
Tan Hill N York 90 E5
Tankerness Ork 147 d4
Tankersley Barns 77 Q4
Tankerton Kent 35 K9
Tannach Highld 151 P7
Tannachie Abers 133 J7
Tannadice Angus 125 J1
Tanner's Green Worcs 53 K6
Tannington Suffk 59 J7
Tannochside N Lans 114 C9
Tansley Derbys 77 Q11
Tansor Nhants 55 Q2
Tantobie Dur 100 F7
Tanton N York 92 B5
Tanwood Worcs 52 G6
Tanworth in Arden
  Warwks 53 L6
Tan-y-Bwlch Gwynd 61 L4
Tan-y-fron Conwy 74 C11
Tan-y-fron Wrexhm 63 J2
Tan-y-grisiau Gwynd 61 M3
Tan-y-groes Cerdgn 48 D10
Taobh Tuath W Isls 152 d6
Taplow Bucks 32 C6
Tarbert Ag & B 111 H11
Tarbert Ag & B 112 C2
Tarbert W Isls 152 e5
Tarbet Ag & B 121 Q12
Tarbet Highld 127 P6
Tarbet Highld 148 E12
Tarbock Green Knows 75 M6
Tarbolton S Ayrs 104 H4
Tarbrax S Lans 115 J10
Tardebigge Worcs 53 J7
Tarfside Abers 132 D8
Tarland Abers 132 D3
Tarleton Lancs 83 K11
Tarlscough Lancs 83 K12
Tarlton Gloucs 29 Q3
Tarnock Somset 21 M3
Tarns Cumb 97 M8
Tarnside Cumb 89 L8
Tarporley Ches W 75 P11
Tarr Somset 20 D7
Tarrant Crawford Dorset ..11 M4
Tarrant Gunville Dorset 23 M10
Tarrant Hinton Dorset 11 M4
Tarrant Keyneston Dorset ..11 M4
Tarrant Launceston
  Dorset 11 M4
Tarrant Monkton Dorset ...11 M4
Tarrant Rawston Dorset 11 M4
Tarrant Rushton Dorset 11 M4
Tarrel Highld 146 F3
Tarring Neville E Susx 15 N10
Tarrington Herefs 41 K3
Tarskavaig Highld 127 K2
Tarves Abers 141 L9
Tarvin Ches W 75 N10
Tarvin Sands Ches W 75 N10
Tasburgh Norfk 59 J2
Tasley Shrops 52 C2
Taston Oxon 42 H7
Tatenhill Staffs 65 M8
Tathall End M Keyn 44 B2
Tatham Lancs 83 N2
Tathwell Lincs 80 F7
Tatsfield Surrey 33 M11
Tattenhall Ches W 75 M12
Tatterford Norfk 70 C6
Tattersett Norfk 70 C6
Tattershall Lincs 80 D12
Tattershall Bridge Lincs 68 D1
Tattershall Thorpe Lincs ...80 D11
Tattingstone Suffk 47 K4
Tattingstone White
  Horse Suffk 47 L4
Tatton Park Ches E 76 D7
Tatworth Somset 9 Q3
Tauchers Moray 140 B6
Taunton Somset 21 K8
Taunton Deane Services
  Somset 21 K9
Tavelty Abers 133 K1
Taverham Norfk 70 H9
Taverners Green Essex 45 Q8
Tavernspite Pembks 37 N8
Tavistock Devon 7 N10
Taw Green Devon 8 E5
Tawstock Devon 19 L7
Taxal Derbys 77 J8
Tay Bridge C Dund 124 H7
Tain Highld 146 F3

Taychreggan Hotel
  Ag & B 121 K8
Tay Forest Park P & K 130 E12
Tayinloan Ag & B 111 P12
Taynton Gloucs 41 L7
Taynton Oxon 42 F9
Taynuilt Ag & B 121 J6
Tayport Fife 125 J7
Tayvallich Ag & B 111 Q4
Tealby Lincs 80 C5
Tealing Angus 124 H5
Team Valley Gatesd 100 G5
Teangue Highld 127 M2
Teanord Highld 137 Q3
Tebay Cumb 89 Q6
Tebay Services Cumb 89 P5
Tebworth C Beds 44 E6
Tedburn St Mary Devon 8 F6
Teddington Gloucs 41 Q5
Teddington Gt Lon 32 H8
Tedstone Delamere
  Herefs 52 C9
Tedstone Wafer Herefs 52 C9
Teesport R & Cl 92 B2
Teesside Park S on T 91 Q3
Teeton Nhants 54 G7
Teffont Evias Wilts 23 L7
Teffont Magna Wilts 23 L7
Tegryn Pembks 37 P4
Teigh Rutlnd 67 L9
Teigncombe Devon 8 C7
Teigngrace Devon 8 F10
Teignmouth Devon 8 H10
Telford Wrekin 64 C10
Telford Services Shrops 64 D10
Tellisford Somset 22 H2
Telscombe E Susx 15 M10
Telscombe Cliffs E Susx 15 M10
Tempar P & K 122 H1
Templand D & G 97 M1
Temple Cnwll 6 H10
Temple Mdloth 115 P9
Temple Balsall Solhll 53 N5
Temple Bar Cerdgn 49 J9
Temple Cloud BaNES 29 J10
Temple Ewell Kent 17 N2
Temple Grafton Warwks 53 L9
Temple Guiting Gloucs 42 C6
Temple Herdewyke
  Warwks 54 C10
Temple Hirst N York 86 B10
Temple Normanton
  Derbys 78 C10
Temple of Fiddes Abers ...133 K8
Temple Sowerby Cumb 89 Q1
Templeton Devon 20 D10
Templeton Pembks 37 M8
Templetown Dur 100 E8
Tempsford C Beds 56 D10
Tenbury Wells Worcs 51 Q7
Tenby Pembks 37 M10
Tendring Essex 47 L7
Tendring Green Essex 47 L6
Tendring Heath Essex 47 K7
Tenpenny Heath Essex 47 K7
Tenterden Kent 16 F4
Terling Essex 46 D8
Ternhill Shrops 64 B6
Terregles D & G 97 J3
Terrington N York 86 C1
Terrington St Clement
  Norfk 69 K8
Terrington St John Norfk ...69 K8
Terry's Green Warwks 53 L6
Teston Kent 34 C11
Testwood Hants 24 F10
Tetbury Gloucs 29 P3
Tetbury Upton Gloucs 29 P3
Tetchill Shrops 63 L5
Tetcott Devon 7 L5
Tetford Lincs 80 F9
Tetney Lincs 80 G3
Tetney Lock Lincs 80 G3
Tetsworth Oxon 43 P11
Tettenhall Wolves 64 G12
Tettenhall Wood Wolves ...64 G12
Teversal Notts 78 D11
Teversham Cambs 57 J9
Teviothead Border 107 L8
Tewin Herts 45 K8
Tewin Wood Herts 45 K8
Tewkesbury Gloucs 41 P5
Teynham Kent 34 G9
Thackley C Brad 85 J7
Thackthwaite Cumb 88 F2
Thackthwaite Cumb 89 L2
Thainstone Abers 141 J12
Thakeham W Susx 14 G7
Thame Oxon 43 P10
Thames Ditton Surrey 32 H9
Thamesmead Gt Lon 33 N6
Thamesport Medway 34 F7
Thanington Kent 35 L11
Tharston Norfk 59 J2
Thatcham W Berk 31 L9
Thatto Heath St Hel 75 N5
Thaxted Essex 45 R5
Theakston N York 91 M9
Thealby N Linc 86 G11
Theale Somset 21 N4
Theale W Berk 31 N8
Thearne E R Yk 87 K8
The Bank Ches E 76 F12
The Beeches Gloucs 42 B11
Theberton Suffk 59 N7
The Blythe Staffs 65 K6
The Bog Shrops 51 K1
The Bourne Worcs 52 H9
The Braes Highld 135 J9
The Bratch Staffs 52 F3
The Broad Herefs 51 N8
The Broads 71 F9
The Brunt E Loth 116 F4
The Bryn Mons 40 C9
The Bungalow IoM 102 d4
The Burf Worcs 52 F7
The Butts Gloucs 41 Q9
The Camp Gloucs 41 Q9
The Chequer Wrexhm 63 M3
The City Bed 56 B9
The City Bucks 31 B3
The Common Oxon 42 G9
The Common Wilts 24 D7
The Common Wilts 30 B5
The Corner Kent 16 C2
The Cronk IoM 102 d3
The Deep C KuH 87 L9
The Den N Ayrs 113 L11
The Forge Herefs 51 K9
The Forstal Kent 16 G2
The Fouralls Shrops 64 C6
The Green Cumb 88 G10
The Green Cumb 88 G3
The Green Essex 46 D8
The Green N York 92 H5
The Green Wilts 23 J6
The Grove Worcs 41 P3

The Haven W Susx 14 F5
The Haw Gloucs 41 N6
The Headland Hartpl 101 M11
The Hendre Mons 40 F9
The Hill Cumb 88 G10
The Holt Wokham 32 A7
The Hundred Herefs 51 N8
Thelbridge Cross Devon 8 E2
The Leacon Kent 16 H4
The Lee Bucks 44 C11
The Lhen IoM 102 d2
Thelnetham Suffk 58 F5
The Lochs Moray 139 P3
Thelveton Norfk 58 H4
Thelwall Warrtn 76 C6
The Marsh Powys 51 K1
Themelthorpe Norfk 70 F7
The Middles Dur 100 F7
The Moor Kent 16 C6
The Mumbles Swans 26 F5
The Murray S Lans 114 B10
The Mythe Gloucs 41 P5
The Narth Mons 40 H10
The Neuk Abers 132 H5
Thenford Nhants 43 L3
Theobald's Green Wilts 29 R8
The Quarry Gloucs 29 L2
The Quarter Kent 16 F2
The Reddings Gloucs 41 P7
Therfield Herts 45 L4
The Rhôs Pembks 40 A5
The Ross P & K 123 K8
The Sands Surrey 14 C2
The Shoe Wilts 29 N7
The Smithies Shrops 52 C1
The Spring Warwks 53 P6
The Square Torfn 28 C3
The Stair Kent 15 R1
The Stocks Kent 16 F5
The Straits Hants 25 N5
The Strand Wilts 29 Q10
Thetford Norfk 58 C4
Thetford Forest Park 57 Q3
Thethwaite Cumb 98 D9
The Towans Cnwll 2 E7
The Vauld Herefs 51 P10
Theydon Bois Essex 33 N2
Theydon Mount Essex 33 P2
Thickwood Wilts 29 N7
Thimbleby Lincs 80 E9
Thimbleby N York 91 Q7
Thingwall Wirral 75 J7
Thirkleby N York 91 Q11
Thirlby N York 91 R10
Thirlestane Border 116 D11
Thirn N York 91 L9
Thirsk N York 91 Q10
Thirtleby E R Yk 87 M8
Thistleton Lancs 83 K7
Thistleton Rutlnd 67 M8
Thistley Green Suffk 57 M5
Thixendale N York 86 F3
Thockrington Nthumb 99 Q2
Tholomas Drove Cambs 68 H11
Tholthorpe N York 85 P2
Thomas Chapel Pembks 37 L9
Thomas Close Cumb 98 E10
Thomastown Abers 140 E8
Thompson Norfk 58 D1
Thong Kent 34 B8
Thongsbridge Kirk 77 M2
Thoralby N York 90 H9
Thoresby Notts 78 G9
Thoresthorpe Lincs 81 J8
Thoresway Lincs 80 D4
Thorganby Lincs 80 D3
Thorganby N York 86 C6
Thorgill N York 92 E7
Thorington Suffk 59 N6
Thorington Street Suffk 46 H4
Thorlby N York 84 E5
Thorley Herts 45 N8
Thorley IoW 12 F7
Thorley Houses Herts 45 N7
Thorley Street IoW 12 F7
Thormanby N York 91 R11
Thornaby-on-Tees S on T ..91 Q3
Thornage Norfk 70 F5
Thornborough Bucks 43 Q5
Thornborough N York 91 M10
Thornbury C Brad 85 J8
Thornbury Devon 7 M3
Thornbury Herefs 51 Q8
Thornbury S Glos 29 K4
Thornby Cumb 98 B6
Thornby Nhants 54 F6
Thorncliff Staffs 77 J12
Thorncombe Dorset 10 B4
Thorncombe Street
  Surrey 14 E2
Thorncott Green C Beds 56 C11
Thorncross IoW 12 G8
Thorndon Suffk 58 H7
Thorndon Cross Devon 7 N4
Thorne Donc 78 H1
Thorne Coffin Somset 10 E2
Thornecroft Devon 5 N3
Thornehillhead Devon 18 H11
Thorner Leeds 85 M7
Thornes Staffs 65 K1
Thorne St Margaret
  Somset 20 H9
Thorney Bucks 32 E6
Thorney C Pete 68 F11
Thorney Notts 79 L9
Thorney Somset 21 P8
Thorney Hill Hants 12 B5
Thorney Island W Susx 13 N4
Thorney Toll Cambs 68 G11
Thornfalcon Somset 21 K8
Thornford Dorset 22 E10
Thorngrafton Nthumb 99 J6
Thorngrove Somset 21 M7
Thorngumbald E R Yk 87 N10
Thornham Norfk 69 P3
Thornham Magna Suffk 58 G6
Thornham Parva Suffk 58 G6
Thornhaugh C Pete 68 C12
Thornhill Caerph 27 N6
Thornhill Cumb 88 D5
Thornhill D & G 105 R12
Thornhill Derbys 77 M7
Thornhill Kirk 85 L11
Thornhill Stirlg 114 B1
Thornhills Calder 84 H10
Thornholme E R Yk 87 L1
Thornicombe Dorset 11 L4
Thornley Dur 100 F9
Thornley Dur 101 J10
Thornliebank E Rens 113 Q9
Thorns Suffk 57 N9
Thornsett Derbys 77 J5
Thornthwaite Cumb 97 K9
Thornthwaite N York 85 J4
Thornton Angus 124 G1
Thornton Bucks 43 Q6
Thornton C Brad 84 H8
Thornton E R Yk 86 E6

Thornton Fife 115 P2
Thornton Lancs 82 H7
Thornton Leics 66 D10
Thornton Lincs 80 E10
Thornton Middsb 91 Q4
Thornton Nthumb 117 L11
Thornton Pembks 36 H9
Thornton Sefton 75 K3
Thornton Curtis N Linc 87 K11
Thorntonhall S Lans 113 R10
Thornton Heath Gt Lon 33 L8
Thornton Hough Wirral 75 J7
Thornton-in-Craven N York 84 D5
Thornton in Lonsdale N York 89 R12
Thornton-le-Beans N York 91 P8
Thornton-le-Clay N York 86 C2
Thornton-le-Dale N York 92 G10
Thornton le Moor Lincs 79 P4
Thornton-le-Moor N York 91 P9
Thornton-le-Moors Ches W 75 M9
Thornton-le-Street N York 91 P9
Thorntonloch E Loth 116 G6
Thornton Rust N York 90 F9
Thornton Steward N York 91 K9
Thornton Watlass N York 91 M9
Thornwood Common Essex 45 N10
Thornydykes Border 116 E11
Thornythwaite Cumb 89 L2
Thoroton Notts 67 J4
Thorp Arch Leeds 85 N6
Thorpe Derbys 65 M2
Thorpe E R Yk 87 J4
Thorpe Lincs 81 J7
Thorpe N York 84 F3
Thorpe Norfk 59 N1
Thorpe Notts 67 J2
Thorpe Surrey 32 E8
Thorpe Abbotts Norfk 59 J5
Thorpe Acre Leics 67 K8
Thorpe Arnold Leics 67 K8
Thorpe Audlin Wakefd 85 N2
Thorpe Bassett N York 92 H12
Thorpe Bay Sthend 34 G5
Thorpe by Water Rutlnd 55 M1
Thorpe Common Rothm 78 C5
Thorpe Constantine Staffs 65 N10
Thorpe End Norfk 71 K10
Thorpe Green Essex 47 L2
Thorpe Green Lancs 83 N10
Thorpe Green Suffk 58 D9
Thorpe Hesley Rothm 78 B4
Thorpe in Balne Donc 78 F2
Thorpe Langton Leics 55 J2
Thorpe Larches Dur 91 P2
Thorpe Lea Surrey 32 E8
Thorpe le Fallows Lincs 79 P9
Thorpe-le-Soken Essex 47 L7
Thorpe le Street E R Yk 86 F6
Thorpe Malsor Nhants 55 L5
Thorpe Mandeville Nhants 43 K5
Thorpe Market Norfk 71 K5
Thorpe Marriot Norfk 58 D10
Thorpe Morieux Suffk 58 D10
Thorpeness Suffk 59 P8
Thorpe on the Hill Leeds 85 L10
Thorpe on the Hill Lincs 79 N9
Thorpe Park Surrey 32 E8
Thorpe St Andrew Norfk 71 K10
Thorpe St Peter Lincs 81 J11
Thorpe Salvin Rothm 78 E7
Thorpe Satchville Leics 67 J10
Thorpe Thewles S on T 91 P3
Thorpe Tilney Lincs 80 C12
Thorpe Underwood N York 85 P3
Thorpe Underwood Nhants 55 K4
Thorpe Waterville Nhants 55 N4
Thorpe Willoughby N York 86 A9
Thorpland Norfk 69 M10
Thorrington Essex 47 K7
Thorverton Devon 8 H4
Thrales End C Beds 44 G8
Thrandeston Suffk 58 G5
Thrapston Nhants 55 P5
Threapland Cumb 97 N10
Threapwood Ches W 63 M3
Threapwood Staffs 65 J4
Threapwood Head Staffs 65 J4
Threave S Ayrs 104 F8
Three Ashes Herefs 40 G2
Three Bridges W Susx 15 K3
Three Burrows Cnwll 3 J5
Three Chimneys Kent 16 E3
Three Cocks Powys 40 A4
Three Crosses Swans 26 E3
Three Cups Corner E Susx 16 B7
Three Gates Worcs 52 C8
Threehammer Common Norfk 71 L8
Three Hammers Cnwll 7 J7
Three Holes Norfk 69 K12
Threekingham Lincs 68 B5
Three Leg Cross E Susx 16 B4
Three Legged Cross Dorset 11 Q4
Three Mile Cross Wokham 31 P9
Threemilestone Cnwll 3 K5
Threemiletown W Loth 115 K6
Three Oaks E Susx 16 E8
Threlkeld Cumb 89 J2
Threshers Bush Essex 45 P10
Threshfield N York 84 E12
Thrigby Norfk 71 P9
Thringarth Dur 90 H2
Thringstone Leics 66 C8
Thrintoft N York 91 N8
Thriplow Cambs 45 N2
Throapham Rothm 78 E6
Throckenhalt Lincs 68 G10
Throcking Herts 45 L6
Throckley N u Ty 100 E5
Throckmorton Worcs 52 B11
Throop BCP 11 Q6
Throop Dorset 11 K6
Throphill Nthumb 100 E1
Thropton Nthumb 108 G9
Throsk Stirlg 114 F3
Througham Gloucs 41 Q10
Throughgate D & G 96 H1
Throwleigh Devon 8 G6
Throwley Kent 34 H11
Throwley Forstal Kent 34 H11
Thrumpton Notts 66 E6
Thrumpton Notts 78 H7
Thrumster Highld 151 P7
Thrunscoe NE Lin 80 F2
Thrunton Nthumb 108 H7
Thrupp Oxon 30 G3
Thrupp Gloucs 41 P11
Thrupp Oxon 43 K8
Thrushelton Devon 7 N7
Thrussington Leics 66 G9
Thruxton Hants 24 D4
Thruxton Herefs 40 F5

Thrybergh Rothm 78 D5
Thulston Derbys 66 C6
Thundersley Essex 34 D5
Thurcaston Leics 66 F10
Thurcroft Rothm 78 E6
Thurdon Cnwll 7 K3
Thurgarton Norfk 71 J5
Thurgarton Notts 66 H2
Thurgoland Barns 77 P3
Thurlaston Leics 66 E12
Thurlaston Warwks 54 D6
Thurlbear Somset 21 L9
Thurlby Lincs 68 B9
Thurlby Lincs 79 M11
Thurlby Lincs 81 J8
Thurleigh Bed 55 Q9
Thurlestone Devon 5 L8
Thurloxton Somset 21 L7
Thurlstone Barns 77 N3
Thurlton Norfk 59 N1
Thurlwood Ches E 76 G12
Thurmaston Leics 66 G11
Thurnby Leics 66 G11
Thurne Norfk 71 N9
Thurnham Kent 34 E10
Thurning Nhants 56 B4
Thurning Norfk 70 G6
Thurnscoe Barns 78 D3
Thursby Cumb 98 C8
Thursden Lancs 84 D8
Thursford Norfk 70 E5
Thursley Surrey 14 C3
Thurso Highld 151 K3
Thurstaston Wirral 74 H7
Thurston Suffk 58 D7
Thurston Clough Oldham 76 H2
Thurstonfield Cumb 98 C7
Thurstonland Kirk 77 M2
Thurston Planch Suffk 58 D8
Thurton Norfk 71 L12
Thurvaston Derbys 65 N5
Thuxton Norfk 70 F10
Thwaite N York 90 E7
Thwaite Suffk 58 G7
Thwaite Head Cumb 89 K8
Thwaites C Brad 84 G7
Thwaite St Mary Norfk 59 L2
Thwaites Brow C Brad 84 G7
Thwing E R Yk 87 K1
Tibbermore P & K 123 Q8
Tibbers D & G 105 Q10
Tibberton Gloucs 41 M7
Tibberton Worcs 52 G9
Tibberton Wrekin 64 C8
Tibenham Norfk 58 H3
Tibshelf Derbys 78 D11
Tibshelf Services Derbys 78 D11
Tibthorpe E R Yk 86 H4
Ticehurst E Susx 16 C5
Tichborne Hants 25 J7
Tickencote Rutlnd 67 N10
Tickenham N Som 28 F8
Tickford End M Keyn 44 C3
Tickhill Donc 78 F5
Ticklerton Shrops 51 N2
Ticknall Derbys 66 B7
Tickton E R Yk 87 K7
Tidbury Green Solhll 53 L5
Tidcombe Wilts 30 G10
Tiddington Oxon 43 N10
Tiddington Warwks 53 N9
Tiddleywink Wilts 29 P7
Tidebrook E Susx 16 C5
Tideford Cnwll 4 E5
Tideford Cross Cnwll 4 E5
Tidenham Gloucs 28 H3
Tideswell Derbys 77 M8
Tidmarsh W Berk 31 N7
Tidmington Warwks 42 F4
Tidpit Hants 23 N9
Tidworth Wilts 24 D4
Tiers Cross Pembks 36 H8
Tiffield Nhants 54 H10
Tigerton Angus 132 E11
Tigh a' Ghearraidh W Isls 152 b8
Tigharry W Isls 152 b8
Tighnabruaich Ag & B 112 E7
Tigley Devon 5 M4
Tilbrook Cambs 55 Q7
Tilbury Thurr 34 B7
Tilbury Dock Thurr 34 B7
Tilbury Green Essex 46 D3
Tilbury Juxta Clare Essex 46 D4
Tile Cross Birm 53 L3
Tile Hill Covtry 53 P5
Tilehouse Green Solhll 53 M5
Tilehurst Readg 31 N7
Tilford Surrey 14 B2
Tilgate W Susx 15 K4
Tilgate Forest Row W Susx 15 J4
Tilham Street Somset 22 D6
Tillers Green Gloucs 41 L5
Tillicoultry Clacks 114 G2
Tillietudlem S Lans 114 E12
Tillingham Essex 46 H11
Tillington Herefs 40 G3
Tillington W Susx 14 D6
Tillington Common Herefs 40 F3
Tillybirloch Abers 132 G3
Tillyfourie Abers 132 G2
Tillygreig Abers 141 L11
Tillyrie P & K 124 C11
Tilmanstone Kent 35 N12
Tilney All Saints Norfk 69 L8
Tilney High End Norfk 69 L8
Tilshead Wilts 23 L4
Tilstock Shrops 63 P5
Tilston Ches W 63 M3
Tilstone Bank Ches W 75 P11
Tilstone Fearnall Ches W 75 P11
Tilsworth C Beds 44 D7
Tilton on the Hill Leics 67 J11
Tiltups End Gloucs 29 N3
Tilty Essex 45 Q6
Timberland Lincs 80 C12
Timbersbrook Ches E 76 G11
Timberscombe Somset 20 E5
Timble N York 85 J4
Timewell Devon 20 E8
Timpanheck D & G 98 C3
Timperley Traffd 76 E6
Timsbury BaNES 29 K10
Timsbury Hants 24 E8
Timsgarry W Isls 152 d3
Timsgearraidh W Isls 152 d3
Timworth Suffk 58 C7
Timworth Green Suffk 58 C7
Tincleton Dorset 11 J6
Tindale Cumb 99 J6
Tingewick Bucks 43 N5
Tingley Leeds 85 L10
Tingrith C Beds 44 E4
Tingwall Airport Shet 147 i7
Tingwall Ork 147 c3
Tinhay Devon 7 M7
Tinker's Hill Hants 24 F4
Tinkersley Derbys 77 P10
Tinsley Sheff 78 D7
Tinsley Green W Susx 15 K3
Tintagel Cnwll 6 F7
Tintern Mons 28 H2
Tintinhull Somset 22 C9

Tintwistle Derbys 77 J4
Tinwald D & G 97 K2
Tinwell Rutlnd 67 P11
Tippacott Devon 19 P4
Tipp's End Norfk 57 K2
Tiptoe Hants 12 D5
Tipton Sandw 52 H2
Tipton Green Sandw 52 H2
Tipton St John Devon 9 L4
Tiptree Essex 46 F8
Tiptree Heath Essex 46 F8
Tirabad Powys 39 L3
Tircoed Swans 26 F2
Tiree Ag & B 118 E4
Tiree Airport Ag & B 118 D4
Tiretigan Ag & B 111 Q9
Tirley Gloucs 41 N6
Tiroran Ag & B 119 N7
Tirphil Caerph 39 Q11
Tirril Cumb 89 N11
Tisbury Wilts 23 L7
Tisman's Common W Susx 14 F4
Tissington Derbys 65 M2
Titchberry Devon 18 E8
Titchfield Hants 13 J4
Titchfield Common Hants 13 J4
Titchmarsh Nhants 55 P5
Titchwell Norfk 69 P3
Tithby Notts 66 H5
Titley Herefs 51 K8
Titmore Green Herts 45 J6
Titsey Surrey 33 M11
Titson Cnwll 7 J4
Tittensor Staffs 64 G4
Tittleshall Norfk 70 C8
Titton Worcs 52 F6
Tiverton Ches W 75 P11
Tiverton Devon 20 E10
Tivetshall St Margaret Norfk 58 H3
Tivetshall St Mary Norfk 58 H3
Tivington Somset 20 E4
Tivy Dale Barns 77 P2
Tixall Staffs 64 H7
Tixover Rutlnd 67 N12
Toab Shet 147 i10
Toadhole Derbys 78 C12
Toadmoor Derbys 65 Q2
Tobermory Ag & B 119 N2
Toberonochy Ag & B 120 D11
Tobha Mòr W Isls 152 b10
Tocher Abers 140 H9
Tochieneal Moray 140 D3
Tockenham Wilts 30 B6
Tockenham Wick Wilts 30 B6
Tocketts R & Cl 92 C3
Tockholes Bl w D 83 P10
Tockington S Glos 29 J5
Tockwith N York 85 P5
Todber Dorset 22 H9
Todburn Nthumb 109 J10
Toddington C Beds 44 E6
Toddington Gloucs 42 B5
Toddington Services C Beds 44 E6
Todds Green Herts 45 J6
Todenham Gloucs 42 F4
Todhills Angus 124 H5
Todhills Cumb 98 D6
Todhills Dur 100 G3
Todhills Rest Area Cumb 98 D6
Todmorden Calder 84 D10
Todwick Rothm 78 E7
Toft Cambs 56 G9
Toft Ches E 76 E8
Toft Lincs 67 Q8
Toft Shet 147 i5
Toftwood Norfk 70 E9
Toft Hill Dur 91 K1
Toft Hill Lincs 80 E11
Toft Monks Norfk 59 N2
Toft next Newton Lincs 79 P6
Toftrees Norfk 70 C6
Toftwood Norfk 70 E10
Togston Nthumb 109 L9
Tokavaig Highld 127 L2
Tokers Green Oxon 31 P7
Tolastadh bho Thuath W Isls 152 h2
Toldish Cnwll 3 M3
Tolland Somset 20 H7
Tollard Farnham Dorset 23 L10
Tollard Royal Wilts 23 L10
Toll Bar Donc 78 F2
Tollbar End Covtry 54 B5
Toller Fratrum Dorset 10 E5
Toller Porcorum Dorset 10 E5
Tollerton N York 85 Q2
Tollerton Notts 66 G5
Toller Whelme Dorset 10 D4
Tollesbury Essex 46 G9
Tolleshunt D'Arcy Essex 46 G9
Tolleshunt Knights Essex 46 G9
Tolleshunt Major Essex 46 F9
Tollingham E R Yk 86 F8
Toll of Birness Abers 141 N9
Tolpuddle Dorset 11 J6
Tolworth Gt Lon 32 H9
Tomatin Highld 138 G10
Tomchrasky Highld 129 J2
Tomdoun Highld 128 G4
Tomich Highld 137 K10
Tomich Highld 137 P6
Tomich Highld 145 N4
Tomich Highld 146 C11
Tomintoul Moray 139 M12
Tomlow Warwks 54 D8
Tomnacross Highld 137 N7
Tomnavoulin Moray 139 M10
Tompkin Staffs 64 H2
Ton Mons 28 D2
Ton Mons 28 E3
Tonbridge Kent 15 Q2
Tondu Brdgnd 27 L5
Tonedale Somset 20 H9
Tonfanau Gwynd 61 J11
Tong C Brad 85 J9
Tong Kent 34 G11
Tong Shrops 64 E10
Tong W Isls 152 g3
Tonge Leics 66 C7
Tong Green Kent 34 H11
Tongham Surrey 14 C1
Tongland D & G 96 E7
Tong Norton Shrops 64 E10
Tongue Highld 149 M5
Tongue End Lincs 68 C8
Tongwynlais Cardif 27 M6
Tonmawr Neath 27 J3
Tonna Neath 27 J3
Ton-teg Rhondd 27 P5
Tonwell Herts 45 L8
Tonypandy Rhondd 27 N4
Tonyrefail Rhondd 27 N5
Toot Baldon Oxon 31 M4
Toot Hill Essex 45 P11
Toothill Swindn 30 D6
Tooting Gt Lon 33 J8
Tooting Bec Gt Lon 33 K8
Topcliffe N York 91 P11
Topcroft Norfk 59 K2
Topcroft Street Norfk 59 K2
Top End Bed 55 P8

Topham Donc 86 B11
Top of Hebers Rochdl 76 F2
Toppesfield Essex 46 C4
Toprow Norfk 58 H1
Topsham Devon 8 H7
Top-y-rhos Flints 75 J12
Torbeg N Ayrs 103 N4
Torboll Highld 146 D5
Torbreck Highld 138 B7
Torbryan Devon 5 N3
Torcastle Highld 128 G8
Torcross Devon 5 N8
Tore Highld 137 Q5
Torfrey Cnwll 3 Q4
Torinturk Ag & B 112 B8
Torksey Lincs 79 L8
Torlundy Highld 128 G8
Tormarton S Glos 29 M6
Tormore N Ayrs 103 N3
Tornagrain Highld 138 E6
Tornaveen Abers 132 F3
Torness Highld 137 Q3
Toronto Dur 100 G12
Torpenhow Cumb 97 P10
Torphichen W Loth 114 H7
Torphins Abers 132 F4
Torpoint Cnwll 4 G6
Torquay Torbay 6 A10
Torquhan Border 116 B11
Torr Highld 5 Q4
Torran Highld 135 K6
Torrance E Duns 114 B6
Torranyard N Ayrs 104 F1
Torre Somset 20 G5
Torridon Highld 136 C5
Torridon House Highld 136 B4
Torrin Highld 135 K11
Torrisdale Highld 149 M4
Torrisdale Ag & B 103 L3
Torrish Highld 146 H1
Torrisholme Lancs 83 K2
Torroble Highld 145 N4
Torry C Aber 133 M3
Torryburn Fife 115 J4
Torteval Guern 12 b3
Torthorwald D & G 97 L3
Tortington W Susx 14 E10
Torton Worcs 52 F6
Tortworth S Glos 29 L4
Torvaig Highld 135 J7
Torver Cumb 89 J8
Torwood Falk 114 F4
Torwoodlee Border 107 M3
Torworth Notts 78 G6
Tosberry Devon 18 E9
Toscaig Highld 135 N8
Toseland Cambs 56 E8
Tosside Lancs 84 A4
Tostock Suffk 58 D8
Totaig Highld 134 C6
Tote Highld 134 G6
Tote Highld 135 J4
Tote Hill W Susx 14 B6
Totford Hants 25 J6
Tothill Lincs 80 H7
Totland IoW 12 E7
Totley Sheff 77 P8
Totley Brook Sheff 77 P7
Totnes Devon 5 N5
Toton Notts 66 E5
Totronald Ag & B 118 G2
Totscore Highld 134 G3
Tottenham Gt Lon 33 L4
Tottenhill Norfk 69 M10
Totteridge Gt Lon 33 J3
Totternhoe C Beds 44 D7
Tottington Bury 76 E1
Tottleworth Lancs 83 Q9
Totton Hants 24 F10
Touchen End W & M 32 C7
Toulston N York 85 P6
Toulton Somset 21 K7
Toulvaddie Highld 146 F9
Tovil Kent 34 D11
Towan Cnwll 3 P5
Towan Cnwll 6 C10
Toward Ag & B 112 H7
Toward Quay Ag & B 112 G7
Towcester Nhants 54 H11
Towednack Cnwll 2 D7
Tower of London Gt Lon 33 L6
Towersey Oxon 43 Q10
Towie Abers 132 C2
Tow Law Dur 100 E10
Town End Cambs 56 H2
Town End Cumb 89 L10
Town End Cumb 89 Q2
Townend W Duns 113 M6
Towngate Cumb 98 D9
Towngate Lincs 68 C10
Town Green Lancs 75 L3
Town Green Norfk 71 M9
Town Head Barns 77 M3
Town Head Cumb 89 L6
Townhead Cumb 97 M11
Townhead D & G 97 Q3
Townhead D & G 106 C12
Town Head N York 84 B3
Townhead of Greenlaw D & G 96 C7
Townhill Fife 115 K3
Town Kelloe Dur 101 J11
Townlake Devon 7 M9
Town Lane Wigan 76 C4
Town Littleworth E Susx 15 M7
Town of Lowton Wigan 75 Q4
Town Row E Susx 15 Q5
Townsend Somset 21 P8
Townshend Cnwll 2 F8
Town Street Suffk 57 P3
Townwell S Glos 29 L4
Town Yetholm Border 108 C4
Towthorpe C York 86 B3
Towthorpe E R Yk 86 G3
Towton N York 85 P7
Towyn Conwy 74 D8
Toxteth Lpool 75 K6
Toynton All Saints Lincs 80 H11
Toynton Fen Side Lincs 80 H11
Toynton St Peter Lincs 80 H11
Toy's Hill Kent 33 N12
Trabboch E Ayrs 104 H5
Trabbochburn E Ayrs 104 H5
Traboe Cnwll 3 J9
Tracebridge Somset 20 G9
Tradespark Highld 138 F5
Trafford Park Traffd 76 E4
Trallong Powys 39 M6
Trallwng Cardif 27 M6
Tranent E Loth 115 Q7
Tranmere Wirral 75 K6
Trantelbeg Highld 150 F6
Trantlemore Highld 150 F6
Tranwell Nthumb 100 H1
Trap Carmth 38 G9
Trapp Carmth 38 G9
Traprain E Loth 116 D7
Trap's Green Warwks 53 L7
Trapshill W Berk 30 H9
Traquair Border 107 J3
Trash Green W Berk 31 M9
Trawden Lancs 84 D7
Trawscoed Cerdgn 49 L6
Trawsfynydd Gwynd 61 M5
Trealaw Rhondd 27 N4
Treales Lancs 83 L9

Trearddur Bay IoA 72 D8
Treator Cnwll 6 C9
Tre Aubrey V Glam 27 N8
Trebanog Rhondd 27 N4
Trebanos Neath 38 H11
Trebartha Cnwll 7 K9
Trebarwith Cnwll 6 F7
Trebeath Cnwll 7 J7
Trebetherick Cnwll 6 D9
Treborough Somset 20 F6
Trebudannon Cnwll 3 L2
Trebullett Cnwll 7 L8
Treburgett Cnwll 6 F9
Treburley Cnwll 7 L8
Treburrick Cnwll 6 B10
Trebyan Cnwll 3 Q2
Trecastle Powys 39 L6
Trecogo Cnwll 7 L8
Trecott Devon 8 G4
Trecwn Pembks 37 J4
Trecynon Rhondd 39 N11
Tredaule Cnwll 7 J7
Tredavoe Cnwll 2 D8
Tredegar Blae G 39 Q4
Tredethy Cnwll 6 F10
Tredington Gloucs 41 P6
Tredington Warwks 42 F3
Tredinnick Cnwll 3 B3
Tredinnick Cnwll 4 B3
Tredinnick Cnwll 4 C5
Tredinnick Cnwll 4 C5
Tredinnick Cnwll 6 D10
Tredomen Powys 39 Q5
Tredrissi Pembks 37 L2
Tredrizzick Cnwll 6 D9
Tredunnock Mons 28 E3
Tredustan Powys 39 Q5
Treen Cnwll 2 B10
Treen Cnwll 2 C7
Treesmill Cnwll 3 Q3
Treeton Rothm 78 C6
Trefasser Pembks 36 H3
Trefdraeth IoA 72 G9
Trefecca Powys 39 Q5
Trefeglwys Powys 50 C3
Trefenter Cerdgn 49 K7
Treffgarne Pembks 37 J5
Treffgarne Owen Pembks 36 G5
Treffynnon Pembks 36 G5
Trefil Blae G 39 Q3
Trefilan Cerdgn 49 J9
Trefin Pembks 36 F5
Treflach Wood Shrops 63 J6
Trefnannau Powys 62 H9
Trefnant Denbgs 74 E9
Trefonen Shrops 63 J7
Trefor Gwynd 60 F3
Trefor IoA 72 F7
Treforest Rhondd 27 P5
Trefrew Cnwll 6 G8
Trefriw Conwy 73 N11
Tregadillett Cnwll 7 K8
Tre-gagle Mons 40 H10
Tregaian IoA 72 G7
Tregare Mons 40 F9
Tregarne Cnwll 3 J10
Tregaron Cerdgn 49 L8
Tregarth Gwynd 73 K10
Tregaswith Cnwll 3 L2
Tregatta Cnwll 6 F7
Tregawne Cnwll 6 E11
Tregeare Cnwll 7 J7
Tregeiriog Wrexhm 62 G5
Tregele IoA 72 F5
Tregellist Cnwll 6 E9
Tregenna Cnwll 3 B8
Tregeseal Cnwll 2 B8
Tregew Cnwll 3 K7
Tre-Gibbon Rhondd 39 N10
Tregidden Cnwll 3 J9
Tregiskey Cnwll 3 Q4
Treglemais Pembks 36 F5
Tregole Cnwll 6 H5
Tregolls Cnwll 3 J7
Tregonce Cnwll 6 D10
Tregonetha Cnwll 3 N2
Tregony Cnwll 3 M5
Tregoodwell Cnwll 6 G8
Tregorrick Cnwll 3 Q4
Tregoss Cnwll 3 N2
Tregoyd Powys 40 C5
Tregrehan Mills Cnwll 3 P4
Tre-groes Cerdgn 38 B3
Tregullon Cnwll 3 P2
Tregunna Cnwll 6 D10
Tregunnon Cnwll 7 J8
Tregurrian Cnwll 3 L2
Tregynon Powys 50 F1
Tre-gynwr Carmth 38 B8
Trehafod Rhondd 27 N4
Trehan Cnwll 4 F5
Treharris Myr Td 27 M3
Treharrock Cnwll 6 E9
Trehemborne Cnwll 6 C10
Treherbert Carmth 38 E2
Treherbert Rhondd 27 L3
Trehunist Cnwll 4 E4
Trekenner Cnwll 7 L9
Treknow Cnwll 6 F7
Trelan Cnwll 3 J10
Trelash Cnwll 6 H7
Trelassick Cnwll 3 L4
Trelawne Cnwll 4 C6
Trelawnyd Flints 74 E8
Treleague Cnwll 3 K10
Treleaver Cnwll 3 J11
Trelech Carmth 37 P4
Trelech a'r Betws Carmth 37 P5
Treleddyd-fawr Pembks 36 E5
Trelew Cnwll 3 K7
Trelewis Myr Td 27 M3
Treligga Cnwll 6 E8
Trelights Cnwll 6 D8
Trelill Cnwll 6 E9
Trelinnoe Cnwll 7 K8
Trelion Cnwll 3 M4
Trelissick Cnwll 3 K6
Trelleck Mons 40 G10
Trelleck Grange Mons 28 G2
Trelogan Flints 74 F7
Trelow Cnwll 6 D10
Trelowarren Cnwll 2 H9
Trelowia Cnwll 4 D6
Treluggan Cnwll 4 E5
Trelystan Powys 63 J11
Tremadog Gwynd 61 J4
Tremail Cnwll 6 H8
Tremain Cerdgn 48 C11
Tremaine Cnwll 7 J7
Tremar Cnwll 4 C4
Trematon Cnwll 4 F5
Trembraze Cnwll 4 C4
Tremeirchion Denbgs 74 E9
Tremethick Cross Cnwll 2 C8
Tremore Cnwll 3 N2
Tre-Mostyn Flints 74 G8
Trenance Cnwll 3 L2
Trenance Cnwll 6 C10
Trenance Cnwll 6 D10
Trenarren Cnwll 3 P5
Trench Wrekin 64 C9
Trench Green Oxon 31 N7
Trendeal Cnwll 3 L4
Trendrine Cnwll 2 D7

Treneague Cnwll 6 E10
Trenear Cnwll 2 H8
Treneglos Cnwll 7 J7
Trenerth Cnwll 2 F7
Trenewan Cnwll 4 B6
Treneweth Cnwll 6 H6
Trengune Cnwll 6 H6
Treninnick Cnwll 3 K3
Trenoweth Cnwll 3 K7
Trent Dorset 22 D9
Trentham C Stke 64 G4
Trentishoe Devon 19 M4
Trentlock Derbys 66 D6
Trent Port Lincs 79 L7
Trent Vale C Stke 64 F3
Treoes V Glam 27 L6
Treorchy Rhondd 27 M3
Trequite Cnwll 6 E9
Tre'r-ddol Cerdgn 49 L2
Trerhyngyll V Glam 27 N7
Trerulefoot Cnwll 4 E5
Tresaith Cerdgn 48 D10
Tresawle Cnwll 3 L5
Tresco IoS b1
Trescott Staffs 52 F1
Trescowe Cnwll 2 F8
Tresean Cnwll 3 J3
Tresham Gloucs 29 M4
Treshnish Isles Ag & B 118 H5
Tresillian Cnwll 3 L5
Tresinney Cnwll 6 G8
Treskinnick Cross Cnwll 7 J5
Tresmeer Cnwll 7 J7
Tresparrett Cnwll 6 H6
Tressait P & K 130 E12
Tresta Shet 147 i6
Tresta Shet 147 k3
Treswell Notts 79 K8
Treswithian Cnwll 2 G6
Tre Taliesin Cerdgn 49 L2
Trethevey Cnwll 6 F7
Trethewey Cnwll 2 B9
Trethomas Caerph 28 A4
Trethosa Cnwll 3 M4
Trethurgy Cnwll 3 P3
Tretio Pembks 36 E5
Tretire Herefs 40 G7
Tretower Powys 40 B7
Treuddyn Flints 75 J12
Trevadlock Cnwll 7 K9
Trevalga Cnwll 6 F7
Trevalyn Wrexhm 75 L12
Trevanger Cnwll 6 D9
Trevanson Cnwll 6 E10
Trevarrack Cnwll 2 D8
Trevarren Cnwll 3 M2
Trevarrick Cnwll 3 N6
Tre-vaughan Carmth 38 B7
Trevaughan Carmth 37 N7
Treveal Cnwll 3 K5
Treveighan Cnwll 6 F9
Trevellas Downs Cnwll 3 J4
Trevelmond Cnwll 4 B4
Trevemper Cnwll 3 K3
Treveor Cnwll 3 N6
Treverbyn Cnwll 3 L5
Treverva Cnwll 3 J7
Trevescan Cnwll 2 B9
Trevethin Torfn 40 C11
Trevia Cnwll 6 G8
Trevigro Cnwll 4 E3
Trevilla Cnwll 3 K7
Trevilson Cnwll 3 L3
Treviscoe Cnwll 3 M3
Treviskey Cnwll 3 M6
Trevithick Cnwll 3 L2
Trevithick Cnwll 3 K5
Trevoll Cnwll 3 K3
Trevone Cnwll 6 C9
Trevor Wrexhm 63 J4
Trevorgans Cnwll 2 C9
Trevorrick Cnwll 6 D10
Trewalder Cnwll 6 F8
Trewalkin Powys 39 R5
Trewarmett Cnwll 6 F7
Trewassa Cnwll 6 H7
Trewavas Cnwll 2 F9
Treween Cnwll 7 J8
Trewellard Cnwll 2 B8
Trewen Cnwll 7 J8
Trewennack Cnwll 2 H9
Trewent Pembks 37 K11
Trewetha Cnwll 6 E9
Trewethern Cnwll 6 E9
Trewidland Cnwll 4 D5
Trewillis Cnwll 3 J11
Trewint Cnwll 6 H6
Trewint Cnwll 7 J8
Trewithian Cnwll 3 L7
Trewoodloe Cnwll 7 L10
Trewoon Cnwll 3 N4
Trewoon Cnwll 3 M4
Treworga Cnwll 3 L5
Treworgan Cnwll 3 K4
Treworlas Cnwll 3 L6
Treworld Cnwll 6 G7
Treworthal Cnwll 3 L7
Tre-wyn Mons 40 D7
Treyarnon Cnwll 6 B10
Treyford W Susx 14 B9
Trezaise Cnwll 3 N4
Triangle Calder 84 E10
Trickett's Cross Dorset 11 Q4
Triermain Cumb 98 H5
Triffleton Pembks 37 J6
Trillacott Cnwll 7 K7
Trimdon Dur 101 K11
Trimdon Colliery Dur 101 K11
Trimdon Grange Dur 101 K11
Trimingham Norfk 71 K4
Trimley Lower Street Suffk 47 N4
Trimley St Martin Suffk 47 N4
Trimley St Mary Suffk 47 N4
Trimpley Worcs 52 E5
Trimsaran Carmth 38 C10
Trims Green Herts 45 N8
Trimstone Devon 19 K5
Trinafour P & K 130 D11
Trinant Caerph 28 B2
Tring Herts 44 C9
Tringford Herts 44 C9
Tring Wharf Herts 44 C9
Trinity Angus 132 F12
Trinity Jersey 13 c1
Trinity Gask P & K 123 M6
Triscombe Somset 20 H6
Trislaig Highld 128 G8
Trispen Cnwll 3 L4
Tritlington Nthumb 109 K11
Troan Cnwll 3 L3
Trochry P & K 123 P5
Troedrhiwfuwch Caerph 39 Q10
Troedyraur Cerdgn 48 E11
Troedyrhiw Myr Td 27 M2
Trofarth Conwy 73 Q9
Trois Bois Jersey 13 c1

Troon Cnwll 2 G7
Troon S Ayrs 104 F4
Tropical World Roundhay Park Leeds 85 L7
Trossachs Stirlg 122 E11
Trossachs Pier Stirlg 122 E11
Troston Suffk 58 C6
Troswell Cnwll 7 J6
Trotshill Worcs 52 G9
Trottiscliffe Kent 34 B10
Trotton W Susx 25 N9
Troughend Nthumb 108 D11
Trough Gate Lancs 84 D11
Troutbeck Cumb 89 L1
Troutbeck Cumb 89 L6
Troutbeck Bridge Cumb 89 L2
Troway Derbys 78 C8
Trowbridge Wilts 29 P10
Trowell Notts 66 E4
Trowell Services Notts 66 E4
Trowle Common Wilts 29 N10
Trowley Bottom Herts 44 F9
Trowse Newton Norfk 71 K10
Troy Leeds 85 K7
Trudoxhill Somset 22 G5
Trull Somset 21 K9
Trumfleet Donc 78 F1
Trumpan Highld 134 D4
Trumpet Herefs 41 K4
Trumpington Cambs 56 H9
Trumpsgreen Surrey 32 E9
Trunch Norfk 71 K5
Trunnah Lancs 82 H6
Truro Cnwll 3 K5
Truscott Cnwll 7 K7
Trusham Devon 8 F8
Trusley Derbys 65 N5
Trusthorpe Lincs 81 K7
Trysull Staffs 52 F2
Tubney Oxon 31 J3
Tuckenhay Devon 5 N5
Tuckhill Shrops 52 E3
Tuckingmill Cnwll 2 G6
Tuckingmill Wilts 23 L7
Tuckton BCP 12 B6
Tucoyse Cnwll 3 N5
Tuddenham Suffk 57 P6
Tuddenham Suffk 59 J11
Tudeley Kent 16 A2
Tudhoe Dur 100 H11
Tudorville Herefs 41 J7
Tudweiliog Gwynd 60 D5
Tuesley Surrey 14 D2
Tufnell Park Gt Lon 33 K5
Tufton Hants 24 G4
Tufton Pembks 37 K5
Tugby Leics 67 J12
Tugford Shrops 51 P3
Tughall Nthumb 109 K4
Tullibody Clacks 114 F2
Tullich Abers 132 B5
Tullich Highld 138 B10
Tullich Highld 146 F10
Tulliemet P & K 123 P2
Tulloch Abers 141 J9
Tullochgorm Ag & B 112 G2
Tulloch Station Highld 129 L8
Tullymurdoch P & K 124 D2
Tullynessle Abers 140 E12
Tulse Hill Gt Lon 33 L8
Tumble Carmth 38 E8
Tumbler's Green Essex 46 E7
Tumby Lincs 80 E11
Tumby Woodside Lincs 80 E12
Tummel Bridge P & K 123 K4
Tunbridge Wells Kent 15 Q3
Tundergarth D & G 97 N2
Tunga W Isls 152 g3
Tungate Norfk 71 K6
Tunley BaNES 29 L10
Tunstall C Stke 64 F2
Tunstall E R Yk 87 P9
Tunstall Kent 34 F10
Tunstall Lancs 89 P12
Tunstall N York 91 L7
Tunstall Norfk 71 N10
Tunstall Staffs 64 G6
Tunstall Sundld 101 K7
Tunstall Suffk 59 M9
Tunstead Derbys 77 L8
Tunstead Norfk 71 L7
Tunworth Hants 25 L4
Tupsley Herefs 40 H4
Turgis Green Hants 25 L2
Turkdean Gloucs 42 C8
Tur Langton Leics 55 J2
Turleigh Wilts 29 N10
Turleygreen Shrops 52 E3
Turn Lancs 84 B11
Turnastone Herefs 40 E4
Turnberry S Ayrs 104 D8
Turnchapel C Plym 4 H6
Turnditch Derbys 65 P3
Turner Green Lancs 83 N9
Turner's Green E Susx 16 B7
Turners Green Warwks 53 M7
Turners Hill W Susx 15 L4
Turners Puddle Dorset 11 L6
Turnford Herts 45 L10
Turnhouse C Edin 115 L6
Turnworth Dorset 11 L3
Turriff Abers 140 H6
Turton Bottoms Bl w D 83 Q12
Turves Cambs 56 G1
Turvey Bed 55 N10
Turville Bucks 31 Q4
Turville Heath Bucks 31 Q4
Turweston Bucks 43 M4
Tushielaw Inn Border 107 J6
Tutbury Staffs 65 N6
Tutnall Worcs 53 J6
Tutshill Gloucs 28 H3
Tuttington Norfk 71 J7
Tutwell Cnwll 7 M7
Twatt Ork 147 b3
Twatt Shet 147 i6
Twechar E Duns 114 C6
Tweedmouth Nthumb 117 M10
Tweedsmuir Border 106 E3
Twelveheads Cnwll 3 J6
Twelve Oaks E Susx 16 C7
Twenty Lincs 68 C8
Twerton BaNES 29 L8
Twickenham Gt Lon 32 H7
Twigworth Gloucs 41 P8
Twineham W Susx 15 J7
Twineham Green W Susx 15 J7
Twinhoe BaNES 29 M10
Twinstead Essex 46 E4
Twitchen Devon 20 B7
Twitchen Shrops 51 L5
Twitham Kent 35 N11
Two Bridges Devon 8 E9
Two Dales Derbys 77 P11
Two Gates Staffs 65 N12
Two Mile Ash W Susx 14 H6
Two Mile Oak Cross Devon 5 P3
Two Pots Devon 19 K4
Two Waters Herts 44 F10
Twycross Leics 65 Q11
Twycross Zoo Leics 65 P11

Twyford Bucks 43 N6
Twyford Hants 24 H8
Twyford Leics 67 J10
Twyford Lincs 67 M7
Twyford Norfk 70 F7
Twyford Wokham 31 R7
Twyford Common Herefs 40 G5
Twyn-carno Caerph 39 Q10
Twynholm D & G 96 D7
Twynllanan Carmth 38 H7
Twyning Green Gloucs 41 P4
Twyn-yr-Odyn V Glam 27 Q7
Twyn-y-Sheriff Mons 40 F10
Twywell Nhants 55 N5
Tyberton Herefs 40 E4
Tyburn Birm 53 L2
Tycroes Carmth 38 F9
Ty Croes IoA 72 F8
Tycrwyn Powys 62 F8
Tydd Gote Lincs 69 J8
Tydd St Giles Cambs 68 H8
Tydd St Mary Lincs 68 H8
Tye Hants 13 M4
Tye Green Essex 45 P7
Tye Green Essex 45 Q4
Tye Green Essex 46 B3
Tyersal C Brad 85 J8
Tyldesley Wigan 76 C3
Tyler Hill Kent 35 L10
Tylers Green Bucks 32 C4
Tyler's Green Essex 45 P10
Tylers Green Surrey 33 L12
Tylorstown Rhondd 27 N3
Tylwch Powys 50 D5
Ty-nant Conwy 62 D3
Ty-nant Gwynd 62 B7
Tyndrum Stirlg 121 Q6
Ty'n-dwr Denbgs 62 H4
Tyneham Dorset 11 L8
Tynemouth N Tyne 101 K4
Tyne Tunnel S Tyne 101 J5
Tynewydd Rhondd 27 M3
Tyninghame E Loth 116 E5
Tynron D & G 105 P11
Tyn-y-bryn Rhondd 27 N5
Ty'n-y-coedcae Caerph 28 B5
Tynygongl IoA 72 H7
Tynygraig Cerdgn 49 M7
Ty'n-y-Groes Conwy 73 N9
Tyn-y-nant Rhondd 27 P5
Tyrie Abers 141 M3
Tyringham M Keyn 44 B2
Tyseley Birm 53 L4
Tythegston Brdgnd 27 K6
Tytherington Ches E 76 G8
Tytherington S Glos 29 K5
Tytherington Somset 22 H4
Tytherington Wilts 23 K5
Tytherleigh Devon 9 Q4
Tytherton Lucas Wilts 29 Q7
Tyttenhanger Herts 44 H10
Tywardreath Cnwll 3 Q4
Tywardreath Highway
  Cnwll 3 Q3
Tywyn Conwy 73 N8
Tywyn Gwynd 61 K12

Ubbeston Green Suffk 59 L6
Ubley BaNES 28 H10
Uckerby N York 91 L6
Uckfield E Susx 15 N6
Uckinghall Worcs 41 P4
Uckington Gloucs 41 Q7
Uckington Shrops 63 P10
Uddingston S Lans 114 C9
Uddington S Lans 105 Q3
Udimore E Susx 16 F7
Udny Green Abers 141 L10
Udny Station Abers 141 L11
Uffcott Wilts 30 D7
Uffculme Devon 9 Q10
Uffington Lincs 67 Q10
Uffington Oxon 30 G4
Uffington Shrops 63 N9
Ufford C Pete 68 B11
Ufford Suffk 59 L10
Ufton Warwks 54 C8
Ufton Nervet W Berk 31 N9
Ugadale Ag & B 103 L4
Ugborough Devon 5 L5
Uggeshall Suffk 59 N5
Ugglebarnby N York 92 H5
Ughill Sheff 77 N3
Ugley Essex 45 P6
Ugley Green Essex 45 P6
Ugthorpe N York 92 H4
Uibhist A Deas W Isls 152 c10
Uibhist A Tuath W Isls 152 b8
Uig Ag & B 118 G2
Uig Highld 134 C5
Uig Highld 134 G3
Uig W Isls 152 d3
Uigshader Highld 134 H6
Uisken Ag & B 119 J8
Ulbster Highld 151 P8
Ulcat Row Cumb 89 L2
Ulceby Lincs 80 H9
Ulceby N Linc 81 L12
Ulceby Skitter N Linc 87 L12
Ulcombe Kent 16 E1
Uldale Cumb 97 Q10
Uley Gloucs 29 M3
Ulgham Nthumb 109 L11
Ullapool Highld 144 E6
Ullenhall Warwks 53 L7
Ullenwood Gloucs 41 Q8
Ulleskelf N York 85 Q7
Ullesthorpe Leics 54 E3
Ulley Rothm 78 D6
Ullingswick Herefs 51 Q10
Ullinish Lodge Hotel
  Highld 134 H4
Ullock Cumb 88 E2
Ullswater Cumb 89 L3
Ullswater Steamers
  Cumb 89 L3
Ulnes Walton Lancs 83 L11
Ulpha Cumb 88 G3
Ulpha Cumb 89 M10
Ulrome E R Yk 87 M4
Ulsta Shet 147 j4
Ulting Wick Essex 46 E10
Ulva Ag & B 119 L5
Ulverley Green Solhll 53 L4
Ulverston Cumb 89 J11
Ulwell Dorset 11 N8
Ulzieside D & G 105 P8
Umberleigh Devon 19 M8
Unapool Highld 148 F10
Underbarrow Cumb 89 M8
Undercliffe C Brad 85 J8
Underling Green Kent 16 D2
Underriver Kent 33 Q12
Underwood Newpt 28 E5
Underwood Notts 66 D2
Undley Suffk 57 N4
Undy Mons 28 F5
Union Mills IoM 102 d6
Union Street E Susx 16 C4
Unst Shet 147 k2

Unstone Derbys 78 B8
Unstone Green Derbys 78 B8
Unthank Cumb 98 E8
Unthank Cumb 98 F11
Unthank Cumb 98 H10
Unthank Derbys 77 P8
Unthank Nthumb 117 M11
Upavon Wilts 23 P2
Up Cerne Dorset 10 G4
Upchurch Kent 34 E9
Upcott Herefs 51 K10
Upend Cambs 57 N9
Up Exe Devon 8 H4
Upgate Norfk 70 H8
Upgate Street Norfk 58 G2
Upgate Street Norfk 59 K2
Uphall Dorset 10 E4
Uphall W Loth 115 K7
Upham Devon 8 G3
Upham Hants 25 J9
Uphampton Herefs 51 L8
Uphampton Worcs 52 F7
Uphill N Som 28 D10
Up Holland Lancs 75 N3
Uplawmoor E Rens 113 N10
Upleadon Gloucs 41 M6
Upleatham R & Cl 92 D3
Uplees Kent 34 H9
Uploders Dorset 10 D6
Uplowman Devon 20 F10
Uplyme Devon 9 Q6
Up Marden W Susx 25 N10
Upminster Gt Lon 33 Q5
Up Mudford Somset 22 D9
Upnor Kent 34 D9
Up Nately Hants 25 M3
Upottery Devon 9 N3
Upper Affcot Shrops 51 M3
Upper Arley Worcs 52 E4
Upper Arncott Oxon 43 M8
Upper Astrop Nhants 43 L4
Upper Badcall Highld 148 E8
Upper Basildon W Berk 31 M7
Upper Batley Kirk 85 K10
Upper Beeding W Susx 14 H8
Upper Benefield Nhants 55 N3
Upper Bentley Worcs 53 J7
Upper Bighouse Highld 150 F5
Upper Birchwood Derbys 66 D1
Upper Boat Rhondd 27 Q5
Upper Boddington
  Ches W 63 M3
  Nhants 54 D10
Upper Borth Cerdgn 49 K3
Upper Brailes Warwks 42 G4
Upper Breinton Herefs 40 G4
Upper Broadheath Worcs 52 E9
Upper Broughton Notts 66 H7
Upper Bucklebury W Berk 31 L8
Upper Burgate Hants 23 P10
Upper Bush Medway 34 C9
Upperby Cumb 98 E7
Upper Caldecote C Beds 44 H2
Upper Canada N Som 28 E10
Upper Canterton Hants 24 D10
Upper Catesby Nhants 54 E9
Upper Catshill Worcs 52 H6
Upper Chapel Powys 39 N4
Upper Cheddon Somset 21 K7
Upper Chicksgrove Wilts 23 L7
Upper Chute Wilts 24 E3
Upper Clatford Hants 24 F5
Upper Coberley Gloucs 41 R8
Upper Cotton Staffs 65 K3
Upper Cound Shrops 63 P11
Upper Cudworth Barns 78 C2
Upper Cumberworth Kirk 77 N2
Upper Dallachy Moray 139 Q3
Upper Deal Kent 35 Q12
Upper Dean Bed 55 P7
Upper Denby Kirk 77 N2
Upper Denton Cumb 99 J5
Upper Dicker E Susx 15 Q9
Upper Dinchope Shrops 51 M4
Upper Dounreay Highld 150 H3
Upper Dovercourt Essex 47 M5
Upper Drumbane Stirlg 122 H11
Upper Dunsforth N York 85 N3
Upper Eashing Surrey 14 D2
Upper Eathie Highld 138 E3
Upper Egleton Herefs 41 K10
Upper Elkstone Staffs 77 K12
Upper Ellastone Staffs 65 L3
Upper End Derbys 77 K8
Upper Enham Hants 24 F4
Upper Farmcote Shrops 52 E2
Upper Farringdon Hants 25 M6
Upper Framilode Gloucs 41 M9
Upper Froyle Hants 25 N5
Upper Godney Somset 22 B5
Upper Gravenhurst
  C Beds 44 G4
Upper Green Mons 40 E8
Upper Green Suffk 57 P7
Upper Green W Berk 30 H9
Upper Grove Common
  Herefs 40 H6
Upper Hackney Derbys 77 P11
Upper Hale Surrey 25 P3
Upper Halliford Surrey 32 F8
Upper Halling Medway 34 C9
Upper Hambleton Rutlnd 67 M10
Upper Harbledown Kent 35 K10
Upper Hardres Court
  Kent 35 L12
Upper Hardwick Herefs 51 L9
Upper Hartfield E Susx 15 N4
Upper Hartshay Derbys 66 C2
Upper Hatherley Gloucs 41 Q7
Upper Hatton Staffs 64 F4
Upper Haugh Rothm 78 C4
Upper Hayton Shrops 51 N4
Upper Heaton Kirk 85 J11
Upper Helmsley N York 86 C4
Upper Hergest Herefs 51 J9
Upper Heyford Nhants 54 H8
Upper Heyford Oxon 43 K6
Upper Hill Herefs 51 M10
Upper Hockenden Kent 33 P8
Upper Hopton Kirk 85 J11
Upper Howsell Worcs 52 E11
Upper Hulme Staffs 77 J11
Upper Ifold Surrey 14 E4
Upper Inglesham Swindn 30 E2
Upper Kilcott Gloucs 29 M5
Upper Killay Swans 26 E4
Upper Kinchrackine
  Ag & B 121 M7
Upper Knockando Moray 139 M7
Upper Lambourn W Berk 30 G6
Upper Landywood Staffs 64 F10
Upper Langford N Som 28 F10
Upper Langwith Derbys 78 H8
Upper Largo Fife 124 H12
Upper Leigh Staffs 65 J5
Upper Littleton N Som 28 H8
Upper Lochton Abers 132 H5
Upper Longdon Staffs 65 K9
Upper Ludstone Shrops 52 E2
Upper Lybster Highld 151 N8
Upper Lydbrook Gloucs 41 J8
Upper Lye Herefs 40 G3
Upper Lye Herefs 51 L8
Upper Maes-coed Herefs 40 D5
Upper Midhope Sheff 77 N4

Uppermill Oldham 77 J3
Upper Milton Worcs 52 E6
Upper Minety Wilts 30 B4
Upper Moor Worcs 52 H11
Upper Moor Side Leeds 85 K9
Upper Mulben Moray 139 Q5
Upper Netchwood Shrops 51 Q2
Upper Nobut Staffs 65 K5
Upper Norwood W Susx 14 D8
Upper Padley Derbys 77 N8
Upper Pennington Hants 12 H6
Upper Pollicott Bucks 43 P9
Upper Poppleton C York 85 Q4
Upper Quinton Warwks 42 E2
Upper Ratley Hants 24 F8
Upper Rissington Gloucs 42 E7
Upper Rochford Worcs 51 Q8
Upper Ruscoe D & G 96 B6
Upper Sapey Herefs 52 C8
Upper Saxondale Notts 66 H4
Upper Seagry Wilts 29 Q6
Upper Shelton C Beds 44 E3
Upper Sheringham Norfk 70 H4
Upper Skelmorlie N Ayrs 113 J6
Upper Slaughter Gloucs 42 D7
Upper Soudley Gloucs 41 K8
Upper Spond Herefs 51 K10
Upper Standen Kent 17 M3
Upper Stanloe Bed 56 C8
Upper Stoke Norfk 71 L10
Upper Stondon C Beds 44 H5
Upper Stowe Nhants 54 G9
Upper Street Hants 23 P9
Upper Street Norfk 71 L8
Upper Street Norfk 71 L8
Upper Street Norfk 71 L8
Upper Street Suffk 47 L5
Upper Street Suffk 57 P10
Upper Street Suffk 58 G10
Upper Strensham Worcs 41 P4
Upper Sundon C Beds 44 F6
Upper Swell Gloucs 42 E6
Upper Tankersley Barns 77 Q4
Upper Tean Staffs 65 J4
Upperthong Kirk 77 L2
Upperthorpe Derbys 78 D7
Upperthorpe N Linc 79 J4
Upper Threapwood
  Ches W 63 M3
Upperton W Susx 14 D6
Uppertown Derbys 65 N2
Uppertown Dur 100 D10
Upper Town Herefs 51 P11
Uppertown Highld 151 Q1
Upper Town N Som 28 H9
Upper Town Suffk 58 D7
Upper Tumble Carmth 38 F9
Upper Tysoe Warwks 42 H3
Upper Ufford Suffk 59 K10
Upperup Gloucs 30 B3
Upper Upham Wilts 30 E7
Upper Victoria Angus 125 M5
Upper Vobster Somset 22 F3
Upper Wardington Oxon 43 K3
Upper Weald M Keyn 44 A4
Upper Weedon Nhants 54 G9
Upper Welland Worcs 41 N3
Upper Wellingham E Susx 15 N8
Upper Weybread Suffk 59 J5
Upper Wick Worcs 52 F10
Upper Wield Hants 25 K5
Upper Winchendon
  Bucks 43 Q8
Upperwood Derbys 77 P12
Upper Woodford Wilts 23 P6
Upper Wootton Hants 25 J3
Upper Wraxall Wilts 29 M7
Upper Wyche Worcs 41 M3
Uppincott Devon 8 H4
Uppingham Rutlnd 67 L12
Uppington Dorset 11 N3
Uppington Shrops 63 Q10
Upsall N York 91 Q9
Upsettlington Border 117 K12
Upshire Essex 33 N3
Upstreet Kent 35 M9
Up Sydling Dorset 10 F4
Upthorpe Suffk 58 E6
Upton Bucks 43 Q8
Upton C Pete 68 D11
Upton Cambs 56 D5
Upton Ches W 75 L10
Upton Cnwll 7 J4
Upton Cnwll 7 J4
Upton Cumb 98 C10
Upton Devon 5 Q8
Upton Devon 10 H8
Upton Dorset 11 N6
Upton Dorset 11 N6
Upton E R Yk 87 L4
Upton Halton 75 M6
Upton Hants 24 F10
Upton Hants 24 E2
Upton Leics 66 B12
Upton Lincs 79 L6
Upton Norfk 71 M8
Upton Notts 67 J1
Upton Notts 67 K2
Upton Oxon 31 L5
Upton Oxon 42 D8
Upton Pembks 37 K9
Upton R & Cl 92 F3
Upton Slough 32 D6
Upton Somset 21 P8
Upton Somset 21 P8
Upton Wakefd 78 D1
Upton Warwks 42 E2
Upton Wilts 23 J7
Upton Bishop Herefs 41 K6
Upton Cheyney S Glos 29 L8
Upton Cressett Shrops 52 C2
Upton Crews Herefs 41 K6
Upton Cross Cnwll 7 K10
Upton End C Beds 44 G5
Upton Grey Hants 25 M4
Upton Heath Ches W 75 L9
Upton Hellions Devon 8 H4
Upton Lovell Wilts 23 K6
Upton Magna Shrops 63 P9
Upton Noble Somset 22 F6
Upton Pyne Devon 8 G5
Upton St Leonards
  Gloucs 41 P8
Upton Scudamore Wilts 23 J4
Upton Snodsbury Worcs 52 H9
Upton Towans Cnwll 2 F6
Upton-upon-Severn
  Worcs 41 N4
Upton Warren Worcs 52 H7
Upwaltham W Susx 14 D8
Upware Cambs 57 K6
Upwell Norfk 69 J11
Upwey Dorset 10 G7
Upwick Green Herts 45 N7
Upwood Cambs 56 E4
Urchfont Wilts 30 B11
Urdimarsh Herefs 51 N9
Ure Bank N York 91 N12
Urlay Nook S on T 91 P4
Urmston Traffd 76 E5

Urpeth Dur 100 G7
Urquhart Moray 139 P3
Urquhart Castle Highld 137 P10
Urra N York 92 B6
Urray Highld 137 N5
Usan Angus 125 P2
Ushaw Moor Dur 100 F7
Usk Mons 28 E2
Usselby Lincs 80 B5
Usworth Sundld 100 H7
Utkinton Ches W 75 P10
Utley C Brad 84 F6
Uton Devon 8 H4
Utterby Lincs 80 F5
Uttoxeter Staffs 65 K5
Uwchmynydd Gwynd 60 B7
Uxbridge Gt Lon 32 F5
Uyeasound Shet 147 k3
Uzmaston Pembks 37 J7

Vale Guern 12 c1
Valley IoA 72 D8
Valley End Surrey 32 D9
Valley Truckle Cnwll 6 H8
Valtos Highld 135 J3
Valtos W Isls 152 e3
Vange Essex 34 C5
Varteg Torfn 40 C10
Vatsetter Shet 147 j3
Vatten Highld 134 E7
Vaynor Myr Td 39 P9
Vazon Bay Guern 12 b2
Veensgarth Shet 147 i7
Velindre Powys 40 B4
Vellow Somset 20 H5
Velly Devon 18 E8
Venngreen Devon 7 M2
Vennington Shrops 63 K10
Venn Ottery Devon 9 K6
Venny Tedburn Devon 8 H5
Venterdon Cnwll 7 L10
Ventnor IoW 13 J9
Venton Devon 5 J5
Vernham Dean Hants 30 H11
Vernham Street Hants 30 H11
Vernolds Common
  Shrops 51 N4
Verwood Dorset 11 Q3
Veryan Cnwll 3 M6
Veryan Green Cnwll 3 M6
Vicarage Devon 9 N3
Vickerstown Cumb 82 F1
Victoria Barns 77 N1
Victoria Blae G 40 A10
Victoria Cnwll 3 N3
Vidlin Shet 147 j5
Viewfield Moray 139 P3
Viewpark N Lans 114 C9
Vigo Kent 34 D11
Village de Putron Guern 12 c3
Ville la Bas Jersey 13 a1
Villiaze Guern 12 b3
Vinehall Street E Susx 16 D7
Vines Cross E Susx 15 Q7
Virginia Water Surrey 32 E9
Virginstow Devon 7 M6
Vobster Somset 22 F4
Voe Shet 147 i6
Vowchurch Herefs 40 E4
Vulcan Village St Hel 75 P5

Waberthwaite Cumb 88 E8
Wackerfield Dur 91 K2
Wacton Norfk 58 H2
Wadborough Worcs 52 G11
Waddesdon Bucks 43 Q8
Waddesdon Manor Bucks 43 Q8
Waddeton Devon 5 N6
Waddicar Sefton 75 L4
Waddingham Lincs 79 N6
Waddington Lancs 83 Q6
Waddington Lincs 79 N11
Waddon Devon 8 H8
Waddon Dorset 10 F7
Waddon Gt Lon 33 K9
Wadebridge Cnwll 6 H9
Wadeford Somset 9 Q3
Wadenhoe Nhants 55 P4
Wadesmill Herts 45 L8
Wadhurst E Susx 16 B4
Wadshelf Derbys 77 P9
Wadswick Wilts 29 M8
Wadworth Donc 78 E4
Waen Denbgs 74 D11
Waen Denbgs 74 F10
Waen Powys 62 H8
Waen Fach Powys 62 F8
Waen-pentir Gwynd 73 K10
Waen-wen Gwynd 73 K10
Wagbeach Shrops 63 L11
Wainfelin Torfn 40 C10
Wainfleet All Saints Lincs 81 J12
Wainfleet Bank Lincs 81 J12
Wainfleet St Mary Lincs 81 J12
Wainford Norfk 59 M3
Wainhouse Corner Cnwll 6 H6
Wainscott Medway 34 C8
Wain's Hill N Som 28 E8
Wainstalls Calder 84 F9
Waitby Cumb 90 B5
Waithe Lincs 80 H5
Wakefield Wakefd 85 M11
Wakehurst Place W Susx 15 L5
Wakerley Nhants 67 N12
Wakes Colne Essex 46 F6
Walberswick Suffk 59 P6
Walberton W Susx 14 D9
Walbottle N u Ty 100 F5
Walbutt D & G 96 F4
Walby Cumb 98 F6
Walcombe Somset 22 D4
Walcot Lincs 67 Q5
Walcot N Linc 86 G11
Walcot Shrops 51 K4
Walcot Swindn 30 D5
Walcot Warwks 42 E2
Walcote Leics 54 F3
Walcot Green Norfk 58 H4
Walcott Lincs 80 C12
Walcott Norfk 71 M5
Walden N York 90 G10
Walden Head N York 90 F10
Walden Stubbs N York 85 Q11
Walderslade Medway 34 D9
Walderton W Susx 13 N3
Walditch Dorset 10 D6
Waldley Derbys 65 L5
Waldridge Dur 100 G8
Waldringfield Suffk 47 N3
Waldron E Susx 15 P7
Wales Rothm 78 D5
Wales Somset 22 D8
Walesby Lincs 80 D5
Walesby Notts 78 H8
Walford Herefs 40 H6
Walford Herefs 51 L6

Walford Shrops 63 M8
Walford Staffs 64 F5
Walford Heath Shrops 63 M8
Walgherton Ches E 64 C2
Walgrave Nhants 55 K6
Walhampton Hants 12 E5
Walkden Salfd 76 D3
Walker N u Ty 100 H5
Walkerburn Border 107 K2
Walker Fold Lancs 83 P7
Walkeringham Notts 79 J5
Walkerith Lincs 79 K5
Walkern Herts 45 K6
Walker's Green Herefs 51 N11
Walker's Heath Birm 53 K5
Walkerton Fife 115 N1
Walkford BCP 12 C6
Walkhampton Devon 4 H3
Walkington E R Yk 87 J9
Walkley Sheff 77 Q6
Walk Mill Lancs 84 C9
Walkwood Worcs 53 J7
Wall Nthumb 99 P4
Wall Staffs 65 L11
Wallacetown S Ayrs 104 E5
Wallacetown S Ayrs 104 E6
Wallands Park E Susx 15 M8
Wallasey Wirral 75 J5
Wallasey (Kingsway)
  Tunnel Wirral 75 K5
Wall End Cumb 88 H10
Wall End Herefs 51 M9
Wallend Medway 34 F7
Waller's Green Herefs 41 K4
Wallhead Cumb 98 F6
Wall Heath Dudley 52 G3
Wall Houses Nthumb 100 D4
Wallingford Oxon 31 M4
Wallington Gt Lon 33 K9
Wallington Hants 13 K3
Wallington Herts 45 K5
Wallington Heath Wsall 65 K5
Wallis Pembks 37 K5
Wallisdown BCP 11 P6
Walliswood Surrey 14 G3
Walls Shet 147 h7
Wallsend N Tyne 100 H5
Wallthwaite Cumb 89 K1
Wall under Haywood
  Shrops 51 N2
Wallyford E Loth 115 Q7
Walmer Kent 35 Q12
Walmer Bridge Lancs 83 L10
Walmersley Bury 76 E1
Walmestone Kent 35 N10
Walmley Birm 53 L2
Walmley Ash Birm 53 L2
Walmsgate Lincs 80 G8
Walney Cumb 82 E2
Walpole Somset 21 M5
Walpole Suffk 59 M5
Walpole Cross Keys Norfk 69 K8
Walpole Highway Norfk 69 K8
Walpole St Andrew Norfk 69 J8
Walpole St Peter Norfk 69 J8
Walrow Somset 21 M4
Walsall Wsall 53 J1
Walsall Wood Wsall 65 K11
Walsden Calder 84 D11
Walsgrave on Sowe
  Covtry 54 C4
Walsham le Willows
  Suffk 58 E6
Walshaw Bury 76 E1
Walshford N York 85 N4
Walsoken Norfk 69 J9
Walston S Lans 115 K12
Walsworth Herts 44 H5
Walter's Ash Bucks 32 B3
Walters Green Kent 15 Q2
Walterston V Glam 27 P8
Walterstone Herefs 40 E6
Waltham Kent 17 K1
Waltham NE Lin 80 E3
Waltham Abbey Essex 33 M2
Waltham Chase Hants 25 J9
Waltham Cross Herts 33 L2
Waltham on the Wolds
  Leics 67 K7
Waltham St Lawrence
  W & M 32 B7
Waltham's Cross Essex 46 C5
Walthamstow Gt Lon 33 L4
Walton C Pete 68 D11
Walton Cumb 98 G5
Walton Derbys 78 B10
Walton Leeds 85 N6
Walton Leics 54 F3
Walton M Keyn 44 C4
Walton Powys 51 J9
Walton Somset 21 M5
Walton Suffk 47 N4
Walton Wakefd 85 M5
Walton Warwks 42 F3
Walton W Susx 13 P4
Walton Wrekin 64 A9
Walton Cardiff Gloucs 41 P5
Walton East Pembks 37 K6
Walton Elm Dorset 22 H9
Walton Grounds Nhants 43 L5
Walton Highway Norfk 69 J9
Walton-in-Gordano
  N Som 28 F7
Walton-le-Dale Lancs 83 M9
Walton-on-Thames
  Surrey 32 G9
Walton-on-the-Hill
  Staffs 64 H8
Walton-on-the-Hill
  Surrey 33 J11
Walton-on-the-Naze
  Essex 47 N7
Walton on the Wolds
  Leics 66 F8
Walton-on-Trent Derbys 65 N8
Walton Park N Som 28 E8
Walton West Pembks 36 G8
Walworth Darltn 91 L3
Walworth Gate Darltn 91 L3
Walwyn's Castle Pembks 36 G8
Wambrook Somset 9 P3
Wampool Cumb 97 P7
Wanborough Surrey 14 D1
Wanborough Swindn 30 E6
Wandon End Nhants 44 F7
Wandsworth Gt Lon 33 J7
Wangford Suffk 59 P5
Wanlip Leics 66 F8
Wanlockhead D & G 105 R7
Wannock E Susx 15 Q9
Wansford C Pete 67 Q12
Wansford E R Yk 87 K4
Wanshurst Green Kent 16 D2
Wanstead Gt Lon 33 M5
Wanstrow Somset 22 F5
Wanswell Gloucs 29 K2
Wantage Oxon 31 J4
Wants Green Worcs 52 D9

Wapley S Glos 29 L6
Wappenbury Warwks 54 B7
Wappenham Nhants 43 N3
Warbleton E Susx 15 Q7
Warborough Oxon 31 M4
Warboys Cambs 56 F5
Warbreck Bpool 82 H7
Warbstow Cnwll 7 J6
Warburton Traffd 76 C6
Warcop Cumb 90 B4
Warden Kent 35 J8
Warden Nthumb 99 P5
Ward End Birm 53 L3
Ward Green Suffk 58 F8
Ward Green Cross Lancs 83 P8
Wardhedges C Beds 44 F4
Wardington Oxon 43 K2
Wardle Ches E 75 Q12
Wardle Rochdl 84 D11
Wardley Gatesd 100 H6
Wardley Rutlnd 67 L12
Wardlow Derbys 77 M8
Wardsend Ches E 76 H7
Wardy Hill Cambs 57 J4
Ware Herts 45 L8
Wareham Dorset 11 M7
Warehorne Kent 16 H4
Warenford Nthumb 109 J4
Waren Mill Nthumb 109 J3
Warenton Nthumb 109 J4
Wareside Herts 45 M8
Waresley Cambs 56 E9
Waresley Worcs 52 F6
Ware Street Kent 34 D11
Warfield Br For 32 C8
Warfleet Devon 5 N7
Wargate Lincs 68 E6
Wargrave Wokham 31 R6
Warham Herefs 40 G4
Warham Norfk 70 D3
Wark Nthumb 99 N3
Wark Nthumb 108 D2
Warkleigh Devon 19 M9
Warkton Nhants 55 M5
Warkworth Nhants 43 K4
Warkworth Nthumb 109 L8
Warlaby N York 91 M8
Warland Calder 84 E11
Warleggan Cnwll 6 H7
Warley Town Calder 84 F9
Warlingham Surrey 33 L10
Warmbrook Derbys 65 P1
Warmfield Wakefd 85 M11
Warmingham Ches E 76 D11
Warmington Nhants 55 Q1
Warmington Warwks 54 C11
Warminster Wilts 23 J4
Warmley S Glos 29 L7
Warmsworth Donc 78 E4
Warmwell Dorset 11 J7
Warndon Worcs 52 G9
Warner Bros. Studio
  Tour 32 F2
Warnford Hants 25 K8
Warnham W Susx 14 H4
Warnham Court W Susx 14 H4
Warningcamp W Susx 14 E9
Warninglid W Susx 15 J5
Warren Ches E 76 G9
Warren Pembks 36 H11
Warrenby R & Cl 92 C2
Warrenhill S Lans 106 B2
Warren Row W & M 32 A6
Warren's Green Herts 45 K6
Warren Street Kent 34 H11
Warrington M Keyn 55 M10
Warrington Warrtn 76 B6
Warriston C Edin 115 N6
Warsash Hants 12 H3
Warslow Staffs 77 K12
Warsop Vale Notts 78 E10
Warter E R Yk 86 G5
Warthermaske N York 91 L11
Warthill N York 86 C4
Wartling E Susx 16 B8
Wartnaby Leics 66 H7
Warton Lancs 83 K3
Warton Lancs 89 M12
Warton Nthumb 108 D2
Warton Warwks 65 P11
Warwick Warwks 53 P7
Warwick Bridge Cumb 98 F6
Warwick Castle Warwks 53 P7
Warwick-on-Eden Cumb 98 F7
Warwick Services
  Warwks 53 Q9
Warwicksland Cumb 98 G3
Wasbister Ork 147 c3
Wasdale Head Cumb 88 G5
Wash Derbys 77 K7
Washall Green Herts 45 N5
Washaway Cnwll 6 H9
Washbourne Devon 5 L6
Washbrook Somset 21 N4
Washbrook Suffk 47 K3
Washfield Devon 20 E10
Washfold N York 90 H6
Washford Somset 20 G5
Washford Pyne Devon 8 F2
Washingborough Lincs 79 P9
Washington Sundld 101 J7
Washington W Susx 14 G8
Washington Services
  Gatesd 100 H7
Washwood Heath Birm 53 L3
Wasing W Berk 31 L9
Waskerley Dur 100 D9
Wasperton Warwks 53 Q9
Wasps Nest Lincs 79 Q10
Wass N York 92 B11
Wast Water Cumb 88 G5
Watchet Somset 20 G5
Watchfield Oxon 30 F3
Watchfield Somset 21 M4
Watchgate Cumb 89 N7
Watchill Cumb 97 N9
Watcombe Torbay 5 Q3
Watendlath Cumb 89 J3
Water Devon 8 E3
Water Lancs 84 C10
Waterbeach Cambs 57 J7
Waterbeach W Susx 14 C7
Waterbeck D & G 97 Q3
Waterden Norfk 70 C4
Water Eaton Oxon 43 L9
Water Eaton Staffs 64 G10
Water End Bed 56 B11
Water End E R Yk 86 E6
Water End Essex 45 Q4
Water End Herts 44 E9
Water End Herts 44 H10
Waterfall Staffs 65 J2
Waterfoot Ag & B 103 L2
Waterfoot E Rens 113 Q8
Waterford Herts 45 K8
Waterhead Cumb 89 J5
Waterheads Border 115 N11
Waterhouses Dur 100 F10
Waterhouses Staffs 65 K2
Wateringbury Kent 34 C11
Waterlane Gloucs 41 Q10
Waterloo Cnwll 6 G10
Waterloo Derbys 78 C11
Waterloo Herefs 51 K11
Waterloo Highld 135 K11
Waterloo N Lans 114 E10
Waterloo Norfk 71 J8
Waterloo P & K 123 Q5
Waterloo Pembks 37 J10
Waterloo Sefton 75 K4
Waterloo Cross Devon 20 G10
Waterloo Port Gwynd 72 H11
Waterlooville Hants 13 L3
Watermead Bucks 44 B8
Watermillock Cumb 89 M2
Water Newton Cambs 56 B1
Water Orton Warwks 53 M2
Waterperry Oxon 43 N10
Waterrow Somset 20 G8
Watersfield W Susx 14 E7
Waterside Bl w D 83 Q10
Waterside Bucks 32 D2
Waterside Cumb 97 P9
Waterside Donc 86 G9
Waterside E Ayrs 104 H8
Waterside E Ayrs 105 L3
Waterside E Duns 114 C6
Water's Nook Bolton 76 C3
Waterstein Highld 134 B6
Waterstock Oxon 43 N10
Waterston Pembks 36 H9
Water Stratford Bucks 43 N5
Water Street Neath 27 J4
Waters Upton Wrekin 64 B8
Water Yeat Cumb 89 J9
Watford Herts 32 G3
Watford Nhants 54 G7
Watford Gap Services
  Nhants 54 F7
Wath N York 84 H2
Wath N York 91 N11
Wath upon Dearne
  Rothm 78 C3
Watlington Norfk 69 M10
Watlington Oxon 31 P3
Watnall Notts 66 E3
Watten Highld 151 N6
Wattisfield Suffk 58 E6
Wattisham Suffk 58 E10
Watton Dorset 10 C6
Watton E R Yk 87 J3
Watton Norfk 70 D12
Watton-at-Stone Herts 45 K8
Watton Green Norfk 70 D12
Wattons Green Essex 33 P3
Wattston N Lans 114 D7
Wattstown Rhondd 27 N4
Wattsville Caerph 28 B4
Wauldby E R Yk 86 H9
Waulkmill Abers 132 G6
Waunarlwydd Swans 26 F3
Waunfawr Cerdgn 49 K4
Waunfawr Gwynd 73 J12
Waungron Swans 38 E11
Waunlwyd Blae G 40 A10
Wavendon M Keyn 44 C4
Waverbridge Cumb 97 P8
Waverton Ches W 75 M11
Waverton Cumb 97 P9
Wawne E R Yk 87 K8
Waxham Norfk 71 N7
Waxholme E R Yk 87 Q9
Way Kent 35 P9
Wayford Somset 9 R3
Waytown Dorset 10 D5
Way Village Devon 8 G3
Way Wick N Som 28 E10
Weacombe Somset 20 H5
Weald Oxon 42 G10
Wealdstone Gt Lon 32 H4
Weardley Leeds 85 L6
Weare Somset 21 N3
Weare Giffard Devon 19 J9
Wearhead Dur 99 N10
Wearne Somset 21 P8
Weasdale Cumb 90 B4
Weasenham All Saints
  Norfk 70 C7
Weasenham St Peter
  Norfk 70 C7
Weaste Salfd 76 E4
Weatheroak Hill Worcs 53 K6
Weaverham Ches W 75 Q9
Weaverslake Staffs 65 L8
Weaverthorpe N York 86 H1
Webbington Somset 21 N2
Webb's Heath S Glos 29 K7
Webheath Worcs 53 J7
Webton Herefs 40 F4
Wedderlairs Abers 141 K9
Wedding Hall Fold N York 84 E6
Weddington Warwks 54 B2
Wedhampton Wilts 30 C11
Wedmore Somset 21 N4
Wednesbury Sandw 53 J2
Wednesfield Wolves 64 H12
Weecar Notts 79 L10
Weedon Bucks 44 A8
Weedon Bec Nhants 54 G9
Weedon Lois Nhants 43 M2
Weeford Staffs 65 L11
Week Devon 5 N4
Week Devon 19 L8
Week Devon 19 P10
Weeke Devon 8 E3
Weeke Hants 24 H6
Weekley Nhants 55 M4
Week St Mary Cnwll 7 J6
Weel E R Yk 87 K8
Weeley Essex 47 L7
Weeley Heath Essex 47 L7
Weem P & K 123 L6
Weeping Cross Staffs 64 H6
Weethley Warwks 53 K9
Weeting Norfk 57 P3
Weeton E R Yk 87 Q9
Weeton Lancs 83 J8
Weeton N York 85 L5
Weetwood Leeds 85 K7
Weir Lancs 84 C10
Weirbrook Shrops 63 K7
Weir Quay Devon 4 F4
Weisdale Shet 147 i6
Welborne Norfk 70 F10
Welbourn Lincs 67 N1
Welburn N York 86 D2
Welbury N York 91 P6
Welby Lincs 67 M4
Welches Dam Cambs 57 J3
Welcombe Devon 18 E9
Weldon Nhants 55 M3
Weldon Bridge Nthumb 109 J11
Welford Nhants 54 G3
Welford W Berk 31 J6
Welford-on-Avon
  Warwks 53 L10
Welham Leics 55 L3
Welham Notts 79 J7
Welham Green Herts 44 H9
Well Hants 25 N4
Well Lincs 80 H8

Well – Willenhall 183

Well N York 91 M10
Welland Worcs 41 M4
Wellbank Angus 125 J5
Well End Bucks 32 C5
Well End Herts 32 H3
Wellesbourne Warwks 53 P9
Wellesbourne Mountford Warwks 53 P9
Well Head Herts 44 H6
Well Hill Kent 33 P9
Wellhouse W Berk 31 L8
Welling Gt Lon 33 N7
Wellingborough Nhants 55 M7
Wellingham Norfk 70 C8
Wellingore Lincs 79 N12
Wellington Cumb 88 E6
Wellington Herefs 51 N11
Wellington Somset 21 J9
Wellington Wrekin 64 C10
Wellington Heath Herefs 41 L4
Wellington Marsh Herefs 40 G2
Wellow BaNES 29 L10
Wellow IoW 12 F7
Wellow Notts 78 H10
Wellpond Green Herts 45 M7
Wells Somset 22 D4
Wellsborough Leics 66 B11
Wells Green Ches E 64 C1
Wells Head C Brad 84 G8
Wells-next-the-Sea Norfk 70 D3
Wellstye Green Essex 46 B8
Well Town Devon 8 G3
Welltree P & K 123 N8
Wellwood Fife 115 K3
Welney Norfk 57 K2
Welshampton Shrops 63 M5
Welsh Bicknor Herefs 41 J8
Welsh End Shrops 63 N5
Welsh Frankton Shrops 63 K5
Welsh Hook Pembks 36 H5
Welsh Newton Herefs 40 G8
Welshpool Powys 62 H10
Welsh St Donats V Glam 27 N7
Welton Cumb 98 D9
Welton E R Yk 86 H9
Welton Lincs 79 P8
Welton Nhants 54 F7
Welton le Marsh Lincs 81 J10
Welton le Wold Lincs 80 E6
Welwick E R Yk 87 Q11
Welwyn Herts 45 J8
Welwyn Garden City Herts 45 J9
Wem Shrops 63 N6
Wembdon Somset 21 L6
Wembley Gt Lon 32 H5
Wembury Devon 4 H7
Wembworthy Devon 8 C3
Wemyss Bay Inver 113 J7
Wenallt Cerdgn 49 L6
Wendens Ambo Essex 45 P4
Wendlebury Oxon 43 M8
Wendling Norfk 70 D9
Wendover Bucks 44 B10
Wendron Cnwll 2 H8
Wendron Mining District Cnwll 2 H8
Wendy Cambs 56 F11
Wenfordbridge Cnwll 6 F9
Wenhaston Suffk 59 N5
Wennington Cambs 56 E5
Wennington Gt Lon 33 P6
Wennington Lancs 83 N1
Wensley Derbys 77 N11
Wensley N York 90 H9
Wentbridge Wakefd 85 P11
Wentnor Shrops 51 L2
Wentworth Cambs 57 J5
Wentworth Rothm 78 C4
Wentworth Castle Barns 77 Q3
Wenvoe V Glam 27 Q8
Weobley Herefs 51 L10
Weobley Marsh Herefs 51 L10
Wepham W Susx 14 F9
Wereham Norfk 69 N11
Wergs Wolves 64 F12
Wern Gwynd 61 J4
Wern Powys 39 Q8
Wern Powys 63 J9
Wern Shrops 63 J5
Werneth Low Tamesd 76 H5
Wernffrwd Swans 26 D3
Wern-y-gaer Flints 74 H10
Werrington C Pete 68 C11
Werrington Cnwll 7 L7
Werrington Staffs 64 H3
Wervin Ches W 75 M9
Wesham Lancs 83 K8
Wessington Derbys 78 B12
West Aberthaw V Glam 27 N9
West Acre Norfk 69 P9
West Allerdean Nthumb 117 L12
West Alvington Devon 5 M8
West Amesbury Wilts 23 P5
West Anstey Devon 20 C8
West Appleton N York 91 L8
West Ashby Lincs 80 E9
West Ashling W Susx 13 P3
West Ashton Wilts 23 J2
West Auckland Dur 91 K2
West Ayton N York 93 K9
West Bagborough Somset 21 J6
West Bank Blae G 40 B10
West Bank Halton 75 N7
West Barkwith Lincs 80 C7
West Barnby N York 92 G4
West Barns E Loth 116 F6
West Barsham Norfk 70 D5
West Bay Dorset 10 C6
West Beckham Norfk 70 H4
West Bedfont Surrey 32 F7
Westbere Kent 35 M10
West Bergholt Essex 46 G6
West Bexington Dorset 10 E7
West Bilney Norfk 69 N9
West Blatchington Br & H 15 K9
West Boldon S Tyne 101 J6
Westborough Lincs 67 L3
Westbourne BCP 11 P6
Westbourne W Susx 13 N3
West Bourton Dorset 22 G7
West Bowling C Brad 85 J9
West Brabourne Kent 17 K2
West Bradenham Norfk 70 D10
West Bradford Lancs 83 R6
West Bradley Somset 22 D6
West Bretton Wakefd 77 P1
West Bridgford Notts 66 F5
West Briscoe Dur 90 F3
West Bromwich Sandw 53 J2
Westbrook Kent 35 P8
Westbrook W Berk 31 J8
Westbrook Wilts 29 Q9
West Buckland Devon 19 M7
West Buckland Somset 21 J9
West Burrafirth Shet 147 h6
West Burton N York 90 G9
West Burton W Susx 14 E8
Westbury Bucks 43 N4
Westbury Shrops 63 K10
Westbury Wilts 23 J3
Westbury Leigh Wilts 23 J3
Westbury-on-Severn Gloucs 41 L9
Westbury-on-Trym Bristl 28 H7
Westbury-sub-Mendip Somset 22 C3
West Butsfield Dur 100 E9
West Butterwick N Linc 79 L3
Westby Lancs 83 J9
West Byfleet Surrey 32 F10
West Cairngaan D & G 94 G12
West Caister Norfk 71 P10
West Calder W Loth 115 J8
West Camel Somset 22 D8
West Chaldon Dorset 11 J8
West Challow Oxon 30 H5
West Charleton Devon 5 M8
West Chelborough Dorset 10 E4
West Chevington Nthumb 109 L10
West Chiltington W Susx 14 F7
West Chinnock Somset 21 P10
West Chisenbury Wilts 23 P3
West Clandon Surrey 32 F11
West Cliffe Kent 17 P2
Westcliff-on-Sea Sthend 34 F5
West Coker Somset 22 C10
West Combe Devon 5 M4
Westcombe Somset 22 F5
West Compton Somset 22 D5
West Compton Abbas Dorset 10 E6
Westcote Gloucs 42 E7
Westcote Barton Oxon 43 J6
Westcott Bucks 43 P8
Westcott Devon 9 J4
Westcott Surrey 14 G1
West Cottingwith N York 86 C7
Westcourt Wilts 30 E10
West Cowick E R Yk 86 C11
West Cross Swans 26 F4
West Curry Cnwll 7 K6
West Curthwaite Cumb 98 C8
Westdean E Susx 15 P11
West Dean W Susx 14 B8
West Dean Wilts 24 D8
West Deeping Lincs 68 B10
West Derby Lpool 75 L5
West Dereham Norfk 69 M12
West Ditchburn Nthumb 109 J5
West Down Devon 19 K5
Westdown Camp Wilts 23 M4
Westdowns Cnwll 6 F8
West Drayton Gt Lon 32 F6
West Drayton Notts 78 H8
West Dunnet Highld 151 M2
Wested Kent 33 P9
West Ella E R Yk 87 J9
West End Bed 55 N10
West End Br For 32 B8
West End Caerph 28 B3
West End Cambs 56 F7
West End Cumb 98 C6
West End E R Yk 86 G9
West End E R Yk 87 M9
West End E R Yk 87 P9
Westend Gloucs 41 M10
West End Hants 24 H10
West End Hants 25 L6
West End Herts 45 J10
West End Herts 45 L10
West End Lancs 83 Q9
West End Leeds 85 K7
West End Lincs 80 G4
West End N Som 28 F8
West End N York 85 Q7
West End Norfk 70 D10
West End Norfk 71 P10
West End Oxon 31 M5
West End S Glos 29 L5
West End Somset 22 F6
West End Surrey 32 D10
West End Surrey 32 G9
West End W & M 32 B7
West End W Susx 14 H7
West End Wilts 23 K8
West End Wilts 23 L8
West End Wilts 29 R7
West End Green Hants 31 N10
Westend Town Nthumb 99 M5
Westenhanger Kent 17 K3
Wester Aberchalder Highld 137 P11
Westerdale Highld 151 L6
Westerdale N York 92 D5
Westerfield Suffk 58 H11
Westergate W Susx 14 D10
Westerham Kent 33 N11
Westerhope N u Ty 100 F5
Westerland Devon 5 P4
Westerleigh S Glos 29 L6
Western Isles W Isls 152 e6
Wester Ochiltree W Loth 115 J6
Wester Pitkierie Fife 125 L11
Wester Ross Highld 143 P9
Westerton W Susx 14 C9
Westerton of Rossie Angus 125 N2
Westerwick Shet 147 h7
West Ewell Surrey 32 H9
West Farleigh Kent 34 C11
West Farndon Nhants 54 E10
West Felton Shrops 63 K7
Westfield BaNES 22 F3
Westfield Cumb 88 C1
Westfield E Susx 16 E8
Westfield Highld 151 J4
Westfield N Lans 114 D6
Westfield Norfk 70 E10
Westfield W Loth 114 G7
Westfields Dorset 10 H3
Westfields Herefs 40 G3
Westfields of Rattray P & K 124 D3
Westfield Sole Kent 34 D10
West Flotmanby N York 93 M11
Westford Somset 20 H9
Westgate Dur 99 P10
Westgate N Linc 79 K2
Westgate Norfk 70 E4
Westgate Hill C Brad 85 J9
Westgate-on-Sea Kent 35 P8
Westgate Street Norfk 71 J8
West Ginge Oxon 31 J5
West Grafton Wilts 30 F10
West Green Hants 31 Q11
West Grimstead Wilts 24 C8
West Grinstead W Susx 14 H6
West Haddlesey N York 85 R10
West Haddon Nhants 54 G6
West Hagbourne Oxon 31 L5
West Hagley Worcs 52 G4
Westhall Suffk 59 N4
West Hallam Derbys 66 C4
West Hallam Common Derbys 66 C4
West Halton N Linc 86 G11
Westham Dorset 10 G9
Westham E Susx 16 B10
West Ham Gt Lon 33 M5
Westham Somset 21 N4
Westhampnett W Susx 14 C9
West Handley Derbys 78 C8
West Hanney Oxon 31 J4
West Hanningfield Essex 34 C2
West Harnham Wilts 23 P7
West Harptree BaNES 28 H11
West Harting W Susx 25 N9
West Hatch Somset 21 L9
West Hatch Wilts 23 K8
West Haven Angus 125 L6
Westhay Somset 21 P5
Westhead Lancs 75 M2
West Head Norfk 69 L11
West Heath Birm 53 J5
West Heath Hants 31 M10
West Helmsdale Highld 147 J2
West Hendred Oxon 31 J5
West Heslerton N York 93 J11
West Hewish N Som 28 E9
Westhide Herefs 41 J3
Westhill Abers 133 K3
West Hill Devon 9 K6
Westhill Highld 138 D7
West Hoathly W Susx 15 L4
West Holme Dorset 11 L7
Westholme Somset 22 D5
Westhope Herefs 51 M10
Westhope Shrops 51 M3
West Horndon Essex 34 A5
Westhorp Nhants 54 E10
Westhorpe Lincs 68 D6
Westhorpe Suffk 58 F7
West Horrington Somset 22 D4
West Horsley Surrey 32 F11
West Horton Nthumb 108 G4
West Hougham Kent 17 N3
Westhoughton Bolton 76 C2
Westhouse N York 89 R12
Westhouses Derbys 78 C12
West Howe BCP 11 P5
West Howetown Somset 20 E6
Westhumble Surrey 32 H12
West Huntingtower P & K 124 B8
West Huntspill Somset 21 M4
West Hyde C Beds 44 G8
West Hyde Herts 32 E4
West Hythe Kent 17 K4
West Ilkerton Devon 19 N4
West Ilsley W Berk 31 K6
West Itchenor W Susx 13 P4
West Keal Lincs 80 G11
West Kennett Wilts 30 C8
West Kilbride N Ayrs 113 J11
West Kingsdown Kent 33 Q9
West Kington Wilts 29 N7
West Kirby Wirral 74 H6
West Knapton N York 92 H11
West Knighton Dorset 10 H7
West Knoyle Wilts 23 J7
West Kyloe Nthumb 108 H2
Westlake Devon 5 K6
West Lambrook Somset 21 P9
Westland Green Herts 45 M7
West Langdon Kent 17 P1
West Lavington W Susx 14 C7
West Lavington Wilts 23 M3
West Layton N York 91 J5
West Leake Notts 66 E7
West Learmouth Nthumb 108 D2
West Lees N York 91 Q6
West Leigh Devon 8 C4
Westleigh Devon 19 J7
Westleigh Devon 20 G10
West Leigh Somset 20 H7
Westleton Suffk 59 N7
West Lexham Norfk 70 B8
Westley Shrops 63 K10
Westley Suffk 58 B8
Westley Waterless Cambs 57 M9
West Lilling N York 86 C2
Westlington Bucks 43 Q9
West Linton Border 115 L11
Westlinton Cumb 98 E5
West Littleton S Glos 29 M7
West Lockinge Oxon 31 J5
West Lulworth Dorset 11 K8
West Lutton N York 86 H1
West Lydford Somset 22 D7
West Lyn Devon 19 P4
West Lyng Somset 21 M7
West Lynn Norfk 69 L8
West Malling Kent 34 B10
West Malvern Worcs 41 M2
West Marden W Susx 25 N10
West Markham Notts 79 J9
Westmarsh Kent 35 N10
West Marsh NE Lin 80 E2
West Marton N York 84 D5
West Melbury Dorset 23 J9
West Melton Rothm 78 C3
West Meon Hants 25 L8
West Meon Hut Hants 25 L8
West Meon Woodlands Hants 25 L8
West Mersea Essex 46 H9
Westmeston E Susx 15 L8
West Mickley Nthumb 100 D6
West Midland Safari Park Worcs 52 E5
Westmill Herts 45 L6
Westmill Herts 45 L8
West Milton Dorset 10 D5
Westminster Gt Lon 33 K6
Westminster Abbey & Palace Gt Lon 33 K6
West Molesey Surrey 32 G8
West Monkton Somset 21 L7
West Moors Dorset 11 P4
West Morden Dorset 11 L6
West Morriston Border 107 P2
West Morton C Brad 84 G6
West Mudford Somset 22 D9
Westmuir Angus 124 G2
West Ness N York 92 E11
West Newbiggin Darltn 91 N3
Westnewton Cumb 97 N9
West Newton E R Yk 87 M7
West Newton Norfk 69 N6
West Newton Somset 21 L7
West Norwood Gt Lon 33 K8
Westoe S Tyne 101 K5
West Ogwell Devon 5 N3
Weston BaNES 29 L9
Weston Ches E 64 D2
Weston Devon 9 M5
Weston Devon 9 M7
Weston Dorset 10 G10
Weston Halton 75 N7
Weston Hants 25 M9
Weston Herefs 51 L9
Weston Herts 45 J5
Weston Lincs 68 F7
Weston N York 85 J6
Weston Nhants 43 M2
Weston Notts 79 K10
Weston Shrops 51 K6
Weston Shrops 51 Q2
Weston Shrops 63 J6
Weston Staffs 64 H7
Weston Suffk 59 N3
Weston W Berk 31 J7
Weston Beggard Herefs 41 J3
Westonbirt Gloucs 29 P4
Weston by Welland Nhants 55 K2
Weston Colley Hants 24 H5
Weston Colville Cambs 57 L10
Weston Corbett Hants 25 M4
Weston Coyney C Stke 64 H3
Weston Favell Nhants 55 K8
Weston Green Cambs 57 M10
Weston Heath Shrops 64 E9
Weston Hills Lincs 68 E8
Weston in Arden Warwks 54 C3
Westoning C Beds 44 E5
Weston-in-Gordano N Som 28 F7
Westoning Woodend C Beds 44 E5
Weston Jones Staffs 64 E7
Weston Longville Norfk 70 G9
Weston Lullingfields Shrops 63 M7
Weston-on-Avon Warwks 53 M10
Weston-on-the-Green Oxon 43 L8
Weston Park Staffs 64 E10
Weston Patrick Hants 25 M4
Weston Rhyn Shrops 63 J5
Weston-sub-Edge Gloucs 42 D3
Weston-super-Mare N Som 28 D10
Weston Turville Bucks 44 B9
Weston-under-Lizard Staffs 64 E10
Weston under Penyard Herefs 41 K7
Weston-under-Redcastle Shrops 63 P6
Weston under Wetherley Warwks 54 B7
Weston Underwood Derbys 65 P4
Weston Underwood M Keyn 55 L10
Weston-upon-Trent Derbys 66 C6
Westonzoyland Somset 21 M6
West Orchard Dorset 22 H10
West Overton Wilts 30 D9
Westow N York 86 D2
West Panson Devon 7 L6
West Park Abers 133 J5
West Parley Dorset 11 Q5
West Peckham Kent 34 B11
West Peeke Devon 7 L6
West Pelton Dur 100 G7
West Pennard Somset 22 D5
West Pentire Cnwll 3 J2
West Perry Cambs 56 C7
West Pinchbeck Lincs 68 D7
West Porlock Somset 20 D4
Westport Somset 21 N9
West Pulham Dorset 10 H3
West Putford Devon 18 G10
West Quantoxhead Somset 20 H5
Westquarter Falk 114 G5
Westra V Glam 27 Q8
West Raddon Devon 8 G4
West Rainton Dur 101 J9
West Rasen Lincs 79 Q6
West Ravendale NE Lin 80 E4
Westray Ork 147 c2
Westray Airport Ork 147 c1
West Raynham Norfk 70 C7
West Retford Notts 78 H7
Westridge Green W Berk 31 M6
Westrigg W Loth 114 G8
Westrop Swindn 30 E4
West Rounton N York 91 P6
West Row Suffk 57 N5
West Rudham Norfk 70 B6
West Runton Norfk 71 J4
Westruther Border 116 E11
Westry Cambs 56 H1
West Saltoun E Loth 116 B8
West Sandford Devon 8 F4
West Sandwick Shet 147 j4
West Scrafton N York 90 H10
West Sleekburn Nthumb 100 H1
West Somerton Norfk 71 P8
West Stafford Dorset 10 H7
West Stockwith Notts 79 K5
West Stoke W Susx 13 P3
West Stonesdale N York 90 E6
West Stoughton Somset 21 P4
West Stour Dorset 22 H9
West Stourmouth Kent 35 N9
West Stow Suffk 57 Q6
West Stowell Wilts 30 D10
West Stratton Hants 25 J5
West Street Kent 34 F11
West Street Kent 35 P11
West Street Medway 34 C7
West Street Suffk 58 E6
West Tanfield N York 91 M11
West Taphouse Cnwll 4 A4
West Tarbert Ag & B 112 C8
West Tarring W Susx 14 G10
West Thirston Nthumb 109 K10
West Thorney W Susx 13 N4
Westthorpe Derbys 78 D8
West Thorpe Notts 66 G7
West Thurrock Thurr 33 Q7
West Tilbury Thurr 34 B7
West Tisted Hants 25 L7
West Torrington Lincs 80 C7
West Town BaNES 28 G10
West Town Hants 13 M5
West Town Herefs 51 M8
West Town N Som 28 G8
West Town Somset 22 C6
West Town Somset 22 F5
West Tytherley Hants 24 D7
West Walton Norfk 69 J9
Westward Cumb 98 C9
Westward Ho! Devon 18 H7
Westwell Kent 16 H1
Westwell Oxon 42 E9
Westwell Leacon Kent 16 G1
West Wellow Hants 24 D9
West Wembury Devon 4 H7
West Wemyss Fife 115 P2
Westwick Cambs 56 H7
Westwick Dur 90 H4
West Wick N Som 28 E10
Westwick Norfk 71 K7
West Wickham Cambs 57 L10
West Wickham Gt Lon 33 M9
West Williamston Pembks 37 K9
West Winch Norfk 69 M9
West Winterslow Wilts 24 C7
West Wittering W Susx 13 N5
West Witton N York 90 H9
Westwood Devon 9 J5
Westwood Kent 33 R8
Westwood Kent 35 Q9
Westwood Notts 66 D2
Westwood Nthumb 99 L5
Westwood Wilts 29 N10
West Woodburn Nthumb 108 E12
West Woodhay W Berk 31 J9
Westwood Heath Covtry 53 P5
West Woodlands Somset 22 H4
Westwoodside N Linc 79 J4
West Worldham Hants 25 M6
West Worthing W Susx 14 G10
West Wratting Cambs 57 L10
West Wycombe Bucks 32 B3
West Wylam Nthumb 100 E5
West Yatton Wilts 29 P7
West Yoke Kent 33 Q9
West Youlstone Cnwll 18 E10
Wetham Green Kent 34 E8
Wetheral Cumb 98 F7
Wetherby Leeds 85 N5
Wetherby Services N York 85 N5
Wetherden Suffk 58 E8
Wetheringsett Suffk 58 H7
Wethersfield Essex 46 C5
Wetherup Street Suffk 58 H8
Wetley Rocks Staffs 64 H2
Wettenhall Ches E 76 B11
Wetton Staffs 65 L1
Wetwang E R Yk 86 H3
Wetwood Staffs 64 E5
Wexcombe Wilts 30 F10
Wexham Slough 32 E6
Wexham Street Bucks 32 E6
Weybourne Norfk 70 G4
Weybourne Surrey 25 P3
Weybread Suffk 59 K4
Weybread Street Suffk 59 K5
Weybridge Surrey 32 F9
Weycroft Devon 9 P5
Weydale Highld 151 L4
Weyhill Hants 24 E4
Weymouth Dorset 10 G9
Whaddon Bucks 44 A5
Whaddon Cambs 45 L2
Whaddon Gloucs 41 N9
Whaddon Wilts 24 C8
Whaddon Wilts 29 P10
Whale Cumb 89 N2
Whaley Derbys 78 E9
Whaley Bridge Derbys 77 J7
Whaley Thorns Derbys 78 E9
Whaligoe Highld 151 P8
Whalley Lancs 83 Q8
Whalley Banks Lancs 83 Q8
Whalsay Shet 147 k5
Whalton Nthumb 100 E2
Whaplode Lincs 68 F7
Whaplode Drove Lincs 68 F9
Wharf Warwks 54 C10
Wharfe N York 84 B1
Wharles Lancs 83 K8
Wharley End C Beds 44 D3
Wharncliffe Side Sheff 77 P5
Wharram-le-Street N York 86 F2
Wharton Ches W 76 C10
Wharton Herefs 51 N9
Whashton N York 91 K5
Whasset Cumb 89 N10
Whatcote Warwks 42 G3
Whateley Warwks 65 N12
Whatfield Suffk 47 J2
Whatley Somset 10 B3
Whatley Somset 22 G4
Whatley's End S Glos 29 K6
Whatlington E Susx 16 D7
Whatsole Street Kent 17 K2
Whatstandwell Derbys 65 Q1
Whatton-in-the-Vale Notts 67 J4
Whauphill D & G 95 M8
Whaw N York 90 G6
Wheal Peevor Cnwll 2 H5
Wheal Rose Cnwll 2 H5
Wheatacre Norfk 59 P2
Wheatfield Oxon 31 P2
Wheathampstead Herts 44 H9
Wheathill Shrops 52 B4
Wheathill Somset 22 D7
Wheatley Calder 84 G10
Wheatley Hants 25 N5
Wheatley Oxon 43 M10
Wheatley Hill Dur 101 K10
Wheatley Hills Donc 78 F3
Wheatley Lane Lancs 84 C7
Wheaton Aston Staffs 64 F9
Wheddon Cross Somset 20 E5
Wheelbarrow Town Kent 17 L2
Wheeler End Bucks 32 A4
Wheeler's Green Wokham 31 Q8
Wheelerstreet Surrey 14 D3
Wheelock Ches E 76 D12
Wheelock Heath Ches E 76 D12
Wheelton Lancs 83 N11
Wheldale Wakefd 85 P10
Wheldrake C York 86 C6
Whelford Gloucs 30 D3
Whelpley Hill Bucks 44 E10
Whelpo Cumb 98 C10
Whelston Flints 74 H8
Whempstead Herts 45 K7
Whenby N York 86 B1
Whepstead Suffk 58 B9
Wherstead Suffk 47 L3
Wherwell Hants 24 F5
Wheston Derbys 77 L8
Whetsted Kent 16 B2
Whetstone Gt Lon 33 J4
Whetstone Leics 54 F1
Wheyrigg Cumb 97 P8
Whicham Cumb 88 F10
Whichford Warwks 42 G5
Whickham Gatesd 100 G6
Whiddon Devon 7 N5
Whiddon Down Devon 8 C6
Whigstreet Angus 125 J4
Whilton Nhants 54 G7
Whimble Devon 7 L4
Whimple Devon 9 K5
Whimpwell Green Norfk 71 M6
Whinburgh Norfk 70 E10
Whin Lane End Lancs 83 J7
Whinnieliggate D & G 96 E8
Whinnow Cumb 98 C8
Whinnyfold Abers 141 P9
Whinny Hill S on T 91 P3
Whippingham IoW 12 H6
Whipsnade C Beds 44 E8
Whipsnade Zoo ZSL C Beds 44 E8
Whipton Devon 8 H6
Whirlow Sheff 77 P7
Whisby Lincs 79 M10
Whissendine Rutlnd 67 K9
Whissonsett Norfk 70 D7
Whistlefield Ag & B 113 J3
Whistlefield Inn Ag & B 112 H3
Whistley Green Wokham 31 R7
Whiston Knows 75 N5
Whiston Nhants 55 L8
Whiston Rothm 78 D6
Whiston Staffs 64 G9
Whiston Staffs 65 J3
Whiston Cross Shrops 64 E11
Whiston Eaves Staffs 65 K3
Whitacre Fields Warwks 53 N2
Whitbeck Cumb 88 F10
Whitbourne Herefs 52 D9
Whitburn S Tyne 101 K6
Whitburn W Loth 114 H8
Whitby Ches W 75 L8
Whitby N York 92 H4
Whitbyheath Ches W 75 L9
Whitchester Border 116 G9
Whitchurch BaNES 29 J9
Whitchurch Bucks 44 A7
Whitchurch Cardif 27 R6
Whitchurch Devon 7 P10
Whitchurch Hants 24 H4
Whitchurch Herefs 40 H8
Whitchurch Oxon 31 N7
Whitchurch Pembks 36 F5
Whitchurch Shrops 63 P4
Whitchurch Canonicorum Dorset 10 B6
Whitchurch Hill Oxon 31 N6
Whitcombe Dorset 10 H7
Whitcot Shrops 51 L2
Whitcott Keysett Shrops 51 J4
Whiteacre Kent 17 K1
Whiteacre Heath Warwks 53 N2
Whiteash Green Essex 46 D5
White Ball Somset 20 H9
Whitebridge Highld 129 N1
Whitebrook Mons 40 H10
Whitebushes Surrey 15 K1
Whitecairns Abers 141 M12
Whitechapel Gt Lon 33 L6
White Chapel Lancs 83 M7
Whitechurch Pembks 37 M3
Whitecliff Gloucs 40 H9
White Colne Essex 46 F6
White Coppice Lancs 83 N11
Whitecraig E Loth 115 Q7
Whitecroft Gloucs 41 J10
Whitecrook D & G 94 H7
Whitecross Cnwll 2 E7
White Cross Cnwll 2 H10
Whitecross Cnwll 6 D10
Whitecross Falk 114 H6
White End Worcs 41 M5
Whiteface Highld 146 C7
Whitefarland N Ayrs 103 M1
Whitefaulds S Ayrs 104 E8
Whitefield Bury 76 E2
Whitefield Devon 19 N6
Whitefield Somset 20 G7
Whitefield Lane End Knows 75 M6
Whiteford Abers 140 H10
Whitegate Ches W 76 B10
Whitehall Hants 25 N3
Whitehall Ork 147 e3
Whitehall W Susx 14 G6
Whitehaven Cumb 88 C3
Whitehill Kent 34 H10
Whitehill Leics 66 C10
Whitehill and Bordon Hants 25 N6
Whitehills Abers 140 G3
Whitehouse Abers 132 F1
Whitehouse Ag & B 112 B9
Whitehouse Common Birm 53 L1
Whitekirk E Loth 116 E5
White Kirkley Dur 100 C11
White Lackington Dorset 10 H5
Whitelackington Somset 21 N10
White Ladies Aston Worcs 52 G10
Whiteleaf Bucks 44 B10
White-le-Head Dur 100 F7
Whiteley Hants 13 J3
Whiteley Bank IoW 13 J8
Whiteley Green Ches E 76 G8
Whiteley Village Surrey 32 F10
Whitemans Green W Susx 15 K6
White Mill Carmth 38 C7
Whitemire Moray 138 H5
Whitemoor C Nott 66 E4
Whitemoor Cnwll 3 N3
Whitemoor Derbys 66 B3
Whitemoor Staffs 76 G11
Whiteness Shet 147 i7
White Notley Essex 46 D8
Whiteoak Green Oxon 42 H9
White Ox Mead BaNES 29 L10
Whiteparish Wilts 24 D8
White Pit Lincs 80 G8
Whiterashes Abers 141 K11
White Roding Essex 45 Q9
Whiterow Highld 151 Q7
Whiterow Moray 139 J4
Whiteshill Gloucs 41 N10
Whitesmith E Susx 15 P8
White Stake Lancs 83 M10
Whitestaunton Somset 9 P3
Whitestone Devon 8 G6
White Stone Herefs 40 H3
Whitestone Cross Devon 8 G6
Whitestreet Green Suffk 46 H4
Whitewall Corner N York 86 E1
White Waltham W & M 32 B7
Whiteway BaNES 29 L9
Whiteway Gloucs 41 Q9
Whitewell Lancs 83 P6
Whiteworks Devon 8 B10
Whitfield C Dund 125 J6
Whitfield Kent 17 N2
Whitfield Nhants 43 M4
Whitfield Nthumb 99 M7
Whitfield S Glos 29 K4
Whitfield Hall Nthumb 99 M7
Whitford Devon 9 P5
Whitford Flints 74 G8
Whitgift E R Yk 86 E10
Whitgreave Staffs 64 G6
Whithorn D & G 95 N10
Whiting Bay N Ayrs 103 Q4
Whitkirk Leeds 85 M8
Whitland Carmth 37 N7
Whitlaw Border 107 M7
Whitletts S Ayrs 104 G5
Whitley N York 85 R11
Whitley Readg 31 P8
Whitley Sheff 77 Q5
Whitley Wilts 29 P9
Whitley Bay N Tyne 101 J4
Whitley Chapel Nthumb 99 P7
Whitley Heath Staffs 64 F7
Whitley Lower Kirk 85 J11
Whitley Row Kent 33 P11
Whitlock's End Solhll 53 L5
Whitminster Gloucs 41 M10
Whitmore Dorset 11 P3
Whitmore Staffs 64 E4
Whitnage Devon 20 G10
Whitnash Warwks 53 Q8
Whitney-on-Wye Herefs 40 C2
Whitrigg Cumb 97 P10
Whitrigg Cumb 97 P6
Whitrigglees Cumb 97 P7
Whitsbury Hants 23 P9
Whitsome Border 117 J11
Whitson Newpt 28 E6
Whitstable Kent 35 K9
Whitstone Cnwll 7 K5
Whittingham Nthumb 108 H7
Whittingslow Shrops 51 M3
Whittington Derbys 78 C8
Whittington Gloucs 42 B7
Whittington Lancs 89 P11
Whittington Norfk 69 N12
Whittington Shrops 63 K6
Whittington Staffs 52 F4
Whittington Staffs 65 M10
Whittington Warwks 65 P12
Whittington Worcs 52 G10
Whittington Moor Derbys 78 B9
Whittlebury Nhants 43 P3
Whittle-le-Woods Lancs 83 N11
Whittlesey Cambs 56 E1
Whittlesford Cambs 57 J11
Whittlestone Head Bl w D 83 Q11
Whitton N Linc 86 G10
Whitton Nthumb 108 H9
Whitton Powys 51 J7
Whitton S on T 91 P2
Whitton Shrops 51 P6
Whitton Suffk 58 H11
Whittonditch Wilts 30 G8
Whittonstall Nthumb 100 D7
Whitway Hants 31 K10
Whitwell Derbys 78 E8
Whitwell Herts 44 H7
Whitwell IoW 13 J9
Whitwell N York 91 M7
Whitwell Rutlnd 67 M10
Whitwell-on-the-Hill N York 86 D2
Whitwell Street Norfk 70 G8
Whitwick Leics 66 D9
Whitwood Wakefd 85 N10
Whitworth Lancs 84 D11
Whixall Shrops 63 N5
Whixley N York 85 N4
Whorlton Dur 91 J4
Whorlton N York 91 Q6
Whyle Herefs 51 P8
Whyteleafe Surrey 33 L10
Wibdon Gloucs 28 H3
Wibsey C Brad 84 H9
Wibtoft Warwks 54 D3
Wichenford Worcs 52 E8
Wichling Kent 34 G11
Wick BCP 12 B6
Wick Devon 9 M4
Wick Highld 151 Q6
Wick S Glos 29 L8
Wick Somset 21 K4
Wick Somset 21 N8
Wick V Glam 27 L8
Wick W Susx 14 E10
Wick Wilts 23 Q9
Wick Worcs 41 Q3
Wicken Cambs 57 L6
Wicken Nhants 43 Q4
Wicken Bonhunt Essex 45 P5
Wickenby Lincs 80 B7
Wick End Bed 55 N10
Wicken Green Village Norfk 70 B6
Wickersley Rothm 78 D5
Wicker Street Green Suffk 46 H3
Wickford Essex 34 D4
Wickham Hants 13 K2
Wickham W Berk 31 J8
Wickham Bishops Essex 46 E9
Wickhambreaux Kent 35 M10
Wickhambrook Suffk 57 P9
Wickhamford Worcs 42 C3
Wickham Green Suffk 58 G7
Wickham Green W Berk 31 J8
Wickham Heath W Berk 31 J8
Wickham Market Suffk 59 L9
Wickhampton Norfk 71 N11
Wickham St Paul Essex 46 E4
Wickham Skeith Suffk 58 G7
Wickham Street Suffk 57 P10
Wickham Street Suffk 58 G7
Wickhurst Green W Susx 14 G5
Wick John o' Groats Airport Highld 151 Q6
Wicklewood Norfk 70 G11
Wickmere Norfk 70 H5
Wick St Lawrence N Som 28 E9
Wicksteed Park Nhants 55 L5
Wickstreet E Susx 15 P9
Wickwar S Glos 29 L5
Widdington Essex 45 P5
Widdop Calder 84 D8
Widdrington Nthumb 109 L10
Widdrington Station Nthumb 109 L11
Widecombe in the Moor Devon 8 D9
Widegates Cnwll 4 D5
Widemouth Bay Cnwll 7 J4
Wide Open N Tyne 100 G4
Widford Essex 46 C10
Widford Herts 45 M8
Widham Wilts 30 C5
Widley Hants 13 L3
Widmer End Bucks 32 C3
Widmerpool Notts 66 G6
Widmore Gt Lon 33 M8
Widnes Halton 75 N6
Widworthy Devon 9 N5
Wigan Wigan 75 P3
Wigborough Somset 21 P10
Wiggaton Devon 9 L6
Wiggenhall St Germans Norfk 69 L9
Wiggenhall St Mary Magdalen Norfk 69 L10
Wiggenhall St Mary the Virgin Norfk 69 L9
Wiggenhall St Peter Norfk 69 L9
Wiggens Green Essex 46 B3
Wiggenstall Staffs 77 K11
Wiggington Shrops 63 K5
Wigginton C York 86 B3
Wigginton Herts 44 D9
Wigginton Oxon 42 H5
Wigginton Staffs 65 N11
Wigginton Bottom Herts 44 D10
Wigglesworth N York 84 B4
Wiggonby Cumb 98 C7
Wiggonholt W Susx 14 F7
Wighill N York 85 P6
Wighton Norfk 70 D4
Wightwick Wolves 52 F1
Wigley Derbys 77 P9
Wigley Hants 24 E10
Wigmore Herefs 51 L7
Wigmore Medway 34 D9
Wigsley Notts 79 L9
Wigsthorpe Nhants 55 P4
Wigston Leics 54 G1
Wigston Fields Leics 66 F12
Wigston Parva Leics 54 D3
Wigthorpe Notts 78 F7
Wigtoft Lincs 68 E5
Wigton Cumb 97 Q8
Wigtown D & G 95 N7
Wigtwizzle Sheff 77 N4
Wike Leeds 85 M7
Wilbarston Nhants 55 K3
Wilberfoss E R Yk 86 D5
Wilburton Cambs 57 J6
Wilby Nhants 55 L7
Wilby Norfk 58 F3
Wilby Suffk 59 K6
Wilcot Wilts 30 D10
Wilcott Shrops 63 L8
Wilcrick Newpt 28 F5
Wilday Green Derbys 77 Q9
Wildboarclough Ches E 76 H10
Wilden Bed 56 B9
Wilden Worcs 52 F6
Wilde Street Suffk 57 N5
Wildhern Hants 24 F3
Wildhill Herts 45 J10
Wildmanbridge S Lans 114 E10
Wildmill Brdgnd 27 L6
Wildmoor Hants 25 L2
Wildmoor Worcs 52 H5
Wildsworth Lincs 79 K4
Wilford C Nott 66 F5
Wilkesley Ches E 64 B4
Wilkhaven Highld 146 G8
Wilkieston W Loth 115 L7
Wilkin's Green Herts 44 H10
Wilksby Lincs 80 F11
Willand Devon 9 K3
Willards Hill E Susx 16 C6
Willaston Ches E 64 C2
Willaston Ches W 75 K8
Willen M Keyn 44 C3
Willenhall Covtry 54 B5

Willenhall Wsall 52 H1
Willerby E R Yk 87 J9
Willerby N York 93 K11
Willersey Gloucs 42 C4
Willersley Herefs 40 D2
Willesborough Kent 17 J2
Willesborough Lees Kent 17 J2
Willesden Gt Lon 33 J5
Willesleigh Devon 19 L7
Willesley Wilts 29 N5
Willett Somset 20 H6
Willey Shrops 64 C12
Willey Warwks 54 E4
Willey Green Surrey 32 D12
Williamscot Oxon 43 K3
Williamstown Rhondd 27 N4
Willian Herts 45 J5
Willicote Warwks 53 M10
Willingale Essex 45 Q10
Willingdon E Susx 15 Q10
Willingham Cambs 56 H6
Willingham by Stow Lincs 79 L7
Willingham Green Cambs 57 M10
Willingham St Mary Suffk 59 N4
Willington Bed 56 C10
Willington Derbys 65 P6
Willington Dur 100 G11
Willington Kent 34 D11
Willington N Tyne 101 J7
Willington Warwks 42 F4
Willington Corner Ches W 75 N10
Willitoft E R Yk 86 D8
Williton Somset 20 G5
Willoughby Lincs 81 J9
Willoughby Warwks 54 E7
Willoughby Hills Lincs 68 G3
Willoughby-on-the-Wolds Notts 66 G7
Willoughby Waterleys Leics 54 F2
Willoughton Lincs 79 M5
Willow Green Ches W 75 Q8
Willows Green Essex 46 C8
Willsbridge S Glos 29 K8
Willsworthy Devon 7 P8
Willtown Somset 21 N8
Wilmcote Warwks 53 M9
Wilmington BaNES 29 L10
Wilmington Devon 9 N5
Wilmington E Susx 15 Q10
Wilmington Kent 33 P8
Wilmslow Ches E 76 F7
Wilpshire Lancs 83 Q8
Wilsden C Brad 84 G8
Wilsford Lincs 67 P4
Wilsford Wilts 23 P5
Wilsford Wilts 30 C11
Wilsham Devon 19 P4
Wilshaw Kirk 77 L2
Wilsill N York 85 J2
Wilsley Green Kent 16 D3
Wilsley Pound Kent 16 D3
Wilson Herefs 40 H7
Wilson Leics 66 C7
Wilsontown S Lans 114 H10
Wilstead Bed 44 F3
Wilsthorpe Lincs 68 B9
Wilstone Herts 44 C9
Wilstone Green Herts 44 C9
Wilton Cumb 88 D4
Wilton Herefs 41 J7
Wilton N York 92 H10
Wilton R & Cl 92 C3
Wilton Wilts 23 N7
Wilton Wilts 30 F10
Wilton Dean Border 107 M7
Wimbish Essex 45 Q4
Wimbish Green Essex 45 R5
Wimbledon Gt Lon 33 J8
Wimblington Cambs 56 H2
Wimboldsley Ches W 76 C11
Wimborne Minster Dorset 11 N5
Wimborne St Giles Dorset 11 P2
Wimbotsham Norfk 69 M11
Wimpole Cambs 56 G10
Wimpstone Warwks 53 N11
Wincanton Somset 22 G7
Winceby Lincs 80 F10
Wincham Ches W 76 C8
Winchburgh W Loth 115 K6
Winchcombe Gloucs 42 B6
Winchelsea E Susx 16 F7
Winchelsea Beach E Susx 16 F7
Winchester Hants 24 H7
Winchester Services Hants 25 J6
Winchet Hill Kent 16 C3
Winchfield Hants 25 N2
Winchmore Hill Bucks 32 D3
Winchmore Hill Gt Lon 33 K3
Wincle Ches E 76 H10
Wincobank Sheff 78 C5
Winder Cumb 88 D3
Windermere Cumb 89 L7
Windermere Jetty Cumb 89 L7
Winderton Warwks 42 G3
Windhill Highld 137 P6
Windlehurst Stockp 76 H4
Windlesham Surrey 32 D9
Windmill Cnwll 6 C9
Windmill Derbys 77 M8
Windmill Hill E Susx 16 B8
Windmill Hill Somset 21 M10
Windrush Gloucs 42 E9
Windsole Abers 140 E4
Windsor W & M 32 D7
Windsor Castle W & M 32 D7
Windsoredge Gloucs 29 N2
Windsor Green Suffk 58 C9
Windygates Fife 115 Q1
Windyharbour Ches E 76 F9
Windy Hill Wrexhm 63 J1
Wineham W Susx 15 J7
Winestead E R Yk 87 P10
Winewall Lancs 84 D7
Winfarthing Norfk 58 G4
Winford IoW 13 J8
Winford N Som 28 H8
Winforton Herefs 40 C2
Winfrith Newburgh Dorset 11 K8
Wing Bucks 44 C7
Wing Rutlnd 67 M11
Wingate Dur 101 K11
Wingates Bolton 76 C2
Wingates Nthumb 108 H10
Wingerworth Derbys 78 C10
Wingfield C Beds 44 E6
Wingfield Suffk 59 J5
Wingfield Wilts 29 N11
Wingfield Green Suffk 59 J5
Wingham Kent 35 M11
Wingland Lincs 69 J7
Wingmore Kent 17 L2
Wingrave Bucks 44 B8
Winkburn Notts 78 H12
Winkfield Br For 32 C8
Winkfield Row Br For 32 C8
Winkhill Staffs 65 K2
Winkhurst Green Kent 15 P1
Winkleigh Devon 8 B3

Winksley N York 85 K1
Winkton BCP 12 B5
Winlaton Gatesd 100 F6
Winlaton Mill Gatesd 100 F6
Winless Highld 151 P6
Winllan Powys 62 H8
Winmarleigh Lancs 83 L6
Winnall Hants 24 H7
Winnersh Wokham 31 Q8
Winnington Ches W 76 B9
Winscales Cumb 88 D2
Winscombe N Som 28 F11
Winsford Ches W 76 C10
Winsford Somset 20 D6
Winsham Devon 19 K5
Winsham Somset 10 B3
Winshill Staffs 65 P7
Winshwen Swans 26 G3
Winskill Cumb 98 H11
Winslade Hants 25 L4
Winsley Wilts 29 M10
Winslow Bucks 43 Q6
Winson Gloucs 42 C10
Winsor Hants 24 E10
Winster Cumb 89 L8
Winster Derbys 77 N11
Winston Dur 91 J3
Winston Suffk 58 H8
Winstone Gloucs 41 Q9
Winswell Devon 19 J10
Winterborne Came Dorset 10 H7
Winterborne Clenston Dorset 11 K4
Winterborne Herringston Dorset 10 H7
Winterborne Houghton Dorset 11 K4
Winterborne Kingston Dorset 11 L5
Winterborne Monkton Dorset 10 G7
Winterborne Stickland Dorset 11 K4
Winterborne Tomson Dorset 11 L5
Winterborne Whitechurch Dorset 11 K5
Winterborne Zelston Dorset 11 L5
Winterbourne S Glos 29 K6
Winterbourne W Berk 31 K8
Winterbourne Abbas Dorset 10 F6
Winterbourne Bassett Wilts 30 C7
Winterbourne Dauntsey Wilts 24 B6
Winterbourne Earls Wilts 24 B6
Winterbourne Gunner Wilts 24 B6
Winterbourne Monkton Wilts 30 C8
Winterbourne Steepleton Dorset 10 F7
Winterbourne Stoke Wilts 23 N5
Winterbrook Oxon 31 M5
Winterburn N York 84 D3
Winteringham N Linc 86 H10
Winterley Ches E 76 D12
Wintersett Wakefd 85 M12
Winterslow Wilts 24 C7
Winterton N Linc 86 H11
Winterton-on-Sea Norfk 71 Q8
Winthorpe Lincs 81 L10
Winthorpe Notts 79 K12
Winton BCP 11 Q6
Winton Cumb 90 C5
Winton E Susx 15 P10
Winton N York 91 Q7
Wintringham N York 92 H12
Winwick Cambs 56 B4
Winwick Nhants 54 G6
Winwick Warrtn 75 Q5
Wirksworth Derbys 65 P1
Wirral 75 J6
Wirswall Ches E 63 P3
Wisbech Cambs 69 J10
Wisbech St Mary Cambs 68 H10
Wisborough Green W Susx 14 F5
Wiseman's Bridge Pembks 37 M9
Wiseton Notts 79 J6
Wishanger Gloucs 41 Q9
Wishaw N Lans 114 E10
Wishaw Warwks 53 M2
Wisley Surrey 32 F10
Wisley Garden RHS Surrey 32 F10
Wispington Lincs 80 D9
Wissenden Kent 16 F3
Wissett Suffk 59 M5
Wissington Norfk 57 M1
Wissington Suffk 46 G5
Wistanstow Shrops 51 M4
Wistanswick Shrops 64 C6
Wistaston Ches E 64 C1
Wistaston Green Ches E 64 C1
Wisterfield Ches E 76 F9
Wiston Pembks 37 K7
Wiston S Lans 106 C3
Wiston W Susx 14 G8
Wistow Cambs 56 E4
Wistow Leics 54 G1
Wistow N York 86 B8
Wiswell Lancs 83 R7
Witcham Cambs 57 J5
Witchampton Dorset 11 N3
Witchford Cambs 57 J5
Witcombe Somset 21 Q9
Witham Essex 46 E9
Witham Friary Somset 22 G5
Witham on the Hill Lincs 68 B9
Witham St Hughs Lincs 79 M11
Withcall Lincs 80 F7
Withdean Br & H 15 K9
Witherenden Hill E Susx 16 B6
Witheridge Devon 20 C10
Witherley Leics 53 Q1
Withern Lincs 80 H7
Withernsea E R Yk 87 R9
Withernwick E R Yk 87 M7
Withersdale Street Suffk 59 M4
Withersfield Suffk 57 M11
Witherslack Cumb 89 L10
Withiel Cnwll 6 E11
Withiel Florey Somset 20 F7
Withielgoose Cnwll 6 E11
Withington Gloucs 42 B8
Withington Herefs 40 H5
Withington Manch 76 F5
Withington Shrops 63 P9
Withington Staffs 65 J5
Withington Green Ches E 76 F9
Withington Marsh Herefs 40 H3
Withleigh Devon 20 C10
Withnell Lancs 83 P10
Withnell Fold Lancs 83 N10
Withybed Green Worcs 53 J7
Withybrook Warwks 54 E5
Withycombe Somset 20 F5
Withyham E Susx 15 P3
Withy Mills BaNES 29 K11
Withypool Somset 20 C6

Withywood Bristl 28 H9
Witley Surrey 14 D3
Witnesham Suffk 58 H10
Witney Oxon 42 H9
Wittering C Pete 67 Q11
Wittersham Kent 16 F5
Witton Birm 53 K2
Witton Norfk 71 L10
Witton Norfk 71 L6
Witton Gilbert Dur 100 G9
Witton Green Norfk 71 L11
Witton le Wear Dur 100 F12
Witton Park Dur 100 F12
Wiveliscombe Somset 20 H8
Wivelrod Hants 25 L6
Wivelsfield E Susx 15 L7
Wivelsfield Green E Susx 15 L7
Wivelsfield Station W Susx 15 L7
Wivenhoe Essex 47 J7
Wivenhoe Cross Essex 47 J7
Wiveton Norfk 70 F4
Wix Essex 47 L6
Wixams Bed 44 F3
Wixford Warwks 53 K9
Wix Green Essex 47 L6
Wixhill Shrops 63 P6
Wixoe Suffk 46 C3
Woburn C Beds 44 D5
Woburn Safari Park C Beds 44 D5
Woburn Sands M Keyn 44 C4
Wokefield Park W Berk 31 N9
Woking Surrey 32 E10
Wokingham Wokham 32 A8
Wolborough Devon 8 F10
Woldingham Surrey 33 L11
Wold Newton E R Yk 93 L12
Wold Newton NE Lin 80 E4
Wolfclyde S Lans 106 C3
Wolferlow Herefs 52 C8
Wolferton Norfk 69 M6
Wolfhampcote Warwks 54 E7
Wolfhill P & K 124 D6
Wolf Hills Nthumb 99 L6
Wolf's Castle Pembks 37 J5
Wolfsdale Pembks 36 H6
Wollaston Dudley 52 G4
Wollaston Nhants 55 M8
Wollaston Shrops 63 K9
Wollaton C Nott 66 C4
Wollaton Hall & Park C Nott 66 C4
Wolleigh Devon 8 F8
Wollerton Shrops 64 B6
Wollescote Dudley 52 H4
Wolsingham Dur 100 D10
Wolstanton Staffs 64 F3
Wolstenholme Rochdl 84 C12
Wolston Warwks 54 C5
Wolsty Cumb 97 M8
Wolvercote Oxon 43 K9
Wolverhampton Wolves 64 G12
Wolverhampton Halfpenny Green Airport Staffs 52 F2
Wolverley Shrops 63 M6
Wolverley Worcs 52 F5
Wolverton Hants 31 L10
Wolverton Kent 17 N2
Wolverton M Keyn 44 B4
Wolverton Warwks 53 N8
Wolverton Wilts 22 H7
Wolverton Common Hants 31 M10
Wolvesnewton Mons 28 F9
Wolvey Warwks 54 C3
Wolvey Heath Warwks 54 D3
Wolviston S on T 91 Q2
Wombleton N York 92 D10
Wombourne Staffs 52 G2
Wombwell Barns 78 C3
Womenswold Kent 35 M12
Womersley N York 85 Q11
Wonastow Mons 40 G9
Wonersh Surrey 14 E2
Wonford Devon 8 H6
Wonson Devon 8 C7
Wonston Dorset 10 H3
Wonston Hants 24 H5
Wooburn Bucks 32 C5
Wooburn Green Bucks 32 C5
Wooburn Moor Bucks 32 C5
Woodacott Devon 7 M3
Woodale N York 90 G11
Woodall Rothm 78 D7
Woodall Services Rothm 78 D7
Woodbank Ches W 75 K9
Woodbastwick Norfk 71 L9
Woodbeck Notts 79 K8
Wood Bevington Warwks 53 K10
Woodborough Notts 66 G3
Woodborough Wilts 30 C10
Woodbridge Devon 9 M6
Woodbridge Suffk 59 K10
Woodbury Devon 9 J7
Wood Burcote Nhants 43 P2
Woodbury Salterton Devon 9 J7
Woodchester Gloucs 41 N11
Woodchurch Kent 16 G4
Woodchurch Wirral 75 J6
Woodcombe Somset 20 E4
Woodcote Gt Lon 33 K10
Woodcote Oxon 31 N6
Woodcote Wrekin 64 E9
Woodcote Green Worcs 52 H6
Woodcott Hants 24 G2
Woodcroft Gloucs 28 H3
Woodcutts Dorset 23 L10
Wood Dalling Norfk 70 G7
Woodditton Cambs 57 M9
Woodeaton Oxon 43 L9
Wood Eaton Staffs 64 F8
Wooden Pembks 37 M9
Wood End Bed 44 E2
Wood End Bed 56 B6
Wood End C Beds 44 D3
Wood End Cambs 56 G6
Wood End Gt Lon 32 G6
Woodend Highld 127 P12
Woodend Nhants 54 G11
Woodend Staffs 65 M7
Woodend W Loth 114 G7
Woodend W Susx 13 P3
Wood End Warwks 53 L6
Wood End Warwks 53 N1
Wood End Warwks 53 P3
Wood Enderby Lincs 80 E11
Woodend Green Essex 45 Q6
Woodfalls Wilts 24 C9
Woodford Cnwll 18 G10
Woodford Devon 5 N6
Woodford Gloucs 29 L3
Woodford Gt Lon 33 M4
Woodford Nhants 55 N5
Woodford Stockp 76 G6
Woodford Bridge Gt Lon 33 M4
Woodford Green Gt Lon 33 M4
Woodford Halse Nhants 54 E10
Woodford Wells Gt Lon 33 M4
Woodgate Birm 53 J4

Woodgate Devon 20 H10
Woodgate Norfk 70 C9
Woodgate Norfk 70 E8
Woodgate W Susx 14 D10
Woodgate Worcs 52 H8
Woodgreen Hants 24 B10
Woodgreen Oxon 42 H9
Woodhall Herts 45 J9
Woodhall Hill Leeds 85 J8
Woodhall Spa Lincs 80 D11
Woodham Bucks 43 P8
Woodham Dur 91 M1
Woodham Surrey 32 F9
Woodham Ferrers Essex 34 D2
Woodham Mortimer Essex 46 E10
Woodham Walter Essex 46 E10
Wood Hayes Wolves 64 H11
Woodhead Abers 141 J8
Woodhill Shrops 52 D4
Woodhill Somset 21 M8
Woodhorn Nthumb 109 M12
Woodhorn Demesne Nthumb 109 M12
Woodhouse Leeds 85 L8
Woodhouse Leics 66 E9
Woodhouse Sheff 78 C7
Woodhouse Wakefd 85 M11
Woodhouse Eaves Leics 66 E9
Woodhouse Green Staffs 76 G11
Woodhouselee Mdloth 115 N8
Woodhouselees D & G 98 C3
Woodhouse Mill Sheff 78 C6
Woodhouses Cumb 98 C8
Woodhouses Oldham 76 G4
Woodhouses Staffs 65 K10
Woodhouses Staffs 65 M8
Woodhuish Devon 5 Q6
Woodhurst Cambs 56 F5
Woodingdean Br & H 15 L9
Woodkirk Leeds 85 K10
Woodland Abers 141 L11
Woodland Devon 5 N5
Woodland Devon 5 Q5
Woodland Dur 90 H1
Woodland Kent 17 L3
Woodland S Ayrs 104 C10
Woodland Head Devon 8 E5
Woodlands Abers 133 J5
Woodlands Donc 78 E2
Woodlands Dorset 11 P3
Woodlands Hants 12 E2
Woodlands Kent 33 Q10
Woodlands N York 85 L4
Woodlands Somset 21 J5
Woodlands Park W & M 32 B6
Woodlands St Mary W Berk 30 G7
Woodland Street Somset 22 C6
Woodland View Sheff 77 P6
Wood Lane Shrops 63 L5
Wood Lane Staffs 64 E2
Woodleigh Devon 5 M7
Woodlesford Leeds 85 M9
Woodley Stockp 76 H5
Woodley Wokham 31 Q7
Woodmancote Gloucs 29 M3
Woodmancote Gloucs 41 M6
Woodmancote Gloucs 42 B10
Woodmancote W Susx 13 J8
Woodmancote W Susx 15 J8
Woodmancott Hants 25 J4
Woodmansey E R Yk 87 K7
Woodmansgreen W Susx 25 Q8
Woodmansterne Surrey 33 K10
Woodmanton Devon 9 J7
Woodmarsh Wilts 23 J2
Woodmill Staffs 65 L8
Woodminton Wilts 23 M9
Woodnesborough Kent 35 P11
Woodnewton Nhants 55 P2
Wood Norton Norfk 70 E6
Woodplumpton Lancs 83 J8
Woodrising Norfk 70 E11
Wood Row Leeds 85 M9
Woodrow Worcs 52 G5
Wood's Corner E Susx 16 B7
Woods Eaves Herefs 51 J11
Woodseaves Shrops 64 C6
Woodseaves Staffs 64 E7
Woodsend Wilts 30 E7
Woodsetts Rothm 78 F7
Woodsford Dorset 11 J6
Wood's Green E Susx 16 B4
Woodside Br For 32 D8
Woodside Cumb 97 L11
Woodside Essex 45 N11
Woodside Fife 124 H11
Woodside Gt Lon 33 L9
Woodside Hants 12 E6
Woodside P & K 124 D5
Woodside Green Kent 34 F11
Woodstock Oxon 43 K8
Woodstock Pembks 37 K5
Woodston C Pete 56 D1
Wood Street Norfk 71 M8
Wood Street Village Surrey 32 D12
Woodthorpe Derbys 78 D9
Woodthorpe Leics 66 E9
Woodthorpe Lincs 80 H7
Woodton Norfk 59 K2
Woodtown Devon 18 H8
Woodvale Sefton 75 K2
Woodwall Green Staffs 64 E6
Wood Walton Cambs 56 D4
Woodyates Dorset 23 M9
Woody Bay Devon 19 N4
Woofferton Shrops 51 N7
Wookey Somset 22 C4
Wookey Hole Somset 22 C4
Wool Dorset 11 K7
Woolacombe Devon 19 J5
Woolage Green Kent 17 M1
Woolage Village Kent 35 M12
Woolaston Gloucs 29 J2
Woolaston Common Gloucs 29 J2
Woolavington Somset 21 M5
Woolbeding W Susx 14 C5
Woolbrook Devon 9 L7
Woolcotts Somset 20 F7
Wooldale Kirk 77 L2
Wooler Nthumb 108 G4
Woolfardisworthy Devon 18 G9
Woolfardisworthy Devon 8 F2
Woolfold Bury 76 F1
Woolfords S Lans 115 J10
Woolhampton W Berk 31 M9
Woolhope Herefs 41 J4
Woolland Dorset 11 J3
Woollard BaNES 29 K9
Woollensbrook Herts 45 L9
Woolley BaNES 29 M8
Woolley Cambs 56 C5
Woolley Cnwll 18 E10
Woolley Derbys 78 C11
Woolley Wakefd 77 Q1
Woolley Edge Services Wakefd 85 L12

Woolley Green W & M 32 B6
Woolmere Green Worcs 52 H8
Woolmer Green Herts 45 J8
Woolmerston Somset 21 L6
Woolminstone Somset 10 C3
Woolpack Kent 16 E5
Woolpit Suffk 58 E8
Woolpit Green Suffk 58 E8
Woolscott Warwks 54 E7
Woolsgrove Devon 8 F4
Woolsington N u Ty 100 G5
Woolstaston Shrops 51 M1
Woolsthorpe by Belvoir Lincs 67 L5
Woolsthorpe-by-Colsterworth Lincs 67 M7
Woolston C Sotn 12 G3
Woolston Devon 5 M8
Woolston Shrops 51 M3
Woolston Shrops 63 K7
Woolston Somset 20 H5
Woolston Somset 22 E6
Woolston Warrtn 76 C5
Woolstone Gloucs 41 Q5
Woolstone M Keyn 44 C4
Woolstone Oxon 30 G4
Woolton Lpool 75 M6
Woolton Hill Hants 31 J10
Woolverstone Suffk 47 L4
Woolverton Somset 22 G4
Woolwich Gt Lon 33 N6
Woonton Herefs 51 K9
Woonton Herefs 51 P8
Wooperton Nthumb 108 G6
Woore Shrops 64 D4
Wootten Green Suffk 59 J6
Wootton Bed 44 E3
Wootton Herefs 51 J9
Wootton IoW 13 J6
Wootton Kent 17 M2
Wootton N Linc 87 K12
Wootton Nhants 55 J9
Wootton Oxon 43 J7
Wootton Oxon 43 K11
Wootton Shrops 63 K6
Wootton Staffs 64 F7
Wootton Staffs 65 L3
Wootton Bassett Wilts 30 C5
Wootton Bridge IoW 13 J6
Wootton Broadmead Bed 44 E3
Wootton Common IoW 13 J6
Wootton Courtenay Somset 20 E5
Wootton Fitzpaine Dorset 10 B5
Wootton Rivers Wilts 30 D10
Wootton St Lawrence Hants 25 K3
Wootton Wawen Warwks 53 M8
Worcester Worcs 52 F9
Worcester Park Gt Lon 33 J9
Wordsley Dudley 52 G3
Worfield Shrops 52 D2
Worgret Dorset 11 L7
Workhouse End Bed 56 B10
Workhouse Green Suffk 46 F4
Workington Cumb 88 D1
Worksop Notts 78 G8
Worlaby Lincs 80 G8
Worlaby N Linc 87 J11
Worlds End Bucks 44 B10
Worlds End Hants 25 L11
World's End W Berk 31 K7
Worlds End W Susx 15 L7
Worle N Som 28 E9
Worleston Ches E 76 C12
Worlingham Suffk 59 N3
Worlington Devon 19 Q10
Worlington Suffk 57 N6
Worlingworth Suffk 59 J7
Wormald Green N York 85 L2
Wormbridge Herefs 40 F5
Wormegay Norfk 69 M10
Wormelow Tump Herefs 40 G5
Wormhill Derbys 77 L9
Wormhill Herefs 40 F4
Wormingford Essex 46 G5
Worminghall Bucks 43 N10
Wormington Gloucs 42 B4
Worminster Somset 22 C5
Wormit Fife 124 H7
Wormleighton Warwks 54 D10
Wormley Herts 45 L10
Wormley Surrey 14 D3
Wormleybury Herts 45 L10
Wormley Hill Donc 86 C12
Wormshill Kent 34 F11
Wormsley Herefs 40 F3
Worplesdon Surrey 32 D11
Worral Sheff 77 P5
Worrall Hill Gloucs 41 J8
Worsbrough Barns 78 B3
Worsbrough Bridge Barns 78 B3
Worsbrough Dale Barns 78 B3
Worsley Salfd 76 D4
Worstead Norfk 71 L7
Worsthorne Lancs 84 C8
Worston Lancs 84 A6
Worth Kent 35 P11
Worth Somset 22 C4
Worth W Susx 15 K3
Wortham Suffk 58 G5
Worthen Shrops 63 K11
Worthenbury Wrexhm 63 M3
Worthing Norfk 70 E8
Worthing W Susx 14 G10
Worthington Leics 66 C8
Worth Matravers Dorset 11 N9
Worthybrook Mons 40 G9
Worting Hants 25 K3
Wortley Barns 77 P4
Wortley Gloucs 29 M4
Wortley Leeds 85 K8
Worton N York 90 H7
Worton Wilts 23 J2
Wortwell Norfk 59 K4
Wotherton Shrops 63 J12
Wothorpe C Pete 67 P11
Wotter Devon 5 K5
Wotton Surrey 14 G1
Wotton-under-Edge Gloucs 29 M4
Wotton Underwood Bucks 43 P8
Woughton on the Green M Keyn 44 C4
Wouldham Kent 34 C9
Woundale Shrops 52 D2
Wrabness Essex 47 L5
Wrafton Devon 19 J6
Wragby Lincs 80 C8
Wragby Wakefd 85 M11
Wramplingham Norfk 70 G11
Wrangaton Devon 5 M5
Wrangbrook Wakefd 78 E1
Wrangle Lincs 68 H1
Wrangle Common Lincs 68 H1
Wrangle Lowgate Lincs 68 H1
Wrangway Somset 20 H9
Wrantage Somset 21 M8
Wrawby N Linc 79 P2
Wraxall N Som 28 G8

Wraxall Somset 22 E6
Wray Lancs 83 N2
Wray Castle Cumb 89 K6
Wraysbury W & M 32 E7
Wrayton Lancs 89 P12
Wrea Green Lancs 83 J9
Wreaks End Cumb 88 H9
Wreay Cumb 89 N12
Wreay Cumb 98 E8
Wrecclesham Surrey 25 P4
Wrekenton Gatesd 100 H6
Wrelton N York 92 F9
Wrenbury Ches E 63 Q3
Wrench Green N York 93 K9
Wreningham Norfk 70 H11
Wrentham Suffk 59 P4
Wrenthorpe Wakefd 85 L10
Wrentnall Shrops 63 M11
Wressle E R Yk 86 D9
Wressle N Linc 79 N2
Wrestlingworth C Beds 56 E11
Wretton Norfk 69 N11
Wrexham Wrexhm 63 K2
Wrexham Industrial Estate Wrexhm 63 L2
Wribbenhall Worcs 52 E5
Wrickton Shrops 52 B3
Wrightington Bar Lancs 75 P1
Wright's Green Essex 45 P8
Wrinehill Staffs 64 D3
Wrington N Som 28 G9
Writhlington BaNES 22 F2
Writtle Essex 46 B10
Wrockwardine Wrekin 64 B9
Wroot N Linc 79 J3
Wrose C Brad 85 J8
Wrotham Kent 34 B10
Wrotham Heath Kent 34 B10
Wrottesley Staffs 64 F12
Wroughton Swindn 30 C6
Wroxall IoW 13 J9
Wroxall Warwks 53 N6
Wroxeter Shrops 63 P10
Wroxham Norfk 71 L8
Wroxton Oxon 43 J3
Wyaston Derbys 65 M4
Wyatt's Green Essex 33 Q2
Wyberton Lincs 68 F3
Wyboston Bed 56 C9
Wybunbury Ches E 64 C2
Wychbold Worcs 52 G7
Wych Cross E Susx 15 M3
Wychnor Staffs 65 M9
Wychwood Ches E 76 D2
Wyck Hants 25 N5
Wyck Rissington Gloucs 42 E7
Wycliffe Dur 91 J4
Wycoller Lancs 84 D7
Wycomb Leics 67 K7
Wycombe Marsh Bucks 32 C4
Wyddial Herts 45 L5
Wye Kent 17 J1
Wyesham Mons 40 G9
Wyfordby Leics 67 K8
Wyke Devon 8 G5
Wyke Dorset 22 G8
Wyke Shrops 63 P11
Wyke Surrey 32 C11
Wyke C Brad 85 J9
Wyke Champflower Somset 22 E6
Wykeham N York 93 K10
Wyken Covtry 54 B4
Wyken Shrops 52 E1
Wyke Regis Dorset 10 G9
Wykey Shrops 63 L7
Wykin Leics 54 A2
Wylam Nthumb 100 F5
Wylde Green Birm 53 L2
Wylye Wilts 23 M6
Wymeswold Leics 66 G7
Wymington Bed 55 N8
Wymondham Leics 67 L8
Wymondham Norfk 70 G12
Wyndham Brdgnd 27 M4
Wynford Eagle Dorset 10 F5
Wynyard Park S on T 91 Q2
Wynyard Village S on T 91 P1
Wyre Piddle Worcs 52 H11
Wysall Notts 66 G7
Wyson Herefs 51 N7
Wythall Worcs 53 K5
Wytham Oxon 43 K10
Wythburn Cumb 89 J4
Wythenshawe Manch 76 F6
Wythop Mill Cumb 97 N12
Wyton Cambs 56 E6
Wyton E R Yk 87 M8
Wyverstone Suffk 58 F7
Wyverstone Street Suffk 58 F7
Wyville Lincs 67 L6

Yaddlethorpe N Linc 79 M2
Yafford IoW 12 G8
Yafforth N York 91 N8
Yalberton Torbay 5 P5
Yalding Kent 34 C12
Yanwath Cumb 89 N1
Yanworth Gloucs 42 C9
Yapham E R Yk 86 E5
Yapton W Susx 14 D10
Yarborough N Som 28 E10
Yarbridge IoW 13 K7
Yarburgh Lincs 80 G5
Yarcombe Devon 9 N3
Yard Devon 19 P9
Yardley Birm 53 L3
Yardley Gobion Nhants 43 Q3
Yardley Hastings Nhants 55 L9
Yardley Wood Birm 53 L5
Yardro Powys 50 H9
Yarford Somset 21 J7
Yarkhill Herefs 41 J3
Yarley Somset 22 C4
Yarlet Staffs 64 G6
Yarlington Somset 22 E7
Yarm S on T 91 P4
Yarmouth IoW 12 F7
Yarnacott Devon 19 M7
Yarnbrook Wilts 23 J3
Yarner Devon 8 E9
Yarnfield Staffs 64 F6
Yarnscombe Devon 19 L8
Yarnton Oxon 43 K9
Yarpole Herefs 51 M7
Yarrow Border 107 K4
Yarrow Somset 21 M4
Yarrow Feus Border 107 J5
Yarrowford Border 107 L4
Yarsop Herefs 40 F2
Yarwell Nhants 55 P2
Yate S Glos 29 L6
Yateley Hants 32 B9
Yatesbury Wilts 30 C7
Yattendon W Berk 31 L7
Yatton Herefs 51 M7
Yatton N Som 28 F9
Yatton Keynell Wilts 29 P6
Yaverland IoW 13 K7
Yawl Devon 9 Q6
Yawthorpe Lincs 79 M5
Yaxham Norfk 70 E9

Yaxley Cambs 56 D2
Yaxley Suffk 58 G6
Yazor Herefs 40 E2
Yeading Gt Lon 32 G6
Yeadon Leeds 85 J7
Yealand Conyers Lancs 89 N11
Yealand Redmayne Lancs 89 N11
Yealand Storrs Lancs 89 M11
Yealmbridge Devon 5 J6
Yealmpton Devon 5 J6
Yearby R & Cl 92 D3
Yearngill Cumb 97 N9
Yearsley N York 92 C11
Yeaton Shrops 63 M8
Yeaveley Derbys 65 M4
Yeavering Nthumb 108 F4
Yedingham N York 92 H11
Yelford Oxon 42 H10
Yell Shet 147 j4
Yelland Devon 19 J7
Yelling Cambs 56 E8
Yelvertoft Nhants 54 F5
Yelverton Devon 4 H3
Yelverton Norfk 71 K11
Yenston Somset 22 G9
Yeoford Devon 8 E5
Yeo Mill Devon 20 C8
Yeo Vale Devon 18 H8
Yeovil Somset 22 D9
Yeovil Marsh Somset 22 D9
Yeovilton Somset 22 D8
Yerbeston Pembks 37 L9
Yesnaby Ork 147 b4
Yetlington Nthumb 108 G8
Yetminster Dorset 10 F3
Yetson Devon 5 N5
Yettington Devon 9 K7
Yetts o'Muckhart Clacks 115 J12
Yews Green C Brad 84 G9
Yew Tree Sandw 53 J2
Y Felinheli Gwynd 73 J10
Y Ferwig Cerdgn 48 C10
Y Fôr Gwynd 60 F4
Yielden Bed 55 P7
Yieldingtree Worcs 52 G5
Yieldshields S Lans 114 F11
Yiewsley Gt Lon 32 F6
Y Nant Wrexhm 63 J2
Ynysboeth Rhondd 27 P3
Ynysddu Caerph 28 A4
Ynysforgan Swans 26 G2
Ynyshir Rhondd 27 N4
Ynyslas Cerdgn 49 K2
Ynysmaerdy Rhondd 27 N5
Ynysmeudwy Neath 38 H10
Ynystawe Swans 26 G2
Ynyswen Powys 39 K9
Ynysybwl Rhondd 27 M3
Ynysymaengwyn Gwynd 61 K11
Yockenthwaite N York 90 E11
Yockleton Shrops 63 L10
Yokefleet E R Yk 86 F9
Yoker C Glas 113 P7
York C York 86 B5
York Lancs 83 Q8
Yorkletts Kent 35 K9
Yorkley Gloucs 41 K10
Yorkshire Dales National Park 90 E10
York Town Surrey 32 B10
Yorton Heath Shrops 63 N7
Youlgreave Derbys 77 N11
Youlthorpe E R Yk 86 E4
Youlton N York 85 P3
Youngsbury Herts 45 L9
Young's End Essex 46 C8
Yoxall Staffs 65 L8
Yoxford Suffk 59 M7
Y Rhiw Gwynd 60 C7
Ysbyty Cynfyn Cerdgn 49 N5
Ysbyty Ifan Conwy 61 Q3
Ysbyty Ystwyth Cerdgn 49 N6
Ysceifiog Flints 74 F9
Ysgubor-y-Coed Cerdgn 49 L2
Ystalyfera Neath 39 J11
Ystrad Rhondd 27 N3
Ystrad Aeron Cerdgn 49 K4
Ystradfellte Powys 39 M9
Ystrad Ffin Carmth 39 N4
Ystradgynlais Powys 39 J9
Ystrad Meurig Cerdgn 49 N6
Ystrad Mynach Caerph 27 P3
Ystradowen V Glam 27 N7
Ystumtuen Cerdgn 49 M5
Ythanbank Abers 141 M10
Ythanwells Abers 140 G9
Ythsie Abers 141 M9

Z

Zeal Monachorum Devon 8 D4
Zeals Wilts 22 H7
Zelah Cnwll 3 K4
Zennor Cnwll 2 D7
Zoar Cnwll 3 J10
Zouch Notts 66 E7
ZSL London Zoo Gt Lon 33 K6
ZSL Whipsnade Zoo C Beds 44 E8